Edited by
Alain-G. Gagnon
McGill University

Nelson Canada

Published in 1993 by
Nelson Canada,
A Division of Thomson Canada Limited
1120 Birchmount Road
Scarborough, Ontario M1K 5G4

Cover photograph courtesy of CANAPRESS.

Canadian Cataloguing in Publication Data
Main entry under title:

Québec: state and society

2nd ed.
Includes bibliographical references.
ISBN 0-17-603533-8

1. Québec (Province) – Politics and government – 1960–1976.* 2. Québec (Province) – Politics and government – 1976–1985.* 3. Québec (Province) – Social conditions. I. Gagnon, Alain-G. (Alain-Gustave), 1954– .

FC2925.Q74 1993   971.4'04   C92–095227–5
F1053.2.Q74 1993

Acquisitions Editor   Dave Ward
Supervising Editor   Nicole Gnutzman
Senior Editor   Linda Collins
Developmental Editor   Patty Riediger
Art Director   Bruce Bond
Design/Cover Design   Julia Hall

Printed and bound in Canada
1 2 3 4   96 95 94 93

CONTENTS

Part IV: Demography, Ethnicity, and Language 279

Part V: Québec Economy 389

NOTES ON THE CONTRIBUTORS

Pierre Anctil, Director, French Canada Studies Programme, McGill University (1988–91).

Fredrick Appel, Ph.D. candidate, Department of Political Science, McGill University.

Louis Balthazar, Professor, Department of Political Science, Université Laval.

André-J. Bélanger, Professor, Department of Political Science, Université de Montréal.

Louis Bélanger, Ph.D. candidate, Department of Political Science, Université Laval.

Yves Bélanger, Professeur, Department of Political Science, Université du Québec à Montréal.

Luc Bernier, Professeur, École nationale d'administration publique, Montréal.

Jerome H. Black, Associate Professor, Department of Political Science, McGill University.

Jacques Bourgault, Professeur, Department of Political Science, Université du Québec à Montréal.

Harold Chorney, Associate Professor, Department of Political Science, Concordia University.

Roch Denis, Professeur, Department of Political Science, Université du Québec à Montréal.

Serge Denis, Associate Professor, Department of Political Science, Université d'Ottawa.

Stéphane Dion, Associate Professor, Department of Political Science, Université de Montréal.

Scott Evans, Ph.D. candidate, Department of Political Science, Carleton University.

Alain-G. Gagnon, Professor, Department of Political Science, McGill University.

Guy Gosselin, Associate Professor, Department of Political Science, Université Laval.

Éric Gourdeau, Consultant, Québec City.

James Iain Gow, Professor, Department of Political Science, Université de Montréal.

David Hagen, Graduate student, Department of Political Science, McGill University.

Jacques Henripin, Professor, Department of Demography, Université de Montréal.

Daniel Latouche, Professor, Institut National de la Recherche Scientifique, Montréal.

Kenneth McRoberts, Professor, The Robarts Centre for Canadian Studies, York University.

Henry Milner, Professeur, Department of Political Science, Vanier College.

Andrew Molloy, Assistant Professor, Department of Political Science, Concordia University.

Alain Noël, Assistant Professor, Department of Political Science, Université de Montréal.

Marc Raboy, Professor, Department of Communications, Université Laval.

François Rocher, Associate Professor, Department of Political Science, Carleton University.

Ronald Rudin, Professor, Department of History, Concordia University.

A. Brian Tanguay, Associate Professor, Department of Political Science, Wilfrid Laurier University.

Charles Taylor, Professor, Department of Philosophy and Political Science, McGill University.

Jean-Philippe Thérien, Associate Professor, Department of Political Science, Université de Montréal.

Tim Thomas, Ph.D. candidate, Department of Political Science, Carleton University.

François Vaillancourt, Professor, Department of Economics, Université de Montréal.

Reginald A. Whitaker, Professor, Department of Political Science, York University.

ACKNOWLEDGMENTS

Several people have contributed to the completion of this volume. I wish to thank all the contributors, who participated with great enthusiasm at all stages of the project. This second edition innovates with the introduction of a peer-review process, and I would like to express my gratitude to everyone who accepted to serve in such a capacity, thus making the final product much better. My thanks go to Frances Abele, Caroline Andrew, Michael Behiels, Luc Bernier, Daniel Bonin, Stephen Brooks, Dorval Brunelle, Alan C. Cairns, Gary Caldwell, Jean-Pierre Collin, Daniel Drache, Joseph Garcea, Elisabeth Gidengil, Hubert Guindon, Sid Ingerman, Jack Jedwab, Jane Jenson, Guy Laforest, Carmen Lambert, Jeanne Laux, Vincent Lemieux, Henry Milner, Daniel Monnier, Claude Morin, Kenneth McRae, Kenneth McRoberts, Jean Mercier, Michel Paillé, Susan D. Phillips, Maurice Pinard, Louise Quesnel, François Rocher, Guy Rocher, Gladys L. Symons, A. Brian Tanguay, Dale Thomson, Hugh Thorburn, Gaëtan Tremblay, James Tully, Yves Vaillancourt, Éric Waddell, Harold Waller, Morton Weinfeld, Reginald Whitaker, and Robert Young. I wish to thank Lance Dadey for his much-appreciated assistance in proposing stylistic comments to some contributors. I would like to thank David Ward, Acquisitions Editor with Nelson Canada, who provided continued support and encouragement throughout the preparation of the book. Finally, I would also like to thank the publisher's assessors who provided constructive suggestions in making this textbook a better one: David Cameron, University of Toronto; Laurent Dobuzinskis, Simon Fraser University; and Garth Stevenson, Brock University.

INTRODUCTION

Over the years, French Canada has gradually been replaced by Québec as a field of research in political science. Pioneering works of the Chicago school, such as the research done by Horace Miner and Everett Hughes, inspired Québec researchers to carry further the political analysis. Among others, the work in Marcel Rioux and Yves Martin's *French-Canadian Society* was the turning point that called specifically for a study of Québec. Influenced by decolonization and liberation movements, Québec's political scientists, in turn, influenced the study of Québec. Several publications have contributed to make Québec a major field of research in its own right, including *Le Québec et la question nationale* (1979), *Le système politique québécois* (1979), *Pratique de l'État au Québec* (1984), *Québec: Social Change and Political Crisis*, 3rd. ed. (1988), and *Québec: Beyond the Quiet Revolution* (1990).

This completely revised edition of *Québec: State and Society* builds on the interdisciplinary perspective that characterizes much of the best of the Canadian social science tradition, and stresses a pluralist interpretation. This book is organized with a view to discuss fully the key issues and themes that constitute present-day Québec politics. The principal aim of this second edition is to be comprehensive in its coverage of the main challenges confronting Québec, and to give access to the basic knowledge and ideas of specialists at the cutting-edge of the field of study.

This second edition of *Québec: State and Society* is intended to provide students of Québec and Canadian politics with a better and more complete understanding of the environment and premises for state action. *Québec: State and Society* is composed of over twenty original essays on the major topics, written by prominent and widely published experts in areas as diverse as political science, sociology, economics, demography, and history.

Politically, socially, economically, and culturally, Québec has experienced significant transformations in the last thirty years in particular. The establishment of CEGEPs to replace classical colleges, following recommendations made by the Parent Commission, the implementation of party financing practices in line with high principles of morality, the establishment of a Québec Charter of Rights and Freedoms in 1975, which, in many respects, goes beyond the 1982 Canadian Charter of Human Rights and Freedoms, and the decision to establish, in 1977, the first antiscab legislation by a government in Canada are all examples of these transformations.

The last thirty years have also witnessed fundamental changes in Québec–Canada relations, and although Québec has made some important gains in several policy areas, most of the time these have been contained by the Canadian government; for example, with the Canadian Charter of Rights and Freedoms and the Constitution Act of 1982 with its main amending formula based on the seven provinces and 50 percent of the Canadian population (7/50) equation, which often renders Québec powerless in the Canadian political setting. Nevertheless, the Québec government has over the years fought to obtain significant powers from Ottawa to better equip itself to face international competition: the setting up of the *Caisse de dépôt et placement* in 1965 is a case in point. Several initiatives were taken over the years to improve Québec's place in the continental economy as well, and to find ways to narrow the gap between Québec and Ontario in particular.

Economically, Québec has made some headway in modifying the ownership pattern of its industrial base. However, the argument that Québec became interventionist once and for all in 1960 with the election of Jean Lesage does not hold as firmly as was once thought by many authors. In 1966, when Daniel Johnson came to power, the government proposed a return to private capital as a way to get out of the economic difficulties that prevailed at that time, which in turn were reflected in high levels of unemployment and diminishing foreign investments. Québec had few instruments at the time to deal with the weaknesses in its economic structure. Now, market forces appear to be dictating the course of history, and politicians in Québec and elsewhere are becoming gradually dependent on their economic success for their own political survival. With the 1982 recession, Québec's economic strategy of interventionism was challenged with the appearance of neoliberalism, compounded with the election of Brian Mulroney in Ottawa in 1984 and the election of the Liberals in Québec in 1985. Privatization and deregulation became the new leitmotifs of the decision-makers, with citizens embracing this change with relative ease. The privatization of provincially owned public enterprises and the pressure for restraint and even dismantling of government-supported social programs signalled the adoption of a new state strategy openly favouring a strengthened entrepreneurial class.

In my view, the area of ideological developments in Québec requires a more nuanced account, in particular as relates to the roots of liberalism, neoliberalism, and social democracy as integral parts of Québec's ideological spectrum. In addition, the works of such *avant-gardistes* as Thérèse Casgrain, Saint-Denys Garneau, Robert Charbonneau, Robert Élie, Roger Duhamel, and Jean-Charles Harvey remind us that the rule of "supposed" unanimity was challenged by several intellectual circles before 1945 and after, questioning a certain orthodoxy among Québec experts.

This book underscores the relationship between the state/state actors and the societal and intermediating actors (political parties, unions, social movements, etc.). In this second edition, an attempt is made to expand the treatment of the state by introducing discussions of the central agencies (Premier's Office, Treasury Board, Executive Committee) and the line departments—the structures of the administrative state—as well as discussions of subjects as relevant and diverse as the Canadian Constitution, economic strategies, municipal politics, immigration policies, educational reforms, and international relations.

Contemporary Québec politics often fuses the concepts of state and society, bringing together the national consciousness and the institutions of the Québec state. This is clearly demonstrated in the policy sectors of education, language, immigration, and the economy. The evolving relations between state and society in Québec are most significant in the development of nationalism in the province, especially from 1960 onward. Indeed, this reveals the extent to which nationalism has been shaped by the consolidation of the Québec state.

Also central to this book is the principle that Québec cannot be discussed in isolation: the linkages with the rest of Canada, the continent, and the international political milieu are discussed throughout the book. The economic component, shaped by politics, is fully explored. Issues such as uneven development (centre-periphery), deficit, language conflicts, demographic trends, patterns of migration and immigration, responsibleness of unions, depolarization of political parties, the aboriginal issue, and the need to build alliances outside traditional forms of political representation are all analyzed in this new edition.

The book is organized in a thematic manner and offers an overview of the dominant interpretations of Québec politics. The volume is composed of five parts: (1) Québec nationalism, (2) symbols, ideologies, culture, and communications; (3) state, society, and politics; (4) demography, ethnicity, and language; and (5) Québec economy.

PART I: QUÉBEC NATIONALISM

Central to any study of Québec state and society is the perennial issue of nationalism, to which four chapters have been contributed in Part I, bringing together macro and micro level interpretations as authors stress local, national, and international infuences on the ups and downs of this 20th-century phenomenon.

In the first part, a historical account of Québec nationalism is provided, as well as various interpretations of its origin and nature.

Louis Balthazar introduces the concept of nationalism in terms of either a movement toward the promotion of the nation or toward the establishment of such a nation if it does not exist. There is an important theoretical discussion of the transformation of a French-Canadian into a Québécois nationalism, with a focus on the 1980s "market nationalism" that has swiftly gained prominence throughout Québec. Balthazar defends the idea that Québec nationalism is founded on a territorial dimension, not an ethnic one. This departure is promising and gives support to the view that Québécois are willing to build a full nation-state incorporating all of its diverse ethnic components.

Reginald A. Whitaker presents a survey of political changes in Québec before 1984, with special emphasis on the forms of Québec nationalism and their relation to class structure and the economy. Challenges posed to the Parti Québécois by the Constitution Act of 1982 and the strains of economic recession are assessed. As a complement to his outstanding contribution to the first edition of *Québec: State and Society,* Whitaker examines, through a review of developments specific to present-day Québec and Canada, why the phenomenon of globalization strengthened Québec nationalism instead of weakening it, and makes for a more complicated Canadian cauldron.

Daniel Latouche draws our attention to the many lives of Québec nationalism, and indicates the extent to which the phenomenon in Québec, rather than being self-centred, is open to the outside world and to the forces of transition. Latouche stresses the fact that Québec and Canadian nationalisms depend on each other for their dynamism, and that Québec nationalism constitutes a real opportunity to partake in the new global culture as it opens the way to as yet unforeseen challenges. In Latouche's words: "The more the new globalism forces nation-states and their central decision apparatus to fine-tune their intervention, the more the national identity and nationalism will be called upon to help in the process of effectively mobilizing resources."

Delving into Québec's distant past, **Harold Chorney** and **Andrew Molloy** question the progressive nature of Québec nationalism and challenge most experts by focusing on antisemitism, which constitutes a subtle undercurrent in Québec nationalism. To do so they examine boss politics in Montréal and conclude to the existence of an authoritarian culture. They state: "Whatever authoritarian tendency there is in Québec society appears to grow in part from the need to advance the interests of the insecure and economically deprived French majority in Montréal." Using a post-modernist framework of analysis, they argue that this tendency is always ready to resurface, even though democracy has acquired a solid base in Québec. Their model leads them to believe that historical process does not necessarily mean progress, and from there comes a warning.

PART II: SYMBOLS, IDEOLOGIES, CULTURE, AND COMMUNICATIONS

Contributions made to Part II illustrate the centrality of symbols, ideologies, culture, and communications in the construction of existing or aspiring nation-states. Each of those elements needs to be well understood if one is to comprehend how political regimes come and disappear. In addition to the better-known aspects of culture and ideologies, it was felt that some important dimensions had been left out in the first edition. Both symbols and communications need to be examined closely considering the role they have in identity-building.

This section of the book provides a basic understanding of how the symbols and myths, ideologies, and culture have varied over time, and examines the policy sector of communications. Contributions to this part are intended to focus more attention on areas that are often left out in the study of Québec politics.

Charles Taylor provides an insightful analysis of the constitutional crisis by looking at historical relationships between Québec and Canada-outside-Québec (COQ). Taylor's interpretation is that Québec stands for a liberal nationalism whereas COQ represents liberal individualism, making it difficult for the two communities to reach a compromise that is acceptable to all. While it is debatable that the two traditions are as geographically clear-cut as Taylor suggests, his interpretation allows for coalition-building between the two political entities. Taylor makes a plea for the accommodation of diversity in Québec and Canada, a diversity that goes beyond the French/English dichotomy, and encourages governments to accommodate a second level of diversity that recognizes the presence and legitimacy of a mosaic identity both in Québec and in Canada-outside-Québec.

Alain-G. Gagnon analyses the political and historical forces that underlie the constitutional crisis, and points to the fact that during the last three decades Québec has developed a de facto special status. Following the Meech Lake debacle and the 1992 referendum, English Canada (perceived in toto) finds it no longer acceptable that different political arrangements be made between Ottawa and the provinces. Asymmetry has become a dirty word. Gagnon indicates that the notion of a "distinct society" has rapidly become a symbol to be fought for in Québec and is simply not acceptable for the rest of Canada. It is clear that accommodation will be particularly difficult to achieve considering that political actors have to work with a Constitution that has yet to be supported by Québec.

Kenneth McRoberts states that English Canadians have yet to come to terms with the idea that Québec forms a distinct sociological and cultural entity. Over the years, McRoberts argues, Québec has adhered to the view that it forms a national collectivity, while English Canadians have gradually become opposed to any admission of this reality, and have demanded instead that the equality of provinces principle alone be recognized. Trudeau is said to have had a deleterious influence on the potential coming together of Québec and Canada-outside-Québec due to a concurrent push in favour of linguistic equality in provincial affairs, multiculturalism, and uniform federalism. This situation was further complicated by the entrenchment in 1982 of the Canadian Charter of Rights and Freedoms.

Fredrick Appel assesses instrumentalist and interpretative approaches as two main competing ways of studying political culture. Appel believes Canada's distinct cultural traditions have an impact on the current political process, and that it is a lack of understanding that puts the future of Canada at risk. The author argues that the English-Canadian political leadership is not willing to recognize at the political level a distinct Québec culture, and presents a complementary argument suggesting that nevertheless the Québécois identity has been positively influenced by the Canadian political order.

André-J. Bélanger defends the thesis that Québec was never isolated from outside influences, and that a close scrutiny of ideological developments in Québec confirms this interpretation. In other words, Québec has been thoroughly inspired by the ideological movements that were felt elsewhere in Western Europe and in North America. Bélanger warns us, however, not to fall prey to a reading that depicts each society as being different from one another, and stresses instead a comparative approach that allows for a study of recurrent patterns in various countries, modified in each setting by a set of social and historical conditions that give special colouration to each situation.

Marc Raboy's analysis of the media in Québec provides key information on the nature of federalism through an examination of the legal and regulatory framework prevailing in Canada. Raboy shows the extent to which Québec constitutes a distinct society, and speaks of the rootedness of Québec in North America. Raboy argues that media systems reflect the societies in which they develop, informing us as to the political and the economic factors that feed the media, and providing ammunition for the realization of "social projects." The author concludes by saying that media have a role to play as "institutions of the public sphere" and that, as such, they should render services to the population notwithstanding the question of ownership.

PART III: STATE, SOCIETY, AND POLITICS

Part III attempts to improve on the first edition by examining more closely Québec politics per se, making the links between state and society more obvious. This is done in part by looking at political parties, unions, and state structures. International relations are included to emphasize the dynamics between state actors in a federal country.

Part III contains studies of relations between state and groups by focusing on party competition, labour movement, and state structures. This new focus in the second edition is intended to provide the reader with information less easily available in the English language, as well as to give a more balanced account of sociological and institutional considerations.

A. Brian Tanguay maintains that the re-election of the Parti Québécois in 1981 challenged the dual polarization of the party system that characterized Québec politics since the election of the Parti Québécois in 1976, and reveals a politics of consensus emerging in Québec rather than a politics of convergence as it is too often argued by other specialists. The recession of the early 1980s and the referendum defeat of May 1980 are well-known components of causes of this transformation. Tanguay elaborates on the disappearance of other political forces (e.g. the Créditistes and the Union Nationale) and the mobilization around federalist and sovereigntist forces, resulting in a more defined, and narrow, political spectrum.

Roch Denis and Serge Denis offer a solid overview of state–labour relations since 1945. The authors indicate the extent to which structural changes in the economy, compounded by economic difficulties, led to profound transformations in the union movement. This contribution stresses the view that the ultimate goal of the labour movement is not to toe the government's line, but rather to have a positive influence on the policies emanating from the government. This chapter provides important information on state/society dynamics from the end of World War II to 1990, and suggests that to become politically relevant the unions need to rethink their role in partisan politics, and not associate themselves blindly with established parties.

Jacques Bourgault, Stéphane Dion, and James Iain Gow contribute a chapter on the role of central agencies in planning, coordinating, and controlling the administration of the Québec state. The Department of the Executive Council, the Department of Finance, the Treasury Board, and the Premier's Office are examined. This chapter reveals that one's comprehension of state/society relations is improved through an understanding of the central agencies. Such an examination allows for a better understanding of government transition phases, governing party influence, and the central role occupied by the premier in the policy process. The authors conclude that there has been a movement toward centralization of government activities during the last three decades in an attempt to rationalize government decisions.

Luc Bernier contributes a chapter on state-owned enterprises in Québec that meshes particularly well with the contribution on central agencies in making the reader more aware of the operative principles of the Québec state. Elaborating on the province-building literature, Bernier discusses the place of state-owned enterprises in Québec's economy. As the author assesses the choice of policy instruments on the part of state managers, he provides us with an important discussion of the Caisse de dépôt et placement, Société générale de financement, Société de développement industriel, and of the Sidérurgie québécoise. In light of the increasing popularity in the 1980s of the neoliberal agenda, Bernier suggests that it is by associating their presence to the mythical Quiet Revolution that managers of state-owned enterprises were able to stop the drive toward their once-expected dismantlement. The push and pull between pro-market ideology and interventionism during those years is also felt throughout the chapter.

Jean-Philippe Thérien, Louis Bélanger, and Guy Gosselin argue that the development of Québec's external affairs since the mid-1960s has "helped consolidate the 'reserves of legitimacy' binding the state to civil society." Following a review of Québec relations with the *Francophonie* (especially France) and the United States, the issues of external trade and immigration are closely examined as representing key components of future initiatives on the part of Québec. In the end the authors state that Québec's impressive development in the area of external relations is directly related to a double phenomenon of state-building and nation-building pursued by Québec during the last thirty years.

PART IV: DEMOGRAPHY, ETHNICITY, AND LANGUAGE

Part IV adds several new dimensions to the first edition, and makes the study of Québec something more what previous studies have accustomed us to. It innovates in the areas of intercommunal relations between aboriginal peoples, the Montréal Jewish community, the anglophones, and the francophone majority. It offers new insights in scrutinizing educational and immigration policies as well as demographic trends in an effort to understand better how Québec is facing new challenges associated with a rapidly globalizing world.

Part IV of the book deals with the evolution of immigration and educational reforms, provides an account of the demographic changes facing Québec, and gives a significant analysis of English-speaking Québécois, the issue of aboriginal communities, and the place of the Jewish community in Québec.

Taking a historical perspective, **Jerome H. Black** and **David Hagen** address the issue of immigration, and reveal that the Québec government favours an interventionist approach to assert its authority over a policy sector that has been dominated for a long time by Ottawa. According to Black and Hagen recent gains made in immigration, a situation that is depicted as being unique among federal states, is an indication that Canadian federalism accommodates Québec's special needs. The authors point to several challenges that could have a major impact on future changes to immigration policy, among which are economic benefits, humanitarian obligations, out-migration due to economic opportunities elsewhere, and demographic tendencies to be corrected.

Jacques Henripin's chapter meshes particularly well with the previous chapter, as he discusses population trends in Québec. The author suggests that it is more and more difficult for communities to blend freedom, affluence, and the raising of children. Indeed, behind these three objectives, one finds a fundamental debate on state capacities and societal goals to be achieved, making the state/society link more prominent. As is the case with immigration policy, the Québec government gives signs of wanting to be interventionist, as it attempts to elaborate a natalist policy that would allow for population growth that is commensurate with the needs of the province. To encourage a higher fertility rate among women, imaginative policies that would provoke reorganization of the workplace have to be implemented.

Henry Milner adds an important piece on education and politics, education being a key policy area that reflects state priorities in Québec over the years, in particular as it moved from a "traditional" and religious to a "modern" and secular society. Current reforms in the educational sector are proposed in Bill 107, which is intended to replace Catholic and Protestant school boards with French and English ones to adapt to a new political reality. Milner also points to the failure of current structures to address adequately Montréal's complex ethnolinguistic reality, and calls for immediate redress. Deconfessionalization and restructuring of the educational system are said to be necessary to allow for fundamental transformation of what is perceived to be a sector in need of intensive care.

Three chapters follow on the place and significance of the English-speaking minority (the population that has English as its mother tongue), the native peoples, and the Jewish community in Québec. **Ronald Rudin** argues in his chapter on the English-speaking minority that signs of disillusionment are more frequently expressed since the return of the Liberals in 1985, leading to the emergence of the Equality Party in 1989 that came to fill a void in Québec's party politics. The decision of the Bourassa government to renege on its promise to water-down language regulations is said to be disappointing to English speakers, who are said to have gradually accommodated to their recently discovered minority status in Québec. According to Rudin, disillusionment comes from an increase in the will of the English speakers to work in a French environment, coupled with a lack of progress on their recognition as first-class Quebeckers. This, in turn, is said to lead to a further weakening of the English-speaking community that is experiencing a steady erosion, and looking for opportunities elsewhere.

Éric Gourdeau provides a solid overview of Québec—aboriginal relations, along with key documents such as the Mohawk agreement and additional policy statements made by the government of Québec. Gourdeau states that Québec, probably more than any other provincial government, has demonstrated a will to recognize the rights of Québec's native peoples that goes beyond what has been proposed by other governments in Canada, though in fairness the Ontario government has lately emulated Québec's earlier initiatives. Indeed, he argues that the Québec government is willing to guarantee the rights of native peoples to self-government, to own and control land, and among other things, to have their own language, culture, and traditions. In closing, Gourdeau mentions that Québec economic difficulties, not political commitment, contributed to delaying the settling of the native peoples–Québec government land claims issue.

Pierre Anctil concludes this section with an important account of the Montréal Jewish community and its relations to the Québec state over the years. Fragmentation within the Jewish community is discussed, through an analysis of, for instance, the Sephardim (francophone Jews coming mainly from Morocco) and the Ashkenazic (anglophone Jews coming from Eastern Europe) components of the Jewish community. Anctil indicates the extent to which Jews were brought into the debate confronting French and English communities in Québec, a debate that they wanted little to do with. In conclusion, the author reviews the constitutional imbroglio following the failure of Meech Lake, and the setting up of the Bélanger-Campeau Commission where representation was made by Jews who defined themselves as Québécois and demanded that democratic principles be upheld, that individual rights be secured, and that Québec be defined as a pluralistic society.

PART V: QUÉBEC ECONOMY

Part V is intended to give readers a comprehensive understanding of the Québec economy, and concretize the links that exist between state and society. A significant and welcome corrective is made to the view that Québec capitalism emerged only recently with a contribution to the effect that Québécois capitalism has deep historical roots. Other important contributions are made in the area of political economy, demonstrating the usefulness of this approach for a more thorough understanding of Québec state and society.

Part V of this book looks at several aspects of the Québec economy: the economic transformations of the business class, the changing economic status of the francophones, the high unemployment brought by current economic policies, and continentalization.

Yves Bélanger argues that a key development in Québec since 1960 has been the consolidation of a business class, a "garde montante," that began as family enterprise to become big business. Bélanger stresses that Québec businesses have been unsuccessful at penetrating the Canadian market and should look elsewhere for new opportunities. Federal–provincial conflicts are said to be detrimental to Québec businesses, and demonstrate the urgent need to come to terms with the issue of Québec within or without Canada.

François Vaillancourt contributes a detailed empirical chapter on the economic status of the French language and francophones in Québec, and shows the extent to which major improvements took place between 1960 and 1990. The changes are not unrelated to the implementation of language laws that provided incentives for businesses to make French the language of work. In turn, the language of work is assisted by markets, ownership, and management decision. The last twenty years have seen an increase of the French-speaking market for Québec firms, an improvement of ownership figures by francophones, and the transformation in hiring practices for management positions. These factors have helped to make French an economic asset and to create an economic good.

Alain Noël argues that lower wages and higher unemployment in Québec compared to Ontario could benefit from a political economy interpretation. Québec's early rural poverty, and "unequal beginning" created a situation propitious for high unemployment and a low-wage labour market in a high-wage continent. This condition did not encourage capital formation and, by extension, diversification of Québec's economy. Basing his premises on the "historical conditions" argument, Noël proposes three models for present-day Québec to find its own way out of its precarious situation. Free market liberalism (the United States), neocorporatist tradition (Germany), and the social democratic experience that supports full employment (Sweden) are assessed, and their potential for Québec are closely examined. Noël is of the opinion that the free market economy model can only be detrimental to a peripheral economy, and he favours a model based on "concertation", or neocorporatism, as a preferable option for job creation and capital formation in a small state.

François Rocher closes this section with a key contribution on the place of Québec in the continental economy. His study of the internal political dynamic, referring to Québec–Ottawa relations, reveals that institutions matter. Rocher goes on to show how Québec has attempted, although with relatively limited success, to remove constraints imposed by the federal government on its attempts to become a full continental player. Québec's economic dependence on the United States and Canada is made clear, and the limitations imposed by such a reality are discussed. The author also speaks of a growing maturity of the francophone business class that orchestrates new initiatives to conquer distant markets. It is felt, however, that Québec's business class, due to Québec's position in the continental economy, will continue to require state support to be successful.

To conclude the volume, an annotated bibliography prepared by **Scott Evans** and **Tim Thomas** is appended with a view to provide the reader with complementary additional readings for the study of Québec. The main areas covered are: Québec economy; identity, symbols, and visions; Québec nationalism; state, society, and politics; forms of representation; demography, ethnicity, and language; and Québec and comparative politics. Finally, the Québec Charter of Human Rights and Freedoms, which may be largely unknown to students of Québec, and particularly Canadian politics, closes the volume.

I feel this book constitutes a major improvement over its predecessor, and that it provides a thorough understanding of Québec state and society suited for the 1990s.

A.-G. Gagnon,
Montréal, November 30, 1992

PART 1

QUÉBEC NATIONALISM

The Faces of Québec Nationalism

Louis Balthazar
Université Laval

Québec nationalism is one of the most misunderstood phenomena among English-speaking Canadians. With striking regularity, it has been dismissed as a remnant of the past, a temporary outburst of emotion brought about by radical social change, an exaggerated manifestation of regionalism, or a deep-seated illusion nurtured by power-hungry elites. Hence the tendency to interpret Québec nationalist dynamics as a bluff destined to subside, if and when properly called. How many times in the last thirty years have we heard about the end of Québec nationalism!

And yet there is hardly an expression of the French Québec collective ethos that has come across more constantly and more forcefully in recent times. It seems that nationalism has the virtue of reappearing at the very times when it is generally discounted. This is true not only in Québec, but also the world over. Anthony Smith wrote in 1983: "All the evidence suggests that we shall be witnessing many more ethnic upsurges and nationalist movements in the decades to come" (1983:xxxvi). The sudden collapse of many communist regimes has made that statement more accurate than anyone would have thought. For better or for worse, nationalism is alive and reinforced by its contagion, in Québec as well as in various regions of the world.

To assess the nationalism particular to Québec, it is first necessary to establish the meaning of words too often understood only vaguely, such as "nation" and "nationalism," and to emphasize the multifaceted nature of this phenomenon. It may also be useful to examine some theoretical accounts of its development. This will help us understand the evolution from a "French-Canadian" to a "Québécois" nationalism. The former fits well enough within the traditional mode of nationalism. The latter corresponds to the dynamics of the Quiet Revolution. In its moderate version, it can be described as a consensual nationalism, espoused by a majority of the Québec population. Recent developments, in the course of the 1980s, have added new dimensions to this majority nationalism.

Thus the topics discussed in this chapter will be: definitions and theories, traditional French-Canadian nationalism, Québec nationalism in the 1960s, the tenets of a moderate consensus, and recent transformations.

WHAT IS NATIONALISM?

There are many definitions of nationalism, quite different from one another, some of which even contradict each other. Most of these definitions are negative, relating to pernicious doctrine, fanatic behaviour, irrational devotion to the nation seen as an all-encompassing whole, generating hatred toward all who do not belong. Such definitions are not very useful for a Canadian analyst, given that most persons who willingly accept to be considered nationalists in Canada, be they devoted to a Canadian, a French-Canadian, a Québec, or an aboriginal nation, do not seem committed to such reckless ideology or behaviour.

One cannot deny, however, that nationalism has often produced horrible results, especially in the right-wing fascist regimes of Europe in the first part of this century. Therefore, the best definition is one that will not prejudge the bad or good effects of the phenomenon. Anthony Smith has offered the following neutral definition: "an ideological movement for the attainment and maintenance of autonomy, cohesion and individuality for a social group deemed by some of its members to constitute an actual or potential nation" (1976:1).

That brings us to the word "nation." Here is a concept that is even more fluid than nationalism. As understood by our contemporaries, it is a rather recent word having acquired its present meaning only 200 years ago, when the Rousseauist model of the social contract was applied to the French revolutionary state. The Valmy cry of "Vive la nation" almost instantly became a powerful myth soon to be reverberated throughout Europe and eventually the whole world.

The nation was understood by some, especially the Germans, as a natural concept rooted in history. But the French—and the Americans before them—saw it much more as a result of free will. According to this latter understanding, nations are the result of the association of free citizens. Of course, like the French Revolution itself, this was much more an ideal than reality. But it offered a new model of belonging, based upon citizenship and equality. A century later, Ernest Renan would define that belonging as "un plébiscite de tous les jours."

The *nation* is such an arbitrary concept that it can be said to exist "when a significant number of people in a community consider themselves to form a nation, or behave as if they formed one" (Seton Watson, 1977:5). However, if we look at the factors that allow people to consider themselves as belonging to a nation, we are led to observe that this occurs, in most instances, among people who have been related to each other by culture, i.e., habits of living, for a certain time, thus sharing a common history. So, without hardening the concept of nation and depriving it of its obvious subjective aspects, we must recognize in it some objective elements such as a common culture, common history, common aspirations, a certain territory, and almost inevitably, at least an embryonic political organization.

It has become fashionable in some intellectual circles to define the nation as the "imaginary" effect of a mere construction of the mind. Many authors, taking advantage of the relative fluidity of the concept of nation, would totally reduce it to an illusion entertained by voracious and cynical leaders who are interested in enslaving populations to national belonging at the expense of these people's freedom and development. We can easily concede that nations are artificial constructions, although they reveal themselves to be quite enduring and resilient, and usually rest on specific sociological foundations. Some other theories may make this case convincing, while accounting for the advent of nationalism or the passage from one form of nationalism to another.

For Karl Deutsch (1966, 1979) nationalism is essentially an effect of modern communications, more specifically, of "social mobilization," which is "the shift of people away from a subsistence economy and local isolation into [*sic*] exposure to the demonstration effects of more modern technology and practices, to exposure to mass media of communication" (Deutsch 1979:302). As long as populations are not mobilized, as long as they cluster in villages where individuals communicate little with just a few others, national belonging is not very relevant. But when great numbers of people are subject to urban-type communication (although not necessarily living in cities), it becomes impossible for them to rely on old forms of solidarity such as the family, religious affiliation, the village, or the region. They tend to look for new forms of allegiance. They rely more and more on a common language and a common culture, that is, a common set of meanings. The national setting responds to this need. "The greater the need for people to communicate in order to make a living, the greater is the importance of language in their lives, and the greater is their potential motivation to prefer a language of their own" (Deutsch, 1979:303). We shall see later how well this fits with the rapid urbanization of Québec in the postwar period. It is easy to see for the moment how nationalism can result from the shock of a recently mobilized population when communications are dominated by people who do not speak its language.

Ernest Gellner also refers to the importance of a "school-mediated ... idiom" in the production of nationalism. "It is the establishment of an anonymous, impersonal society ... in place of a previous complex structure of local groups, sustained by folk cultures ..." (Gellner, 1983:57). For Gellner, nationalism may be a construction, but it reflects the *real* phenomenon of modernization and urbanization: "when mobility and context-free communication come to be of the essence of social life, the culture in which one has been taught to communicate becomes the core of one's identity" (1983:61). Thus nations may be fostered, consolidated, and created, but they usually rest on old cultural links and on a fresh need for people to regroup themselves in order to find their way in a forest of necessary communications.

Such theories may account for the rise of modern nationalism in industrialized societies, but they do not tell us anything about traditional forms of nationalism. For this, we must look at the model of Eastern European nationalisms in the 19th century, such as depicted by Hans Köhn. While the French Revolution had promoted an egalitarian nation based on enlightened concepts and civil rights, the Germans and East Europeans reacted with a consciousness of national identity resting mainly on cultural traditions and the "Volksgeist" as the nonpolitical provider of energy and solidarity (Köhn, 1956:4). This traditional type of reaction to modernity corresponds well enough to what was called nationalism in Québec between 1840 and 1960. Let us look at what was left of it during the years prior to the Quiet Revolution.

FRENCH-CANADIAN NATIONALISM

Traditional nationalism was pervasive yet questioned in Québec during the period following World War II. It was still the prevailing ideology, although it appeared more and more in contradiction with the day-to-day life of most Quebeckers. An ideology conceived for a stable, rural society was bound to become an empty shell among an urbanized population subject to the effects of industrialization.

It is, in fact, rather amazing that such an ideology endured so long when we consider that Québec was one of the first Canadian provinces to undergo the Industrial Revolution. The majority of its population was urban as early as 1921. But French-Canadian clerical and "petit bourgeois" elites could keep alive the traditional ideal for some thirty years, partly because the old parish structure (conceived for rural life) was reproduced in cities, and partly because consciousness of the new conditions of life was very slow to mature within a population not culturally attuned to capitalist enterprise. Industrialization was considered as the realm of "les Anglais" while French Canadians were encouraged to concentrate on "survivance," i.e., the preservation of their culture mainly expressed in language and religion. Of course, this official gospel was not followed by everyone. It was always questioned and criticized by some, but it was never seriously challenged by any other well-structured ideology until the 1950s.

This traditional nationalism had several characteristics. First, it was predominantly cultural, not political. This is not to say that it did not reach the electoral pulpits and the governmental milieux: French-Canadian nationalists made themselves heard in Parliament in Ottawa as well as in the legislature in Québec City. We can only remember the struggles of Honoré Mercier, Henri Bourassa, and many others. It is revealing, however, that this nationalism rarely reached the level of political realization in that it never produced a strong, effective political organization. Bourassa's nationalist party in the 1910s, the "Action libérale nationale" in the 1930s, and the "Bloc populaire" in the 1940s were not very successful organizations. It is noteworthy that the most prestigious leader of the nationalist movement in Québec during these years was a priest, Lionel Groulx, who spoke of a French state, but always kept from getting involved in politics. Maurice Duplessis was the one who skilfully reaped political benefits out of nationalism, but he was much more of a politician than a genuine nationalist.

Second, French-Canadian nationalism was not concerned with the economic dimension. It would not encourage its supporters to engage in economic activities for the promotion of national interests. It is true that some nationalist voices (Errol Bouchette, Édouard Montpetit) were calling for attention to economic issues, but they were mostly preaching in the desert. Alphonse Desjardins had a better fate with his cooperative movement, but it was long confined to small-scale organizations without much effect on the Québec economy as a whole. Some nationalists addressed the vital sector of natural resources and called for the nationalization of electric power in the 1930s, but they failed to obtain anything until the 1940s when their program was only partially realized with the creation of a small Hydro-Québec.

Religion was on the nationalist agenda much more than the economy. The fact that the French-Canadian identity was closely linked to Catholicism can be considered as a third feature of traditional nationalism in Québec. Again, though, there were dissident voices: free thinkers were always present, sometimes even quite active in French-Canadian society. Nonetheless, it is almost impossible to imagine a nationalist message before the late 1950s without the obliged reference to Catholic traditions. The French language was considered the "guardian of the faith," and as late as the early 1960s, a respected nationalist writer could still affirm that "French Canada will be Catholic or will not be."

Fourth, French-Canadian nationalism was basically inward-looking. Again, this is not a universal characteristic: the Québec government had representatives in Paris, London, and Brussels, for long periods. Some Québec premiers, such as Chapleau and Mercier, travelled extensively. Others, such as Gouin and Taschereau, were very open-minded toward British and American industrialists. But nationalist leaders were generally not interested in international developments; they were, above all, concerned with the protection of French Canadians against outside pressures such as anglophone North America, immigration, and secular Europe. Catholic France, the Vatican, and missionary enterprises were the only windows in the tight edifice of French Canada.

Consequently, as a fifth characteristic, the French-Canadian nation was not open to newcomers. It assimilated a few elements, particularly some Catholic Irish, but it was usually not easy to integrate into French Canada. The nation was conceived as an ethnic entity and its racial homogeneity was often stressed, although it was much less homogeneous than was thought. There had been, in particular, quite a few marriages between French Canadians and Indians.

Such was the French-Canadian nation, as it was still defined by Québec elites between 1945 and 1960, but this image was less and less accepted by the general population. Nationalist leaders were not very popular during that period, especially among the youth. Although this image was routinely projected by the Duplessis government, it did not correspond to a society that was becoming more and more complex and dynamic.

Those five aspects of nationalism were challenged, criticized, and contradicted in social life in Québec during the postwar years. Many talked about doing more than preserving provincial jurisdictions for the government of Québec, favouring a more meaningful autonomy. In the early 1950s the "Chambres de Commerce" pressured Duplessis into creating a provincial income tax and instituting a commission on constitutional problems. It turned out that the report of the commission, headed by Judge Thomas Tremblay (Québec, 1956), tabled in 1956, would become the constitutional Bible of the Quiet Revolution. In this document, two options were already formulated for the future of Québec: decentralization of federal power or special status. The fate of the French-Canadian nation was being associated with the province of Québec.

As exemplified by the action of the Chambers of Commerce and the importance given to taxation power, more and more interest was taken in financial and economic matters. As prosperity raised the standard of living to unprecedented levels, people became more materialistic and disenchanted with the ethereal message of traditional nationalism. On the religious front, the challenge was less direct: collusion between some clerical authorities and political power was denounced, but it was much more the use of religion for secular ends that was criticized than the omnipresence of religious leaders. There was opposition to clericalism while religious pluralism was discreetly advocated.

French Canadians were slowly coming out of their cocoons: young elites were travelling in Europe and studying in France. Television was opening windows on the whole world. A young reporter, René Lévesque, was conducting a very popular show ("Point de mire") dealing chiefly with international affairs. As French Canadians were becoming more affluent, they found more frequent opportunities to travel out of their region. Their ethnic consciousness was also questioned as they came in contact with English-speaking compatriots, and with immigrants in Montréal. For some it meant assimilation; for others it created an aspiration to a new form of self-assertion where the word "culture" would supersede the word "race," which was not to be used after the revelation of Nazi Germany's horrors.

There were two attitudes taken toward the old nationalism that was still being kept alive by aging elites. One was total rejection and criticism in the name of liberalism: this was the antinationalism well represented by the periodical *Cité libre* and its most well-known writers, Pierre Elliott Trudeau and Gérard Pelletier. Some in this group advocated social democracy, and others, a small minority, were advocating socialism. Federal institutions such as the CBC, the National Film Board, and the Canada Council seemed to them much more appealing for the development of a francophone culture than the old-fashioned Québec organizations still dominated by the church.

Another attitude consisted in countering the traditional French-Canadian nationalism with another form of nationalism that would be political, concerned with economics, secular, outward-looking, and territorial. People such as André Laurendeau, Jean-Marc Léger, and Michel Brunet were representing this trend in *L'Action nationale* and *Le Devoir* while the federalists were more present in Radio-Canada and the Faculté des sciences sociales at Laval University (see Behiels, 1985).

The Quiet Revolution in the 1960s was to be, in the beginning at least, an amalgam of these two attitudes. Both federalists and nationalists were ardently calling for and supporting the long-needed reforms of Québec society and politics. It is only with the progress toward a new form of nationalism that some federalists would depart from the trend.

THE SHAPING OF QUÉBEC NATIONALISM

This new nationalism may be seen as a continuation of the traditional French-Canadian ideology. It is dedicated, as much as the latter if not more, to the preservation of a francophone nation in North America. But in more than one way, it is radically different from its predecessor. In fact, for many of its followers, this nationalism could not be espoused without the total rejection of the old one. A dose of antinationalism was needed before adopting the Québec nationalism of the 1960s. How can we account for the rapid rise of this movement among people who had rejected the nationalist doctrine of their forefathers? The theories developed by Karl Deutsch and Ernest Gellner may be particularly helpful in answering this question.

In a sense, French-speaking Quebeckers had been undergoing "social mobilization" for quite some time before the Quiet Revolution, as they had been urbanized since the beginning of the century. But, as mentioned above, they had not yet manifested a real consciousness of that change. They were more or less living in clusters and had not yet become involved in frequent and intense social commu-nication. Two phenomena would accelerate this movement during the period fol-lowing World War II: the generalized use of the automobile and the expansion of television. By the 1950s, the majority of French Canadians had moved into the world of communications. They realized, more vividly than ever, that Canadian communications were controlled by the English-speaking majority. Long-distance phone calls, railway transportation, air travel, staying in large urban hotels, eating in restaurants, shopping in downtown Montréal, doing business—all of these activities required the use of the English language, even in the very French prov-ince of Québec.

As Deutsch has shown, this alienation of an entire population submitted to the use of an unfamiliar language can produce assimilation. And this has occurred in Québec as well as in other Canadian provinces. However, according to figures col-lected by Deutsch, assimilation progresses five times more slowly than social mobilization. "This means that, on the average, for every five persons mobilized only one becomes assimilated by the predominant ... language or culture, while four become potential supporters or potential recruits for some self-assertive nationalist movement" (Deutsch, 1979:305). In the case of Canada, we could say that, among socially mobilized French-speaking minorities outside Québec, assimilation may be produced almost as fast as mobilization, given the small pro-portion of francophones in the communication area. Thus, when St. Boniface becomes a suburb of Winnipeg, it is submitted to intense pressures to assimilate. Hence the law regarding French-speaking minorities in Canada: the further they are from Québec, the higher their assimilation rate.

In Québec, given the mass of francophones, social mobilization has more often produced nationalism rather than assimilation. In the mid-1950s, for example, as more and more French-speaking artists were finding an outlet in Radio-Canada, they flocked in large numbers on what was then Dorchester Boulevard, in its west-ern part, at what had been formerly the Ford Hotel, between Mackay and Bishop streets, where the new CBC studios were. This was an area of Montréal where the French language was almost as foreign as in Victoria, British Columbia (Québec was officially bilingual!). How could these communicators *par excellence* not be shocked when they met the wall of English unilingualism as they moved through surrounding restaurants and bars. René Lévesque dates his nationalism to that period, especially the strike of 1958, when francophone artists became aware of the CBC's two solitudes.

Ironically enough, Radio-Canada, a federal institution devised to bring Canadi-ans closer to each other, was one of the institutions that contributed the most to the development of Québec nationalism. When television was established in Canada in 1952, there was no way to avoid creating two networks, and there was no way to escape the harsh reality: the French-Canadian population was concentrated in Québec. It would have been totally extravagant to extend the network all across Canada during the 1950s. As a result, for all practical purposes, the French net-work of the CBC became a Québec network. What it did was bring French-speak-ing Quebeckers closer to one another, sending them daily, in Chicoutimi and Gaspé as well as in Hull, a mirror of themselves forming a nation. If the Québec nation has been created, constructed, imagined, this has been done, in great part, within an institution regulated by the government of Canada. Radio-Canada did not even bring English-speaking Quebeckers closer to the francophone majority, as anglophones generally turned down this occasion to integrate into Québec, learn the French language, and appreciate the Québec culture. To this day, there are more francophones in Québec who watch English television than the other way around.

Thus French Canadians living in Québec saw the need to create and consolidate their own communication network, or in other words, to organize and promote their own nationhood. They also came to realize, as the example of Radio-Canada shows clearly, that this network was almost coextensive with the territory of the province of Québec and had little future outside Québec. For all practical purposes, French Canada had to be equated with Québec if it was to be a modern, dynamic network. This is, in all likelihood, what Jean Lesage meant when he said in 1964: "Québec is the political expression of French Canada and it plays the role of a homeland for all those who speak our language in Canada" (*Le Devoir*, 20 September 1964; Morin, 1973:67–68).

Jean-Jacques Bertrand sent the same message when he said: "Without Québec, there could be French minorities, but there would not be a French Canada" (Morin, 1973:69). Only in Québec could there be a real, well-organized, and authentic modern French-speaking society. This is how French-Canadian nationalism came to be superseded by Québec nationalism.

Thus were laid the foundations for the actions of the Québec state. There is no doubt that the main protagonist of the new nation was the government of the province of Québec. As the reforms of the Quiet Revolution took place, under the supervision of a revamped civil service, a new middle class was rising and looking for a means to legitimize its authority. It found a fertile ground in the new sense of community acquired by French-speaking Quebeckers and immediately endeavoured to foster and promote this new Québec allegiance. A special role could be conceived for the government of Québec because it was presiding over the development of a unique, specific culture, because it was the only truly francophone goverment in North America. "Quebeckers have only one powerful institution: their government. Now they want to use this institution to build a new era...." Such was the language of Jean Lesage in 1963 (*Le Devoir*, 10 October, 8). Obviously, Québec's political leaders were well engaged in nation-building if not nation-creating. A new nationalism was developed around the existence of the provincial state, which typically ennobled itself with the new designation: "L'État du Québec."

Ernest Gellner points out quite appropriately that "nationalism emerges only in milieux in which the existence of the state is already very much taken for granted" (1983:4). Let us go one step further and assert that the more the state is present, powerful, and interventionist, the more intense nationalism will be. This may mean that nationalism will be fostered by the state to rationalize its interventions. It may also mean that a national consciousness will arise as a resistance to state intervention and its invariable efforts to create homogeneity.

When we look at the rise of the Québec state during the Quiet Revolution, we may be so impressed by this dynamism that we tend to overlook the broader context of the Canadian state and its gigantic progress during the period following World War II. There had been a "quiet revolution" in Ottawa during these years, although it was less sudden and dramatic than the one in Québec. A whole class of civil servants, intellectuals, and politicians had been involved for quite some time, since the 1930s, after Canada gained its sovereignty, in building a Canadian nation. The Rowell-Sirois Report, tabled in 1940, responded to the aspirations of this Ottawa class when it proposed that the federal government take over provincial responsibility in order to pursue "national" goals such as equalization of standards of living and unemployment insurance.

After World War II, that program would be implemented in an atmosphere of rising Canadian nationalism. Canadian citizenship was established in 1947. Under a French-Canadian prime minister, Louis St. Laurent (1948–57), Canada was becoming a middle power, the Canada Council was created, and the federal government moved aggressively in the fields of culture and education. More and more, the words "nation" and "national" became part of the current vocabulary in Ottawa and, to some extent, throughout English Canada. As a result of the new governmental assertiveness and intervention, a Canadian nation was in the making.

The Tremblay Commission, mentioned above, was created by Québec as a counterpart to Ottawa's new policies and sense of nationhood. Obviously, French Canadians, at least those living in Québec, did not feel comfortable in the Canadian "nation," which did not reflect their feelings of togetherness. Thus the Quiet Revolution can be seen very much as a response to the conception of the welfare state and its corresponding nationalism elaborated in Ottawa in the postwar years. Almost all new policies that came from Québec may be analyzed as responses to what Ottawa was doing. In fact, many of the new policy-makers in Québec had been trained in Ottawa.

Ironically again, just as in the case of the CBC, a Canadian "national" enterprise turned out to be instrumental in fostering Québec nationalism. One could even go so far as to say that the more you try to unite Canada, the more you unite Québec. Québec nationalism is the illegitimate child of Canadian nationalism. The Canadian nation-state gave rise to the Québec nation-state.

This may constitute the striking paradox of Canadian history: that the greatest architects of "national" unity, the Liberal prime ministers from Québec, Wilfrid Laurier, Louis St. Laurent, and Pierre Trudeau, have all been more successful in uniting English Canada than in creating a new Canadian consciousness among their fellow French-speaking Quebeckers. Not that they were unpopular in Québec. They regularly delivered the vote from their province and filled Parliament with French-Canadian faithful. But they ended up reinforcing nationalism in Québec. Henri Bourassa's nationalist party was a result of Laurier's policies, and as we noted above, the Tremblay Report and the nationalist spirit of the Quiet Revolution were a direct response to St. Laurent's new Canadianism. As for Pierre Trudeau, it has become obvious that his concept of a united bilingual Canada and his Charter of Rights and Freedoms have received a much better reception outside Québec than within, and that post–Meech Lake nationalism in Québec is a belated but vigorous reaction to Trudeau's manoeuvres of 1981–82.

The irony might be carried even further by asserting that the new Canada that has resulted from this contemporary evolution is more "French," in a special way, than the pragmatic federation that evolved through the turn of the century. Borrowing this idea from Christian Dufour (1989), I mean that Canada has become less pragmatic, and more declaratory, stressing principles such as in an official

Charter of Rights and Freedoms, in the French tradition. Thus, by moving closer to the Jacobin model of indivisible sovereignty, Canada is throwing gasoline on the fire of Québec nationalism that may, in turn, develop a Jacobinism of its own. What is even more obvious is that Canada, paradoxically, resembles more than ever the United States, the very model that it was to repudiate in the very beginning. There would be no Canada today if French Canadians, content with being recognized as a distinct society by the Québec Act of 1774, had not refused the offer to join the American Revolution and if the Loyalists had not separated from the enterprise of creating an American nation. There would be no Canada if British subjects to the north had not refused to form a nation.

Quebeckers are willing to subscribe to some form of Canadian federation, but their nationalism will always oppose an ideal that would have them "pledge allegiance to one nation, indivisible" on the American model, unless it would be a Québec nation. Even the latter, however, does not correspond to the aspirations of most Québec nationalists, for the type of nationalism that developed during the 1960s around the claims of the Québec government did not lead to the ideal of total sovereignty. Of course, the "indépendantistes" can claim to represent the clear expression of Québec nationalism and that comes close to the textbook definition, but that never corresponded to the wishes of the majority of Quebeckers. What were these wishes?

THE TENETS OF QUÉBEC MAJORITY NATIONALISM

Oddly enough, the majority of Quebeckers never accepted, during the 1970s and the 1980s, the ideals proposed by their two most venerated political leaders. Pierre Trudeau and René Lévesque were certainly among the most respected politicians Québec has ever known. The first may have been more admired than loved, but he succeeded in rallying the Québec vote in all his electoral battles, including the most important one, the 1980 referendum. Yet Quebeckers never endorsed his conception of Canada, bilingual but multicultural or, more to the point, monocultural, with a strong centre, a *nation* that meant more than the sum of its parts. The referendum slogan was "Mon NON est québécois," so that Quebeckers felt they would not be giving up their Québec allegiance by saying no to sovereignty-association. Trudeau was wrong in announcing the end of Québec nationalism the day after the referendum. Claude Ryan, his temporary ally, could have corrected the prime minister if he had dared to consult him. The same Ryan, a loyal federalist, also strongly opposed the patriation process and refused, as leader of the Québec Liberal Party, to attend the signing of the new Constitution on 17 April 1982. Through the voice of their representatives in the National Assembly (freshly elected in April 1981), Quebeckers repudiated Trudeau's new Canada.

René Lévesque was immensely popular in Québec. He would form a government in 1976 and again, in spite of the referendum defeat, in 1981. But Quebeckers, despite the confidence they had in him, turned down his sovereignty-association project for which he had fought for thirteen years.

As a consequence, during the whole decade of the 1970s, Quebeckers were polarized by their leaders between two options that a majority of them repudiated. What was then the ideal that suited this majority? What were the tenets of this consensus nationalism? The idea, as it was phrased by Jean Lesage, that "Québec is the political expression of French Canada" (quoted above) is already an answer. It comes close to saying that Québec claims to be a "national state" for the French Canadians within Canada. Daniel Johnson, for his part, has given, in 1966, one of the clearest replies to the relentless question, "What does Québec want?":

> As a basis for its nationhood, it wants to be master of its own decision-making in what concerns the human growth of its citizens—that is to say education, social security, and health in all their aspects—their economic affirmation—the power to set up the economic and financial institutions they feel are required—their cultural development—not only the arts and letters, but also the French language—and the Québec community's external development—its relations with certain countries and international bodies. (Morin, 1976:97)

This is the kind of autonomy deemed necessary for Québec by a majority of its citizens. It takes the form of nationalism because this was constantly denied by Ottawa and most other provinces. Claude Morin expressed it well:

> [All Québec premiers] have borne unrelenting faith ... to what might be termed "a certain idea of Québec." And basically, that "certain idea of Québec" is no more than the badly-expressed and hesitant notion of a "Québec that is certain." In any case, it has nothing to do with lingering regionalism. This, however, Ottawa has never understood, and in all probability quite honestly.... But Québec nationalism, that age-old and instinctive quest for the "land of Québec," has absolutely nothing in common with the elements of the usual federal equation. (Morin, 1976:96)

Almost twenty years after these lines were written, they remain as valid and relevant as they were in the early 1970s. In the summer of 1991, the "certain idea of Québec" is less recognized than ever by the rest of Canada. Yet, the theme of "the distinct society" has been recurrent in Canada's history since the Québec Act of 1774. It had been emphasized by the *Preliminary Report of the Royal Commission on Bilingualism and Biculturalism* (1965) through the concept of the two majorities. It was again reasserted by the *Report of the Task Force on National Unity* (Pepin-Robarts) in 1979: "Québec is distinctive and should, within a viable Canada, have the powers necessary to protect and develop its distinctive character; any political solution short of this would lead to the rupture of Canada" (87).

Only in 1987 was this distinctiveness officially endorsed by the federal government, as well as the nine other provincial premiers. We know it was rejected in 1990, not so much by two recalcitrant legislatures as by a majority of the Canadian population. Premier Bourassa had no choice but to declare, on that fateful eve of Québec's national holiday, that "Quebeckers are free to assume their own destiny, to determine their political status and to assure their economic, social and cultural development." Beyond the technicalities that denied the implementation of the Meech Lake agreements, it is the new Canada, with its Charter spirit, that rejected, so to speak as a foreign body, the minimal expression of the modern idea of Québec. It is no wonder that nationalism was aroused.

The Commission on the Political and Constitutional Future of Québec, chaired by Michel Bélanger and Jean Campeau, became the channel *par excellence* of Québec nationalists' aspirations during the fall and winter of 1990–91. It produced a consensus that may be seen as reflecting the nationalism of the majority: at long last, there must be a choice—either Québec's claims will be recognized or

Quebeckers will have to opt for sovereignty, which is still not considered their first choice. The Bélanger-Campeau Report, in contrast to the Québec Liberal Party's Allaire Report tabled a month before, does not offer a long list of powers that are needed for Québec. It nevertheless enumerates parameters that may be seen as an echo of Daniel Johnson's claims twenty-five years before. Necessary changes to the Constitutions must have in common:

- the necessity of creating a new relationship between Québec and the rest of Canada, based on the recognition of and respect for the identity of Quebeckers and their right to be different;
- a division of powers and responsibilities that assures Québec of exclusive authority over those matters and domains that already fall under its exclusive jurisdiction;
- the exclusive attribution to Québec of powers and responsibilities related to its social, economic, and cultural developments as well as to language (*Report of the Commission on the Political and Constitutional Future of Québec*, 1991:48).

To sum up, Québec majority nationalism consists of the struggle of the French-speaking Quebeckers to exist collectively and to have this collective existence recognized politically. In the event of meaningful recognition, if the French character of Québec is seen as secured, that nationalism would be satisfied and Quebeckers would be quite willing to give their allegiance to Canada. When public opinion polls reflect a rise in the popularity of the idea of sovereignty, it only means that Quebeckers' secular claim to political recognition is felt as not being likely to be accepted by the rest of Canada. Québec nationalists, in their majority, definitely consider sovereignty as a means to an end, not as an end in itself. Moreover, given social developments during the 1980s, the concept of a strong Québec, as well as the concept of sovereignty, has come to be regarded in a different way. By the early 1990s, Québec nationalism has taken a new shape.

A NEW NATIONALISM IN THE 1980S

The 1980 referendum brought relief throughout Canada. In Québec itself, however, it turned out to produce a malaise, not only among wounded supporters of the "yes" side, but also within the "victorious" majority, for that victory soon appeared to be rather meaningless. Quebeckers had said no to a project, but they had not said yes to anything. The Québec boat had no direction. When René Lévesque committed himself to preserving a status within Canada, he was no more credible than Trudeau who pretended to respect provincial autonomy. The November 1981 *coup de force*, when Chrétien isolated the Québec delegates overnight from their allies in seven other provinces, took Quebeckers by surprise and found them more dispirited than shocked. The April 1982 Constitution proclamation was largely unattended and ignored by Quebeckers. Coupled with the most severe economic recession since World War II, it left them in a state of torpor and morosity that may be compared to the Canadiens' state of mind after the failure of the rebellions of 1837 and 1838. Like these events, it signalled the failure of a political class. The Parti Québécois did not die like the Parti Patriote of 1838. However, the political spirit of the Quiet Revolution was waning. Quebeckers may not have been as outraged by the 1982 Constitution as their ancestors by the Durham Report, but the radical effects of the Charter on the idea of Canada turned out to be felt as strongly as Lord Durham's recommendations.

Just as in 1840, a new elite would take over as the guiding light of the French-Canadian collectivity. The rising business class of Québec would take over the role of politicians and civil servants like the church leaders replaced the Patriot elite in the 19th century. The atmosphere of the 1980s was one of disenchantment with the role played by the state of Québec. The referendum was a "no" to sovereignty-association. The Constitution was a "no" to a strong Québec within Canada. The recession also meant a "no" to significant government leadership. Québec nationalism had revolved around a Keynesian Québec state born out of the Quiet Revolution, a state that claimed to play a "national" role with the possible option of sovereignty if that failed. By 1982, all of that was gone and Québec's political class was suddenly losing its prestige. In an international neoliberal context, Quebeckers would turn to the leaders of private enterprise as a source of inspiration. Unexpectedly, this new elite would eventually inspire a new nationalism.

In fact, Québec's new entrepreneurial class was a natural fruit of the nationalism of the Quiet Revolution. The latter was seen by many, probably wrongly, as being coupled with a spirit of social democracy. If looked at more closely, the great economic endeavours of the 1960s were much more liberal in their intent than they were social democratic. True, they were launched by the state and heralded a mixed economy, but most of them were not so much aimed at income redistribution or social solidarity as at creating and consolidating francophone private enterprises. Hydro-Québec is a state corporation, but it contributed to the rise of the entrepreneurial spirit among Québec engineers and managers. The General Investment Society (Société générale de financement) was created to help small and medium-sized firms subsist. The Québec Deposit and Investment Fund (Caisse de dépôt et placement) was also created for the same purpose and contributed to spectacular takeovers by francophone business people. SIDBEC also became semi-private, and so did many government-inspired corporations.

Québec nationalism was associated, during these years, with its outspoken cultural and political manifestations. Its economic dimension appeared less striking; for it had to evolve more slowly. But its effects were to be enduring and would fully manifest themselves only in the 1980s. So, quite naturally, some high civil servants who were the pride of the Quiet Revolution became the great financiers of the 1980s.

Like all private entrepreneurs, Québec business people would tend to downplay the role of the state in society, though they owed a lot to that state. They would not forget, however, their allegiance to Québec society at large, especially when they were confronted with the traditional English-speaking Canadian business elite. Just as the Quiet Revolution created a general communication network, there is a new francophone economic network in Québec that allows many business people to express their allegiance to Québec through their actions. Not that these people are all outspoken nationalists, not that they are all ready to commit themselves to a strong Québec government, but they undeniably show a willingness to stress their francophone collective existence and the relevance of the recognition of Québec as a distinct society.

The cooperative movement has evolved in a somewhat parallel way. It has been a very special private enterprise that, due to its original intent, has always been coloured with some nationalism. The rise of the entrepreneurial spirit in the 1980s has given a new aura to the Desjardins movement, which has become a symbol of Québec's achievement and economic confidence. No doubt its leaders are more naturally inclined to take a nationalist position.

Business people, who are undeniably very influential over the government, especially the Liberal government but also, to a great extent, the Parizeau-Landry wing of the Parti Québécois, have gradually given a new orientation for Québec nationalism. As they are the interpreters of contemporary world trends, particularly the rising economic interdependence in the global economy, they tend to emphasize a side of Québec nationalism that has brought a majority of Quebeckers to value association with other states and international dialogue. As a consequence, even sovereignty had to be coupled with economic association. Free trade with the United States had to be supported, and eventually, for most members of Québec's new elite, a Canadian union will have to be preserved.

This view of things seems to be well reflected within a majority of the Québec population. It produces a new type of identity for Quebeckers: a people proud of their achievements, protective of their identity, but more outward-looking than ever. In 1988, for instance, in the same breath, Quebeckers could pressure Bourassa into taking a strong stand on the language of commercial advertising (Bill 178) and support the Mulroney government on free trade with the United States. There is certainly a link between this openness to the outside and the tendency to insist on securing a linguistic identity.

It has become obvious that Québec's best economic achievements are related to exports and a dynamic presence abroad. Successes of firms such as Bombardier, Cascades, Teleglobe, Vidéotron, SNC, not only in North America, but in Europe and around the world, have persuaded nationalists that a better status for Québec (within or without Confederation) has to be coupled with strong links with the outside world. Given the momentum of institutions such as the General Agreement on Tariffs and Trade (GATT) and the Canada–U.S. Free Trade Agreement (even if it has to be renegotiated by a sovereign Québec), it is now almost impossible to envisage an isolated Québec, whatever happens to its constitutional status.

While Québec nationalism is connected with a form of internationalism, it is also more and more compatible with pluralism at home. As such, the passage from the ethnic nature of French-Canadian nationalism to a territorial conception of the nation indicated a departure such that, in its very dynamic, Québec nationalism became incompatible with an ethnic definition of the nation. Nonetheless, Québec nationalists were slow to open their nationhood to anglophones and newly migrated people. Many nationalists in Québec tended to exclude, in deed if not in word, those not considered as real French Canadians. Given Québec's low birthrate and the necessity of making French the main language of communication in Québec, it became necessary to call for the integration of immigrants and, to some extent, of anglophones into French Québec. Again, however, Québec nationalists were more negative than positive, that is, they condemned the unwillingness of some groups to speak French and integrate, but did little to encourage them to do so.

The irrational and counterproductive nature of that attitude appeared more and more obvious by the 1980s, when the new generation of Quebeckers tended to be much more liberal than their parents in their definition of Québec. Some of those who went to school in Montréal under Bill 101 no longer defined a Québécois as a French Canadian. It is true that some schools have been polarized along racial or linguistic lines in spite of their official French character, but that does not seem to be the case for the majority of educational institutions. Some immigrant children's resistance to speaking French may come from the fact that their parents are still unable to speak the official language. This may change when the effect of Bill 101 is felt on an entire generation, but at this point there are certainly many more Québec nationalists willing to define their social belonging in pluralistic terms than just ten years ago.

Whatever the situation is, it is fair to say that Québec nationalism has no sense and no future if it is defined in ethnic terms. This does not mean that it will be easy for Quebeckers to follow the American and the French tradition of pluralistic nation-building. This path will be difficult for a small people like Québec, speaking a language that has such a minority status in North America and even in the world at large, although the French language has kept a remarkable aptitude to express universality. It will be especially difficult at a time when both the French and the Americans are showing signs of fatigue and decadence in their multiethnic ideal. France no longer seems to be the "terre d'asile" it was considered for years. And the recognition of ethnic groups in the United States, if carried too far through a dogmatic "political correctness," may engender the dissolution of national cohesion. Québec may follow suit in stressing multiculturalism, but that should not prevent integration, which, properly understood, is still the only viable social model.

The aboriginal populations are not to be included in this process. Through their leaders' discourse, they refuse integration and demand, in the same vein as Quebeckers, more autonomy. Québec nationalists should not oppose such a claim, and it seems that they do not. The Parti Québécois, for instance, produced a very liberal platform at its convention in the winter of 1991, in respect to aboriginal nations' political autonomy. Nationalists in the Liberal Party may have a harder time reconciling the Great Whale/James Bay project with respect for the Cree populations, but it seems that a growing number of young Liberal nationalists, as sensitive to the environment as they are to national aspirations, are not comfortable with Hydro-Québec's megaprojects.

The Oka Crisis of 1990 was perceived by the anglophone media as a confrontation between First Nations and Québec nationalists. This was not the case, although some Indian Mohawks confused Québec nationalism with white supremacy, and the behaviour of some Quebeckers did reinforce this view. The situation was more complex and the old tradition of accommodation between the French Canadians and the Indians, dating back to the early days of colonization through the formation of a large Métis population and the support for Louis Riel, is still alive. It seems that the Québec population, by and large, feels closer to the aboriginal peoples than the rest of Canadians, although racism and injustice always threaten to resurface (see Philpot, 1991). It is true that nationalisms often tend to oppose each other, but there is great potential for mutual respect between Quebeckers and native peoples.

Québec nationalism has grown quite strong in 1990, and public opinion in Québec has come to endorse sovereignty to an unprecedented degree. However, nationalism has taken a new form, and is now tempered by an international consciousness and a growing recognition of pluralism at home. Even if Quebeckers come to endorse sovereignty, that sovereignty is likely to be envisaged as being limited by the necessities of the contemporary world, as they are perceived by Quebeckers.

If nationalism can be defined as an intemperate manifestation of chauvinism, this is less and less true of contemporary Québec nationalism. As we have seen, the passage from a French-Canadian traditional national consciousness to the new idea of a Québec allegiance has meant a gradual redefinition of Quebeckers' identity and a move from ethnic to territorial nationalism. As it was defined by the majority, this nationalism was content with claiming political recognition within Canada. The new nationalism that took shape in the 1980s is even more moderate in its conception, although it may be pushed toward sovereignty by the recently "chartered" Canadians.

REFERENCES

Behiels, Michael, 1985, *Prelude to Québec's Quiet Revolution*, Montréal: McGill-Queen's University Press.
Canada, 1965, *A Preliminary Report of the Royal Commission on Bilingualism and Biculturalism*, Ottawa: Queen's Printer.
Deutsch, Karl, 1966, *Nationalism and Social Communication*, Cambridge, Mass.: M.I.T. Press.
Deutsch, Karl, 1979, *Tides Among Nations*, New York: The Free Press.
Dufour, Christian, 1989, *Le défi québécois*, Montréal: L'Hexagone.
Gellner, Ernest, 1983, *Nations and Nationalism*, Ithaca, N.Y.: Cornell University Press.
Köhn, Hans, 1956, *The Idea of Nationalism*, New York: Macmillan.
Morin, Claude, 1973, *Le combat québécois*, Montréal: Boréal Express.
Morin, Claude, 1976, *Québec versus Ottawa: The Struggle for Self-Government*, Toronto: University of Toronto Press.
Philpot, Robin, 1991, *Oka: dernier alibi du Canada anglais,* Montréal: VLB.
Quebec, 1956, Royal Commission of Inquiry on Constitutional Problems. Report. 5 volumes. Quebec: Queen's Printer.
Quebec, 1991, *Report of the Commission on the Political and Constitutional Future of Québec*, Québec: National Assembly.
Seton Watson, Hugh, 1977, *Nations and State, An Enquiry into the Origins of Nations and the Politics of Nationalism*, Boulder, Col.: Westview Press.
Smith, Anthony D., ed., 1976, *Nationalist Movements*, London: Macmillan.
Smith, Anthony D., 1983, *Theories of Nationalism*, London: Duckworth.
The Task Force on National Unity, A Future Together, Observations and Recommendations, 1979, Ottawa: Supply and Services Canada.

From the Québec Cauldron to the Canadian Cauldron

Reginald A. Whitaker
York University

The Quiet Revolution, the FLQ, "bilingualism and biculturalism," "special status," égalité ou indépendance," the 1970 October Crisis and the War Measures Act, the Parti Québécois and "sovereignty-association," the May 1980 referendum—for twenty years Québec has been constantly in the headlines, a bomb always seemingly about to explode, an enigma and a question mark always hovering on the Canadian horizon. "What does Québec want?" has become a cliché of English-Canadian political discourse in the 1960s and 1970s, and no doubt will continue through the 1980s. It is surely impossible, if not absurd, to try to understand the dynamic and the rhythm of Canadian political development without understanding the forces that have gone into the Québec upheaval.*

The first problem is inherent in the question, what does Québec want? With remarkable consistency, while working at complete cross-purposes, both the Québec nationalists and their English-Canadian opponents have operated on the assumption that there is something called "Québec"—a monolithic, collective leviathan that speaks with the united voice of six million Québécois. Whether as a mythical construct of nationalist yearnings or the equally mythical nightmare of anglophone bigotry, "Québec" does not in reality have a concrete, material existence any more than does "Canada." This is not to say that one cannot speak of a Québec nation, which we surely can; nor does it mean that we cannot speak of Québec nationalism as a force and a passion that far surpasses Canadian nationalism, for it certainly does. It is to say that the dynamic of events in Québec, the explanation of the vast changes during the past two decades, can only be understood when "Québec" is viewed as a forum or framework within which conflict and struggle between contending forces, class, linguistic, and ethnic, have taken place and continue to take place. Far from being a monolith, Québec's extraordi-

*This paper is an updated version of an article published in Alain-G. Gagnon, ed., *Quebec: State and Society* (Toronto: Methuen, 1984), pp. 70–91.

nary dynamic in recent years derives from its status as a battleground for conflicts perhaps more bitter and more profound than the contentions that have riven English Canada.

Any analysis of Québec that locates events solely within the framework of nationalism tends to be tautological and ultimately void of explanatory power. Nationalism, in the sense of a strong feeling of national identity and, at least since 1960, a tendency to formulate demands on the political system grounded in concepts of the national interest, is a force that permeates almost all areas of Québec life and cuts across class and other social divisions. But to explain why Québec has become such a disruptive and contentious force within the Canadian Confederation since 1960, "nationalism" tells us very little. After all, Québec nationalism can be truthfully called a constant of Québec history. The real question is why nationalism has taken the particular forms it has assumed since 1960. And to answer that question, one must examine the conflicting forces at work within Québec and how various formulations of nationalism have expressed the class and other interests of these conflicting forces. Thus, when one analyst of Québec politics writes that the Parti Québécois is not merely a party but "the embodiment of the national identity and the collective will,"[1] he is writing nonsense. And those who assumed that the evolution of Québec was an inevitable, irresistible flowering of the Québec nation into the status of sovereignty failed to remember that history is innocent of "inevitabilities" imposed on it by ideologists. At the same time, it would be equally fallacious (and equally tempting to those seeking simple answers) to assume that the 60 percent "no" vote in the 1980 referendum means that "Québec" has single-mindedly rejected sovereignty-association and the independence option. The forces continue to contend and the options remain open.

Let us begin where Québec itself begins as a nation—with the Conquest of New France by the British in 1763. A possible fate of the French-speaking Catholic inhabitants was assimilation or worse by their English-speaking Protestant conquerors. After all, such has indeed been the fate of numerous other people unlucky enough to have fallen under foreign military domination. In the event, the French language and certain French customs, such as the Civil Code, were preserved, along with the Catholic Church and the educational system, which went along with the church's domination of Québec cultural life. As a result, what had begun as a tiny colony four centuries ago is today a modern, wealthy, and confident nation poised, many would say, at the brink of national sovereignty. This long odyssey from conquered colony to a nation within the Canadian Confederation might seem to speak well of the tolerance and generosity of the conquerors. In fact it rather speaks more strongly of the courage and tenacity of this small people who would not give up what has made them distinctive in North America. For the survival of Québec, and of French Canada, has been above all a story of *resistance* to pressure for assimilation or repression, resistance that has forced the English and then the English-speaking Canadians to make compromises and concessions over time that have taken form in various shifting accommodations. The simple reality of New France at the time of the Conquest was, as Pierre Trudeau once wrote, that the French were too weak to become themselves an independent nation, yet too strong to be crushed by the conquerors. There is a sense in which this basic paradox has remained true down to the present day.

By examining the bases of the various accommodations that have been arrived at over time, one can begin to understand the logic of Québec's relation to Canada. And these accommodations have been above all economic accommodations of class alliances cutting across the two ethnic and linguistic communities. Following the Conquest, tacit alliance was struck between the English military and the English-speaking merchants who had come in the wake of the Conquest, on the one hand, and the Catholic clergy and the seigneurial landlords who benefited from the feudal land-tenure system of New France. The core of this alliance was to be founded on a fateful trade-off of mutual elite interests: the English were to be left formal political control and major economic activity—that is, the "dream" of opening up a transcontinental economy along the "empire of the St. Lawrence"— the clergy would be left with "cultural" matters, such as religion and education. This arrangement guaranteed that the two dominant elites of New France would retain their privileges, but at the expense of economic development. At the same time, the English bought economic superiority at the expense of leaving the major institutions of the conquered people intact. Under these circumstances, Québec would find it difficult to develop the indigenous bourgeoisie so necessary for autonomous capitalist development and would be saddled with elites who depended on the English and who had a vested interest in fostering economic backwardness and political subservience among the mass of the population.

The first and greatest manifestation of discontent spilling over into revolution against the English came with the rebellions of 1837–38, which were much more serious and sustained than the rebellion in Upper Canada, where discontent lacked the reinforcement of ethnic division. But the rebellions themselves were the desperate product of a growing resistance symbolized by the deadlock in the government of the colony between the ruling anglophone clique and the assembly dominated by francophones. The latter group were led by a class element generated by the anomalies of the accommodation referred to above: professionals such as lawyers and doctors who had been educated above their largely peasant origins but who could find no place in state administration controlled by anglophone patronage. Forced to return to their places of origin, these "new middle class" elements remained close to the people, but had the voice and education to agitate on behalf of French grievances in the assembly.

When worsening economic conditions and growing reaction among the English and the ruling clique finally forced matters to open rebellion, left and right were further polarized within the rebellious *Patriote* movement itself. Just as in the American Revolution over a half-century earlier, events drove many rebels toward more radical liberal and democratic views—although in this case always within the context of a strong sense of nationalism, which reinforced in some *Patriotes* a radical drive to overthrow the internal elites who were perpetuating their national subservience.

The movement failed, however, to develop the kind of mass base that could eventually drive out the English. The final defeat of the rebellion in 1838 had fateful consequences: not only did it confirm English hegemony in Québec, but it also confirmed the dominance of the church over Québec life, a dominance that was to last for well over a century. For this period, French-Canadian nationalism was largely stripped of the liberal-democratic promise of 1837 and was instead characterized by social and political conservatism, under the close tutelage of the church, which had become perforce the only institutionalized defender of the French language and culture. The general aversion of clerical nationalism to anything smacking of economic "radicalism" left the English-speaking capitalists more or less free rein. And the latter were only too happy to leave the church in charge of educating a population that was more and more to provide a cheap and docile labour force for English, American, and English-Canadian capital.

At the same time, French Canadians were showing considerable skill in using English parliamentary institutions to ensure national survival. The legislative union of Upper and Lower Canada in 1840 was designed to sink the francophone majority in Lower Canada into an overall minority, but this scheme immediately foundered on the capacity of the French members to act as a cohesive ethnic bloc that had to be accommodated by the warring partisan factions among the anglophone members, if they wished to form a government. It was partially out of a desire to break this stranglehold that anglophone politicians finally agreed to set out on the road to the Confederation agreement of 1867, but along the way they were forced to concede provincial status to Québec, along with considerable powers over education and culture, and recognition of the French language in Québec at least.

Moreover, it was soon apparent that in practice a French-Canadian presence would have to be granted in the makeup of the federal cabinet and other federal institutions, since any national government without Québec support would prove precarious. Yet the old economics–culture trade-off, implicit in the tacit bargain struck after the Conquest and made explicit in the provisions of the British North America Act—which granted almost all important economic responsibilities and all important revenue sources to the national government—was itself reinforced in the elite accommodation of the cabinet: until the 1960s no important economic portfolio was given to a French-Canadian minister. Indeed, it was well over a century until a francophone was appointed minister of finance, in the late 1970s. In addition, the two greatest crises of English–French relations in Canada's first half-century—the hanging of Louis Riel and the imposition of conscription on an unwilling Québec population during World War I—demonstrated that the West would be an exclusively anglophone preserve (thus clearly tilting the balance of Confederation) and that, when an issue sharply divided the two communities, the English majority would always win. These events also sealed the fate of the Conservative Party as a vehicle of accommodation of francophone political elites, thus ultimately ensuring that only one party, the Liberals, could effectively play this role.

By the early 20th century, two main variants of nationalist ideology had emerged. One was symbolized by Henri Bourassa, politician, journalist, and founder of *Le Devoir*; the other by the historian, Canon Lionel Groulx. The former was founded on the vision of *French Canada* and saw the best protection for the French-Canadian nation in equal partnership with English Canada along bilingual and bicultural lines. The latter variant increasingly saw *Québec* as the only viable basis of French-Canadian nationhood and often looked to right-wing corporatist and authoritarian movements as the way to success—as opposed to the more liberal politics of Bourassa. Yet both variants finally failed to address themselves to the real core of the problem of French-Canadian inferiority: their economic subservience. And it must be said that Bourassa's pan-Canadian liberalism, just as much as Groulx's more inward-looking nationalism, drove English Canadians to near violent opposition—as during the World War I conscription crisis.

Consequently, by the 1940s and 1950s Québec was increasingly the scene of insupportable contradictions. The francophone majority was manifestly worse off than the anglophone minority by virtually any measure one wished to use. At the same time they were mired in an ideology that had little or no connection with reality, a backward-looking rural vision of Catholic and antimaterialist values. The irony was that Québec had early in the century become the most heavily urbanized of all the Canadian provinces. Yet in this case urbanization did not mean modernization; instead, it meant the aggregation of a cheap labour force for English-Canadian and American capital.

There was a saying that in Québec capital speaks English and labour speaks French. This not only caught the essence of the situation, but also indicated exactly how, in the long run, class and nationality would become mutually reinforcing characteristics. But so long as the traditional elites—the clergy, the politicians, and the local notables and petite bourgeoisie—kept up their tacit alliance with English-Canadian capital and the Canadian state, the situation remained frozen. Thus, under Maurice Duplessis's Union Nationale government (1936–39, 1944–60), political corruption, patronage, and intimidation helped maintain a regime that in fact challenged capital and the Canadian state only at the rhetorical level. Rural votes were mobilized to maintain a regime that was turning its energies to selling out Québec's natural resources and encouraging industry seeking low labour costs.

Yet enormous changes were in the making. The 1949 asbestos strike drew 5,000 miners out in defiance not only of the American company but also of the Duplessis government in a four-month confrontation widely viewed at the time as quasi revolutionary, and which drew the support of a number of journalists, labour leaders, and academics—presaging in a small but dramatic way the coming cataclysm of the 1960s.

This was on the surface. Underneath were far-reaching changes in the very structure of Québec society. As industrialization and urbanization proceeded, it was inevitable that the political and ideological superstructure would suffer increasing tension and pressure from new forces with no place in the antiquated world of politics. Corporate capital requires a certain kind of labour force; it also requires a growing middle stratum of technical and professional white-collar workers. Slowly, inefficiently, the Québec educational system was beginning to respond to the demand for more technical, professional, and commercial skills.

Yet the emergent new middle class found precious little scope for their ambitions and talents. The corporate world was strongly anglophone and largely impervious to the advancement of francophones past the middle range, at best. The Canadian state presented an equally hostile face. And the Québec provincial state under Duplessis presented little scope to any technical-professional middle class, whether francophone or anglophone, since it avoided economic intervention of the Keynesian variety and left social programs to the church and the private sector. In fact, it was very much in this latter location that the new middle class was taking shape. The church-controlled educational and health sectors required the services of a growing number of lay persons with technical qualifications to staff the schools, hospitals, and other social institutions that in English Canada were under public jurisdiction. These persons were generally underpaid and had very little say in running the institutions they staffed. During the 1950s there was a notable increase in the number of Catholic lay organizations seeking a voice in the direction of their society. Much of this activity remained largely apolitical and well within the bounds of Catholic orthodoxy. Yet even in the 1950s—the era later became known as *la grande noirceur* (the dark ages)—there were those who began to question more deeply. The revue *Cité libre* carried on a long war with clerical and political reaction, featuring a roster of future "stars" of Québec life in the 1960s and 1970s from Pierre Elliott Trudeau to future *indépendantiste* intellectuals. And the Québec Liberal Party, shut out by Duplessis as well as by the federal Liberal Party in Ottawa, began a democratization of the party structures in the late 1950s, which had the effect of opening up the party to the new forces brewing beneath the surface.

The death of Maurice Duplessis in 1959 was like the breaking of a spell. First, the Union Nationale under Duplessis's successor, Paul Sauvé, appeared to be about to undergo changes itself, but Sauvé's untimely death left the UN without new direction, and in 1960 the Liberals under Jean Lesage returned to power after sixteen years of opposition. For once, a change in government was much more than a mere change in faces at the top and patronage to supporters below. The Liberal victory signalled the Quiet Revolution, a massive *déblocage* that opened up Québec's great springtime. The Lesage government drastically revised the role of the provincial government in Québec life, from the nationalization of private hydroelectricity (under then-Liberal minister René Lévesque) to the secularization of the educational system, to the reform of the civil service, to the setting of a whole new host of demands on Confederation that shook Canadian federalism to its roots. But this was by no means a period of change from the top down. Political events moved to a new rhythm: the seething demands and desires of a population suddenly liberated from generations of constraint and backwardness. For a while it seemed as if everything was in question and that everything was possible. All the promise of modernity that had lain before English Canadians for so long appeared as a kind of revelation to this people so long repressed. Young people, intellectuals, and artists in particular responded: the early 1960s became a festival of innovation in culture and ideas. It also became a time of violence, when radical demands for independence took the form of demonstrations and even terrorist groups like the FLQ, which took to bombs.

Revolutions, quiet or otherwise, are in the nature of things more or less civil wars. Not everyone in Québec was swept away by enthusiasm for what was happening. Many elements—particularly from the older, rural, and more traditional Québec—were increasingly worried by the onrush of change and by their place in the new Québec. In part this was masked by the fact that the new regime clothed its policies in the garb of nationalism, now given a brighter and more modern hue by a willingness to dispense with the age-old tacit bargain that had traded off economics for culture, and to make demands that struck at the very heart of the "unequal union," in Stanley Ryerson's phrase, of English and French in Canada. To this extent the Lesage Liberals were the most potent champions of the fundamental desire for national survival who had yet appeared on the scene; they were thus able to mobilize widespread support behind policies that might otherwise have proven highly divisive. In retrospect, however, it is apparent that the nationalism of the Quiet Revolution was above all a nationalism of the new middle class, who expressed their demands for a place in the sun in a language that was no doubt sincerely nationalist in its cultural identification but at the same time an expression of their self-interest as a class or, more precisely, a class fraction.

In fact, the entire logic of the modernization of the Québec state and its transformation from a laissez-faire operation of local notables to Keynesian interventionism was predicated on the ascent of the new middle class. Locked out from both the corporate world and the national state, the francophone middle class would build a state in Québec that would be open to its talents. The nationalization of hydro, for example, created Hydro-Québec, a vast state enterprise staffed from top to bottom by a francophone technical and professional middle class. The reform of the civil service, the attack on the old patronage system of appointment, and the expansion of technical tasks on the state's agenda all served to transform the provincial state apparatus into a pole of attraction for ambitious young francophone university graduates. The demands of the Lesage Liberals for control of the pension plan and medicare legislation being introduced by the federal Liberal government in the 1960s arose not so much from a traditional Québec aversion to state social services, but from a desire to control the vast investment funds that come with such schemes so as to strategically influence the economic development of the province.

This *étatist* orientation not only effectively renegotiated the terms of accommodation between the elites of English and French Canada, but it also tended to redefine the very subject of nationalism itself. "French Canada" increasingly began to give way to "Québec" in nationalist discourse. In part this reflected a realization that the future of francophone communities outside Québec was dim and that efforts would be best concentrated on the one jurisdiction where francophones formed an indisputable majority and could control the machinery of government. But in a deeper sense it was a reflection on the ideological level of the fact of the Québec state's emergence as a powerful bureaucratic actor on the Canadian stage. That nationalism would increasingly be seen as Québec rather than French-Canadian nationalism symbolized the drawing together of nationalist ideology with the interests of the new middle class and other elements who saw their interests closely identified with the Québec state. The interpretation of nationalism in generalized cultural or ethnic terms fails to grasp the specific class interests that had appropriated nationalist discourse for statist purposes.

If we accept this nationalist-statist discourse on its own terms, we simply see a kind of collective self-fulfilment, and *épanouissement* or flowering and the popular slogan *maîtres chez nous* (masters in our own house). In reality we find class conflict and the heightening of contradictions. Just who were to be the new *maîtres*? The 1960s saw the growth of working-class consciousness and increasing labour militancy, as the previously excluded workers sought their own share. Ironically, given the statist orientation of Québec development, this increasing labour militancy bore most heavily on the swollen state sector, so that by the 1970s the political leadership in Québec, including the PQ after 1976, found themselves in an adversarial position with the teachers and other organized state employees. It is impossible to disentangle the developing class consciousness of Québec workers from their developing national consciousness; in many ways the two were mutually reinforcing phenomena. Yet it would also be a mistake to subsume simply working-class consciousness under the rubric of nationalism: first, because nationalist demands articulated by the working class always differ in significant ways from nationalist demands articulated by the new middle class; second, because the confrontation with the Québec state as employer pitted working-class francophones against a francophone elite, with both sides appealing to public opinion. This is a familiar enough scenario elsewhere in the Western world, but it fits rather uneasily into a simplistic nationalist schema.

In fact, the Québec union movement has displayed an even more adversarial attitude toward the Québec state than many English-Canadian unions have displayed toward the federal or provincial states. This has remained true even when the PQ, closer to a social-democratic party than any previous provincial party, came to power. Why this should be so may become clearer when we examine the deepest failing of the Quiet Revolution and its successors, the inability actually to confront the structures of English-Canadian and American capital in any significant way. Apart from the nationalization of hydro, which indeed only followed the example of the Conservative government of Ontario that had created Ontario Hydro a half-century earlier, the Lesage Liberals did not make any real inroads into the power of capital. Like moderate reform governments everywhere, they were cowed by the necessity to maintain business confidence, to retain their credit rating in the bond markets, to encourage investment, and to prevent flights of capital and consequent disappearance of jobs.

The Québec Liberal Party was in no way a vehicle for the mobilization of a mass working-class movement that might have formed an alternative centre of pressure and direction. The long-term result was that *maîtres chez nous* became an empty slogan when matched against the commanding power of "foreign" capital in making the really crucial decisions about the shape of Québec development. To be sure, the Québec state gained a greater leverage than before in setting guidelines, regulating, and in exercising its own voice in deploying the investment funds it now controlled. But this was a long way from mastering the Québec economy in the name of the people who elected the provincial government. It also meant that the Quiet Revolution ultimately satisfied neither the new-middle-class elite of strongly nationalist persuasion nor the working class who began more and more to see the Québec state as an ally of their enemies, or in some cases as the enemy itself.

In any event the Lesage Liberals were themselves driven out of office in 1966 by a revivified Union Nationale under Daniel Johnson, who had quietly built up an alliance of all the elements in Québec society that had reason to fear and mistrust the Liberal thrust toward modernization, especially in the rural areas and small towns. Johnson's problem, and that of his successor following his death, Jean-Jacques Bertrand, was an inability to construct a viable modern version of the old UN nationalism. With a social base in the old Québec and no means of building a new base on the forces unleashed by the Quiet Revolution, the UN remained suspended uneasily between rhetorical nationalism and aggressive demands for equal partnership in Confederation. (*Egalité ou l'indépendance* was the name of a book that Johnson authored.) This came out most acutely in the crisis set off by the UN's attempt to enact language legislation with the ostensible purpose of strengthening the position of French: in fact, they ended by antagonizing both francophone and anglophone without meeting either set of demands.

Meanwhile, another event of historic significance had taken place in 1965 when Pierre Elliott Trudeau, Jean Marchand of the CSN union federation, and the journalist Gérard Pelletier announced their adherence to the federal Liberal Party and were elected to Parliament in the federal election of that year. This act indicated in a dramatic way that the new middle class was by no means united in its nationalist ideology. Some elements of the provincial Liberals, such as René Lévesque, were clearly moving in the inexorable direction of *indépendantisme*, the logical result of the philosophy of *maîtres chez nous*. Trudeau, Marchand, and Pelletier went to Ottawa to create a federalist counterpole of attraction.

When Trudeau won the leadership of the Liberal Party three years later and a landslide victory in the general election that followed, this became in effect the official policy of the national government. The passage of the Official Languages Act and the promotion of bilingualism in the federal civil service were two prongs of a policy of attempting to renegotiate a new basis of elite accommodation between English and French Canada. Another was the concerted attempt to revitalize the federal Liberal Party in Québec, to appoint francophones to economic portfolios in the cabinet hitherto reserved to anglophones, and to promote a francophone presence at the highest levels of the federal public service. Underlying all this was an ideological appeal to *French-Canadian* nationalism, as opposed to *Québec* nationalism, and an appeal to the pride of francophones to seek their fulfilment within the wider sphere of a federal system in which the rights of the French language and French-Canadian culture would be guaranteed. The figure of Pierre Trudeau himself, the francophone who became one of Canada's most electorally successful prime ministers and a statesman of world status, was assiduously cultivated to symbolize the potential for French Canadians within the federal system. And, indeed, opinion polls over the last decade had consistently shown Trudeau to be the most respected public figure among francophone Québécois.

The new-found confidence in Ottawa was parlayed into a new toughness on behalf of federal interests in negotiation with Québec governments, putting an end to the apparent slide of the Pearson Liberals toward giving Québec de facto special status. In some ways, the Trudeau style rather belied the reality that Québec did continue to be treated somewhat differently from other provinces, in recognition that it is, after all, in Trudeau's own phrase, the "homeland and centre of gravity of the French-Canadian nation." But there would be no *formal* recognition of special constitutional status: Trudeau has always been adamant on the fundamental philosophical point that the best guarantees of the French-Canadian language and culture are through *individual* rights, unlike recognition of *collective* rights, which would be discriminatory and illiberal.

When René Lévesque left the provincial Liberal Party in 1967 to form a new group that ultimately became the Parti Québécois, he tended to take away with him not only the more nationalist elements of the Liberal Party, but also the more socially progressive as well. This left the Liberals as a much more right-wing group than before, as most of the dynamic thrust of the Quiet Revolution left with Lévesque. But it also serve to realign Québec politics. Lévesque incorporated two fringe groupings, the RIN, a left-wing separatist force that had contested the 1966 election, and the small right-wing RN. As well, some of the more nationalist elements of the UN joined in. Yet, even in its initial formulations, the PQ was notably moderate in its version of independence: the idea of linking political independence with economic association was not a later adjustment to political reality, but a founding idea.

Shortly after the PQ had contested its first election in 1970—the same election that saw the Liberals under Robert Bourassa come back to power in a landslide—a series of events unfolded that dramatically highlighted the forces at play in the Québec cauldron and indicated the direction of the 1970s. What has been called the October Crisis began when the terrorist FLQ kidnapped a British diplomat and later kidnapped and murdered the Québec minister of labour, Pierre Laporte. The response of the federal government in invoking the War Measures Act against an "apprehended insurrection" and the subsequent arrests and incarceration of numerous persons, few of whom had anything to do with the FLQ, remains a hotly debated question of public policy. What is relevant here is that the entire affair was in fact played out among different factions of Québécois: the federal Liberals, the Bourassa regime, and the Montréal government of Mayor Jean Drapeau on the one side; and, on the other, the FLQ and their public sympathizers, such as the labour leader Michel Chartrand and the revolutionary theorist Pierre Vallières. In the event, the clear superiority of the federal government over the provincial state was demonstrated. Moreover, the might the federal government could thus array in effect broke the back of the tiny terrorist organization, which failed to mobilize popular resistance or even much public support. By the end of the crisis the field had at least been cleared. The PQ, with its moderate, constitutionalist approach of respecting the democratic electorate and observing due process, would be henceforth the only voice of *indépendantisme*.

The Bourassa regime turned to an economic-development strategy that emphasized above all the attraction of private investment and the promotion of large public-works projects—one of which, the James Bay Hydro development, was an immense success that gives Québec a solid renewable energy resource base for the future and another of which, the Olympic Games project, turned out to be a financial disaster and administrative fiasco. In a sense, the Bourassa regime represented a reversion to the Duplessis era, inasmuch as everything was subordinated to the encouragement of private investment and business was given a distinctly privileged place in dealings with the provincial government; at the same time, union bashing became more or less official policy. Another aspect of Duplessism came to the fore as well: political patronage and corruption. Moreover, the apparent servility of Bourassa to his "big brothers" in Ottawa began to grate on the nerves of nationalists, even those who were far from being separatists. This was particularly true when an antibilingual backlash developed in English Canada, calling the viability of Trudeau's national bilingualism into question, a dilemma symbolized by the strike of airline pilots over the use of French in air traffic control in Québec and by the apparent capitulation of the federal government in the face of an anti-French backlash.

When the Québec Liberals were still able to paint the PQ as a dangerous party that threatened the economic stability of Québec by their "separatist" designs, they were able to mobilize public support, winning a huge landslide in 1973. But when the PQ hit on the strategy of promising a referendum on sovereignty-association and ran on the platform of competence and honesty in government, as well as on a mildly social-democratic program, an electorate sick of scandals and sellouts turned the Liberals out of office. The coming of the PQ signalled the gravest crisis yet of Canadian federalism.

The PQ government that took office in 1976 appeared on the surface to be the true heirs of the Quiet Revolution; the cabinet was a who's who of the Québec political, administrative, academic, and media elites. It must be said that the PQ has in its terms of office largely delivered on its promise of good government, in the sense of administrative competence and efficiency, along with a reasonable degree of public honesty. A pursuit of the policy of *maîtres chez nous* was now given a much more hard-nosed economic and political thrust than it had in the days of Lesage. Attempting to pursue the goal of sovereignty while operating a provincial government within the context of the existing Canadian federation is not, however, without its ironies.

One of the greatest ironies of all is that what may be the PQ's most enduring achievement probably undermined its own independence option. The PQ language legislation succeeded where the Liberals and the UN had failed before them: to secure the position of the French language in Québec life. By contrast with its predecessors, Camille Laurin's language act was clear in intention and followed through its aims with rigorous consistency, avoiding the anxiety-producing uncertainties of earlier acts. A wild uproar in the anglophone community led to streams of affluent refugees fleeing to Toronto and parts west. Among those who stayed there is now a much greater acceptance of the predominantly French character of Québec. The immigrants, despite long simmering conflicts with Montréal working-class francophones with whom they were competing, have adjusted for the most part with surprisingly good grace. Once the situation was made clear, those who had already made a decision to live their lives in a new language showed that they could adapt as well to French as to English. And since it was above all the immigrants overwhelmingly adopting English who had been the real threat to the linguistic balance, the PQ thus neatly defused what had been an explosive situation of ethnic conflict.

Now the francophones of Québec feel a new security: Québec is to remain unmistakably French in character. Hence, the mere existence of an anglophone minority tied to an anglophone majority outside Québec began to lose the threatening quality it once posed to the integrity of Québécois culture and identity. In short, the PQ reversed what had been one of the most significant weaknesses of Trudeau's official languages policy: a cultural and linguistic insecurity it had actually encouraged in Québec. The profound irony for the PQ is that this achievement may well be seen as a necessary condition for Québec's continued place within Confederation. Without it, the case for independence would certainly have been much stronger. With the substantive and psychological victory of the language law, Québec may well feel more confident about playing a continued role in Confederation.

In economic policy, the PQ's approach has been severely restrained, even to the extent of mitigating in office its moderate social-democratic philosophy. In part this reflects a general disillusion with the statist ventures of the Lesage period, many of which (Hydro-Québec aside) have proven to be particularly ineffective. Partly it reflects the unpleasant economic realities of the 1970s and 1980s when inflation and unemployment have combined to discredit much of the earlier Keynesian interventionism. But above all it represents the conundrum of a party dedicated to seeking a major structural change in the national and constitutional status of Québec. Since business fears uncertainty more than anything else and since the PQ project was premised on the maintenance of existing living standards and investment levels in Québec, the PQ government was forced to go to greater lengths to reassure business than less "dangerous" governments have to. The PQ's fiscal and monetary policies have thus turned out to be cautious and conservative.

In the case of its economic-development strategy, the PQ represents, if anything, a step back from the Quiet Revolution. Apart from the more or less symbolic nationalization of the asbestos corporation (a ritual bow to the memory of the strike of 1949?), which was in any event a declining industry, the PQ has been notably loath to engage in direct state intervention. In fact, its development strategy has been largely along the lines inscribed by Bourassa's Liberals: a heavy reliance on private investment by multinationals based on the availability of natural resources and energy (James Bay), state agencies as facilitators of private enterprise, and a reduction of regulatory and control devices over business. The one area where they have differed from the Liberals is in the vast program of assistance and encouragement of small and medium enterprises (which of course are those most strongly francophone in ownership). Even this emphasis, strong in their first term, has begun to weaken in their second, with the realization that small and medium enterprises make only a small dent in the unemployment picture. As well, they have begun emphasizing that the rationalization and consolidation of certain aging sectors of the economy will also be necessary, even at the cost of short-term dislocations. In short, they seem to be moving more and more into the kind of development strategy, heavily dependent on large multinational capital and tied to resource sectors, that is characteristic of other provincial governments in Canada.

This raises another crucially important point about the nature of the PQ project for sovereignty: its economic base. Some have viewed the PQ as *merely* a vehicle for new-middle-class nationalism, rooted in the state elite. Yet the PQ has not behaved as if it were a mere reflection of a bureaucratic class fraction. Is this just a failure of will in the face of the power of "foreign" capital? It was, in fact, no longer true in the 1970s that francophones were shut out of the corporate sector. The emergence of a francophone bourgeoisie—not located in the small-business sector alone—is obviously of critical importance for evaluating the relationship of Québec to its Canadian, and North American, environment. That elements of a francophone bourgeoisie do exist is no longer a matter of much dispute; the hotly debated question has to do with its relationship to North American capitalism. Is it a "French-Canadian" bourgeoisie linked to a pan-Canadian economy, a regional Québec bourgeoisie offering a potential base for sovereignty-association, or is it itself divided into different fractions, with fragmented political plans?[2] These and other questions (such as the relationship between this bourgeoisie and the state elite located in such crucial positions as Hydro-Québec and the various investment funds) await definitive answers. Suffice to say for now that the PQ plan for a sovereign Québec seems to have been predicated on some concept of a francophone bourgeoisie, assisted by the state, developing its place in the sun through a renegotiated settlement with English Canada and even, perhaps, through an eventual common market with the United States. A sovereign Québec was not seen as a socialist Québec—although there have always been minority elements in the PQ who have retained more radical perspectives than the conservative and technocratic leadership. In any event, the support of business, including francophone business, for the "no" side of the referendum was not a sign that this emergent bourgeoisie saw itself as having *indépendantiste* aspirations, at least at this time.

If the PQ has not seen its role as that of a socialist party mobilizing the working class against foreign capitalist domination, it did see its role in relation to the organized working class as distinct from that of the Liberals. The PQ began with a more conciliatory line in labour relations, including the passage of antiscab law more progressive than anything existing in any other North American jurisdiction. While it has generally shown more adroitness and finesse in handling labour relations than its predecessors, it has not gained the formal allegiance of the unions, who have no official affiliation with the party—although the majority of working-class voters appear to vote PQ. The fiscal crisis of the Québec state, in part exacerbated by the PQ's studied largesse in encouraging its state-sector supporters in the years leading up to the referendum on sovereignty-association, came home to roost in 1982–83 when the PQ was forced into confrontation with its own employees, which has done severe damage to its image as progressive in labour relations. While the federal and other provincial governments have frozen or limited salaries of public employees, the Québec government actually rolled back wages, under the authority of special legislation. The refusal of teachers to accept the government's terms brought down on their heads one of the most draconian pieces of special antilabour legislation passed in recent years in any Canadian legislature, including the specific exemption of the legislation from the provisions of both the federal and Québec charters of rights. It now seems doubtful whether the PQ can repair its relations with organized labour in time for the next election.

The PQ has attempted to reconcile the contradictions of its labour policy by pushing for a series of quasi corporatist-style government-business-labour advisory bodies. Although they hoped that common nationalist aspirations might overcome class divisions, not much has in fact come of these initiatives, nor is much likely to come. Nationalism does not in fact override the structural division of a capitalist economy, when bread and butter issues, as opposed to nationalist symbolism, are in question. On the other hand, the reaction from the labour leaders and from the political left in the wake of the PQ's cutbacks and special antilabour legislation has gone to such extremes as to label the party as a reactionary betrayer of the working class. Since the PQ did not claim to be a worker's party in the first place, the degree of disillusion seems exaggerated.

Indeed, in continuity with its past, the PQ today seems to be pursuing a populist line, in which it portrays itself as the defender of the "little guys" against the special interests, even where these interests include the unions, especially when they include the "privileged" ranks of the state employees. Of course, this may damage its support among the new middle class, particularly the participation of new middle class activists in the party organization. On the other hand, the party may become a different kind of organization, eschewing its former role as a mass party, instead coming to resemble a kind of modernized version of the old Duplessis Union Nationale: nationalist, populist, firmly rooted in a network of local supporters tied together by patronage and shared partisan identity, and solidly under the control of *le chef*. Of course, there are many differences with the old UN, but so too are there some striking similarities.That the PQ began as a reformist party is no surprise; so did the UN. (Duplessis was allied with young left-wing nationalists and promised the nationalization of hydroelectric power.) In both cases, nationalism was the predominant thrust; in both cases, social reformism was always secondary. It might be added that, in the case of the UN, the combination of populism and nationalism was sustained by substantial working-class support at the polls, even in the face of repressive antilabour activities by the state.

If the PQ has a blurred conservative image in its economic and social policies, its constitutional formulation of its nationalist position has been even more riven with hesitation and contradiction. Despite hysterical anglophone allegations that the PQ is "racist" and that its independence project resembled some variant of "fascism," the truth is far different. Faced with the thorny problem of expressing a francophone nationalist vision in a society where about one in five does not share in this cultural and linguistic identity, the PQ (not without some hesitations and self-deceptions) has not officially supported an *exclusionary* definition of nationality, but instead generally has chosen a *liberal* interpretation, which left membership open to all those willing to participate voluntarily in the national culture, along with guarantees for minorities. Indeed, the entire ethos of the PQ has been so permeated with a full acceptance of liberal-democratic principles as to make any allegations of totalitarianism laughable—as well as to differentiate sharply the PQ from older reactionary and authoritarian expressions of Québec nationalism. A close reading of the official documents produced by the PQ in power—from the constitution to culture to economics—indicates a liberal-democratic discourse to which various nationalist themes are rhetorically wedded in an uneasy and contradictory manner. In some cases, as in the official economic-development strategy (*Bâtir le Québec*), nationalist themes virtually disappear. In others, like the White Paper on sovereignty-association, the tension is reflected in glaring inconsistencies.

Partly out of its basic inability to define clearly its own nationalist direction, partly out of the constraints of trying to reassure business and voters, the PQ's constitutional option was blurred. Since it has insisted on linking political sovereignty with economic association—that is, to argue that national independence was a constitutional superstructure unrelated to the economic base—it has in effect put a double proposition to the voters: first, that there was a will to seek political sovereignty; second, that this will to independence was linked to the continuance of existing economic relations with English Canada, in some cases on a new basis, in some cases on a basis suspiciously like the present. The problem with this duality was that the first part could be a unilateral expression, with which English Canada would have to deal; the second was a matter for negotiation, which cannot be unilateral. Yet the first was linked to the second. The paradox for the PQ was that Québec opinion, as revealed in the government's own polls, was contingent on English Canada's reaction; this was summed up neatly in a cartoon in *Le Devoir* showing Québec as a boxer in the corner saying, "We're ready to come out and fight, if English Canada allows us to win." Trudeau paraphrased the referendum question as: "Do you want to have your cake and eat it too?" Even worse was the PQ's promise that the economic association would be based on the principle of equality (*égal à égal*). Why English Canada, representing 70 percent of the population should agree to a 50–50 relationship with 30 percent of the population in Québec was never obvious. Presumably the *formal* equality involved in bilateral relations between sovereign nations would be in effect, but formal equality between materially unequal nations is an empty equality.

The referendum result revealed an underlying reality of Québec's relationship to Canada, which appears to have escaped the attention of the most militant *indépendantistes*. Quebeckers have a long history—and, doubtless, a long future—of demanding more power and autonomy for the province. *Péquistes* made the mistake of assuming that this was a cumulative process that would inevitably lead to sovereignty. But demands made *in the provincial sphere* for provincial goals are not the same as demands made *in the federal sphere*. Hence, the sometimes bizarre contrasts between provincial and federal voting in Québec (*Péquistes* to Québec City and Liberals to Ottawa). In pursuing apparently divergent ideological and constitutional paths in federal and provincial politics, Quebeckers are not necessarily being irrational. Quite the contrary. A strong voice for the province of Québec in federal–provincial negotiations need not be a contradiction of a strong Québec presence in Ottawa—the irrationality may perhaps be discerned in the *structures* of federalism, which set one political elite from Québec against another elite in an adversarial bargaining confrontation, but that is another story. Pierre Trudeau *and* René Lévesque were both perceived by the bulk of voters in Québec as champions of Québec interests. And so they were.

The PQ's fatal error was to demand in effect that the people of Québec be forced to choose, definitively, between two levels of government to which they were still by and large attached. If the federalist option had been successfully portrayed as a unitary centralism, within which the Québec provincial state would inevitably disappear, the PQ's option could have won considerably greater support. A small number of *Péquiste* zealots aside, such a scenario could gain little credibility. Anyone with much of a memory could see tangible evidence that the Québec state, under federalism, had gained enormously in fiscal power and responsibility over the twenty years since 1960. The real choice was between federalism, with its two levels of government, and sovereignty, with its one level. Of course, the PQ hastened to muddy this with its arguments about sovereignty-association and its curious re-creation under different names of federalist structures (although as decided *bureaucratic* structures without the legitimation of direct popular election). But, in order to mobilize support for the "yes" vote, it was necessary to identify rhetorically loyalty to Québec exclusively with a sovereign Québec, thus excluding the notion of attachment to the federal dimension.

When the "no" strategists devised the slogan "*Je suis fier d'être québécois et canadien*," they quite brilliantly distilled the quintessence of the reluctance of the mass of the population to make the choice demanded by the PQ. Although a vast majority unsurprisingly agreed with a mid-referendum questionnaire statement that "I am profoundly attached to Québec," it was perhaps less expected that 76 percent of the same sample agreed with the statement "I am profoundly attached to Canada"—including an extraordinary 47 percent of those who intended to vote "yes."[3]

As the "no" campaign gained in confidence, an interesting phenomenon came to the fore. The display of Canadian flags and the singing of "O Canada" became features not only in predominantly anglophone gatherings, but in francophone ones as well. The point to be made here is not that Québec francophones are really Canadians first; rather, it is that the steady growth over recent years of popular identification as "Québécois" has not necessarily meant that "Canadien" has suffered an equivalent elimination. Obviously, for a body of *indépendantiste* activists and perhaps for certain occupational categories such as intellectuals and artists, Québec and Canada have tended to become mutually exclusive categories. But, for a sizable section of the population, the intensification of emotional, nationalistic attachment to Québec that began with the Quiet Revolution did not in itself subvert an attachment to federalism and a Canadian identification that no doubt lacks the warmth and sentimentality of loyalty to Québec, but maintains tenacious roots. Perhaps Pierre Trudeau's notion that passionate national loyalties to French Canada are matched by a cooler, more "rationalist" or functionalist base of loyalty to Canada as a whole may have some relevance here.

This raises another question. It has been argued, especially by left-wing independence supporters, that the "no" campaign was largely one of fear, in which pro-federalist forces combined with the big corporations to intimidate working-class and vulnerable middle-class voters into backing away from sovereignty-association under the threat, implied or direct, of a flight of capital. This charge has an element of truth, but it can be exaggerated. The PQ hardly posed a radical alternative to capitalism in its referendum question. Moreover, it suggests a deep contempt of the Québec people themselves to argue that federal anti-alcohol ads with the theme "*non merci*" somehow stampeded impressionable voters into the "no" side. In any event, the PQ had four years of control over government advertising in the media to drive *its* point home.

Despite some rather tortured attempts to argue that the majority of francophone voters had actually voted *yes* (it being necessary to assume a sharply higher turnout among anglophones than among francophones and an extraordinarily high *no* percentage among all nonfrancophones), it seems likely that in fact more francophones voted *no* than voted *yes*. It should also be obvious that the percentage of francophones who did vote *yes* was quite high, even if not a clear majority. Although the referendum was run on a simple majority basis, with no distinctions formally being made between francophones and anglophone voters, the political reality was, of course, quite different. An overall "no" majority of, say, 51 percent would clearly have lacked any legitimacy, since under such circumstances it would have been obvious that the francophones had voted decisively "yes." The resulting crisis would have been extremely volatile and dangerous for relations between the two communities in Québec and would have left matters hanging intolerably for the rest of Canada. A clear result, one way or another, was obviously preferable and was in fact produced.

The question remains whether the result of the referendum can be seen as *definitive*. Predictions about the long run are best left to astrologers, but there has been a growing sense in the years since the referendum that in the short run—say, the next decade or so—the results will be determining. Despite the increasingly ritualistic reiterations by government leaders that sovereignty remains just around the corner and despite repeated promises to run the next general election as a referendum on sovereignty, there is a pervasive feeling in Québec that *indépendantisme* is yesterday's issue. There are a number of reasons for the waning of this question that so dominated Québec politics for so many years.

The referendum was, in some ways, a moving example of a people undertaking a collective decision that would determine their destiny for the future. The debate penetrated into levels of society normally left untouched by party politics, and in some senses represented a moment of true democracy rarely witnessed in Québec or elsewhere. The other side of this coin is that it was a traumatic event for many, to those whose families and personal relations were rent by political divisions, and above all to those who threw themselves body and soul into the "yes" campaign, then saw their dream rejected by 60 percent of their fellow citizens. The historic moment arrived and the vision suddenly shattered. It may be difficult for this generation of *indépendantiste* activists to put themselves again through that kind of traumatic public vulnerability for some time.

Apart from psychological suppositions, there are deeper reasons to suspect that the referendum has settled matters for a good while. For instance, growing evidence suggests that the ancient complaint of francophones that they have no future in the corporate sector is becoming less credible as capitalism adjusts to making profits in French as well as in English. Moreover, there is a marked shift among francophone students toward commerce and business administration, which is eliminating the differences in career orientation that until recently had separated anglophone from francophone. A study published in 1981 under the sponsorship of the *Conseil de la langue française* revealed that, when age is taken into account, there is little if any evidence of higher income among anglophones than among francophones in their 40s and younger in similar occupations in Québec; indeed, there is marginal evidence that some francophones now make more than their anglophone counterparts.[4] In short, the generation who came of age at the time of the Quiet Revolution has moved through a historic alteration of the old pattern of unequal accommodation between the two language groups. The generation coming of age in the 1980s faces fewer of the blatant aggravations that galvanized an earlier generation into militant *indépendantiste* politics. Lévesque claimed on referendum night that his sovereignty-association option had been defeated by "*le vieux Québec.*" The assertion that the younger voters are naturally *indépendantistes* and that opposition to the PQ option will pass away with time— an assertion repeated once again for the benefit of the French media on Lévesque's 1983 visit to France—appears to be another comforting, but insubstantial, PQ myth. PQ support is in fact weakening among the very youngest voters; 18- to 21-year-old voters appear to have divided pretty much in the same proportions as their elders on the referendum's question.

The problematic character of Québec youth's attachment to independence was dramatically highlighted in August of 1983 when a summit meeting of youth organizations voted against a resolution expressing support for an independent Québec. As some of the delegates made clear, this result arose perhaps not so much out of positive support for Canadian federalism as from disillusion with an *indépendantiste* government that, instead of solving problems whose solution already lay within provincial jurisdiction, persisted in trying to use these problems as a means of mobilizing support for sovereignty as a panacea.

The backdrop to the referendum and to the subsequent confrontation between the PQ government and Ottawa over the new Constitution has, of course, been the continued economic recession that has cut even more deeply into Québec than into some other parts of Canada, given the historically limited nature of Québec's industrialization. The PQ has attempted to fix the blame for this squarely on the federal government's policies and to argue that salvation can come only through independence. Yet, far from intensifying popular support for sovereignty, hard economic times seem to have deepened uninterest in nationalist adventures. In part this lack of interest derives from fear of more political uncertainty driving out investment and jobs; in part it derives from a desire to see both levels of government stop their petty conflicts over place and prestige and get down to the job of cooperating for economic recovery.

The PQ's role in the constitutional negotiations following the referendum must also be critically scrutinized to understand their waning prestige within Québec as the defenders of the Québec nation. Having misfired their own constitutional option, the PQ proved singularly inept at negotiating a new constitutional arrangement within Canada. Lévesque actually signed an accord with the premiers in opposition to Trudeau's unilateral initiative, which failed to recognize a special veto for Québec on amendments (the federal government's proposals did include a Québec veto), then bitterly denounced Ottawa for denying Québec's "historic" right to a veto when the accord to which he had agreed was accepted. At a premiers' conference in the 1970s, Lévesque had offered a reciprocal exchange of minority-language rights in education with the English-Canadian premiers—then vehemently denounced the exact same agreement, when written into the new Constitution, as an attack on Québec's linguistic rights.

Lévesque's negotiating tactics make sense only if they are seen as resulting from *une politique du pire*—that is to say, a policy of ensuring defeat in order to demonstrate that things are so bad under federalism that sovereignty is the only salvation. If that were indeed the plan, the effect on public opinion may have been badly misjudged. Québec voters have always wanted their provincial government to stand up for Québec in federal–provincial relations. While some may interpret the Constitution Act of 1982 as a sign that there is no future for Québec within Canada, a great many more may well conclude that the PQ is simply a poor negotiator on behalf of Québec interests. Moreover, while the absence of a Québec veto is dangerous in a binational state, things are not so dark as the PQ would have people believe. Provinces can, after all, opt out of constitutional amendments of which they disapprove and, where such amendments have to do with educational or cultural matters, they can receive fiscal compensation—a clear indication of a special status for Québec. The main lines of the Québec language law (French as the language of work, French for signs and advertising, and the assimilation of the nonanglophone immigrants into French-language education) are now preserved by the Constitution, with only such marginal matters as bilingual statutes and debate in the National Assembly, and the right of anglophones coming from other provinces to send their children to English schools open to change by constitutional interpretation. In exchange, there has been a major concession to French language rights in education in English-Canadian provinces, and the extension of official bilingualism to New Brunswick, with its large Acadian minority.

In fact, the new Constitution does clearly recognize the linguistic and cultural duality of Canada—that is, the duality of English and French Canada. But it does not recognize duality of the Québec and Canadian *states*, as states. In short, the constitutional resolution of 1982 was a victory for Pierre Trudeau's longstanding belief that the question was one of individual rights of English and French Canadians, and a defeat for the *Péquiste* position that linguistic and cultural survival demands a sovereign state as its only sure guarantee. Time alone will tell if the Trudeau solution will actually work; just as obviously, it is requisite to the PQ's survival as a force that it *not* work. The conundrum for the PQ is whether *la politique du pire* is defensible strategy to sell to the people. For instance, the PQ, alone among the provincial governments, has decided to invoke the "notwithstanding" clause on each and every piece of legislation it introduces into the National Assembly, thus exempting Québec from the Charter of Rights. Can it, in the long run, justify to its own citizens the denial of the protection of individual rights, in the name of a (negative) defence of the rights of the Québec state?

The difficulties encountered by a government attempting this kind of strategy were painfully highlighted in the immediate aftermath of the constitutional accord, at a PQ congress. After escalating the rhetorical level to suggest that Québec was being virtually raped by the federal government and the English-Canadian provinces, Lévesque in effect incited the extreme nationalist wing of the party to push for an out-and-out sovereignty position. Aware at the same time that this extreme reaction would be rejected by the voters, Lévesque refused to accept the majority decisions of the congress, and subjected the party to the humiliating exercise of a mailed ballot (the so-called *"Renérendum"*), in which party members were asked to recant their views or to force *le chef* to resign. Obedience to *le chef* won over party democracy. The confusion in all this is profound and the contradictions may well be insupportable. Certainly doubts must remain that the PQ will actually fulfil its stated determination to fight the next provincial election on the sovereignty issue. Or, if it does, that it can be anything other than a suicidal decision. In 1970, 1973, and 1980 the PQ was the party of sovereignty, and was rejected by the voters. In 1976 and 1981, it was the party of good government, and was endorsed.

An interesting feature of the 1981 election was the decline in ethnic polarization. More anglophones and especially other ethnics voted PQ than before, and two anglophones were elected as PQ members in predominantly francophone seats. In the Montréal civic elections of 1982, ethnic and linguistic polarization seems to have broken down entirely under the counterpressure of a struggle between the old Jean Drapeau machine and a francophone-anglophone reformist party. It is possible that Québec politics will become more oriented toward economic and social issues and less dominated by an overarching concern for nationalism without social content. Ironically, the PQ will have helped bring this about, both through creating a legislative framework conducive to the enhanced position of francophone identity in Québec and by finally stretching the nationalist issue nearly to the breaking point. How well the PQ can itself survive its ironic success is another matter.

Beyond party politics, there remains the deeper and more significant question of the relationship of Québec society to Canada and to North America. The problem to be addressed in the 1980s is that of the integration of Québec into the economic structures of North American capitalism. To what extent this process will continue, to what effect on the class structure of Québec, and to what effect on Québec culture and identity—these questions will ultimately determine whether the referendum of 1980 was the last gasp of the kind of nationalism unleashed by the 1960s or merely another shot in a gathering campaign. Of course, English Canada's *political* responses to Québec will play a role in this, but not so important a role as the structural changes in Québec itself. To return to where this essay began: one thing alone is certain, that Québec nationalism will continue; what specific form and expression that nationalism will take will ultimately be a product of forces deeper than politics alone.

POSTSCRIPT: THE CANADIAN CAULDRON

This essay was originally written shortly after the referendum on sovereignty-association in 1980 and then revised in 1984. At the time it was generally believed, within Québec as well as without, that the sovereigntist project had suffered a very serious, if not fatal, setback. This was a view that my essay shared, at least in part. Now in the early 1990s, a sovereign Québec, while by no means a certainty, is probably closer to realization than ever before.

It is of course impossible to answer in a few pages the intriguing question of how this stunning reversal of fortune has come about. I would, however, like to point to some important factors that have served to undermine the conditions that a decade ago seemed to be conspiring to kill the sovereignty movement. In my 1984 piece, I argued that "nationalism" was a constant factor of Québec history, but that its specific forms at particular historic moments were shaped by the forces of economics and class conflict. The modernization of Québec, its transformation into a liberal capitalist North American society, has proceeded apace through the 1980s. But this process has quite contradictory implications.

It is no doubt a high historical irony that the Quiet Revolution's attempt to save the particularity of traditional Québec values and culture by developing appropriately "modern" means of nationalist defence should have resulted in the replacement of that traditional society. Today Québec is much less distinguishable, as an economy, society, and culture, from its North American neighbours than it was thirty years ago—apart from the all-important difference of language. But the spread of corporate capitalist organization on a global scale, and the growing prevalence of internationalized mass culture, has clearly not served to undermine small nationalisms. On the contrary, and this is apparently true across the globe and not merely in Québec, "modernization" has proved a Janus-faced phenomenon: on the one side, cultural homogenization and economic globalization; on the other, enhanced capacity and will of small nationalities to construct more autonomous political spaces for themselves.

Neither the diminution and even disappearance of the real economic and social grievances that gave rise to an earlier era of Québec nationalist demands nor the ever-closer integration of Québec into the continental corporate economy have lessened the thrust within Québec toward political disentanglement from the Canadian federal state. Whether this disentanglement takes the form finally of a clear rupture, or simply of a further accentuation of the scope for autonomous political action within a looser and more decentralized, or more asymmetrical, federalism is still an open question. But the direction seems much more decisive than it was in the years immediately following the 1980 referendum.

If national identity has been sharpened and clarified, rather than weakened, by the pressures of globalization, it nevertheless required a conjuncture of specific developments and events to bring the sovereignty project once more to a head. These events may be very briefly summarized as follows:

(1) Meech Lake and the famous "distinct society" clause was endorsed by the Canadian political elite, left before the country for three years of acrimonious debate, and then failed. Quebeckers felt rejected.

(2) The free trade agreement with the United States was imposed upon an unwilling English Canada in 1988 largely as a result of Québec support for the

Conservatives. Bitterness toward Québec remains among English-Canadian nationalists.

(3) Having demonstrated their relative confidence in open borders over free trade, Quebeckers showed their own particular national vulnerability when the Supreme Court struck down the sections of the Québec language law that forbade the use of English on commercial signs. When the Québec government invoked the "notwithstanding" clause to pass a new language law that banned English on outside signs, the reaction in English Canada was overwhelmingly hostile. Quebeckers spoke of their *collective* right to protect their language, and thus their culture and nationality within Québec. English Canadians, by and large, spoke about *individual* rights that must be protected equally in every part of Canada.

(4) The Québec business class has emerged in a clear leadership position within Québec society. Québec capital's orientation toward sovereignty is now treated as a viable potential option by many influential sections of Québec business. So long as the French language is secure, Québec society is relatively confident of its ability to compete economically on the world stage—more confident than English Canada, which lacks the natural protection of linguistic difference from the United States. Québec labour is now apparently quite willing to play a supporting role to business in any move to sovereignty.

(5) Free trade has radically altered the economic context within which Québec views the potential difficulties and dangers of going it alone politically. Instead of having to work out a form of institutionalized economic association with English Canada, Québec can now contemplate membership within a North American free trade zone.

(6) The political context for the sovereignty debate is different than in 1980. In Québec, sovereignty has become less associated as a partisan issue with the Parti Québécois, and is more an option open to all factions of Québec political life, including the Bourassa Liberals. On the federal stage, the rise of the Bloc Québécois is a radical development, potentially eliminating the counterbalance of a strong federalist option favoured by Québec federal voters (as with Trudeau). In the context of the catastrophic decline in national support for the Conservatives under Mulroney and the likely fragmentation of English-Canadian votes among four parties (including Reform) in the next election, dramatic leverage could be exercised by the BQ.

These do not, of course, exhaust all the relevant factors in the present conjuncture. But two points particularly stand out. First, the internal dynamic of Québec society—to which I made extensive reference in my essay—has attained a certain level of stability relative to a more turbulent and divisive past, in which something like a consensus has formed behind a business-led "market nationalism." Unlike the earlier *étatiste* nationalism of the 1960s, market nationalism intersects more effectively with the larger continental and global forces of capitalism while at the same time creating a potentially more viable space for political disentanglement from the Canadian state, while in the short run at least lessening the degree of internal social conflict. This diminution of social conflict may well be a temporary phase, but in the critical conjuncture of the constitutional crisis of the early 1990s, it is an important new factor that greatly strengthens the hands of the sovereigntists.

The second main point of difference from the first phase of the sovereignty debate is that English Canada is now becoming a more active and assertive player.

In 1984 I wrote that "English Canada's *political* responses to Québec will play a role [in the shaping of Québec nationalism], but not so important a role as the structural changes in Québec itself." While that statement remains broadly true, English-Canadian actions, as opposed to reactions, now have to be weighed more seriously by Quebeckers than in the past. This is because English Canada has developed its own stronger sense of nationalism (evident in the free trade debate and in the Meech Lake fiasco). This newly awakened pan-Canadian nationalism has meant the emergence of a specifically English-Canadian constitutional agenda (around issues such as reforming the Senate, aboriginal self-government, and strengthening Charter rights) that collides directly with the Québec agenda for further enhancing Québec's power and autonomy and reducing the role of the federal government. A constitutional solution that pleases all sides now seems more remote and unobtainable than ever.

This new English-Canadian self-absorption has also encouraged a substantial, if still minority, section of English-Canadian opinion to contemplate the departure of Québec with something approaching equanimity, if not in some cases downright enthusiasm. Unlike 1980, this support for Québec sovereignty proceeds less from a desire to grant Québec's right to national self-determination (which in any event has been recognized, in effect, by all three leading Canadian political parties) than from a calculation of the benefit to be gained by an English Canada freed at long last of a Québec-driven agenda. Thus developments both within Québec and within the rest of Canada are in effect conspiring to strengthen the case for Québec's separation from Confederation.

None of this means, to be sure, that sovereignty is a certainty for the near future. If economics is at the heart of the powerful reassertion of the sovereignty project, it may also be its Achilles heel. A business-led market nationalism may in the end quail at the prospect even of short-run economic costs of disruption, uncertainty, and loss of investor confidence. Capitalists are not, after all, much given to political adventurism, unless the alternative of the status quo is even more laden with costs (which is by no means clear).

Whether nationalist sentiment or the corporate bottom line will win out is the key question for the immediate future of Québec. Another variable, as relevant now to Quebeckers as to Canadians elsewhere, is whether the newly self-conscious, populist, and cantankerous English-Canadian nation will be willing to buy a constitutional solution that retains Québec as an integral member of the political community at the cost of lessening a regional and social egalitarianism that many Canadians have learned to value. What I called the "Québec cauldron" in the early 1980s has now become the "Canadian cauldron."

NOTES

1. Henry Milner, *Politics in the New Quebec* (Toronto: McClelland and Stewart, 1978), p. 148.
2. Some of this debate has been translated into English in *Studies in Political Economy*. See Jorge Niosi, "The New French-Canada Bourgeoisie," I (Spring 1979); Gilles Bourque, "Class, nation, and the Parti québécois," II (Fall 1979); Pierre Fournier, "Parameters of the new Quebec bourgeoisie," III (Spring 1980).
3. Maurice Pinard and Richard Hamilton, poll reported in *Le Devoir* (17 May 1979), p. 9.
4. Robert Lacroix and François Vaillancourt, *Les revenus et la langue au Québec (1970–1978)* (Quebec, 1981).

"Québec, see under Canada"[1]: Québec Nationalism in the New Global Age

Daniel Latouche
Institut National de la Recherche Scientifique

At regular intervals, social scientists and politicians take stock of a phenomenon known as "Québec nationalism." This is usually a time when old definitions are sharpened, when past events are recalled, and when, finally, a prognosis is offered as to the health of the patient. To see nationalism as essentially a disease of the body politic encourages such stock-taking. Rare are those analyses of Québec nationalism that do not share in this medical paradigm (Juteau-Lee, 1979; Gingras and Nevitte, 1984). Most nationalisms, especially those of the subnational (Catalonia, Corsica) and Third World variety, are usually considered as "symptoms" of wider phenomena.

This article has very little to say about definitions (see Balthazar, in this volume). It deals almost exclusively with the present and with those coloured glasses through which Québec nationalism is being scrutinized. We will complete, rather than supersede, the many theoretical constructs that have attempted to explain why Québec nationalism appears unwilling to fade away.

THE SEVEN LIVES OF QUÉBEC NATIONALISM

One of the surprising aspects of Québec nationalism is how often it has been diagnosed as terminally ill. Since 1959, it has been declared "dead on arrival" on no less than six occasions. Obviously, it has also been declared well and alive on an equal number of occasions. *Noblesse oblige.* You must be reborn if you are to die again.

The first such pronouncement came in 1959 when Maurice Duplessis passed away and the Union Nationale stood a good chance of losing its grip on power, especially after the sudden death of Duplessis's popular successor, Paul Sauvé. It was widely believed at the time that the old clerical backward nationalism would disappear with the Unionist dynasty. As this traditional nationalism was then the only known form of Québec nationalism, everyone also concluded that all traces of the said phenomenon would soon disappear. Curiously, nobody, in Québec or elsewhere, foresaw the emergence of the Quiet Revolution and of its own special brand of nationalism.

So opposed was he at the time to any form of nationalism that René Lévesque even agreed to run for the Québec Liberal Party in the 1960 election, in part because there was little chance for this party ever to espouse the traditional nationalist cause. The provincial Liberal leader, Jean Lesage, had a reputation of being one of the least nationalist French Canadians in the Louis St. Laurent federal cabinet. Not surprisingly, the 1960 Liberal provincial platform specifically condemned the sterile nationalist battles of the past. Its program was exclusively one of administrative, economic, and social renewal of Québec.[2]

Six years later, the electoral defeat of the same Liberal Party was welcomed by many and deplored by still more as the beginning of the end of what had become known in the meantime as Québec's "new" nationalism. It was widely expected that the Union Nationale under the direction of Daniel Johnson would turn back the nationalist clock to its rural, clerical, and defensive time-zone of pre-1960 fame. Jean-Jacques Bertrand who, following the 1960 defeat, had run for the Union Nationale leadership on a nationalist and progressive platform had been soundly defeated by Daniel Johnson, whose coming to power both in the party and in Québec City was taken as a signal of difficult times ahead for the Quiet Revolution and for the positive forward-looking nationalism it carried with it.

Two years later a similar diagnosis was produced, but this time the diagnosis followed the death of Daniel Johnson, whose antinationalist and anti–Quiet Revolution feelings had apparently been greatly exaggerated. By 1969, it was the coming of political age of Johnson's successor, Jean-Jacques Bertrand, the same man whose previous political defeat had been heralded as the end of nationalist politics, which was interpreted as a sign of the coming demise of nationalism. Suddenly, M. Bertrand was judged to be more federalist-oriented than Jean-Guy Cardinal, his opponent at the National Union 1969 leadership convention. Over the years, Québec nationalism has known a curious assortment of the "undertaken."

But many would argue that the third death of Québec nationalism had actually taken place a few months before with the election in Ottawa of arch antinationalist Pierre Trudeau, whose wide support within Québec was considered a sure indication that the Québécois had tired of the nationalist game in any shape and form and would be content from now on to play a diluted version of the French-Canadian nationalist game in Ottawa. There is still some confusion as to whether or not the April 1970 election of Robert Bourassa and his impressive defeat of the charismatic Parti Québécois leader, René Lévesque, constituted a distinct death for Québec nationalism or should be considered as part of the high-mortality 1968–70 period.

There is no such confusion regarding the October Crisis and the FLQ episode of 1970. The swift and violent reaction of Prime Minister Trudeau, his complete disregard of due process, and the large degree of acceptance received by such measures both in English- and French-speaking Canada was considered at the time as the final fatal blow to the prospects of a democratic and electorally conducted drive toward that ultimate nationalist goal, Québec sovereignty. Nationalism, this time in its independentist incarnation, had died a fourth time! The 1973 massive electoral collapse of the Parti Québécois—René Lévesque was defeated again in his own riding—was considered a mere confirmation that all was indeed very quiet on the Québec nationalist front. Clearly, nothing could bring the nationalist corpse back to political life.

Between 1976 and 1980, Québec nationalism, which had been resurrected through the PQ electoral victory, underwent its longest stretch without a single death. Now in its fourth or perhaps fifth reincarnation, it survived happily under the form of "progressive" neonationalism only to suffer its most serious death, that of the referendum defeat of 1980. Pierre Trudeau, who in the past had happily proclaimed Québec's nationalism to be dead, could do so one more time.

The same proclamation was again issued in 1982 with the adoption of the Canadian Charter of Rights and Freedoms, which put Canada and Québec on an individual rather than a collective course. The accompanying new Constitution also put an end to Québec's pretence of having its own nationalist cake while eating it too. The rebirth of Québec nationalism following the stunning PQ electoral victory of 1981 had indeed been a short one. The idea could die peacefully one more time.

The resignation and the death of René Lévesque and the decision of the new *Péquiste* leader Pierre-Marc Johnson to come back to a placid nonseparatist form of nationalism—not unlike that of his father, Daniel Johnson—were widely interpreted as additional signatures on the seventh nationalist death certificate. So was the eviction of even this moderate leader and his replacement by radical Jacques Parizeau. By announcing that the Parti Québécois would no longer campaign on sovereignty-association but would espouse the more radical goal of total sovereignty, with or without an economic association with the rest of Canada, M. Parizeau was perceived as moving his party to the fringe with little hope of ever coming back from the political cold. As many analysts then pointed out, ideological political parties such as the PQ never die, they simply radicalize themselves out of the political spectrum. The stunning comeback of Robert Bourassa, the ease with which he could sell his compatriots on a Meech Lake deal, which he himself described as constituting the maximum Québec could hope for after years of self-defeating nationalist-inspired policies, was also taken as proof that the nationalist tide had completely receded. Not only was nationalism dead, it was only a memory.

By 1990, of course, Québec nationalism had been reborn again, and the only thing that can safely be predicted is that it will eventually die for an eight or ninth time within the next few years. But could it be that nationalist-watchers have consistently missed the beat on Québec nationalism and that by tying its fortunes too closely with the fate of parties, leaders, constitutional proposals, or even economic conditions, they fail to see that it is even more closely connected with a changing global geopolitical environment? Even those who, at one moment or another, can claim to have uncovered a rebirth of Québec nationalism often fall victim to this obsession with local episodes. Paradoxically, Québec nationalists themselves have repeatedly fallen in the same trap. They are often the first to proclaim, as they did in the aftermath of the 1980 referendum, that having refused to proceed to its logical conclusion, i.e., political sovereignty, Québec nationalism could only go the Cajun way. After the collapse of the Meech Lake agreement, they were also the first to point to a renewal of their good fortune, only to be disappointed once more in 1992 with the rising prospect of a new constitutional deal.

Each rebirth of nationalist feelings is thus greeted with a mixture of relief and apprehension. "Will it last?", "Is this time the good time?" are questions that lie, if not at the heart, at least in the background of the nationalist vision. To be a nationalist in Québec is to worry, almost as much as if you are an antinationalist. "Will it come back?"

A look at the "big picture" would help put things in perspective. Québec nationalism, it is suggested, cannot be understood if we only look at it as an ingrown reaction, either positive or negative, to a set of social, political, and economic features of Québec society at a certain given time. The meanders of electoral and constitutional politics, the "ups and downs" of the economic situation, and the coming and going of charismatic and not-so-charismatic leaders can perhaps go a long way in explaining the confusing life history of Québec nationalism. They do not go all the way.

THE BIG PICTURE

Could it be that nationalism is a permanent fixture of the Québec political landscape? In the quarter century between 1966 and 1990, 7 640 709 Quebeckers cast a ballot at one time or another in the seven general elections held during that period for a party advocating one form or another of political sovereignty for Québec (Table 3.1). This represents an average of 32.7 percent at each election, with a total of slightly more than a million votes each time (1 091 530). This is a surprising result that is often lost, preoccupied as we all are with the mutation of a nationalism that often comes back under a different semantic disguise: separation, sovereignty, and sovereignty-association. Nevertheless, this permanence should tell us something of the underlying reality.

First, it confirms the electoral staying-power of the nationalist idea in its most radical proposition, that of independence for Québec. There has been no other similar situation anywhere in the world for the last quarter of a century. Of course, other Western and non-Western countries have witnessed the emergence of nationalist-inspired parties, but none has achieved such consistent results over such a length of time and such a diversity of conditions. Some have burst onto the political scene and have disappeared rapidly having partially succeeded or most likely miserably failed in their objectives. Others have languished in the 5 to 10 percent interval, often saved from extinction by a system of proportional representation that provides them with the parliamentary representation denied to them by the electorate. In Québec, the Parti Québécois has succeeded over the years in electing 218 members in the National Assembly. On two occasions, 1976 and 1981, it has had a majority of seats, and even its average thirty-five seats in each legislature makes for a performance that would be envied by ethnonationalist parties everywhere, not to mention third parties such as the Canadian federal NDP, which has had difficulties in breaking the parliamentary barrier even with a less economic and certainly a less radical constitutional program than that of the Parti Québécois.

As shown in Table 3.1, independentist nationalism in Québec has from the start been a question of numbers, with the Parti Québécois successful in exerting a near-perfect monopoly on the separatist vote. More than 97 percent of the seven million votes ever cast for political sovereignty were obtained by this party. There have been splinter parties, but no other independentist party ever achieved more

Table 3.1
Electoral Support for Québec Independentist Parties, 1966–90

YEAR	PARTY*	%	VOTES NUMBER	% INCREASE	NUMBER
June 1966	RIN	5.4	129 045		
	RN	3.1	74 670		
	PSQ	0.0	1 090		
	Total	8.5	204 805		
April 1970	PQ	22.6	662 404		
	PQ ("independent")	0.1	2 998		
	Total	22.7	665 402	+14.2	+460 597
October 1973	PQ	29.7	897 809	+7.0	+232 407
November 1976	PQ	40.5	1 390 351	+10.7	+507 458
May 1980	OUI	39.7	1 485 851	–0.8	+95 500
April 1981	PQ	48.7	1 773 237	+9.0	+287 386
December 1985	PQ	38.1	1 320 008		
	PI	0.4	15 423		
	Total	38.5	1 335 431	–10.2	–437 806
September 1989	PQ	40.2	1 369 067		
	PI	0.1	4 607		
	Total	40.3	1 373 674	+1.8	+38 243

*PQ: Parti Québécois
RIN: Rassemblement pour l'indépendance nationale
PSQ: Parti socialiste du Québec
PI: Parti indépendantiste
RN: Ralliement national

than 0.4 percent of the nationalist vote. The baseline support of the party passed the one million mark in 1976 and has never fallen below this since then. In fact, the PQ's performance in 1985 and in 1989, when on both occasions the party lost to the Liberal Party, was roughly equivalent, vote-wise, to its historic 1976 victory when it shook Canada and became the first secessionist government of modern-day Canada.

Since 1976 and including the 1980 referendum, the radical nationalist option has always obtained the support of approximately 40 percent of the total Québec electorate, which translates roughly into a 50 percent support among francophone Québec voters. True, this support has not always been one of strict fidelity to independence. In 1976, for example, a sizable proportion of the *Péquiste* electorate was made up of voters who wanted to shake Canada out of its complacency or who were tired of the Bourassa regime. The platform of the PQ has changed over the years. In 1970, 1973, 1976, and 1981, when it received its highest percentage of the vote, sovereignty-association and not strict political sovereignty was the order of the day. But except in 1976 and 1981, a vote for the PQ and sovereignty-association has most often been interpreted as a vote for a party supporting the idea of Québec becoming an independent country. In 1985, the PQ ran on a platform of "national affirmation" for Québec, but did not do as well as the most radical-ever *Péquiste* program of 1989.

It has not always been easy to follow the semantic hesitations of the Parti Québécois as it moved from independence to sovereignty to sovereignty-association and back to sovereignty. However, one cannot but marvel at the relative ease with which the party has retained its hold on the radical side of the nationalist spectrum. Its promise to hold a referendum and the fact that such a referendum was actually held, and lost, no doubt contributed to increase rather than decrease the legitimacy of the party as it moved through various definitions of what sovereignty actually means. But clearly, the PQ seems to have been in tune with the nationalist mood of the day.

Support for the Parti Québécois, however, is not equivalent to support for independence. Most independentists vote for this party and a vast majority of the party's electorate is also in favour of the idea (however one defines it). Nevertheless, the correlation is far from being perfect. In 1973, for example, there was approximately an equal number of *Péquistes* who did not look favourably upon the idea of independence as non-*Péquistes* who were supportive of the idea (Latouche, 1976). One of the reasons for the PQ staying-power has been its capacity to retain and even increase to its maximum its share of the pro-independence vote while retaining a substantial portion of the non-independentist vote. Such a result has even been achieved while the party radicalized its nationalist stand. One could have expected the PQ to have lost either its non-independentist support as it grew more radical under the leadership of M. Parizeau or its independentist support as the non-independentist retain their relative place within the party. On the question of independence and popular support, the Parti Québécois has apparently been able to have its cake and eat it too.

A study of 153 polls and surveys conducted between 1960 and 1991 offers another view of the "big picture" of Québec nationalism.[3] Between surveys, support for independence necessarily varies a great deal. The context is often different, the question is not exactly the same, and pollsters rarely follow the same techniques. Longitudinal analysis is thus difficult to achieve and rarely attempted. Figure 3.1 does precisely that. It plots the average by option and by period of the 153 measures accumulated over the years. Intraperiod differences are thus smoothed away. Although one should be careful not to extrapolate too much from such data, certain observations are again in order.

First, the four measures plotted here have constantly maintained their semantic "distinctiveness" among the Québec electorate.[4] Separation, independence, sovereignty-association, and a mandate to negotiate sovereignty-association (as was the case in the 1980 referendum question) have managed to keep their distance from one another. Clearly, these measures do not tap exactly the same underlying reality. With one exception, the ranks of the four options have remained the same at both ends of the time period.[5] It would seem that the Québec electorate has no difficulty in understanding the nuances between them. It could also mean that over any length of time, these formulations tap the same underlying attitude.

The differences between the various options have grown smaller rather than larger over the years. This is also surprising since the overall movement of the various curves is upward. One could have expected the distance to increase rather than decrease as more and more people join each camp. Apparently this has not been the case. With the passing of time, Quebeckers have continued to differentiate between these various formulations, but they have also tended to see them as part of the same movement. This further confirms the hypothesis of an underlying attitude.

Figure 3.1
Support for the Sovereignty Idea in Québec (1960–90)

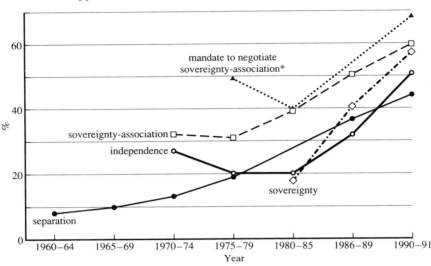

*The 1980 referendum question.
Note: For each time interval, the average support for each formulation was calculated and plotted.
Source: Édouard Cloutier, Jean H. Guay, and Daniel Latouche, *Le virage,* Montréal: Québec-Amérique, 1992.

The upward trend of all four indicators is undoubtedly the most dramatic result of this graphic summary, but it is not the only one. The constant and cumulative nature of the evolution of the four curves is also instructive. Movements downward are rare over these five-year intervals, but they do exist. For example, the "mandate to negotiate" indicator has gone down after its peak during the 1975–79 period. Clearly, this option lost much of its credibility after its startling failure in the referendum.[6] Could it be that the Québec electorate can recognize a "losing" formulation when it experiments with one?

When looking at these curves and their seemingly inexorable movement, one is at a loss to understand the logic behind the many death certificates that have been so generously awarded to the nationalist option over the last twenty-five years. But one should also refrain from making conclusions as to any inevitability. Never has a majority of the entire Québec electorate given its support to the Parti Québécois. Surveys and elections are indeed two distinct realities. On the basis of the trends illustrated in Figure 3.1, Québec should have attained a sovereign status sometime ago. It has not. If there is a message to be drawn from this "big picture" of Québec nationalism it is not so much its apparently unstoppable climb toward the magic 50 percent mark, but more appropriately its inability to do so when so many structural forces push it in this direction. Can a close-up on more recent events provide us with more satisfactory answers?

THE RECENT PICTURE

As expected, the failure of the Meech Lake Accord had a significant impact on political attitudes in Québec. The upward movement is clearly apparent toward the end of the graph in Figure 3.1. The much-heralded argument that a refusal by certain provinces to ratify the deal would be interpreted by Quebeckers as a rejection by English Canada was indeed confirmed, much to the chagrin of those who had worked hard for its ratification and who pointed out that provinces with more than 90 percent of the population of the rest of Canada had indeed ratified the agreement.

In the end, such clarifications as well as the denials, sincere or not, of those whose actions contributed to the final collapse of the process—native leaders as well as the Manitoba and Newfoundland political leadership—could not prevent the image of rejection from taking hold. Publication of numerous public opinion polls showing a majority of non-Quebeckers either ignorant of or against the agreement, coupled with the unthinkable (in the eyes of Quebeckers at least), that is, the decision by some provincial premiers to renege on duly-affixed signatures, had a more important impact than the collapse of the deal itself, which until the end had never enjoyed widespread support either in the population or among the Québec political elites.

But the June 1990 failure of the Meech Lake Accord is only part of the picture. More important perhaps in terms of public opinion is the linguistic crisis of December 1988, a crisis triggered by the Supreme Court of Canada decision to declare as unconstitutional some of the few remaining provisions of Bill 101. The impact of Premier Bourassa's decision to make use of the "notwithstanding" clause is well known. It served to undermine one of the major arguments in favour of Meech Lake, that in effect such an agreement did not provide Québec with anything else than a symbolic and theatrical recognition of its distinct nature. One of the provisions of the Meech Lake deal specified that the Québec National Assembly and the government of Québec had a special responsibility to defend and to promote as it saw fit the status of the French language and the French culture within its boundaries and areas of jurisdiction. If Québec could make use of the "notwithstanding" clause to go around a Supreme Court ruling that stated restrictions on language could not be considered acceptable exceptions under the Canadian Charter of Rights, what would a Québec government be able to achieve if the distinct society clause not only legitimized ahead of time any such actions but actually encouraged them?

The reactions of English Canada to the Québec decision to make use of the clause had probably a more important effect on Québec nationalist attitudes, moving them further along the radical continuum, than the Meech Lake fiasco itself. Scenes of the Québec flag being stamped upon, the decision of the Sault Sainte Marie City Council to declare itself unilingually English, followed by similar gestures across the country, all contributed to an exacerbation of nationalist feelings in Québec. By the fall of 1989, such nationalist sentiments were running at an all-time high in Québec. They were further helped along the way by the farce-like manoeuvres of the following spring to save the foundering Meech Lake Accord.

But the apparent close association between events taking place in the public realm, however dramatic they should be,[7] and the evolution of public opinion and of the nationalist sentiment should not be exaggerated. Not only did support for the various forms of political nationalism not vanish after the 1980 referendum, a noticeable resurgence of public support became apparent sometime after 1985, precisely at the time when all had been deemed to be quiet on the nationalist front. Nationalism runs in unexpected ways. The intensity of its media presence following important political conflagrations—and the linguistic crisis of 1988 and the Meech Lake failure of the following year certainly qualify as such—cannot be taken as the sure sign of a shift in the world view of the Québécois. Such events often provide new justifications for old reasonings or simply confirm the wisdom of the path already taken.

English-Canadian sense of betrayal at the Québec use of the "notwithstanding" clause was judged to be both ill-founded and sheer hypocrisy by many Québécois. The inclusion of this clause in the 1982 constitutional package was achieved not at Québec's insistence, but to placate some premiers, notably from Western Canada, who requested such a clause in order to retain their own manoeuvring ability. The decision of the Québec government to make use of a clause that had clearly been intended to be used was seen by most Quebeckers as only natural. In fact, the English-Canadian sense of outrage deprived Québec federalists of one of their most effective arguments in favour of the federal framework, that of the large degree of latitude enjoyed by Québec to achieve all of its cultural objectives within the present constitutional framework. Why, it was widely argued in Québec, was it deemed unacceptable for Québec to make use of a perfectly legitimate provision that the rest of the country had agreed upon no more than seven years before?

Nor was the "English-Canadian" sense of outrage at Bill 178 well received, since the new language laws, even after the "notwithstanding" clause, were less restrictive than before, thus indicating that Québec was moving—perhaps not rapidly, but nevertheless moving—in the same direction as the rest of the country, which, for its part, had still a very long way to go before providing its French minorities with a set of benefits even remotely as generous as the ones already enjoyed by Québec anglophones, even under the so-called harsh treatment of Bill 101.

Nationalism, we will argue, is an attempt to make sense of the world and of the place of one's national group within it. It gives meaning to past events, the good times and the bad times alike. It provides a summary for what happened. As such, it can only be reinforced when outside events follow an apparently incoherent logic and thus threaten the future of the group. Having agreed to undertake a round of constitutional negotiation to bring Québec back in the Canadian constitutional realm, having agreed to a plan to that effect, why was it then that English Canada suddenly changed course in the middle of the delicate constitutional passage? Québécois were never provided with a satisfactory answer to this troubling question. In a rapidly evolving political situation—turbulence would perhaps be a better term—the electorate has to give meaning to a host of ever-changing and contradictory events. Ever since 1988, Quebeckers have had to work hard to make sense of a political universe that, after the initial ease with which the Meech Lake agreement was arrived at, never unfolded according to plan. When asked to summarize and draw their own conclusions, they show no hesitation in registering their feelings on the most widely available thermometer, the "attitude-toward-sovereignty" one, but they do so depending on their present reading of the situation.

On September 24, 1991, the federal government made public its proposals to renew the federal framework, taking into account the traditional grievances of Québec as well as the demands by native groups and Western Canada for increased political recognition. These proposals were immediately denounced by Québec nationalist leaders as not only less generous than the Meech proposals but as a threat to the integrity of a host of Québec economic institutions. Polls taken in the wake of these proposals revealed that the all-time highs enjoyed by the sovereignty option following the Meech Lake failure had not been undermined by the new federal initiatives. In October 1991, roughly 60 percent of the Québec francophone voters were inclined to support either full independence or sovereignty-association for their province. These results are understandable and should not be taken as a sign of a closed mind and a lack of generosity by Québécois and their blind nationalist leaders. It is more a case of a rational response to a situation deemed to be increasingly turbulent if not irrational. Following the Meech Lake fiasco, Prime Minister Mulroney had hinted at new proposals that would transform Canada to the point of making it unrecognizable. Many Québécois had come to expect proposals that would even turn the country into a republic with equal power-sharing at the top. The timidity of the initial set of constitutional proposals proved not only a disappointment, but also a source of apprehension. The final report of the joint parliamentary committee—the Beaudoin-Dobbie Committee—did nothing to alleviate these fears. Its suggestion that Québec be given additional constitutional powers over marriage, divorce, and inland fisheries was received with much derision by both pro-sovereignty and pro-federalism forces. Further concessions and attempts to make such proposals more acceptable to the "average" Québécois will no doubt have a positive impact on Québec public opinion, but will also reinforce the belief that the federal government is but following the mood of the country and must consequently be considered as an unpredictable player.

Support for independence will undoubtedly continue to fluctuate as each electoral *rendez-vous* forces Québécois to take stock of who they are and what they want to achieve. The October 26th referendum on the Charlottetown Accord that was rejected by 57 percent of the Quebec electorate only confirms the difficulty of gauging correctly the sovereignty sentiment through mechanisms, in this case a pan-Canadian referendum, where multiple calculus were involved. No doubt, the next federal election, scheduled for spring 1993 and the following provincial one will further increase the confusion as to where the Québécois really stand. At first, a success or a failure of the *Bloc Québécois* and the Parti Québécois will be interpreted as a victory or a defeat for the nationalist cause, only to discover later that the issue has not been settled either way. Electoral confrontations tell us little as to where this nationalism is going. As exemplified by the uproar raised by Ottawa's proposals to centralize all economic decision-making instruments at the federal level, this nationalism is no longer limited to a simple question of language and culture. Over the years, Québec has come to see itself as a "distinct society" not only because of its Civil Code, but mainly because of its economic regime with its intricate web of formal and informal arrangements between government, trade unions, employers' associations, state corporations, private business, and various regional bodies. These views were widely expressed during the hearing of the *Commission sur l'avenir politique et constitutionnel du Québec* (the Bélanger-Campeau Commission) and served as the core of the so-called Québec model (Gagnon, Latouche, 1991). By the early 1990s, Quebeckers had come to believe, rightly or wrongly, that their economic regime was not only more responsive to their needs, but constituted a more efficient avenue to join in the so-called "new international economic order."

Québec nationalism is fuelled and tempered by events taking place on the Canadian political scene. The burning of the Québec flag, the rejection of Québec as a "distinct society," and anti-French feelings will undoubtedly exacerbate tensions and increase support for sovereignty. Similarly, gestures of good will, the constitutionalization of a "distinct society clause," or economic bad times will serve to lower the sovereignty thermometer. Depending on the exact timing of any referendum—not to mention the wording of the question asked—one will get 35 percent, 40 percent, 48 percent, 53 percent, or 60 percent support for sovereignty, sovereignty-association, or renewed federalism. But these results should be interpreted for what they are: instant reaction to short-term events.

THE SYMBOLIC CONSTRUCT THAT REFUSES TO DIE

Until the late 1950s, studies of nationalism bore titles such as *The Dangers of Nationalism*, *The Myth of Nationalism*, and on a more hopeful note, *The End of Nationalism*. The case against nationalism was such that few people even dared present a defence. The excesses of the French Revolution, World War I, and the horrors of Nazi Germany, a series of human catastrophes closely associated with nationalism, effectively convinced most social scientists to stay away from nationalism except to denounce it.[8] Quite naturally, nationalist outbreaks within otherwise quite "normal" nation-states have been considered either as aberrations or as surprising exceptions worthy of further investigation. The Basques, the Scots, the Bretons, the Welsh, the Walloons, and of course the Québécois thus became travelling companions in the "Great Ethnonationalist Revival Trek," which led to a number of stimulating explanations and some ambitious theories as to why apparently modern, developed, and civilized societies were suddenly fallen victim to nationalist agitation.

Summarizing the literature on ethnonationalism, Arend Lijphart has listed eight such explanations: (1) a decrease in assimilation and integration following a rapid increase in social and communication transactions. As two societies come to know more about one another, they often find new reasons for not wanting to share the same nation-state; (2) the "horizontalization" of ethnic groups, which under the pressures of modernization find themselves more and more integrated and no longer able to live in the splendid isolation so favourable to ethnic peace and coexistence; (3) the growth of state activities that provide disadvantaged ethnic groups with further reasons for dissatisfaction and for agitation in favour of their own state; (4) the decreasing salience of other conflicts, mostly religious and class, have made ethnic conflicts the only ones left on the block, thus their increase in relative salience; (5) the stimulus to ethnic demands brought about by the increasing concern for a more complete and responsive democracy; (6) the growth of post-bourgeois values and their insistence on a sense of belonging and collective as well as individual self-fulfilment; (7) the universal acceptance and the general-ization of the principle of self-determination, which was first meant to apply to colonies and has grown to become relevant for all form of social groupings; (8) the demonstration effect of ethnic demands by small and insistent groups.[9]

This post-facto explanation is nevertheless as suspect as the previous indiffer-ence. How could so many scholars of nationalism be so blind to so many forces and not see ahead of time that nationalism would simply not go the way of magic, child labour, and slavery?

The theoretical harvest in the Québec case has been equally productive, with internal colonialism as one of the early and best-known candidates to explain why nationalism has remained a permanent fixture of the modernizing Québec scene. Québec, it has been argued, was nothing but an economic and political colony exploited by a central government that behaved much in the same way as London and Paris did in the 19th century (Hechter, 1975; McRoberts, 1979). Not surpris-ingly, the Québécois are said to have reacted against this subjugation and in the process developed further their own national consciousness. In this vision, no longer prevalent, Québec nationalism was but a national liberation struggle under a more peaceful and subdued name.

Other explanations have pointed out that the inevitable disappearance of nationalism was not contradicted by ethnonationalist revival movements. Although they exhibit all exterior signs of social and political modernity, many groups still have a long way to go before being considered fully modernized. The modernization process is not without setbacks and tensions as old habits are being replaced by new ones.[10] Nationalism only reflects, much as the body temperature does, the difficulties associated with a rapid change in the political and social cli-mate. Thus, ethnic tensions are but the other face of a grinding modernization pro-cess.

As the dependence explanation became popular to explain the languishing state of many post-colonial societies, it was also seized upon to explain the resurgence of ethnonationalism in more developed countries. When the development of a society (Canada) requires the underdevelopment of another (Québec), it should come as no surprise that the distortion and imbalances that appear in the depen-dent society give rise to rejection movements.[11] Québec's nationalist agitation is no different from the passionate uproar that has also affected those Canadian peripheral regions whose development has been distorted by the needs of Ontario for high tariffs and American investments. But, as many critics of this thesis have pointed out, Québec is not a periphery; it is at the core of the Canadian economic enterprise.

As expected, Marxism and class analysis have also been made to contribute their own brand of explanatory power to the Québec case. During the 1960s and 1970s variants of the class explanation from Hubert Guindon's[12] "new middle class" to Anne Légaré's and Gilles Bourque's "national class" became the domi-nant explanations in a field already crowded with theses and counter-theses (Bourque and Légaré, 1979; Bourque and Laurin-Frenette, 1970). All variants of the class explanation agree that the Quiet Revolution is essentially the creation of a new Québec elite with nationalism—and this is where controversies set in—as either a tool for imposing their hegemonic control over other classes or as an instrument around which to build a common front.

For a phenomenon supposedly on the decline and bound to disappear, Québec nationalism has always generated a lot of intellectual, not to mention political, passion. In fact, rare are those pre-theories, paradigms, and approaches of the last twenty years that have not at one point or another been called upon to explain the resurgence of nationalism. Paradoxically, most of these explanations of the Québec situation make little use of the world-wide nature of the ethnonationalist phenomenon. True, the previously mentioned explanations, from internal colonialism to class analysis, all have had an international flavour inasmuch as the re-emergence and the direction taken by Québec nationalism was deemed to be explained through processes that were also at work in other regions of the world.

But most of these explanations go no further than to point out the simultaneity of certain conditions and processes. For example, after reviewing specific conditions that have led Québec and other subnational regions to experiment with separatist politics, Mary Beth Montcalm concludes that similar factors produce similar results.[13] To insist as she and others do on macroeconomic change as it affects "all western society in general and Canada in particular"[14] is to provide only a partial glimpse of the impact of the new global context. Logically, one could argue that the Québec case can be unique and still be shaped by international factors.[15] One should not confuse the diffusion of a phenomenon across continents with the global forces that are shaping the phenomenon.

The idiosyncrasies of the Québec situation as well as the sheer quantity of information available have even served to limit the contributions of other "cases" to the understanding of Québec nationalism, which, we might argue, has little to do with any revival process but more with a changing strategic response to a changing environment. Students of Québec, should they be Québécois or Canadians, have too much at stake politically to be able to make constructive use of the international literature. For their part, outside observers of the Québec nationalist scene do not fare much better; they most often make only passing references to the Québec case, as if its unpredictable course and its shifting evolution make it hazardous to use as an aid in understanding the nationalist revival everywhere.[16] Among the few international perspectives on Québec, O'Sullivan See's (1986) theory of resource competition under the direction of the state, Olzak's approach (1982) through the concept of ethnic mobilization, and Gourevitch's (1979) vision of a political leadership failure when confronted with economic growth stand alone as providing both general and Québec-specific explanations.

The variety of these explanations should alert us to the perpetuity and the richness of the phenomenon under investigation. Clearly, Québec nationalism is amenable to all possible forms of theoretical life. Ethnic nationalism exists in many societies. In this sense, it can be said to be an international phenomenon. What makes the Québec case a challenging one is its mixture of revivalism and globalism. True, there is a process of cultural division of labour at work behind the Québec nationalist scene. Various social classes are also actively involved in trying to shape this nationalism. But such explanations do not tell the whole story. Québec nationalism is also a societal nationalism where society is mobilized to attain certain objectives deemed necessary in this age of global competition. Thus, Québec nationalism is about English–French relations and about settling historical scores, much as is the case for Irish and Scottish ethnonationalism, but it is also about finding the optimal formula for inserting Québec into the new global age. It is through its nationalism that Québec can best claim to have access to a certain universality. The mixture of distinctiveness and similarity that has come to characterize Québec society remains its best entry point in the new global order. This is also the only way this ethnic-based nationalism can someday evolve into a more civic one, incorporating anglophones, allophones, and aboriginal peoples in a societal project where they feel they can play an active and not uniquely defensive role. How well Québec moves away from one form of nationalism to another may well determine how successful its insertion in the new world community will be.

THE MISSING COMPONENTS

The various incarnations of nationalism in Québec through the ages have been well documented. Until now, the dominant historical interpretation has been that of Léon Dion (1964, 1969, 1975). Expanding on two of his previous articles on the "pessimistic" and "growth" varieties of nationalism, Dion has identified four nationalist "projects," each corresponding to a historical period: a *conservative* nationalism with its traditional and clerical definition of what French-Canadian society should be; a *liberal* nationalism either in its anticlerical 19th-century or modernist mid-20th-century incarnation and which has suggested that Québec adapt itself to the dominant liberal ideology of its North American environment; a *social-democratic* nationalism with its obsession of building a strong and interventionist Québec state; and finally a resolutely *socialist* nationalism, more radical in its socioeconomic program and proposing a break with the dominant capitalist ideology. Dion's presentation of a pre-1960 and a post-1960 break in the nationalist continuum has been one of the credos of the Quiet Revolution paradigm and has never been challenged.

Balthazar also identifies a traditional, a modern (i.e., liberal), and a state-oriented nationalism (in both its social democrat and socialist version). What is more interesting is the chronology associated with each of these phases. Balthazar points out that Québec nationalism in its first incarnation was a thoroughly modern phenomenon and not as is often assumed a reactionary, church-ridden and rural-oriented phenomenon as has been popularized by Pierre Trudeau.[17] Contrary to Trudeau's analysis, Québec's first brush with nationalism came through politics and parliamentary politics, and not because of any romantic, backward predisposition. Far from being an alternative to the world-wide phenomenon of liberalism, this first wave of Québec nationalism actually brought the infant political society of the 1800s in contact with visions of the world that for the first time were not limited to the pre-revolutionary vision of the *ancien régime*. Could we not hypothesize that Québec nationalism, far from being a purely ingrained product, controlled by the church, the new elites, or the intellectual "workers" of the day (Pinard and Hamilton, 1981), is but the privileged mode of access to the rest of the planet? Seen in this light, the content of the nationalist project would be but the sum of those codes and keys judged necessary by Québécois to integrate themselves in what they perceive is going on in the rest of the world.

Far from being enclosed on itself, the nationalist project is an attempt to come to terms with the outside. As such, it has never been the totalitarian ideology often described. For one, antinationalism has always had a strong and visible presence on the Québec ideological spectrum. One measure of its success has been the reluctance of most intellectuals and social scientists to identify too closely with either nationalism or its most radical extensions, political independence and the Parti Québécois. Pierre Trudeau has been the most eloquent and certainly the most theoretical of these antinationalist thinkers, but he has not been the only one.[18] In addition to the numerous ills of nationalism in general, antinationalist thinkers have singled out a number of Québec-induced problems associated with even a small dose of nationalism. For example, nationalism is criticized for its association with political failure and the high costs of such failures (Dufour, 1989). It is a masochistic self-defeating machine that feeds upon real and imaginary defeats. It stifles artistic creativity by imposing "Québécitude" as the official dogma. It complicates debates on every possible issue by imposing a nationalist grid even when one is not called for. New ways of thinking—feminism, ecology, peace—are unduly set back and have to wait on the sidelines until the "question nationale" is solved. Nationalism has given undue power to certain groups who use their own capacity to manipulate its symbols to their advantage (Taylor, 1970). Nationalism produces what Paul-André Comeau, a former managing editor of *Le Devoir*, has called the Train Syndrome: Québec is always late in latching onto the passing intellectual and political trains, but when it finally gets on board, it usually overshoots its station by a few stops.

Nationalism is a symbolic construct. It singles out a certain definition of the group and what lies outside the group. But this symbolic engineering feeds upon its own negation. In its attempts at hegemony and at universality, Québec nationalism has always been forced to take notice of those who have refused its ecclesiastical pretensions. It seeks to integrate them by either incorporating or neutralizing their arguments. Both antinationalists and nationalists are caught in a mirror dynamics of one another.[19]

Nor is Québec nationalism entirely free from the evolution of its old nemesis, Canadian nationalism. We are used to evaluating the impact of Québec and its nationalism on the evolution of Canada. When we speculate on the political future of the country, the forces for change are always assumed to come, mostly in the form of a threat, from Québec. Occasionally, Canadian politicians of various persuasions are heard to complain that the rest of the country should follow the Québec example. In some cases this is meant as a compliment to Québec, as when references are made to the specific Québec mixture of state capitalism, aggressive private entrepreneurship, and inclusive networking. Most often, the admonition is meant as a reminder to Canadians from other regions and provinces that Québec should not be alone in its pretension of wanting to be more equal than others.

One of the most important keys to understanding Québec nationalism lies not only within the complexities of Québec society itself, its class organization, its cultural division of labour, but in the ways the rest of the country has seen itself over the years. Québec nationalism makes little sense outside of this dynamic interference with this other nationalism, the Canadian one. When defining themselves, Quebeckers take into account what other Canadians, the so-called English Canadians, think of themselves and how they define the rest of Canada as well as the whole of Canada.

LIFE AND DEATH ON THE QUÉBEC NATIONALIST TRAIL

The last "death" of Québec nationalism, that which followed the referendum defeat and the signing of the 1982 constitutional deal, is a particularly telling one. In one of 1990's most popular essays, *Bilan du nationalisme au Québec*, Louis Balthazar (1990) concluded that not only is the end in sight for Québec nationalism, it is already upon us. This assessment is typical of most of Québec intellectual production in the mid-1980s. Within a few short years, there were as many books and articles on the irreversibility of the nationalist downfall as there had been, a few years before, books praising the Québec soul and collective identity.

Québec nationalism died, wrote François Ricard, because we had too much of it. We had an overdose of identifying symbols, from the flag to the food. Now, even the idea of Québec is a banal one. It generates no pathos, and without pathos, Québec nationalism, any nationalism, is doomed (Ricard, 1984a, 1984b). Death occurred because of the symbolic hijacking of the word "Québec," has suggested Paul Painchaud (1982). Originally, the word had only a territorial and at best a geopolitical meaning. Over the years, nationalists loaded the word with so many cultural meanings that it became top-heavy. The referendum defeat forced a conceptual readjustment on reluctant nationalists. Presumably, Québécois are now freeing themselves of the shackles of their old nationalist vision and realizing that there is no future either for their backward vision or for their garrison mentality.

The list of what went wrong in Québec is apparently without end. It is part of the "liquefaction" of politics laments Marc Henry Soulet, a fact that explains why Québec intellectuals have suddenly grown silent (Soulet, 1987). And without intellectuals and their passion for words, no nationalism can take root. Even when they are not as desperate, other analysts complain that Québec nationalism has switched side. It is now in "the service of conformity and even repression" argues Dominique Clift, one of the early proponents of the "death of nationalism" thesis (Clift, 1982). The epitaph suggested by Kenneth McRoberts, one of Canada's foremost students of Québec politics, makes it clear that even the foundations of the neonationalist project are close to crumbling:

> Much of the force of the neo-nationalist project, especially its social-democratic variant, had derived from belief in the efficacy of state intervention to solve social and economic problems. Once this premise was placed in question, let alone dismissed, the neo-nationalist project was gravely compromised. (McRoberts, 1988:341)

What did the "good doctors" predict for the post-nationalist age? Many show no hesitation in proclaiming an era of individual liberation, soft political ideologies, and personal growth. The Québec countercultural movement has always been ill at ease with its surrounding nationalist environment: "too heavy" was the general feeling. The end of nationalism is thus seen as the beginning, at last, of the Aquarius moment. It is the first step to the New Age, declared Pierre Vallières.[20]

Balthazar, for one, sees a return to a more discreet, less state-oriented, and less politicized nationalism as the most likely outcome of the post-1985 situation. The signs are all over the wall, he claims: the 1982 constitutional fiasco and the acquiescence manifested by both the population and the elites, the passing of

René Lévesque, the 1985 election of the Québec Liberal Party and its 1989 re-election, the new orientation of the Parti Québécois, the election of the Conservative government, the new passion for the stock market, the return of Robert Bourassa. But because all the objectives of the "old" neonationalism have not been attained and because some gains, notably in the economic sphere, are fragile ones, nationalism will not entirely disappear. A "new" neonationalism is already here.

This new version will be of the "provincial autonomy" variety, slightly antistate and open to certain forms of international and continental integration. Québec will come to resemble more and more the United States and Canada in its ethnic composition and multicultural heritage. Like them, it will seek to keep in touch with its historical roots while building a new and distinct culture. But there remains something mysterious in nationalism, so much so that most authors who have diagnosed a terminal illness feel obliged to conclude that it might very well make a comeback. One is never too prudent with nationalism.

First, as McRoberts points out, the Québec sense of identity, which is a prerequisite to any nationalism, is in no immediate danger of disappearing in Québec. "A sense of identity and distinctiveness can rest as much on separateness as on difference," he points out (McRoberts, 1988:437). A group does not have to be totally at odds with its social environment to retain a sense of identity. Thus, contrary to William Coleman, McRoberts sees no problem in the fact that the French spoken in Québec is increasingly being "invaded" by technical terms imported from France so that it "is losing its traditional roots and becoming like the language of advanced capitalism in North America, English" (Coleman, 1984:209). In doing so, Quebeckers are increasingly talking the same language as the rest of North America, but they do so in French, which only accentuates the differences of their situation.

Second, McRoberts insists on the dynamism and the richness of the symbolic construction and reconstruction that has always characterized the Québec process of self-definition. Quoting Léon Dion, he insists on the mythical texture of this definition and on the capacity of old myths to accommodate themselves to new ones, especially those produced by the newcomers to the Québec scene.[21] But this potential identity is no sufficient guarantee of resurgence of nationalism. The declining presence of Québec within federal institutions because of slow demographic growth is bound to have political repercussions and render obsolete the dream of a strong French presence in Ottawa. Increasingly, Quebeckers will have to count on their state and their government as their sole institutional ally. Furthermore, the implementation of a free trade agreement with the United States will undoubtedly diminish the perceived costs of moving out of the Canadian federal system. Not only is the American market much larger than the Canadian one, but any attempt by Canada to discriminate against Québec products would immediately threaten the entire free trade agreement and its acceptability within the GATT framework.

Yet these and other similar speculations tell us little of a nationalist renewal, like the one Québec has been experiencing almost exactly from the moment these severe diagnoses were being announced. At best, they list the background factors to such a renewal. They are perhaps necessary, but certainly not sufficient conditions.

IS THE NATION-STATE OBSOLETE?

The verdict of the literature on this question is a resounding yes and has been so for the last twenty years. Apparently, the fact that only one such nation-state, the German Democratic Republic, has officially accepted this verdict has not deterred analysts from making the same prediction with more certainty year after year.[22]

The "end-of-the-nation-state" tradition has a long history, almost as long as the "death-of-nationalism" one. To a large extent, they both feed upon one another, although the nation-state is judged to be doomed for a number of reasons of its own. Above all, it has come to be seen as nonindispensable, as illustrated by the much-quoted statement that nation-states are too big for the small problems of this world and too small for the really big problems. In the first category, one finds anything from the quality of hospital care, the sclerosis of our schools, or the financing of arts infrastructures. In the second category, pollution, drugs, energy conservation, the ozone layer, world financial stability, and terrorism are seen as the vanguards of those new global problems that will require global solutions that are only possible if the nation-state fades away. In short, the "size" of the problem determines the size of the agency or the decision-making authority deemed optimum to solve it. At best, these proponents of the size principle—the bigger the more serious—will agree that it is necessary to think globally and act locally. No one has ever made it clear why the contrary would not be a better option.

If it is indeed true that nation-states have become the dinosaurs of the new global agenda, then it is indeed probable that Québec nationalism will have run its independentist course and will opt instead for the "provincial autonomy" orientation predicted by Balthazar and others.

We cannot even hope to summarize all the "unmistakable" signs that taken together confirm the coming end of the nation-state. The rise of multinational corporations, the increasing scope of transnational forces of all kinds, the end of the Cold War, the growing irrelevancy of weapons of total annihilation, the increasing interdependency of all nations, especially those with historical feuds, the growth of international trade, the increasing relevancy of the United Nations, the crisis of the modern state, the overload situation in which all Western governments now find themselves, the increasing complexities and global nature of problems in need of urgent attention, all of these have, at one point or another, been identified as key elements in the story-line of the end of the nation-state. In Canada, no "sign on the wall" has been more frequently used to confirm the ahistorical, almost ridiculous nature of a sovereign Québec as that of the growing unification of Europe.[23]

But this is not the only reading possible. One can also argue that the structures and issues that are likely to characterize the emerging global system favour not only the consolidation of nation-states, but are likely to encourage the latter to play a more active role in this emerging system. True, nation-states no longer have a monopoly of "seats" at the international table. Since 1945, they have had to share this monopoly first with international organizations and multinational corporations and recently with drug cartels, banks, cities, and terrorist networks. But nation-states remain the most important actors, and with each increase in the number of international actors, the relative importance of nation-states may decline somewhat, but its marginal impact is necessarily increased. No international regimes can be established without the active cooperation of nation-states. They are the best-organized and best-prepared actors, and in many instances, Germany for example, participation in supranational experiences has only reinforced the national overtones of a given foreign policy.

Few predictions can be safely made about this new global order, except that it will be economy-driven and that this world economy, in the Wallerstein sense, will be a capitalist and market-oriented one. Following Ian Wallace (1990:6–7), what is already apparent in this new capitalist cycle is the extent of the "uncoupling" that has already taken place. First, many have already noticed how primary products have become uncoupled—to the chagrin of Third World countries—from an industrial economy that certainly needs such resources, but that has been able to neutralize effectively its dependency on resource-producing countries. This form of first-level uncoupling will likely go on as more and more Third World countries are left behind in the race for competitive advantages. Second, in all industrial countries, employment has also been uncoupled from production so that full employment and industrial reconversion have become incompatible objectives. Thus within countries, entire regions, racial groups, and even city-blocks are already being left behind. Third, capital, especially financial capital, is no longer related to the other means of production or to the immediate production of goods and services. It moves by itself, and these movements are the major determinants of economic growth. Finally, economic growth has also uncoupled itself from the traditional ideas of material progress and development. One can no longer assume that more factories, more highways, more high-tech centres will automatically produce "winners" in the international economic race. There is more to growth and to staying on top—or even in the race—than to simply pile up one upon the other the various individual ingredients deemed necessary.

In this turbulent world economy, nation-states are the only actors capable of bringing a sense of order. Contrary to multinationals, technology, or financial capital, they are anything but footloose. Nation-states provide a geographical closure to political and economic debates. They determine where the "buck" will finally stop and how certain groups will try to maximize their own advantages over a given territory.

Nation-states and their central government are in the best position to aggregate effectively demands and adjudicate conflicting claims on resources while disaggregating the costs and allocating the benefits of certain decisions affecting the citizenry. They are no longer at the apex of the decision-making chain, and there is no doubt that the responsibilities that they agree to push upstairs to the level of international organization are unlikely to ever come back down to them.[24] But such "losses" only modify the relative position of the nation-state within the chain of command. In no way does it affect its pivotal role. In short, the nation-state is fast becoming the "non-commissioned officer" of the new order, which in no way should be taken as a diagnosis of irrelevancy.[25]

In the context of permanent economic warfare, only the nation-state is able to exact from the various social partners the necessary concessions to arrive at a social contract without which any society cannot hope to compete effectively at the global level. The pulp and paper firms of Québec or the mining concerns of northern Ontario can no longer improve their strategic position solely by lowering their costs or improving on their technology. The key to their successes increasingly lies outside of their high-tech walls. Environmental constraints, manpower training pressures, and R&D requirements have little to do with job security, and benefits, the traditional issues of contention between management and workers. Such externalities can only be taken into account outside the firm. Society alone can organize such externalities in any optimal fashion. The rise of societal issues (drugs, death, genetic engineering, etc.) is already a defining characteristic of the new order. Heads of state now meet to discuss the plight of children. But who will speak for society? Who else than the political institutions of nation-states?

Nation-states have survived both the diminished importance of security issues and of territoriality with which they have been closely associated ever since the Treaty of Westphalia, which set the foundations of the modern international relations regime. As it becomes increasingly difficult to identify the frontier between the domestic and the international arenas,[26] national governments find themselves dealing increasingly with "adjustment" issues of many varieties. Domestic political and socioeconomic structures must be constantly adjusted so as to allocate more efficiently, and it is hoped more equitably, the benefits and the costs imposed by changing geostrategic conditions. Market forces can record such changes; they can rarely put together the social pact necessary if the new conditions can be successfully internalized.

As pointed out earlier in this chapter, it has often been said that nation-states have become too "small" for the so-called big issues of today's interdependent world (pollution, climate control, energy, etc.) and have for some time been too "big" for the problems of hospital management, school reform, and highway construction. Presumably, what is meant by this attractive formula is that the instruments normally available to sovereign countries (treaty-making, fiscal control, and legislative exclusivity) are of little use when trying to find local solutions to local problems or global ones for more encompassing problems. But such a view presumes that local and global problems operate in two different worlds with little interaction between the two. Surely, the new interdependence era so much celebrated in the speeches of presidents and prime ministers is characterized by precisely the contrary phenomenon. The role of national governments is increasingly one of finding the appropriate entry point at which to intervene. In some cases, this means allocating more resources at a local level; in other situations, it means pooling resources and transferring part of its own decision-making authority, permanently or not, at a higher level. To maintain the proper equilibrium between the two has become the raison d'être of national governments. When they fail to do so—as is the case in the post-Maastricht European situation—extremist parties of all kinds find a very fertile ground to grow.

The size of the territory and of the population that should fall under the equilibrium responsibility of one national government rather than the other can be decided based upon legal principles (the right of self-determination), the rule of force, historical precedents, or even moral or scientific pretences. Throughout history all of these rules have been used and adapted so as to legitimize territorial expansions or in order to support just and not-so-just causes. But clearly, without a sense of collective identification, political units, should they be empires, kingdoms, republics, or utopian communities, cannot hope to survive.

National identity is but one such form of collective identification. It might not be the final word on the question of identity, nor is it incompatible with other collective identities, more local or more global in nature. But not only has it shown remarkable resilience, its capacity to coexist with other forms of identification and to transcend—not always, unfortunately—its limited linguistic, religious, or ethnic origins has increased over time. In Québec, as in 170 other similar situations, nationalism offers the best hope of joining and contributing effectively to the new global culture. The more the new globalism forces nation-states and their central decision-making apparatus to fine-tune their intervention, the more national identity and nationalism will be called upon to help in the process of effectively mobilizing resources. As stressed by Anthony Smith, one of the foremost students of nationalism and one who began his study of nationalism using the prevalent medical metaphor (1971):

> Nationalism may not be responsible for the many instances of reform and democratization of tyrannical regimes, but it is a frequent accompanying motive, a source of pride for downtrodden peoples and the recognized mode for joining and rejoining democracy and civilization. It also provides the sole vision and rationale for solidarity today, one that commands popular assents and elicits popular enthusiasm. All other visions, all other rationales appear wan and shadowy by comparison. They offer no sense of election, no unique history, no special destiny. (1991:176)

In this sense, Québec nationalism is here to stay, not because, as so many have asserted, French Québec is isolated in an English-speaking continent and is threatened by the new global world, but precisely because this world offers challenges and opportunities never before available. The shape and form of this nationalism, the precise mixture of societal, civic, and ethnic elements as well as the constitutional status of its state apparatus, will no doubt vary. Some of these variations will undoubtedly be interpreted as further occurrences of the "Death-Revival Syndrome." One can even imagine a sovereign Québec state with little ethnonationalist content to it or a dynamic societal nationalism with little support from the Québec state. But nationalism in one form or another is likely to remain. It is much too important to be left to nationalists.

Quebeckers will probably go on arguing as to the best way to meet these challenges and tap the opportunities of the new age. Should their membership in the new global age be mediated by their participation in the Canadian federal structure, or should they "go at it" directly, without an intermediary? Nothing best illustrates this question than the ongoing debate about trade negotiations. Which is the better road: to let Ottawa defend Québec's interests or for Québec to speak for itself. As a founding member of GATT and member of the G-7 group, Canada has certainly more "clout" than a sovereign Québec could ever achieve. But, is it not better to defend your own interests, strike your own bargains, and make your own concessions?

However, the "global" issues are not limited to trade. Paradoxically, by opening itself to international forces and considering the "big issues," Québec is already confronting the issues of the next century. The transformation of Québec nationalism from an ethnic-based phenomenon to a more civic and cosmopolitan one has already begun. It will not be an easy task, as the temptation will be strong to fall back on the traditional ethnolinguistic definition of who the collective "nous" includes. These, then, are the issues that will constitute the future "très belles heures" of Québec nationalism.

NOTES

1. Quoted from the index entry in E.J. Hobsbawn, *Nations and Nationalism since 1780*, Cambridge: Cambridge University Press, 1990.

2. Constitutional issues were only a secondary component of this program and included a call for "patriating" the Canadian Constitution. In 1982, this initial wish was indeed granted, but this time conditions had changed and the National Assembly refused to join in the Canada Act.

3. This analysis as well as the data borrow extensively from Cloutier, Guay, and Latouche, 1992.

4. These measures are for the entire Québec electorate and not only the francophone one.

5. This is no doubt explained by the fact that during the Meech Lake debate sovereignty and sovereignty-association increasingly became associated in the mind of the public and as sovereignty-association became a more popular option it drew with it support for sovereignty as a stand-alone option.

6. One can also understand why such option found itself on the ballot on 20 May 1980. Its support until then clearly put it in a class by itself.

7. We have also left out Québec's support for free trade, which publicly manifested itself during the 1988 federal election and which certainly contributed to the re-election of the Mulroney government. English-Canadian elites and intellectuals, especially those that had always prided themselves on being open-minded and sympathetic to Québec's interminable demands, saw this support and especially Québec's evident lack of appreciation for their own cultural concerns as a sign of rejection and of an exclusive sense of self-interest on the part of Quebeckers. See Resnick (1989).

8. So pervasive is this belief that one of Québec's foremost students of nationalism feels obligated to remind his readers that although he has "a certain sympathy for the Québec nationalism in its moderate version, he nevertheless has a profound repulsion towards fanaticisms of all shades and colors" (my translation, Balthazar, 1990:13). No similar disclaimers would be expected in a study of the environment, of democracy or liberalism.

9. Taken from Lijphart, 1977:46–64.

10. This approach is no longer "in fashion" but some of its basic texts are still worth going back to (Mayer, 1972; and Binder, 1971). For a more specifically ethnic perspective, see Enloe, 1973. The political development literature as it applied to Québec has been extensively covered by Bernier, 1976.

11. Popular in Latin America, this explanation was not received as well as could have been expected by Québec scholars and intellectuals who objected, somewhat childishly, to the characterization of Québec as a dependent or peripheral society. See Savaria, 1975; Van Schendel, 1971.

12. His classic 1960 piece "The Social Evolution of Québec Reconsidered" and his 1964 "Social Unrest, Social Class, and Québec's Bureaucratic Revolution" are reprinted in Guindon (1988). Guindon's thinking is interesting not only because of the insights that he provided very early on as well as by his intuition that the Québec case was a promising one theoretically, but also because with Marcel Rioux he stands alone among the original *Cité libre* group to have come out on the side of independence for Québec.

13. "The findings noted here about the coincident postwar growth in a new middle class in Québec, Scotland and Wales, Brittany, Flanders and Wallonia, and the Basque area as well as escalation in separatist demands suggest that commonly experienced conditions in developed states underlie this escalation" (Montcalm, 1984:55).

14. Montcalm, ibid., p. 56.

15. In fact, references to other cases of so-called ethno-regionalism could be seen as an attempt to normalize, scholarly at least, the Québec case by associating it with a host of similar occurrences, some of which were not too respectable. Canadian comparative scholars have been known to have their own ideological agenda.

16. This is especially true of some of the most recent, and well-received, publications on nationalism. See E.J. Hobsbawn's quote at the beginning of this article. Ernest Gellner (1983:70) has eight words to say about Québec, all in the context of a comparison with Ruritania and Iboland; Peter Alter (1989), on his part, has absolutely nothing to say.

17. Curiously, Trudeau's vision of Québec history begins in the late 19th century, probably corresponding to his interest in the period's British political thinking. For example, his analysis of the intellectual background of the Asbestos Strike really begins with turn-of-the-century French-Canadian thinkers. See his "Québec on the Eve of the Asbestos Strike," in Ramsay Cook, ed., *French Canadian Nationalism* (1969), 32–63. In fact, Trudeau insists in saying that one of the problems of Québec, and certainly one of the explanations for its obsession with nationalism, is its impermeability to all new political ideas (except those of German romantic nationalism)

generated at the time of the French, American, and Industrial revolutions. See his famous 1958 article "Some Obstacles to Democracy in Québec" (reprinted in Trudeau, 1968).

18. Michael Behiels (1985) has documented the diversity of the antinationalist arguments before 1960. Antinationalists could be found everywhere: in Catholic youth organizations such as the Jeunesse étudiante catholique, in the universities, notably the Faculty of Social Sciences of Laval University, among journalists and the media in general, notably at Radio-Canada, in unions, and in writers' associations.

19. This analysis was developed more extensively in Latouche (1970).

20. No one has better articulated this perspective than Pierre Vallières who as a *Cité libre* editor, FLQ intellectual in residence, PQ supporter, and gay activist has undergone a remarkable number of ideological conversions (Vallières, 1982).

21. In 1987, Léon Dion produced the first volume of what will undoubtedly become the classic examination of the Québec condition (Dion, 1987).

22. For the 1991 General Assembly of the United Nations alone, seven new nation-states have applied for official membership: the two Koreas, Estonia, Lithuania, Latvia, Micronesia, and the Marshall Islands, raising to 166 the number of "doomed" entities. In 1992, they were joined by all of the ex-Soviet Republics.

23. Paradoxically, in the United States the same European sign is seen as indicating the necessity for the United States to become a genuine nation-state with an active central government and all of the paraphernalia of the modern nation-state: an industrial policy, a national education policy, a science and technology policy, etc., etc.

24. They could come back to local and regional governments as is already the case in Western Europe where certain delegated powers are now being devolved from Brussels to local governments.

25. We are light years away from the pronunciamentos of only twenty years ago when nation-states were judged to be absurdities, obsolescences living off the parochialism of their reactionary commitments to independence. They had not even noticed having been passed by transnational corporations. For a good summary of this view, see Barnet and Muller, 1974.

26. For an early view of the domestication of international politics, see Hanrieder (1978). Already in 1957, John Herz was commenting on the rise and the fall of the territorial state.

REFERENCES

Peter Alter, *Nationalism*, London: Edward Arnold, 1989.

Louis Balthazar, *Bilan du nationalisme au Québec*, Montréal: L'Hexagone, 1990.

R.J. Barnet and R.E. Muller, *Global Reach: The Power of the Multinational Corporations*, New York: Simon and Schuster, 1974.

Michael Behiels, *Prelude to Québec's Quiet Revolution*, Montréal: McGill-Queen's University Press, 1985.

Gérald Bernier, "Le cas québécois et les théories de la modernisation," in Edmond Orban, ed., *La modernisation politique du Québec*, Sillery: Boréal Express, 1976, 19–54.

Leonard Binder, et al., *Crises and Sequences in Political Development*, Princeton, N.J.: Princeton University Press, 1971.

Gilles Bourque and Nicole Laurin-Frenette, "Classes sociales et idéologies nationalistes au Québec, 1760–1970," *Socialisme québécois* 20 (1970), 13–55.

Gilles Bourque and Anne Légaré, *Le Québec: la question nationale*, Paris: Maspero, 1979.

Dominique Clift, *Québec Nationalism in Crisis*, Montréal: McGill-Queen's University Press, 1982.

Édouard Cloutier, Jean H. Guay, and Daniel Latouche, *Le virage. Comment le Québec est devenu souverainiste*, Montréal: Québec-Amérique, 1992.

William Coleman, *The Independence Movement in Québec, 1945–1980*, Toronto: University of Toronto Press, 1984.

Léon Dion, "Genèse et caractères du nationalisme de croissance," in Congrès des affaires canadiennes, *Les nouveaux Québécois*, Québec: Les Presses de l'Université Laval, 1964, 59–76.

Léon Dion, "Pessimistic Nationalism: Its Source, Meaning and Validity," in Ramsay Cook, ed., *French Canadian Nationalism*, Toronto: Macmillan, 1969, 294–303.

Léon Dion, *Nationalismes et politiques au Québec*, Montréal: Hurtubise HMH, 1975.

Léon Dion, *À la recherche du Québec*, Québec: Les Presses de l'Université Laval, 1987.

Christian Dufour, *Le défi québécois*, Montréal: L'Hexagone, 1989.

Cynthia Enloe, *Ethnic Conflict and Political Development*, Boston: Little, Brown and Co., 1973.

Alain-G. Gagnon and Daniel Latouche, *Allaire, Bélanger, Campeau et les autres*, Montréal: Québec-Amérique, 1991.

Ernest Gellner, *Nations and Nationalism*, Ithaca: Cornell University Press, 1983.

François-Pierre Gingras and Neil Nevitte, "The Evolution of Québec Nationalism," in Alain-G. Gagnon, ed., *Québec: State and Society*, Toronto: Methuen, 1984, 2–15.

Peter Gourevith, "The Reemergence of Peripheral Nationalism: Some Comparative Speculations on the Spatial Distribution of Political Leadership and Economic Growth," *Comparative Studies in Society and History* 21, 3 (1979), 303–22.

Hubert Guindon, *Québec Society: Tradition, Modernity, and Nationhood*, Toronto: University of Toronto Press, 1988.

Wolfram F. Hanrieder, "Dissolving International Politics: Reflections on the Nation State," *American Political Science Review* 72, 4 (1978), 1276–87.

Michael Hechter, *Internal Colonialism: The Celtic Fringe in British National Development*, Berkeley: University of California Press, 1975.

John H. Herz, "The Rise and Demise of the Territorial State," *World Politics* 9, 4 (1957), 473–93.

Daniel Juteau-Lee, "The Evolution of Nationalism in Québec," in J.L. Elliott, ed., *Two Nations, Many Cultures*, Scarborough: Prentice-Hall, 1979, 60–74.

Daniel Latouche, "Anti-séparatisme et messianisme au Québec," *Revue canadienne de science politique* 3, 4 (1970), 559–79.

Daniel Latouche, "La composition de l'électorat péquiste," in D. Latouche, G. Lord, and J.-G. Vaillancourt, eds., *Le processus électoral au Québec*, Montréal: Hurtubise HMH, 1976, 187–212.

Arend Lijphart, "Political Theories and the Explanation of Ethnic Conflict in the Western World: Falsified Predictions and Plausible Explanations," in Milton J. Esman, ed., *Ethnic Conflict in the Western World*, Ithaca: Cornell University Press, 1977, 46–64.

L.C. Mayer, *Comparative Political Inquiry*, Homewood, Ill.: Dorsey Press, 1972.

Kenneth McRoberts, "Internal Colonialism: The Case of Québec," *Ethnic and Racial Studies* 2, 3 (1979), 293–318.

Kenneth McRoberts, *Québec: Social Change and Political Crisis*, 3rd ed., Toronto: McClelland and Stewart, 1988.

Mary Beth Montcalm, "Québec Separatism in a Comparative Perspective," in Alain-G. Gagnon, ed., *Québec: State and Society*, Toronto: Methuen, 1984, 45–58.

Susan Olzak, "Ethnic Mobilization in Québec," *Ethnic and Racial Studies* 5, 3 (1982), 253–75.

Katherine O'Sullivan See, *First World Nationalisms. Class and Ethnic Politics in Northern Ireland and Quebec*, Chicago: University of Chicago Press, 1986.

Paul Painchaud, "Un autre univers de référence," *Le Devoir*, 4 February 1982.

Maurice Pinard and Richard Hamilton, "Le référendum québécois: les intellectuels québécois et le projet souverainiste," *Options politiques* 2 (1981), 39–44.

Philip Resnick, *Letters to a Québécois Friend*, Montréal: McGill-Queen's University Press, 1989.

François Ricard, "Indépendance du discours et discours de l'indépendance," *Liberté* 153 (1984a), 16–17.

François Ricard, "Quelques hypothèses à propos d'une dépression," *Liberté* 153 (1984b), 40–48.

Jules Savaria, "Le Québec est-il une société périphérique?" *Sociologie et sociétés* 7, 1 (1975), 115–28.

Anthony D. Smith, *Theories of Nationalism*, 2nd ed., New York: Harper and Row, 1983 (first published in 1971).

Anthony D. Smith, *National Identity*, New York: Penguin Books, 1991.

Marc Henry Soulet, *Le silence des intellectuels*, Montréal: Editions Saint Martin, 1987.

Charles Taylor, "Nationalism and the Political Intelligentsia: A Case Study," in W.E. Mann, ed., *Social and Cultural Change in Canada*, Vancouver: Copp Clark, 1970, 274–87.

Pierre Elliott Trudeau, *Federalism and the French Canadians*, Toronto: Macmillan, 1968.

Pierre Vallières, "Vers un Québec post-nationaliste? Idéologies et valeurs: oppositions, contradictions et impasses," in Serge Proulx and Pierre Vallières, eds., *Changer de société*, Montréal: Québec-Amérique, 1982, 21–56.

Michael Van Schendel, "Impérialisme et classe ouvrière au Québec," *Socialisme québécois* 21–22 (1971), 156–209.

Ian Wallace, *The Global Economic System*, London: Unwin Hyman, 1990.

Boss Politics in Montréal and Québec Nationalism, Jean Drapeau to Jean Doré: From the Pre-modern to the Post-modern

Harold Chorney and Andrew Molloy
Concordia University

INTRODUCTION

The relationship between the political culture of Québec and its largest metropolis parallels that in other provinces. To an extent metropolitan culture transcends political boundaries. The very mass nature of the modern metropolis inevitably affects the nature of daily experience, which in turn profoundly shapes the public mind of urban citizens (Chorney, 1990a; Gottdiener, 1987).

Nevertheless, every metropolis has its own peculiar character, history, and sensibility. Therefore, there are aspects of Montréal's political history that are rooted to a large extent in the specific political character of Québec society. Much of the recent history of Québec and therefore of Montréal revolves around the theme of modernization. Indeed, the national movement is inextricably linked to this phenomenon (McRoberts, 1988).

However, the linkage is more complicated than often supposed. On the one hand, the Quiet Revolution was clearly a movement of modernization. On the other hand, the resurgence of nationalism can be seen as a reaction to the fear of absorption into the anonymous culture of post-industrial modern North American society. Max Weber pointed out many years ago that modernization inevitably leads to disenchantment. In a society like Québec, and perhaps also elsewhere in Canada, such disenchantment can create mass insecurity. In Québec, nationalism is the beneficiary of such insecurity. In the rest of Canada, particularly the West, right-wing populism appears to be the principal beneficiary. Thus it is ironic that the current incarnation of Québec nationalism is led largely by the technocratic and business class feeding on an essentially captive body politic. It is unlikely that such a strange coalition can last, unless it is united by a variant of authoritarian corporatism. Perhaps the roots of authoritarian tendencies in Québec politics lie in this uneasy symbiosis.

The very insecurity of the Québec masses in the face of the dissolving culture of North American mass society provides the political base for an elite-dominated nationalist politics. This is particularly so in the absence of a successful social democratic alternative. Despite a long history of effort, the New Democratic Party in Québec remains a marginal party and the national question confounds whatever social democratic tendencies there are in the Parti Québécois (Lévesque, 1984). In the West, similar authoritarian politics can develop around populist themes—witness the Social Credit movement in Alberta and British Columbia (Finkel, 1989). In Western Canada, however, this variant of populism is propelled by quasi-national regional resentments (Chorney and Hansen, 1985; Finkel, 1989; Molloy, 1992). However, the presence of ethnically defined nationalist passions in the politics of Québec society provides a dimension that is of little importance to western regionalism, although red-neck and racist sentiments are found among fringes of the populist movement of the West.

MUNICIPAL POLITICS IN MONTRÉAL AND TORONTO

If we compare the history of municipal politics in Toronto with that of Montréal, we will note certain similarities. For example, both cities suffer from low rates of political participation in local elections as compared to provincial ones (Higgins, 1989). On the other hand, there are definite differences. For example, Montréal appears to have had longer-serving, more charismatic, and one might even say more authoritarian mayors and less emphasis upon citizen participation than Toronto has had. Whereas Jean Drapeau and Camillien Houde could easily fall under the rubric of boss politics, few would say the same about Arthur Eggleton, John Sewell, Phillip Givens, William Denison, Jimmy Simpson, and David Crombie.

Neither Crombie nor Eggleton, who were long-serving mayors, matched Drapeau or Houde for longevity or sheer populist appeal. The one mayor who might have, Sam Mcbride, served only for a brief period. Perhaps the most authoritarian and effective Toronto politician, "Big Daddy" Fredrick Gardiner, served as Metro Chairman, rather than as mayor. Gardiner served from 1953 to 1961, a period far shorter than the tenure of Drapeau or Houde (Sancton, in Magnusson and Sancton, 1983). The current Montréal mayor, Jean Doré, at first blush seems to be much closer to the Toronto reform model. But we believe that he still is closer to the spirit of Drapeau than his reform rhetoric would suggest.

The question to be answered, however imperfectly, is whether or not this difference that we observe between the mayors in the two largest Canadian metropoles during the past sixty years is the product of something specific in the political culture of Montréal and possibly Québec. Or rather is the observed difference simply a consequence of a different stage in the development of the two societies?

MONTRÉAL AND TORONTO: A TALE OF TWO CITIES

There are definite differences in the political economy of the two metropoles. Prior to the current recession the unemployment rate in Toronto was consistently below that of Montréal. During this recession Toronto has suffered from severe unemployment that approaches the chronic levels of unemployment from which Montréal normally suffers. On the whole, however, the economic circumstances of Toronto have been considerably more favourable. Montréal has experienced for the last several decades a decline in its economic position in relation to Toronto

(Naylor, 1990). This can be seen in statistics that compare head office locations, stock market volumes, property values, and unemployment rates. Over the period 1950 to 1991 the unemployment rate in Montréal has exceeded the national unemployment rate by several percentage points (Chorney, 1990b; Gagnon and Montcalm, 1990).

Table 4.1 compares unemployment rates in Montréal and Toronto from 1966 until 1991, the period for which reliable metropolitan data are available. It clearly shows that Montréal has suffered from much higher rates of unemployment.

Table 4.1

Unemployment in Montréal and Toronto, 1966–91

	MONTRÉAL	TORONTO
1966	3.4%	2.0%
1967	4.0	2.7
1968	5.4	3.0
1969	5.8	2.5
1970	6.8	3.9
1971	7.1	5.1
1972	7.0	4.6
1973	6.0	3.9
1974	5.4	3.6
1975	6.4	6.5
1976	6.6	4.8
1977	9.4	7.1
1978	10.3	7.0
1979	8.3	5.5
1980	9.3	5.9
1981	9.4	5.1
1982	13.5	8.7
1983	14.4	9.7
1984	12.3	7.4
1985	11.8	6.8
1986	10.1	6.4
1987	10.2	5.2
1988	9.2	3.7
1989	9.3	3.7
1990	8.9	3.9
1991	11.9 (July)	11.1

Note: Rates for the period 1966 to 1972 are annual rates. Rates for other years are the June rates. The census metropolitan areas are used for both Montréal and Toronto.
Source: Statistics Canada, 1966–91.

It is thus not surprising that Montréal also has a lower average per capita income and more people with poverty-level incomes and fewer with upper incomes than does Toronto. For example, in the 1988 tax year the average income for all those who filed a tax return in Montréal was $19,540. The same statistic in Toronto was $28,181. When one examines the distribution of incomes by income class for tax filers the results are equally striking.

Table 4.2 simply reinforces the status of Montréal as a much poorer metropolis than Toronto. Because of this poverty and higher unemployment, there is greater

Table 4.2
Income Tax Filers by Income Class, Toronto and Montréal, 1988

INCOME CLASS	TORONTO	MONTRÉAL
	Number of filers	Number of filers
under $2,500	67,040	91,760
2,500–5,000	45,150	52,680
5,000–7,500	50,110	62,230
7,500–10,000	49,090	61,880
10,000–12,500	48,290	58,020
12,500–15,000	46,360	53,090
15,000–17,500	45,170	48,650
17,500–20,000	43,690	44,750
20,000–25,000	80,440	76,810
25,000–30,000	65,240	55,420
30,000–35,000	51,400	42,220
35,000–40,000	37,880	28,340
40,000–50,000	45,300	32,680
50,000+	75,830	37,570
Total number of filers	750,999	746,090

Source: *Taxation Statistics*, 1990 edition, Revenue Canada.

pressure on municipal administrations to address the issue of employment gener-ation. Also, the higher unemployment undoubtedly plays a role in fuelling nation-alist passions (Chorney, 1991).

During the current recession the unemployment rate in Montréal proper, as opposed to the metropolitan area, has approached 20 percent and even higher in certain *quartiers*, while in the Toronto area proper it is somewhat lower. In the course of the current recession that began in the last quarter of 1990 Montréal has suffered a net loss of some 42,000 jobs. Most job losses have occurred in older manufacturing sectors of the economy that were vulnerable to the restructuring pressures of the free trade agreement once a recession was unleashed (Statistics Canada, 20 September 1991). Manufacturing has been hit hard in Ontario as well, but the city of Toronto starts from a stronger base than does Montréal.

This economic difference has made concern over local employment and eco-nomic development in Montréal very central to the political strategy of its leading politicians. The need for strong measures of intervention in the economy or, fail-ing this, some other equally strong pole of attraction, such as expositions and spectacular events or major public works that generate construction activity and employment, is more pressing. In addition, the higher rate of unemployment is in itself a cause of legitimate grievance that fuels the political debate at the local, provincial, and federal levels. There are those who also argue that Québec nation-alism has contributed to the economic decline. However, we would rather argue that the higher unemployment is what fuels nationalism, not the other way around. What is actually responsible for this unemployment is quite another and larger matter that has been extensively discussed elsewhere (see, for example, Chorney, 1989, 1990b; Durocher and Linteau, 1980; McCallum, 1991; Naylor, 1990).

In this essay we can reach no definitive conclusion about the role that economic difference has played. But some speculation about the nature of the political differences between the two metropolises is in order. Clearly the issue of different rates of development does play a role. For example, Toronto had universal enfranchisement in 1958. Montréal, on the other hand, had to wait until the 1970s for the elimination of the special seats reserved for property owners (McKenna and Purcell, 1980; on stages of development, see Gagnon and Montcalm, 1990; Trofimenkoff, 1983; McRoberts, 1988). Beyond differences that are traceable to differing stages of development and divergent value systems and cultural traditions, we come finally to forces that appear to be promoting some sort of convergence between the two metropolises. Broadly speaking, we could group these forces under the post-modern umbrella of political life.

A number of writers have argued that Western society and its metropolises appear to be leaving the modern epoch and entering the century of post-modernism (Boyne and Rattansi, 1990; Harvey, 1990). In this post-modern world it is argued that there may well be a convergence of politics and modern daily experience around the values of spectacle, imagery, and media-driven surreal entertainment. What begins as serious political reform ends not in the classical situation of a degraded authoritarian politician, but in the post-modern farce of a politician posing as a reformer but practising authoritarian politics without any of the convincing grandeur of the modernist boss politician. Instead of drama the result may be comic opera.

But what exactly is post-modernism and can it help us make sense out of what has transpired in local politics in Montréal? It begins with the idea that history does not necessarily represent progress. Instead, the exponents of post-modernism argue that the historical process is really an exercise in myth-making and linguistic game playing.

The modern project in the words of one of post-modernism's most important interpreters, Jean-François Lyotard, has failed (Boyne and Rattansi, 1990). The era of the grand narrative is over. By grand narrative is meant an ideological overview of society and how it can progress if it adopts a certain program of action. For example, Marxism, liberalism, or conservatism would be considered grand narratives. Instead, it is claimed that a multitude of smaller events, none of which has a totally consistent meaning in the context of an overall world view, dominate the landscape (Molloy, 1992). We are not totally convinced by this concept, but it does provide an intriguing perspective on political life in Montréal.

In this essay we explore the history of Montréal politics from the modern epoch that began with the arrival of Jean Drapeau in office in 1954 to the present regime of the Montréal Citizens' Movement (MCM) under Jean Doré. In doing so we seek to draw some political insights about the nature of Montréal's political culture as both a great Canadian metropolis and as the leading metropolis in Québec society. As well, we will discuss the role that Québec nationalism has played in shaping the culture of urban politics in Québec. Finally we will explore to what extent, if at all, the post-modern approach can explain some of the current character of Montréal politics.

This character has been shaped in the age of reform and national *épanouissement* under the big top of the spectacle, but now minus its most impressive circus master of the modern epoch, Jean Drapeau. Put simply, Jean Doré, while Drapeau's successor and despite his credentials as a reformer, falls well short of the mark. His repudiation of strong grassroots democratic participation as excessive utopianism, and the zeal with which he has embraced the trappings of office, may belie as much the nature of the post-modern world as they do his own ambiguous heritage in the politics of Québec nationalism.

MONTRÉAL CITY POLITICS: THE COMING OF DRAPEAU

From 1914 until the present Montréal has been governed by eight mayors. These included: Médéric Martin from 1914 until 1924 and again from 1926 to 1928; Charles Duquette from 1924 to 1926; Camillien Houde from 1928 until 1932, and again from 1934 to 1936 and 1938 to 1940. During the years 1932 to 1934, Ferdinand Rinfret replaced Houde. Adhemar Reynault served as mayor from 1936 to 1938 because of Houde's imprisonment under the War Measures Act, and he served again from 1940 to 1944.

Houde was returned (from internment for opposing conscription) to power from 1944 until 1954. From 1954 until 1957 and from 1960 until 1986, Jean Drapeau served as mayor. Sarto Fournier replaced Drapeau in 1957 and served until Drapeau's return in 1960. Jean Doré was elected mayor in 1986 and re-elected for another four years in 1990. His term, therefore, will be at least eight years and probably longer should he wish to stay on. In other words, from 1914 until the present, Montréal has had nine mayors with an average tenure of about ten years each. During this seventy-seven-year period, three men, Médéric Martin, Camillien Houde, and Jean Drapeau, governed for a total of fifty-four years or an average of eighteen years each.

Drapeau, of course, was the longest-serving mayor—a total of almost thirty years! None of these men, despite the reputation of both Drapeau and Doré for being reformers, could be considered to have governed in a very open and democratic fashion. Some observers would protest that it is too soon and unfair to include Doré in this company. However, there is considerable evidence to suggest that his style of government is, despite much rhetoric and some practice to the contrary, rather more closely tied to the authoritarian tradition in Montréal politics. Also we have almost five full years of Doré's term in office as mayor on which to base our assessment.

The two major politicians who preceded Drapeau to the position of mayor, Médéric Martin and Camillien Houde, were clearly part of the "boss" tradition of municipal politics. In this tradition power tends to be concentrated in the hands of an all-powerful figure, aided by a circle of lesser persons. Both Martin and Houde appealed to populist instincts in the electorate. In this respect they were cousins of figures such as Mayor Fiorella Laguardia in New York and Mayor Richard Daley in Chicago—tough, charismatic, and populist in approach. Both Martin and Houde were also strong Québec nationalists. Martin was elected in 1926 on the slogan "No more English Mayors here." This was at a time when the English-speaking population of Montréal Island was about 32 percent (Magnusson and Sancton, 1985:67; Rumilly, 1973:49; Masson and Anderson, 1972:97).

As for Houde, he was one of the leaders of the anticonscription fight during World War II and a heroic figure for Québec nationalists and for many French Montréalers generally. Nonetheless, when he announced his support for Mussolini in 1939 most nationalists disassociated themselves from his statements (Lévesque and Migner, 1978:159; McKenna and Purcell, 1980). This is not surprising when among Houde's outrageous claims was the declaration that "French-Canadians in the province of Québec are fascists by blood if not by name" (Lévesque and Migner, 1978:159). Houde later distanced himself from some of these statements.

Of course, French-Canadian personalities were not the only public figures who expressed admiration for fascistic politics. Mackenzie King himself was apparently impressed by both Mussolini and Hitler during the 1930s. As well, antisemitism was commonplace among many members of the Anglo-Canadian elite right up until the mid-1960s (Abella, 1982).

DRAPEAU AND THE QUIET REVOLUTION

Drapeau, of course, was at the centre of nationalist politics before he came to power in 1954. His victory was seen by many as the opening shot in the Quiet Revolution in Québec. During the war, however, he was briefly associated with the right-wing Catholic views of Québec's Lionel Groulx and the fascistic views of Charles Maurras. Even as late as 1959 Drapeau would quote Groulx's views on the survival of French Canadians with approval. Groulx played an important role in encouraging French Canadians to be proud of their past, but he was a virulent antisemite, an extreme reflection of the anti-Jewish perspective common throughout the Catholic world before World War II. Groulx also embodied right-wing Catholicism's rejection of modernity (Delisle, 1992). Drapeau, to his credit, was later embarrassed by his youthful right-wing associations. And to be fair to him it must be said that most of the Canadian establishment and masses, anglophone and francophone, expressed antisemitism and racism during this period.

Like most Quebeckers, Drapeau retained his commitment to Québec nationalism. Stripped of the antisemitism of Groulx, Drapeau's nationalism became a more robust ideology that had appeal well beyond the borders of Québec. But because of its origins in the ideology that Groulx had helped shape, it unfortunately retained a predisposition to corporatist and authoritarian methods. Given the economic circumstances of Montréal, in which unemployment above the national average has been a chronic problem, public construction works of a grand scale played an important role in the policy options favoured by Drapeau (Roy and Weston, 1990). As Karl Wittfogel and Maynard Keynes himself had pointed out, such a predisposition toward large-scale public works favoured a kind of corporatism and inevitable reliance upon the state to supervise the construction (Wittfogel, 1957; Keynes, 1936).

When he first came to power in 1954, Drapeau was supported by many of the people who later played an important role in the Quiet Revolution. Indeed, his first campaign for city hall was fought on the theme of cleaning up the city and ridding city hall of crime and corruption, making it a classic case of the politics of the social revolution that swept Québec in the following decade. One may question the effectiveness of Drapeau in accomplishing his original aims, but few could question his sincere devotion to this cause. After his defeat in 1957 and his period of exile, he re-entered politics a somewhat chastened figure and probably a good deal less naive, or some would say more cynical, about the nature of the political process. His third campaign was in that sense more manipulative of the media and the political forces of the city. Once in office he set about to ensure that he would never lose power again. This overarching objective, alongside his stated objectives of political reform and advancing the cause of Québec nationalism by constructing a model Québec metropolis that would show the whole world the achievements of the French Canadians in North America, led him to become a withdrawn and isolated political figure—the very antithesis of what he set out to accomplish. In this sense, politics in Montréal, as perhaps in all spheres of life, follows the dictum that one should beware the curse of getting what one wished for! But, given Drapeau's hubris, he probably never saw himself suffering this fate.

Abe Limonchik, one of the MCM's more proficient councillors and political analysts, made the case some years ago (Roussopoulos, 1982) that Drapeau's program could only be understood in the context of his devotion to the cause of Québec nationalism. Each of Drapeau's major accomplishments as he himself saw them—the Métro, Expo 67, the Expos, the Olympic Games, La Floralie, the various grandiose art exhibitions that he organized—was part of his scheme for enhancing Montréal's prestige as a city of world-class importance.

They may pale in significance now and in the future as the wind-swept and concrete sights of their former glories fade into the obscurity of the past (or fall to the ground in extreme cases), but for Drapeau what counted was their spectacular quality, their capacity to bestow pride of accomplishment, and their intimate connection to the non-Anglo-Saxon values of patrimony and aesthetic. Only the Montréal Expos—in the eyes of some, Drapeau's most enduring accomplishment, and in the eyes of others his most faded—is purely North American. The others are European or worldly in inspiration, something grander and more grandiose than what his fellow English-Canadian mayors could have accomplished.

Furthermore, these grand spectacles all involved substantial employment opportunities and capital investments, including the great metropolitan underground transit system, the Métro, and major roadworks such as the Décarie expressway, the Ville Marie, and the Métropolitain. Drapeau's final gesture, which thankfully he never accomplished, was the construction of a major tower atop Mont Royal, the monument to top monuments, to rival la tour Eiffel in grandeur and imaginative dominance of the landscape, a kind of secular equivalent to the sacred cross atop the mountain that had become for many the very symbol of Montréal and that would clearly surpass by its daring the substantial hunk of concrete, the CN Tower, that the "Anglo-Saxons" had erected on the waterfront in Toronto.

This final grand geste, hopefully to have borne his name, was snuffed out by his political retirement and the defeat of his political successors. Had it been built in the true tradition of the monumentalists who had inspired him, his career as the builder of the French-Canadian metropolis would have been crowned in glory. No one who succeeded him could have accomplished more in this respect. The Baron Haussmann of Montréal would have left office a contented man.

It is no accident that Drapeau retired to work as ambassador to UNESCO in Paris. For him it was a totally appropriate appointment for someone who had built his career around the theme of patrimony. Of course, with the monuments, the capital works, and glory came cost overruns, the whiff of scandal and corruption, and most importantly the Olympic debt and the misplaced priorities that crippled the civic administration in meeting many of its other more plebian needs.

These needs included good quality housing for all income classes and not just for the wealthy; proper recreational, park, and cultural facilities that were accessible for participation and not just spectatorship; a well-maintained system of roads and public transportation that wasn't starved of operating funds; a sense of neighbourhood that was inviolate against the inroads of development projects that coveted its land; a fair property tax system that did not overtax tenants while sparing the wealthiest property owners. Finally and perhaps most importantly, there was a need for a democratic city hall, first in the sense of a civic administration accessible to all citizens wanting participation in the level of government closest to their daily concerns, and second in the sense of a functioning opposition with access to resources.

All of the above were sacrificed so that Drapeau could promote his monumentalism and his linked vision of Québec nationalism. In the end Drapeau largely succeeded in his mission. Thirty years of authoritarianism at city hall produced an electorate at once riddled with apathy yet proud of the achievements of the mayor. Even with his effective defeat, his monuments stand and will shape, as he well understood, the urban landscape well into the next century and possibly beyond. Like all monument-builders he will not have to live with the consequences nor witness what later generations will do to his work. The sands of time may cover some of his glories, but some of them will last and be identified with Montréal far into the future.

Drapeau, of course, was not that different from other boss politicians of his epoch, such as Richard Daley, mayor of Chicago. Both figures were committed to authority and governance and ruled by the power of their machine and their populist appeal. But perhaps Drapeau more accurately resembles that of other great monumentalist in North America, Robert Moses of New York. Like Moses, Drapeau finally retired from his position a largely rejected and disrespected man. But in truth it could be said of him, as it is said of Moses, that he changed the face of his city. Unlike Moses, Drapeau was a politician rather than an appointed official. Furthermore, Drapeau, unlike either Daley or Moses, was driven by his commitment to the nationalist cause. His desire to put French Canada on the map became a cause and overshadowed any other objectives he might have had. Obviously, boss politicians are not limited to Québec, but Québec nationalism has helped sustain the boss politician if for no other reason than the fact that nationalism in Québec has produced a political culture that is very supportive of populist politics of a conservative variety. In this sense there is a good fit between boss politics and conservative nationalism.

JEAN DORÉ: THE POLITICS OF DEMOCRATIC REFORM AND DISILLUSIONMENT

In the final years of Jean Drapeau's reign, civic activists and reformers had a keen sense of momentous change in the politics of Montréal. All those who had opposed the regime of Drapeau as authoritarian, antidemocratic, and unprogressive mobilized in the ranks of the opposition parties led by the Montréal Citizens' Movement. Begun largely by anglophone activists and built out of the ruins of the FRAP opposition that Drapeau had destroyed in the election of 1970, the MCM had high hopes for the major changes they expected the party to bring about when it conquered city hall after Drapeau's retirement.

The party had built itself patiently and thoroughly from the small number of activists who had struggled to change the face of civic politics in Montréal from its traditional authoritarian approach. The party was formed in May 1974 from a broad coalition of forces, including former FRAP militants, partisans of the Parti Québécois, members of the Montréal council of the major trade unions, the Québec wing of the federal New Democratic Party, independent radicals, and a significant number of anglophone intellectuals. One of its founding members, Marc Raboy, described it in 1982:

> The significance of the alliance of groups at the origin of the MCM should not be underestimated.... It was an alliance between the most progressive elements of very diverse and often conflicting political and social groups, and represented a degree of unity on the left with little precedent.... Particularly noteworthy was the MCM's ability to bring together English- and French-speaking activists, to an extent which no group in Québec had achieved. (Raboy in Roussopoulos, 1982:237–38)

At its founding congress the MCM endorsed the principle of grassroots democracy, including the establishment of neighbourhood councils with considerable decision-making authority; the municipalization of land and the provision of greatly increased co-operative housing; increased public transportation and the eventual elimination of fares; a large increase in expenditures on public recreation and parks. The party established itself on the anglophone side of town where some of its leading councillors were first elected in 1974. From this strong base the MCM by 1986 had established itself as the obvious successor to the Drapeau regime. During that period of time it also went through several transformations from the radical grassroots party it began life as. With each transformation it moved further and further away from an urban social movement with radical policies and closer and closer to a pragmatic liberal reform political party. By the time it came to power in 1986 it had almost completely abandoned its radical roots and many of its initial activists.

An important part of the process of cleansing the party was the selection of Jean Doré as its candidate for mayor. Doré, like the party itself, had started out as part of the radical social movement in Québec. During the late 1960s and early 1970s he had actively participated in the nationalist independence movement. Indeed, he was the co-author of a book published in this period that sought to expose RCMP intelligence activity directed against nationalist activists in Québec (Doré, 1978).

When the Parti Québécois came to power in 1976, Doré was brought to Québec City by René Lévesque where he worked as his special assistant for several years. Like many other 1960s activists, Doré had become much more pragmatic by the time he ascended to the head of the MCM. Proclaiming his commitment to the democratic and reform goals of the MCM, he nevertheless distanced himself and thereby the party from some of its more "utopian" objectives. Like his mentor Michael Fainstat who served as the party's chief apparatchik and later chief of the executive committee at city hall, Doré saw himself as a tough but pragmatic politician determined to obtain power and to exercise it effectively.

Despite the promise of more open government linked to grassroots democratic neighbourhood councils, the actual government that Doré leads is, in practice, rather centralized, secretive, and hierarchical. Instead of government from below it continues much of the tradition of government from above. It does so, however, with the rhetoric and to a certain extent the trappings of greater citizen involvement and openness.

For example, although the party under the urging of Doré and Fainstat had dropped its commitment to introduce neighbourhood councils during its first term in office, it did hold extensive hearings on the issue of local democracy. It ultimately introduced district advisory committees, largely powerless local advisory groups, as part of the process by which local residents could have some input into city hall. But these groups fell far short of what the party had originally promised. The party, to its credit, did introduce a public question period during council meetings and generally increased public access through neighbourhood information offices and greater attention paid to public liaison. But the executive committee and Doré himself continued the tradition of secretive and autocratic rule. Executive committee meetings were where the real decisions were taken. In the first years of the new regime these decisions included several that critics alleged showed the MCM was rather closer to developers than it liked to admit. The fact that the decisions took place behind closed doors simply made the sense of disappointment and betrayal worse.

Despite his populist platform, once in power Doré appointed a number of senior officials, mostly from Parti Québécois backgrounds, to highly paid positions at city hall. One such official, Pierre Le François, was appointed to a top job at a salary of $125,000. This appointment disillusioned a number of MCM partisans because it seemed to smack of the habits and ways of doing business of the old Drapeau regime (Bennett, 1990).

Like his predecessor Jean Drapeau, Doré had come to power on a wave of public expectation of substantial reform. Largely unknown to the public, however, was the sometimes apparently ruthless way in which Fainstat and Doré had asserted their control over what had started out as a grassroots movement. The truth was that neither Doré nor Fainstat or other key executive members had much patience for grassroots democracy. Like other social democratic parties before them, they fairly quickly succumbed to the iron law of oligarchy.

Once in power Doré, like Drapeau before him, began to display high-handed and authoritarian behaviour that had been familiar to his opponents within the party but unknown to the general public. Rather soon after their landslide victory in 1986, squabbles broke out between the secretive and autocratic executive committee and several dissident councillors with a long history of party activism on behalf of the MCM. By 1987 these squabbles were out in the open, and the basis for a new political party ostensibly committed to the original program of the MCM was laid.

The break between these dissident councillors and their backers, the "Jodoin club," revolved around a series of policy disputes during the MCM's first term in office. These included: the eviction of tenants from a low-cost rental housing project at the behest of a developer who intended to replace the units with a much more expensive project, but ended up abandoning the project after the tenants had been evicted and their units destroyed—the "Overdale project"; the planning approval granted to an arms manufacturer's expansion of its parking facilities at the expense of forest land—the "Matrox project"; several other development deals that involved destruction of either heritage buildings or site clearance and then abandonment of the development plan, resulting in large, unsightly open lots in the central downtown; the watering down of neighbourhood democracy; several examples of excessive waste and foolish expenditure plans by high-handed members of the executive committee; the general secrecy with which the executive committee behaved and their clear hostility for the idea that the party ought to have significant input into political and administrative decisions.

By 1988 the dissident councillors and their supporters found themselves more and more at odds with the party's executive—in reality with Doré and Fainstat and their immediate circle. Many of the other councillors who had been recent converts to the MCM as it approached power in 1986 were more than content to follow the lead of the executive, secure in the knowledge that to do so would ensure reward from the centre. By the end of 1988 four of the dissidents had resigned their position in the MCM caucus and announced their intention to sit as independent MCM councillors.

After a series of skirmishes with the party executive over their right to do so and to continue as MCM members, the four quit the party in the fall of 1989 and together launched a new party, the Democratic Coalition, to contest the 1990 election on a platform that closely resembled the original MCM objectives. Some of their rank and file supporters followed them into this party. Others who had been very critical of Doré and Fainstat for having betrayed the original aims of the MCM were drawn into a new grouping around green themes, Écologie Montréal. Both parties contested the fall election, and while the ecologists elected no members and the Democratic Coalition elected only three, their efforts were still judged to be successful by many of those who had supported them. The Doré-Fainstat group dismissed them as irrelevant, but privately conceded that they had indeed a support base in English-speaking Montréal, in particular.

POST-MODERNISM OR THE IRON LAW OF OLIGARCHY?

How is one to judge the evolution of Montréal urban politics from the time of Drapeau? The experience of the MCM has definitely disillusioned a large number of former political activists. Others, such as those connected to the Democratic Coalition or Écologie Montréal, soldier on confident that this time things will be different and that their particular brand of reform will succeed and not fall victim to the practical demands of power and the cultural vacuum that constitutes mass politics at the local level in North America (Gottdiener, 1987; Chorney, 1990).

A long time ago, in 1911 to be exact, Roberto Michels in a different context had predicted what has befallen the MCM in his classic study of the German social democrats from which the phrase "the iron law of oligarchy" is drawn (Michels, 1970). The thesis was deceptively simple. Mass parties, particularly social democratic parties drawn from larger social movements, were inevitably prey to the kind of bureaucratic conservatism that appeared necessary to the parties' very successful functioning as vote-getting machines. The only problem was that the very ingredient necessary to their electoral success was also responsible for their ultimate failure as movements for social change and reform. Certainly there is much in the argument that has explanatory power.

There is also something to the argument that the particular culture of Québec politics, despite the great strides that have been made in modernization and the introduction of fair electoral practices and fundraising, is still susceptible to authoritarian politics. But perhaps in this era of spectacular politics and image politicians and government by opinion polling, given the traditions of Montréal that placed a lot of emphasis upon the charismatic authority figure, we can draw from a more recent approach an alternative explanation of what has happened. This approach is post-modernism.

From a perspective of post-modernism there is a general disillusionment in practical politics that is felt by many in contemporary society. The steady diet of nihilistic events that our media-driven mass society is fed constantly conveys the image that, in the end, it is power and nothing else that counts. Even with the collapse of the power system of totalitarian Eastern Europe this insight still dominates the public's perception.

The Doré regime was elected on a program that was supposed to mark a radical departure from the Drapeau regime that preceded it. But in practice it has disappointed many of its former supporters, and its promises seem to have dissolved into language games and empty rhetoric (Melançon, Rotrand, Goyer, Boskey, and Bastien in Roy and Weston, 1990). The result is that disillusionment and nihilism gain greater acceptance. The modernist project of enlightenment and social reform through the application of reason and passion for political advance fades like the political posters in tatters on the urban wallscape.

From the post-modern perspective, political parties, politicians, and personalities come and go and life goes on. How can we speak any longer of emancipation, democracy, liberty, and progress in the light of all we have witnessed in this century? The disappointments of Montréal city politics are but small setbacks in the century that has produced Auschwitz, Cambodia, famine in Africa, or Saddam Hussein, the numerous wars, and the depression of the 1930s and of the past decade.

The disillusionments of the Doré epoch, and of the Drapeau era before it, and perhaps even of the Houde one before that—what do they mean, if not to shatter the possibility of a well-grounded belief in political and social reform? All politics is nothing but a grand game of deception and games playing. There is no ultimate truth or historical progress, only power and the games required to exercise it.

Take the real situation of Montréal and its current rate of unemployment and the suffering and poverty that it creates. If the project of enlightenment meant anything, surely this poverty and suffering would not continue, let alone last a period of years. And yet it goes on. The longer it continues, political cynicism grows deeper. Even the national project of Québec's intelligentsia in the eyes of some former partisans has been degraded into a simple grab for power by Québec's business and technocratic class. There are no more sacred causes. All seems profaned by the exercise of power.

Thus it would be relatively easy to accept the post-modern verdict on what has come to pass in Montréal. But the problem with post-modernism is both its ambivalence and its tendency to reduce complex events to a nihilistic set of lyrical prescriptions. As social theory as art, it works very well indeed. But in terms of its capacity to speak pragmatically to the practical difficulties of evolutionary reform and social change, it is largely silent. At best it can offer individual acts of resistance or nonconformism, or even small group projects of this kind. Perhaps in its most optimistic guise it can form the rationale for social movements of one kind or the other (Hamel, 1991).

However, it seems to us that a belief in the efficacy of social movements violates the inherent pessimism of post-modernism about grand narratives. Therefore, given the likely increase in pessimism and a turning away from political action that post-modernism would promote, one must assess the consequences of such an increase in pessimistic outlook. In effect, a vacuum is created in the political system at the level of practical politics.

Perhaps Québec is no more or less susceptible than any other part of Canada to the kind of politics that often flows from a body politic that has become cynical and nihilistic. But there remains a nagging doubt. Political disillusionment and loss of efficacy can breed undemocratic politics. Much of the populist reaction on the right of the spectrum in recent years in Canada has been born of this kind of disillusionment. In Québec nationalism in recent years has been the movement of the progressive left and social democrats who have incorporated it as part of a strategy of decolonization. Certainly this is how Drapeau formulated it in his book in the 1950s (Drapeau, 1959). As part of this strategy, a variant of corporatism, long a part of Québec's political culture (Archibald, 1984), has resurfaced in the approach of the contemporary elite. For example, the labour unions, business, and the state have shared a common cause on the national question and have also recently held congresses on the issue of full employment and economic development under the umbrella of the "Forum pour le plein emploi."

But one cannot forget that nationalism also has had a right-wing stream that in the past was xenophobic. Since the modernization of Québec politics in the era from 1960 onward, most of this xenophobic tendency in Québec nationalism has been banished by its leadership. Nevertheless, the national project, because it is so intimately bound up with treating the collective insecurity of the French majority, is vulnerable to the kind of vacuum and political disillusionment that a post-modern world may deliver.

Whatever authoritarian tendency there is in Québec society appears to grow in part from the need to advance the interests of the insecure and economically deprived French majority in Montréal. Even when this issue is not part of the agenda, the style of politics that has often been associated with it has become part of the political culture. Even in as democratically inclined a politician as Jean Doré this tendency is never far from the surface. No one should think for a moment that Jean Doré is at all sympathetic to xenophobia. But he has shown himself thus far not to be immune from authoritarian behaviour (Melançon, Rotrand, Goyer, Boskey, and Bastien, 1990).

In the end, the era of boss politics in Montréal may not, despite the election of the MCM, have truly ended. The next few years will tell us more definitively if Montréal politics has moved from the pre-modern to the post-modern and the consequences that this will have had for the face of democracy in Québec.

REFERENCES

Abella, Irving (1982). *None is Too Many: Canada and the Jews of Europe*, Toronto: Lester and Orpen Dennys, 1982.

Archibald, Clinton (1984). "Corporatist Tendencies in Quebec," in A. Gagnon, ed., *Quebec: State and Society*, Toronto: Methuen, pp. 353–64.

Bennett, Arnold (1990). "Why I stayed in the M.C.M.," in J. Roy and B. Weston, *Montreal: A Citizen's Guide to Politics*, Montréal: Black Rose Books, pp. 164–80.

Boismenu, Gérard et al. (1983). *Espace régional et nation*, Montréal: Boréal Express.

Boyne, Roy, and Ali Rattansi, eds. (1990). *Postmodernism and Society*, London: Macmillan.

Chorney, Harold (1989). *The Deficit and Debt Management: An Alternative to Monetarism*, Ottawa: Canadian Centre for Policy Alternatives.

Chorney, Harold (1990a). *City of Dreams: Social Theory and the Urban Experience*, Toronto: Nelson Canada, pp. 90–98.

Chorney, Harold (1990b). "Urban Economics—The Challenge of Full Employment," in J.H. Roy and B. Weston, *Montreal: A Citizens Guide to Politics*, Montreal: Black Rose Books.

Chorney, Harold (1991). "The Economic and Political Consequences of Canadian Monetarism," paper presented to the Annual Meeting of the British Association of Canadian Studies, University of Nottingham, 12 April.

Chorney, Harold, and Phillip Hansen (1985). "Neo-Conservatism, Social Democracy and 'Province Building': The Manitoba Experience," *Canadian Review of Sociology and Anthropology*, Vol. 22, no. 1, pp. 1–29.

Delisle, Esther (1992). *Le Traître et le Juif: Lionel Groulx, Le Devoir et le délire du nationalisme d'extrême-droite dans la province de Québec 1929–1939*, Montréal: Éditions l'Étincelle.

Doré, Jean et al. (1978). *La police secrète au Québec: la tyrannie occulte de la police*, Montréal: Éditions Québec/Amérique.

Drapeau, Jean (1959). *Jean Drapeau Vous Parle*, Montréal: Les éditions de la Cité.

Durocher, R., and P.-A. Linteau (1980). *Le retard du Québec et l' infériorité économique des Canadiens francais*, Montréal: Boréal Express.

Finkel, Alvin (1989). *The Social Credit Phenomenon in Alberta*, Toronto: University of Toronto Press.

Gagnon, A., and M. Montcalm (1990). *Québec: Beyond the Quiet Revolution*, Toronto: Nelson Canada.

Gottdiener, Mark (1987). *The Decline of Urban Politics*, London: Sage Library of Social Research.

Hamel, Pierre (1991). *Action collective et démocratie locale*, Montréal: Les Presses de l'Université de Montréal.

Harvey, D. (1990). *The Condition of Post Modernity*, Oxford: Basil Blackwell Ltd.

Higgins, Donald (1989). *Urban Canada*, Toronto: Macmillan.

Keynes, John Maynard (1936). *The General Theory of Employment Interest and Money*, London: Macmillan.

Lévesque, Andrée (1984). *Virage à gauche interdit*, Montréal: Boréal Express.

Lévesque, R., and R. Migner (1978). *Camillien et les années vingt suivi de Camillien au Goulag*, Montréal: Les Éditions des Brûlés.

Limonchik, Abe (1982). "The Montreal Economy: The Drapeau Years," in D. Roussopoulos, *The City and Radical Social Change*, Montreal: Black Rose Books, pp. 179–206.

Linteau, Paul-Andre (1985). *The Promoter's City*, Toronto: James Lorimer.

Magnusson, Warren (1983). "Toronto," in W. Magnusson and A. Sancton, *City Politics in Canada*, Toronto: University of Toronto Press, pp. 94–139.

Masson, Jack, and James Anderson (1972). *Emerging Party Politics in Urban Politics*, Toronto: McClelland and Stewart.

Mathews, George (1990). *Quiet Resolution: Quebec's Challenge to Canada*, Toronto: Summerhill Press.

McCallum, John (1991). "Agriculture and Economic Development in Québec and Ontario until 1870," in G. Laxer, *Perspectives on Canadian Economic Development*, Toronto: Oxford University Press, pp. 10–20.

McKenna, Robert, and Susan Purcell (1980). *Drapeau*, Toronto: Clarke, Irwin.

McRoberts, Kenneth (1988). *Quebec: Social Change and Political Crisis*, 3rd ed., Toronto: McClelland and Stewart.

Melançon, P., M. Rotrand, P. Goyer, S. Boskey, P. Bastien (1990). "Resignations-MCM Councillors' Letters," in J. Roy and B. Weston, eds., *Montreal: A Citizen's Guide to Politics*, Montréal: Black Rose Books, pp. 156–63.

Michels, Roberto (1970). *Political Parties*, New York: Free Press.

Molloy, Andrew (1992). "Art, Culture, Regionalism and the Representational: Populist *Ressentiment* and William Kurelek," in A. Molloy, *The Political Economy of Western Canadian Regionalism*, Ph.D. thesis, Concordia University, pp. 190–235.

Naylor, Tom (1990). "Business Prospects—Decline and Fall," in J. Roy and B. Weston, eds., *Montreal: A Citizen's Guide to Politics*, Montréal: Black Rose Books, pp. 70–74.

Pelletier, Gérard (1991). "Du pain avant les jeux," *Cité libre*, Vol. XIX, numero 1, July-August.

Raboy, Marc (1982). "The Future of Montréal and the MCM," *The City and Radical Social Change*, edited by Dimitrios Roussopoulos, Montréal: Black Rose Press, pp. 235–59.

Renaud, Jacques (1991). "Les géants-villages, réflexions sur une notion familière: la nation," *Cité libre*, Vol XIX, numero 1, July-August.

Roussopoulos, Dimitrios (1982). *The City and Radical Social Change*, Montréal: Black Rose Books.

Roy, Jean-Hugues, and Brendan Weston, eds. (1990). *Montreal: A Citizen's Guide to Politics*, Montréal: Black Rose Books.

Rumilly, Robert (1973). *Maurice Duplessis et son temps*, Montréal: Éditions Fides.

Sancton, Andrew (1983). "Montreal," in W. Magnusson and A. Sancton, *City Politics in Canada*, Toronto: University of Toronto Press, pp. 58–93.

Trofimenkoff, Susan (1982). *The Dream of Nation*, Toronto: Gage.

Wittfogel, Karl (1957). *Oriental Despotism*, New Haven, Conn.: Yale University Press.

P A R T

2

SYMBOLS, IDEOLOGIES, CULTURE, AND COMMUNICATIONS

The Deep Challenge of Dualism*

Charles Taylor
McGill University

I

The Meech fiasco could perhaps be taken as the final failed attempt to express in the Constitution a form of dualism that could accommodate Québec. The "distinct society" was a new avatar of the spirit that had animated such formulae as Canada as a pact between "two nations," or "two founding peoples." These formulae always seemed in the end to cause more confusion than clarity. In the end, the controversy around the misunderstandings they generated ended up eclipsing whatever merit they might have had in formulating the issue of Québec in Canada. The same fate seemed to have overtaken Meech. It's one of the mysteries of the Canadian political process that the issues always in the end become muddied; because at bottom the demands of Québec in this department don't seem hard to understand, even if they are in some respects complex and nuanced.

It was somewhat complex first of all because the dualism Québec sought was meant to exist at two levels. First, it meant (1) that French had to be recognized as a language along with English in the federation. That is, French had to be given a status clearly different from that of an ethnic immigrant language, even if it were the most important among these. And second, it meant (2) that *la nation canadienne-française*, or its major part, had to have some autonomy, some ability to act as a unit. Both these features were built to some degree into the original Confederation pact, but in the case of (1) in partial and somewhat grudging form. Points (1) and (2) are separate requirements, but also in a sense they are related. There is a certain degree of complementarity, in that the more freely and completely (1) is granted, in theory the less the need will be felt for autonomous action. It is perhaps

---

*This contribution draws on an argument I made in "Shared and Divergent Values," in R.L. Watts and D. Brown, eds., *Options for a New Canada* (Toronto: University of Toronto Press, 1991), pp. 53–76.

the tragedy of Canada that (1) was eventually granted too late, and too grudgingly, and that this established a high and irreversible pattern of demands on (2).

Both these requirements have been a source of difficulty. The extension of (1) beyond its original limits raised a problem, because Canada-outside-Québec (COQ)[1] in its developing multiculturalism was naturally led to accord English the status of a common language, and to split language from culture. That English was the main language was not meant to imply that people of English descent had privileges or were somehow superior. The hegemony of English had to be justified in purely utilitarian terms. Within this framework, the case for putting French along-side English was impossible to make. Outside Québec, a special status for French was rarely justified by numbers, and certainly not by its indispensability as a medium of communication. It seemed like indefensible favouritism.

Second, both (1) and (2) met with resistance because of a perceived difference of Québec from the values of the rest of Canada. This starts off as a dark prejudice in the mind of Orange Protestants, but it continues on in many another milieux because of the supposed appeal of illiberal modes of thought in Québec. In particular, this militated against further concessions in the area of (2).

It has been one of the remarkable achievements of the last thirty years, and particularly of the Trudeau government, to have established (1) almost integrally. There has been a certain cost in resentment in some areas, and this may be fateful in the forthcoming negotiations. I want to return to this below. But there is no doubt that a big change has been brought about. On (2) as well, great progress has been made. First, the Canadian federation has proven a very flexible instrument, giving lots of powers to the provinces. And second, where Québec's needs have been different from the other provinces, a large de facto special status has been developed. Québec has its own pension plan, levies its own income tax, has a special immigration regime, and so on.

But where things have become blocked is on the recognition of this. Giving Québec the autonomy it needs, without disbalancing the Canadian federation, would involve giving Québec a different kind of relation to the federal government and institutions. Although this has worked de facto to a remarkable extent, there are powerful resistances to according it recognition in principle. This is because there is a deep clash of purpose between the two sides of Canada. Where the old clash of values seems to have disappeared, a new conflict of purposes—of answers to the question, "What is a country for?"—has surfaced.

The demands of (2), of a special status for Québec, run against those of regional equality as these are conceived by many in COQ, and against a widespread understanding of the Canadian Charter of Rights and Freedoms. Regional equality has come to be defined for some as entailing an equality of the provinces. The great moral force of the principle of equity between regions has been mobilized behind the rather abstract juridical issue of the relative constitutional status of provinces. Now regional equity seems to be flouted if all provinces aren't placed on the same footing. A special status can be presented as a breach in this kind of equality.

More grievously, the special status for Québec is plainly justified on the grounds of the defence and promotion of *la nation canadienne-française*. But this is a collective goal. The aim is to ensure the flourishing and survival of a *community*. Now the new patriotism of the Charter has given an impetus to a philosophy of rights and of nondiscrimination that is highly suspicious of collective goals. It can only countenance them if they are clearly subordinated to individual rights, and to provisions of nondiscrimination. For those who take these goals seriously, this subordination is unacceptable. The Charter and the promotion of the nation, as understood in their respective constituencies, are on a collision course. The reactions to Bill 178, and much of the Meech Lake debate, were eloquent on this score.

This difficulty arises with (2), where it didn't for (1). The provisions for bilingualism in federal legislation can be justified in terms of individual rights. They concern the guarantee that francophones can be dealt with and obtain government services in their language. Once French is given this status along with English, what is protected are the rights of individuals. The collective goal goes beyond this. The aim is not only that francophones be served in French, but that there still be francophones there in the next generation; this is the objective of *survivance*. It can't be translated into an assurance of rights for *existing* francophones. Indeed, pursuing it may even involve reducing their individual freedom of choice, as Law 101 does in Québec, where francophone parents must send their children to French-language schools.

So if the two halves of Canada have come onto a collision course it is because of the conflict in their respective answers to the question, "What is a country for?" In particular, this conflict is between regional equality as widely understood and the Charter as a symbol of unity, on one hand, and (2) (Québec autonomy) on the other. But before examining more closely how this conflict works out in the case of the Charter, I want to look at the history of our national misunderstanding, in order to see what is special about the present conjuncture.

II

One might well ask, why the collision course now? Surely the old "English" Canada, before the legislation about bilingualism and the Trudeau revolution, was even more inhospitable to the demands of Québec. It balked not only at (2), but at (1) as well. Moreover, it penetrated much more within Québec. In those days, the English minority, backed often by the federal government or pan-Canadian institutions such as the CPR, maintained its own English-only forms of operation, excluding or marginalizing or downgrading the French language. Why didn't things fly apart then?

The answer is that separation didn't seem a realistic option back then for all sorts of reasons. It started with a clear-sighted appreciation of the relation of forces, and a sense of what the English-Canadian majority would tolerate. There was also a greater commitment to the francophone minorities outside the province than there now is. Moreover, an extremely important factor was the restricted economic role of French Quebeckers. The English still had a preponderant role in the economy. Big business spoke English; anglophones dominated the ranks of management, and had more than their share of certain key economic professions such as engineering. This was a source of grievance on many levels. In particular, it permitted the English minority to arrogate to itself a place in the province that demographics would never justify. To take just one instance, before the Quiet Revolution, again and again, union leaders would have to bargain in English with management on behalf of a work force that was 100 percent francophone. At the same time, this imbalance contributed to a climate in which Québec society felt incomplete, in which essential functions were being filled by outsiders. The relation was never articulated in this way at the time, but it helped to keep the option of a total break off the agenda. Separation wasn't a real option before 1960, even though it seems to have been toyed with as an eventual long-term destination by Abbé Groulx.

Paradoxically, as some of the most crying grievances were resolved, as the insulting and sometimes threatening marginalization of the French language was reversed, as francophone Quebeckers began to take their full place in the economy, at first through the public and para-public sectors (e.g., Hydro-Québec) and then the private sector, precisely in the wake of all these successes, the demand for independence gained strength; until it became one of two major constitutional options, on a par with its federalist rival, and, in the first nine months after Meech, even ahead. And all this while outside Québec at the federal level, bilingualism is advancing, and Quebeckers wield more power than ever before. These are the years of "French power." Some westerners have the feeling that the federal government is run by Quebeckers. Why does breakup loom now? How does one explain this paradoxical and even perverse result?

Part of the answer, implicit in the above, is that now for the first time the option looks conceivable, possible, and even safe. In this regard, even the last decade has seen a change. In 1980, most Quebeckers still found sovereignty a somewhat frightening prospect. The referendum revealed that clearly. In 1990, this no longer seems to be so. A great deal of the difference seems to stem from the now perceived high profile of francophones as big players in our economic life. This is something that has been happening over a number of decades, but as is the way with media-driven public perceptions, the realization has come all in a rush. And with this realization, a great flush of confidence. As often with these media-driven perceptions, we go easily from one exaggeration to another. Quebeckers weren't as powerless before, and they aren't as powerful now as they think. Separation risks being much more economically costly than they now believe, even as it would have been less catastrophic than many thought in 1980. And we may even be in for another swerve of opinion as the present recession dims expectations. But the basic change is undeniable. Separation is really thinkable.

But that can't be the whole explanation. To claim this would be to say that Quebeckers never really wanted anything else, that they were just waiting for the moment when they could dare go for it. And nothing could be more incorrect than that. A great deal attached francophone Quebeckers to this country: first of all, the sense that the larger entity was the home of *la nation canadienne-française*, whose whole extent included more than Québec; then a certain *attachement* to a constitutional home that had become familiar, and that their leaders had had a hand in building. But what was always missing was a genuine patriotism for Canada. That kind of sentiment was reserved for *la nation canadienne-française*. It has lately been transposed onto Québec, as the viable segment of that nation, but never managed to spread from there onto the whole political unit.

That is why people have often spoken of Canada as being for Quebeckers a "*mariage de raison*." This somewhat understates the case, because it doesn't take account of the multiform attachment to Canada I have just described, but it is emotionally true in this negative sense, that a genuine patriotism for a bilingual, two-nation Canada never developed.

But this by itself still doesn't explain the strength of the independentist option today. After all, if Canada was a *mariage de raison*, why abandon it when it has never been so reasonable, when the deal seems the most favourable ever? Of course, many federalist Quebeckers are pleading the cause of Canada today in just these terms. But why doesn't it have more success? Why are even those who are making the plea profoundly ambivalent about it?

Here one can easily be misled, because the opponents of these partisans of "profitable federalism" seem to want to engage them on their own ground, and strive to prove that Confederation is a bad deal for us. But in fact, the emotional drive behind independence is elsewhere. It is much more a failure of *recognition*. For decades, Québec leaders explained that Confederation was a pact between two founding peoples, two nations. This was never the way the matter was understood outside the province. But the claim was not so much to the effect that this was the plain sense of the Confederation pact, somehow perversely forgotten by the others—although this is how it was often put. It was much more an expression of the profound sentiment that this was the only form in which Confederation could be ultimately acceptable to French Canadians, in a way that could engage their hearts and respect their dignity.

In fact, in the real world it was necessary to live with compromises, in which the duality principle was given a rather limited and grudging expression. It was necessary to operate in a country that for many purposes was run much more as a nation with one hegemonic culture, with more or less generous provision for minorities on a regional basis. Present-day Canadians, some of whom still may want to complain about the number of languages on their corn flakes boxes, have no idea of how exiguous the place of French was in the bad old days. In the 1930s even the money was still unilingual English.

Canada had to be accepted, but never so as to engage the heart, or respect dignity. It could not be accepted "*dans l'honneur et l'enthousiasme*," to use a phrase that has been so often repeated during the drama of Meech Lake. Below the rational acceptance of the marriage of reason, these denials bite deep. This is easy to overlook, because those who are frustrated in their desire for recognition understandably don't want to present their case in those terms. It is only when one is recognized that one is happy to avow the desire. So the phrase "*dans l'honneur et l'enthousiasme*" emerges when it looked as though that aspiration was at last met. But when it is denied, the opponents of federal Canada will pretend that no one was ever interested in mere symbols, that the calculus of independence is made in the realistic terms of power and prosperity, that the attitudes of the English-Canadian partner mean nothing to them. In all this, they do protest a little too much.

The present strength of independence is thus due in part to the new confidence of Quebeckers; in part to the fact that Canada never gelled as a nation for them; yet in large part to the continued denial of their understanding of Canada, of the only terms on which it could have been fully accepted by them. These were articulated, among other forms, in the "two-nations" view of the country. Of course, this was unacceptable as it stood to the rest of the country, which didn't itself feel like a "nation." Here there was an attempt by French Canadians to foist a symmetrical identity on their partners. And this attempt is not yet abandoned, as one can see from much of the discussion in Québec today, which I will return to below. But there was a basic demand that could be disintricated from this presumptuous definition of the other. This was the demand that *la nation canadienne-française* be recognized as a crucial component of the country, as an entity whose survival and flourishing was one of the main purposes of Canada as a political society. If this had been granted, it wouldn't have mattered how the rest of the country defined itself.

De facto, the country has come to arrange itself not at all badly for this purpose, through federal bilingualism, through advances made by some French-speaking minorities elsewhere, and through a de facto administrative special status for Québec. But what was missing was a clear recognition that this was part of our purpose as a federation. This is why Meech Lake was so important, and why its failure will have such dire consequences. If one just listens to what people say in Québec, this can seem strange. Lots of Quebeckers either did not admit that they were in favour of Meech or expressed lukewarm support. Basically, all the independentists took this line. Those who were sceptical about English Canada hedged their bets; they never wanted to allow that recognition mattered to them. But the depth of the reaction to its demise shows how little this represented how they felt.

Meech was important because it was the first time that Canada was writing into a statement of what it was about a recognition of Canadian duality and the special role of Québec. The fact that the accord conferred no additional powers largely narrowed its significance to this one clear declaration of intent. The importance of this declaration can be understood only in the light of the years of nonrecognition, of the marriage of reason that failed to engage the heart and reflect dignity. It can be understood in the context of a present generation that is quite free of the timidity of its ancestors before a possible break, which is even a little surprised, sometimes a trifle contemptuous of their predecessors, for having put up with nonrecognition for so long. And its refusal when it was *just* this, a declaration of pure intent, takes on fateful significance. (That's the point of the oft-repeated phrase that Meech constituted Québec's *"conditions minimales."*)

With the demise of Meech, something snapped. I think it can be rather simply described. Quebeckers will no longer live in a structure that does not fully recognize their national goals. In the early 1980s, after the defeat of the "yes" in the referendum, many toyed with the idea of accepting the marriage of reason, and making a go of it with or without recognition. The new confidence could also have motivated this rather different stance, which marginalized the issue of recognition. After all, if you know your own worth, why do you need the other? But in a sense, Meech wiped out this possibility, just because it raised the hope of recognition. And now we are irretrievably on another track. (Not that I think the "reasonable" track could have lasted very long anyway; it was always at the mercy of some new development.)

What remains to be explained is the extraordinary euphoria that all observers noted among the crowds celebrating Québec's national holiday, the St. Jean 1990. Why did Quebeckers feel so united, and so relieved at being united, almost as though the demise of Meech had taken a great weight off them? I think it's because the long division and hesitation, between the "reasonable" acceptance of a structure that didn't recognize them, and the insistence on having their national purposes openly accepted, had at last been resolved. This was felt as a division between Quebeckers, and especially painfully at the time of the 1980 referendum, when families were often split. But it also divided many Quebeckers within themselves. At last the long conflict, the long hesitation, the long ambivalence was over. Quebeckers were clear what they wanted to ask of any future political structure on the northern half of this continent. Consensus was recovered, but also a kind of psychic unity. A certain kind of compromise was forever over.

But what does this mean for the future? It means that demand (2) has become imperious and virtually non-negotiable. And this brings a real danger of breach between the two parts of the country. For it follows that Quebeckers will not accept any structure in which their collective aspirations are not fully and overtly recognized. Already this is expressing itself in the requirement that negotiation be one-on-one, because this is felt to reflect in itself the acknowledgment of Québec's status as a distinct society. But all this is happening at the moment that COQ's new-found Charter patriotism is making it less capable of acknowledging the legitimacy of collective goals; and as regional alienation is lending further strength to the principle of the equality of provinces. The common ground seems to be shrinking fast.

III

From the preceding discussion we can see that the impact of the Charter on our impending potential breakup fits into an already distressingly familiar pattern. What Québec or French Canada has felt is essential to its recognition seems in COQ to violate one of the conditions of national unity on a fair basis. Just as bilingualism seemed to many an unconscionable favouritism to one minority language, just because they saw Canada as a multicultural mosaic united around a single lingua franca, English, so the recognition of collective goals for one province seems to violate the status of the Charter as the framework of rights enjoyed equally by all Canadians. And in fact the anti-Meech majority in COQ brought together these two kinds of opposition under one roof, even though many Charter patriots had been vigorous and courageous defenders of bilingualism.

But do we have to fight over the Charter? Is it all perhaps based on a misunderstanding? It is time to delve into the philosophical and political sources of the dispute.

At first sight, it might appear that the disagreement could have been avoided. Those who drafted the Charter were aware of the complexity of the Canadian political scene. They tried to strike a balance between individual rights and collective goals. The Charter not only entrenches the internationally recognized list of immunities. It also deals with language rights, which, although they do not strictly figure as collective rights, derive their political significance from the existence of communities striving to secure their survival. In addition, the document recognizes "aboriginal rights," which, although as yet undefined, will clearly have to incorporate some that are collective in nature.

But as the Charter entered public consciousness, this balance was progressively lost. This is not surprising if we take into account the whole movement toward entrenched rights and judicial retrieval that has been proceeding throughout Western societies, and to some extent even on a world scale, since World War II.

The Canadian Charter in fact follows the trend of the last half of the 20th century, and gives a basis for judicial review on two basic scores. First, it protects the rights of the individual in a variety of ways. And second, it guarantees equal treatment of citizens in a variety of respects; or alternatively put, it defends against discriminatory treatment on a number of irrelevant grounds, such as race or sex. There is a lot else in the Charter, as I have just mentioned, but the two themes I singled out dominate in the public consciousness.

This is no accident. These two kinds of provisions are now quite common in entrenched schedules of rights that provide the basis for judicial review. In this sense, the Western world, perhaps the world as a whole, is following American precedent. The Americans were the first to write out and entrench a bill of rights, which they did during the ratification process of their Constitution and as a condition of its successful outcome. One might argue that they weren't entirely clear on judicial retrieval as a method of securing those rights, but this rapidly became the practice. The first amendments secured individuals, and sometimes state governments,[2] against encroachment by the new federal government. It was after the Civil War, in the period of triumphant Reconstruction, and particularly with the Fourteenth Amendment, which called for "equal protection" for all citizens by the laws, that the theme of nondiscrimination becomes central to judicial review. But it is by now on a par with the older norm of the defence of individual right, and in public consciousness even perhaps ahead.

Now for a number of people in COQ, a political society's espousing certain collective goals threatens to run against both of these basic provisions of the Charter, or indeed any acceptable bill of rights. First, the collective goals may require restrictions on the behaviour of individuals that may violate their rights. For many nonfrancophone Canadians, both inside and outside Québec, this feared outcome had already materialized with Québec's language legislation. Law 101 prescribes, for instance, the type of school to which parents can send their children; and in the most famous instance, it forbids certain kinds of commercial signage. This latter provision was actually struck down by the Supreme Court as contrary to the Québec Charter of Rights, as well as the Canadian Charter, and only re-enacted through the invocation of the "notwithstanding" clause.

But second, even if this were not the case, espousing collective goals on behalf of a national group can be thought to be inherently discriminatory. In the modern world it will always be the case that not all those living as citizens under a certain jurisdiction will belong to the national group thus favoured. This by itself could be thought to involve some discrimination. But beyond this, the pursuit of the collective end will in all likelihood involve treating insiders and outsiders differently. Thus the schooling provisions of law 101 forbid (roughly speaking) francophones and immigrants sending their children to English-language schools, but allow Canadian anglophones to do so.

This sense that the Canadian Charter clashes with basic Québec policy was one of the strong grounds to opposition in COQ to the Meech Lake Accord. The worry here concerned the distinct society clause, and the common demand for amendment was that the Canadian Charter be "protected" against this clause, or take precedence over it. There was undoubtedly in this a certain amount of old-style anti-Québec prejudice, the continuing echoes of the old image of "priest-ridden Québec." Thus various women's groups in COQ voiced the fear that Québec governments in pursuit of higher birthrates might adopt Ceausescu-type policies of forbidding abortions or making birth control more difficult. Yet, even when one factors out the silliness, contempt, and ill-will, there remains a serious point. Indeed, there are two kinds of serious point. First, there is a genuine difference in philosophy concerning the bases of a liberal society. And second, there is a difference in view about the basis for national unity.

Let's take the philosophical difference first. Those who take the view that individual rights must always come first and, along with nondiscrimination provisions, must take precedence over collective goals are often speaking out of a view of a liberal society that has become more and more widespread in the Anglo-American world. Its source is, of course, the United States, and it has recently been elaborated and defended by some of the best philosophical and legal minds in that society, for instance, John Rawls, Ronald Dworkin, Bruce Ackerman, and others.[3] There are various formulations of the main idea, but perhaps the one that encapsulates most clearly the point that is relevant to us is Dworkin's way of putting things in his short paper entitled "Liberalism."[4]

Dworkin makes a distinction between two kinds of moral commitment. We all have views about the ends of life, about what constitutes a good life, which we and others ought to strive for. But then we also acknowledge a commitment to deal fairly and equally with each other, regardless of how we conceive our ends. We might call these latter "procedural" commitments, while those that concern the ends of life are "substantive." Now Dworkin claims that a liberal society is one that as a society adopts no particular substantive view about the ends of life. The society is rather united around strong procedural commitments, to treat people with equal respect. The reason why the polity as such can espouse no substantive view, cannot, for instance, allow that one of the goals of legislation should be to make people virtuous in one or other meaning of that term, is that this would involve a violation of its procedural norm. For, granted the diversity of modern societies, it would unfailingly be the case that some people and not others would be committed to the favoured conception of virtue. They might be in a majority; indeed, it is very likely that they would be, for otherwise a democratic society would probably not espouse their view. But nevertheless, this view would not be everyone's, and in espousing this substantive outlook the society would not be treating the dissident minority with equal respect. It would be saying to them, in effect, "your view is not as valuable, in the eyes of this polity, as that of your more numerous compatriots."

There are profound philosophical assumptions underlying this view of liberalism, which is influenced by the thought of Immanuel Kant. Among other features, this view understands human dignity to consist largely in autonomy, that is, in the ability of each person to determine for him/herself a view of the good life. Dignity, that is, is connected less with any particular understanding of the good life, such that someone's departure from this would be a derogation from his/her own dignity, than it is with the power to consider and espouse for oneself some view or other. We are not respecting this power equally in all subjects, it is claimed, if we raise the outcome of some people's deliberations officially over that of others. A liberal society must remain neutral on the good life, and restrict itself to ensuring that however they see things, citizens deal fairly with each other and the state equally with all.

The popularity of this view of the human agent as primarily a subject of self-determining or self-expressive choice helps to explain why this model of liberalism is so strong. There is also the fact that it has been urged with great force and intelligence by liberal thinkers in the United States, and precisely in the context of constitutional doctrines of judicial review.[5] And so it is not surprising that the idea becomes accredited, well beyond those who might subscribe to a specific Kant-derived philosophy, that a liberal society cannot accommodate publicly espoused notions of the good. This is the conception, as Michael Sandel has called it, of the "procedural republic,"[6] which has a strong hold on the political agenda in the United States, and which has helped to place increasing emphasis on judicial review on the basis of constitutional texts at the expense of the ordinary political process of building majorities with a view to legislative action.

A society with collective goals like Québec violates this mode. It is axiomatic for Québec governments that the survival and flourishing of French culture in Québec is a good. Political society is not neutral between those who value remaining true to the culture of our ancestors and those who might want to cut loose in the name of some individual goal of seif-development. It might be argued that one could after all capture a goal like *survivance* for a proceduralist liberal society. One could consider the French language, for instance, as a collective resource that individuals might want to make use of, and act for its preservation, just as one does for clean air or green spaces. But this can't capture the full thrust of policies designed for cultural survival. It is not just a matter of having the French language available for those who might choose it. This might be seen to be the goal of some of the measures of federal bilingualism over the last twenty years. But it is also a matter of making sure that there is a community of people here in the future that will want to avail itself of this opportunity. Policies aimed at survival actively seek to create members of the community, for instance in assuring that the rising generations go on identifying as French-speakers or whatever. There is no way that they could be seen as just providing a facility to already existing people.[7]

Quebeckers therefore, and those who give similar importance to this kind of collective goal, tend to opt for a rather different model of a liberal society. In this view, a society can be organized around a definition of the good life, without this being seen as a depreciation of those who do not personally share this definition. Where the nature of the good requires that it be sought in common, this is the reason for its being an object of public policy. According to this conception, a liberal society singles itself out as such by the way in which it treats minorities, including those who do not share public definitions of the good; and above all by the rights it accords to all its members. But in this case, the rights in question are conceived to be the fundamental and crucial ones that have been recognized as such from the very beginning of the liberal tradition: such rights as to life, liberty, due process, free speech, free practice of religion, and the like. On this model, there is something exaggerated, a dangerous overlooking of an essential boundary, in speaking of fundamental rights to things like commercial signage in the language of one's choice. One has to distinguish the fundamental liberties, those that should never at any time be infringed, and that therefore ought to be unassailably entrenched on one hand, from privileges and immunities that are important, but that can be revoked or restricted for reasons of public policy—although one needs a strong reason to do so—on the other.

A society with strong collective goals can be liberal, on this view, provided it is also capable of respecting diversity, especially when it concerns those who do not share its goals; and provided it can offer adequate safeguards for fundamental rights. There will undoubtedly be tensions involved, and difficulties, in pursuing these objectives together, but they are not uncombinable, and the problems are not in principle greater than those encountered by any liberal society that has to combine, for example, liberty and equality, or prosperity and justice.

Here are two incompatible views of liberal society. One of the great sources of our present disunity is that they have come to square off against each other in the last decade. The resistance to the "distinct society" that called for precedence to be given to the Canadian Charter came in part from a spreading procedural outlook in COQ. From this point of view, attributing the goal of promoting Québec's distinct society to a government is to acknowledge a collective goal, and this move had to be neutralized by being subordinated to the existing Charter. From the standpoint of Québec, this attempt to impose a procedural model of liberalism not only would deprive the distinct society clause of some of its force as a rule of interpretation, but bespoke a rejection of the model of liberalism on which this society has come to be founded. There was a lot of misperception by each society of the other throughout the Meech Lake debate, as I mentioned above. But here both saw something right about the other—and didn't like it. COQ saw that the distinct society clause legitimated collective goals. And Québec saw that the move to give the Canadian Charter precedence imposed a form of liberal society that is alien, and to which Québec could never accommodate itself without surrendering its identity. In this context, the protestations by Charter patriots that they were not "against Québec" rang hollow.

This was one source of deep disagreement. There was also a second one, which was interwoven with it. The Charter has taken on tremendous importance in COQ not only because of the growing force of procedural liberalism, but also because in the steadily increasing diversity of this multicultural society, people are looking for new bases of unity. COQ has also seen its reason for existence partly in terms of its political institutions. Even though the Charter offers a relatively weak answer to the distinctness question, because it makes us more like the United States, it nevertheless can provide a convincing answer to the unity question. The two motives for Charter patriotism come together here. As the country gets more diverse, we are more and more acutely aware of the divergences in our conceptions of the good life. It then appears that what can and ought to bind us together are precisely the procedural norms that govern our interaction. Procedural liberalism not only begins to look more plausible in itself, but it also seems to be the only unquestionable common ground.

But if it is really serving as this, then it is hard to accept that its meaning and application may be modulated in one part of the country by something like the distinct society clause, differently from the way it applies in others. The resistance to this clause of the Meech Lake Accord came partly from the sense that the Charter of all things had to apply in the same way to all Canadians. If the procedural bond is the only thing that can hold us together without ranking some above others, then it has to hold without exception.

IV

Can this conflict be arbitrated? In a sense not. One side insists on holding the country together around a model of liberalism that the other cannot accept. If there is to be agreement, this first side has got to give way. But ought it to give way? I can only offer an answer to this question by deserting all appearance of neutrality and taking an openly partisan stance. So let me throw off the mask and state my position.

It seems to me that the claim of proceduralist thinkers to define the very essence of liberalism is erroneous and in a sense arrogant. We have to acknowledge (1) that there are other possible models of liberal society. This becomes pretty evident once one looks around at the full gamut of contemporary free societies in Europe and elsewhere, instead of attending only to the United States. At the same time, it should be evident to procedural liberals in COQ that (2) their francophone compatriots wish to live by one such alternative. This should be clear to anyone with a modicum of knowledge of Québec history and politics.

But once you accept (1) and (2), then it is clear that the attempt to make procedural liberalism the basis of Canadian unity is both illegitimate and doomed to failure. For it represents an imposition of one society's model on another, and in the circumstances of late-20th-century Canadian democracy this cannot succeed. The only way we can coexist is by allowing ourselves to differ on this. Does this mean that we can only coexist as two independent societies, perhaps loosely linked by supranational institutions? That is the thesis of Québec sovereigntists. But this has never seemed to me to be self-evident. It becomes true only to the extent that procedural liberals stand so firmly on principle that they cannot bear to share the same country with people who live by another model. Rigidity of this kind began to be evident during the Meech Lake debate. If this were to be COQ's last word, then indeed, the independentists are right, and there is no solution short of sovereignty-association.

But do they have to be right? Is there something wrong with accommodating difference in this way?

In a way, accommodating difference is what Canada is all about. Many Canadians would concur in this. That's why the recent bout of mutual suspicion and ill-will in the constitutional debate has been so painful to many of our compatriots. It's not just that the sources of difference I have been describing are becoming more salient. Old questions may be reopened. To some extent Trudeau's remarkable achievement in extending bilingualism was made possible by a growing sympathy toward the French fact among political and social elites in COQ. They pushed the process faster than many of their fellow citizens were happy with. For many people lower down in the hierarchy, French was being "stuffed down their throats," but granted the elite-run nature of the political accommodation process in this country, they seemed to have no option but to take it.

During the Meech debate the procedures of elite negotiation came under sharp criticism and challenge. Moreover, the COQ elites were themselves split on how to respond to the new package, in a way they hadn't been on bilingualism. It was therefore not surprising that we began to see a rebellion against the accommodation of French. This might be the harbinger of greater resistance to come. Already one hears westerners saying that Canadian duality is an irrelevancy to them, that their experience of Canada is of a multicultural mosaic. The very bases of a two-language federation are being questioned again. This important axis of difference is under threat.

But more fundamentally, we face a challenge to our very conception of diversity. Many of the people who rallied around the Canadian Charter and multiculturalism to reject the distinct society are proud of their acceptance of diversity. And in some respects rightly so. What is enshrined here is what one might call first-level diversity. There are great differences in culture and outlook and background in a population that nevertheless shares the same idea of what it is to belong to Canada. Their patriotism or manner of belonging is uniform, whatever their other differences, and this is felt to be a necessity if the country is to hold together.

But this is far from accommodating all Canadians. For Quebeckers, and for most French Canadians, the way of being a Canadian (for those who still want to be) is via their belonging to a constituent element of Canada, *la nation québécoise*, or *canadienne-française*. Something analogous holds for aboriginal communities in this country. Their way of being Canadian is not accommodated by first-level diversity. And yet many people in COQ are puzzled by the resulting sense of exclusion, because first-level diversity is the only kind they are sensitive to, and they feel they fully acknowledge that.

To build a country for everyone, Canada would have to allow for second-level or "deep" diversity, where a plurality of ways of belonging would also be acknowledged and accepted. Someone of, let's say, Italian extraction in Toronto, or Ukrainian extraction in Edmonton, might indeed feel Canadian as a bearer of individual rights in a multicultural mosaic. His/her belonging would not "pass through" some other community, although the ethnic identity might be important to him/her in various ways. But this person might nevertheless accept that a Québécois(e), or a Cree, or a Dene, might belong in different ways; that they were Canadian through being members of their nations. And reciprocally, the Québécois(e), Cree, or Dene would accept the perfect legitimacy of the "mosaic" identity.

Is this utopian? Could people ever come to see their country this way? Could they even find it exciting and an object of pride that they belong to a country that allows deep diversity? Pessimists say no, because they don't see how such a country could have a sense of unity. The model of citizenship has to be uniform, or people would have no sense of belonging to the same polity. Those who say this tend to take the United States as their paradigm, which has indeed been hostile to deep diversity, and has sometimes tried to stamp it out as "un-American."

But these pessimists should bear in mind three things.

First, deep diversity is the only formula on which a united federal Canada can be rebuilt—once we recall the reasons why we all need it.

Second, in many parts of the world today, the degree and nature of the differences resemble Canada's rather than those of the United States. If a uniform model of citizenship fits better the American image of the liberal state, it is also true that this is a strait jacket for many political societies. The world needs other models to be legitimated, in order to allow for more humane and less constraining modes of political cohabitation. Instead of pushing ourselves to the point of breakup in the name of the uniform model, we would do our own and some other peoples a favour by exploring the space of deep diversity. To those who believe in according people the freedom to be themselves, this would be counted a gain in civilization. In this exploration we would not be alone. Europe-watchers have noticed how the development of the European Community has gone along with an increased breathing space for regional societies—Breton, Basque, Catalan—that were formerly threatened with the steamroller of the national state.

Third, after dividing to form two polities with uniform citizenship, both successor states would find that they had failed after all to banish the challenge of deep diversity; because the only way that they can do justice to their aboriginal populations is by adopting a pluralist mould. Neither Québec nor COQ could succeed in imitating the United States, or the European national states in their chauvinist prime. Why not recognize this now, and take the road of deep diversity together?

NOTES

1. In Québec we speak blithely of "English Canada," but the people who live there don't identify with this label. We need a handy way of referring to the rest of the country as an entity, even if it lacks for the moment political expression. In order to avoid the clumsy three-word hyphenated expression, I plan to use "COQ" henceforth in this chapter. I hope the reader won't take this as a sign of encroaching barbarism, or Québécois self-absorption (although it might partake in small measure of both).

2. For instance, the First Amendment, which forbade Congress from establishing any religion, was not originally meant to separate state and church as such. It was enacted at a time when many states had established churches, and it was plainly meant to prevent the new federal government from interfering with or overruling these local arrangements. It was only later after the Fourteenth Amendment, following the so-called "Incorporation" doctrine, that these restrictions on the federal government were held to have been extended to all governments, at whatever level.

3. John Rawls, *A Theory of Justice*, Oxford University Press, 1971; "Justice as Fairness: Political not Metaphysical," *Philosophy and Public Affairs*, vol. 14, 1985; Ronald Dworkin, *Taking Rights Seriously*, London: Duckworth, 1977; "Liberalism," in Stuart Hampshire, ed., *Public and Private Morality*, Cambridge: Cambridge University Press, 1978; Bruce Ackerman, *Social Justice in the Liberal State*, New Haven: Yale University Press, 1980.

4. Dworkin, "Liberalism."

5. See, for instance, the arguments deployed by Lawrence Tribe in his *Abortion: The Clash of Absolutes*, New York: Norton, 1990.

6. Michael Sandel, "The Procedural Republic and the Unencumbered Self," *Political Theory*, vol. 12, 1984.

7. An ingenious argument has recently been put forward by Will Kymlicka in his brilliant book, *Liberalism, Community and Culture*, Oxford: Clarendon Press, 1989. He argues that what I have been calling procedural liberalism can be made compatible with the defence of collective rights and cultural survival in certain cases. Kymlicka, unlike the major American authors, writes in full knowledge of the Canadian scene, and with a strong commitment to the defence of aboriginal rights in this country. While espousing a politics of "neutral moral concern," that is, a view of the liberal state as neutral between conceptions of the good life (p. 76), he nevertheless argues that collective cultural rights can be defended on the grounds that the members of certain threatened communities would be deprived of the conditions of intelligent, self-generated decisions about the good life, if the "cultural structures" through which they can grasp the options are undermined (p. 165). If Kymlicka's argument really went through, it would close the gap between the two models of liberalism that I am contrasting in these pages.

C H A P T E R

6

Québec–Canada: Constitutional Developments, 1960–92*

Alain-G. Gagnon
McGill University

During the last decade, Canada has experienced significant transformations, starting in 1981 with the patriation of the Constitution and the federal government's decision to append to it a Charter of Rights and Freedoms. Insertion of the Charter was a severe blow to parliamentary democracy and to executive federalism, as it gave added powers to the judiciary. In the course of the 1980s, the political dynamics of Québec have changed fundamentally, with nationalist elements going through shades of popularity, undeniably growing support for sovereignty in the electorate following Meech Lake's failure and, in the spring of 1990, the formation at the federal level of a new political voice, the Bloc Québécois.

Options being discussed are reminiscent of earlier debates, and tend to get more complicated and intermingled as the positions of various political actors are articulated. The deliberations of the Keith Spicer Citizens' Forum, the Bélanger-Campeau Commission, the Beaudoin-Edwards Committee, Castonguay-Dobbie/ Dobbie-Beaudoin, and other commissions struck throughout the country to assess the crisis are attempting to influence the agenda surrounding the expected renegotiation of the Canadian federal union. The challenge for these commissions is major, if only due to the fact that English Canada has undergone substantial transformation during the last decades. Among the changes, one notes an increased significance given to entrenched rights and freedoms, a growing admission of a native and multicultural heritage, a mounting recognition of the equality of provinces principle, ascending regionalism, and a growing disenchantment with exec-

*This chapter draws on an argument I made in "Everything old is new again: Canada, Québec and Constitutional Impasse," pp. 63–105 in Frances Abele, ed. (1991), *How Ottawa Spends 1991–92: The Politics of Fragmentation* (Ottawa: Carleton University Press). For helpful comments, I am most grateful to Frances Abele, Daniel Drache, François Rocher, Richard Simeon, and Reginald Whitaker.

utive federalism. In addition to these factors, there has been the impact of an increasing pull of the continental economy and its dangers for Canada's survival. This chapter will first discuss earlier negotiations between Québec and the other constitutional partners, starting with the Quiet Revolution. Second, the potential for success of Québec's pursuit of constitutional objectives is evaluated using domestic and external factors.

THE HISTORIC LEGACY, 1960–92

What have we learned from the last thirty years of our common existence? With the beginning of the Quiet Revolution, Québec championed special arrangements with the declared aim of increasing and, at a minimum, consolidating the province's power and resources. During this entire period, Québec sought recognition of its special status, and ultimately at the end of the period under review, asked that special status be entrenched through the Meech Lake Accord.

During the 1960s, there were more concerted efforts by Québec and the other provinces to deal with the federal government as a bloc. At Lesage's invitation, the provincial premiers met annually in conferences intended to lessen the possibility for unilateral actions by the federal government in areas of provincial interest. Indeed, federal–provincial conferences took place more frequently, broadening the range of issues discussed and creating subcommittees and ministerial committees to deal with outstanding problems and administrative matters. Simultaneously, and respecting the Gérin-Lajoie doctrine of provincial autonomy (Morin, 1987),[1] Québec began developing relationships with international organizations and other governments outside Canada. Québec recognized that external affairs was a federal responsibility, but asserted its right to act abroad in areas of provincial jurisdiction, which brought about several battles with Ottawa. Québec was particularly successful between 1964 and 1966 in signing a series of agreements, covering youth, education, and cultural affairs. Constitutional reforms were unavoidable as pressures mounted from Québec and other parts of Canada for a "renewed federalism." The main stumbling block at the time was the lack of an amending formula in the British North America Act of 1867 (see Thérien et al. in this volume).

During Lesage's tenure (1960–66), two proposals for constitutional reform regarding amending formulas were rejected, and there was a perceptible change in the Liberals' approach to the issue. In 1961, Lesage turned down the Davie Fulton (then Minister of Justice) amending formula because the federal government would not circumscribe the powers it had acquired in 1949, powers that allowed for unilateral amendment of the Constitution in areas of exclusive federal jurisdiction. Moreover, Québec would have had no voice in deciding reforms to central institutions such as the monarchy, the Senate, and the Supreme Court. Similarly, in 1966, Lesage rejected the Fulton-Favreau formula, whereby constitutional amendments would have required the approval of the federal government and all other provincial governments for provisions respecting provincial powers, use of the English and French languages, denominational rights in education, and representation in the House of Commons. Other provisions respecting the monarchy, Senate representation, and the like could be amended by Ottawa with the concurrence of two-thirds of the provinces comprising more than half the population (Simeon and Robinson, 1990:204).

An amending formula based on unanimity was strongly opposed in Québec because it could threaten the possibility of attaining agreements between Québec and the federal government in such a culturally sensitive area as language policy, and could discourage transfer of powers from the federal to the provincial order. However, the central issue for Québec was not the amending formula, but rather the overhaul of the Constitution and a new division of powers.[2] Faced with the prospect of a provincial election, Lesage could not consent to proposals that would run against strong provincialist and nationalist sentiments in the province. Lesage refused to consider patriation or an amending formula unless this was combined with a clear definition of Québec's powers and responsibilities, and protection of the French language and francophone culture. He thus established the framework that would guide future Québec governments in discussion of constitutional reform.

Québec's position on the Constitution underwent significant transformations. For instance, during the 1966 election, Lesage, afraid of being outflanked by Daniel Johnson, adopted a more nationalist political platform by demanding a special status for Québec instead of advocating simple equality among the provinces. While Lesage was strengthening the provincial position, he also sought to influence the federal government. In the 1966 Québec budget, the government went so far as to suggest that the province should participate directly in areas of exclusive federal jurisdiction, by being associated in the development and execution of fiscal, monetary, and trade policies. The federal government resisted such intervention (Smiley, 1967:68–70; Morin, 1972; Simeon, 1972).

The Lesage administration was resolute in pushing for reform, ready to risk entangling relationships with Ottawa if this could enhance Québec's economic and political power and status. In 1964 the Québec government was granted control of its own public pension plan. At that time, the federal government attempted unsuccessfully to convince other provinces to follow Québec's lead, so that the latter would not appear to have gained special status. The establishment of the Québec Pension Plan gave the province greater fiscal autonomy, allowing for new initiatives without continued federal involvement. The Québec Pension Plan constituted a major gain as it assisted building the most important investment pool in the country, the *Caisse de dépôt et placement*, the gem of Québec financial institutions.

The push for constitutional reform and greater autonomy that commenced under Lesage continued with the governments of Daniel Johnson (1966–68) and Jean-Jacques Bertrand (1968–70). Recognizing the success of the Liberals, the Union Nationale government continued to use an interventionist approach to domestic policy and federal–provincial relations. Johnson's theme for the 1966 election campaign—*Égalité ou indépendance*—was in fact a stronger attempt to appeal to nationalist forces than the Liberals were ready to make at that time. Johnson went one step further than the previous government by making reference to the binational character of Canada, and by putting forward a tentative proposal for special status for Québec (Gagnon, 1991:173–81). Johnson, and subsequently Jean-Jacques Bertrand, tended to concur with the *Report of the Royal Commission of Inquiry on Constitutional Problems* (the Tremblay Commission) that the division of powers and revenues between the provinces and the federal government should be based on the Québec interpretation of the British North America Act of

1867. Under such a proposal, the Union Nationale demanded limits on federal government transfer payments to individuals through pan-Canadian social programs, and complete federal withdrawal if these were run on a shared-cost basis. The spending power of the federal government was perceived as having a negative influence on the maintenance of federalism since it did not respect a watertight division of powers between the two orders of government. Johnson argued that programs such as family allowance, pensions, social assistance, health services, and labour force training should be the sole responsibility of Québec. Johnson went on to stress that the uniqueness of Québec warranted bilateral arrangements between Québec and Ottawa that were not contingent upon the federal government's relations with other provinces. In short, this was an early call for asymmetrical federalism as a means to respond to Québec's special needs, and was a major bone of contention during all of Trudeau's reign in Ottawa, as he refused to concede to Québec what he was unwilling to give to the other provinces.

Pursuing his demand for constitutional reform, and benefiting from the momentum provided by the Royal Commission on Bilingualism and Biculturalism (the Laurendeau-Dunton Commission), Johnson developed a binational solution to Canada's constitutional problems. The way out of the already looming constitutional crisis was based on an interpretation that would depict the country as a compact between the French and English. Under Duplessis, the Union Nationale had already sought to protect the existing division of powers from federal encroachment. The party, led by Johnson, asked for additional powers to protect francophones within, and to some extent outside, Québec. The modifications were seen to be commensurate with Québec's responsibilities as the primary protector of the French-speaking community in Canada. The government under Jean–Jacques Bertrand continued to argue that the distinctiveness of Québec deserved full recognition in a new Canadian Constitution.

Québec was not completely stonewalled during the second half of the 1960s. For example, several deals were made with Ottawa on tax revenues, and an opting-out formula was implemented. In addition, Québec started to play an important role in *la francophonie*, while an informal agreement with the federal government allowed Québec to expand the small immigration bureau established during Lesage's mandate into a legitimate department (see Black and Hagen, in this volume). This departure from established practice opened the way for an asymmetrical federalism. Under the successive governments of Robert Bourassa (1970–76 and 1985–) and René Lévesque (1976–85), Québec and Ottawa reached more formal agreements broadening the province's responsibilities in the areas of immigration and, to a lesser extent, international relations. It should be stressed that neither Ottawa nor the other provinces have agreed to constitutional entrenchment of Québec's rights in these domains, granting only the possibility of making administrative arrangements that are nothing more than reversible deals.

During the 1970s, the Québec government continued its search for greater autonomy by urging that it be given additional powers and the necessary revenues to exercise them with a view to preserving and promoting Québec's distinct society and culture. It is in this context that Robert Bourassa has been pursuing the objectives of *profitable federalism*, *cultural sovereignty*, and, of late, *shared sovereignty*. At first, Bourassa was not particularly concerned with the entrenchment of Québec's national aspirations in the Constitution, and looked instead for a revision of the federal system that would assign Québec the requisite powers and resources needed for the "preservation and development of the bicultural character of the Canadian federation" (Bourassa quoted in Roy, 1978:205). At the Victoria Conference in 1971, it appeared that the constitutional debate would be successfully resolved, but at the last minute, when the time came to sign a formal document, Québec declined. The reason given for this reversal was the imprecision of the text surrounding Article 94A, outlining responsibility for pensions and other social programs. For Québec, 94A was said to be a test of the extent to which its constitutional partners were willing to push for a significant new sharing of powers. Moreover, there was intense political pressure in Québec regarding the proposed amending formula that would have given a veto to Québec, Ontario, as well as one to the western provinces collectively and one to the eastern provinces. The package deal proposed by Ottawa failed to guarantee Québec control over cultural and social policies. This resulted in a mobilization of nationalist forces in the province, and as opposition mounted in Québec, forced Bourassa to turn down the Victoria proposals.[3]

Negotiations were reopened in 1975, with the federal government's suggestion that the issue of the division of powers be set aside in favour of simple patriation with an amending formula. This implied that any discussion of a new division of powers would be the subject of future multilateral and bilateral bargaining among Québec, the other provinces, and the federal government. Ottawa recognized that in modifying the federal sharing of powers, the protection and promotion of linguistic and cultural concerns were of primary interest to Québec. This was presented at the time as a recognition of Québec's demand for "special status" (Stevenson, 1982:210). Québec made public then that it was prepared to accept this approach providing that its linguistic and cultural concerns be entrenched in the Constitution (Trudeau, 1977:140–69). It is evident that the federal government did not want to give ammunition to the Parti Québécois, which was rapidly gaining popularity among the Québec electorate.

In exchange for patriation, Bourassa asked that the following provisions be included in a new Constitution: the right for Québec to veto future constitutional amendments; control of policies in the fields of education and culture in the province; the right to opt out of federal programs with compensation; a more important role in immigration, especially aspects dealing with selection and integration of immigrants into Québec society; and limits on the federal government's declaratory and spending powers in areas of provincial jurisdiction (Saywell, 1977:43, 93–94).

The 1975 federal initiative also included a threat of unilateral patriation by Ottawa. Bourassa used this in the fall of 1976 to call an election. The PQ swept to power on 15 November 1976, with a program for sovereignty-association. Under René Lévesque and, for a short time in 1985, Pierre-Marc Johnson, the PQ government was committed to acquiring full political sovereignty for Québec, with an economic association (later replaced by the notion of economic union) between Québec and the rest of Canada. Following Lévesque's election in 1976, the federal government continued to press for patriation of the Constitution with an amending formula.

In 1978, Ottawa introduced Bill C-60, the Constitutional Amendment Bill, containing terms very similar to the 1971 Victoria formula. The renewed federalism of the Trudeau Liberals, proposed under Bill C-60, called for intrastate modifications that would strengthen provincial representation at the federal level, and be accompanied by a Charter of Rights and Freedoms (it was conceived at the outset as an "opt-in" arrangement for the provinces) and a constitutional amending formula. According to Bill C-60, these transformations would have involved replacing the Senate with a House of the Federation, with half its proposed 118 members selected by provincial assemblies and the other half selected by the House of Commons. This would have been accompanied by entrenched representation of Québec in the Supreme Court. In addition, the ability of the House of the Federation to veto changes to language legislation could be reduced to a sixty-day suspensive veto, but could be overturned with the support of two-thirds of the House of Commons (Verney, 1986:367). In a reference decision, the Supreme Court of Canada ruled in 1979 that the Parliament of Canada was not empowered to modify itself in a manner that may affect the provinces. It was argued by the court that despite the power of amendment in section 91(1), the House of the Federation, in substituting for the Senate, was affecting an institution that was of interest to the provinces. According to Douglas Verney, the Supreme Court based its decision on a 1965 federal White Paper that recognized a "provincial role in amendments to the BNA Act beyond those matters exclusively assigned to the provinces" (Verney, 1986:367).

The Québec government showed no interest in this new initiative, as it was then preparing its White Paper, *Québec–Canada: A New Deal* (1979). This option argued for the formation of "Two Communities" where nine provinces would reconstitute Canada and the tenth, that is Québec, would exist as a separate state but part of the new Canadian economic union. From a Québec point of view, the sovereignty-association option had the advantage of dealing directly with the enduring issue of duality, whereas in the rest of the country it was perceived as ignoring the emerging equality of provinces principle especially claimed by provinces outside central Canada.

An important federal initiative was the Task Force on Canadian Unity, struck in 1977. Known as the Pepin-Robarts Task Force, it was based on three elements: the existence of different regions, the predominance of two cultures, and equality of two orders of government. The main thrust of the proposed changes was the institutionalization of *asymmetrical federalism*, suggesting that all provinces are not equal and the same. While avoiding a de jure special status for Québec, Québec's special relationship to the rest of Canada was said to be de facto, recognized in the arrangements that had been offered to all provinces but in which Québec had been the only participant. The Québec Pension Plan is the most potent example. This recognition of special status and asymmetry was extended to language, where it was admitted that each province had the right to determine provincial language policy. Major institutional innovations included proposals for transforming the Senate, an expanded Supreme Court, and changes to certain federal powers such as the abolition of the federal powers of reservation and disallowance. Concurrency was proposed for federal declaratory, spending, and emergency powers. The task force also proposed replacement of the Senate by an eighty-member Council of the Federation entirely composed of delegates nominated by the provinces. Moreover, seats based on proportional representation would be added to the House of Commons to redress the imbalances of the political parties. Expanding and dividing the Supreme Court into specialized "benches" (designed to address deficiencies in the ability of the courts to rule in various jurisdictions) was also among the proposals. In an attempt to reconcile western alienation and Québec nationalism, the task force tackled the issues of provincial autonomy, provincial control over language policy, representation of provincial interests in Ottawa, and recognition of Québec's special status. The main recommendations of the task force were largely ignored by Prime Minister Trudeau, who pursued his own agenda.

In May 1979, Canada elected its first Conservative government since 1963. Prime Minister Joe Clark was better disposed than Trudeau toward a decentralized federalism, expressed in the conception of Canada as a "community of communities." At that time, Canada was in both a debilitating economic recession and continuing constitutional crisis. Despite the change in the federal position, the Québec government remained committed, following the election of the Parti Québécois in 1976, to holding a referendum on sovereignty-association. Then, unexpectedly, the cards were reshuffled. The Conservatives were forced to call an election, and the Trudeau Liberals returned to power in February 1980 with a renewed desire to crush the "separatists" and little interest in finding solutions to Québec's claims. These claims were centred around the perennial notion that Québec constitutes a distinct society in North America. Québec, with its French-speaking majority, demanded sufficient powers to protect and preserve its character. This was felt to be especially important in policy sectors of communications, culture, education, immigration, international relations, language, and manpower training.

At the same time, under the influence of Claude Ryan, the Québec Liberal Party proposed a more *decentralized federalism* as an alternative to Québec sovereignty-association. Under these arrangements, more powers would be allocated to the provinces, two sovereign jurisdictions recognized, and more direct provincial influence on federal activities accomplished through a provincially appointed intergovernmental body, called the Federal Council. Inspired by the German Bundesrat, this was an effort to meet Québec's legitimate aspirations in the context of a Canadian federalism where the equality between the "two founding peoples" would be affirmed, and popular approval of change would take place in the context of an explicit agreement between the two historic communities comprising Canada (Verney, 1986:374). Proposed changes involved the replacement of the Senate by a provincially appointed structure capable of curbing federal powers, proportional representation in the House of Commons, and the abolition of the monarchy. The proposed Federal Council would link the provinces, have its own source of funding, and be free from federal manipulation and intrusion. Its roles would include the approval of federal appointments, ratification of treaties affecting provinces, a veto on federal emergency and spending powers, and an advisory role in matters of fiscal, monetary, and transportation policy. In legislation regarding language and culture it would operate on a double majority principle. The Federal Council would also be responsible for federal–provincial relations, thereby making federal–provincial conferences obsolete. A Canadian Charter of Rights and Freedoms was also proposed.

During the 1980 referendum campaign, Trudeau challenged Québec independentists, and sent his Québec-based ministers to campaign for the "no" forces. Trudeau Liberals had promised that defeat of the referendum would not be interpreted as endorsement of the status quo, undertaking to elaborate policies that would respond to Québec's special needs and concerns. Many supporters of this option during the referendum campaign were made to believe that renewed federalism meant an official recognition of Québec as a distinct society/people, and that new powers commensurate with this admission would be given to Québec. One will remember that federalists of different persuasions had rallied around Pierre Elliott Trudeau to defeat Québec's claim for a new agreement between Québec and Ottawa.

Québec's federal MPs, in an ultimate attempt to convince Québécois to vote against the PQ's proposal for independence, said they were putting their seats on the line. This was generally believed to mean that a genuine desire by the federalists to accommodate Québec culturally and linguistically existed. Unfortunately for the proponents of renewed federalism, this option was completely discredited in Québec during the tenure of the Trudeau Liberals in Ottawa, as they failed to deliver on early promises. Instead of being granted special recognition, Québec was weakened by the federal order. The federal government took the initiative by patriating the Constitution with a Charter of Rights and Freedoms against Québec's will. This move was repudiated both by Québec nationalists and federalists active provincially, including federalists that in May 1980 were on Trudeau's side. These federalists felt betrayed. Trudeau's victory turned sour as opinion leaders who once fought for the federalist cause (such as Claude Ryan, Robert Bourassa, and the business community at large) called for corrective measures to be implemented rapidly to keep Canada together.

The federal government took the 1980 referendum's result only as an indication that Québec wanted to remain in Confederation. Ottawa proposed to continue constitutional discussions determined to be tougher than ever before since the so-called "separatists" were disorganized and demoralized. Trudeau challenged provincialism and decentralization as views of the past, and proposed a centralist vision. The PQ was in disarray, the Québec Liberal Party had fought a tough campaign against independence along with Ottawa, the Trudeau Liberals had a majority government, the state of the economy was abysmal, and a neoliberal ideology was gaining support.

Trudeau lost no time after the referendum and planned a constitutional conference for September 1980. Afraid of the possibility of a unilateral move by Ottawa if talks failed, Québec was busy forging alliances with other provinces. The first ministers' conference failed due to a confrontation between two competing visions of Canada: centralization versus decentralization. The federal government kept the initiative by introducing on 2 October 1980 a "Proposed Resolution for Address to Her Majesty the Queen Respecting the Constitution of Canada." Québec and seven other provinces—the Gang of Eight—opposed the move, preparing reference cases in the Québec, Manitoba, and Newfoundland appeal courts that proved disappointing for the provincialist forces. Ultimately, the case reached the Supreme Court of Canada, which ruled on 21 September 1981:

> that it would be legal for the Parliament to act without provincial consent, but that this would still be unconstitutional since it would breach an established convention of substantial provincial consent.... The only way out was to return to the intergovernmental table. But now there was a critical difference: the convention, said the Court, did not

mean unanimity; it required only "substantial consent." Two provinces was clearly not "substantial consent," but one province could no longer stop the process. The groundwork for a settlement without Québec had been laid. (Simeon and Robinson, 1990:278)

Taking advantage of these circumstances, a constitutional conference was called by Trudeau for November 1981. With the support of the Québec National Assembly and seven provincial premiers (Ontario and New Brunswick excepted), Premier Lévesque expressed opposition to the central government's plans to reform and patriate the Constitution unilaterally. Initially and strategically, Lévesque agreed to the principle of provincial equality. At the same time, he continued to oppose patriation in the absence of agreement on an amending formula and a new division of powers, demanded that Québec be recognized as a culturally and linguistically distinct society, and asked for the responsibilities and resources that that implied. In return for Québec's acceptance of the equality of provinces notion, the premiers confirmed Québec's veto right. It was believed by the Québec delegation that this would have allowed the province to press for increased autonomy within a revised federal system, and would ultimately legitimize the Parti Québécois' pursuit of independence as defined under international law (Rémillard, 1985:115-17).

Opposing any form of special status for Québec, be it entrenched in the Constitution or through international recognition, Trudeau shut Québec out. On 5 November 1981, in the absence of Premier Lévesque, the other premiers agreed to patriation with a Charter of Rights and Freedoms. With agreement came their preferred amending formula,[4] and the right to opt out of the secondary provisions of the Charter, which were entrenched in the Constitution. The opting-out (or "notwithstanding") clause ensured the western premiers' support of the package deal. Québec was isolated, with no other course of action but to make use of the notwithstanding clause, which it did systematically until the election of the Québec Liberals in December 1985. The decision to patriate with an entrenched Charter of Rights and Freedoms proved to be a major assault on Québec's vision of its own collective aspirations in an environment that was growing hostile to any protective measures. According to most centralist federalists, time would heal everything. Ten years after patriation, the healing process is far from complete.

Before the election of Brian Mulroney's Conservative government in 1984, no new constitutional initiatives to appease Québec were undertaken by Ottawa. Following the election of a Conservative government, and the stated intention of Prime Minister Mulroney to reintegrate Québec into the constitutional family with "honour and enthusiasm" (Mulroney, 1984), Premier Lévesque spoke of *un beau risque*, and went on in May 1985 to present the new federal prime minister with a "Draft Agreement on the Constitution"[5] that embodied twenty-two claims made by Québec to settle the constitutional crisis (Gagnon and Montcalm, 1990:162–63). Differences between the Parti Québécois government, after the defeat of the 1980 referendum, and Robert Bourassa's Liberals, following his re-election in 1985, were small. These were differences of degree, not of kind. It is to be noted that between 1981 and 1985 Lévesque, having lost the referendum, negotiated from a position of weakness. This changed somewhat when Bourassa, a bona fide federalist, came back as premier.

The Draft Agreement was used by the Québec Liberals as a bottom line during subsequent negotiations.[6] The five conditions to be entrenched in the Constitution were:

- the explicit recognition of Québec as a distinct society;
- increased power to Québec in immigration regarding recruitment, administration, and integration;
- appointment of three Supreme Court judges with expertise in Québec civil law;
- containment of the federal spending power; and
- a full veto for Québec in any new modifications to be considered to the Canadian Constitution.

The Meech Lake proposals (1987–90) attempted to deal with most of these claims but failed due, at least in part, to a lack of openness to difference and a reform process (amending formula) that is insensitive to Québec's distinct character.

For Ottawa, Meech Lake reflected a constant preoccupation with uniformity in Canadian federalism, except for the distinct society clause. By providing all the other provinces that which had been granted to Québec, Ottawa intended to give what the other provinces demanded and remove any impression of giving Québec a special status. In turn, the federal government would have obtained a major concession from Québec, as it was willing to recognize for the first time the federal spending power in spheres of exclusive provincial jurisdictions. In Québec, the federal spending power was viewed as federal intrusion, but was still accepted by the Québec government, to the great disenchantment of autonomists and nationalists. In the rest of Canada, there was a general understanding to the effect that the provinces had too much room to manoeuvre, as they were allowed to opt out of federal arrangements under certain conditions.

Several contingencies made it impossible for all premiers to agree on Meech Lake, despite these interlocking concessions (Fournier, 1990, Denis, 1990). Support for Meech was difficult to secure in Canada outside Québec considering that several issues were said to be left unresolved. As the Meech Lake negotiations began (supposedly intended to bring Québec back into the pan-Canadian family as a full participant), other interests organized with the aim of defeating Québec's vision of federalism. In the process, Québec's claims became secondary to natives, have-not provinces, equality of provinces, universality of social programs, etc. All of these reasons combined to deny Québec recognition of its distinct character. It became an all-or-nothing issue: Meech Lake died.

Following the failure of the Meech Lake Accord in June 1990, the government of Québec no longer had, however, a mandate to negotiate its reinsertion in the Canadian federation. This forced the Québec Liberal Party to elaborate a new policy platform (the Allaire Report), and convinced the Québec government to set up the Commission on the Political and Constitutional Future of Québec (the Bélanger-Campeau Commission).

The Allaire Report, entitled *A Québec Free to Choose*, released 28 January 1991, proposed to diminish the federal government's scope and to transfer significant powers to the provinces. The federal government would be left with jurisdiction over defence, equalization payments, monetary policy and customs, and debt management. Exclusive jurisdiction for the provinces is proposed in twenty-two fields, among which are: labour, natural resources, communications, health, agriculture, unemployment insurance, regional development, energy, environment, industry and commerce, language, research and development, public security, and income security. Shared jurisdictions are demanded for native affairs, taxation and revenue, immigration, financial institutions, fisheries, justice, foreign policy, post office, telecommunications, and transport.

The Allaire Report refers also to "a new structure" that would allow for Québec's special status to be recognized, and proposes to accommodate the other provinces that wish to assume additional responsibilities. If they do not want such powers, the possibility to delegate them to Ottawa is open. Predictably, Québec is demanding jurisdiction in all twenty-two domains identified as of provincial interest. Giving Québec what it demands would allow for asymmetrical federalism to take a significant hold in Canada. The Allaire Report also proposes changing the amending formula, requiring, among other things, a Québec veto. In addition, the report recommends the abolition of the Senate, the establishment of a community tribunal to oversee compliance with a new Constitution to be drafted, and a regionally sensitive central bank. Finally, an argument is made for a Québec Charter of Rights and Freedoms to be entrenched in a Québec Constitution. This Charter would prevail, it is assumed, over the Canadian Charter in Québec.

In response to the failure of Meech Lake to confirm Québec's distinct status, a democratization process that goes beyond anything we have experienced so far in Canada was launched, with the establishment of the Bélanger-Campeau Commission that was formed by a broad coalition of interests (see Gagnon and Latouche, 1991). The recent Commission on the Political and Constitutional Future of Québec in Canada (the Bélanger-Campeau Commission) sought "a new definition of the relation between Québec and Canada—and of Québec's place within or at the side of Canada." This constitutes a unique moment in Canadian history. A province, through its governing party and with the full backing of the official opposition, decided to assess the appropriateness of its continued association with the rest of the country of which it was a founding member, renewing the 1981 unanimity that had condemned unilateral patriation of the BNA Act without Québec's consent.

Following the tabling of the Bélanger-Campeau Report that was recommending the setting up of two special National Assembly committees, Bill 150 was enacted to confirm such a proposal. The Québec government intended to maintain the pressure on the other governments (provincial and federal) with these two public forums as renewed federalism and sovereignty are confronted on a daily basis.

The Bélanger-Campeau Commission asked that a referendum on the future of Québec in Canada be held no later than 26 October 1992. So as to regain the initiative, Ottawa released on 24 September 1991 a discussion paper to propose, against all expectations, a restructured federation along the lines of a centralized economic model, and set up a joint parliamentary committee (Castonguay-Dobbie, later Dobbie-Beaudoin) to, once more, examine the perennial issue of Québec's relations with the rest of Canada.

Contrary to all expectations, the federal government and the nine anglophone provinces reached a consensus on 7 July 1992 stating that asymmetrical federalism was not the order of the day. The essence of the deal was later confirmed in the 28 August 1992 Consensus Report on the Constitution (Charlottetown

Accord). Far from recognizing Québec's distinct status in Canada, and proceeding to a devolution of powers, the agreement proposed an increase of powers for the central government through the constitutionalization of its spending power, and the strengthening of central institutions, such as the Senate. Instead of transferring powers to the provinces, as has been demanded by Québec, the Charlottetown Accord proposed instead to make room for the provinces in the Senate and to consolidate the powers of the federal government to intervene in spheres of exclusive provincial jurisdiction. The Charlottetown Accord also included a Canada clause that gave equal weight to the distinct society clause, the equality of provinces principle, and the obligation for Canadians and their governments to promote Québec's anglophone minority. A major section of the proposed accord dealt with native rights to self-government.

The Accord was soundly defeated in Québec, as it was in Manitoba, Saskatchewan, Alberta, British Columbia, and to a much lesser extent, in Nova Scotia. In addition, the Accord was rejected by Native communities throughout the country, to the great disappointment of Ovide Mercredi, whose leadership was shaken. The defeat of the Charlottetown Accord constituted an unprecedented dismissal of the political class, as Canadians throughout the country said NO to a package deal cobbled behind closed doors. This also represented a major setback for Robert Bourassa who had, according to his closest constitutional advisers, "caved in" as he failed to defend Québec's traditional demands and political *acquis*. The Québec premier did not even secure the five minimal conditions of the Meech Lake proposals that were to be met before Québec could agree to re-enter formal constitutional negotiations. In short, Québec had made no gains in the sharing of powers, and saw the centralization of power as being further ensconced, since the federal government could negotiate five-year reversible deals with individual provinces, and Ottawa confirmed and potentially expanded its capabilities on intervention in areas of exclusive provincial jurisdiction (Bariteau, et. al., 1992).

IS THE CANADIAN FEDERATION A VIABLE OPTION?

Since the failure of Meech Lake, the positions of political actors and of Canadians in general have hardened. Nothing points to an easy resolution of the current, and possibly fatal, constitutional crisis. It is difficult to see how Québec's aspirations can be formally recognized, and very tough to imagine how the injustice of 1981 could ever be corrected. As Richard Simeon perceptively pointed out in his interpretation of the Meech Lake failure:

> Conspicuously missing ... was a response to the Québec agenda, which had always stressed the need for greater provincial autonomy. Indeed it could be argued that after 1982, Québec had less rather than more authority: it had gained no new powers, had lost the veto over future constitutional change which most political actors assumed it always had and was now to be subject to a Charter which, in the public mind at least, was intrinsically hostile to collective rights and which opened the possibility of broad legal challenges to Québec's attempts to shape its linguistic makeup through its language laws. Most telling, the *Act* had been passed over the objections not only of the Parti Québécois government, but also of Québec federalists. The Supreme Court subsequently rejected Québec's claim that the constitutional convention of "substantial provincial consent" should be read to include Québec. (Simeon, 1990:17–18)

To assess the viability of the Canadian federation, it is essential to consider domestic and external factors, including the Charter of Rights and Freedoms, economic and fiscal considerations and, not to be discounted, the capacity for constitutional engineering on the part of key political actors.

The Charter of Rights and Freedoms

To most students of Canadian federalism, the last thirty years demonstrate that Québec has been able to exercise some autonomy as long as special arrangements were made on an ad hoc basis and, more importantly for the other provinces, that these were not constitutionally entrenched. Indeed, as the first part of this chapter shows, several initiatives were taken by the government of Québec without fundamentally challenging the existence of the Canadian federal system. What changed the political dynamics, I believe, is the insertion in 1982 of a nonfederal document into the Constitution Act of 1982, namely the Canadian Charter of Rights and Freedoms, and to a lesser extent, the emerging view, as James Mallory put it,

> ... that a province is a province is a province. Whatever their strength, size or lack of same, provinces are the basic units of the system. (Mallory, 1990)

This interpretation is substantiated by Charles Taylor (see also Taylor in this volume) who identified at least two irreducible collision courses endangering the country's survival. He refers to:

(1) the conflict between the Charter of Rights and the recognition of Québec as a distinct society, which raises the question of the procedural approach, implying that the Charter might well be differently interpreted in specific cases, and

(2) the irreconcilable issue of equality between provinces in contrast to the special status demanded by Québec. (Taylor, 1990)

These two elements (the existence of a Charter of Rights and Freedoms that provides a definition of rights that are nonterritorially based conflicts with the "distinct society" view, and the equality of provinces principle clashes with Québec's continued claim for special status) make it impossible to solve the present constitutional crisis within the present constitutional framework, and point in the direction of the sovereignty-association option, or a variant, as the only realistic course of action for the Québécois. Following the failure of the Meech Lake Accord, such a prospect is not totally out of the question, as it would have the potential of bringing the federation together again in a newly formed alliance between Québec and the rest of Canada (or perhaps its successor states formed by the regions of Ontario, the West, the Atlantic, and eventually the North). Asymmetry or special status for Québec during the Meech Lake debate (and in its aftermath) proved to be a highly objectionable option to the rest of Canada. The Charter of Rights and Freedoms, perceived by most Canadians residing outside of Québec as providing equal treatment without regard to territorial specificity, makes it difficult for French-speaking Québécois to accept its application.

The tension between group and individual rights in an increasingly rights-fixated society indicates that this will constitute a major stumbling block in any new federal arrangement. In Canada, a "Charter culture" has developed and is having a significant impact on how Canadians outside of Québec view intergroup relations and the role of the state in citizens' affairs. The issue of rights is wrapped in the discourse of individual protection, and despite being applicable to groups, the Charter might well work against collective interests of those who predominate in a given region or province. In other words, the Canadian Charter of Rights and Freedoms has the potential to undermine effectively territorial diversity, especially in Québec. A *renegotiated federalism*, if it is still possible, must take into account the legitimating power of the "Charter" culture, but be willing to build institutions that are still capable of ensuring a greater degree of territorial autonomy than what is possible at the present time. The debate over the "distinct society" clause in the Meech Lake Accord, the Charlottetown Accord, and Québec sign legislation (Bill 178) demonstrates the potential cleavage that such an issue is capable of generating. To avoid being trapped in a debate of individual versus collective rights,[7] one will have to take into account concurrently the question of territoriality so fundamental to Québec's existence, and consider the collective goals pursued by both Québec and the rest of Canada with a view to reaching a political compromise (e.g., the social charter).

In light of recent constitutional negotiations, an emerging minoritarian tradition that is concerned with aboriginals, multicultural communities, women's rights, and other interests, displacing the notion of founding people as the principal pillar of Canadian society, has developed. The immediate consequence of this has been to undermine the leadership granted to elected representatives, and stress the new status accorded to groups via the Charter of Rights and Freedoms (Cairns, 1990:71–96). An important caveat, however, is that the Charter of Rights and Freedoms weakens parliamentary supremacy, leaving the notwithstanding clause as the only instrument available to the Québec government to protect its distinct character. In the process, the Canadian Parliament becomes more responsive to special interests that are not territorially based (e.g., natives, women, ethnic communities, and similar groups).

Economic Considerations

Whatever the recommendations elaborated respectively by federalist and sovereigntist forces, these will have to take into account the existence of a staggering federal debt. The accumulated deficit is such that collaboration between Québec and the rest of Canada is compulsory if the two protagonists are to be taken seriously by international creditors. The federal government is burdened by an enormous deficit that deters it from any significant initiatives to respond to Québec's challenge. This predicament must be taken seriously since the federal government has less financial leeway than it had in 1980 when it fought against Québec's separation. In the end, economic considerations may well force Québec and the rest of Canada to listen to each other. Economic considerations are likely to play a significant role in the current crisis. But, as the economist Pierre Fortin remarked:

> In previous rounds of constitutional debate in Québec, the drive for a greater measure
> of autonomy was constantly restrained by the general apprehension that any such
> occurrence would reduce the province's average standard of living. The main

arguments were, first, that Québec's economy was internally weak and highly dependent on external ownership, finance, manpower and technology; second, that any unilateral move by the province to appropriate greater constitutional powers would meet with swift trade retaliation from outside; and, third, that Québec drew substantial net economic benefits from its participation in the federation. Today, all three arguments stand on their heads…. (Fortin, 1990)

To substantiate his position, Fortin stresses that Québec gradually narrowed the productivity gap with its traditional competitor, Ontario; that the province has introduced major financial innovations, starting with deregulation in the financial sector, encouraged collaboration between the private and public/parapublic sectors, and developed a more competitive tax system; that the business-community involvement in the constitutional discussions has given credibility to Québec's potential for independence; that trade retaliation in an international economy entering globalization would not be advisable, and would probably be challenged under the General Agreement on Tariffs and Trade (GATT), or the free trade agreement with the United States; and, finally, that the federal deficit is so high that the government's capability to resolve the crisis is seriously undermined (Fortin, 1990).

The business community in Québec involved itself on the pro–Meech Lake side, providing an unexpected ally to forces asking for a new package deal with the rest of Canada. During the Bélanger-Campeau Commission hearings, the business community (through the Desjardins Movement, the Chamber of Commerce of the Province of Québec, and the Montréal Chamber of Commerce, and to a lesser extent, the Montréal Board of Trade) has asked for decentralization of several powers to the province. The business community seeks political stability to achieve bigger profits. If this means decentralization, so be it. Indeed, the status quo (meaning current federalism) is viewed as unacceptable by most economic actors.[8] In sharp contrast with the 1980 Québec referendum, the current impasse will not be debated, or resolved, around the economic issues. The federal government is viewed as moribund by most economic and political actors, and the place of Québec in the new international economy is perceived as respectable. As Pierre Fortin argued:

> With increased globalization, economic boundaries transcend political boundaries as countries have to comply with international treaties. The correlation between income per capita and population size among industrial countries is almost exactly zero. The size of the Québec economy is actually equal to or greater than that of Austria, Belgium, Denmark, Finland, New Zealand, Norway, and Switzerland, and not much smaller than that of Sweden. (Fortin, 1990)

Constitutional Engineering and Politics

For some time, Québec nationalists went unchallenged, but the federalist forces regrouped for the final assault. To be credible, federalists had to integrate in their counterattacks two crucial aspects that arose time and again in the briefs presented to the Bélanger-Campeau Commission: the need for Québec to operate within a more functional system and the economics-based definition of the new Québec–Canada relationship. It is believed that concessions to Québec would be acceptable to the rest of Canada only if these are perceived as bona fide cultural demands with little financial implication.

A series of interventions by Prime Minister Brian Mulroney and challenger Jean Chrétien in the latter part of 1990 called for a new division of powers between the federal and the provincial orders, with the combined objective of putting an end to overlapping jurisdictions and revising power-sharing arrangements with a view to transferring powers to the provinces as long as guarantees of national standards and universality are provided (Tyson, 1990:1, 4). These propositions are reminiscent of promises made during the 1980 referendum debate in Québec, and have accordingly been received with great suspicion by sovereigntists (Léger, 1991:11).

Under the concepts of *flexible and functional federalisms*, the federalist forces are elaborating a normalization scenario, as suggested by recent initiatives put forward both on the Québec and federal fronts.[9] For example, the deal reached in December 1990 between Québec and Ottawa on the immigration issue indicates a political will to remove irritants between Québec and Ottawa. It is intended to resolve the issue of control of settlement and adaptation programs, and improve the likelihood immigrants will be better integrated into a French milieu (Cauchon, 1990; Oziewicz, 1991).

Following the immigration deal, Québec has intensified pressures on the federal government to vacate fields of shared federal–provincial jurisdictions, and turn over responsibilities and powers related to, among others, the Canada Health Act, post-secondary education, unemployment insurance, and labour force training. Québec's strategy appears to be operating at two levels: on the one hand, fundamental changes are proposed via the Allaire Report and the Bélanger-Campeau Commission while, on the other hand, Ottawa and Québec are trying to come up with deals that would demonstrate to Québécois the extent to which there is flexibility in the system.

Ottawa released on 24 September 1991 a set of proposals aimed at resuming constitutional talks. Contrary to all predictions, the suggested package was highly centralist. For instance, section 91A (1) was to stipulate that "without altering any other authority of the Parliament of Canada to make laws, the Parliament of Canada may exclusively make laws in relation to any other matter that it declares to be for the efficient functioning of the economic union." This issue, in addition to the issues of "national" standards and universality, resurfaced again during the negotiations leading to the Charlottetown Accord since Canadians outside of Québec have come to see programs such as medicare as defining characteristics of what it is to be a "Canadian."

CONCLUSION

The record indicates that since 1960 Québec has been most successful in bilateral negotiations. Through a strong presence within the federal governing party, Québec was usually able to obtain some concessions at the administrative level, but failed to translate these to formal arrangements. Time and time again changes have been incremental and have failed to bring about a fundamental redefinition of the Canadian federation that could accommodate Québec in the long haul. Once concessions were obtained, these were then offered to all other provinces so that no asymmetrical federalism would ever develop in Canada. The convention against asymmetry has proven to be "problematic" during the Meech Lake discussions as well as the referendum campaign of 1992. Symmetrical federalism was often perceived by Meech opponents as the only valid doctrine from which to conduct federal–provincial negotiations in Canada. Whatever the end result of the current constitutional crisis, it surely cannot be resolved without an explicit recognition of Québec's distinct presence and role in the Canadian federation. Given the new rules of the constitutional game in Canada (imposed by the Constitution Act of 1982), special status cannot be achieved in the present context. However, bilateral deals through section 43 of the Constitution Act of 1982 are possible.[10] Backlash from other players is anticipated, though, making asymmetrical federalism untenable and demonstrating once again the extent to which the Constitution has become a strait jacket for Québec.

The failure of Meech demonstrates the urgency of crafting political institutions that are sensitive to both individual rights and collective goals, at least if the intent is to propose enduring solutions. If Canada is to survive as a plural society, there is an immediate need to stop approaching federalism in reductivist ways. Instead of symmetry, consideration of a more generous kind of federalism is necessary, based on a vision that accepts asymmetry, as the Pepin-Roberts Task Force had already proposed in 1979. An acceptable solution for Québec requires significant changes, allowing at a minimum for the recognition of asymmetrical federalism. With the Charter culture gradually taking hold in the rest of Canada, however, asymmetrical federalism will not be easily achieved.

The future of Canada depends on a variety of factors, among which are the imagination of its leaders, the will to accept Québec's special place in Canada, and more importantly, the capacity of these leaders to find devices that subsume the application of the Canadian Charter of Rights and Freedoms under a territorial formula to account for Québec's special and unique needs in the Canadian federation. This will be difficult to achieve due to:

- the rapid demise of first ministers' conferences (and executive federalism), which are perceived as too elitist;
- profound distrust of traditional forms of representation (for example, the major political parties) complicated by the emergence of regional blocs such as the Reform Party and the Bloc Québécois;
- the rapidly acquired faith in the Charter of Rights and Freedoms in English-speaking Canada, complicated by Québec's cultural insecurity; and
- the equality of provinces precept that gained prominence with the growing popularity of province-building in the 1970s.

All of these factors coalesce in making a recognition of Québec as a distinct society difficult. In fact, the combination of these elements makes a solution to the present crisis improbable. First, Québec will never agree to define itself as a *province comme les autres*. Second, Québec cannot accept that the Canadian Charter of Rights and Freedoms undermines the supremacy of Québec's National Assembly. Québec, as the only province that has a francophone majority, cannot accept having English-speaking Canadians decide the fate of the most important and viable French-speaking community in North America. The situation is further compounded by the fact that Québec's conventional right of veto was denied by its

Canadian partners when the time came to patriate the Constitution in 1981, and that so far no corrective measures have been implemented. It is ludicrous to imagine a country such as Canada that has not yet been able to obtain the consent of its second most populous province for its primary symbolic document, the Constitution Act of 1982. The legitimacy of the Constitution Act of 1982 is put in question due to the fact that Québec is the only region of Canada where French has a majority status.

There remain several intangibles that could still have a crucial impact on the future of Canada. First, the capacity of political leaders to craft political solutions that tackle Québec's distinct status, aimed at finding a territorial solution to the Canadian Charter of Rights and Freedoms. Second, the circulation of political leaders at the provincial level with the election of Bob Rae in Ontario, Michael Harcourt in British Columbia, and Roy Romanow in Saskatchewan and the departure of Don Getty and Joe Ghiz should bring some fresh air into the process of constitutional negotiations. In addition, the recession may create a climate that encourages Canadians living outside of Québec to be more receptive to a federalism that nourishes diversity, instead of a federalism that stresses universal truths. Alternatively, the recession may discourage Québec itself from taking the next logical step.

Failure to accept Québec's distinct status, and its need for a constitutional veto, may have brought Canada to a point of no return, to be restructured around a new set of values rather than the ones that brought about its creation. In the end, the only available option for the rest of Canada may be to define its common values around the Charter of Rights and Freedoms, which has gained the adherence of English-speaking Canadians, and let Québec go its own way. In this regard, there is growing support on the part of the rest of Canada to let Québec do so. If this is the conclusion reached, then Québec and the rest of Canada should find ways to continue their economic association (Drache and Perin, 1992; and Gagnon and Rocher, 1992) as the Bélanger-Campeau Commission recommended, and encourage economic solidarities that transcend political niceties.

NOTES

1. This principle recognized, for instance, the provincial right to enter into negotiations with international organizations in matters exclusively assigned by the BNA Act of 1867 to the provinces.
2. Ironically, Québec agreed to unanimity in 1980 as a last-resort effort to block the federal government's patriation package.
3. We learned that Mr. Bourassa was saying different things to the electors and to the federal government. In fact, during the week that preceded the Victoria Conference, Mr. Bourassa had committed his government (via the government's principal secretary, Mr. Julien Chouinard) only to achieve practical results in the field of social policy rather than pushing for constitutional objectives. A memorandum prepared by Gordon Robertson, then Clerk of the Privy Council, and made public 24 October 1991, reveals this "double-play" on the part of Mr. Bourassa: "Mr. Chouinard said that Mr. Bourassa had managed, at the Cabinet meeting yesterday [3 February 1971] to get agreement that the fundamental thing for the Québec government (and for Mr. Castonguay) is to achieve the practical results that are contemplated in the Castonguay-Nepveu report. He apparently persuaded the Cabinet that the constitutional aspect is secondary and that the question whether constitutional change is necessary should depend on and emerge from discussions with Ottawa as to the ways and means of achieving the practical results in terms of social policy toward which the Commission was looking" (Robertson, 1991, B-10).
4. The amending formula stipulates that constitutional changes can be made with the support of seven provinces totalling 50 percent of the Canadian population, and indicates that the formula,

along with a limited set of other changes, can be modified only with unanimity. This situation was forced onto Québec, which, against its consent, has to abide by rules that were set by others.

5. The Draft Agreement on the Constitution was largely inspired by a key document prepared by the Department of Intergovernmental Affairs, during the first mandate of the Parti Québécois. See, *Les positions constitutionnelles du Québec sur le partage des pouvoirs (1960–76)* (Québec: Éditeur officiel du Québec, 1978).

6. Before coming to power in 1985, the Liberals had prepared a series of policy papers that pointed to areas where compromises needed to be reached. See, Québec Liberal Party, *A New Canadian Constitution* (1980), *A New Political Leadership for Québec* (1983), and *Mastering Our Future* (1985), which set the five conditions that would eventually constitute essential conditions for the Meech Lake Accord. These conditions were made public 9 May 1986.

7. Alan Cairns and Cynthia Williams provide a convincing argument concerning the impact the Charter has on both political culture and citizen–state relationships. If Cairns and Williams (1985) are correct in their assessment, the discourse of rights, either collective or individual, must be confronted in a *renegotiated federalism* to be perceived as legitimate by the public.

8. To name a few, the Royal Bank, Canadian Pacific, Bell Canada, the Conseil du Patronat, the Québec wing of the Canadian Manufacturers' Association, the Forum de l'emploi. Some, such as the Desjardins Movement, did not hesitate then to go as far as proposing full independence for Québec. This reading emerged clearly out of the briefs presented at the Bélanger-Campeau Commission. (See, Gagnon and Latouche, 1991).

9. This possibility was suggested by both David Milne and Peter Meekison at the 16 January 1991 Business Council on National Issues' special meeting held in Toronto on Constitutional Options for Canada.

10. Section 43 stipulates that "an amendment to the Constitution of Canada in relation to any provision that applies to one or more, but not all provinces" may be decided by Parliament and the relevant province(s) alone. This is available to all provinces, but gives some flexibility to the federal government to enter into some constitutional negotiations with Québec.

REFERENCES

Bariteau, A., A. Bernard, G. Boismenu, H. Brun, A.-G. Gagnon et al. (1992). *Les objections de 20 spécialistes aux offres féderales: Référendum, 26 octobre 1992.* Montréal: Éditions Saint-Martin.

Cairns, Alan (1990). "Constitutional Minoritarianism in Canada," in Ronald Watts and Douglas Brown, eds., *Canada: The State of the Federation, 1990* (pp. 71–96). Kingston: Institute of Intergovernmental Relations.

Cairns, Alan, and Cynthia Williams (1985). "Constitutionalism, Citizenship and Society in Canada: An Overview," in Alan Cairns and Cynthia Williams, eds., *Constitutionalism, Citizenship and Society in Canada* (pp. 1–50). Toronto: University of Toronto Press.

Cauchon, Paul (1990a, December 22). "Plus de pouvoirs au Québec en immigration: entente Québec–Canada sur le projet de Meech," in *Le Devoir*, pp. A-1, A-4.

Cauchon, Paul (1990b, December 28). "Québec françisera seul ses immigrants," *Le Devoir*, pp. 1, 4.

Denis, Roch, ed. (1990). *Québec: Dix ans de crise constitutionnelle.* Montréal: VLB éditeur.

Drache, Daniel, and Roberto Perin, eds. (1992). *Negotiating With a Sovereign Quebec.* Toronto: Lorimer.

Fortin, Pierre (1990, November 17). "Québec's Forced Choice," Remarks prepared for the Conference on the Future of Québec and Canada. Faculty of Law, McGill University.

Fournier, Pierre (1990). *Autopsie du lac Meech: la souveraineté est-elle inévitable?* Montréal: VLB éditeur.

Gagnon, Alain-G. (1991). "Egalité ou indépendance: un tournant dans la pensée constitutionnelle du Québec," in Robert Comeau, dir., *Daniel Johnson: Rêve d'égalité et projet d'indépendance* (pp. 173–81). Sillery: Presses de l'Université du Québec.

Gagnon, Alain-G., and Daniel Latouche (1991). *Allaire, Bélanger, Campeau et les autres: les Québécois s'interrogent sur leur avenir.* Montréal: Québec/Amérique.

Gagnon, Alain-G., and Mary Beth Montcalm (1990). *Québec: Beyond the Quiet Revolution.* Toronto: Nelson Canada.

Gagnon, Alain-G., and François Rocher, eds. (1992). *Répliques aux détracteurs de la souveraineté du Québec.* Montréal: VLB éditeur.

Mallory, James (1990, November 9). "Comments: The Future of Canadian Federalism," Canadian Study of Parliamentary Group: Ottawa.

Morin, Claude (1972). *Québec Versus Ottawa: The Struggle for Self-Government, 1960–1972.* Toronto: University of Toronto Press.

Morin, Claude (1987). *L'art de l'impossible: la diplomatie québécoise depuis 1960.* Montréal: Boréal.

Mulroney, Brian (1984, August 6). "Notes pour une allocution de l'honorable Brian Mulroney." Sept-Îles.

O'Neill, Pierre (1990, June 27). "Peterson et Bourassa jettent les bases d'un nouveau partenariat économique," in *Le Devoir,* pp. 1, 8.

Oziewicz, Estanislas (1991, February 6). "Québec calls immigration pact model for future," *The Globe and Mail,* p. A-4.

Rémillard, Gil (1985). *Le fédéralisme canadien: le rapatriement de la constitution.* Montréal: Québec/Amérique.

Report of the Constitutional Committee of the Québec Liberal Party (Allaire Report) (1991, January 28). *A Québec Free to Choose.*

Robertson, Gordon (1991, October 24). "Le mémorandum du 4 février 1971," *Le Devoir,* p. B-10.

Roy, Jean-Louis (1978). *Le choix d'un pays: le débat constitutionnel Québec-Canada, 1960–1976.* Ottawa: Leméac.

Saywell, John, ed. (1977). *1976 Canadian Annual Review of Politics and Public Affairs.* Toronto: University of Toronto Press.

Séguin, Rhéal (1990, December 13). "Give Canada a Last Chance, Grit Adviser Tells Québec," in *The Globe and Mail,* p. A-5.

Simeon, Richard (1972). *Federal-Provincial Diplomacy: The Making of Recent Policy in Canada.* Toronto: University of Toronto Press.

———. (1990). "Why Did the Meech Lake Accord Fail?" in Ronald Watts and Douglas Brown, eds. *Canada: The State of the Federation, 1990* (pp. 15–40). Kingston: Institute of Intergovernmental Relations.

Simeon Richard, and Ian Robinson (1990). *State, Society and the Development of Canadian Federalism.* Toronto: University of Toronto Press.

Smiley, Donald (1967). *The Canadian Political Community.* Toronto: Methuen.

Stevenson, Garth (1982). *Unfulfilled Union: Canadian Federalism and National Unity.* Toronto: Gage Publishing.

Taylor, Charles (1990, November 16). "Keynote address: Collision Courses Québec-Canada," Conference on the Future of Québec and Canada, Faculty of Law, McGill University.

Trudeau, Pierre Elliott (1977). "1976 Correspondence to all provincial premiers," in Peter Meekison, ed., *Canadian Federalism: Myth or Reality* (pp. 140–69). Toronto: Methuen.

Tyson, Marie (1990, December 17), "Mulroney promet un nouveau partage des pouvoirs," in *Le Devoir,* pp. 1, 4.

Venne, Michel (1990, December 19). "Québec dit oui au libre-échange entre les provinces," *Le Devoir.*

Verney, Douglas (1986). *Three Civilizations, Two Cultures, One State: Canada's Political Traditions.* Durham: Duke University Press.

C   H   A   P   T   E   R   7

English-Canadian Perceptions of Québec*

Kenneth McRoberts
York University

Historically, English Canadians have never fully confronted, let alone recognized and accepted, the conception that French Canadians have held of themselves as a people and of Canada. Few English Canadians have ever come to terms with the notion that French Canadians constitute a distinct people, let alone a nation. And they have been just as unlikely to accept the French-Canadian belief that Confederation constituted some sort of pact or arrangement between two founding peoples.

In fact, through most of Canada's history many English Canadians did not even know that French Canadians harboured such notions. And, by and large, French Canadians did not insist that English Canada recognize their vision. Periodically, as with the hanging of Louis Riel or the conscription crises, English Canadians and French Canadians would find themselves fundamentally divided on major issues of the day. But this rarely led to any questioning of the political order itself. The two groups simply continued to view the same country in different terms.

With the 1960s, however, Québec francophones began to demand that English Canada come to terms with their vision and that it be recognized formally within the institutions of Confederation. Initially, some English Canadians struggled to find ways to do so. With the 1970s, however, English-Canadian resistance to the Québec question hardened, thanks in large part to the leadership of Pierre Elliott Trudeau. Thus, as Québec francophones have become more and more insistent on some recognition of their vision, English Canada has become more and more resistant to making any room for it—as the Meech Lake Accord debacle clearly demonstrated.

---

*This article is based in part on my *English Canada and Quebec: Avoiding the Issue*, the Sixth Annual Robarts Lecture, which has been published by the Robarts Centre for Canadian Studies, York University. The underlying argument is elaborated in a book-length study soon to be published by McClelland and Stewart.

With English Canada and French Québec more committed than ever to their separate visions of Canada, and aware of the differences between them, it has become much more difficult to devise ways to accommodate both within Confederation.

HISTORICAL ATTITUDES REGARDING QUÉBEC

Before the 1960s English Canadians were relatively untroubled in their belief that Canada was essentially an English-speaking country. In 1964, Frank Underhill, one of English Canada's leading historians, shrewdly noted that English Canadians needed to beware of their "unconscious or subconscious assumption," born of the Conquest and of English Canada's majority status, that:

> Canada is fundamentally an English-speaking community and [that] our English-Canadian habits, methods, forms of social organization, and way of life generally, must in the end be accepted by the French-Canadians as their way of life also. This is a tendency natural to all comfortable majorities.[1]

Initially, the English-Canadian view of Canada derived from Canada's role as an integral part of the world's greatest power, the British Empire. To be sure, this Empire had come to embrace a wide variety of languages, cultures, and races. But Canada's English-speaking majority bestowed upon it a special status. It was one of the White Dominions, in which British settlers had sought to reproduce British society in the New World. Thus, Canada's membership in the British Empire naturally privileged the country's English-speaking roots.

Not surprisingly, many English Canadians responded accordingly. As J.W. Dafoe noted at the turn of the century:

> English-speaking Canadians were more British than the British, they were more loyal than the Queen.... Imperialism, on the sentimental side, was a glorification of the British race.... Moreover, it gave them a sense of their special importance here in Canada, where the population was not "homogeneous in blood, language, and religion"; it was for them, they felt, to direct policy and control events.[2]

As Carl Berger documents in his *The Sense of Power*, some English-Canadian imperialists were quite explicit in the view that there was no place at all for a French fact in Canada. Imperial Federation League president D'Alton McCarthy declared in 1889 that language rights had grown to "monstrous proportions" and that if a French Canadian were to be a true Briton, "he must learn to cherish, not only our institutions, but our glorious past and look forward with us to a still more glorious future."[3]

However, some English-Canadian imperialists were more subtle in their approach to French Canada. Instead, they interpreted the French-Canadian presence in ways that made it more compatible with Canada's role within the Empire. Thus French Canadians were extolled for their loyalty to the British Crown and more generally were portrayed as a conservative and rural folk. Nonetheless, they were a minority and were destined to become even more so in the future. The imperialists believed that French-Canadian

> opposition to imperialism, however, was of small consequence and could only be significant temporarily because the rapid growth of the English-speaking section of the

population, including the "foreigners" who would be assimilated to the prevailing ideals, would in the end exert a total dominance over the Canadian nationality.[4]

During this century, the decline of the British Empire meant that Canada was drawn into the sphere of a new world power that was also English-speaking, the United States. Once again Canada's English-speaking society was privileged. Moreover, American historical development had been closely shaped by the ideal of an English-speaking "melting pot." As English-speaking Canadians became increasingly integrated with American society, they could only be strengthened in the belief that Canada was itself essentially an English-speaking country.

For that matter, some Americans would not hesitate to express this view themselves. It was recently revealed that in a 1942 letter to Prime Minister Mackenzie King, U.S. President Franklin D. Roosevelt wondered

whether by some sort of planning Canada and the United States, working toward the same end, cannot do some planning—perhaps by unwritten planning which need not even be a public policy—by which we can hasten the objective of assimilating the New England French Canadians and Canada's French Canadians into the whole of our respective bodies politic.[5]

To be sure, their rejection of French-Canadian claims of nationhood did not prevent English Canadians from tolerating or even supporting some limited recognition of Canadian duality. After all, Sir John A. Macdonald had warned English Canada in a celebrated phrase: "Treat them [French Canadians] as a nation and they will act as a free people generally do—generously. Call them a faction and they become factious."[6]

Thus, historically there was a certain acceptance of bilingualism in Parliament and on Canadian currency and official documents. Under the terms of the British North America Act, French was to have equal status to English within Parliament and federal courts. By the same token, since the days of Laurier one national party, the Liberal Party, has followed a practice of alternating its leadership between an English Canadian and a French Canadian. At least some English-Canadian Liberals must have supported this practice, although there is no direct evidence to this effect.[7]

But there were very clear limits to this toleration of duality.[8] It was not to be extended from Parliament to the federal bureaucracy. There, only the norms of personal merit and administrative efficiency were to prevail; they precluded any concern with bilingualism. For that matter, if French Canadians could expect a roughly proportional share of cabinet portfolios, they were effectively excluded from the powerful economic ministries. Until the 1970s, no French Canadian held the portfolios of Finance and Trade and Commerce.

And English Canadians fully expected that when they differed on policy issues from the French-Canadian minority, their majority will would prevail. Within their fundamentally liberal world view the polity was composed of individuals, not collectivities. For that matter, the parliamentary tradition was itself based upon rule by the majority. Thus, there was no sense that French Canadians or Québécois might have any special say over federal policies.

Accordingly, in 1885 the federal government yielded to English-Canadian pressure to allow the execution of Louis Riel, over the fierce objections of French

Canada. And during the two world wars most English Canadians insisted that the federal government override French-Canadian objections to the imposition of conscription for overseas service. Three years into World War I the government of Robert Borden broke its pledge not to impose conscription, provoking French-Canadian demonstrations and riots in the process. For its part, the World War II government of Mackenzie King used a national referendum to release the government from a commitment King had made during the 1939 Québec provincial election not to impose conscription for overseas service. Predictably, the vast majority outside Québec (79 percent) approved the proposition; the vast majority within Québec (72 percent) opposed it.[9] Finally, in the fall of 1944, under relentless English-Canadian pressure, the government imposed the measure.

In short, recognition for duality in federal affairs consisted of a carefully circumscribed official role for the French language. With the exception of Québec, this same principle was not to be applied at all at the provincial level. By the 1920s any role for French within provincial governments or public schools had been eliminated.

By the same token, English Canadians came to embrace the principle of federalism that French-Canadian leaders had insisted upon at the time of Confederation. In fact, during the first few decades after Confederation the provincial government of Ontario was in the forefront of the struggle to protect provincial autonomy. And English Canadians usually accepted that the Québec provincial government would represent the wishes of its French-Canadian majority.

However, there was little support in English Canada for the notion that the Québec government should exercise any special rights as a consequence. Most English Canadians believed that if Québec's approval was judged to be necessary for constitutional amendment, this was only because the approval of *all* provinces was necessary for such amendments.

By the same token, if Québec should decide through an excessive concern with provincial autonomy not to participate in an initiative of the federal government, it followed naturally that Québec would be deprived of the benefits. In the fiscal year 1959–60 Québec lost $82 million through the refusal of the Duplessis government to participate in several federal–provincial schemes and to allow such institutions as universities to receive federal funds.[10]

Typically, English Canadians presumed that Québec's zealous defence of provincial autonomy reflected the continued hold of conservative forces within Québec, especially the church. In effect, these forces were fighting a doomed battle to hold Québec in its backwardness. Once they were replaced by progressive elements, it was presumed, Québec would join the mainstream of Canadian society and its government would behave like all the other provincial governments.

Until the 1960s, the dominant elements in French Québec were generally prepared to accept these parameters. Typically, French-Canadian nationalists would call for a closer adherence to the terms of the British North America Act, not for a renegotiation of them. Clearly, they had a different reading of these terms than did most English Canadians. Not only was control over all areas of provincial jurisdiction sacrosanct, and these jurisdictions were interpreted in a generous manner, but Confederation was seen as a pact between two nations. Yet, since no demands for substantial constitutional change flowed from this reading, English Canadians could easily ignore it.

RESPONSES TO THE NEW NATIONALISM OF THE 1960S

With the 1960s this all changed. The 1960 provincial election placed the Québec government under the influence of social and political forces that had heretofore been largely undetected in English Canada. Unlike the Duplessis regime, with its strong electoral base in rural Québec and close links to small-town elites and the clergy, the Liberal Party of Jean Lesage had strong roots in urban Québec.

In particular, Liberal policies responded to a new middle class of salaried professionals that had arisen in universities, the media, church-controlled social service and health organizations, and even French-owned enterprises, but was seriously underrepresented in the anglophone corporations that dominated Québec's economy. Within their resolutely secular vision of Québec, the Québec state had to become much more interventionist so as to raise the level of public services available to francophones and to carve out a new role for francophones within the Québec economy. This new emphasis upon state intervention placed the Québec state at the centre of French-Canadian nationalism. In fact, it necessitated a resolutely *Québec* nationalism. The Québec state was to become a truly national state.

This new Québec nationalism had in turn radical implications for the Canadian constitutional order. Canadian federalism had to be revised so as to give the Québec state the additional powers and status that were needed for it to fulfil its special responsibilities as a nation-state. And federal-level institutions had to be explicitly organized on the basis of equality between Québec and English Canada. Nothing less would do given the centrality of the state to this new nationalism.

Initially, a good number of English-Canadian intellectual and political leaders tried to grapple with the new demands emanating from Québec. First, the notion that Canada is composed of two founding peoples or nations was endorsed by all three federal parties. In 1963 the Liberal government of Lester B. Pearson created a Royal Commission on Bilingualism and Biculturalism with the mandate to recommend "what steps should be taken to develop the Canadian Confederation on the basis of an *equal partnership between the two founding races* ['peoples' in the French-language version], taking into account the contribution made by other ethnic groups to the cultural enrichment of Canada."[11]

For their part, the Conservatives struggled with the notion of "two nations." In 1967, a thinkers conference at Maison Montmorency in Québec adopted the position that Canada is composed of "deux nations," which was rendered "two founding peoples" in English. At the subsequent leadership convention, John Diefenbaker angrily denounced the proposition, but none of the other leadership candidates supported him, and the motion was "tabled."[12] The New Democratic Party had already confronted the issue at its founding convention in 1961, incorporating in its program the statement that Canada was created by the association of two nations.[13]

As for the status of Québec itself, during the early 1960s Prime Minister Pearson openly recognized Québec's distinctiveness with such statements as:

> While Quebec is a province in the national confederation, it is more than a province because it is the heartland of a people: in a very real sense it is a nation within a nation.[14]

Moreover, during this period the Pearson government allowed Québec to exercise a de facto particular status by opting out of a large number of joint federal–provincial cost-shared programs and even exclusively federal programs.

With its commitment to state intervention, the New Democratic Party recognized that the federal government could not assume its proper role if Québec had to be included in all its initiatives. Thus, at its 1967 convention the party forthrightly endorsed special status for Québec:

> In fields of government which touch a community's way of life—fields such as social security, town planning, education and community development—Quebec must have the right and the fiscal resources to adopt its own programmes and policies in place of those designed and financed by the federal government. At the same time, the federal government must be able to play an increased role in these fields where this is desired by the people of other provinces.[15]

During the 1968 election campaign, Tommy Douglas vigorously defended this position, declaring:

> The NDP takes the position that we must have a strong federal government. It must have power it has never had before to grapple with modern problems that are conspicuously beyond the grasp of the provincial and municipal governments…. Thus, it may mean that in any area such as education and housing, where Quebec feels that a strong federal power may erode provincial rights, it may be necessary to have two programs—one for English-speaking Canada and one for Quebec.[16]

He bitterly decried the fact that "anyone who talks about particular status for Québec or any negotiation is automatically called a separatist" by the new Liberal leader, Pierre Elliott Trudeau.[17]

For their part, the Progressive Conservatives apparently did not take an explicit position on the question of Québec's status, although party leader Robert Stanfield evoked sufficient openness to the notion to receive the support of *Le Devoir* editor Claude Ryan during the 1968 federal election—in opposition to Québec's ostensible favourite son, Pierre Trudeau.[18]

Probably, neither of these positions commanded clear majority support among English-Canadian political and intellectual elites. In all three parties, each was vigorously challenged. John Diefenbaker's final act as Conservative Party leader was to lead a campaign against the "two nations" thesis. The NDP's evocation of "two nations" precipitated Eugene Forsey's departure, and its endorsement of special status for Québec caused Ramsay Cook and Kenneth McNaught to leave it.[19]

But at least the "two nations" thesis and special status for Québec were viewed as legitimate positions for discussion, and had advocates in English Canada. In the process, English Canadians for the first time were confronting directly the French-Canadian vision of Canada.

IMPACT OF THE TRUDEAU VISION

This new English-Canadian effort to respond directly to Québec's vision of Canada proved to be short-lived. By the early 1970s, opinion had shifted decisively to an alternative that was most forcefully articulated by Pierre Elliott Trudeau, elected prime minister in 1968.

Trudeau contended that any formal recognition of the claims of Québec nationalists would be a fatal error. Rather than restoring a semblance of national unity, it would have the effect of strengthening the forces of Québec separatism. Moreover, he argued, the forces of Québec nationalism could be effectively undermined through a series of measures that, rather than recognizing Québec's distinctiveness, sought to incorporate Québec within a pan-Canadian perspective.

Foremost among these measures was official bilingualism. Not only was the federal government to become rigorously bilingual in its own operations, but the provincial governments were, to varying degrees, to afford equality to both languages. Québec's language regime of de facto equality between French and English was to be the ideal to which the other provinces were to aspire. In effect, Québec was to become a province "like the others" by making the other provinces like Québec.

Once this was done, Trudeau would declare, there would no longer be a need to recognize Québec's constitutional demands because Québec could no longer claim to be speaking for the French-Canadian nation. As Trudeau contended in 1968:

> If minority language rights are entrenched throughout Canada then the French-Canadian nation would stretch from Maillardville in BC to the Acadia community on the Atlantic Coast.... Québec cannot say it alone speaks for French Canadians ... Mr. Robarts will be speaking for French Canadians in Ontario. Mr. Robichaud will be speaking for French Canadians in New Brunswick. Mr. Thatcher will speak for French Canadians in Saskatchewan. Nobody will be able to say, "I need more power because I speak for the French-Canadian nation."[20]

The Trudeau response to Québec did require a recognition of duality that was much more thoroughgoing than in the past. However, it shared the essential limitations of past conceptions of duality. Formal equality was to be established between the English and French languages, not the speakers of these languages. There was no sense that English Canada and French Canada, as collectivities, should be in a position of equality. Nor was there a sense that their members within the federal government should assume equality. Thus, during the Trudeau years the federal government made an unprecedented effort to increase the presence of francophones in the upper levels of the public service, but the explicit objective always was a proportional representation, in which the presence of francophones in the public service would reach their proportion (25 percent) within the Canadian population as a whole.

By the same token, the Trudeau government rejected the B&B Commission's twin notion of biculturalism, fearing that to go beyond language to culture might indeed serve to sanction the ideal of two nations. These fears are evident in a mid-1960s article that several of Trudeau's fellow antinationalists published in *Cité libre*. Severely criticizing the B&B Commission's Preliminary Report, the authors declared that:

> [the government and the Commission] voluntarily abandon the linguistic dimension (which provides some concepts which are nonetheless applicable) so as to slip into "biculturalism" and to talk of equality of citizens in as much as they participate in one of two cultures.... And what is the meaning in practice of a Confederation which "develops according to the principle of equality between the two cultures"?...

Once again, political science is very familiar with the idea of equality between individuals within the same state, but the idea of equality between peoples underlies the concept of national sovereignty, and it would have been interesting to see how the Commission intends to interpret its mandate without being led necessarily to propose the division of Canada into two national states.[21]

Thus, in 1971 the Trudeau government declared that it would pursue a policy of "multiculturalism within a framework of bilingualism." Trudeau was explicit in his rejection of biculturalism:

The very title of the Royal Commission whose recommendations we are now in the process of implementing seems to suggest that bilingualism and biculturalism are inseparable. But the term biculturalism does not accurately depict our society; the word multiculturalism is more precise in this respect.[22]

In effect, then, French Canada's language may be one of two official languages, but its culture is only one of a vast multitude of "cultures," many of which have at best a very nebulous existence.

So as to reinforce further its notion of linguistic duality, the Trudeau government sought to entrench language rights within a new charter of rights. Back in 1968 Trudeau had declared that, along with patriation, such an entrenched charter of rights should be the first objective of constitutional revision, with reform of federal-level institutions the second. Only when these two matters had been resolved should attention turn to the division of powers—the primary concern of Québec nationalists.

The 1982 constitutional revision, engineered by the Trudeau government, was faithful to this strategy: revision was indeed restricted primarily to patriation and a charter of rights. Moreover, the Canadian Charter of Rights and Freedoms was faithful to the Trudeau conception of language rights. There can be little doubt that the primary purpose of the Charter was the entrenchment of the right to minority-language education. Moreover, this right is conceived in a resolutely pan-Canadian fashion. Applying equally to all provinces, the right to minority-language education is qualified only by the numerical presence of official-language minorities.[23]

Finally, reflecting its rejection of Québec nationalism, the Trudeau government was insistent on the principle of equality among the provinces. Early in his political career Trudeau had staked out his opposition to any arrangement through which Québec might be ascribed additional powers under the Constitution. As prime minister he remained steadfast in his opposition to the scheme.

With its emphasis upon official bilingualism and entrenchment of language rights, its substitution of multiculturalism for biculturalism, and its insistence upon the formal equality of all the provinces, the Trudeau strategy was to have a profound effect on English-Canadian perceptions of Québec, and of the sources of Québec nationalism.

By the early 1970s, most English-Canadian political and intellectual leaders were fully confirmed in the belief that the essential concern of Québec francophones was with the reinforcement of the status of French outside Québec, whether in federal institutions or among the provinces. In effect, Québec francophones simply wanted to be fully incorporated, as individuals, within Canadian society. For many English Canadians the validity of this view was regularly demonstrated by the Liberals' massive electoral victories in Québec. (Yet, Trudeau's electoral success in Québec appears to have been based less on any popular attachment to his vision of Canada than upon preference for a fellow Québec francophone, running against two English-Canadian leaders of predominantly English-Canadian parties.)

Within this perspective, there was no need to address the specific demands of the Québec government for additional powers. The concerns of Québec francophones really bore upon the other governments of Canada. Moreover, to accede to the Québec government's demands would only serve to reinforce a Québécois identity, which otherwise would fade through the integration of Québec francophones, and their language, within Canada as a whole. In effect, English Canadians were confirmed in the belief that, in the last analysis, most Québec francophones are not Québécois, but French Canadians, and in fact French-speaking Canadians. Those few Québec francophones who do not see themselves in these terms could be induced to do so through the appropriate policies.

To be sure, English-Canadian confidence in this analysis of Québécois' "true" aspirations was shaken by the 1976 election of the Parti Québécois to the Québec government. Many English Canadians had come to believe that "separatism is dead." But confidence was restored by the victory of federalist forces in the 1980 Québec referendum. Widely viewed in English Canada as "a vote for Canada," the referendum result was generally credited to Trudeau's intervention in the referendum campaign. (The reality appears to have been considerably more complex.[24])

Ultimately, the initiatives of the Trudeau era were to affect not just how English Canadians see Québec, but how they see the Canadian polity itself. In particular, the Canadian Charter of Rights and Freedoms has had a profound effect upon English-Canadian political culture. The primary purpose of the Charter might have been to placate Québec, through the provisions entrenching French-language rights,[25] but the primary impact of the Charter has been upon English Canada.

The many provisions of the Charter that do not deal with language have assumed an importance to English Canadians that relatively few commentators anticipated. Beyond wedding English Canadians more closely than ever before to the ideal of equality in individual rights, the Charter has given them a sense of constitutional proprietorship. No longer concerned just with the division of powers among government, which is essentially a concern of politicians, the written Constitution now defines the rights of all citizens. In the potent phrase of the Trudeau government, the 1982 constitutional revision constitutes a "people's package." Finally, by delimiting rights that all Canadians enjoy, the Charter has served as a powerful new focus of Canadian nationalism.

By the same token, the Trudeau government's insistence that Québec must have the same status as the other provinces has helped to reinforce English-Canadian attachment to the principle of equality among the provinces. In western Canadian hands the principle has been turned against Ontario as well. Thus, by 1975 the governments of Alberta and British Columbia were no longer satisfied with the amendment formula, which they had supported during the 1971 Victoria Conference: the formula explicitly guaranteed a veto to Québec and Ontario but to no other province. A 1975 interprovincial meeting in Edmonton reiterated the principle of equality among *all* provinces. By the same token, in the current debate over

Senate reform the most popular scheme in Western Canada, "Triple E," requires that all provinces have exactly the same number of seats.

This change in English Canada's political culture has made it even more difficult for English Canadians to see Québec in anything other than pan-Canadian terms. If both individuals and provincial governments are to enjoy absolute equality in status and rights, Québec can only be "a province like the others" and its residents can only be "Canadians like the others." The Québec government must have exactly the same jurisdictions as the other governments, and in discharging these jurisdictions it must respect the same constraints and obligations as must all other provincial governments.

These attitudes were clearly manifested in English Canada's response to Bill 178, the 1988 measure of the Bourassa government that restored the provision of Bill 101 requiring that outdoor signs be in French only. The Canadian Supreme Court had declared that the provision violated guarantees of freedom of speech under the Charter. For its part, the Québec government claimed that as the only province with a predominantly French-speaking population, it had a special responsibility to ensure the pre-eminence of French. Moreover, in restoring the sign law it used the "notwithstanding" clause, a provision of the Charter that had been inserted at English-Canadian insistence. But these subtleties were lost on most English Canadians. For them, the Québec government had precisely the same obligations as all other provincial governments, and the rights of individuals in Québec could be no different than the rights of all other Canadians. By 1988, use of the notwithstanding clause had become an illegitimate attack on a central element of Canadian nationhood.

Yet, however much they may have reshaped the English-Canadian conception of Canada, and of Québec, the policies of the Trudeau era manifestly did not have the anticipated effect of incorporating Québec francophones within a pan-Canadian perspective. After twenty-five years of official bilingualism and nine years of the Canadian Charter of Rights and Freedoms, Québec francophones seem to be more wedded than ever to the notion that they constitute a distinct entity, even a nation. As English Canadians became more and more deeply entrenched in a perspective that denies Québec's specificity, Québec francophones have become more and more attached to that specificity. This fundamental contradiction was fully revealed in the debate surrounding the Meech Lake Accord (see, Taylor in this volume).

THE MEECH LAKE DEBACLE AS THE LOGICAL OUTCOME

In terms of its specific provisions, the Meech Lake Accord appeared to many close observers of Canadian federalism to be a relatively modest document. After all, it emerged from the Bourassa government's attempt to define the minimal conditions upon which Québec could formally adhere to the Constitution. It was presented in a serious attempt to secure an agreement at a time when Québec's bargaining position was at an all-time low given the 1980 referendum defeat. In fact, the five conditions presented by Québec fell considerably short of the formulations of previous post-1960 Québec governments. And most of the elements of the accord had long circulated among the political and intellectual elites that concerned themselves with Canadian federalism. Some of the elements of the accord, including provincial participation in the selection of senators and Supreme Court justices and restriction on use of the federal spending power in exclusive provincial jurisdictions, had even been proposed at various times by the Trudeau government, although in different formulations than those appearing in the accord.

However, one element of the accord was relatively new to constitutional discussions: the declaration that Québec constituted a "distinct society." (The term itself was not new, however. It can be traced back to the Preliminary Report of the B&B Commission.[26]) It is here that we can find the primary basis of English-Canadian opposition to the accord.

Soon after the accord had been reached a survey demonstrated that among all the specific provisions of the accord the "distinct society" clause received the lowest level of support (46.3 percent) among English-speaking Canadians. And a detailed analysis of public opinion in late 1988 clearly showed the centrality of the "distinct society" clause to English-Canadian opposition to the accord. Blais and Crête found that when respondents were informed that the accord contained such a clause they were much more likely to oppose the accord (opposition rose by twenty-eight percentage points). Mention of no other element in the accord had such an effect. It is essentially on this basis that opposition to the accord rose from 27 percent in April 1988, to 51 percent in March 1990. Blais and Crête conclude:

> There is hardly any doubt that rejection of the Meech Lake Accord reflected the majority sentiment in English Canada. The mobilization of opposition to the Accord can be explained essentially in terms of reaction to the distinct society clause.... The opponents of the Accord simply had to focus attention upon the distinct society clause, which they clearly did, to mobilize an opposition which initially was latent.[27]

Yet, for many constitutional scholars even this provision of the accord was quite modest in its potential effect. After all, it was preceded by a "duality clause" that evoked the presence of English-speaking Canadians and French-speaking Canadians as a "fundamental characteristic" of Canada. And it was followed by a provision declaring that the "distinct society" clause could not cause a shift in powers or prerogatives from one level of government to another.[28]

Clearly, for most English Canadians who opposed the distinct society clause their discontent lay less in the specific wording of the provision than in the very fact that it declared Québec to be a "distinct society." As such, it evoked a vision of Québec, and of Canada, that directly contradicted the vision that many English Canadians had acquired during the 1970s and that had been entrenched in the 1982 constitutional revision. For them, any reference to Québec's specificity, however carefully circumscribed, could only be a step backward.

PRESENT CONSTITUTIONAL DISCUSSIONS

In sum, whereas Québec francophones have grown increasingly attached to the idea that Québec constitutes a national collectivity, English-speaking Canadians have become increasingly resistant to any formal recognition of Québec's specificity. Thanks in particular to the leadership of the Trudeau government and its key initiatives, there is little trace left in English Canada of the 1960s attempts to respond directly to the aspirations of Québec nationalism. In part, this reflects simple antagonism to Québec, with the belief that Québec has already received more than its fair share of attention and benefits. But English-Canadian rejection of Québéc's demands also follows logically from the new principles of Canadian political life, which effectively exclude any direct recognition of the political vision held by most Québec francophones.

Thanks to official bilingualism and the ideal of linguistic equality, French is seen to enjoy privileged status throughout Canada, denying Québec any distinctiveness. Moreover, many English Canadians understand the expansion of French-language services outside Québec as having been a direct response to the demands of Québec francophones—and a very expensive one at that. Thus, they have been understandably angry to discover that since 1974 French has been the only official language of the province. In effect, Québec appears to have been acting in bad faith, insisting on linguistic equality in the rest of Canada, but refusing to recognize it within its own territory. Not only that, but after receiving such substantial "concessions," Québec francophones demand even more: enhancement of Québec's constitutional position. The difficulty, of course, is that for most Québécois the primary concern had always been with the status of French in Québec rather than in the other provinces. And such concerns as these continued to fuel demands for expansion of Québec's powers, however much French may be reinforced in the rest of Canada.

Thanks to multiculturalism, it is now difficult for many English Canadians to comprehend the cultural dimension of the Québec question. Canada is now seen as being composed of a multiplicity of cultural groups. Thus, two Liberal MPs, Charles Caccia and Sergio Marchi, chose these terms to condemn the Meech Lake Accord's references to Canadian duality. The accord constitutes:

> a rear-view mirror vision which may have been valid two generations ago, an outdated [definition of Canada] ... primarily satisfied with only depicting our people's past and our country's history.... Millions of Canadians are left out who do not identify with either English or French. They have no place in the Accord, and they are outside the Constitution.[29]

Finally, it is now very difficult to comprehend the political dimension of the Québec issue thanks in large part to the Trudeau government's approach to federal–provincial relations, but also to the reconfiguration of power in English Canada toward the West. English Canadians are now firmly wedded to the idea that all provinces must have equal status. Measures such as the Victoria Charter amendment formula, which were acceptable twenty years ago, are no longer so.

The effects of these three policies, linguistic equality in provincial affairs, multiculturalism, and uniform federalism, have each been reinforced by the Canadian Charter. The Charter reinforced linguistic equality by entrenching a limited form of minority-language rights, within Québec as well as the rest of Canada. It reinforced the effect of multiculturalism by giving constitutional status to a wide range of non-official language groups. And it has reinforced uniform federalism by specifying that rights must be the same in all parts of Canada. All provincial governments are to be bound by exactly the same constraints and obligations in dealing with their citizens.

As English Canadians and Québec francophones enter the post-Meech round of constitutional discussions they are more divided than ever before in their conceptions of each other, and of the country. Accommodations of Québec's aspirations that might have been feasible in the 1960s are no longer so. Clearly, the options have narrowed.

NOTES

1. Frank H. Underhill, *The Image of Confederation*, The Massey Lectures (Toronto: CBC Publications, 1964), 48.
2. J.W. Dafoe, *Laurier, a study in Canadian Politics*, p. 74, as cited in Underhill, *The Image of Confederation*, 37.
3. *Equal Rights Association of Ontario: D'Alton McCarthy's Great Speech Delivered at Ottawa, December 12th, 1889* (Toronto, n.d.), 26 as quoted in Carl Berger, *The Sense of Power* (Toronto: University of Toronto Press, 1970), 135.
4. Berger, *The Sense of Power*, 152.
5. Letter from Franklin Roosevelt to Mackenzie King, May 18, 1942, as reproduced in Jean-François Lisée, *Dans l'oeil de l'aigle: Washington face au Québec* (Montréal: Éditions du Boréal, 1990), 454–55.
6. As quoted in Ramsay Cook, *Canada and the French-Canadian Question* (Toronto: Macmillan, 1966), 172–73.
7. Peter Regenstreif, "Note on the 'Alternation' of French and English Leaders in the Liberal Party of Canada," *Canadian Journal of Political Science*, II: 1 (March 1969), 118–22.
8. See the discussion of English-Canadian attitudes toward dualism in Douglas V. Verney, *Three Civilizations, Two Cultures, One State* (Durham: Duke University Press, 1986), 212–29.
9. Herbert F. Quinn, *The Union Nationale*, 2nd ed. (Toronto: University of Toronto Press, 1979), 108.
10. Donald V. Smiley, "Constitutional Adaptation and Canadian Federalism Since 1945," *Documents of the Royal Commission on Bilingualism and Biculturalism*, No. 4 (Ottawa: Queen's Printer, 1970), 72.
11. Royal Commission on Bilingualism and Biculturalism, *Preliminary Report* (Ottawa: Queen's Printer, 1965), 151 (my emphasis). (In the French text of the mandate, "races" appeared as "peoples.")
12. See the account in *The Canadian Annual Review, 1967*, 32–38.
13. Desmond Morton, *The New Democrats, 1961–1986: The Politics of Change* (Copp Clark Pitman, 1986), 25.
14. This was contained in a 1963 statement to a meeting of the Canadian French-Language Weekly Newspapers Association at Murray Bay, Québec. It is similar to a 1964 statement made to English Canada, on CBC television, that Québec is "in some respects not a province like the others but the homeland of a people." Both are quoted in Peter C. Newman, *The Distemper of Our Times* (Toronto: McClelland and Stewart, 1968), 320.
15. Morton, *The New Democrats*, 77.
16. *Canadian Annual Review, 1968*, 60–1.
17. "PM Creating Great Division, Douglas Says," *The Globe and Mail*, June 21, 1968, 10.
18. See *Canadian Annual Review, 1968*, 37–38. On the other hand, Simeon and Robinson claim that he personally disliked the idea; Richard Simeon and Ian Robinson, *State, Society and the Development of Canadian Federalism*, Vol. 71, Research Studies, Royal Commission on the Economic Union and Development Prospects for Canada (Toronto: University of Toronto Press, 1990), 190. Indeed, during the election campaign Stanfield not only refused to endorse either two nations or special status, but bitterly complained about a Liberal advertisement that associated him with the two concepts ("Stanfield Continues Feud with PM on PC constitutional position," *The Globe and Mail*, June 21, 1968).
19. Morton, *The New Democrats*, 77–78. See also André Lamoureux, *le NPD et le Québec, 1958–1985* (Montréal: Éditions du Parc, 1985), 97. Forsey's opposition is elaborated in Eugene Forsey, "Canada: two nations or one?" *Canadian Journal of Economics and Political Science*, XXVII: 4, November, 1962.
20. Speech to Québec Liberal Convention, January 28, 1968, reported in *Ottawa Citizen*, January 29, 1968, as quoted in George Radawanski, *Trudeau* (Scarborough: Macmillan—NAL Publishing Ltd., 1978), 286.
21. Comité pour une politique fonctionnelle, "Bizarre algèbre," *Cité libre*, XX: 82 (décembre, 1965), Albert Breton, Claude Bruneau, Yvon Gauthier, Marc Lalonde, Maurice Pinard, p. 14. (Trudeau played an instrumental role in preparing the piece, but did not sign it apparently because of his entry into federal politics.) As Raymond Breton, brother of one of the co-authors, has recently

noted: "Multiculturalism turned out to be instrumental to the Trudeau government's political agenda. Indeed, the terms of the royal commission could be interpreted as lending support to the 'two nations' view of Canada. A policy of cultural pluralism would help to undermine a notion that was seen as dangerously consistent with the Quebec independence movement." Raymond Breton, "Multiculturalism and Nation-Building," Alan Cairns and Cynthia Williams, eds., *The Politics of Gender, Ethnicity and Language in Canada*, Vol. 34, Research Studies, Royal Commission on the Economic Union and Development Prospects for Canada (Toronto: University of Toronto Press, 1986), 47.

22. This constitutes a translation of extracts from the French text, as reproduced in *Le Devoir*, October 13, 1971.

23. Charter of Rights and Freedoms, section 23(3).

24. For instance, see the analysis of the referendum campaign in McRoberts, *Quebec: Social Change and Political Crisis*, 324–27.

25. See the discussion in McRoberts, *English Canada and Quebec*, 15.

26. Royal Commission, *Preliminary Report*, 111.

27. André Blais and Jean Crête, "Pourquoi l'opinion publique au Canada anglais a-t-elle rejeté l'Accord du lac Meech?" in Raymond Hudon and Réjean Pelletier, eds., *L'engagement intellectuel: mélanges en l'honneur de Léon Dion* (Québec: Les Presses de l'Université Laval, 1991), p. 398 (my translation).

28. See the discussion in Peter W. Hogg, *Meech Lake Constitutional Accord Annotated* (Toronto: Carswell, 1988), ch. 4.

29. Alan Cairns, "Citizens (Outsiders) and Governments (Insiders) in Constitution-Making," 124.

Instrumentalist and Interpretive Approaches to Québec Political Culture: A Critical Analysis*

Fredrick Appel
McGill University

INTRODUCTION

An examination of recent developments on the Canadian and Québec political scene has shown us that discussions of political culture are much more than abstract, academic exercises with little relevance to the world of practical politics. Indeed, I would argue that the inability in much of Canada outside Québec to appreciate Québec political culture has contributed to the failure of the Meech Lake Accord in the summer of 1990, to the Charlottetown Accord of 1992, and to the continuing suspicion of (and, in some quarters, hostility toward) the Québec government's constitutional proposals. The reflections in this article are part of the continuing attempts of the author, himself a former resident of a predominantly English-speaking Canadian province, (a) to come to grips with that political culture, and (b) to search for an appropriate conceptual framework for the understanding of political culture and nationalism in general.

In covering both (a) and (b) in the same discussion, I am suggesting that an examination of Québec's—or of any society's—political culture cannot be detached from an analysis and assessment of the various treatments of politics and culture associated with the rival theoretical models that uneasily coexist within the social science community. Why is this necessarily the case? In large part because, consciously or unconsciously, overtly or tacitly, we all invoke some version of one or more of these models in our own efforts at explaining social and political reality to ourselves and to others. Political culture, after all, is not a "thing" to which we can attain unproblematic access through simple empirical observation, as labora-

*I would like to thank Ruth Abbey, Lance Dadey, Professors Alain-G. Gagnon and Stephen Brooks, and the participants of a faculty-student forum held in McGill University's Department of Political Science in April 1991 for their thoughtful comments on earlier versions of this chapter. I also gratefully acknowledge the financial assistance of the Social Sciences and Humanities Research Council of Canada.

tory scientists can examine bacteria under a microscope. Numerous philosophers of the social sciences have argued over the past few decades that our understanding of the culture and politics of particular societies is dependent in many ways upon our theory-laden understanding of the human condition; of what it means to be a human being, of the relationship between human beings and society, and of the very nature of society and politics (see Taylor, 1985:58–90).

In light of the theory-laden nature of my topic, I will begin this discussion with an examination of two rival approaches to the analysis of culture and politics that appear regularly within the social science literature on Québec politics and society, approaches that emerge out of competing traditions of social science practice that I shall term "instrumentalist" and "interpretive" for reasons to be explored presently. I shall then put forward an argument for the superior merits of the latter tradition over the former, without claiming to make a definitive case.

Competing theoretical traditions are far from the hermetically sealed fortresses that some might lead us to believe. This point may become clear in the course of my discussion of interpretive approaches to Québec politics and culture, where I note how such approaches have greatly benefited from a critical encounter with some of the more useful elements of their instrumentalist rival.

THE INSTRUMENTALIST APPROACH

Instrumentalism as a Concept

I suggested above that our understanding of Québec and other political cultures is tied to and largely shaped by some of our implicit answers to certain, basic questions concerning the nature of human beings, society, and the relation between the two. Let me try to illustrate this in a concrete manner by recalling a number of typical reactions in Canada outside of Québec to the resurgent *indépendantiste* movement in Québec. On the one hand, we find the familiar optimistic suggestion (optimistic, that is, from a federalist point of view) that a rational examination of the economic consequences of political separation from Canada will eventually dissuade Québec's political leadership from taking an *indépendantiste* course (as if such decisions were taken with the detached, calculating *sang-froid* of an accountant examining a balance sheet). On the other hand, those more pessimistic about the long-term future of a Canadian federation that includes Québec insist that such "bottom-line" considerations cannot stop the driving force of what they consider to be an essentially irrational phenomenon, a Québécois nationalism that they equate with narrow-minded, xenophobic doctrines propagated by an opportunistic and self-serving political leadership. Finally, a third camp, one that can be set apart from these optimistic and pessimistic scenarios, includes those Canadians outside of Québec who are tired of (or disgusted with) constitutional matters; settle this business quickly, they seem to say, so we can return to what *really* matters, i.e., questions of economic growth, job creation, interest rate policy, etc.

Is there a common denominator to these three disparate positions? I think so. All three, by implying (a) that political reality is driven primarily by considerations of economic or material self-interest and (b) that political movements and ideologies are fundamentally the creation of and driven by self-interested individuals or groups who use them for their own (individual or collective) ends, suggest a particular vision of politics that I will refer to as "instrumentalist." While others label such positions as "materialist," I prefer this more encompassing term, since it seems most accurately to reflect the notion of politics as being, first and foremost, a logical outgrowth or accompanying expression of some "deeper," more important reality, however that reality is defined.

As we shall see, the influence of instrumentalist visions of politics has not been limited to popular, layperson views of Canadian and Québec political reality; they have also shaped much of the writing on Québec politics and society within the social sciences. I am thinking in particular of the research that has emerged from the very influential political economy literature over the last quarter century in English and French Canada.

The instrumentalist stance embodied in these political economy writings is indeed materialist in the sense that the "deeper" reality of social life is identified with a material sphere—the sphere of "real life," work, economic reality, or material interests—which supposedly dominates or sets the agenda for an epiphenomenal sphere of culture, symbols, ideas, ideology, and so on. To use the jargon of empirically minded social scientists, culture and politics in an instrumentalist approach are seen as dependent variables relative to a "deeper" material reality that serves as the independent variable.

Instrumentalist Accounts of Québec Political Culture

By way of illustration, let us briefly examine some standard political economy treatments—both Marxist and non-Marxist—of that constant of the Québec political landscape, the phenomenon of Québécois (or, in its earlier incarnation, French-Canadian) nationalism.

Political economy treatments of this phenomenon tend to be undergirded by a desire to unmask the "real interests" said to underlie discourses about the nation. In most versions of Marxist theory, for example, the concepts of nation and nationalism are identified as ideological constructs designed to promote particular class interests. As Gilles Bourque and Nicole Laurin-Frenette have argued:

> [t]he nation is the effect of certain economic, political and ideological features of the structure of the capitalist mode of production.... Nationalist ideologies can only be class ideologies. A nationalist ideology only makes sense through the class which becomes its propagandist. (Bourque and Laurin-Frenette, 1972:192–93)

This class-based means of analysis has had a tremendous impact on all political economy accounts of Québec politics. This will become clear in an examination of the standard political economy treatment of traditional French-Canadian, pre–Quiet Revolution nationalism.

Two major themes may be associated with this treatment. First, political economists tend to emphasize how the nationalist ideology perpetuated by the traditional French-Canadian elite (composed of members of the clergy, small merchants, professionals, and politicians) contributed significantly to the development and perpetuation of the capitalist economic system in Québec. William Coleman, for example, in a neo-Marxian account of pre-1960 Québec, argues that the nostalgic, idealized visions of pre-industrial society found in the traditional nationalist ideology served to rule out all but a laissez-faire approach to the newly industrial economic order on the part of the state, an approach adopted by every Québec provincial government up to and including the Duplessis regime and one that was conducive to the needs of industrial capitalism in its early, competitive stage (Coleman, 1984a:388–409).

Second, political economy accounts stress both the dependent or retarded nature of capitalist development in Québec and the benefits accrued by the indigenous francophone elite from this dependency and/or arrested development. The stability and longevity of the traditional nationalist ideology is said to have been the result of a largely unspoken agreement between the leadership of English Canada and the French-Canadian elite to erect and maintain a "cultural division of labour" within Québec, a bargain in which the English merchant class's control over economic affairs in Québec was to be left uncontested in exchange for the preservation of the francophone elite's areas of cultural autonomy (Gingras and Neville, 1984:2–14; Whitaker, 1984:72). In other words, the traditional nationalist ideology's legitimization of the continued exclusion of francophones from the ranks of the *grande bourgeoisie*, while serving to retard the economic development and political strength of the francophone majority, at the same time worked to the benefit of the indigenous francophone elite whose status as protector and champion of traditional French-Canadian culture remained unchallenged (Dofny and Rioux, 1964; Simard, 1979:26; Whitaker, 1984:72). Coleman has suggested in this context that

> ... the whole emphasis in the colleges on the classics, on religion, and on intellectual and spiritual matters fostered an antipathy toward the material and corrupting world of business. The ... system was not likely to orient its graduates toward challenging directly the economically subordinate position held by French Canadians.[1]

From this perspective, the traditional francophone elite's use of the political process to defend French-Canadian culture and religion served primarily to deflect criticism from both the economic dominance of the Anglo-Saxon merchants of Montréal and the exploitation of cheap French-Canadian labour by American and Anglo-Canadian enterprises (McRoberts, 1988:57).

Marxist and non-Marxist political economists are generally agreed that the continued hegemony of the Québec anglophone and traditional francophone elites came to an end in the late 1950s and early 1960s. Fundamental changes in Québec's economic "base," associated with urbanization and industrialization, are said to have been largely responsible for innovations at the level of the "superstructure," namely the crumbling of the old nationalist ideology and its replacement by new nationalist ideologies more attuned to the new stage of economic development. Dominique Clift echoed a familiar refrain in describing the traditional nationalist ideology as being "... incapable of integrating urbanization and industrialization into its system of thought, except in a negative fashion as trends to be condemned and resisted."[2] In effect, the political economy argument tends to adhere to the following lines. The traditional nationalist ideology became increasingly untenable (a "fetter" on the mode of production, in Marxian language) as its nostalgic, pre-industrial portrait of an idealized francophone society came into ever more glaring contradiction with the reality of a modernizing, industrializing Québec society (see Whitaker, 1984:74–75; Coleman, 1984b:65;

Houle and Hamel, 1987; Trudeau, 1974). The social tensions created by this disjunction between culture and reality reached a breaking point, leading to the political and economic reforms associated with the "neonationalistic" Quiet Revolution of the early 1960s, a revolution understood in the literature essentially as a badly needed "catching up" (*rattrapage*) of politics and ideology to the new economic reality.

Under this broad canopy, Marxist and non-Marxist political economy accounts of the ideological innovations of the Quiet Revolution sometimes diverge, stressing different angles. Marxian versions tend to explain the ideological shift of the postwar era in terms of the "needs" of an increasingly monopolistic capitalist system for a more activist state, and hence for an ideological discourse that could legitimate such state activism (see Coleman, 1984b:63; Gagnon and Montcalm, 1989:68). Non-Marxist political economy accounts, by contrast, have interpreted the Quiet Revolution in one of two ways: some have relied on conventional modernization theory to describe the shift in political discourse and action in the early 1960s as a normal, systemic readjustment from "traditionalist" to "modern" modes of behaviour more appropriate to an industrial society (e.g., Trudeau, 1974; Behiels, 1985:20). Others place emphasis on the self-interest of what has often been called the "new middle class" (or the "technocratic petty bourgeoisie"; Bourque and Legaré, 1979) of highly educated, francophone white-collar workers who, having been largely shut out of the modern, anglophone-dominated economy, allegedly came to champion the cause of greater political autonomy for Québec in order to profit from the increased employment opportunities that would result from an expanded provincial government sector in the province (Guindon, 1964:155; Breton, 1964; Gourevitch, 1979:245; Hechter, 1987:414–26).

Notwithstanding these divergences, much cross-fertilization is evident in the political economy literature between Marxian and non-Marxian approaches. The Marxian-influenced writing on Québec, for example, is rife with discussion of the new middle class, borrowing extensively from the Hubert Guindon/Albert Breton thesis, which focuses on this class as the originator and main beneficiary of the new "neonationalism" of the 1960s (e.g., Montcalm, 1984:51; M. Fournier, 1987:72–73; Whitaker, 1984:176; Bourque and Laurin-Frenette, 1972:200). There has been much discussion within the Marxian camp of how this new middle class has functioned as a "new clergy" in Québec, having effectively replaced the old nationalist ideology with a more modern, "technocratic" variety that serves both to justify its own class power and to perpetuate the capitalist system (Simard, 1979:32; Brooks and Gagnon, 1988:61). Those influenced by the postwar "Frankfurt school" of German social theory have adopted very dark readings of this ideological "changing of the guard," seeing it primarily in terms of an inexorable encroachment of bureaucratic rationality on ever-increasing areas of life (e.g., Renaud, 1984:179).

This recurring emphasis on the new middle class has not been welcomed, however, by all within the camp of Marxian political economy. Increasingly it has been suggested that while the francophone new middle class may indeed have benefited from the reforms of the Quiet Revolution during the 1960s and 1970s, a francophone *grande bourgeoisie* has supplanted it as the hegemonic element in the Québec class structure in the last decade. The terrain for francophone bourgeois ascent, it is argued, was being prepared even in the early days of the Quiet Revolution, with the direct and indirect benefits for Québec capital accrued through the modernization of the province's economic infrastructure (Renaud, 1984:174; P. Fournier, 1984:224). "For many years," suggest Gagnon and Montcalm,

> ... the correlation between Québec's state strategy and the interests of its business class was obscured, first by the enhanced role played by Québec's new middle class in the state apparatus, and subsequently by the social democratic image [of the Parti Québécois].[3]

Despite its association with the new middle class, adds Whitaker, the Parti Québécois has not behaved as if it were a mere reflection of a bureaucratic "class fraction"; "... the PQ plan for a sovereign Québec seems to have been predicated on some concept of a francophone bourgeoisie, assisted by the state, developing its place in the sun through a renegotiated settlement with English Canada...."[4]

In this light, even the language policies of successive Québec governments since the early 1960s are seen as a means of consolidating the hegemony of the rising francophone bourgeois class, and hence of the capitalist system. Coleman, taking his cue from Marxian theorists such as Claus Offe and James O'Connor, understands Québec language policies in terms of the capitalist state's "legitimation function." From this perspective, Québec government language policies emerging in the 1960s and early 1970s helped to maintain "diffuse support" for capitalist economic institutions and for the political regime, since the "French face" subsequently adopted by English-dominated private businesses deflected potential criticism of their foreign (and presumably capitalist) character (Coleman, 1984a:390–92).

It should be noted once again that this instrumentalist tendency to reduce contemporary Québec nationalism to an ideological pillar for the edifice of Québec-based capitalism is not restricted to the Marxian fold; indeed, numerous Marxian political economists have pointed to the writings of Canadian policy analyst (and non-Marxist) Thomas Courchene and his concept of "market nationalism" as a veritable confirmation of their theses (see Courchene, 1986:7–12). Moreover, Québec nationalism has been treated in a similar vein from the standpoint of "rational choice theory," an increasingly popular non-Marxian outgrowth of the political economy tradition that gives analytic priority to the notion of the utility maximizing individual and to conceptions of means–ends, instrumental rationality (see Olson, 1965; Rogowski, 1985; Laitin, 1986; Hechter, 1987; Meadwell, 1989).

The contributions of the political economy tradition to our understanding of Québec society should not be underestimated. Its most important contribution, its sensitivity to the class-mediated nature of political discourse and action, has served as a valuable corrective to rather simplistic "culturalist" explanations of Québec society that were popular in the 1950s and early 1960s, explanations that blithely associated capitalism with Anglo-Saxon culture and argued that the dearth of French Canadians in positions of economic power could be attributed largely to a Catholic culture and value system that precluded anything resembling materialistic avarice or risk-taking (see Rioux, 1964; N.W. Taylor, 1964).[5] As I will suggest below, however, the strengths of a political economy approach can be incorporated into a framework that offers a richer, more nuanced account of political action and discourse.

INTERPRETIVE APPROACHES

Identity, Culture, and Interpretation

While the instrumentalist treatment of politics and culture associated with the political economy tradition dominates contemporary social science treatments of Québec, other roads may be and have been taken in the assessment of the Québec political landscape. In what follows I wish to outline an alternative, interpretive approach, one that can be distinguished from its instrumentalist rival primarily in its treatment of the question of identity.

How relevant are questions of social identity in social science treatments of politics and culture? Political economists rarely see the question of identity as terribly important, for they assume that social actors have either a clear sense of who they are and what they want from the beginning (in, for example, rational choice approaches) or are in possession of "objective" sets of interests and identities that can be discerned by others in a better position to perceive them (as in numerous Marxian approaches).[6]

For theorists working within an interpretive framework, however, questions of identity form the very heart of the inquiry. Far from being considered unproblematic (either self-evident or readily discernible through the application of some scientific method), the identities of individual and collective actors are said to be formed and reformed through a continual process of self-interpretation and self-definition. This process is in turn inextricable from the identity formation and reformation of the communities that, to a large degree, shape the range of possible identities available to the actors in question (MacIntyre, 1984; Geertz, 1973 and 1983).

Rather than dismissing these self-understandings as superstructural ideology derivative of "real," supposedly "deeper" material interests, those working within the interpretive tradition see them as crucial, ongoing contributions to the actual maintenance and reconstruction of political and social reality. Culture is thus understood as *constitutive of* rather than *instrumental to* social life; instead of being imagined reductively as an arsenal of symbolic weapons that self-interested actors draw upon in the pursuit of (already defined and/or supposedly scientifically objective) material interests, culture is posited as a matrix of tacit, commonly held and widely shared knowledge that serves as the point of departure both for political action and theoretical discourse.[7] As Benedict Anderson has suggested in a recent, penetrating analysis of modern nationalism, communities are "imagined" into reality to a much greater degree than we would think (Anderson, 1991).

Interpretive Approaches to Québec Political Culture

In the following exploration of how representatives of the interpretive tradition portray the history of Québec nationalism, I intend to limit my discussion primarily to the work of Québec authors Fernand Dumont and Christian Dufour.[8] Let us begin by comparing their assessments of traditional French-Canadian nationalism with those of the political economists.

At first glance, their writings appear to echo many of the themes we encountered earlier, notably in their acknowledgment of the undeniable link between political discourse and the material conditions of the population. Dumont, for example, sees the profound social, political, and economic marginalization of the *Canadiens* as largely responsible for the compensatory, often otherworldly nature of their traditional discourses:

> When a people has been dispossessed of its country in so many ways, without any real political or economic control over its destiny, how could it not resort to compensatory dreams? How could it not have found a refuge in ideology?[9]

The traditional francophone intelligentsia, on the defensive in the face of English political and economy hegemony, engaged in an interpretive rearguard action by portraying the dependent, marginal status of traditional Québec society as its greatest asset. Materially poor, the French-Canadian nation was deemed to have a historical vocation of spiritual magnitude. Excluded from major economic decision-making, the nation was exhorted to turn to more noble pursuits associated with idealized visions of pre-industrial agrarian society. These visions, propagated with increasing intensity toward the end of the 19th century, are explained by authors like Dumont less in terms of false consciousness and mystification than as the products of a people uncertain of its destiny, a people attempting to cushion itself against the upheavals and dislocations of capitalist industrialization (Dumont, 1974:8).

Both Dumont and Dufour suggest that the often-dismissive treatment of these traditional ideologies found in the instrumentalist social sciences impedes a true appreciation of how they reflected a genuine need in French Canada to deal with the collective traumas associated with the aftermath of the Conquest of 1759 and the aborted rebellions of 1837–40. As Dufour suggests, the flight into religion enabled the French-Canadian identity to save face and maintain its psychological integrity in the wake of dramatic military and political defeats (Dufour, 1990:67). He draws a provocative parallel between the economic nationalism of Québécois entrepreneurs of the 1980s and the partisans of the traditional, defensive nationalism of the late 19th century; in both cases, francophone leaders of stature propagated a type of nationalist discourse partly as a means of saving the collectivity's sense of honour in the wake of a traumatic political defeat (Dufour, 1990:120–122).[10] In each of these two very different historical periods, Dufour relates the indigenous francophone nationalist discourse to the state of what could be called the "national psyche."

Now to speak in terms of a national psyche or consciousness need not preclude a consideration of the social class variable and more generally an incorporation of the political economy literature's sensitivity to the class-mediated nature of nationalist discourse. Dumont, for example, has followed the political economists in tracing how the clergy's social position was bolstered in the wake of a military conquest that left the Catholic Church as one of the few social structures of the old order unscathed. The church, suggest both Dumont and Dufour, served as a substitute for the state in the eyes of the francophone population, a circumstance all the more understandable given the underdevelopment of municipal and provincial political structures and the political and military defeat of Papineau's secular-minded rebels at the hands of the English (Dumont, 1987:251; Dufour, 1990:35). The fortuitous combination of these elements made it relatively easy for the clergy to become a privileged carrier of nationalist discourse in French Canada from the mid-19th to the mid-20th century.

Of course, the traditional nationalist discourse was not formulated and promulgated exclusively by the clergy. Members of the old middle class, educated by and maintaining close social contact with the clergy, also played an important role. Men and women of modest backgrounds, they maintained close ties with rural life and the peasantry. Admittedly, as political economists have stressed, their unceasing stress on cultural matters (questions of language, law, education, social institutions, and the general cultural *épanouissement* of the French-Canadian nation) and their adherence to an agrarian vision of French-Canadian society represented, at least in part, a form of compensation for their exclusion from the lucrative managerial positions in finance and manufacturing in the cities (Dumont, 1973:104). But to limit one's analysis of traditional nationalist discourse in Québec by speaking strictly in terms of "clerical domination" or of the material self-interest of the petite bourgeoisie or old middle class would block one's appreciation of the resonance of this religio-nationalist discourse within the populace during this period. "Québec society," argues Dumont, "... not only experienced religious power: it subsisted as a religious society. That was its self-consciousness and its uniqueness."[11] Catholicism was at the core of the identity of the *Canadiens* at a time when religion occupied a considerable portion of the political realm (Dufour, 1990:36). Even Papineau's anticlerical *Patriotes* came to appreciate how Catholicism impregnated the French-Canadian national identity; how the parish, at the centre of everyday existence, was commonly identified with *la patrie* (Dumont, 1987:253).

Given this undeniable *complicité* between church hierarchy and laity, it is doubtful whether the clerico-petty bourgeois nationalist discourses of the 19th and early 20th centuries could be understood simply in terms of class exploitation, as representing nothing more than an elaborate smoke screen for certain "real" interests, economic or otherwise:

> ... the professional bourgeoisie defended its own interests in exalting the collectivity's institutions; the people were in accord, since they sensed in a partial, confused manner that the legal conditions of its own traditional way of life were at stake.[12]

In other words, while the francophone leadership did indeed universalize its own social condition in its conceptualization of the French-Canadian nation, its relative ease in doing so can be explained by the kinship of its situation, its attitudes, and its problems with those of the people (Dumont, 1971:2).

More than one commentator on Québec political culture has noticed the close relationship between the "spiritual" focus of the dominant nationalist discourses of the 19th and early 20th centuries and a pervasive, generalized contempt for the secular political realm, a contempt that effectively blocked large-scale state-initiated economic and social reforms before the 1950s. Dumont in particular has perceptively noted how French-Canadian popular culture before the Quiet Revolution tended to associate the entire political realm with an image of the corrupt, self-interested, patronage-seeking politician. The popular disgust with the politician furnished one of the major themes of this epoch's ideologies (Dumont, 1974:11). This widely shared distaste for politics and politicians may have fuelled the widespread support for corporatist political ideologies during the 1920s and 1930s, ideologies that championed a notion of political authority that somehow side-steps the pettiness of party politics. As Ralph Heintzman argues, the distaste for patronage politics led many nationalist writers of the interwar years to "[yearn] for a political leader (*'le chef'*) who would somehow be above the low form of politics they saw around them.... They called for government action ... which would nevertheless be insulated from the political process."[13]

Heintzman builds upon Dumont's discussion of traditional French-Canadian "apoliticism" to suggest that part of the essence of the Quiet Revolution involved an important attitudinal change within the Québec intelligentsia in the postwar years, namely the willingness of a new generation of Québec intellectuals to imagine the state as a legitimate expression of social, economic, and national development. From an interpretive perspective, this change of attitude is seen not as the product of "underlying" structural forces that allowed ideology to "catch up" to the level of economic life, but rather as an occurrence made possible by a new generation of reform-minded intellectuals who used the resources of their cultural heritage to integrate innovative ideas, concepts, and practices emanating from abroad.[14]

While acknowledging the key role played by the new middle class in the Quiet Revolution, interpretive approaches refuse to see the conduct of middle-class nationalist leaders strictly in terms of the rational calculations of individual or class interest. Of course, political economists have been quite right to point out how the underrepresentation of these highly educated, white-collar francophones in the upper-level managerial ranks of the Québec economy formed an important part of the background to the political changes of the early 1960s. Exclusively instrumentalist accounts have been unable, however, to explain satisfactorily why the new middle class expressed itself politically in terms of Québec *nationalism*.

Why, one might ask, did the majority of this francophone elite not follow in the footsteps of cosmopolitan-minded intellectuals such as Pierre Elliott Trudeau, Gérard Pelletier, et al. of *Cité libre* fame and renounce French-Canadian or Québécois nationalism as inherently retrograde in a world allegedly run more and more by technocratic principles? How is it, McRoberts wonders,

> that with the 1960s the Québec state came to be perceived ... not only as the essential instrument to respond to and even accelerate social and economic change, but as the central institution of a distinct Québécois nation? How is it that social and economic development became a national project?[15]

McRoberts suggests in his questioning that strictly instrumentalist accounts fail to make clear why the Québec state, rather than the federal state, became the privileged focus of attention of the new middle class. Nor have such accounts been able to explain adequately the existence of nationalist sentiments among blue-collar workers, who have not faced the occupational barriers and pressures to operate in English of their white-collar, managerial compatriots (McRoberts, 1988:432), or among members of the new Québécois entrepreneurial class, who no longer suffer the effects of the old cultural division of labour between anglophones and francophones in the big business sector.

From an interpretive perspective, then, instrumentalist explanations have failed to explain the resilience of Québec nationalism. This failure, I would suggest, can be traced back to the clearly inadequate instrumentalist treatment of the question of identity. Those working within the interpretive tradition argue that nationalism has much to do with the existence of a collective identity, perpetually reformulated in the narrative discourses that make up a people's collective memory. As we have seen, these discourses can and often are used by individuals and groups for material or other gain, and political economy research has quite rightly drawn our attention to this. Before nationalism can be exploited in this instrumental fashion, however, there must first be something deeply rooted to exploit; a narrative tradition rooted in a particular community and way of life that can be tapped into and appropriated, a tradition whose stories "... envelop us and form our pictures of ourselves and our past, more than we are usually aware."[16]

In the contemporary Québec context, the continuing project of preserving and promoting the French language has been at the centre of nationalist sentiment, serving as a vital link with the struggles of the past. As McRoberts suggests,

> ... the knowledge that so many generations of Francophones fought so hard to maintain the viability of French-language institutions within Québec ... is bound to support a strong normative commitment to [defend] the pre-eminence of French within Québec.[17]

Surely this sense of continuity with a longstanding collective project explains in a manner more compelling than any instrumentalist argument why, as Dufour perceptively notes,

> ... nationalism is a permanent feature of Quebeckers' collective and individual lives, intimately linked to their geopolitical situation in North America. Far from being the prerogative of a political party or a social class, the phenomenon affects the whole of Québec society, to varying degrees and in various forms. There will be no more nationalism in Québec when there are no more Québécois.[18]

Québécois nationalism, it would appear, is not simply the result of a haphazard, transitory convergence of the aspirations and sentiments of a majority of individual Quebeckers. The common aspiration for the survival of a francophone national identity in Québec may be seen as a communally sustained backdrop against which all political debate in the province is conducted. Consciously-held nationalist ideologies can and have been propagated by particular self-interested social groups against this backdrop, but while particular ideological formulations come and go, the backdrop remains a ubiquitous presence on the Québec political landscape, a common aspiration that serves as one of the common reference points of all public debate in Québec society (Taylor, 1985:38–39).[19]

QUÉBEC POLITICAL CULTURE AND THE CONSTITUTIONAL CRISIS

I began this paper by suggesting that the pertinence of studying political culture has become increasingly apparent to many observers of Canada's latest constitutional crisis. In my closing, all too brief reflections on current constitutional developments I hope to leave the reader with a sense of how an interpretive theoretical analysis can make a contribution to everyday political discourse and practice.

We noted above that the collective aspiration for the continued survival and promotion of a viable French-language nation in the northern half of North America has been and remains one of the central items on the Québec political agenda.

From a Québec perspective, then, continued allegiance to the Canadian federation makes sense only if that federation demonstrates its willingness to contribute to this collective project. Historically, and with increasing insistence since the 1960s, Québec has asked the federation to show its commitment to this project by insisting (1) that the federation recognize French as a language with a status equal to that of English in Canada, and (2) that the federation allow the Québec government—the only government in North America in which francophones hold a majority—enough autonomy to enact measures in line with its special responsibilities for the safeguarding of the French language and culture. Without minimizing the importance of point (1)—official bilingualism—it is fair to say that the second point—the according of some degree of political autonomy to Québec—has become increasingly important over the years for Quebeckers, perhaps in part because of their perception that the grudging, half-hearted acceptance of official bilingualism in much of the rest of Canada reflects a half-hearted commitment (at best) to the preservation and promotion of the French fact in Canada.

On the political autonomy front, Québec has not done badly over the last few decades. As Taylor has noted, the Canadian federation has proven itself flexible enough in practice to accommodate many of Québec's demands for special status, i.e., for a relation to the federal government and institutions that other provinces do not necessarily share (Taylor, 1991:60). Québec has its own pension plan, levies its own income tax, has partial control over immigration, and so on. This system of "asymmetrical federalism," as Cairns and others have termed it (Cairns, 1991), has been the rule, not the exception. The Québec government's demands during the constitutional negotiations of 1990 and 1992 for formal recognition of Québec as a "distinct society" within the Canadian federation simply represented an attempt to entrench this de facto special status into the de jure language of the Canadian Constitution.

The formal recognition of this political reality, however, remains blocked. The Meech Lake Accord was rejected in 1990 after the Manitoban and Newfoundland provincial governments refused to ratify the document in their legislatures by the June 1990 deadline. Moreover, as the recent popular rejection of the Charlottetown Accord of 1992 has shown, opposition to the inclusion of a "distinct society" clause in a reformed Constitution remains strong, especially among partisans of the western-based Reform Party and political supporters of former prime minister Pierre Elliott Trudeau.

This opposition to a formal recognition of our asymmetrical federalist system, of the fact that Québec has political responsibilities not shared by other provincial governments, appears to be rooted in a particular vision of the country that has gained widespread support in the predominantly English-speaking provinces in the last decade, and particularly since the entrenchment of the Charter of Rights and Freedoms in the Constitution Act of 1982. Proponents of this vision hold tenaciously to two fundamental principles: the absolute primacy of individual rights over collective goals or projects, and the equality of the provinces.

Proponents of the primacy of individual rights quite rightly point out that their view does not prevent individuals from choosing to protect and promote particular collective identities; in our multicultural society, they maintain, we are allowed to maintain the heritage of our cultural group and celebrate our differences as Icelandic Canadians, Japanese Canadians, Ukrainian Canadians, and so on. They believe, however, that these group identities ought not to impede our common status as rights-bearing individuals with the same relationship to the Constitution in general and the Charter in particular (see Cairns, 1988 and 1991; Taylor, 1991). From their perspective, any attempt on the part of governments to promote or favour the projects of a particular linguistic or cultural group may run roughshod over the rights of individuals, and hence cannot be tolerated.

Now it is obvious that a society like Québec violates this principle. While contemporary Québec political culture has shown itself to be perfectly compatible with the respect of the most fundamental of individual rights (to freedom of speech and assembly, to liberty, the practice of religion, due process, etc.), it is clear that Québec governments cannot remain neutral with respect to the preservation and promotion of the French language. Pursuing this collective goal may entail the reduction of individual freedom of choice, as Law 101 does by insisting that francophone parents send their children to French-language schools (Taylor, 1991; Cairns, 1991).

Canadians both inside and outside Québec who cling to the absolute primacy of individual rights also tend to reject the reality of our de facto asymmetrical federalist system in favour of an idealized, symmetrical model in which every provincial government has exactly the same constitutional status as all the others. All ten provincial governments, it is claimed, must be equal in their jurisdictions and powers; any other arrangement would violate the principle of provincial equality. Moreover, since many of the proponents of this notion of provincial equality also are in favour of a strong, central government in Ottawa, they are reluctant to support constitutional proposals that would give Québec new jurisdictional powers. Québec's assumption of a wider range of responsibilities, in their view, would have to be coupled with a similar devolution of powers to all the other provinces. In effect, the efforts of constitutional negotiations in 1990 and 1992 to accommodate the equality of the provinces principle inadvertently gave the most zealous partisans of this principle an opening to attack the Meech Lake and Charlottetown Accords. By raising (and, arguably exaggerating) the prospect of excessive balkanization of the country, opponents of the Meech Lake and Charlottetown packages in English-speaking Canada successfully contributed to the downfall of these most recent attempts at constitutional reform.

It would be unfair, however, to claim that all the blame for our constitutional problems lies with politically intransigent and intolerant elements in the predominantly English-speaking provinces. Ironically, their lack of appreciation for and tolerance of important elements of Québec political culture may be matched by a similar level of intolerance and incomprehension among elements within the *indépendantiste* movement within Québec itself. In belittling the importance of the political gain that Meech Lake and Charlottetown potentially represented for Québec and in actively working for its subversion, the leaders of the *indépendantiste* movement showed themselves either unable or unwilling to consider how the Canadian political order may have contributed (and could continue to contribute) to the flourishing of the Québécois identity.

Dufour notes in a similar vein that many *indépendantistes* refuse to consider the possibility that the contemporary Québécois identity, bound historically to the self-conception of Canada and Canadians as a whole, may have a greater chance of long-term survival in the context of a continued political union with the predominantly English-speaking provinces, just as the *Canadiens* and United Empire Loyalists needed one another in the 19th century to survive the birth and initial aggressiveness of an expansionist American republic to the south (Dufour, 1990:57, 109, 122). The dream of political independence may be blinding some Québec nationalists to the commonality of interests that continues to exist in the northern half of North America: just as the Québécois fear assimilation into a continental, anglophone melting pot, so are English Canadians fearful of being swallowed up by the United States.

It remains to be seen whether the climate of acrimony and mutual suspicion stirred up by recent constitutional debates will triumph in the long run, deflecting Canadians and Quebeckers from an appreciation of their common history and common interests, and impeding the accommodation of a distinctive Québec political culture within a broader Canadian federalist project.

NOTES

1. William Coleman, *The Independence Movement in Québec: 1945–1980* (Toronto: University of Toronto Press, 1984), p. 63. See also similar remarks in Alain-G. Gagnon and Stephen Brooks, *Social Scientists and Politics in Canada: Between Clerisy and Vanguard* (Kingston and Montréal: McGill-Queen's University Press, 1988), p. 24.

2. Dominique Clift, *Québec Nationalism in Crisis* (Kingston and Montréal: McGill-Queen's University Press, 1982), pp. 7–8.

3. Alain-G. Gagnon and Mary Beth Montcalm, *Québec: Beyond the Quiet Revolution* (Scarborough, Ont.: Nelson Canada, 1989), p. 69.

4. Reg Whitaker, "The Québec Cauldron: A Recent Account" (1981), in *Québec: State and Society*, ed. Alain-G. Gagnon (Toronto: Methuen, 1984), p. 83.

5. Gilles Houle and Jacques Hamel discuss the "culturalist" thesis at length in "Une nouvelle économie politique québécoise francophone," *Canadian Journal of Sociology*, 1–2, 1987, pp. 42–63.

6. The Marxian notion of "false consciousness" accounts for the possibility of class actors being unaware of their real interests, interests that may be discerned by those with the scientific insight to penetrate bourgeois ideology and perceive the true nature of the relationship between class actors and the mode of production.

7. The philosophical explorations of this field by such 20th-century thinkers as Michael Polanyi (1966), Ludwig Wittgenstein (1968), and Hans-Georg Gadamer (1990) have laid the groundwork for this hermeneutic or interpretive tradition of social inquiry. See also the work of Charles Taylor (for example, 1985, 1987, 1989).

8. For another interpretive approach to Québec political culture, see Stanley Ryerson (1972, 1984).

9. Fernand Dumont, *Le sort de la culture*, p. 242. All of the English translations of passages from Dumont's work in this paper are my own.

10. The political defeat that Dufour sees as the background to the economic nationalism of the 1980s is, of course, the referendum result of 1980.

11. Dumont, *Le sort de la culture* (Montréal: Éditions de l'Hexagone, 1987), p. 250.

12. Dumont, *Chantiers: Essais sur la pratique des sciences de l'homme* (Montréal: Éditions Hurtubise HMH, Ltée, 1973), p. 104.

13. Ralph Heintzman, "The Political Culture of Québec, 1840–1960," *Canadian Journal of Political Science*, XVI;1 (March 1983), p. 48.

14. Cf., for example, the various discussions of the intellectual evolution of Québec nationalist André Laurendeau in *André Laurendeau: un intellectuel d'ici*, ed. Robert Comeau and Lucille Beaudry (Québec: Presses de l'Université du Québec, 1990). Some of these traditional cultural resources were provided by the famous *collèges classiques*, institutions much vilified in later years as carriers of reactionary thought and practice.

15. Kenneth McRoberts, *Québec: Social Change and Political Crisis*, 3rd ed. (Toronto: McClelland and Stewart, 1988), p. 144

16. Charles Taylor, *Sources of the Self* (Cambridge, Mass.: Harvard University Press, 1989), pp. 415–416.

17. McRoberts, *Québec*, p. 438.

18. Christian Dufour, *A Canadian Challenge—Le défi québécois* (Lantzville, B.C. and Halifax, N.S.: Oolichan Books and The Institute for Research on Public Policy, 1990), p. 121.

19. The focus of this paper has been on the enduring power of nationalism in Québec through time, and not on the important changes in nationalist discourse with the onset of modernity, changes that have led to shifts in the very identity and self-understanding of the Québécois people over the last thirty years. An analysis of the important shifts from traditional French-Canadian to modern Québécois identity, however, would go beyond the limited scope of this chapter.

REFERENCES

Abbey, Ruth. *Approaches to Québec Neo-Nationalism: A Survey.* Unpublished manuscript, McGill University Department of Political Science, 1989.

Anderson, Benedict. *Imagined Communities: Reflections on the Origin and Spread of Nationalism*, 2nd ed. London: Verso Books, 1991.

Behiels, Michael. *Prelude to Québec's Quiet Revolution: Liberalism versus Neo-nationalism, 1945–1960.* Kingston and Montréal: McGill-Queen's University Press, 1985.

Bourque, Gilles, and Nicole Laurin-Frenette. "Social Classes and National Ideologies in Québec," *Capitalism and the National Question*, ed. G. Teeple. Toronto: University of Toronto Press, 1972, pp. 185–210.

Bourque, Gilles, and Anne Legaré. *Le Québec: la question nationale.* Paris: Maspero, 1979.

Breton, Albert. "The Economics of Nationalism," *Journal of Political Economy*, 72 (4), 1964:376–86.

Brooks, Stephen, and Alain-G. Gagnon. *Social Scientists and Politics in Canada: Between Clerisy and Vanguard.* Kingston and Montréal: McGill-Queen's University Press, 1988.

Cairns, Alan C. "Citizens (Outsiders) and Governments (Insiders) in Constitution-Making: The Case of Meech Lake," *Canadian Public Policy*, XIV, 1988:s122–s141.

Cairns, Alan C. "Constitutional Change and the Three Equalities," *Options for a New Canada*, ed. Ronald L. Watts and Douglas M. Brown. Toronto: University of Toronto Press, 1991, pp. 77–100.

Clift, Dominique. *Québec Nationalism in Crisis.* Kingston and Montréal: McGill-Queen's University Press, 1982.

Coleman, W.D. "The Class Bases of Language Policy in Québec, 1949–1983," *Québec: State and Society*, ed. Alain-G. Gagnon. Toronto: Methuen, 1984a, pp. 388–409.

Coleman, William. *The Independence Movement in Québec: 1945–1980.* Toronto: University of Toronto Press, 1984b.

Courchene, Thomas. "Market Nationalism," *Policy Options*, 7 (8), October 1986:7–12.

Descent, David, Louis Maheu, Martin Robitaille, and Gilles Simard, eds. *Classe sociales et mouvements sociaux au Québec et au Canada: Essai-Synthèse et Bibliographie.* Montréal: Les Éditions Saint-Martin, 1989.

Dofny, Jacques, and Marcel Rioux, "Social Class in French Canada," *French-Canadian Society*, eds. Y. Martin and M. Rioux. Toronto: McClelland and Stewart, 1964, pp. 307–18.

Dufour, Christian. *A Canadian Challenge—Le défi québécois.* Lantzville, B.C. and Halifax, N.S.: Oolichan Books and The Institute for Research on Public Policy, 1990.

Dumont, Fernand. "Quelques réflexions d'ensemble," *Idéologies au Canada Français: 1850–1900*, ed. Fernand Dumont, Jean-Paul Montminy, and Jean Hamelin. Québec: Les Presses de l'Université Laval, 1971, pp. 1–12.

Dumont, Fernand. *Chantiers: Essais sur la pratique des sciences de l'homme.* Montréal: Éditions Hurtubise HMH, Ltée, 1973.

Dumont, Fernand. "Du début du siècle à la crise de 1929: un espace idéologique," *Idéologies au Canada Français: 1900–1929*, ed. Fernand Dumont, Jean Hamelin, Fernand Harvey, and Jean-Paul Montminy. Québec: Les Presses de l'Université Laval, 1974, pp. 1–11.

Dumont, Fernand. "Les années 30: la première Révolution tranquille," *Idéologies au Canada Français: 1930–1939*, ed. Fernand Dumont, Jean Hamelin, Jean-Paul Montminy. Québec: Les Presses de l'Université Laval, 1978, pp. 1–18.

Dumont, Fernand. *Le sort de la culture.* Montréal: Éditions de l'Hexagone, 1987.

Fournier, Marcel. "Culture et politique," *Canadian Journal of Sociology*, 12 (1–2), 1987:64–82.

Fournier, Pierre. "The New Parameters of the Québec Bourgeoisie," *Québec: State and Society*, ed. Alain-G. Gagnon. Toronto: Methuen, 1984, pp. 201–27.

Gadamer, Hans-Georg. *Truth and Method*, 2nd rev. ed. New York: Crossroad, 1990.

Gagnon, Alain-G., and Mary Beth Montcalm. *Québec: Beyond the Quiet Revolution.* Scarborough, Ont.: Nelson Canada, 1989.

Geertz, Clifford. *The Interpretation of Cultures: Selected Essays.* New York: Basic Books, 1973.

Geertz, Clifford. *Local Knowledge: Further Essays in Interpretive Anthropology.* New York: Basic Books, 1983.

Gingras, François-Pierre, and Neil Neville, "The Evolution of Québec Nationalism," *Québec: State and Society,* ed. Alain-G. Gagnon. Toronto: Methuen, 1984, pp. 2–14.

Gourevitch, Peter. "Québec Separatism in Comparative Perspective," *The Future of North America: Canada, the United States, and Québec Nationalism,* eds. E.J. Feldman and N. Nevitte. Cambridge, Mass.: Center for International Affairs, 1979, pp. 237–52.

Guindon, Hubert. "Social Unrest, Social Class, and Québec's Bureaucratic Revolution," *Queen's Quarterly,* 71 (2), 1964:150–62.

Hamel, Jacques, and Gilles Houle. "Une nouvelle économie politique québécoise francophone," *Canadian Journal of Sociology,* no. 1–2, 1987:42–63.

Hechter, Michael. "Nationalism as Group Solidarity," *Ethnic and Racial Studies,* 10 (4), October 1987: 414–26.

Heintzman, Ralph. "The Political Culture of Québec, 1840–1960," *Canadian Journal of Political Science,* XVI(1) March 1983:3–59.

Laitin, David D. *Hegemony and Culture.* Chicago: University of Chicago Press, 1986.

MacIntyre, Alasdair. *After Virtue: A Study in Moral Theory,* 2nd ed. Notre Dame, Indiana: University of Notre Dame Press, 1984.

McRoberts, Kenneth. *Québec: Social Change and Political Crisis,* 3rd ed. Toronto: McClelland and Stewart, 1988.

Meadwell, Hudson. "Cultural and Instrumental Approaches to Ethnic Nationalism," *Ethnic and Racial Studies,* 12 (3), July 1989.

Montcalm, Mary Beth. "Québec Separatism in a Comparative Perspective," *Québec: State and Society,* ed. Alain-G. Gagnon. Toronto: Methuen, 1984, pp. 45–58.

Olson, Mancur. *The Logic of Collective Action.* Cambridge: Harvard University Press, 1965.

Polanyi, Michael. *The Tacit Dimension.* New York: Doubleday, 1966.

Renaud, Marc. "Québec New Middle Class in Search of Social Hegemony," *Québec: State and Society,* ed. Alain-G. Gagnon. Toronto: Methuen, 1984, pp. 150–85.

Rioux, Marcel. "Remarks on the Socio-Cultural Development of French Canada," *French-Canadian Society,* eds. Y. Martin and M. Rioux. Toronto: McClelland and Stewart, 1964, pp. 162–77.

Rogowski, Ronald. "The Causes and Varieties of Nationalism: A Rationalist Account," *New Nationalisms of the Developed West,* eds. Ronald Rogowski and Edward A. Tiryakian. Boston: Allen and Unwin, 1985, pp. 87–108.

Ryerson, Stanley. "Québec: Concepts of Class and Nation," *Capitalism and the National Question,* ed. G. Teeple. Toronto: University of Toronto Press, 1972, pp. 212–27.

Ryerson, Stanley. "Disputed Claims: Québec/Canada," *Québec: State and Society,* ed. Alain-G. Gagnon. Toronto: Methuen, 1984, pp. 59–67.

Simard, Jean-Jacques. *La longue marche des technocrates.* Laval: Éditions coopératives Albert Saint-Martin, 1979.

Taylor, Charles. "Interpretation and the Sciences of Man," *Philosophy and the Human Sciences: Philosophical Papers 2.* Cambridge: Cambridge University Press, 1985, pp. 15–57.

Taylor, Charles. "Overcoming Epistemology," *After Philosophy: End or Transformation?,* eds. K. Baynes, J. Bohman, and T. McCarthy. Cambridge, Mass.: MIT Press, 1987, pp. 464–88.

Taylor, Charles. *Sources of the Self: The Making of the Modern Identity.* Cambridge, Mass.: Harvard University Press, 1989.

Taylor, Charles. "Shared and Divergent Values," *Options for a New Canada,* eds. Ronald L. Watts and Douglas M. Brown. Toronto: University of Toronto Press, 1991, pp. 53–76.

Taylor, Norman W. "The French-Canadian Industrial Entrepreneur and His Social Environment," *French-Canadian Society,* eds. Y. Martin and M. Rioux. Toronto: McClelland and Stewart, 1964, pp. 271–95.

Trudeau, Pierre Elliott. "The Province of Québec at the Time of the Strike," *The Asbestos Strike,* ed. Pierre Elliott Trudeau. Toronto: James Lewis and Samuel, 1974, pp. 1–81.

Waddell, Éric. "State, Language and Society: The Vicissitudes of French in Québec and Canada," *The Politics of Gender, Ethnicity and Language in Canada,* eds. Alan Cairns and Cynthia Williams. Toronto: University of Toronto Press, 1984, pp. 67–110.

Whitaker, Reg. "The Québec Cauldron: A Recent Account" (1981), in *Québec: State and Society,* ed. Alain-G. Gagnon. Toronto: Methuen, 1984, pp. 70–91.

Wittgenstein, Ludwig. *Philosophical Investigations.* New York: Macmillan, 1968.

Québec: Not that Unique, nor that Alone*

André-J. Bélanger
Université de Montréal

"Comparative sociology is not a particular branch of sociology; it is sociology itself..."
–Emile Durkheim

Québec is usually considered to be an isolated case in the course of Western ideological history. Severed from the European world by being cut off from France its motherland, and from the rest of North America by the language barrier, Québec has all the trappings of an isolated entity that can only be understood from the inside. Observers, for a long time now, have banked on *la différence* to explain it. Already in the 18th century, people from New France were identifying themselves as *Canadiens* to distinguish themselves from the people of France. In the 19th century, two liberals of different roots, Alexis de Tocqueville and Lord Durham, were struck, after a visit to Lower Canada, by the specific character of French Canadians (Dion, 1990), who appeared to have no resemblance whatsoever to their French counterparts, nor to other North Americans. Durham saw French Canadians as debilitated remnants of the *ancien régime* that had to be shaken out of their stagnant culture. Durham was not, as he has often been labelled by French-speaking Quebeckers, against French Canadians as such. His purpose was, in his mind, merely to bring light to the unenlightened. We may agree or disagree with the means he advocated, but that is another question.

As time passed, French Canada came to be identified as a distinct entity. Local traditionalists such as Jules-Paul Tardivel, Henri Bourassa, and later on, Lionel Groulx emphasized its distinctness, if only to keep it as it was. This was, it was thought, the best way to safeguard the culture from the external influences of economic and political liberalism. It is interesting to note that observers from the outside would readily agree with a reading of French Canada as a distinct entity.

*I wish to thank my colleague Alain Noël for his useful comments on the preliminary draft of this article.

All societies are indeed subject to this treatment: they all have characteristics of their own that make them distinct. Whether one considers, for instance, France, Great Britain, Italy, or, let us say, the United States, the main thing that they all have in common is that they have little in common. Their respective ideological situations put them in different categories. France's history is one of legitimacy problems; Great Britain's has to do with the development of opposed ideologies within a liberal matrix; Italy's is made up of a totalitarian experience and recent access to liberal democracy; American history is one of acculturation into a common liberal ideology. They all represent different ways in which cultures are constituted so that they appear absolutely unique in their own right.

If analysts were to abide by this apparent evidence, they would have to be satisfied with descriptive monographs, and explanations of events solely from within the inner dynamics of each respective culture. The temptation would be to search for a presumed essence proper to each society. Collectivities would therefore produce their own frameworks of explanation, and the analyst's work would be, by investigating from within, to reveal their true natures. The same mode of thinking can be discerned among global social movements: labour, feminist, and ecological movements, for instance, have all had at one time or another the propensity to explain and legitimate their own actions based on approaches that are deemed intrinsic to the movements themselves.

Another approach, which is the one I wish to adopt, tries to understand events from a comparative perspective. Instead of isolating events solely within the context of one society's history, it attempts to understand events from within the context of that society's perspective, as well as from other perspectives. The emphasis is put upon what a society has in common with others as well as the degree to which it is also different. This approach induces the observer to concentrate on recurrent patterns and thereafter show the diversity in their applications. By so doing the analyst is likely to adopt a more heuristic strategy. Within this point of view, events gain their significance from their relatedness with, or departure from, trends that are common to a number of societies.

We should make no exception for Québec in this respect. Kenneth McRoberts (1988), for one, has based his analysis on a number of parameters: the degree of development in terms of urbanization, secularization, mass education, and economic growth, as well as notions of dependence, class division, and national consciousness. In this case, the analysis proceeds from universal categories that are applied to Québec. It does not purport to express the true inner nature of this society, but rather stakes out an area of observation based on specific criteria. The monograph, then, is not a mere idiographic endeavour, since it at least intends to make possible comparisons with other societies based on similar criteria.

Having said this, it is necessary to move further in the direction of a decidedly comparative approach. The purpose is not to produce a drab image of Québec, but to show instead that this society reacted to conditions that were not entirely unique. If one looks carefully at Québec's ideological evolution, one should be able to notice comparable trends in societies with analogous conditions.

Before going any further, it would be appropriate to clarify the usage of the concept *ideology*. It serves, in my mind, to designate a construed structure of forms that, through signs and symbols, legitimates a collective order of values (Bélanger, 1985:50). Ideology refers to a rational construct of society, whereas culture refers to accepted forms of functioning whose legitimacy raises no problem. Ideology and conflict work together, for the former serves to legitimate actions involved in the latter. Let us take an example. With the end of the 18th century, Western societies were torn by conflicts regarding their own social fabrics. They were therefore submitted to the clashes of ideologies, one claiming the advent of new modes of functioning, the liberal, and the other, the conservative, sustaining the maintenance of the status quo. This is indeed a simplification, but it serves to situate the nature of the conflict.

Let us now observe how ideological clashes have progressed in Québec; how, in other words, they have emerged, how they have developed, and also how they have modified their courses under new social conditions.

THE LIBERAL REVOLUTION

After the advent of parliamentary institutions introduced by the Constitutional Act of 1791, there emerged in the early 19th century a certain form of political liberalism in Québec (which, at the time, was called Lower Canada). For an author like Pierre Elliott Trudeau, these instruments of ruling were alien to the *Canadiens'* mentality, and were to remain alien to them until very late in their history, for in 1958 he described the situation as being virtually unchanged (Trudeau, 1958). Of a similarly pessimistic point of view, historian Fernand Ouellet (1980) insisted upon the unliberal claims of the 1830s *Patriotes*. The first *aperçu* of this liberalism in the making has often been negative: the *Patriotes* being seen largely as tainted by basically retrograde interests. This is a reading that is not foreign to Lord Durham's.

The *Patriotes* were largely professionals and shopkeepers who professed liberal ideas regarding politics while at the same time being lukewarm, if not hostile, to the current commercial capitalism that was carried on by the English merchants. The *Patriotes'* discourse may not have been dominated by liberalism, especially on economic matters, but its main political thrust was one it held in common with the rest of the Western Hemisphere at the time. The 1830s in Lower Canada witnessed the rise of politicians whose views were derived from a widespread understanding of the right of nations to self-determination. The idea by that time was an accepted view among progressive people. It grew in the wake of the French Revolution (1789) and of a series of successful moves toward independence in America. The United States had severed from Great Britain in 1783, and most of the Latin American countries had separated from Spain and Portugal, between 1811 and 1825. All these events, by themselves, may or may not have affected Lower Canada's domestic politics to the same degree, but the ideas were not new.

The independence of the United States was due to a movement whose liberal content was well rooted in Protestant individualism. In the case of Latin American countries, emancipation took place in entirely different circumstances. The tradition in their case was basically Catholic, influenced by the Enlightenment. It is generally recognized that independence there amounted to the creole (American-born Spaniards) landowners taking over from the European aristocracy. Independence as such was not a revolutionary but a conservative event. Nonetheless, it had a double consequence for the formation of ideologies: it entailed reflection regarding the legitimacy and workings of the new political institutions replacing the colonial regime and reflection regarding the identity of these nascent societies. The adoption of the newly acquired liberalism's tenets was selective, leaving room for values inherited from the Latin American tradition. This did not prevent, at the time, the thinkers' high admiration for the United States' institutions.

Now, if we turn back to the ideologies that came out of the 1837–38 rebellion in Québec, we can readily notice an opposition shaping up that was to lead to a zero-sum game encounter, one where the winner's gains amount to the loser's losses. Who were then to be the protagonists? The answer is clear: the *Rouges* who were the outgrowth of the *Patriotes* and the Catholic clergy. Between the two stood a conservative petite bourgeoisie, which was later epitomized by George-Étienne Cartier.

The *Rouges'* presence in Québec politics was significant during the period of the Union (1840–67). Not only did they have ideological influence; they were also recognized as a component to be reckoned with in the political arena. More than a movement, it was a political party with newspapers to promote its actions, *l'Avenir* being the most representative. Thus when one speaks of the *Rouges* one refers to a well-established tradition in 19th-century Québec. They were somewhat the counterpart of the Grits of Upper Canada. Wilfrid Laurier was to be one of the *Rouges'* immediate and mellowed successors.

Political parties, at the time, were more a gathering of politicians with similar opinions on what they considered essential matters, than the well-structured organizations we know today. Politics was for politicians a more individualistic endeavour: candidates had commitments of their own they would set on personal electoral platforms. So one should not be surprised by the diversity of views among the *Rouges* as among any other parties.

The *Rouges* in their most radical expression were probably closer to the republican or even Jacobin traditions in France than to the liberal tradition of the American continent. Economic considerations were limited and political ones were highlighted. Closely associated with *L'Institut canadien*, which served as a sort of think-tank, the *Rouges* produced articulate discourses whose gist provided for the promotion of a rising petite bourgeoisie of lawyers, notaries, physicians, and the like that had emerged in the 1790s. They were also likely to be landowners of varying importance. Their demands would focus on the importance of providing "democratic" institutions based on the sovereignty of the (male) people and freedom of the press. This was matched with a strong anticlericalism, especially on matters of tithe and education. Favourable at one time to annexation with the United States, the *Rouges* opposed Confederation (1867), and from then on withered away as a formal political movement. Many of their ideas remained.

Some aspects of the literature they left are still relevant to contemporary political thought. Here I think of Louis-Antoine Dessaulles's *Six lectures sur l'annexion du Canada aux États-Unis*, which, more than a mere apology for the cause, amounts to a complete depiction of the radical political liberalism of the time. The text was reprinted in 1968. It is worth reading, as it is provocative as well as characteristic of a certain type of political thought. Dessaulles belongs to a rationalist individualism that foresees indefinite progress in all respects, so long as reason is left unfettered in its quest for truth. The argument is not without affinities with what was to become the *Radical* ideology of France's Third Republic. Nor is it alien to the sort of anticlerical rationalism that became widespread at the same time in Latin America.

The model, therefore, is far from being unique: it fits very well the categories of intellectual struggles that, in Catholic countries, pitted a clergy protective of its cultural hold on the masses against a petite bourgeoisie who was ready to assume the functions of socialization and lawmaking as well. The argument being put forward was a rationalist one that aimed at substituting religion with reason while also substituting arbitrary authority with an enlightened one. The rationale served to bolster a new rising class. This was the case in Latin America, France, Italy to some extent, and Québec.

THE COUNTER-REVOLUTION

The clergy in Québec did not remain on the defensive. On the contrary, one might even say that it took the offensive, even before the rebellion of 1837–38. From the turn of the century to the early 1840s, the church's influence was in constant decline. There were proportionately fewer priests, and more people, especially from the bourgeoisie, were keeping their distance from the church. The impressive recovery that took place at the time owes its success to the initiative of two archbishops, Lartigue and Bourget, who focused on instruments of socialization, such as education, recreational activities, and social welfare, thus strengthening the church's presence by expanding extensively its clergy. Lartigue founded the *Grand Séminaire* in Montréal whereas Bourget, after him, welcomed numerous male and female recruits from France while at the same time encouraging the establishment of new congregations of priests and nuns.

The ideology shared by the upper clergy was influenced by the reactionary thinkers of Restoration in France: De Bonald, de Maistre, and later, the journalist Louis Veuillot. The ideology, called ultramontane, reached its apex of influence in Québec between 1848 and 1878 (Gadille, 1985). Its main tenets provided for the immediate ascendancy of the Roman Catholic Church, as operated from Rome, on all matters of religion and morality. It strongly opposed liberalism, especially in its political forms.

The French authors put forward the idea of a return to the *status quo ante* (which is why they were called reactionary): a sort of monarchy as it had existed to some extent under the *ancien régime*. Such was definitely not the case for Québec ultramontanes such as Jules-Paul Tardivel, who had to content themselves with watered-down solutions. Nobody could envisage for Québec a political apparatus that would be consistent with full-fledged ultramontanism. The ultramontanes had to operate within the confines of a political and economic system that was alien to them and that could hardly be modified.

The clerical ideology, as it is usually called, developed within specific boundaries. It had to make do with a gradually industrializing environment of a capitalist nature, and with a political landscape dominated by liberal democracy. The only area where the clergy could make its influence fully felt was within the ideological sphere, and it made every effort to do just that. The church managed to exercise a monopoly over education as a whole, thus becoming the sole official agent of socialization for over a century. In 1875 the abolition of the fledgling Ministry of

Education (created in 1867) deprived the state of any real say in matters of education until the early 1960s.

Through the instruments of education and other incidental means the clergy succeeded in reducing the area of political discussion, developing a more consensual outlook on life in society. The model was simple and has often been exposed and derided since. Suffice it to say that it provided for a static understanding of society: Québec was conceived as a privileged entity that had been spared the qualms of modernity. Severed from France at the right time, it did not have to undergo the Revolution; and distinct from Anglo-Saxon Protestantism, it had been shielded from the rampant individualism of liberal ideas. The clerical ideology furnished an idealized and traditional picture of Québec where people, speaking the same language and belonging to the same faith, were called upon to pursue a rural life, as we say in French, "*à l'ombre de leur clocher*," in the shade of the church steeple. This remained, indeed, an idealized picture, one that developed the myth of a rural calling from the colonial era, and the pursuance of a static way of life. The model was ahistorical: it was situated outside any consideration of evolution, and was meant to remain identical to itself at all times.

It is interesting to note through the successive writings of representative authors how the clerical ideology little by little replaced the liberal discourse of the *Rouges*. If one looks at the route followed by authors such Arthur Buies, Errol Bouchette, and Edmond de Nevers, one easily grasps the progressive ascendancy of an ideology coming of age. Arthur Buies started as a flamboyant radical with rationalism as his standard, and ended as secretary of the Curé Labelle. Errol Bouchette is illustrative, at the turn of the century, of a liberal mind on economic and political questions, but of a traditional mind regarding some aspects of the organization of society. This led him to propose a reconciliation of industrialization with traditionalism, by considering a form of economic development in the countryside that would not upset the demographic proportion of rural populations. Finally, with Edmond de Nevers, we witness the extolling of the nation and its traditions. But whatever the direction taken by these three authors, there remained in their respective works constant references to European thinkers, such as Tocqueville, for instance, with whom they felt a link should be preserved.

With the turn of the century, ideas were being narrowed in their perspective, so much so that with Henri Bourassa at the beginning of the century, and later on with Canon Lionel Groulx, we find ourselves in the midst of an autarkic world where the clerical ideology is self-sustaining, in that it is in no need of external sources of rejuvenation. There are no more references to European thinkers, and French Canada is seen as in a state of complete ideological isolation and self-sufficiency.

This very sketchy outlook calls for a number of comments and reservations. To start with, this form of isolationism was far from being uncommon at the time among former colonies. Though it may seem surprising, if not far-fetched, the French-Canadian era of ideological confinement, which extended to the threshold of World War II, is similar to isolationism in the United States and in other Latin American countries. In the latter, the period at the turn of the century came to be one of profound soul-searching, intellectuals pondering about the national identity of their respective countries. After a period of partial liberalism followed by a "positivist" era, Latin American societies set off—to use Martin S. Stabb's own booktitle (1967)—in "quest of identity." This amounted to a rediscovery of America as a social entity distinct from the motherlands, Spain and Portugal, one leading to *indigenismo* and a messianism to be found in *Mexicanidad*, *Perunidad*, and *Argentinidad*.

Louis Hartz recognized in this process of ideological crystallization the consolidation of fragments of European ideologies that, without the dialectic dynamics of opposing ideologies, kept indefinitely their own momentum in the colonies. My purpose is not to elaborate on Hartz's thesis, but simply to underline the comparable aspects of identical trends.

In Québec, the ideological climate was propitious to a religious comeback, for the isolation at the level of values and the social identity that these values projected were likely to lay the groundwork for a return to a supposedly original condition. In fact, the clergy constituted the only authentic institution remaining from the French regime. The clerical ideology was best positioned to contrast with the English-speaking Protestant environment, and in this respect Québec achieved a clear distinctness. Henri Bourassa could, like many others, put forward the idea of "*La langue gardienne de la foi*": the language guardian of the faith. This isolationism also applied to Québec's relationship with the mother country: the secularized France of the Third Republic could no longer be considered the "eldest daughter of the church" as it used to be; it had become by then a reprobate daughter. By the turn of the century, France aroused no feelings of belonging on the part of French Canada. With the first and the second world wars, it became obvious that English-speaking Canadians were ready to fight for their mother country, whereas their French-speaking counterparts felt little concern for "les vieux pays"—the old countries of Europe. Most Quebeckers were by then French-speaking North Americans who considered themselves untouched by European affairs, just as Americans from the United States remained aloof until that country was forced by circumstances. With Pearl Harbor, the Americans had no choice but to enter into the conflict. French Canadians could easily have adopted the assertion of Speaker Champ Clark in the House of Representatives about the draft: "In the estimation of Missourians there is precious little difference between a conscript and a convict" (1917).

The clerical ideology reached its apex in the 1920s. Just as generations of immigrants get acculturated to their adopted country, so did French-speaking Quebeckers gradually adopt clerical values through socialization. Thanks to its ascendancy over education as a whole, the clergy exercised a growing influence that reinforced itself as generation after generation passed through the educational system.

It must be made plain that this influence, though overpowering, remained by and large strictly at the level of symbolic values. It did not impinge significantly on the economic and political behaviour of Quebeckers. It did not modify their migration to the cities or even to the United States. Colonization of the forestland was perhaps the only concrete manifestation of the ideology. It apparently had a limited impact on the political scene, but it certainly contributed in severely limiting the state's propensity to intervene in matters of education and even welfare. On the other hand, the ideology served as a matrix for the emergence of a nationalist movement, though this nationalist trend of a traditionalist nature never really made it in the political arena.

The clerical ideology developed through the years into a nationalist one with Lionel Groulx (who was not always appreciated by the church hierarchy). The problem with this traditionalist mode of nationalism was that it was not conducive to any specific conception of politics. Democratic liberalism was simply alien to the clerics' basic principles, as it was readily considered a by-product of Protestant individualism. The institution that would have been compatible with clerical ideology would have been the monarchy prior to Louis XIV, but this would have been dismissed as nostalgia. While fascism was considered, it exercised a very limited attraction, as it would have impinged on the clergy's privileged sphere of influence.

Traditional nationalism was not initially meant to be political, but rather mystical. Lionel Groulx was adamant, his action was intended to reach the souls where the national conversion was expected to take place. It was a question of national salvation leading to a national communion where politics was secondary if not nonexistent. One may refer to his thinking as one of anarchism, but from the right (Bélanger, 1977:187–89; 1974:191ff).

Traditional nationalism was based on the premise that you must change the social before you could alter the political. Moral regeneration had to precede institutional renewal. It amounted by and large to a symbolic discourse without any political implications; it suited the clerical purpose of keeping lay people at arm's length from any immediate involvement in matters regarding the inner fabric of society. This discourse was at the lofty level of socialization. It permeated the education system as well as clerical and para-clerical means of diffusion such as *l'Action catholique* and *Le Devoir*. It remained, on the whole, at the strict level of symbolic communication. The church and especially the Jesuits supported a form of corporatism outside the authority of the state. One should not forget that throughout the movement's existence, the nationalists kept on complaining about the lack of interest it aroused in the masses. It was elitist in its pretentions and saw its influence largely confined to an intellectual elite of people such as André Laurendeau and Roger Duhamel. The masses were more subdued by a clerical culture where nationalism had very little to say. They were nonetheless affected by a number of newspapers of a more worldly nature.

Political parties, at the time, had their own means of diffusion. Such dailies as *Le Canada* in Montréal and *Le Soleil* in Québec City were leading papers acting as official mouthpieces of the Liberal Party of Canada. Their point of view was decidedly different from the current clerical message, and was basically adapted to the political expediency of the moment. This reality introduced a discrepancy between the traditional mode of socialization in the hands of the clergy and mass media, which were usually more mundane in their pursuits.

THE QUIET AND LESS QUIET REVOLUTIONS

The depression years of the 1930s marked an important watershed. One could say that the Quiet Revolution of the 1960s is rooted in the ideological reconsiderations aroused by the dire economic conditions of the 1930s. The depression induced at least two opposite readings. For the traditionalists, it vindicated their opposition to modernity: industrialization and the urbanization it entailed. For some members of the younger generation, the depression, on the contrary, triggered a reflection that broke the barriers that defined the inner world of Québec. Periodicals such as *La Relève* and movements such as *La Jeunesse étudiante catholique*, whose influence reached the early 1960s, represent a renewal that was noticeable in literature too. Modern literature in Québec started with novels such as *Trente arpents* by Ringuet and poems such as those of Alain Grandbois. Right from that time, one can discern a gradual split between the traditionalists, whose demise would be more obvious after World War II, and the modernists, who will later group together in an informal network that expressed itself through the journal *Cité libre*, Radio-Canada, *L'Institut canadien des affaires publiques*, and others.

This intellectual movement in Québec was concomitant with other upheavals that could be seen at the same time throughout the Western world. The depression brought about reformist movements such as the New Deal in the United States, radical ones such as the CCF in Canada, formation of Popular Fronts in France and Spain, and totalitarian movements as in Germany. This shaking-up could not leave Québec indifferent, so much so that marginal groups could be found that embraced the communist faith or the fascist belief.

Cité libre in the 1950s revived a liberal trend that had been muted by traditionalist intellectuals. To be sure, some liberal voices had been heard since Dessaulles. Jean-Charles Harvey, Albert Pelletier, and Philippe Panneton (Ringuet) around a review called *Les Idées* (1935–39) had vented their discontent, especially regarding the educational system. The liberal premier Godbout (1939–44) had introduced measures in favour of compulsory attendance to primary schools and free access to textbooks, as well as extending voting rights to women. Many of these moves were contrary to the clerical ideology.

With *Cité libre* the discussion resumes around a rationalist construction of society. Reason is again in the forefront after decades of obfuscation. The individual is opposed to the totalitarian conception of thinkers that Pierre Elliott Trudeau, for one, would later try to identify with the nationalists. The discussions of the 1950s set the groundwork for the policies that were to be adopted in the decade that followed. The idea of the social and educational responsibility of the state toward society as well as the idea of a functional organization of government are well rooted in the period that preceded the Quiet Revolution. Interestingly enough, the Quiet Revolution meant, at the political level, the implementation of policies whose principles had already been voiced. The real change was in the way French-speaking Quebeckers would define themselves.

The idea of an independent Québec is not an invention of the 1960s. Tardivel, at the turn of the century, had made subtle references to a separate French Canada. The Francoeur motion in the Québec Legislative Assembly in 1918 served as a reminder that if the rest of Canada felt that Québec was an impediment to Canada's progress, Québec was ready to put an end to the federal pact. Rodrigue Villeneuve, who was to become cardinal a decade later, belonged to the 1922 movement, whose program elicited in *L'Action française* (January issue) the possibility of a separation imposed by the "necessity" and "hazards" of history. The depression years were even more conducive to the development of *indépendantiste* ideas: Lionel Groulx toyed with the idea in sibylline terms, whereas, more explicitly, *La Nation* (1936–39) linked *indépendance* with a fascist project. Dostaler O'Leary's *Séparatisme* (1937) also provided for a corporatist organization. But these were isolated cases of no real consequence.

As a matter of fact, the *indépendantiste* movement that emerges in the early days of the Quiet Revolution is part and parcel of a modern conception of society and has little in common with the nationalism formerly voiced. After World War II the traditional nationalism à la Groulx had little to say for the new generations, and was already dead before *Cité libre* took over. Significantly, people such as André Laurendeau were not at ease with the new expression of nationalism in the 1960s.

The *indépendantiste* movement of the Quiet Revolution must be understood in the context of the decolonization discourse, which was *the* discourse of French intellectuals at the time. Thus Québec's intellectuals shared a general concern that found fertile ground among themselves. A periodical such as *Parti pris* expressed this quest for liberation from the colonial yoke as identified with English Canada. It posed the problem of identity, which it had in common with the newly decolonized countries from Africa. The situation induced the kind of psychological intro-spection that Frantz Fanon had done, whereby the colonized is seen as alienated from the colonizer. *Indépendance* appears as a cathartic movement of emancipa-tion for the individual as well as the collectivity. With a supposedly Marxist inter-pretation of domination, it expressed a strictly intellectual reading of the situation. *Parti pris*, whose real influence spanned a limited period, 1963 to 1967, triggered a mode of reasoning that brought together socialism and nationalism.[1]

THE SILENT REVOLUTION[2]

The period that follows is permeated with divergent ideologies that were shared by the rest of the Western world: counterculture as proposed by the American West Coast mingled with Maoist cultural revolution as conveyed by activist groups in France. Nationalism remained a common denominator, but took diverse forms.

As these ideologies shared by the baby boomers were receding so also was nationalism fading as a mobilizing force. The Parti Québécois contributed to some extent in dedramatizing the movement. By being in power it institutionalized the latter and therefore reduced the ideology's incantatory power of attraction. The defeat during the referendum of 1980 may have had a demoralizing effect, but it did not prevent the Parti Québécois from getting re-elected the following year.

More interesting to observe is the dulling effect the party had over the ideolog-ical enthusiasm of its beginnings. It toned down its most radical aspects, helping, ironically, to bring the party into the liberal fold. As finance minister in 1982, Jacques Parizeau imposed stringent budgetary cuts on civil servants, teachers, and hospital staffs, opening the way to conformity with neoliberalism as it was under-stood in the Western world.

In hindsight, it is striking that the transition from the Parti Québécois to Robert Bourassa's Liberals in 1985 did not constitute a major ideological break. Both par-ties agreed, for instance, with the idea of a free trade agreement with the United States. In addition to this, Bourassa's government has paid more and more heed to the increasing disillusion of the public regarding the rest of Canada, especially after the failure of the Meech Lake Accord.

This rapprochement between nationalism and liberalism may sound awkward at first glance, for nationalism is rooted in emotional dispositions of belonging, whereas liberalism, whether economic or political, is based on a contractual understanding of social relations. Times are now conducive to a return to what appears natural; and both free market and the nation do appear "natural" (Bélanger, 1990). They seem to be products of the true nature of social life, whereas the state and its interventions stand out as artificial contrivances. This trend is not exclusive to Québec: it can be seen as well in Eastern Europe. The flow of events taking place in Québec forms a pattern that can easily be detected elsewhere. Neoliberalism is still by far the most pervasive, and is as noticeable in Québec as nationalism, as is the case with numerous other societies and ethnic groups that have been integrated into greater wholes by the force of political circumstances.

This time *indépendance* is seen as flowing in a natural course of evolution. It formerly was the product of intense mobilization on the part of intellectuals, artists, and the Parti Québécois. Now, the movement is not seen by the new generation as an ideological decision to be discussed and defended, but rather as a goal determined by the nature of things. It has become part of the culture itself where consensus operates from the spontaneous values of a collectivity. Just as neoliberalism can claim to be a mere return to the true nature of the market, so too can the new sovereigntist trend claim to abide by the true nature of collectivities. It *appears* to signal the end of ideologies at both the economic and political levels.

It is therefore fruitful to observe what a specific collective entity has in common with others while continuing to underline the differences. In the case of Québec, what is interesting is the disjunction that existed for decades between, on the one hand, the political arena together with the economic market and, on the other hand, the socialization area where a clerical ideology was imposed, becoming very nearly a culture unto itself. The progressive movements that followed, such as *Parti pris*, remained strictly at the level of ideologies, that is, on the outskirts of the political arena. In this, they were consistent with previous expressions of traditionalism, sustained by an antiliberal intelligentsia that frowned on the murky world of politics (Bélanger, 1977). In fact, it is only with the advent of the Parti Québécois that the three levels of the social structure (economics, politics, and ideology) gradually became integrated. This process ultimately led to a sort of recognition of liberalism, in stark contrast with the radical views expressed by some members when the party was at its incipient stage.

The consensus that has grown around sovereignty since 1990 tends to blur other social divisions, just as in Eastern Europe. The political climate now tends more toward the expression of voices in unison. Divisions will reappear when the fruition of (economic) liberalism and nationalism reaches its ultimate stage.

NOTES

1. The ideological structure leading to a form of anarchy in *Parti pris* exhibited an interesting resemblance to the nationalist thinking of Lionel Groulx, even though the former was apparently totally alien to the latter (Bélanger, 1977: 187).
2. No relationship to Ronald Inglehart's thesis.

REFERENCES

Behiels, Michael D. 1985. *Prelude to Québec's Quiet Revolution*. Kingston and Montréal: McGill-Queen's University Press.

Bélanger, André-J. 1974. *L'Apolitisme des idéologies québécoises*. Québec: Presses de l'Université Laval.

Bélanger, André-J. 1977. *Ruptures et Constantes*. Montréal: Hurtubise HMH.

Bélanger, André-J. 1985. *Framework for a Political Sociology*. Toronto: University of Toronto Press.

Bélanger, André-J. 1988. "Les Idéologies politiques dans les années 1950," in J.-F. Léonard, ed., *Georges-Émile Lapalme*. Sillery: Presses de l'Université du Québec, 121–32.

Bélanger, André-J. 1990. "Political Science: *Die Frau ohne Schatten*, or the Challenges of Liberalism and Nationalism," *Canadian Journal of Political Science*, XXIII, 4 (December):643–52.

Bernard, Jean-Paul. 1971. *Les Rouges*. Montréal: Presses de l'Université du Québec.

Dessaulles, Louis-Antoine. 1968 (1851). *Six Lectures sur l'annexion du Canada aux États-Unis*. Montréal: P. Gendron. Johnson Reprints, Mouton.

Dion, Stéphane. 1990. "Tocqueville, le Canada français et la question nationale," *Revue française de science politique*, 40, no. 4 (August):501–19.

Dumont, Fernand, J. Hamelin, and J.P. Montminy. 1971–81. *Idéologies au Canada français*, 5 vols. Québec: Presses de l'Université Laval.

Gadille, Jacques. 1985. "L'Ultramontanisme français au XIXème Siècle," in N. Voisine and J. Hamelin, *Les Ultramontains canadiens-français*. Montréal: Boréal Express. 27–66.

Hartz, Louis, ed. 1964. *The Founding of New Societies*. New York: Harcourt, Brace and World.

Lemieux, Lucien. 1989. *Histoire du catholicisme québécois, Les XVIII et XIX Siècles, Les années difficiles (1760–1839)*. N. Voisine, ed. Montréal: Boréal.

McRoberts, Kenneth. 1988. *Québec: Social Change and Political Crisis*, 3rd ed. Toronto: McClelland and Stewart.

Monière, Denis. 1981. *Idéologies in Québec*. Toronto: University of Toronto Press.

Ouellet, Fernand. n.d. *Papineau*. Québec: Presses de l'Université Laval.

Ouellet, Fernand. 1980. *Lower Canada, 1791–1840*. Toronto: McClelland and Stewart.

Stabb, Martin S. 1967. *In Quest of Identity*. Chapel Hill, N.C.: University of North Carolina Press.

Trudeau, Pierre E. 1958. "Some Obstacles to Democracy in Québec," *Canadian Journal of Economics and Political Science*, XXIV, no. 3 (August):297–311.

Vigod, Bernard L. 1986. *The Political Career of Louis-Alexandre Taschereau*. Kingston and Montréal: McGill-Queen's University Press.

Voisine, Nive, and Jean Hamelin. 1985. *Les Ultramontains canadiens-français*. Montréal: Boréal Express.

C H A P T E R *10*

The Media in Québec

Marc Raboy
Université Laval

In the past few decades, in Québec as in other modern societies, the media of mass communication have become the central institutions of public life. Press, radio, television—and increasingly, new services delivered by cable and satellite technologies—occupy an ever greater place in people's lives, as sources of information and means of recreation.

Sixty percent of Quebeckers read a newspaper every day, more than half of them spending upward of forty minutes at the task (Québec, 1986). Two-thirds read weekly or monthly periodicals regularly (Québec, 1986). But it is radio and television consumption that really occupies their time: three hours a day listening to the radio and more than three and a half hours daily spent watching television *on average* (Québec, 1986). In 1987, francophone Quebeckers watched more television than any other national group in the world, except for the Americans and British (Canada without Québec was sixth) (Québec, 1989a). Seventy percent of Québec households subscribe to cable.

On the basis of these figures alone, the media merit our attention. But media consumption is a particular form of consumer activity, insofar as it takes place in the sociocultural sphere. For governments, business people, social groups, and ordinary citizens, media constitute a privileged arena of struggle, where opposing conceptions of society confront one another, and different interpretations of reality are played out. Media take on particular importance in periods of crisis, but even in "normal" times, they set the public agenda, tell us what to think about, and present a certain way of looking at the world.

In Québec as elsewhere, these social and cultural institutions are politically and economically driven—that is to say, the structures, practices, and products of the media, as well as the way they are received, are essentially the result of economic and political factors.

Media systems are a reflection of the societies in which they take root and flourish. In this sense, the distinctive characteristics of Québec's media system are part of what makes Québec a distinct society, while the similarities with North

American media in general clearly show Québec's rootedness in North America. Finally, the structural dependence of Québec media on the Canadian legal and regulatory framework poses certain difficulties symptomatic of the general problem of Canadian federalism.

SOME HISTORICAL BACKGROUND

There were no media of mass communication in the colony of New France. However, the oldest existing newspaper not only in Québec, but in all of Canada, is *The Gazette* of Montréal, founded in 1778 by a bilingual printer from Philadelphia, Fleury Mesplet, who was set up in business by Benjamin Franklin in an attempt to gain support for the newly formed republic to the south. *The Gazette*'s fortunes fluctuated as Mesplet was in and out of grace with the British authorities (who would put him in jail one day and offer him a printing contract the next). The relationship between media and the state in Québec, as well as the American connection (see Lamonde, 1984) thus goes back to the earliest years following the British Conquest.

The press played an important role in the struggles for political democracy of the early 19th century in both Upper and Lower Canada. The "journals of opinion" of this era gave way to mass-circulation "news" papers by about 1869, and with the spread of literacy, urbanization, industrialization, and European immigration, a commercial press, in English and in French, was well established by the early decades of the 20th century (De Bonville, 1989; Hamelin and Beaulieu, 1966).

In Québec, however, a tradition of partisan, ideological "journaux de combat" persisted well into the 1920s, particularly in promotion of various approaches to French-Canadian nationalism. One of these papers, *Le Devoir*, founded in 1910, remains the only independent daily newspaper in Québec today, and is distinguished by a unique ownership structure and a self-appointed role as a journal of conscience. In the 1970s, this tradition also spawned a short-lived newspaper, *Le Jour*, with close ties to the Parti Québécois. *Le Jour* was unable to survive a combination of advertiser hostility and political intrigue, and published for only two years (1974–76) (Raboy, 1984).

Examples such as these—abundant in Europe—are not to be found elsewhere in North America other than in Québec. On the other hand, newspaper publishing in Québec has, since the 1960s, become even more closely associated with big business, exhibiting, for example, a higher degree of concentration of corporate ownership than the rest of Canada. In the new pro-business climate of the late 1980s, concentration of media ownership, including cross-media ownership, came to be seen as an important mechanism for launching major players on the world scene, despite the sustained criticism of social groups concerned about the impact on the quality and independence of information. We shall return to this point later.

Media played an important role in the postwar modernization of Québec culminating in the Quiet Revolution of the 1960s (Roy, 1976). John Porter, in his classic study *The Vertical Mosaic* (1965), noted the preponderance of "intellectual journalists" in articulating the values of change in Québec society, and indeed the mythology of the period and its key events (e.g., the asbestos strike of 1949) is laced with the exploits of legendary journalists and editors such as Gérard

Pelletier, Gérard Filion, André Laurendeau, Judith Jasmin, and René Lévesque. During the 1950s, television became Québec's "window on the world"—and on itself—as distinctive forms of public affairs, dramatic, and variety television programming were created on the public service Radio-Canada network, paradoxically a creation of federal policy. When a labour dispute shut the network down in the winter of 1958–59, Ottawa's sluggish response to the deprivation of service became one of the earliest symbols of the dysfunctions of federalism.

In the 1960s and 1970s, Québec was the setting of some unique examples of social and political uses of media, in the context of the radical questioning of society that marked these years (Raboy, 1984). Social and political movements integrated a critique of mainstream media into their overall philosophies (see, for example, CSN, 1968), and the search for communication "alternatives" was an essential element of movement strategy. The ideological hegemony of media owners and the logic of the marketplace was vigorously contested by professionals working within the mainstream media institutions as well, and rare was the news organization that did not undergo some serious upheaval. Important alternatives, such as the weekly newspaper *Québec-Presse*, were created and sustained for relatively long periods. The most militant group of the period, the Front de Libération du Québec (FLQ), consciously sought to appropriate media space and time, in an attempt to establish direct communication links with the population.

This is the general sociocultural context in which media in Québec have evolved. Shortly, we will look at their present situation, but first we will develop one specific aspect that has particular implications with respect to the constitutional future of Canada and Québec: the legal and regulatory framework of broadcast media.

THE CASE OF BROADCASTING

The influence of the emerging liberal traditions of the United States and Britain kept the state relatively remote from the affairs of the press in 19th- and early 20th-century Canada. No legal restrictions or regulation were applied to newspaper publishing, other than those imposed by the general law of the land (e.g., concerning libel or sedition). But, as in the case of those two "mother countries," the context shifted dramatically with the introduction of radio broadcasting in the 1920s (see Raboy, 1990).

One of the world's first commercial broadcasting enterprises was the Marconi-owned CFCF, in Montréal, which began operating in 1919. By 1921, Montréal had a second station, CKAC, established by the newspaper *La Presse*. In fact, early radio broadcasting was generally the domain of receiving-set manufacturers and newspaper publishers, for whom radio operations were a means of promoting their principal product.

By the mid-1920s, sentiment in English Canada particularly was alarmed at the influence of American broadcasters on the new medium. Canadian stations, including those in Québec, were affiliating with American networks who provided them with cheap, popular programs. The introduction of program sponsorship and advertising seemed to divert broadcasting away from "uplifting" forms such as talks, lectures, and concerts, and toward categories that some segments of society considered of dubious moral value, such as sports matches and soap operas. Third, the lack of a regulatory framework meant that there were no guidelines for controversial (e.g., religious) or politically partisan programming.

Thus, in 1928, the government of Canada decided it was time to intervene with respect to broadcasting. A Royal Commission on Radio Broadcasting boldly recommended nationalization of the commercial stations and establishment of a national public monopoly along the lines of several European countries (Canada, 1929). It also proposed an important measure of decentralization, through a system of provincial commissioners who would be responsible for programs broadcast in each of the provinces. Even before its report was tabled, however, the Québec government of Louis-Alexandre Taschereau passed legislation authorizing Québec to erect and operate its own radio station, as well as produce programs for broadcast by existing commercial stations.

Before acting on the recommendations, Ottawa asked the Supreme Court to determine whether jurisdiction over broadcasting lay with the Dominion or the provinces. Québec argued that broadcasting *as a means of education* was within provincial competence under the British North America Act, but the court ruled in Ottawa's favour on the grounds that the activity extended beyond provincial boundaries.

The Canadian Radio Broadcasting Act of 1932 created a national public service broadcaster, the Canadian Radio Broadcasting Commission (CRBC), which had the additional responsibilities of regulating the activities of the private broadcasters. (This double mandate would be transferred to the CRBC's successor, the Canadian Broadcasting Corporation, in 1936.) The royal commission's proposal for provincial broadcasting commissioners was not retained in the legislation.

The Canadian state thus asserted its legitimacy with respect to broadcasting in the early 1930s, setting up a model half way between the British and U.S. systems—part public, part private, and regulated according to periodically reformulated policy objectives. In spite of the formal "arm's length relationship" with individual broadcasters, the federal government has used its exclusive jurisdiction to fashion the system so that it could be used, as necessary, to promote general policy objectives and, particularly, a centralized conception of "national unity." Meanwhile, broadcasting has remained a sphere of federal–provincial dispute unto this day (see Raboy, 1991).

In the 1960s, the Pearson government publicly identified cultural policy in general and broadcasting in particular as strategic weapons in its struggle against the rising and increasingly radical nationalist movement in Québec (see, for example, Canada, 1964). At parliamentary committee hearings in 1966, Liberal backbenchers from Québec and Radio-Canada middle-management executives sparred over their respective views of the CBC's coverage of "separatism," and when a new broadcasting act was introduced in October 1967, it contained a clause that read as follows: "The national broadcasting service [CBC] should … contribute to the development of national unity and provide for a continuing expression of Canadian identity" (Canada, 1968).

Radio-Canada's interpretation of its mandate to promote national unity led to bizarre incidents such as keeping its cameras trained on the parade at the 1968 Saint-Jean-Baptiste Day celebrations in Montréal, while police and demonstrators fought a bloody battle on the sidelines. During the October Crisis of 1970, the federal cabinet closely oversaw what was and was not broadcast by Radio-Canada, and a few months later a string of management "supervisors" appeared in the corporation's newsrooms, with no apparent function other than political surveillance (see Raboy, 1990:204–8).

The situation culminated with Prime Minister Trudeau's instruction to the Canadian Radio-television and Telecommunications Commission (CRTC), to inquire into CBC news coverage in the wake of the election of the Parti Québécois in Québec in November 1976. After the CRTC report vindicated the CBC, the Liberal government appears to have changed its view of the role of media in Canada's constitutional struggle. By year's end it had created a new agency, the Canadian Unity Information Office, and strategy for containment of the pressures of national fragmentation thereafter flowed through there. Political expectations of the CBC diminished, and in the important run-up to the Québec referendum of 1980, the corporation was left to establish and carry out an internal policy of news coverage according to rigorous journalistic standards and the principle of "the public's right to be informed" (see, for example, CBC, 1979). Ultimately, the referendum campaign was covered by CBC as a straight news event, while the government sought to mobilize its constituency directly, particularly through advertising (Johnson, 1983).

From 1968 on, renewed demands from Québec for constitutional powers in broadcasting highlighted the constitutional debates of the day and marked the evolution of communications in Canada. In its brief to the constitutional conference convened by Lester Pearson in February 1968, Québec claimed the right to play the role of a national state in matters pertaining to language and culture, including broadcasting. In the coming months, debate focused on the question of "educational broadcasting." Returning to Québec from the constitutional conference, Johnson declared that his government had decided to apply a 1945 law (adopted by the Duplessis government but never operationalized) establishing Radio-Québec (Québec, 1968:3). The move was enough to upset Ottawa's design. By the end of 1969, Ottawa and the provinces had settled on a definition of educational broadcasting under which, in the 1970s, provincial public broadcasting agencies would begin operating in four provinces.

The growing complexity of communications in the late 1960s prompted Ottawa to create a Department of Communications in April 1969. Determined to match Ottawa move for move, Québec created its own Ministère des communications six months later. In the early 1970s, negotiating a strong role for Québec in communications policy became one of the hallmarks of Robert Bourassa's program for achieving "cultural sovereignty." In a series of policy statements authored by communications minister Jean-Paul L'Allier, Québec proposed "to promote and maintain a *québécois* system of communications" (Québec, 1971), and to become "master craftsman of communications policy on its territory" (Québec, 1973).

The *Régie des services publics du Québec* began to subject the 160 cable companies then operating in Québec to its own regulation as well as that of the CRTC, but in November 1977 the Supreme Court ruled that the CRTC had the exclusive jurisdiction to regulate cable. Oddly enough, the court split neatly along national lines, the three judges from Québec dissenting from the majority opinion, prompting then constitutional expert Gil Rémillard to write: "On the strictly legal level, both options were defensible. The decision was based on the judges' different conceptions of Canadian federalism" (Rémillard, 1980:349).

Under the Parti Québécois government, Québec did not directly engage with Ottawa over communications policy. The PQ carried over the policy thrust of the Bourassa government, but basically abdicated to its lack of power over communications under the existing system. Paradoxically, the PQ was thus a lot less aggressive than its predecessors in seeking concrete gains from Ottawa in this area. It concentrated instead on developing the programs and policies begun by Union Nationale and Liberal governments: Radio-Québec, now a full-fledged broadcaster, and the particular Québec form of participatory communication known as "community" media.

In both Ottawa and Québec City, government policy with respect to media— and "cultural industries" generally—took on an economic turn in the 1980s. Federal policy since 1983 has been marked notably by a gradual withdrawal of fiscal responsibility for public service broadcasting (CBC budget cuts), privatization of television production (through the Telefilm fund), and the introduction of a wide range of new commercial cable-delivered television signals (pay-TV and nondiscretionary subscriber-funded specialty services). Québec, meanwhile, beginning during the PQ's second mandate, has followed a similar path, reducing support for publicly oriented services (Radio-Québec and the community media), and seeing its main role as lobby and promoter for the development of commercially viable Québec cultural industries domestically, vis-à-vis Ottawa, and abroad (see French, 1987; Tremblay, 1988).

With the election of the Mulroney government and its commitment to "national reconciliation," Québec and Ottawa found themselves on a harmonious political, as well as economic, course by 1985. Brian Mulroney's choice of Marcel Masse to be his minister of communications was an astute one in this regard. As a reputed Québec nationalist who had been involved with the Union Nationale government of the late 1960s in its battle for more provincial power through agencies such as Radio-Québec, Masse was the ideal minister for thawing relations with Québec while applying broad federal policy to communications.

Masse and Québec communications minister Jean-François Bertrand signed an agreement on communications enterprises development under which they jointly provided $40 million in seed-money to stimulate research and job creation by Québec-based communications firms. The industrial thrust of the accord was self-evident, aiming at technical innovation and support for the production, development, and marketing of communications goods and services, especially in export markets (Canada/Québec, 1985a).

It was the first ever communications agreement between Ottawa and Québec since they created their respective communications ministries a few months apart in 1969. Masse and Bertrand also announced the setting up of a permanent joint committee, chaired by their two deputy ministers, to pursue further areas of collaboration. This committee has functioned successfully ever since, making communications one field where Ottawa and Québec actually function *d'égal à égal* (personal interview with MCQ official, 1990).

The committee's first effort produced an important report on "The Future of French-Language Television," made public in May 1985 (Canada/Québec, 1985b). The report's central recommendation was crucial to the developing federal policy with respect to broadcasting, as well as strangely premonitory. It proposed "that the special nature of the French-language television system be recognized within the Canadian broadcasting system, and that government policies and regulations be adapted accordingly" (Canada/Québec, 1985b:2). Such a proposal would recognize, for the first time, the historic reality of parallel development of Canadian broadcasting since the 1930s. It would also mark a major shift in Ottawa's official attitude that there is but one policy for Canadian broadcasting, not two.

In addition, the report proposed general ongoing consultation between Ottawa and Québec. A "harmonization" agreement for the development of French-language television was signed soon thereafter (Canada/Québec, 1986). Between 1985 and 1990, areas of federal–provincial collaboration have included working groups on cable television, children's advertising, and computer software (see Tremblay, 1988), and the idea of tailoring policy to meet the distinct needs of different markets has been reflected notably in CRTC decisions (e.g., CRTC, 1987) and the policies of the Telefilm fund.

The federal task force set up by Masse to recommend a new policy for broadcasting, the Caplan-Sauvageau Task Force, welcomed the proposals of the federal–provincial committee on French-language television, and reiterated many of its key proposals. It proposed "that the distinctive character of Québec broadcasting be recognized both in itself and as the nucleus of French-language broadcasting throughout Canada" (Canada, 1986:223). French- and English-language services within the CBC should be recognized as serving "distinct societies," and be allowed to take "different approaches to meeting the objectives assigned to public broadcasting" (Canada, 1986:217). The CBC's French network budgets should be reviewed "to establish hourly production costs that reflect the role assigned to the French network in the new television environment" (Canada, 1986:253). As for the CBC's national unity mandate, the task force found it "inappropriate for any broadcaster, public or private.... It suggests constrained attachment to a political order rather than free expression in the pursuit of a national culture broadly defined" (Canada, 1986:283–84). The task force proposed to replace it with "a more socially oriented provision, for example, that the service contribute to the development of national consciousness" (Canada, 1986:285).

The government's position was formalized in a policy statement tabled by then minister Flora MacDonald along with new broadcasting legislation in June 1988. Here it was recognized that "the problems and challenges for English-language broadcasting and French-language broadcasting are not the same ... [and that] these differences between the English and French broadcasting environments necessarily require different policy approaches for each" (Canada, 1988b:6–7).

The legislation (Bill C-136) featured a half-dozen clauses referring to the linguistic duality of the system. The key clause, article 3.1.b., specified that "English and French language broadcasting, while sharing common aspects, operate under different conditions and may have different requirements." The CBC's mandate was changed to read that "the programming provided by the Canadian Broadcasting Corporation should ... contribute to shared national consciousness and identity." An amendment introduced later added that it should "strive to be of equivalent quality in English and in French" as well (Canada, 1988c and 1988d).

Bill C-136 died in the Senate on September 30, 1988, as Parliament was dissolved for the national elections (see Raboy, 1990:329–34). It was reintroduced virtually intact, however, and was eventually adopted in February 1991 (Canada, 1991).

Québec's claims for jurisdiction over broadcasting have been reinvigorated by the renewed constitutional debate that has followed the collapse of the Meech Lake Accord. Every important group that mentioned culture and communication before the Bélanger-Campeau Commission called for full repatriation of powers, as did the Québec Liberal Party's Allaire Report. Regardless of the future constitutional arrangement, Québec will clearly have more powers in this area. But as in so many others, little indication has been given so far of what a Québécois communication system will look like. Québec will have to decide about the appropriate relationship between public and privately owned services, the role of the state and the regulatory apparatus, the balance between sociocultural and economic and industrial objectives, and the space available for democratic participation (see Table 10.1). Paradoxically, the broadcasting system built up from Ottawa is still based on a strong public service tradition (however eroded in the past ten years), while Québec City has historically opposed the system on political grounds. The present danger is that the space evacuated by Ottawa will be occupied by commercial business groups whose interest in broadcasting does not extend beyond the bottom line.

Table 10.1
Type of Property, Regulatory Framework, and Financial
Basis of Québec Media Forms

MEDIA	REGULATORY FRAMEWORK	PROPERTY TYPE	FINANCIAL BASIS
1. Press	Unregulated	Privately owned	Advertising, sales
2. Radio	Regulated (federal)	a. Private	Advertising
		b. Public (CBC)	Parliament
		c. Community	Various grants, some ads, public subscription
3. TV	Regulated (federal)	a. Private	Advertising
		b. Public (CBC, Radio-Québec)	Parliament/Ntl. Assembly, advertising
		c. Community	Grants, public cable companies
4. Cable	Regulated (federal)	Private	Subscription

MEDIA IN QUÉBEC: WHO OWNS WHAT

The commercialization and commodification of mass media is a global process from which Québec has not been exempt. If anything, history and politics have combined to concentrate media power in Québec in even relatively fewer hands than elsewhere. The evolution of media ownership patterns and the present degree of concentration bears witness to this fact. As noted earlier, the press in Québec lies entirely in the private sector although, traditionally, it has included newspapers whose principal vocation was sociopolitical rather than commercial. This phenomenon has undergone important change in recent decades.

In Québec and in Canada, discussion of the political economy of mass media has, since the late 1960s, focused invariably on the question of concentration of ownership (see, for example, Canada, 1970; Canada, 1981; Canada, 1978). In Québec, the question burst onto the public agenda in 1967, when the major newspaper, *La Presse*, passed from the hands of the Montréal family that had controlled it since it was founded in 1886 to a company controlled by businessman Paul Desmarais, which already owned three other small dailies (*Le Nouvelliste* of Trois-Rivières, *La Voix de l'Est* of Granby, and *La Tribune* of Sherbrooke).

Concentration of ownership implies a decrease in the number of independent voices with access to the media. The potential danger for freedom of expression and "the public's right to know" was one of the leading causes for the creation, in 1969, of the *Fédération professionnelle des journalistes du Québec*. The Québec government of Jean-Jacques Bertrand, meanwhile, convoked a special commission of the National Assembly to consider the question of press freedom. This commission continued its work during the first term of Robert Bourassa, but never published a final report. However, public opinion was sufficiently alerted that the government intervened in 1973 when Paul Desmarais's Power Corporation indicated its intention to acquire the Québec City daily *Le Soleil*. While armed only with moral authority, government opposition to this deal was enough to cause Power to withdraw in favour of Jacques Francoeur (UniMédia). A similar attempt to oppose the sale of UniMédia to Toronto-based entrepreneur Conrad Black (Hollinger) in 1987 failed, however, provoking some controversial comments that the problem of concentration of ownership was now compounded by that of *foreign* ownership as well.

The 1970s saw the shutdown and sell-off of numerous dailies in Québec. *Montréal-Matin* was acquired by Power Corporation and then closed a few years later; Québec City's *Action catholique* closed its doors after no buyer could be found; the *Chronicle Telegraph* went weekly; Montréal's two large English-language dailies, *The Star* and *The Gazette*, were sold to English-Canadian chains (Southam and FP/Thomson), and *The Star* was closed in 1979.

Alongside this, a remarkable success story: the market penetration and spectacular rise to dominance of the tabloid dailies of Quebecor, founded in 1964 by Pierre Péladeau. By 1980, the daily newspaper sector was dominated by four groups—Power, Quebecor, UniMédia, and Southam—to which one could add two independent papers: *Le Devoir* and the tiny Sherbrooke *Record* (since bought by Quebecor).

Concentration of private ownership has also marked the broadcasting sector, and has taken on increased importance in the past decade in light of the decreasing state support for public and community-based broadcasting undertakings. (Canadian, and hence Québec, radio, as we saw earlier, began in the private sector and has been a "mixed" system since 1932. Television, introduced as a public monopoly, has been "mixed" since 1961. Cable services have always been, and remain, strictly privately owned, albeit regulated, commercial undertakings.)

By the 1980s, press, radio, television, and cable undertakings were tending to come together, particularly through cross-media ownership and competition for audiences and advertising dollars (see Table 10.2). In the unregulated print sector, it was increasingly difficult for anyone to enter the market, even with a highly capitalized financial base, as a number of unsuccessful attempts to do so made clear (*Le Matin*, backed by Southam; Quebecor's *Montreal Daily News*). The significant "alternative" press culture that had flourished in the 1960s and 1970s was virtually

Table 10.2
Québec's Major Media Corporations, 1989
(present in Québec but based outside)

RANK	NAME	REVENUES (,000)	PROFITS (,000)
1	Quebecor	1,755,482	27,589
2	(Southam)	1,677,154	88,100
3	(Maclean-Hunter)	1,426,200	90,300
4	(Hollinger)	754,867	73,087
5	GTC	366,382	7,455
6	Vidéotron	344,880	25,811
7	Power	268,300	221,253
8	Astral	264,452	4,240
9	Télémédia	215,792	2,254
10	Gesca [Power]	198,500	10,087
11	UniMédia [Hollinger]	148,112	(2,358)
12	CFCF	125,185	3,173
13	Télé-Métropole [Vidéotron]	115,983	1,212
14	Reader's Digest	113,314	11,925
15	Cogéco	101,969	3,862
16	Pathonic [Vidéotron]	55,426	4,098
17	Radiomutuel	31,580	(n.a.)

Source: *The Financial Post Magazine*, Summer 1990.

out of business, as popular ventures such as *Le Temps fou* and *La Vie en rose* could not find sufficiently large markets in a climate of rising costs.

Various government commissions (Canada, 1970, 1978, 1981, 1986) have proposed measures to control concentration of ownership, particularly *cross-media ownership* in the same market, but to little avail. The only concrete measure any government in Canada has taken was a 1982 federal cabinet directive to the CRTC prohibiting the awarding of broadcasting licences to newspaper owners in the same market—but this was abrogated by the Conservatives in 1985, and paved the way for a Power Corporation application to purchase Télé-Métropole, Québec's most important, and at the time most lucrative, private television station. The CRTC rejected the Power application (for lack of merit, stating unequivocally that concentration had nothing to do with the rejection), but later approved instead a bid by Vidéotron, Québec's main cable distribution company. This association created a vertically integrated broadcasting conglomerate of unprecedented scale (see Raboy, 1990:313–16).

Under recent federal policy—tacitly approved by Québec and vigorously encouraged by Québec business—the pull of globalization and the desire to launch large corporations on the world market has taken precedence over the needs of the local population. Despite stern warnings from the parliamentary committee responsible for broadcasting, the CRTC has refused to see concentration as a problem, preferring to oversee the "financial viability" of broadcasting undertakings (see Canada, 1988a).

Concentration of ownership is even more remarkable when one looks at it in terms of market share. According to a recent study done for the Ministère des communications du Québec (Québec, 1989b), the largest media groups control an even larger share of their respective markets than is indicated by the number of companies they own. (The authors of this study used as indicators of market share factors such as advertising revenue for radio and television, number of subscribers for cable, total revenue for telephone companies, and circulation for the written press.)

Tables 10.3 and 10.4 provide a highly instructive portrait of the degree of concentration in Québec media. With the exception of radio, more than two-thirds of the Québec market in every sector is controlled by groups, in some cases (daily newspapers) rising to virtual group monopoly. Table 10.3 also shows the tendency toward *cross-media ownership*. Thus, among the thirteen groups shown, seven are active in at least two sectors, and two (Power and Cogéco) are active in four sectors. The Ministère des communications du Québec expects the coming years to be marked by new crossovers involving media and telecommunications companies, as well as companies dealing in computerized information services (not shown in the table).

Table 10.3
Market Share of Principal Communications Groups in Québec, 1988

GROUP	% MARKET SHARE, BY SECTOR						
	tel.	news.	wkly.	mags.	radio	TV	cable
Bell Canada	90.1						
Power (Gesca)		27.3	4.0		2.8	1.4	
Southam		15.9					
Maclean-Hunter				10.3			
Quebecor		39.9	25.4	35.6			
Québec-Téléphone	7.7						
Hollinger (Uni.)		15.4	10.4				
Vidéotron						56.3	56.1*
GTC			11.8				
Télémédia			14.5	16.0	20.1		**
CFCF						28.9	13.1
Cogéco			15.1		9.0	4.9	11.7**
Radiomutuel					14.8		**
TOTALS	97.8	98.5	69.4	73.7	46.7	91.5	80.9

* Does not take into account acquisition of the five-station Pathonic network in 1990.
** Does not take into account participation in specialty TV services.
Source: *La concentration des marchés dans les secteurs des communications au Québec et au Canada depuis 1980*, Québec, Ministère des communications du Québec, 1989.

Table 10.4
A Who's Who of Québec Media

Quebecor Inc.
Vertically integrated press conglomerate controlled by self-made Québec entrepreneur Pierre Péladeau. Enjoys about 44 percent of the French-language daily newspaper market in Québec, and a major player in weeklies, magazines, periodical distribution, printing, and newsprint production.

Southam Inc.
Canada's largest media-only enterprise. Legacy of an early Canadian newspaper family, publisher of fifteen important English-language dailies, including *The Gazette* of Montréal. Major shareholders

Table 10.4 continued

include Torstar Corp. (publishers of *The Toronto Star*) and the financial institution National Trustco. Also active in periodical publication, but its radio and TV interests have been sold off in recent years.

Maclean-Hunter Ltd.
Diversified media conglomerate. Canada's leading publisher of business and consumer magazines, in English and French (e.g., *L'Actualité, Châtelaine*), as well as a major cable company owner. In 1988, carried out the most costly transaction in Canadian broadcasting history, acquiring the interests of Selkirk Broadcasting (Southam) for about $600 million.

Hollinger Inc.
Conrad Black's company. Its interests in Canada include the UniMédia chain of newspapers in Québec (*Le Soleil*), the Sterling chain of newspapers, an important stake in *The Financial Post*, and *Saturday Night* magazine.

GTC Transcontinental Group Ltd.
Vertically integrated Québec press conglomerate, with major interests in direct mail circulars, business periodicals, and distribution.

Groupe Vidéotron Ltée
Vertically integrated Québec electronic media conglomerate, with interests in cable, television broadcasting, production, and post-production services. A leader in research and development, and pioneer of interactive television. Controlled by its founder, André Chagnon, with a major minority shareholder the Caisse de dépôt et placement du Québec (province of Québec employees' pension fund).

Power Corporation of Canada
Management company controlled by Québec entrepreneur Paul Desmarais. The most profitable of the "Financial Post Top 500" Canadian companies, with a return of 82.5 percent in 1989. Publisher of several important daily newspapers (e.g., *La Presse*) and also active in other media sectors (through its subsidiary Gesca).

Astral Inc.
A leading film and video producer and service company controlled by Harold Greenberg and associates. It recently pulled off the coup of hiring retiring CRTC chairman André Bureau as chief executive officer. Astral owns a majority in Viewer's Choice Canada, which has just been awarded a licence to introduce "pay-per-view," an *à la carte* cable subscription service for high-value sporting and cultural events and first-run films.

Télémédia Inc.
Controlled by one of Québec's oldest elite families, the de Gaspé Beaubiens, it owns a radio chain and operates a network in Québec and owns radio stations in Ontario and a string of magazines publishing in both English and French. Also 50 percent owner of a French-language specialty television service, "Réseau des sports."

CFCF Inc.
Named for the CTV affiliate in Montréal, which it owns, and Canada's oldest radio station, which it sold in 1987. Also owns and operates Télévision Quatre Saisons, a French-language television network, and a major cable company, all in Québec.

Télé-Métropole Inc.
French Canada's first and most popular private television station, founded in 1961. Family owned until sold to Vidéotron in 1987, following a controversial CRTC hearing where public intervention focused on the new and unprecedented form of concentration the cable/broadcaster fusion represented.

Table 10.4 continued

Reader's Digest Assoc. (Canada) Ltd.
This wholly owned subsidiary of the U.S. parent publishes the highest circulation magazine in Québec, *Sélection du Reader's Digest.*

Cogéco Inc.
One of the most widely diversified, although still small, Québec media conglomerates, with interests in television, radio, cable, publishing, and specialty TV services (Canal Famille), all in Québec. Owned by the Audet family.

Réseau Pathonic Inc.
Operator of five radio stations and a network serving small metropolitan areas of Québec. Taken over by Vidéotron in 1990, and subsequently dissolved.

Radiomutuel
Radio chain, also 50-percent owner of the rock video cable television service "Musique Plus."

Thus, in Québec today:

♦ four companies (Quebecor, Power, Southam, and Hollinger) control 98.5 percent of daily newspaper circulation;

♦ five (Quebecor, Cogéco, Télémédia, Hollinger, and Power) control 69.4 percent of the weeklies market;

♦ four (Quebecor, Télémédia, GTC, and Maclean-Hunter) control 73.7 percent of magazines;

♦ four (Vidéotron, CFCF, Cogéco, and Power) received 91.5 percent of television advertising (excluding CBC and Radio-Québec);

♦ four (Télémédia, Radiomutuel, Cogéco, and Power) received 46.7 percent of radio advertising;

♦ three (Vidéotron, CFCF, and Cogéco) have 80.9 percent of cable television subscribers;

♦ two (Bell Canada and Québec-Téléphone) control 97.8 percent of the telephone market (destined to become increasingly important as computer-linked telecommunications networks become central to media communication).

CONCLUSION

Virtually all mass media organizations in the world today are directly controlled by either large commercial corporations or agencies of the state. Québec is no different in this respect. But Québec is presently in the unique position of developing a new communication policy in the expectation of new powers. It is thus in a position to innovate. Québec's media traditions and the existing Québec media environment are rich with examples on which to base this policy.

Given the sociocultural importance of media as *institutions of the public sphere*, it appears to this author that communication policy should start from the premise that the media system is one of public service (like health care, or education). This would imply that *all* media, regardless of ownership, should be expected to serve some public service objective. Within a general public service framework, there would be room for commercial and noncommercial media. Mechanisms would be put in place for providing public participation in the system (for example, in the determining of types of services, in the programming of cable systems, through access to the means of expression, in audience assessment, etc.). Access to the marketplace should be as free as possible, but at the same time, market criteria should not be allowed to take precedence over public service ones. This implies not only public subsidies for certain services, but also measures to ensure the viability of small media by redistributing the wealth generated by the system as a whole. The press should be included in the general regulatory framework.

Proposals such as these certainly appear to go against the grain of the times, but they are not merely idealistic. They are essential if the media is to be something more than just another sector of the entertainment industry. Their consideration would place public communication at the centre of the social project that one hopes will emerge in the new Québec of the 21st century.

REFERENCES

Canada (1929). Royal Commission on Radio Broadcasting, *Report*. Ottawa: King's Printer.

Canada (1964). House of Commons, *Debates* (1964–65), pp. 10080–86 (Speech by Hon. M. Lamontagne, Secretary of State).

Canada (1968). "Broadcasting Act," *Statutes of Canada*, 1967–68, c. 25.

Canada (1970). Special Senate Committee on Mass Media, *Report*. Ottawa: Information Canada.

Canada (1978). Royal Commission on Corporate Concentration, *Report*. Ottawa: Minister of Supply and Services Canada.

Canada (1981). Royal Commission on Newspapers, *Report*. Ottawa: Minister of Supply and Services Canada.

Canada (1986). Task Force on Broadcasting Policy, *Report*. Ottawa: Minister of Supply and Services Canada.

Canada (1988a). House of Commons, Standing Committee on Communications and Culture (1986–88), *A Broadcasting Policy for Canada*. Ottawa: Minister of Supply and Services Canada.

Canada (1988b). Communications Canada, *Canadian Voices, Canadian Choices*. Ottawa: Minister of Supply and Services Canada.

Canada (1988c). Unpassed Bills, "Broadcasting Act," Bill C-136, First Reading, 23 June 1988.

Canada (1988d). Unpassed Bills, "Broadcasting Act," Bill C-136, Third Reading, 28 September 1988.

Canada (1991). "Broadcasting Act," *Statutes of Canada*, 38–39 Elizabeth II, c. 11.

Canada/Québec (1985a). *Canada–Québec Subsidiary Agreement on Communications Enterprises Development 1984–1990*. Ottawa and Québec: Government of Canada/Gouvernement du Québec.

Canada/Québec (1985b). Canada/Québec, Federal–Provincial Committee, *The Future of French-Language Television*. Ottawa and Québec: Government of Canada/Gouvernement du Québec.

Canada/Québec (1986). Canada/Québec, "Canada–Québec Memorandum of Understanding on the Development of the French-language Television System." Ottawa and Québec: Government of Canada/Gouvernement du Québec.

CBC (1979). Canadian Broadcasting Corporation, *The CBC—A Perspective*. Ottawa: CBC, pp. 377–424.

CRTC (1987). Canadian Radio-television and Telecommunications Commission, *More Canadian Programming Choices*. Ottawa: CRTC.

CSN (1968). Confédération des syndicats nationaux, *Le Deuxième Front*. Montréal: CSN.

De Bonville, J. (1989). *La presse québécoise de 1884 à 1914: Genèse d'un média de masse*. Québec: Presses de l'Université Laval.

French, R.D. (1987). "The Francophone Summit," *Canadian Journal of Communication*, unnumbered, 47–53.

Hamelin, J., and A. Beaulieu (1966). "Aperçu du journalisme québécois d'expression française." *Recherches sociographiques* 7, 3, pp. 305–48.

Johnson, A.W. (1983). "The Re-Canadianization of Broadcasting," *Policy Options* 4, 2, pp. 6–12.

Lamonde, Y. (1984). "American Cultural Influence in Québec: A One-Way Mirror." In A.O. Hero, Jr., and M. Daneau, eds., *Problems and Opportunities in U.S.–Québec Relations*. Boulder: Westview Press, pp. 106–26.

Porter, J. (1965). *The Vertical Mosaic*. Toronto: University of Toronto Press.

Québec (1968). Legislative Assembly, *Journal des débats*.

Québec (1971). Ministère des communications du Québec, *Pour une politique québécoise des communications*. Québec: MCQ.

Québec (1973). Ministère des communications du Québec, *Le Québec, maître d'oeuvre de la politique des communications sur son territoire*. Québec: MCQ.

Québec (1986). Ministère des communications du Québec, *Le rapport statistique sur les médias québécois*. Québec: MCQ.

Québec (1989a). Ministère des communications du Québec, *La télévision francophone du Québec*. Québec: MCQ.

Québec (1989b). Ministère des communications du Québec, *La concentration des marchés dans les secteurs des communications au Québec et au Canada depuis 1980*. Québec: MCQ.

Raboy, M. (1984). *Movements and Messages: Media and Radical Politics in Québec*. Toronto: Between the Lines.

Raboy, M. (1990). *Missed Opportunities: The Story of Canada's Broadcasting Policy*. Montréal and Kingston: McGill-Queen's University Press.

Raboy, M. (1991). "Canadian Broadcasting, Canadian Nationhood: Two Concepts, Two Solitudes and Great Expectations." In J. Courtney, P. MacKinnon, and D.E. Smith, eds., *After Meech Lake: Lessons for the Future*. Saskatoon: Fifth House Press, pp. 181–97.

Rémillard, G. (1980). *Le fédéralisme canadien: Éléments constitutionnels de formation et d'évolution*. Montréal: Québec-Amérique.

Roy, J.-L. (1976). *La marche des Québécois: le temps des ruptures, 1945–1960*. Ottawa: Leméac.

Tremblay, G. (1988). "La politique québécoise en matière de communication (1966–1986): De l'affirmation autonomiste à la coopération fédérale–provinciale," *Communication/Information* 9, 3, pp. 57–87.

P A R T

3

STATE, SOCIETY, AND POLITICS

C H A P T E R 11

Québec's Political System in the 1990s: From Polarization to Convergence*

A. Brian Tanguay
Wilfrid Laurier University

In their trenchant examination of electoral politics in Canada, the authors of *Absent Mandate* argue that voters in this country "are rarely presented with a clear choice between world views and the political projects that follow from them" (Clarke et al., 1991:9). A quick scan of Canada's electoral history during the past few decades should suffice to convince even the most Panglossian observer of this argument. At the federal level, elections involving a straightforward clash of competing political philosophies seem to occur with about the same frequency as Halley's comet's passage through our solar system. When voters *are* actually confronted with meaningful policy choices in a federal election, this usually takes place in spite of the assiduous efforts of party strategists to orient the campaign around the tried and true—and electorally safe—issues of leadership and patronage, as was the case in the so-called free trade election of 1988 (Salutin, 1989; Tanguay, 1990).

Provincial politics (apart from the Atlantic provinces and, until recently, Ontario) is more likely to involve the kind of ideological confrontation that is so patently lacking at the federal level. This was certainly the case in Québec during the 1970s, when the Québec Liberal Party (QLP), a staunchly federalist and pro-business organization, was pitted against the *indépendantiste* and social democratic Parti Québécois. To be sure, not every election in the province during this decade constituted an unambiguous referendum on these competing world views, especially since the traditional staples of Canadian politics—leadership, patronage, corruption, party image and style—frequently pushed aside the more fundamental issues of policy and ideology. As well, the PQ was forced both to soften its stance on the national question (by promising a referendum on sovereignty some time during its first mandate) and to downplay the more radical socialist planks in its platform in order to cobble together a coalition of voters large enough to propel

---

*The author wishes to thank Susan Phillips and Elisabeth Gidengil for their helpful suggestions.

it into office (which it succeeded in doing in 1976). Despite these concessions to political expediency, however, party competition in Québec during the 1970s was highly polarized[1] and probably came closer to John Porter's ideal of *creative politics* than most other party systems, either federal or provincial, have ever done.[2]

Contrast this image of party politics in Québec during the 1970s with the situation in the early 1990s. Over the past decade the Liberals and the Parti Québécois have gradually crept closer to one another on *both* the national question and socioeconomic issues. While it would not be completely fair to dismiss the two parties as mere clones of each other, the programmatic differences between them are often very subtle indeed, more a matter of emphasis and degree than of substance. For instance, the erstwhile social democratic party, the PQ, now frequently sounds as neoliberal as the Liberals in its zeal to "put the welfare state on a diet" and to trim the rights and privileges of some sections of organized labour (notably public-sector unions). The national question, which after a brief period of quiescence in the middle part of the 1980s[3] has once again erupted onto the political agenda in both English Canada and Québec, has produced a similar, if less complete, convergence between the two major parties. The death of René Lévesque in November 1987, the uproar over the issue of bilingual commercial signs (1988), and the failure of the Meech Lake Accord (June 1990) all served to breathe new life into what only a few years before had appeared to be a moribund nationalist movement. At the same time, these events precipitated a startling ideological transformation of the Liberal Party, driving it in an increasingly nationalist, even *indépendantiste,* direction (though admittedly it is still far more equivocal and hesitant on Québec's constitutional future than the PQ). As a cursory glance at the Liberal Party's latest version of its constitutional policy will attest, it shares with the Parti Québécois a virtually identical analysis of the sources of the present political impasse in Canada (Québec Liberal Party, 1991).

This chapter examines the causes and consequences of this shift from party polarization in Québec during the 1970s to party convergence in the late 1980s. The first two sections focus on the ideology and leadership of the two major parties, the PQ and the Liberal Party. The third section deals briefly with the most important "minor" party in the province, the Equality Party. This anglophone-rights splinter group was formed shortly before the 1989 provincial election to protest the Bourassa government's reneging on its promise to allow bilingual commercial signs, a promise made very explicit during the 1985 campaign in which it defeated the incumbent PQ government. A brief concluding section discusses the impact that the recent trend toward party convergence has had on political discourse and democratic government in contemporary Québec.

THE PARTI QUÉBÉCOIS, 1976–92: THE DIFFICULTIES OF GROWING OLD

In his *Memoirs*, René Lévesque makes a number of wistful observations about the functions of political parties in democratic politics and about the inevitable fate—senescence, sclerosis, and irrelevance—that awaits many of them:

... I believe I could never be a party man, no more Péquiste than Liberal. For me any political party is basically just a necessary evil, one of the instruments a democratic society needs when the time comes to delegate to elected representatives the responsibility of looking after its common interests. But parties that last generally age poorly. They have a tendency to transform themselves into lay churches with power to loose and to bind and can turn out to be quite insupportable. In the long run sclerosis of ideas sets in and political opportunism takes over. Every new party should, in my opinion, write into its statutes a clause anticipating its disappearance after a certain time, perhaps after a generation, certainly no longer. If it goes on past this, no matter how much plastic surgery it undergoes to restore its beauty, one day it will be nothing more than a worn-out old thing blocking the horizon and preventing the future from breaking through. (Lévesque, 1986:216–17)

Lévesque was ostensibly writing about the Québec Liberal Party in the late 1960s and his decision to break from what he considered to be an increasingly sterile, "outmoded" organization. But he no doubt had the more recent example of the Parti Québécois firmly in mind when he wrote that "parties that last generally age poorly." Unceremoniously squeezed out of the leadership of the party that he had founded in 1968, Lévesque was understandably bitter about the treatment he had received at the hands of his impatient successors, and could be forgiven for concluding that "crass opportunism" had taken hold of the Parti Québécois. Yet his comments should not be dismissed as merely another exercise in self-justification, for they perfectly describe the meteoric rise and equally rapid decline of the PQ. In the short span of eight years (from 1968 to 1976) this organization grew from a tiny band of disaffected Liberals, *Créditistes*, and radical separatists to become the governing party of Québec. Throughout this period, the PQ leadership sought to portray the party as the embodiment of youthful vigour, destined to seize power once the grip of an older generation on the reins of government had been pried loose. But it was its tenure in power, and in particular the organizational and ideological strains created by the need to provide an efficient administration while laying the groundwork for the *étapiste*[4] accession to sovereignty, that caused the Parti Québécois to age so rapidly and, to echo Lévesque, so "poorly." By the time Lévesque published his *Memoirs,* the PQ was a mere shell of its former self, having lost much of its previous *élan* and dynamism. And although the party has made a partial recovery under the leadership of Jacques Parizeau, it still fails to attract members and voters in the same numbers that it once did. This section examines the aging of the Parti Québécois, its transformation from a youthful social movement into a tired, somewhat disillusioned opposition party, a *"parti comme les autres,"* which some critics have uncharitably likened to a latter-day version of the old Union Nationale.

The Parti Québécois, 1976–81: Social Democracy in the Service of the Referendum

When the Parti Québécois took office in November 1976 it was faced with a number of daunting problems. How could it mollify a frightened business community (skittish foreign investors, in particular), convince organized labour in the province of the reality of its rhetorical "favourable prejudice toward workers,"[5] defuse an explosive labour relations scene (strike rates in Québec during the Bourassa years had been among the highest in the Western world), and cultivate the proper environment for the passage of the promised referendum on sovereignty-association, all at the same time? To make matters even more difficult, the PQ from its birth had been a fragile coalition of disparate ideological movements, ranging from the extreme right (former *Créditistes* like Gilles Grégoire) to the hard left (Robert Burns and, from time to time, Pierre Bourgault, when he was not resigning from the party). Could the party maintain its tenuous unity during the early years of its mandate, when policies designed to alter the balance of power between labour and capital would have to be implemented if the government was to fulfil certain explicit promises in its program and retain the support of its key allies— organized labour, most notably?

Viewed from the vantage point of the early 1990s, the accomplishments of the first Lévesque administration are quite impressive. One need only compare the PQ's first year in power with that of the current NDP government in Ontario to be struck by the seeming boldness of the Lévesque administration. After all, the Rae government has quietly abandoned many of its pre-election promises, and shied away from implementing any policies that might antagonize the business establishment. By contrast, during its first year in power, the Parti Québécois introduced sweeping reforms of election finance legislation, with the objective of eliminating corruption and undue business influence on government. It revised the Labour Code, strengthening the financial base of trade unions (through the imposition of the Rand Formula),[6] prohibiting the use of replacement workers ("scabs") during legal strikes, and facilitating union certification in the province. It also nationalized part of the province's automobile insurance industry and purchased the American-owned Asbestos Corporation in an ultimately abortive attempt to create more manufacturing jobs in this important industry. These, along with the Charter of the French Language (Bill 101, adopted in 1977), were among the Lévesque government's more innovative and controversial measures.

While some *marxisant* critics of the Parti Québécois have pooh-poohed these policies as mere window dressing on capitalist exploitation, the business world, both foreign and domestic, was clearly unsettled by the new administration's initiatives. In a perceptive article on the class bases of the Parti Québécois's electoral coalition and on the nature of its political and social projects, Richard French (1985:165, 168) observed:

> The nationalist and social democratic consensus shared by the PQ and the opinion-oriented middle class gave short shrift to private enterprise. The business community reacted with shock to the PQ victory of November 1976. It was as entirely unprepared as the new government to undertake constructive discussion. For the first eighteen to twenty-four months, relations went from bad to worse, as the government seemed intent on realizing business' worst nightmares.... Pierre Des Marais II, while president of the Employers' Council in 1978, "reminded the Premier that the members of the Council were also Quebecers and that they resented being treated as persona non grata by their own government. He said that the PQ government had treated businessmen like dirt and that some ministers had virtually declared war on the business world, employers and private enterprise."[7]

French draws attention here to an important sociological characteristic of the Parti Québécois: in terms of both its electoral support and its membership, the PQ was *primarily* (though not exclusively) the vehicle of an ascendant francophone new middle class (what French describes as the "opinion-oriented middle class")—civil servants, journalists, social scientists, and the employees of the state-run health, educational, and welfare bureaucracies whose ranks had been swollen by the growth of the provincial state since the Quiet Revolution. In order to reach out beyond this core group of supporters and forge a broad interclass coalition in favour of Québec sovereignty, the PQ was forced to introduce policies (like the reforms of the Labour Code mentioned above) that would gain the political support of the working class, both organized and unorganized. In this sense, the Parti Québécois's labour policy during its first term in office, to paraphrase von Clausewitz, was the continuation of its nationalist project by other means. At the same time, these reforms were designed to assuage the PQ's restive and vocal left wing, which was constantly on guard against the danger of sacrificing the party's ideological radicalism to the exigencies of power.

The Lévesque administration managed to perform this balancing act until 1980. Along with the antiscab measures described above, which were cautiously endorsed by the main private-sector labour federation, the *Fédération des travailleurs du Québec* (FTQ),[8] there were additional elements in the PQ's consensus-building strategy. The government held regular tripartite economic summit meetings that brought together the peak associations of business and labour with government representatives. These conferences were designed to foster dialogue among the so-called "social partners," to inculcate in organized labour and business a *national consciousness*, a recognition that their own sectional demands were secondary to the fate of the collectivity.[9] By eroding or even dissolving the class distinctions between workers and owners, the government hoped, tripartism would lead to a *new social contract* and transform these sectional groups into *Québécois*, a necessary prelude to the passage of the referendum.[10] Although the hype surrounding these conferences undoubtedly dwarfed their real impact on policy-making, their chief benefit for the government consisted in the wedge that they drove between the radical union leadership, who continually railed against the PQ's "petit bourgeois" reformism, and the more moderate rank and file workers, many of whom were openly sympathetic to the Parti Québécois and its independence project.[11]

The Lévesque government also proved to be remarkably generous in its negotiations with its employees in the public and parapublic sectors. Triennial collective bargaining in Québec's public sector—which since the late 1960s had been highly centralized, politicized, and conflictual—has traditionally been the graveyard of the electoral hopes of incumbent governments. With the deadline for the promised referendum on sovereignty-association rapidly approaching—negotiations took place in 1979, three years into the PQ's mandate—the administration felt that it could not risk rending the social fabric, and possibly jeopardizing the chances for success of the referendum, by precipitating an all-out confrontation with the Common Front.[12] Thus the government's chief negotiator, Finance Minister Jacques Parizeau, made far-reaching concessions to the unions on their demands for isolation pay, improved maternity benefits, and increased job security (which was already pretty much iron-clad).

By the time the referendum was finally held in May 1980, therefore, organized labour in Québec found itself considerably strengthened by a number of legislative measures passed by the PQ—the antiscab laws, a new occupational health and safety regime, minimum standards of work, the Charter of the French Language, which protected the right of workers to use French in the workplace—and by the bargaining concessions made by the Lévesque administration during the 1979 round of public-sector collective bargaining. With the collapse of the PQ's independence project after the referendum, however, the situation changed abruptly and drastically. Not only did the defeat suffered by the "yes" campaign signal the demise of the Parti Québécois's constitutional option, it also prefigured the collapse of most of the social and economic policies pursued by the Lévesque administration from 1976 to 1980. After the referendum, it was no longer necessary to perform the delicate balancing act required before 1980 to reconcile the mutually antagonistic interests of various classes and class fractions in Québec, in the hopes of forging a pro-independence coalition in Québec.

The "Union-Nationalization" of the Parti Québécois, 1981–85

With its twin national and social projects virtually dead, the Parti Québécois underwent a startling metamorphosis, from a programmatic or mass party of the sort described by Maurice Duverger (1954:62–71), to a *parti comme les autres*. Its primary objectives after its surprising re-election in 1981 (which had a great deal to do with widespread satisfaction with Lévesque and his government's performance, combined with a distinct lack of enthusiasm for Claude Ryan[13]) were to cling to power, to defend Québec's interests as jealously as possible within the federal system, and to foster the development of francophone-owned businesses. Regarding this pro-business component of the PQ's new philosophy, Courchene (1986:7) claims that the Lévesque administration "became, after the referendum, the most business-oriented or market-oriented government in Canada." Karniol (1981:120) describes the Parti Québécois after the referendum as the "hero of francophone capitalism," having implemented or promised a welter of programs and incentives to promote the growth and productivity of small and medium-sized firms in the province, the so-called PME (*petites et moyennes entreprises*). These sweeping changes in the philosophy and style of intervention of the second Lévesque government reflected what some observers have called the "Union-Nationalization" of the Parti Québécois. Some critics found it deliciously ironic that the PQ government removed a statue of Maurice Duplessis from storage and erected it in a position of prominence in front of the National Assembly. The erstwhile champion of Swedish-style social democracy in an independent Québec, by the early 1980s, had been transmogrified into a latter-day version of the old Union Nationale, defending Québec's interests within federalism and bashing the unions when it was politically expedient to do so. The rehabilitation of the statue of the autocratic *chef* symbolized this shift in party ideology.

Along with an increased solicitude for the interests of francophone business, the Parti Québécois during its second mandate displayed a growing obsession with the size of the budget deficit, and began to make noises about the need to slash spending ruthlessly in order to restore some sanity to the province's finances. The PQ had been re-elected at the onset of the worst recession during the postwar period, and its fiscal margin for manoeuvre was restricted by the need to pay for the numerous concessions it had made to the Common Front during the 1979 round of negotiations. After 1981, wages and benefits paid to government employees were singled out by the new Parti Québécois as the principal cause of the government's budgetary woes.

Before the 1982–83 round of public-sector bargaining had even got underway, the Lévesque government passed legislation (Bills 70 and 105) that unilaterally opened up the collective agreements signed in 1979 and imposed wage cuts of up to 20 percent on some categories of workers. The government's feeble justification for this extraordinary breach of duly-signed contracts was that "during an economic crisis a social democratic government has the responsibility to spread out the effects of the crisis, just as it has the duty to share the collective wealth during a period of prosperity" (Chevrette, 1989). In a desperate move, therefore, the PQ tried to rob from the public-sector Paul (the "fat-cat," privileged government employees, or so the Lévesque administration's public relations campaign sought to portray them) to pay the private-sector Peter (all other wage-earners and tax-payers).[14]

Although most of the public-sector unions eventually succumbed to the Lévesque government's package of sticks (the threat of coercive measures implicit in Bills 70 and 105) and carrots (special provisions to increase the pay of the lowest categories of public-sector workers), the teachers walked off their jobs for three weeks in January and February 1983. This illegal strike was eventually ended by the enactment of Bill 111, which a highly respected political scientist labelled one of the most draconian pieces of legislation in Québec's history (Bergeron, 1984:158). The passage of Bill 111, by brutally severing the ties between the PQ and its strongest supporters, the public-sector workers, marked the beginning of the end for the Parti Québécois as a governing party. When Bill 111 was being debated, disgruntled civil servants milled about outside the National Assembly, burning Lévesque, Parizeau, et al. in effigy, and making a bonfire of their PQ membership cards. And just weeks after the teachers' strike was ended, a crowd of angry trade unionists interrupted a regional meeting of the PQ national council, and a number of ministers were roughed up in the melee. Despite the premier's false bravado—he welcomed the departure from his party of disaffected "radicals" and boasted that their loss would be more than offset by the arrival of "normal, ordinary" citizens as new members—the Parti Québécois never fully recovered from this confrontation. Its popularity in the polls plummeted, and in the next provincial election (held in 1985), the party's share of the vote among public-sector employees was almost 20 percent lower than it had been in 1981 (Blais and Crête, 1986:22–24). Membership levels in the PQ dropped precipitously, from over 200,000 in February 1982 to a mere 80,000 three years later (February 1985).[15]

The labour movement never really recovered from its bloodletting with the PQ, either. After having been one of the most dynamic and progressive forces in Québec politics in the 1970s, the trade unions lapsed into a profound organizational and ideological funk during the 1980s. Labour has been a marginal actor in Québec politics since 1982–83, incapable of mounting an effective challenge to the neoliberal winds sweeping through the province (manifested in the attempts to downsize the welfare state, increase market discipline, and integrate Québec into a North American free trade zone). It is as though two heavyweights, the PQ and labour, had pounded each other into unconsciousness in 1983, and left the ring wide open to new contenders (the Liberals and a supremely confident francophone business class). In effect, then, the PQ itself fired the first salvo in the neoliberal "counter-revolution" that has shaped political discourse and, to a lesser extent, political practice, in Québec since the mid-1980s.

In the years following the Bill 111 debacle, the Parti Québécois has gamely, if unconvincingly, tried to refurbish its social democratic image. In 1983 the party's *Centre d'animation politique* published a discussion paper entitled *Le Québec et le défi social-démocrate* (Parti Québécois, 1983). Larded with quotations from socialist intellectuals (André Gorz) and politicians (Michel Rocard), the document continues to speak glowingly about the prospects and accomplishments of tripartite concerted action in Québec (despite the unfortunate run-in with the public-sector unions, which receives nary a line of commentary) and links the realization of social democracy with the achievement of Québec sovereignty. The paper also urges social democrats in Québec, if they hope to have any impact on contemporary political and economic debates, to jettison their reflexive Keynesian attitudes and to come up with new ideas on how to create wealth, not merely redistribute it.[16] This sort of soul-searching and ideological retooling has been characteristic of most of the social democratic parties in the Western world during the 1980s, as they have scrambled to respond to the increasingly influential exponents of neoliberalism (who seek to roll back the frontiers of state intervention) and neoconservatism (a call for the return to traditional values and increased law and order to supplement the discipline of the marketplace). By the time *Le Québec et le défi social-démocrate* was published, however, it was painfully obvious that not many of the rapidly dwindling number of social democrats in Québec were listening to the Parti Québécois.

This is not to say that there were no committed social democrats in the Parti Québécois after 1982–83, for there were. Pauline Marois, a former minister of manpower and revenue security in Lévesque's cabinet, is one obvious example. Michel Bourdon, the former head of CSN-Construction, and Robert Dean, the former Québec director of the United Auto Workers union, are others. That social democrats such as these continue to work within the PQ is largely a testimony to the paucity of party alternatives from which to choose. There simply is *no other* credible left-wing party in Québec, and there has not been since the PQ appeared on the scene in the late 1960s. The provincial NDP, to take the most glaring example, despite a brief surge of popularity while Jean-Paul Harney was leader in the mid-1980s, is today little more than a rag-tag and pathetic organization, a monument to political irrelevance. Thus, if social democrats choose to work within the traditional party system, they are almost forced to opt for the Parti Québécois, *faute de mieux*.

Perhaps the greatest obstacle to any resurgence of the PQ's former commitment to social democracy lies in the person of the current party leader, Jacques Parizeau, on whom the label "social democrat" has never fit very comfortably. On many economic and social issues—North American free trade, user fees in the social services, and universal (or "*mur-à-mur*") welfare programs, to name three—Parizeau's views are virtually indistinguishable from those of his Liberal counterpart, Robert Bourassa. When the delegates to the PQ's 1988 national convention passed a number of interventionist and pro-labour resolutions, including one that called for increased welfare benefits for the young and another endorsing an active manpower policy inspired by Swedish practice (sponsored by Robert Dean), Parizeau appeared to repudiate the convention's decisions in his closing remarks. Emphasizing the need to temper the party's rhetorical commitment to social democracy with fiscal realism, Parizeau claimed that he had spent thirty years in public life trying to raise Québec's rate of economic growth, and that he was not about to fight an election on a promise to lower it—which, he contended, would be the inevitable outcome of some of the more interventionist resolutions passed by the convention.[17]

Such are the ambiguities of the Parti Québécois's version of social democracy in the 1980s and 1990s. Since 1985, when faced with the choice between an unambiguously pro-business party, the Liberals, and a party like the PQ, which gives out very mixed signals, many of Québec's voters have opted for the former. One of the PQ's biggest challenges in the foreseeable future will be to define an electoral constituency that is distinct from that of the Liberals, and to formulate a socioeconomic program capable of mobilizing this group. The party is still a long way from doing this.

Looking Back to the Future: The Parti Québécois and the Resurgence of Nationalism

In contrast to the Parti Québécois's increasingly fuzzy thinking on economic and social matters since the mid-1980s, its position on the constitutional question has become progressively clearer during the same period, to the point where it is now a virtual reprise of the hard-line stance it held in the early 1970s. But getting to this relatively unambiguous position in favour of sovereignty for Québec, with no guarantee of an economic association with English Canada, has not been a linear process. It has also exacted a heavy toll on party unity.

The evolution of the PQ's constitutional thinking since the referendum has passed through four distinct phases. The first, encompassing the period from its re-election in 1981 to the defeat of the Liberals in the 1984 federal election, found the Parti Québécois on the defensive, forced to react to the Trudeau government's attempt to patriate the Canadian Constitution and entrench a charter of rights in it. When the so-called "Gang of Eight"—the provincial alliance opposed to the deal—crumbled, Québec was left as the sole opponent of Prime Minister Trudeau's package, without any power to veto it. In the wake of the patriation deal, Lévesque initially uttered some intemperate remarks about Québec having been "screwed" by Trudeau and the other provincial premiers. He hinted that outright independence (with no mention of an economic association with English Canada) was now the best option for Québec, and that the next provincial election should be fought on the question. But these remarks were clearly the product of Lévesque's anguish and humiliation, not a true indication of the direction he wanted the party to take. When the PQ convention, held in December 1982, adopted a hard line on independence, Lévesque was forced to backtrack, fearing that the PQ might become another *Rassemblement pour l'indépendance nationale* (RIN), a relatively marginal (never getting as much as 10 percent of the popular vote) but noisy advocate of unadorned independence in the mid-1960s (Fraser, 1984:309). Lévesque took the unusual step—Fraser called it "an embarrassing display of personal blackmail by the leader" (1984:313)—of holding an internal party referendum to "clarify" the PQ's position on sovereignty-association and the means of achieving it. Sardonically referred to in the press as the "Renérendum," this plebiscite achieved its ostensible purpose of softening the PQ's stance on independence, of bringing it closer to the traditional option of sovereignty-association, although an economic association with English Canada was no longer a *prerequisite* for Québec's sovereignty. But the costs of this process, on party unity and effectiveness, were exceedingly high.

The second phase of the PQ's post-referendum constitutional thinking began with the victory of Brian Mulroney and the Progressive Conservatives in the 1984 federal election, a victory that was aided by a tacit alliance between the Parti Québécois and the Tories in many Québec ridings. Immediately after the election, Lévesque uttered the delphic remark that negotiating with the new government—and thereby postponing yet again the achievement of sovereignty-association—would involve a "beautiful risk." Within a couple of months of the Tory victory, Lévesque and the most important moderate in the PQ, Pierre-Marc Johnson, had completely repudiated the party convention's decision of 1982 to fight the upcoming election on sovereignty. This *volte-face* precipitated a schism within the party, as the hard-line advocates of independence, the so-called *orthodoxes*, either renounced their party membership or resigned from the National Assembly altogether. More than a quarter of the PQ cabinet resigned, including such heavyweights as Jacques Parizeau, Camille Laurin, Jacques Léonard, and Denis Lazure (Fraser, 1984:365).

This rupture in the Parti Québécois was followed in short order by Lévesque's resignation from the leadership in 1985. His departure was ostensibly for health reasons: Lévesque's behaviour during the months following the schism had been increasingly erratic, betraying a profound mental and physical exhaustion. He was succeeded by Pierre-Marc Johnson, who had done very little to conceal the fact that he coveted the premier's job. This inaugurated the third phase of the Parti Québécois's constitutional thinking, during which the party embraced the nebulous and singularly uninspiring notion of *national affirmation*. According to a party document (Parti Québécois, 1987:7–8), the PQ "proposes a process of national affirmation ... in order that Québec again takes the offensive and advances further along the route to sovereignty." Because the party was defeated by the Liberals in the 1985 provincial election, however, Pierre-Marc Johnson had very little time in which to flesh out this concept, which sounded suspiciously like a throwback to the old Union Nationale's defensive nationalism of the 1940s and 1950s.

Johnson did not remain leader of the PQ for very long. He was ousted in a *putsch* in late 1987, just a few weeks after René Lévesque's death had rekindled the smouldering embers of nationalism in the province. Committed *indépendantistes* such as Gérald Godin and Louise Harel compared the bland, technocratic and crypto-federalist policies of Johnson with those of his predecessor and found him wanting. Not wishing to spark the second schism within two years in the PQ, Johnson resigned as leader. He was replaced by the darling of the orthodox faction, Jacques Parizeau.[18] This ushered in the fourth phase of the PQ's post-referendum constitutional thinking, which essentially consisted of a relatively straightforward commitment to sovereignty for Québec. Parizeau succeeded in having inserted into the PQ program a commitment to a "clear and democratic process" for declaring sovereignty, but the ultimate objective of independence was still hedged in with qualifications and contingencies (Parti Québécois, 1989:7). During the 1989 provincial election, Parizeau raised the possibility, if his party were elected, of holding a series of referendums on the repatriation of various state powers from the federal government—death to Confederation by a thousand cuts, instead of in one cataclysmic confrontation.

This position has become even more straightforward in the wake of the rejection of the Meech Lake Accord in June 1990. In a separate comment included as an addendum to the Bélanger-Campeau Report on Québec's political and constitutional future (Commission sur l'avenir politique et constitutionnel du Québec, 1991:95–96), the Parti Québécois states that the best solution to the existing constitutional impasse is sovereignty for Québec, which "is viable and can be achieved in an orderly manner." The PQ calls for a referendum to be held as soon as possible on the question of sovereignty; the issues of economic association, a common currency with English Canada, and so on, are to be resolved *after* sovereignty has been proclaimed.

Future Prospects for the Parti Québécois

While it may be true that the Parti Québécois has aged "poorly," as René Lévesque implied in his *Memoirs*, in a sense it is remarkable that the party has been able to survive at all. Not too long ago, many pundits were confidently predicting the party's demise, either through a prolonged hemorrhage of its most dynamic members or its absorption into a right-of-centre nationalist party (possibly led by Lucien Bouchard, according to speculation in the late 1980s). However, considering that the Parti Québécois in its formative years was as much a full-fledged social movement as it was a traditional political party, interested in changing the world and not merely in exercising power, mere survival has not been enough to dispel the lingering disappointment and melancholy that now afflicts many of the party's former members.

This sense of disappointment and melancholy among the PQ rank and file is bound to be exacerbated by the recent (May 1992) revelations that Claude Morin, one of the key figures in the party up to 1982 and the principal architect of the *étapiste* strategy for achieving independence, had acted as a paid informant for the RCMP in the mid-1970s. Morin attempted to justify his apparent duplicity by claiming that he had acted as a sort of double agent, in order to cull information from the RCMP on *péquiste* sympathizers or militants who were being targeted by the federal security service. In this way, Morin argued, he succeeded in warning a number of people who were the targets of secret surveillance; moreover, he was able to play the part of Santa Claus by donating the money he received from the RCMP (above and beyond his "expenses") to various unnamed charities or Parti Québécois riding associations.

Only the most credulous aficionados of spy fiction seem willing to buy Morin's line. The damage that these startling revelations will eventually cause to the Parti Québécois, in terms of increased cynicism and disillusionment among its members, is quite likely incalculable. Those who are prone to believe that reality is often stranger than a Le Carré novel might well be asking themselves why this information about Morin surfaced at the particular time that it did: Might it have had something to do with the laborious negotiations on Canada's and Québec's constitutional futures? Perhaps some future royal commission will have to sort out this and other questions like it.

THE QUÉBEC LIBERAL PARTY, FROM BOURASSA TO BOURASSA

The story of the Québec Liberal Party since 1976 has two main themes. The first is the astonishing political comeback of Robert Bourassa to regain the party leadership in 1983. This was the same individual who had been widely vilified as the "most hated man in Québec" only seven years earlier, when the Liberals had gone down to a crushing defeat at the hands of the Parti Québécois. The second theme has been the party's gradual drift toward a quasi-*indépendantiste* position on the question of Québec's constitutional future. This shift in party ideology (if this is not too strong a word to describe the very loose set of principles to which the party is committed) has, for the most part, been a belated response to changing public opinion, as the Liberal Party, a quintessentially opportunistic and electoralist organization, has sought to keep up with the increasingly mercurial voters.

The Ryan Years

Graham Fraser (1984:136) writes that when Robert Bourassa hastily resigned as leader of the Québec Liberal Party immediately after the 1976 election debacle, and fled to a self-imposed exile in Europe, he left behind "a demoralized, disorganized, rudderless rump." Certain key figures in the party sought to recruit a new leader who would dispel the bad memories of the Bourassa years, memories of corruption, vacillation (during the October Crisis, and over the Victoria Charter), and the triumph of style over substance (symbolized by Bourassa's personal retinue, which included a hairdresser/bodyguard). Claude Ryan, the ascetic and intellectual publisher of *Le Devoir,* was the person that the Liberals eventually recruited. He handily defeated his only rival for the position, Raymond Garneau, the former minister of finance in Bourassa's cabinet, at a leadership convention in April 1978.

Ryan achieved the leadership despite some obvious political disabilities: a wooden and ponderous manner, a strong sanctimonious and authoritarian streak, and a penchant for vindictiveness that undermined the Liberals' frantic search for party unity.[19] Even more worrisome, for Liberals who styled themselves committed federalists, was the fact that Ryan, in a *Le Devoir* editorial, had urged voters to support the PQ in the 1976 election. In some party quarters, there were grave doubts about the depth of Ryan's commitment to federalism.

The worries about Ryan's aptitude for partisan politics, it turned out, were well founded. Ryan never seemed very comfortable in his new role, and patently failed to excite or capture the imagination of Québec's voters. During his tenure as leader, the party moved further toward a highly decentralized, but still recognizably federalist position on the constitutional question (see Québec Liberal Party, 1980). But in the crucial referendum debate, Ryan was first overshadowed by the passionately articulate advocates of sovereignty-association in the PQ government, and then eclipsed by the federal Liberal "heavy artillery"—Trudeau, Chrétien, and Lalonde, among others—which was brought into the campaign in a desperate bid to secure a win for the "no" side. Ryan then sleepwalked through the 1981 provincial election, seemingly convinced that the referendum victory would automatically translate into an election win. His convincing defeat at the hands of Lévesque and the Parti Québécois brought to an abrupt end his tenure as leader, and he was ultimately succeeded by the man he himself had replaced, Robert Bourassa, the "Rocky" of Québec politics (he has made fewer comebacks than the cinematic hero, but against similar odds).

Bourassa Renascent

With Bourassa's return to the leadership in 1983,[20] the Liberal Party program once again became dominated by economic issues, especially the need to ensure economic growth and to scale down the bloated provincial state. In a working paper published just prior to the 1985 provincial election, the party warned that the welfare state should not "kill personal initiative by trying to manage everything.... [T]he government should stop taking the place of individuals as initiators of development. Instead of levelling social aspirations and trying constantly to play the role of leader, the government should encourage pluralism and diversity" (Québec Liberal Party, 1985:11, 13; my translation). Elsewhere in this document, the party decried the "bureaucratic inflation" that has throttled Québec's political life during the past few years, and inveighed against the overregulation of citizens' lives that ultimately "tramples on individual liberties, restricts the rights of property, and discourages individual initiative" (Québec Liberal Party, 1985:94). The party promised to establish a task force on deregulation once it was in power.

In addition to this enduring economic obsession (which reflected the preoccupations of its leader, Robert Bourassa), the Liberal Party of 1985 exhibited a willingness to relax the restrictive language laws in Québec. In an interview with *Maclean's* immediately after his assumption of the leadership, Bourassa remarked:

> At least 95 per cent of francophone Quebecers want to make Bill 101 more flexible and eliminate its abuses. We must return to common sense. On signs, French could be obligatory and all other languages discretionary.... The law has to be made more flexible but it also has to be applied with more understanding. (Deshaies, 1983)

Bourassa reiterated his commitment to relaxing some of the provisions in the Charter of the French Language after his party had easily defeated the Parti Québécois in the 1985 election.[21] In particular, the prohibition on the use of any language other than French in commercial signs was singled out as unnecessary. Nowhere "in the free world," Bourassa claimed, "is there a country where the minority is prohibited from using its own language on its signs" (cited in Scowen, 1991:36). Bourassa would soon regret having made this comment.

On both of the major themes outlined in the Québec Liberal Party's election program in 1985—the conversion to neoliberal economic doctrine and the relaxation of language policy, in a way that would better balance individual rights against the legitimate aspirations of the francophone collectivity—the Bourassa government's actual accomplishments were either disappointingly timid or, in the case of language laws, an outright repudiation of election promises. On the economic front, the new Bourassa government gave every indication of launching a Québec version of the Reagan/Thatcher revolution. Prominent members of Québec's rising francophone bourgeoisie—Pierre Fortier (an engineer who had worked for the SNC Group), Pierre MacDonald (Bank of Montreal), and Paul Gobeil (formerly of Provigo, the supermarket chain and retail holding company), for example—were named to the cabinet in 1985. Three task forces were set up by the new government in early 1986 to make recommendations on deregulation, privatization, and government reorganization. All three tabled their final reports by June 1986.[22] Among the principal recommendations of the three task forces were:

a) the abolition of a host of consultative committees and other government agencies (*l'Office de planification et de développement du Québec*, and the *Institut national de productivité*, to name just two);

b) decentralization of the administration and financing of the educational and health systems;

c) adoption of a voucher system in education, whereby parents would be able to choose whatever school, public or private, they considered best able to meet the needs of their children;

d) privatization of small and medium-sized hospitals in Québec, along with the creation of a new type of medical centre, patterned after the Health Maintenance Organizations in the United States;

e) adoption of a guaranteed annual income plan;

f) harmonization of Québec's antiscab laws with existing measures in other provinces (which, in effect, would prohibit only the use of professional strike-breakers);

g) deregulation of Québec's construction industry;

h) privatization of ten crown corporations, which had outlived their original purpose (promotion of francophone managers, pursuit of economic nationalism) and turned in a mediocre financial performance.[23]

Courchene (1987:40–41) has noted that these three reports did not receive an overly warm welcome from the Québec public. In fact, among some sectors of the population—those targeted for drastic cutbacks, most notably—the sweeping calls for a return to market discipline, scaled-down government, and deregulation incited a small-scale panic. Nonetheless, Courchene concluded that the recommendations were a much-needed tonic for Québec's economy, and that they represented one way (among others, which he left unspecified) of restructuring the relationship between the individual and the state, a process that was then occurring in almost all advanced industrialized democracies.

Premier Bourassa, the embodiment of the cautious, consensus-seeking politician, did not proceed on these task force recommendations with undue haste, it should be noted. In 1986, the *Raffinerie du sucre du Québec* was sold to private interests, as were, eventually, Québécair, Madelipêche, and some of the holdings of the *Société nationale de l'amiante*. In addition, a number of consultative councils and other government agencies (the *Conseil des Arts du Québec*, for instance, and the *Institut national de productivité*) were abolished. However, these hardly constituted bold steps toward the neoliberal paradise sketched out in the Fortier Report. Moreover, what might be called the "big-ticket" items in the three task force reports—the softening of the antiscab laws, sweeping deregulation and privatization, a guaranteed annual income—are yet to be implemented. In fact, on the question of the antiscab laws, which have frequently raised the ire of the business community in Québec, Premier Bourassa announced that nothing would be done to weaken their impact, for fear of endangering "social peace"—a euphemistic way of saying that he did not wish to antagonize the labour movement on this particular issue (Rouillard, 1989:161).

In short, the neoliberal counter-revolution trumpeted by Liberal Party leaders in the 1985 election campaign, and fleshed out in the Fortier, Gobeil, and Scowen reports, has amounted to something less than a headlong stampede toward unadulterated Thatcherism or Reaganism. More than anything else, implementation of the most radical proposals contained in the task force reports has been blocked by Robert Bourassa's natural inclination to compromise on important issues and to avoid controversy as much as possible. Perhaps symptomatic of the timid swing toward neoliberalism during Bourassa's first term in office (1985–89) was the fact that the three best-known representatives of the new francophone bourgeoisie— Fortier, MacDonald, and Gobeil—all abandoned their political careers before the 1989 election and returned to the private sector. Daniel Latouche wrote caustically of these apostles of laissez-faire: "The market maniacs who so dominated the Bourassa government between 1986 and 1989 are gone, victims of the mess they created and their desire for more money and better limousines" (Resnick and Latouche, 1990:101). And while the allure of the astronomical salaries they could earn in the private sector might well have been one of the factors behind their decision to abandon politics, another was undoubtedly their frustration at the snail-like pace of change preferred by the professional politicians in the Liberal Party.

It would not be entirely accurate to dismiss Bourassa's first term in office as a mere "hiccup" in the neoliberal counter-revolution launched by the Parti Québécois after 1981. For if Bourassa shied away from the more radical measures in the task force reports, his government has nonetheless accelerated the process of redefining the vocabulary of Québec politics that was begun by the PQ. *All* of the major parties in the province are now more interested in creating wealth than in redistributing it. All recognize the primacy of private enterprise, and the subordinate or supplementary role that the provincial state must play in the economy. All are preoccupied by the excessively bureaucratic nature of the welfare state, and are seeking ways of rendering the social welfare apparatus more sensitive to individual needs.[24] But in every case, Bourassa's Liberals have merely continued the trend away from *étatisme* and interventionism that began during the Parti Québécois's second term in office.

The remarkable continuity between the economic policies of the Parti Québécois and those of Robert Bourassa's Liberal government is nowhere more apparent than in the area of labour relations, particularly public-sector labour relations. When he was re-elected leader of the Liberals in 1983, Bourassa had this to say about the poisonous labour relations climate in Québec's public and parapublic sectors:

> If the PQ wants to fight an election on the issue of labor relations I can hardly wait. The people no longer want this tradition of civil disobedience which has existed in Quebec for the past 20 years. We are the only civilized society to live in a climate of broken contracts, violated special legislation, injunctions which are scoffed at, and illegal strikes in the essential services. This tradition has ruined me as it has ... Lesage and ... Johnson. It will also ruin Lévesque. We have to put an end to the parallel power of the unions. (Deshaies, 1983:19)

Bourassa's prediction about the harmful effect that labour relations would have on the PQ's prospects for re-election was right on target. But the new Liberal government did not have to undertake many new initiatives on its own after the 1985 election to curb the "parallel power of the unions." That had already been done by the Parti Québécois itself, through its rollbacks of public-sector wages in the early 1980s (Bills 70 and 105), its internecine conflict with the teachers' unions in the winter of 1982–83, and its enactment of legislation (Bill 37) just before it left office that decentralized the bargaining regime in the public sector and drastically limited the right to strike. The impact of this new legislation was to hasten the decline in union solidarity that had begun with the events of 1982–83. As a result, the 1986 round of public-sector bargaining was the most peaceful and most uneventful in the last twenty years.

Labour policy (along with the language question, as we shall see below), however, has always been something of an Achilles heel for Robert Bourassa throughout his political career. And Bourassa's mishandling of public-sector negotiations in 1989 may well have served to breathe new life into a previously demoralized and disorganized labour movement. Many observers suspected that one of the reasons that Bourassa called a provincial election for September 25, 1989 was to secure a strong mandate before negotiations in the public sector heated up. Bourassa did not expect too many problems during this round of bargaining, what with the provincial economy humming along and public opinion still quite leery of the excessive power of "big labour." But the Liberal government's calculations were upset by the actions of one group that is gaining quite a reputation for militancy across Canada: the nurses. When the nurses walked off their jobs during the election campaign to support their demands for better pay—as a group, nurses in Québec then earned less than their counterparts in any other province, except for New Brunswick—public opinion surprisingly swung behind the workers, and not the government. The nurses' union was able to gain public support for its actions—all the more remarkable since its strike was technically illegal (conciliation not yet having taken place)—by drawing attention to the yawning gap between the occupational responsibilities of nurses and their poor working conditions and low pay, their comparatively low status in relation to other health-care professionals, and their continuing exclusion from the material benefits of Bourassa's vaunted economic revolution. Whether this particular conflict will serve as a catalyst for the rest of the labour movement is at best a dubious proposition, however, inasmuch as the public still has a fairly jaundiced view of organized labour in general. But one ought not to underestimate Bourassa's capacity for breathing new life into previously dormant movements, as his handling of both the nurses' strike and the language issue after 1985 attests.

It was noted earlier that Bourassa and the Liberals campaigned openly in the 1985 provincial election on a promise to relax some of the more irritating aspects of Bill 101. The latter's prohibition on the use of any language other than French in commercial signs was singled out as needlessly oppressive, and unnecessary in a mature, civilized society. Public opinion, even among francophones, seemed to be receptive to bilingual commercial signs. However, since this provision of the Charter of the French Language had already been challenged as unconstitutional—an infringement of the freedom of expression guaranteed under the Charter of Rights and Freedoms—and the case was still before the Québec Court of Appeal, the Bourassa government decided to take no action until a decision had been handed down. But it did take the important symbolic step of passing Bill 142 in December 1986, which guaranteed the right of every English-speaking person "to receive health services and social services in the English language, taking into account the organization and resources of the establishments providing such services..." (Lois du Québec, 1986: ch. 106, s. 5.1).

When the Québec Court of Appeal handed down its decision on December 22, 1986, ruling unanimously that the prohibition on bilingual commercial signs was unconstitutional, the Bourassa government "did not act as it had promised. Instead, it decided to appeal the decision again, this time to the Supreme Court of Canada. With the benefit of hindsight, one can see that any changes to the signs legislation were probably doomed from that day onward" (Scowen, 1991:39). By waiting for two years while the Supreme Court deliberated, the Bourassa government effectively abdicated responsibility for language policy to an increasingly vocal minority opposed to any alteration of Bill 101, which by 1988 had assumed sacrosanct status. With their rallying cry of "Ne touchez pas à la Loi 101," this group succeeded in painting Bourassa into a very cramped corner (of course, the premier's penchant for vacillating and avoiding controversial decisions had already put him there). When the Supreme Court confirmed the lower court decision on the unconstitutionality of this section of Bill 101, the widespread public support for relaxing some of the more intrusive aspects of the language law, which had existed only two years earlier, had by then evaporated.

Bourassa's attempted solution to the language crisis of 1988 was more than a little reminiscent of his earlier botched effort to defuse linguistic tensions in the province, Bill 22 (passed in 1974). Bill 178, hastily enacted in the wake of the Supreme Court decision, and passed with the help of the "notwithstanding" clause in the Canadian Charter of Rights and Freedoms, resembled Bill 22 in that both were compromises that failed abysmally to secure the support of either the militant francophone nationalists or the English community in the province. Bill 178, the so-called "inside/outside" law, permitted the use of English on signs *inside* a commercial establishment, but prohibited any language other than French on signs placed *outside* a store (this in order to preserve the *visage français* of Québec, which had been one of Camille Laurin's fundamental objectives when he first introduced Bill 101 into the National Assembly).

The adoption of Bill 178 precipitated a small schism in the Liberal Party, as three senior English-speaking cabinet ministers—Richard French, Herbert Marx, and Clifford Lincoln—resigned from the government. In his address to the National Assembly, Clifford Lincoln underscored the tension between the Liberal Party's ostensible devotion to individual rights and the commitment to the preservation of collective linguistic rights that is enshrined in Bills 101 and 178:

> In my belief, rights are rights are rights. There is no such thing as inside rights and outside rights. No such thing as rights for the tall and rights for the short. No such thing as rights for the front and rights for the back, or rights for East and rights for West. Rights are rights and always will be rights. There are no partial rights. Rights are fundamental rights. (Québec, Assemblée nationale, 1988:4417)

And lest anyone think that this compromise was terribly popular among francophone nationalists, one need only listen to the imprecations Daniel Latouche uttered against the law: "Bill 178 [is] the most ridiculous piece of legislation ever passed in Canada. It turns Québec into a linguistic Disneyland, French on the outside and English inside.... It takes us back twenty years" (Resnick and Latouche, 1990:89).

Not only did Bill 178 fail to resolve linguistic tensions in Québec, it contributed to the subsequent unravelling of the Meech Lake Accord in June 1990. Many English-speaking Canadians detected in the legislation a simple desire for *revenge*,[25] and wondered out loud why efforts at bilingualism should be made outside Québec when that province was implementing restrictive and seemingly vindictive measures against the minority language. To be sure, at least some of this outrage was purely hypocritical, given that English Canada's treatment of its francophone minorities has hardly been exemplary. Nonetheless, Bill 178, along with the closed and elitist process of bargaining that characterized the entire Meech Lake debacle, has to be considered one of the principal causes of the failure of the accord.

In the aftermath of the failure of the Meech Lake pact, the Québec Liberal Party's position on constitutional matters has undergone a pronounced radicalization, bringing it much closer to the Parti Québécois's traditional stance on such issues. The Liberal Party's constitutional committee issued its position paper on Québec's future place in Confederation, *A Québec Free to Choose*, in January 1991 (Québec Liberal Party, 1991; the document is better known as the Allaire Report, after the chairman of the party's constitutional committee). Affirming that Canada, "in its present form, can only lead ... to a constitutional, political, and even financial and economic impasse," the document calls for a radical decentralization of powers in the federal system. Under the Allaire Report's proposals, which were adopted as party policy at a convention in March 1991, the provinces would assume control over most of the important economic and social functions currently under federal jurisdiction (unemployment insurance, manpower and formation, culture and communications, income security, as well as others). Ottawa would be left with exclusive control only over defence, customs and tariffs, currency, and equalization. The increased powers of the provinces would require "major fiscal rearrangements.... The central government's tax base will be revised and its budgetary practices made subject to institutional constraints, including setting targets designed to severely limit its deficits and restrict its taxation powers.... One of the objectives will be to reduce substantially the size of the central government" (Québec Liberal Party, 1991:38–39). The report calls for a referendum to be held by the fall of 1992 on Québec sovereignty, if negotiations with English Canada for a new deal fail.

Along with its proposals for a sweeping change in the balance of power between Ottawa and the provinces, the Allaire Report is remarkable for its similarity, in tone and analysis, to the Parti Québécois government's White Paper on sovereignty-association, published in 1979 (Québec, Conseil exécutif, 1979). Like the PQ document, the Allaire Report's analysis of the evolution of Canadian federalism is heavily indebted to the Tremblay Report of the 1950s. All three rail against the federal government's ruthless centralization of power and its brazen invasion of provincial spheres of authority. All three make liberal use of the compact theory of Confederation to justify Québec's claim to distinct society status. All three claim that the overlapping jurisdictions inherent in Canadian federalism, and Ottawa's lack of understanding of the regions, are the root cause of the constitutional impasse. Graham Fraser (1991:A15) incisively noted that the Allaire

Report has "much ... in common with the white paper on sovereignty-association produced by the PQ government in 1979. The two documents have a virtually identical reading of Canadian history.... [T]he Liberal Party of Quebec has gone from an essentially federalist logic to one that, regardless of its specific recommendations, leads inexorably to Quebec independence."

The Liberal Party's position on sovereignty during the two years or so immediately after the defeat of the Meech Lake Accord might best be characterized by paraphrasing Mackenzie King's infamous exercise in equivocation: sovereignty if necessary, but not necessarily sovereignty. An editorial cartoon by Bado in *Le Devoir* shortly after the release of the Allaire Report neatly encapsulated the differences in the Parti Québécois' and the Liberals' positions on Québec's constitutional future. Bearing the caption "The Road to Sovereignty," the artist depicts Jacques Parizeau and Robert Bourassa holding aloft what look like traffic indicator signs. On Parizeau's is a simple, straight arrow; on Bourassa's, an unintelligible squiggle, leading in all directions at once, but ultimately arriving at the same destination as Parizeau's. This was probably a fair assessment of the two parties' positions, at least until the summer of 1992, when Bourassa finally "came out of the closet," as it were, and publicly avowed his faith in renewed federalism. But Bourassa's belated conversion to the cause of revamping Confederation, along the lines set out in the complicated *Consensus Report on the Constitution* (dubbed the "Charlottetown Accord" by the media), has alienated the many nationalists within his caucus and the Québec Liberal Party organization. Jean Allaire, the principal author of the report that served as the basis for much of the Bourassa government's constitutional negotiating strategy in the post-Meech period, has repudiated the premier's decision, as has the militant youth wing of the party. Party unity has thus been shattered at a time when it is most essential: in the months leading up to the October referendum, which is to be held *not* on the issue of Québec sovereignty as originally envisaged in Bill 150, but on whether to accept the new package of constitutional reforms cobbled together by Joe Clark and the first ministers.

The increasingly nationalist stance adopted by the Liberals after their 1985 election win succeeded in alienating one of the party's most faithful constituencies: the anglophone community. This important bloc of voters has traditionally been unwavering in its commitment to federalism, and has also tended to emphasize individual over collective rights. Bourassa's mishandling of the issue of bilingual signs, therefore, and his cosying up to the Parti Québécois on constitutional matters, were difficult for Québec's anglophones to stomach. In 1989, as a result of Bourassa's perceived "betrayal" of anglophones, a new English-rights party appeared on the scene in Québec. This represented the most significant break in the past decade in the dominant trend of ideological convergence in Québec politics. The next section of this article examines the causes and consequences of the creation of the Equality Party.

THE EQUALITY PARTY: STEPCHILD OF BILL 178

Québec's English community, quite understandably, felt betrayed by the Bourassa government's reneging on its election promise to allow bilingual commercial signs, and by its use of the Charter's "notwithstanding" clause to pass Bill 178. In 1989, with a provincial election in the offing, two English-rights parties, the Equality Party and the Unity Party, were formed, the former centred in Montréal, the latter in rural Quebec (Scowen, 1991:101). In the November 1989 election, the Equality Party won four seats, all in the heavily English-speaking ridings of west-end Montréal. No one in the new party,[26] however, had the status, credibility, or visibility of the departed anglophone ministers in Bourassa's cabinet—Messrs. French, Marx, and Lincoln. This lack of *presence*, and the inexperience of the party's young leader, Robert Libman, have continued to hobble the Equality Party since the 1989 election.

Two other factors militate against the long-term success of the Equality Party. In the first place, it remains very much a tiny rump of anglophone politicians in the public mind, especially since it has been unable to seize on any issue other than language rights and individual liberties. Apart from a brief flurry of publicity that attended Libman's decision to divulge, under cover of parliamentary immunity, the details of "secret" contracts between Hydro-Québec and a number of industrial consumers (mainly aluminum and magnesium smelting plants), the Equality Party has not succeeded in convincing the electorate that it is deeply interested in anything other than minority-language rights. This suspicion is confirmed by a perusal of party literature, which devotes considerable attention to constitutional matters, and neglects broader economic concerns (see Equality Party, 1991).

The second factor likely to limit the Equality Party's future effectiveness is the obvious lack of party unity. Richard Holden, probably the best known of the four Equality MNAs, has had a running feud with the party leader, Robert Libman, almost from the moment the two were elected. This culminated in a nasty public squabble between the two in October 1991, after which the party expelled Holden from the caucus. At issue was Holden's decision to leak to the press a memorandum he had written on the subject of the Equality Party's continuing ineffectiveness. Entitled "Two Years Before the Mace," the document singled out the party leader, Libman, as the major reason for its inability to develop from a minor protest group into a viable political party. Holden further claimed that over half of the Equality Party's members are "disenfranchised Anglos" who are "anti-Québec" and have a "visceral hatred" for Premier Bourassa and everything he does (Peritz, 1991:A1).

Whether or not Holden is a gadfly and a loose cannon, as Libman has claimed,[27] it must be admitted that his memorandum points to the Equality Party's greatest weakness. It is simply not a credible party alternative for many voters in Québec, even those members of the English-speaking community who are bitterly resentful of the Bourassa government's waffling on linguistic policy. Unless the Equality Party can come up with a broad-based party program capable of addressing the pressing economic and social questions—beyond the issue of minority-language rights—that are confronting Québec, and unless it can attract candidates of stature, it is unlikely to have a very long life. And if the Bourassa government *does* relax certain irritants in existing language legislation, as it has hinted it might do, then the future for the Equality Party is even bleaker. All indications are, then, that most anglophone voters in Québec will gradually make their way back into the Liberal fold, for want of a credible partisan alternative.

CONCLUSION

The dominant trend in Québec party politics since the defeat of the referendum in 1980 has been the shift from ideological polarization to convergence. On economic and social issues, the Parti Québécois has moved closer to the Liberals' traditional territory: both now extol the virtues of the market and call for a dramatic scaling down of the state. Both, most tellingly, have become zealous apostles of North American free trade. This triumph of neoliberal doctrine in Québec parallels ideological developments that are occurring throughout the world, as the traditional Left is in retreat and disarray virtually everywhere. Though the PQ might protest that it has more of a social conscience than the Liberals, that its version of the new economic orthodoxy is both kinder and gentler than that of Bourassa and his business friends, this is cold comfort to those marginalized groups in society who are being left behind in the scramble to embrace the discipline of the market. In Québec, the poor, the marginal, and the powerless are now effectively disenfranchised, as both of the major parties seem eager to sacrifice their needs to the new gods of competitiveness and globalization.

On the national question, the Liberals surprised most observers by briefly abandoning their commitment to federalism after the rejection of the Meech Lake Accord in June 1990, in favour of a position that was scarcely distinguishable from that of the independence-minded Parti Québécois. Constancy, however, has never been one of Robert Bourassa's cardinal virtues. His decision in the summer of 1992 to support renewed federalism exacted a heavy toll on party unity, with Jean Allaire and the young Liberals publicly rejecting the premier's position. Despite Bourassa's return to the federalist fold, therefore, it would be premature at this point to speak of the end of the partisan convergence on the national question that has characterized Québec politics in the 1990s. What happens to Québec's party system after the referendum in October 1992, however, is strictly a matter for speculation.

NOTES

1. As Raymond Hudon (1984:314) observed of this period: "An increasing polarization between workers and employers has been the most significant development in Quebec over the last few decades, especially since the end of the 1960s. This polarization around the vision of Quebec as a society was accompanied by an outwardly comparable trend articulated around the vision of Quebec as a nation.... During the 1970s, this social polarization specifically echoed at the level of political parties through a strained opposition between the Parti Québécois and the Liberals."

2. John Porter, writing in the mid-1960s, lamented the fact that Canadian party politics lacked an ideological dimension, one that revolved around issues of class and the distribution of power in capitalist society. He argued that Canada was "one of the few major industrial societies in which the right and left polarization has become deflected into disputes over regionalism and national unity" (1965:369). Referring specifically to the disconcerting tendency of Canada's major parties to avoid hard issues, to try to be all things to all voters, Porter commented: "... to obscure social divisions through brokerage politics is to remove from the political system that element of dialectic which is the source of *creative politics*. The choice between genuinely radical and genuinely conservative traditions could mean a period of creative politics followed by a period of consolidation as conservatives and radicals oscillated in and out of office" (1965:374).

3. Gow (1985), among others, wondered whether Québec nationalism was a "spent force" in the mid-1980s. To his credit, he answered this rhetorical question with a cautious reminder to those in English Canada who were only too eager to inter Québec nationalism: "For the moment, nationalism is in a decline and relations between francophones and non-francophones are rela-

tively quiet. Events of the past thirty years should teach us not to be categorical in assessing the likely course of future events" (1985:625).

4. A term coined to describe the preferred strategy of the moderate faction within the Parti Québécois (led by Lévesque and Claude Morin, who acted as Minister of Intergovernmental Affairs in the first PQ cabinet) for achieving independence. The central tenet of this approach was that independence could only be achieved after a referendum gave the government a *mandate* to negotiate Québec's sovereignty with Ottawa. This allowed the party to divorce the action of voting for the PQ from support for sovereignty, a key tactical manoeuvre that helped ensure the PQ victory in the 1976 election. The radicals in the party had always maintained that the PQ ought to present itself as an unequivocally *indépendantiste* organization during election campaigns; for this faction, a vote for the PQ would be interpreted as a vote in favour of independence for Québec. This strategy, which was the dominant one before 1974, hindered the PQ's electoral chances, in the eyes of many outside observers and party strategists alike (see, especially, Hamilton and Pinard, 1977).

5. In an interview shortly after the PQ victory, Lévesque claimed that his government "must maintain a favourable prejudice toward workers [*un préjugé favorable aux travailleurs*]" (Lévesque, 1978:76).

6. The Rand Formula stipulates that "non-union employees in [a] bargaining unit must pay the union a sum equal to union fees as a condition of continuing employment. Non-union workers are not, however, required to join the union" (Labour Canada, 1984:18). For a discussion of the PQ's labour legislation during its first term in office, see Tanguay (1987–88).

7. French is quoting a comment made by Des Marais to the *Montreal Star*. The Employers Council to which French refers is the *Conseil du Patronat du Québec*, the most powerful business association in the province, and one of the most cohesive business groups in the entire country (see Coleman, 1985).

8. But they were vociferously opposed by the more militant *Confédération des syndicats nationaux* (CSN) and the teachers' federation, the *Centrale de l'enseignement du Québec* (CEQ). See Tanguay (1987–88:400–401).

9. In the Parti Québécois's most important economic policy statement during its first term in office (Québec, Ministère d'État au Développement économique, 1979:100), tripartite economic conferences are described as necessary for the emergence of "a national consciousness and a desire for concerted action among the economic agents...." This national consciousness, according to the government, was indispensable for Québec's economic, social, and cultural development.

10. This objective behind the PQ government's consensus-building strategy was perceptively noted by Normand Dugas (1980:11), who wrote a highly critical article on the Parti Québécois for the official publication of the teachers' federation, *Ligne directe*: "To listen to the Parti Québécois, it is the entire Quebec 'nation' that will say 'yes,' with a single voice, to the referendum. All groups in society are therefore invited to bury their sectional interests in order to be grafted onto the minimum of national solidarity so well defined by Premier Lévesque.... At the Lord's Table of the referendum, through a fusion that only nationalism can (or perhaps cannot) explain, one will find neither social classes ... nor divergent interests ... but simply the nation as a whole" (my translation).

11. For a good idea of the tensions that were created within the teachers' federation by the election of the PQ and its pursuit of a new social contract, see CEQ (1977).

12. The name given to the bargaining cartel of public-sector unions affiliated with the FTQ, CSN, and CEQ. First formed during the 1972 round of bargaining, the Common Front was born anew during each successive round, until the mid-1980s (when Bourassa and his Liberal Party returned to power after a nine-year hiatus).

13. See McRoberts (1988:343). According to a SORECOM poll cited by McRoberts, Lévesque was considered the party leader best able to govern by 50 percent of respondents, whereas only 23 percent endorsed Ryan.

14. In his inaugural address to open the first legislative session of his second government, Lévesque continually returned to the theme of the enormous gap between the wages and working conditions of public-sector employees and those of their private-sector counterparts. It was no longer ethical, he claimed, to demand that unorganized and less powerful sections of society (whose employers were "not as generous as the state") pay for the privileges of public-sector workers (Québec, Assemblée nationale, 1981:8).

15. On the precipitous slide in party membership, see Angell (1987:374). Not all of this drop can be attributed to disaffection over Bill 111, of course. Another factor in the PQ's declining popularity and vitality after 1981 was its ill-advised flirtation with the old Union Nationale's nebulous

constitutional option of "national affirmation," which certainly lacked the imaginative qualities necessary to revitalize the Parti Québécois as a mass political party (of which more below).

16. A position that echoed James Laxer's critique of federal NDP economic policy. See Laxer (1983).

17. The author was present at the convention as an observer. When the resolution on an active manpower policy was passed by the convention, in a tight vote, one delegate rose to say that she feared that the PQ would become a creature of the unions, just as the Liberals were the dupes of business. Her comments elicited a fair amount of applause from the delegates, indicating that not everyone in the party agrees with Robert Dean's contention that the trade unions are the PQ's natural allies.

18. Parizeau was unopposed for the leadership. Johnson had been elected using a new and ostensibly more democratic leadership selection device: a vote by all party members, instead of the customary delegated convention typical of almost all other political parties in Canada. Media pundits seemed to dislike the new process, dismissing it as "boring," but what it lacks in excitement it more than makes up for in the reduction of the opportunities for squalid vote-rigging that have marred the most recent leadership campaigns in the federal Liberal and Tory parties.

19. Fraser (1984:151) notes that Ryan ostracized Garneau and his supporters after the leadership campaign, leading Garneau, a capable and energetic politician, to resign from the party within a year of his defeat.

20. He easily defeated his two rivals, Daniel Johnson (Pierre-Marc's brother, and Liberal Party finance critic) and Pierre Paradis, a small-town lawyer who was once an organizer for the Union Nationale.

21. The Liberals took ninety-nine seats with 56 percent of the popular vote. The PQ won a mere twenty-three seats with 39 percent of the vote.

22. The three reports were: *De la Révolution tranquille ... à l'an deux mille* (Québec, Comité sur la privatisation, 1986), better known as the Fortier Report after its president, Pierre Fortier; *Rapports* (Québec, Groupe de travail sur la révision des fonctions et des organisations gouvernementales, 1986), or the Gobeil Report; and *Réglementer moins et mieux* (Québec, Groupe de travail sur la déréglementation, 1986), or the Scowen Report (after its president, Reed Scowen). For an analysis of the social and economic significance of these three reports, see Courchene (1987).

23. The ten state enterprises slated for privatization were:
Société générale de financement (SGF);
Société québécoise d'initiatives agro-alimentaires (SOQUIA);
Société québécoise d'exploration minière (SOQUEM);
Société québécoise d'initiatives pétrolières (SOQUIP);
Société de récupération, d'exploitation et de développement forestier du Québec (REXFOR);
Sidérurgie québécoise (SIDBEC);
Société québécoise des transports (SQT, which owned Québécair);
Société nationale de l'amiante (SNA);
Madelipêche;
Société des établissements de plein air du Québec.

24. The Rochon Report on health care, released in February 1988, was one very important contribution to the debate on making the welfare state less bureaucratic and alienating. See Bernard (1989:39–40).

25. Philip Resnick (Resnick and Latouche, 1990:24) wrote that he saw in Bill 178 "a simple desire for vengeance, for paying the Anglos back for their sins of omission and commission.... Would some bilingual signs in the Montreal districts of NDG or Snowdon with English lettering significantly smaller than the French really bring the edifice of French culture in Quebec crumbling down?" Interestingly, opinion among many francophone intellectuals has moved in a similar direction during the past year or so. In a recent editorial, for example, Lysiane Gagnon of *La Presse* questioned the need for Bill 178, and went on to claim that the law made the francophone majority look "so paranoid that it can't bear the sight of another language" (cited in Macpherson, 1991:B3).

26 The Unity Party merged with the Equality Party after the election, keeping the latter name as the official party label. See Scowen (1991:102).

27. Holden's startling decision in August 1992 to join the Parti Québécois (and the PQ's equally surprising willingness to accept him into the fold) would appear to confirm Libman's assessment.

REFERENCES

Angell, Harold. (1987). "Duverger, Epstein and the Problem of the Mass Party: The Case of the Parti Québécois." *Canadian Journal of Political Science* 20:2 (June), 363–78.

Bergeron, Gérard. (1984). *Pratique de l'État au Québec*. Montréal: Éditions Québec/Amérique.

Bernard, André. (1989). "Les politiques gouvernementales." In Denis Monière, ed., *L'Année politique au Québec, 1987–1988* (pp. 33–45). Montréal: Éditions Québec/Amérique. En collaboration avec *Le Devoir*.

Blais, André, and Jean Crête. (1986). "La clientèle péquiste en 1985: Caractéristiques et évolution." *Politique* 10 (Fall), 5–29.

Centrale de l'enseignement du Québec. (1977). *La main tendue et l'oeil ouvert: Réflexions pour une prise de position de la CEQ face au gouvernement du Parti Québécois*.

Chevrette, Guy. (1989). *Interview*. Québec City. May 31.

Clarke, H., J. Jenson, L. LeDuc, J. Pammett. (1991). *Absent Mandate*, 2nd ed. Toronto: Gage.

Coleman, William. (1985). "Québec Nationalism and the Organization of Business Interests." Paper prepared for the Conference on the Regional Organization of Business Interests and Public Policy, McMaster University, Hamilton, May 22–24.

Commission sur l'avenir politique et constitutionnel du Québec. (1991). *Report*. March.

Courchene, Thomas J. (1987). *Les offrandes des Rois mages: État-providence ou État providentiel?* C.D. Howe Institute.

_____. (1986). "Market Nationalism." *Policy Options* 7:8 (October), 7–12.

Deshaies, Guy. (1983). "Revelations from a second-life politician." *Maclean's*, October 24, 19.

Dugas, Normand. (1980). "Et si, en plus d'un pays le gouvernement réservait un syndicat aux travailleurs du Québec." *Ligne directe* 8:5 (April), 11–14.

Duverger, Maurice. (1954). *Political Parties*. Trans. B. North and R. North. London: Methuen.

Equality Party. (1991). *Final Version of Ratified Resolutions*. Montréal. March 17.

Fraser, Graham. (1991). "Radical proposals or borrowings from the past?" *The Globe and Mail*, February 5, A15.

_____. (1984). *PQ: René Lévesque and the Parti Québécois in Power*. Toronto: Macmillan.

French, Richard. (1985). "Governing Without Business: The Parti Québécois in Power." In V.V. Murray, ed., *Theories of Business-Government Relations* (pp. 159–80). Toronto: Trans-Canada Press.

Gow, J. Iain. (1985). "Quebec Nationalism in the 1980s: A Spent Force?" *Canadian Public Administration* 28:4 (Winter), 617–25.

Hamilton, Richard, and Maurice Pinard. (1977). "The Independence Issue and the Polarization of the Electorate: The 1973 Quebec Election." *Canadian Journal of Political Science* 10:2 (June), 215–59.

Hudon, Raymond. (1984). "Polarization and Depolarization of Quebec Political Parties." In Alain-G. Gagnon, ed., *Quebec: State and Society* (pp. 314–30).Toronto: Methuen.

Karniol, Robert. (1981). "Vive l'entreprise libre!" *Canadian Business* 54:9 (September), 120–26.

Labour Canada. (1984). *Glossary of Industrial Relations Terms*, 3rd ed. Ottawa: Minister of Supply and Services.

Laxer, James. (1983). *Rethinking the Economy*. Toronto: NC Press.

Lévesque, René. (1986). *Memoirs*. Trans. Philip Stratford. Toronto: McClelland and Stewart.

_____. (1978). *La Passion du Québec*. Montréal: Éditions Québec/Amérique.

Lois du Québec. (1986). *An Act to again amend the Act respecting health services and social services*. Chapter 106.

Macpherson, Don. (1991). "Undoing Bill 178." *The Gazette*, October 19, B3.

McRoberts, Kenneth. (1988). *Quebec: Social Change and Political Crisis*, 3rd ed. Toronto: McClelland and Stewart.

Parti Québécois. (1989). *Programme du Parti Québécois: Édition 1989*. Adopted at the special national convention, 25–27 November, Saint-Hyacinthe.

_____. (1987). *Parti Québécois*. Montréal: Permanence nationale. September.

_____. (1983). *Le Québec et le défi social-démocrate*.

Peritz, Ingrid. (1991). "Equality dumps Holden." *The Gazette*, October 12, A1.

Porter, John. (1965). *The Vertical Mosaic*. Toronto: University of Toronto Press.

Québec. Assemblée nationale. (1988). *Journal des Débats*. December 20, 4415–419.

_____. Assemblée nationale. (1981). *Journal des Débats*. November 9, 7–8.

_____. Comité sur la privatisation. (1986). *De la Révolution tranquille ... à l'an deux mille*. June. [Scowen Report].

_____. Groupe de travail sur la révision des fonctions et des organisations gouvernementales. (1986). *Rapports*. March and May. [Gobeil Report].

_____. Groupe de travail sur la déréglementation. (1986). *Réglementer moins et mieux*. June. [Scowen Report].

_____. Conseil exécutif. (1979). *Québec–Canada: A New Deal*. Éditeur officiel.

_____. Ministère d'État au Développement économique. (1979). *Bâtir le Québec: Énoncé de politique économique*. Éditeur officiel.

Quebec Liberal Party. (1991). *A Québec Free to Choose*. Report of the Constitutional Committee. January 28.

_____. (1985). *Maîtriser l'avenir. Programme politique*. February.

_____. (1980). *A New Canadian Federation*. Report of the Constitutional Committee.

Resnick, Philip, and Daniel Latouche. (1990). *Letters to a Québécois Friend*. Montréal and Kingston: McGill-Queen's University Press.

Rouillard, Jacques. (1989). "Le mouvement syndical." In Denis Monière, ed., *L'Année politique au Québec, 1987–1988* (pp. 149–64). Montréal: Éditions Québec/Amérique. En collaboration avec *Le Devoir*.

Salutin, Rick. (1989). *Waiting for Democracy*. Markham, Ont.: Viking.

Scowen, Reed. (1991). *A Different Vision*. Don Mills, Ont.: Maxwell Macmillan Canada.

Tanguay, A. Brian. (1990). "Canadian Party Ideologies in the Electronic Age." In Alain-G. Gagnon and James P. Bickerton, eds., *Canadian Politics: An Introduction to the Discipline* (pp. 129–57). Peterborough, Ont.: Broadview Press.

_____. (1987–88). "Business, Labor and the State in the 'New' Quebec." *American Review of Canadian Studies* 17:4 (Winter), 395–408.

Québec Unions in Politics, 1960–90

Roch Denis
Université du Québec à Montréal

and Serge Denis
Université d'Ottawa

INTRODUCTION

Québec unions face many difficult challenges as they enter the 1990s. With a million members, most belonging to one of the three major *centrales* or federations, the labour movement had barely recovered from the 1982 recession, at the time the most serious economic crisis since World War II, when a deep recession struck again in early 1991. The economic problems have rocked the foundations of the movement and shaken its traditions. Some say the unions are in an impasse. These developments coincide with a cooling of the special relationship the unions have enjoyed with the Parti Québécois since the late 1960s. Unions that may have viewed that party as a vehicle to represent them found themselves at the close of the 1980s virtually disoriented and without a political outlet; this too has added to the feeling of helplessness.

Is it possible at this point to draw up a balance sheet of these years? Over the last thirty years, the face of Québec trade unionism has been profoundly modified. The unions have developed from a minority movement into a national force capable of engaging in powerful economic and social actions, with a political weight that no party or government can henceforth ignore. But how did this development come about, and what are its distinguishing features? And how should we assess the current political situation of the labour movement, its perspectives in the medium term? These are the questions we wish to address in this chapter, after the brief analytical reminder that follows.

Political action by the labour movement is always a function of elements that are both indigenous and exterior to its own dialectic of development. For example, it is widely recognized that periods of profound economic difficulty thrust a major share of union activities in the direction of a political reorientation—a *reconversion politique*, as Georges Haupt (1981) describes it—even if the place and meaning of this adaptation are not immediately evident. Similarly, throughout the period that concerns us, the specific developments within Québec nationalism had a direct influence on the forms of workers' political action. Thus, in defining the organizational and political evolution of the unions we must take into account the major aspects of the social, economic, and political context that were reflected in their specific activities.

We note, however, that the labour movement relates to the state in two fundamental ways: first, on the economic plane, through struggles and more or less developed mechanisms of contact that bring the union organizations and the private or state bureaucracies into contact with each other; second, on the level of what could be termed direct political action, through participating in discussions of the general issues of the broader society, during election campaigns for example. Here we find two major trends in the North American union tradition: "nonpartisanship," which—paradoxically—may mean both failure to take a position and active support of a political formation that is not a product of the labour movement; and the so-called third-party orientation, in which the labour movement is summoned to play an initiating or supportive role in the formation of a political party mandated to represent its interests.

So "direct political action" may mean electing candidates sympathetic to the labour movement through the traditional parties, or it may mean taking power as such through the formation of an independent party, while the primary purpose of involvement in participation mechanisms is not to influence the composition of governments, but to orient the operations of particular governmental agencies in the direction of the interests and concerns of "organized labour."

ORGANIZATIONAL DEVELOPMENT

One of the first problems in any study of union political action is to draw connections between data that are not always approached interactively: for example, the evolution in the occupational composition of the employed labour force and the transformation of the general relations between the unions and the state. Similarly, it is necessary to assess the impact of organizational advances on immediate political practices, that is, the effects of the expansion per se of the unions on their political role.

Evolution of the Labour Movement Since 1945

If we draw a portrait of the occupational composition of the employed labour force, the most obvious phenomenon is, of course, the constant progression during the 1960s and 1970s of that sector of the work force concentrated in "services," particularly the public services. At the end of the war, workers in the "tertiary" sector (office, business, transportation, public service, etc.) accounted for 40 percent of the employees in Québec; by 1960 the proportion was 60 percent, by 1970 close to 66 percent, and in the 1980s it accounted for more than two-thirds of the work force (CSN-CEQ, 1984). Between 1945 and 1960, the labour force in the secondary sector remained steady at about 30 percent, while in the primary sector it declined from 25 percent to 10 percent, and was only 5 percent by the end of the 1970s when fewer than 30 percent of workers were employed in manufacturing and construction. It should be noted that while these transformations were taking place, the proportion of women in the work force increased from 30 percent in 1960 to about 33 percent in 1970 and more than 43 percent by 1990.

The overwhelming predominance of the service sector by the end of the 1980s is explained in particular by the expansion of schools, hospitals, and the civil service. For example, in six years alone, from 1960 to 1966, the number of hospital employees increased from about 50,000 to 100,000. Another significant change in the labour force was the remarkable increase in its educational level. In 1960 barely one-half of French-speaking youths had completed ninth grade, while in 1980 the proportion was 95 percent. The percentages for university graduates are 4 and 15 percent, respectively.

Contrary to what is sometimes thought, the concentration of the labour force in the service sector, particularly the public service, does not mean a decline in "manual labour" in favour of those categories of employees that might be combined under the heading of intellectual labour. In a study that specifically addresses this question, Brunelle and Drouilly showed that between 1971 and 1981 "the most significant growth was in manual occupations, which accounted for 69 percent of the total employment created during this period" (Brunelle and Drouilly, 1985:242). As we just noted, in 1981 the so-called tertiary sector accounted for more than two-thirds of the employed labour force in Québec, yet manual workers, all sectors combined, accounted for more than three-quarters of the total labour force. These data suggest that since World War II, and especially in the period we are studying, the employed labour force increased in Québec and extended mainly into the service sector, where most of the jobs created were manual. But the data are also significant in another respect.

If we take into account the fact that within the service sector a large proportion of the labour force was flowing into the public service, it will be observed that tens of thousands of new employees were now being placed in a direct relationship with the state (provincial or municipal governments, schools, hospitals, etc.) in terms of their wages and working conditions. What we were seeing in this mass phenomenon of the "public" employees was the establishment of a new reality—the state as employer or boss. This fact alone had major implications for what has been referred to as the tendency toward growing politicization of labour conflicts.

Emergence of a New Social Force

In 1945 there were 200,000 union members in Québec—20 percent of the work force. By 1960 the number of organized workers had almost doubled, to 375,000 or 30 percent of the work force. Ten years later, in 1970, the number had almost doubled again, to more than 700,000 or close to 40 percent—a remarkably high rate of unionization. In 1977 Québec had almost one million union members (about 900,000); the rate of unionization, after peaking at about 42 percent between 1971 and 1974, tended to fluctuate at around 35 percent in the early 1980s (Fleury, 1984:4; Rouillard, 1989:289), then rise again to 40 percent at the end of the decade, with one million members.

The relative decline in union membership in the early and middle 1980s stemmed from the shutdowns, redundancies, and increased unemployment resulting from the economic crisis that shook the economy. While average employment totals in Québec fell by 145,000 between 1981 and 1982, 73,000 of these positions were lost in the tertiary sector alone (Ingerman, 1983).

Between 1945 and 1960 the majority of Québec union members belonged to international and Canadian unions, and this is still the case today. The Catholic unions, the Confédération des travailleurs catholiques du Canada (Canadian and Catholic Confederation of Labour), which became the Confédération des syndicats nationaux (Confederation of National Trade Unions) in 1959–60, represented one in four union members up to the early 1960s. In the following years they managed to channel the huge wave of unionization that swept through the civil service and the hospitals into their ranks, and by 1970 they accounted for 30 percent of the Québec union membership, some 200,000 workers.

From 1960 to 1970 the membership of the Fédération des travailleurs du Québec (FTQ, or Québec Federation of Labour) grew from 100,000 to 200,000. By the end of the 1970s it was close to 300,000, and it continued to grow subsequently, reaching about 350,000 in the early 1980s and more than 425,000 in the latter half of the decade, according to FTQ figures. It then represented about 95 percent of the Québec membership of unions affiliated to the Canadian Labour Congress (membership in the FTQ is optional), compared with 41 percent in 1961 (Rouillard, 1989:302, 304).

Finally, it should be noted that the Corporation des instituteurs et institutrices catholiques du Québec (the Catholic teachers' union), which had 16,000 members in 1959 and 28,000 in the early 1960s, grew rapidly to more than 80,000 in 1977 and about 100,000 ten years later. It became the Centrale de l'enseignement du Québec (CEQ, or Québec teachers' union) in 1974.

This pronounced growth in union membership was more than a simple quantitative development. It was so strong that it allowed the union movement to cross a qualitative threshold from the standpoint of its existence as an established social force. From a numerically weak group of organizations prior to 1960, it became in a few years a genuine movement composed of the biggest and strongest social organizations in Québec.

To synthesize this evolution, it is important to note the following elements:

1. The outstanding feature in the development of the unions during the 1960s was their expansion into the public sector, in particular the hospitals, the public service, and the educational sector.
2. The unions also expanded into job categories on a national scale, unlike the relatively local or regional character of some components of the labour force in the private sector.
3. Expansion into the public sector thus gave the Québec unions, for the first time, the stature of a national movement. Initially, during the first and second bargaining rounds in 1967 and 1968–69, public sector job action was not really centralized. Then, beginning in 1971, the common fronts were formed to provide public sector employees with a collective national (Québec) strength and impact.
4. The government's intervention in public sector labour conflicts could not be clothed with the same "externality" as its intervention in private sector conflicts. It was immediate and ongoing.

5. There was therefore a tendency toward politicization of union struggles, even though the point of departure might be strictly economic. Accordingly, unions that traditionally had not been placed as frequently in a conflictual relationship with the government now found themselves in frontal confrontations with it, which of course had some influence on their general relationship to the state.

RELATIONSHIP TO POLITICS

Until the mid-1950s the generally predominant trend within the Québec union movement, from the standpoint of its traditions of political action, was to lobby or pressure the existing governments and parties. Of course, there were the industrial unions of the CIO (FUIQ),[1] which recognized the old CCF (Cooperative Commonwealth Federation) as Labour's political arm against the Liberals and Conservatives. But the incipient tendency toward independent political action that they embodied did not have a huge impact, given the numerical and organizational weakness of these unions in Québec.

Labour's Political Traditions and the Quiet Revolution

However, while the nonpartisan tendency for the most part occupied the field of political activity, an important change occurred in the latter half of the 1950s. The first significant indication of a movement in the Québec unions in favour of constituting a "third party" in the province appeared at the FUIQ's convention in Joliette, in 1955, and it gained force in 1958 with the call by the FTQ convention for the founding of a "party of the labouring classes" (Denis, 1979:157–59). There were other indications as well. The CTCC-CSN, at its convention in September 1959, voted to authorize its member unions to support a political formation and even affiliate to a party—a decision that marked a significant departure from its traditions. Several months earlier, its executive had even agreed to participate in "talks … with a view to the founding of a new political party" (the future NDP), while however reiterating their bias in favour of nonpartisanship (CSN-CEQ, 1984:161).

Strikes then developed that focused the unions' increasing opposition to the Duplessis regime, and made them look for a political outlet beyond the dominant parties. This was without a doubt the major factor in the FTQ's appeal, although the creation of this federation one year earlier itself promoted this development, as did the position taken by the Canadian Labour Congress (CLC) in April 1958 in favour of the formation of a new party. The third-party orientation ebbed, however, in the early 1960s after an initial breakthrough under Duplessis. Why did this happen?

It has been argued that the coming to power of the Liberal Party and the development of the national question and nationalism were the major factors in the failure of the third-party movement at that time. But it is necessary to add to these factors the obstacles within the unions themselves, such as the fact that entire contingents of the labour force were excluded from the unions and did not yet have the organizational means of support to get involved even in strictly economic struggles. The substantial weight of Catholic doctrine and conservatism and the traditions of nonpartisanship themselves also worked against a radical reorientation of trade union political action, as did the pleas of the media and the dominant parties, which sought to discourage the emergence of this new political force.

Furthermore, responsibility for organizing a new party would fall most heavily on the unions themselves. It would entail a much higher level of political involvement than the nonpartisan policy did. If an alternative solution appeared to be developing, one that would absolve the unions from the responsibility of themselves providing a way out, the tendency toward a more lobby-oriented tactic would grow.

It was this type of relationship that soon harnessed the unions to the Lesage government, from 1960 to 1964. Even while the FTQ was officially pursuing its efforts to create a labour party, the labour movement was trying to obtain as much as it could from a party, now in government, that had previously served as the major political vehicle for the opposition to Duplessis. This tendency was even encouraged, in a contradictory way, by the new strength the unions were beginning to wield. For the first time they managed to carry out some extremely effective actions in the political and social arenas, reducing, at least temporarily, the belief in the need for an independent party. Trade union political action during this period was characterized by a sympathetic attitude toward the government. It does not necessarily follow that this sympathy meant submission. For example, it is noteworthy that, while in practice giving political support to the Liberals, the union federations mobilized vigorously to force the government to concede the right to organize, bargain collectively, and strike in the public sector.

In other words, their support was "bargained" in exchange for substantive concessions. This relationship with the Liberal government lasted only a few years, however. It was challenged as early as 1965, when, amid a constant stream of social and democratic demands, and the swift development of the nationalist movement, the unions apparently found that the government was no longer the political instrument of progress they had continued to anticipate. After the Duplessis years, the Liberals had managed to tap into the desires for social and political change. But in the 1966 elections, neither they nor the Union Nationale could aspire to that role.

A third space was opening up, but the labour movement failed to claim it. The unions were just emerging from the unsuccessful experience with the NDP and the Parti Socialiste du Québec (PSQ), and this weighed heavily on their political conduct.[2] However, in 1967 a split in the Liberal Party suggested that a significant realignment of political forces was taking shape (around the former cabinet minister René Lévesque), and that it might result in the establishment of a new instrument that for the first time would achieve a fusion between social and national aspirations.

Union political action was at that point in a holding pattern. But, significantly, between 1966 and 1968 the unions did not simply revert to their traditional lobbying strategy. The CSN and CEQ, confronting the Union Nationale (UN) government, tried for the first time to adopt a permanent means of political intervention. In the case of the CSN, this resulted in the opening of a "second front" of struggles, to promote action by the federation on such things as elections, unemployment, and consumer issues, which went beyond the collective agreement, the "first front" of its usual activity. Furthermore, in 1967 relations with the government were overshadowed by the unions' defeat over Bill 25, aimed at the teachers, which dictated their working conditions for eighteen months and imposed a province-wide bargaining structure in the education sector. In early 1968, the CSN created political action committees (CAPs), and the CEQ, grassroots action and education committees.

These initiatives reflected a growing belief in the need for political action. But they were not conceived by their major promoters as a step or stage in the process of establishing a "third party." Rather, they were intended to complement, not replace, the nonpartisan orientation; the idea was to expand and politicize the unions' actions to encompass more than collective bargaining issues. Thus, although the unions armed themselves with the means to engage in more independent political action, it was in fact the coming of the Parti Québécois that put its stamp on their electoral orientation from 1968 on.

Political Action and Nationalism

The Québec nationalism of the recent period has been studied a lot. Here we simply want to outline briefly the major features of its articulation in the labour and community movements. The growth and transformations in the nature of the labour organizations between 1957 and the early 1970s, combined with the enthusiasm and energy aroused by the initial debates, hopes, and reforms of the Quiet Revolution, promoted the political radicalization of a whole series of urban social sectors more or less linked to the petite bourgeoisie and student community—the artists, the Mouvement laïque de langue française, founded in 1961, the Union générale des étudiants du Québec, founded in 1965, etc. It was a context characterized by the objective weight of the national question,[3] which recurrently increased the attraction of nationalist solutions, and less visibly, by the failure of the NDP-PSQ. This in large part explains why a significant layer of these urban elements tended to organize around a radical nationalist project, a sort of leftward extension of the Quiet Revolution. The Rassemblement pour l'indépendance nationale (RIN), formed back in September 1960, appeared to be the main manifestation of this current, with its platform of national independence, secularization, and support for some of the major labour and community struggles.

But this conjuncture soon resulted in other developments. As the only option independent of the "old" parties, nationalism tended to channel other expectations. From a traditional elite movement it developed into a mass phenomenon.[4] As a corollary, it helped define the popular perception of the major political issues and gradually overlapped with and absorbed all aspirations, as a genuine "political envelope" of social and democratic demands.

These processes marked the beginning of a period in which the national question was at the centre of all political issues in Québec, when its impact would challenge the very foundations of the Canadian state, as the Laurendeau-Dunton Commission put it. They illustrated two major changes in comparison with the social maturation of the previous decade. First, in contrast to the 1950s, the organized labour movement was much less involved in action to build and develop a political alternative to the Liberals and Union Nationale. Second, while the political platforms devised and developed by the unions in the final years of Duplessism sought to address national, democratic, and social problems simultaneously, the national question was never assigned the full significance it assumed during the 1960s. The role of the national question and the dynamics of the new nationalism penetrated the entire labour movement, from the base to the summit, as well as the grassroots and community groups, and articulated a specifically "nationalist" consciousness of their relationship to politics and the state.[5] The rapidity of the nationalist upsurge, moreover, confirmed that fundamental social processes were already shaking the traditional bipartism and creating an opening for a new party.

The Parti Québécois was in fact built as a product and a link in this evolution, as both a depositary and an indicator of the trends we have observed. Beginning by establishing its hegemony over the movement of national aspirations, it managed to assume the form of a mass party, strengthening and accentuating the march toward a political formation independent of the Liberals and *Unionistes*.

The development of Québec's trade union movement was itself a precondition to this evolution. In his book *Communisme et anti-communisme au Québec (1920–1950)*, Marcel Fournier noted how the persistence in the urban environment of the solidarity networks issuing from the traditional rural society, based on the family and the parish, was an important factor in the weak impact the major left-wing movements had in Québec in the 1930s. In the 1960s, the combination of urbanization, industrialization, and massive trade unionization overcame this. The new organizations of social solidarity and action hurled tens and then hundreds of thousands of people into militant action against the employers and the government. The grassroots communities in the cities were organized on an ongoing basis in organizations that escaped the control of the traditional political, economic, and clerical elites. They developed confidence in their own forces, and became used to intervening in the major social issues of the day. The development of the unions was a factor of mass politicization that directly contributed to the process of democratization that Québec society was experiencing. The PQ appeared as the progressive political expression of this movement, in a context in which grassroots nationalism had become the primary ideology challenging the traditional bipartism.

In 1974–75, the party membership reached 100,000, and by the 1976 campaign it was slightly over 130,000. The composition of its membership (which roughly overlapped with the composition of its electorate and was based in particular on activists in the grassroots and union movements), and the type of commitment that it demanded of its members, contrasted with those of the old parties. The 1976 victory over Bourassa reinforced these processes. In 1979, for example, the PQ had some 200,000 members, in April 1980, 238,000, and in March 1981 close to 300,000 (Fraser, 1984:391–98; Carlos and Latouche, 1976; Hamilton and Pinard, 1984).

In this sense there are particular aspects to the PQ victory in 1976 that should be emphasized. First, it did not fit within the framework of the traditional bipartism. It went further, for example, than the type of alliance that the CIO established in the 1930s with the Democratic Party in the United States. The U.S. labour movement at that time designated one of the two dominant parties as the vehicle for its political intervention. In Québec in the 1970s, the union support of the PQ broke with bipartism since this party presented itself as an alternative to the two old parties. No one in the leadership of the PQ or the unions presented this formation as a "workers' party." But it is obvious that the PQ, because it had developed out of a split from the Liberals and the Union Nationale, was perceived as playing that role. This not only gave a new impulse to the expectations with regard to the PQ, but it also strengthened confidence in it. In this sense 1976 confirmed and accentuated the monopoly on political representation that the Parti Québécois was to exercise henceforth over the labour movement.

THE UNIONS AND THE PARTI QUÉBÉCOIS

The resulting mechanisms of this relationship produced a qualitative change in the ways the unions operate and exist politically. This is what we will now analyze, by taking a closer look at the key events in this evolution.

The New Alliance

As it entered the 1970s the labour movement was in open opposition to the parties that had traditionally dominated the province, while the structures and institutions of collaboration at the governmental level were generally in disrepute. The Union Nationale government, for example, had created a Conseil général de l'industrie (General Council of Industry) in 1969, with a mandate to advise the government on the province's economic future; it was composed wholly of representatives of the employers (Favreau and L'Heureux, 1984:59). Clinton Archibald recalls that three days after the first meeting of the Conseil consultatif de la planification et du développement (Planning and Development Advisory Council), in December 1970, the FTQ withdrew with the explanation that the workers were "underrepresented" (Archibald, 1983:221). In fact, the political elites proved unable to define the terms of an effective mode of coexistence and collaboration with the labour movement. Another important development, in 1970, was the application of the War Measures Act, which resulted in the formation of a broad labour and democratic opposition front. Coming only a few months after the election of Robert Bourassa, it was a sign of the distrust and hostility toward his government, and helped to increase the opposition. The "Bourassa experience," barely under way, was already being rejected by the unions.

The dynamic promoted by the new social weight of the unions also reinforced the need and the desire to intervene politically in their own name. Thus, the argument[6] that the relationship between the government and big business circles was too close was transmuted into an overt search for union access to the procedures for determining macroeconomic policies.[7] In its "Déclaration de principes" published in 1971, the CSN said that "the ability of workers to participate through their unions in the development of the economic policies that shape the society in which they live" was "a requirement of social justice" (p. 38). Somewhat along the same lines, at the FTQ convention in 1969 Louis Laberge, its president, was harshly criticized for not having committed the federation to the battle against Bill 63 giving parents freedom of choice of the language of education[8]; and the organized workers of St-Jérôme, Baie-Comeau, and Hauterive got involved in municipal election campaigns in 1967–68.

The unions were in fact trying to define the means that would procure some political influence for them commensurate with what they had become. For a while the situation resulted in some contradictory developments, fostered by the tensions that continually arose between the labour movement and the Bourassa government between 1970 and 1976. Thus there emerged a noticeable tendency toward protest actions and radical opposition to the government and institutions. This was the period in which FTQ president Louis Laberge said that the unions should question their participation in governmental "advisory" agencies because in those conditions the economic, judicial, and political authorities tended to combine forces against "us"; in this sense, he explained, what really counts is the "striking force" that "our" organization can muster, and lobbying and working in parliamentary committees cannot be a substitute for the relationship of forces that can result from direct action and demonstrations (Laberge, 1971:7–9, 16–17). He called on the FTQ convention in 1971 to "smash the system" through direct political action. A similar development occurred in the CSN, whose president Marcel Pepin told the 1972 convention that it was necessary to "bring down the Bourassa regime," in particular by setting up "grassroots committees" in each provincial riding.

Not only was "dialogue" not on the agenda, but the points of contact with the governmental bureaucracy had become almost nonexistent. This was reflected in the major union manifestoes adopted in the early 1970s, which sought to seal the break with the Liberal regime and the very rationality of private enterprise: *L'État, rouage de notre exploitation* (FTQ), *Il n'y a plus d'avenir pour le Québec dans le système économique actuel* and *Ne comptons que sur nos propres moyens* (CSN), and *L'école au service de la classe dominante* (CEQ).

It was in this framework, as well, that in the spring of 1970 fifteen major interunion symposiums were held, drawing together some 5,000 active members of the three federations throughout Québec to discuss the conditions of their collective action outside the workplace. And, finally, this was the framework for the CSN's strengthened desire to form *Comités d'action politique*—the CAPs, or political action committees—in all 108 provincial constituencies, and the work of its political action central committee with its "permanent secretariat" (Favreau and L'Heureux, 1984:33–34).

While the CAPs worked primarily to develop the unions' involvement in various social issues, the interunion symposiums were more directly oriented toward independent politics at the municipal level. The leading example of municipal action (of the independent "third-party" type), and the best known, was the creation of the FRAP[9] in Montréal in May 1970, a product of a meeting between the interunion symposium in the Metropolitan area and a local gathering of community associations, the RAP. Its goal was "to elect to City Hall the largest possible number of councillors who would be accountable to the working class,"[10] as its vice-president, Émile Boudreau of the Montréal Labour Council (FTQ), stated. Although confined to the municipal level, the FRAP experience broke with the traditional nonpartisanship. It was the expression of a policy favouring the establishment of a formation issuing as such from the labour movement.

Yet the "third-party" experience did not go beyond this stage. Granted, the major union manifestoes of 1971 and 1972 mark an ideological radicalization of the federations, itself fostered by the social struggles in this period. All three advocated the establishment of a socialist society based on democratic participation. But the "Comité des douze," a committee of twelve leaders of the CSN appointed by its Conseil confédéral to supervise the overall discussion of the federation's manifesto *Ne comptons que sur nos propres moyens* and report back on the results, noted that while all the documents and discussions raised the question of power, no one drew from this a precise orientation with regard to political action, which is all the more astonishing in that this was accompanied by a blanket rejection of the traditional parties (Comité des douze, 1973:43–48). Indeed, the unions soon began marking time in their political evolution, and to take their distance from "third-party"–related actions. They gradually returned to the nonpartisan forms of action, but this time in support of the PQ (regardless, incidentally, of the rhetoric used to present this position).

For a short time these specific forms developed concurrently. The interunion symposiums initially viewed municipal political action as a "learning experience" for struggles for power. But at the same time, for many people, this experience was complementary to the Parti Québécois experience provincially. The PQ was formed in the same year, 1968, that the "second front" was launched. Thus, when it came to hatching a new party, the union symposiums lagged behind the movement led by René Lévesque. The dual nature of the labour movement's political evolution is indicated by the fact that most of the activists involved in designating municipal workers' candidates were also active members of the PQ. This was the case in Montréal, Québec City, and the rest of the province. Close to half the candidates of the FRAP, it seems, were members of local executives of the Parti Québécois. Some union members saw to it that the PQ's program included demands originating in the labour movement. And others, while claiming to be supporters of socialism and a workers' party, had no problem supporting PQ candidates (Favreau and L'Heureux, 1984:60, 99, 102).

It was in this context that the temporary concurrence of the different forms of political action was resolved in favour of nonpartisanship, precisely because the formation of the PQ was grasped by wide sectors of the labour and mass movements as the realization of their own political option. Thus, while the forms of political action by the federations were comparable, from then on, to general nonpartisan practices, the consciousness stemming from these processes is not reducible to such practices. To some extent the actual forms of this action were nonpartisan, but they were to a large degree perceived in the popular consciousness as the realization of the "third party."

To prepare for the 1973 provincial elections, the CSN published a special booklet[11] comparing the positions of the various parties with its own positions. It clearly indicated that the PQ's policies were much closer to the CSN's positions. Louis Laberge, for his part, pointed out that most of the candidates who were union members were running on the PQ label. These initiatives were, of course, each in their own way, typical of the traditional methods of North American nonpartisanship.

Between 1971 and 1974, however, municipal political action underwent a change in course. In Montréal, with the approach of the 1974 elections and in response to an appeal by the remnants of the FRAP, the regional bodies of the three federations decided to again work at forming a party to oppose the municipal party of Mayor Jean Drapeau. But this time the Parti Québécois was involved, and in April 1974 the Rassemblement des citoyens de Montréal (RCM), or Montréal Citizens' Movement, was formed. The RCM addressed itself to the "citizens" of

Montréal, while the FRAP had presented itself as the vehicle of the "employees."[12]

In the 1976 elections nonpartisanship borrowed from another of its traditional methods: propagating its own demands in the form of a political platform, but without identifying with any particular party. The CEQ had previously alluded to the need to circulate the workers' demands and give them public currency, while Louis Laberge stated:

> I think the time has come to bring our scattered demands together ... to pull together an authentic political program of the Québec workers that we can explain to our members and ... put forward during the big public debates that election campaigns represent. (Laberge, 1975:48)

As for the CSN, the Conseil confédéral adopted a resolution in January 1976 that "union members, locally, regionally and nationally, in the workplaces and in the federations, work at developing a political ideology and program by and for the workers" (Pepin, 1976). When the campaign began, the three federations called more or less openly for a vote "for the party that is closest to our interests"—i.e., the PQ. The FTQ also urged its members to work within the Parti Québécois to influence its program, a position that was similar to the type of "nonpartisan" relationship that the AFL-CIO maintains with the Democratic Party. At a news conference on October 26 the FTQ explicitly put the finishing touch to this orientation by declaring its official support to the Parti Québécois (Lamoureux, 1985:16).

After the PQ victory in 1976, the emphasis was put on the idea that it was not in the nature of trade unionism to intervene in setting up a party. CSN president Norbert Rodrigue told the federation's convention in 1977 that *"political action, [to us,] is putting forward our demands at all levels, . . .* developing an alternative line geared to fundamental changes" (CSN, 1977:38). The speech provided conclusive evidence that the initiatives that had been associated with the formation of a workers' party were ebbing. Political action was from now on to take the form of lobbying the PQ in a context in which Lévesque's party was implicitly acknowledged as the political expression of the social movement. This orientation was carried further in the FTQ than in the CSN and CEQ. But in relation to the forms of political action, the attitude was the same.

It is important to analyze more specifically the nature of the political alliance that was achieved in this period between the labour movement and the Parti Québécois. None of the representative organizations of the employers supported the PQ in 1976 or in 1981. Its victory was perceived as a victory of the grassroots against the parties and candidates that the ruling class explicitly acknowledged as its own, even if the PQ was not officially presented by any group as a workers' party. In this sense, its victory in 1976 can be compared, in our opinion, with the political processes of the European "People's Fronts" or popular fronts, and with what the election of governments of this type represented historically.

The Parti Québécois was in fact sustained by the dynamic of the masses' aspirations and the desire for change, which it served to focus and organize through mass electoral action. Its program accepted some social and working-class demands. Moreover, like the People's Fronts, it campaigned as a vehicle for breaking from the traditional formulas of bipartism and government alternance.

The victory over these "formulas" was a victory of the "vote of the masses" by the party they had grasped as their own. But it is also necessary to note the contradictory relationship that was established, as in the case of the People's Fronts, between the voters' aspirations and the type of government that was installed. In this sense it is not sufficient to say that the PQ victory was a product of those aspirations, since it was simultaneously an instrument for channelling and containing them, and it was not long before the PQ government stood in opposition to their implementation.

One of the primary characteristics of the People's Fronts is the coalition of parties originating from the workers' movement (CP, SP, Labour parties, etc.) with parties historically rooted in the movement of other social forces (for example, the republican and secular bourgeoisie in 1930s France and Spain). The resulting governments cannot be characterized as "workers'" governments, although the major electoral force in these coalitions is of working-class and other noncapitalist origins.

The PQ government—not the government of a workers party but relying on the support of the labour movement and seeking the support of many growing sectors of the Québec bourgeoisie and petite bourgeoisie—thus had some of the features associated with popular fronts and the political role they play. The political alliance it pursued may have been "informal," but it was as strong as the formal coalitions observed in other countries. This, in our view, is of primary significance to the 1976 election. At that point the relationship to the PQ's nationalism appeared highly profitable to the labour movement, and the alliance with the PQ seemed even more "natural" and easier to justify.

"Concertation" and Participation

The Parti Québécois program promised a willingness to recognize institutionally the labour movement—through universal application of the Rand Formula and the union shop, multi-employer certifications, etc.—that exceeded anything in the past. In its ideology and practice as a government, this approach turned out to be integrally bound up with the PQ's concern to establish a structured participation of the unions in the determination of particular economic policies, and to attach appropriate mechanisms that would enable the unions to become voluntarily partners in this approach.

At the time the PQ first advanced the idea of provincial "concertation," in 1976, the Québec union federations had unanimously rejected the Canadian Labour Congress's proposed tripartite corporatism on the federal level. However, once the PQ was elected, the federations began to formulate positions that were favourable to concertation with the PQ and even to voluntary restrictions on the unions' demands.[13] When the Lévesque government called its first economic summit, the CEQ's Bureau national spoke of a "political gesture without precedent in Québec" that might contribute to "the consolidation of the government within Québec and its credibility in foreign financial markets" (CEQ, 1977).

In our opinion, there were three major factors behind this sympathetic attitude that was present in each of the Québec union federations. First, the PQ's opening to the unions was genuine, in the sense that its program promised a form of recognition of their existence that seemed quite acceptable to the unions. Second, its concertation proposals were presented not only as involving the labour movement to a substantial degree, but as an attempt to redefine economic and social life in accordance with principles that appeared to be similar to those of the unions. And finally, to the vast majority of union members the party was the new party they had elected, and the promise of change was being implemented, so they were prepared to collaborate with it and they trusted it.

What is perhaps most surprising, then, is that the concertation did not go further and was not more formalized in stable mechanisms. At the outset, the positive attitudes were obvious, both on the union side and in the government. But a number of factors were to combine and compromise this development. First, the economic situation characterized by the recession of the mid-1970s; while the government enacted reforms along the lines of the union positions,[14] it did not commit itself to the type of concessions[15] that might at some point genuinely deepen the process with the unions. Second, the most powerful bastion of the Québec labour movement, the unions in the public and parapublic sector, bargained directly with the state, which tended to result in constant friction with the government. The CEQ's decision not to participate in the second socioeconomic summit, at Montebello in March 1979, was based essentially on the opening of a new round of negotiations involving the Common Front. Finally, the participationist mechanisms were also hamstrung by the fact that the labour movement gradually lost its illusions concerning the nature of the PQ program. Labour organizations had expected economic and social measures[16] and some moves to democratize the structure of government,[17] which would have required a degree of demarcation from the old regime that the PQ government never sought to achieve.

Thus the process of integrating the Québec labour movement did not go very far, despite some attempts in this direction. In 1979 the Lévesque government, like its predecessor, resorted to special laws against particular unions—for example, withdrawing from the Common Front the right to strike. But by that time the impact of such actions on the political attitudes of the organized labour movement and its membership was less significant than might appear at first sight. The status of the Parti Québécois did not primarily depend upon an exact correspondence between its social program and the program of the unions, but on the content that was assigned to the national aspirations, and the monopoly on political representation that it enjoyed in relation to those aspirations. It was the trek toward the referendum that dominated political consciousness at this time.

In this context, the contact mechanisms between the provincial government and the labour movement did not disappear. Rather, they changed their tone. It is indicative that access to the PQ cabinet by men and women linked to the unions appeared to increase at a time when economic summitry was less in vogue. It was almost as if they wanted to establish new paths of preferential relationships between the PQ and the unions, paths whose effectiveness would be determined by the degree to which they were direct and permanent, and immune from public scrutiny, unlike the major summit events.[18]

NATIONAL QUESTION AND SOCIAL QUESTION

The Québec referendum of May 20, 1980, was a highly critical event in, and manifestation of, the crisis of the Canadian state, as were all of the debates surrounding the "repatriation" of the British North America (BNA) Act. The Parti Québécois orientation suffered two defeats, which in turn produced the first real questioning within the unions concerning the merits of their alliance with the PQ. We are unable to analyze this context in this essay, but will confine our remarks to several key elements with some further particulars concerning the high point in the obvious alienation that developed between the labour movement and the PQ after 1982.

An Assessment of Parti Québécois Strategy

In 1980 none of the Québec union federations came out officially in favour of independence, although this is not necessarily true with regard to their intermediate bodies. This may not appear significant, in itself, but it is necessary to understand the context. The mere recognition of the right to self-determination, which was supported by the FTQ, the CSN, and the CEQ, could not represent a comprehensive position on the Québec national question. The political debate had already reached a higher stage, involving the concrete forms in which this right would be exercised. To limit oneself to affirming a principle might be identified increasingly with a refusal to take a position, if not desertion from the cause.

The discussions that had been going on for some years on this subject resulted in a special convention of the CSN, on June 1 and 2, 1979. The federation's Comité d'orientation, supported by a majority of the executive, moved that "in order to wage a successful struggle against national oppression and its various manifestations, the CSN [should join] in the efforts by the people of Québec to appropriate the political, economic and cultural authorities and institutions" (CSN, 1979). Apart from this recommendation, it proposed that the federation not take any specific constitutional position. This orientation prevailed in the face of a strong current proposing that the federation come out for independence.

The same orientation was adopted by the CEQ in a special convention held less than a week later, on June 8 and 9, 1979. After calling on its members and affiliates to struggle against any violation of the right to self-determination, and demanding effective recognition of this right by the federal government, the Conseil général, on a motion by the executive, decided that the CEQ's participation in the public debate on the national question would not be based on a particular constitutional option. As in the CSN, this position was defended not against possible supporters of federalism, but against those who wanted active intervention in support of independence (Rouillard, 1989:369–70).

The FTQ held a convention on the following November 26 to 30. The leadership, which itself presented the national question as one of the major issues to be discussed (cf. *Le Monde ouvrier*, the FTQ newspaper, October 1979), gave the delegates its policy positions at the opening of the proceedings. At the 1977 convention the delegates had urged the federation to defend the workers' interests in the referendum debate, and to conduct a broad consultation on this matter. At the 1979 convention, as the newspapers noted, the proposals defended by Louis Laberge and all of the FTQ leaders were relatively limited. The document they presented, *La FTQ et la question nationale*, repeated the 1977 position and proposed a meeting of the Conseil général or perhaps a special convention "to take a position" once the Lévesque government's referendum question had been released.

The delegates unanimously demanded that such a convention be mandatory. It was a stormy debate. As *Le Devoir* reported, on November 30, 1979: "The FTQ, which yesterday reaffirmed Québec's right to self-determination, to some degree had to restrain many delegates who wanted an immediate discussion on the future of Québec."

Once the Lévesque government's referendum question was known, the three federations supported the PQ's "yes," in more or less official and more or less critical forms.[19] In the months following the referendum, there were a number of criticisms within the Québec unions concerning the policy they had followed at the time. We would like to briefly recall the nature of these analyses by quoting from an initial report prepared by Gérald Larose, then president of the Montréal CSN's Conseil central and now president of the federation. Quite similar comments were circulated within the other two major federations. Writing in the fall of 1980, Larose said that in his opinion the labour movement had "suffered a defeat." "The hope we had of putting ourselves in a better immediate position to continue our struggle for Québec independence within the framework of our fight for a socialist society has been demolished," he said. "May 20, 1980 was a victory for a formidable coalition of the forces of capitalist, employer and federalist reaction in the country."

How was the unions' political orientation up to the referendum to be characterized? Larose's reply was unequivocal:

> Is it necessary to explain that by the turn of the decade the labour movement had to all intents and purposes abandoned the national question to the Parti québécois, and in doing so, left the latter with all the room it needed to carve out a hegemonic role with regard to the rights and status of Québec. This meant that the independentist and progressive character of the national question was rapidly squandered, becoming little more than a vague proposal to reorganize Québec's political structures within a capitalist and still Canadian framework.

In this context it was not easy to define the "paths to follow" in order to regain the initiative in the struggle, but "the labour movement can no longer leave it to the Parti québécois to define the future of Québec's rights and status on its own" (Larose, 1980:62).

It is necessary to add the following observation, which follows, we think, from an examination of the union conventions and positions taken by the federations prior to the referendum: if indeed the labour movement had "abandoned" the Québec national question, this had primarily taken the form of a refusal to adopt a clear position on the issue. Thus it was relatively easy for the PQ's sovereignty-association position and resulting constitutional strategy to remain hegemonic.

Following the referendum, the union federations failed to draw up any official balance sheets of what they had done, although the criticism we have mentioned indicated the need for some reorientation of their strategy. The unions' political intervention and their relationship to the PQ government remained fundamentally the same. The constitutional threats implicit in the federal government's post-referendum initiatives and the march toward unilateral patriation of the Constitution both exerted pressure to maintain the alliance with the PQ, notwithstanding the fact that in October 1980, after the federal announcement of the plan to patriate the BNA Act, CEQ president Robert Gaulin stated:

The Parti québécois government has opened the way to the repatriation of the Constitution.... The PQ has served as a stepping stone for Trudeau's undertakings. It will fall to the various trade union and grassroots organizations to organize the opposition to this undemocratic assault on the people. (CEQ, 1980)

When the Supreme Court of Canada ruled unanimously, on December 6, 1982, that under the Canadian Constitution Québec did not have a right of veto over constitutional amendments, the FTQ, CSN, and CEQ, as part of a common front of various organizations, issued a political statement:

This constitution ... is not, cannot be, and will never be ours. And since we no longer have a constitution, we should now provide ourselves with one. And since the current process always works against us, we should provide ourselves with an appropriate method for determining a constitution: the only one that is appropriate in this democratic era is one that returns the constitution to those to whom it belongs, that is, the people themselves. (CSN-CEQ-FTQ, 1982)

The demand for a constitution developed by the people as an effective rejoinder was put forward within a framework that inferred the convening of a Québec constituent assembly.

There was no immediate follow-up to this call. But it indicated that the PQ's defeat in 1980 and setback in 1982 had led the unions to adopt a more critical stance toward the party's policies and strategies, and produced a desire for greater independence on their part on the national question itself. When the discussions on the Meech Lake Accord began, in 1987, the Québec unions were active participants, this time in a way that reflected these new inclinations.

They lost little time in rejecting the accord on the grounds that the process by which it had been developed and the procedure for adoption were not based on the broad democratic participation of the people, and because its provisions did not satisfy Québec's needs as a nation. Prior to the definitive failure of the accord, the CEQ, CSN, and FTQ came out officially in the spring of 1990 in favour of the independence of Québec and (depending on the specific terms and conditions in each case) for the convening of a constituent assembly of the Québec people.[20]

The Point of Separation

The crisis-ridden conjuncture of 1982–83 brought about a qualitative transformation in the political position of Québec trade unionism. It accelerated a process through which support to the PQ suddenly changed into massive rejection. The "favourable bias toward the workers" gave way to reductions in social programs, cuts in wages, and open confrontation with the unions, in a context in which the PQ government proved incapable of reducing unemployment.

We cannot retrace all the ups and downs that marked the break between the Québec government and the 300,000 employees in the public and parapublic sectors in this period. It should be noted, however, that this was the most important development in the political evolution of the labour movement in the recent period.[21] It was the seminal event in the growing alienation between the unions and the party of René Lévesque.

The process was expressed in several ways. When a vote was taken in favour of a general strike, first in each of the individual public and parapublic sectors, then unanimously by the 800 delegates in the Conseil d'orientation of the Common Front, on January 9, 1983, it was a vote against a government based on a party that had been the focus for the political energy and aspirations of the trade unions. The demonstration of 50,000 in front of the National Assembly on January 29 was an essentially political demonstration. The subsequent harassment of all the government ministers, each time they appeared in public, and the anger toward them expressed by the teachers at the March 1983 meeting of the PQ's Conseil national was an expression of the same disillusionment. Civil servants would disrupt ministerial news conferences chanting "Élections! Élections!" and "PQ battu, vendu [PQ beaten, sold out]," etc.

Demanding the resignation of the government, the CSN and its president explained that the Parti Québécois had "disqualified itself nationally, economically and socially" (CSN, 1982). Louis Laberge of the FTQ stated during the same period that the government was condemned and that the issue was whether there was any further chance of saving the party. He asked the PQ's Conseil national to express its opposition to government policy at a session that opened on March 5. But instead the council supported the government's measures "strict as they are" (*Le Devoir*, March 7, 1983), which was one way of answering the FTQ president's question. Some elements within the FTQ hierarchy appear to have considered intervening within the PQ to increase the unions' influence.[22] But there was no real follow-up. During a CLC symposium in Québec City on March 5–8, 1983, on the theme "Equality Now" (a symposium called to discuss the struggle against the oppression of women), the 600 or so delegates unanimously adopted a resolution stating, in part:

> Be it resolved that the labour movement found a party of workers at the provincial level (Québec), during the next year, for the purpose of running candidates in future elections. The unions should defray the necessary costs involved in establishing this party and ensure its continuance. (CLC, 1983)

Finally, let us note that at a meeting of the Conseil fédéral of the Fédération des affaires sociales of the CSN, also in March 1983, it was decided to organize an "anti-PQ financing campaign" (to oppose the PQ's appeal for funds). Here again, these decisions had no immediate concrete follow-up. But they reflected a development that was to have lasting impact. The special relationship between the Parti Québécois and the unions had just dissolved amid a serious social crisis that directly challenged the very forms of union political action as they had gradually taken shape since the Quiet Revolution. The Parti Québécois could no longer be regarded as the political vehicle and parliamentary mouthpiece for the unions' aspirations. In this sense there was a break, which was made possible because, in the wake of the PQ's defeats in the referendum and the opposition to constitutional patriation, the union forces had questioned the merits of its political hegemony on the national question. Only this time, the PQ strategy had also lost its progressive aura in social matters.

The Québec unions (like the other grassroots movements) were entering a period of redefining their relationship to politics. The historic alliance with the

Parti Québécois, which had lasted some fifteen years, was giving way to a wait-and-see situation. The results of the election of December 2, 1985, which brought the Liberals to power led by Robert Bourassa, demonstrated this in their own way: the PQ's losses were "twice as significant as the Liberals' gains," with an "accompanying increase in abstentions" (Drouilly, 1990a:106). In the election of September 25, 1989, the abstention rate reached "a record level"; since it was primarily registered among the francophone and PQ electorate (Drouilly, 1990b:260–62), it can be assumed to be fresh evidence of the break in the special relationship between the labour and mass movements and the Parti Québécois.

The Return of Bourassa

In economic and social terms, Robert Bourassa's return to power in 1985 produced no abrupt turn in union–government relations. There was a continuation of the same policies and type of activity that had prevailed since the early 1980s. On the one hand, the Liberals embraced some of the key legislative measures of the PQ regime, such as Law 37, which armed the government with new means to stem the conflicts that had become characteristic of bargaining and job action in the public sector. On the other hand, parallel to this preventive legislation, the Bourassa government was quick to resort to repressive laws to curb union militancy. A prime example was the adoption in 1989 of Law 160, used to smash collective action by health sector employees through extremely harsh provisions such as loss of seniority. The government even went so far as to announce a wage freeze in the spring of 1991 for the 400,000 workers in the Québec public sector, reminiscent of analogous action by the PQ government.

The unions, however, responded to these attacks by accelerating the retreat that had begun following the setbacks of the early 1980s. The leaders of the three federations joined in a public denunciation, on May 8, 1990, of the policy of the Bourassa government, which, they said, "is doing its utmost to flout the right to free bargaining in Québec."[23] But instead of trying to develop a systematic confrontation with the government in opposition to this policy, they relied, for example, on negotiations to obtain the repeal of the most draconian features of Law 160, which was ultimately achieved in June 1991. Similarly, after violent denunciations of the government's unilateral wage freeze in the public sector, the union leaders bargained their way to partial relief from, but not repeal of, this decision.

Comparing this attitude to that of the union leadership ten years earlier, a clear evolution is evident. There is every indication that the weight of the defeats, or rather the undelivered victories, has inspired the general staffs of the unions to favour the search for new, more effective forms of action. Major mobilizations and strikes have led, it seems, to an impasse. But while some are prepared to offer this diagnosis, others, in contrast, think that the unions' disappointing setbacks are explained by an insufficient use of mass action. These two positions suffused the union debates as they entered the 1990s.

The overriding policy of the union leadership, nevertheless, seems clearly inclined toward a new approach in their relations with the government and private sector employers, based on *concertation*, economic initiative, and contributing to social development rather than confrontation. The Fonds de solidarité, created by the FTQ in 1983 to channel workers' savings into a corporate investment fund designed to preserve or create jobs, is certainly the most elaborate expression of this orientation at present. But at other levels, too, one is struck by the new involvement of the unions in joint regional development initiatives with the employers, the government, and other economic "partners." This is the case in particular in the regions with the highest unemployment rates, or disadvantaged neighbourhoods such as those in Montréal. In addition to these initiatives, we should note the increasing frequency of joint statements by the unions and the employers' organizations on such issues as the environment, monetary policy, etc.

On the more directly political level, how should the development of the unions' positions under the Bourassa government since 1985 be assessed? First, we should note again the unanimous position of the union federations in opposition to the Meech Lake Accord negotiated by the Liberal government with Ottawa and the premiers of the other provinces in 1987, followed by the positions taken by the FTQ, CSN, and CEQ in May and June 1990 in support of Québec's independence and the defeat of the Meech agreement. These constitute by far the major political developments of the period, and highlight in particular the clear opposition of the unions to the Bourassa government's orientation.[24]

The other major political battle of the unions since 1985 has been over free trade. In Québec this issue, like the constitutional issue, has placed the unions and the Bourassa government in opposing camps. The unions fought the free trade agreement, taking a position identical to that of the unions in the rest of Canada. But despite this opposition from the most massive social organizations, it may have appeared that Québec as a whole supported free trade, in contrast to the rest of Canada. This impression was fostered by the fact that the two parties in the National Assembly, the PQ and the PLQ, took the same position in support of free trade. While this is not sufficient to classify Québec society as a whole in the free-trade camp, it does serve to remind us, once again, that the political positions of the unions and mass organizations are not represented in the Québec parliament. At the end of the 1980s, the struggle against free trade again drew attention to this fact.

* * *

A cycle of political evolution, characterized by the quantitative and qualitative growth of the trade union movement since the mid-1950s, had come to an end. At the beginning of the 1990s the unionized percentage of the work force, which had declined somewhat during the 1980s, again passed the 40 percent mark; however, this seems to be a plateau in the present circumstances, particularly in view of the impossibility of multi-employer certifications. With the disappearance of the Union Nationale, the PQ has become one of the two dominant formations in a reconstituted two-party system; it may yet benefit from the fact that no significant opposition has appeared to rob it of the unique niche it occupies, in the name of nationalism, on the electoral stage. But any support it may solicit anew from the unions will necessarily be negotiated on an ad hoc basis, unlike the support it enjoyed in the 1970s. Nonpartisan agreements could no longer be based on the same relationship of trust. And in that sense, the Parti Québécois' hegemony over the unions is a thing of the past, as we enter the 1990s.

By virtue of its numerical and organizational strength, and the need for recognition of the legitimacy of its demands, the trade union movement must operate effectively in elections and in its ongoing relations with the state. Thus the end of its special relationship with the PQ places it in a period of transition, since it can no longer be content with a return to the limited and relatively unproductive nonpartisan methods prior to the mid-1950s. It therefore finds itself today in a political situation that is, by necessity, unstable.

CONCLUSION: TOWARD A POLITICAL TURN BY THE UNIONS?

At the beginning of this chapter we noted that the trade unions of the 1950s were led by the course of events to confront the problem of their own political representation even before entire sections of the labour force had managed to win the right to organize and bargain collectively. It would be a mistake to attribute the failure of the initial attempt to establish a new political party based on the unions to this factor. But the subsequent expansion of trade unionism, the quantitative increase in its numerical and organizational strength, effectively gave it a political influence and weight that it had never previously had. Its relationship with the state also became more intense, by the very fact that a large section of its new membership came from the public service and was active on a national, Québec level.

Yet the new strength of the unions, which might, at least in theory, have facilitated their pivotal role in the emergence of an independent political formation, did not initially have that effect. Instead, it encouraged the labour movement to act as a political force in its own name, drawing the maximum benefit from the opening provided by the post-Duplessis conjuncture. To the extent that its action seemed to enable it to modify the relationship of forces in favour of the working population, the issue of an independent political party as an extension of bread-and-butter unionism seemed less significant. The ideology of a self-sufficient unionism gradually infused all of its activities, so that the PQ's entry on the scene appeared to be an opening to increase the direct influence of the unions on the government's activities.

In practice, however, a political orientation like this is conditioned by two essential factors: on the one hand, the effective possibility of winning substantial concessions from the government and the employers; on the other, the possibility that the political system and the prevailing forces will themselves produce one or more alternatives to represent change and openness in opposition to "worn out" and "discarded" parties and governments. As one might imagine, if neither of these conditions exists, the situation is much more propitious for attempts to structure the political self-representation of the working class in forms that go qualitatively further than mere nonpartisanship.

Since the 1989 re-election of the Bourassa government, it has been evident that progressive reforms are not on the agenda, and that no component of the labour movement regards the Liberals as the instrument for new advances on the social and national plane in the wake of the break from the PQ. Accordingly, how and on what bases can the line of union nonpartisanship be maintained and practised in the coming years? While it is impossible to predict the precise political evolution of the unions, which in any case cannot be envisaged as a linear process, one thing at least seems obvious. The political question will tend to reappear in the unions, not as it did twenty-five years ago, before the experience with the Parti Québécois, but on the very basis of that experience. This, in the long term, is an additional maturation factor, because it is hard to conceive of a more solid and extensive nonpartisan relationship than the one that developed in the 1970s with the PQ. It would appear that Québec trade unionism is now faced with a choice between accepting a decline in its economic and political influence or committing itself more directly to the formation of a new partisan instrument for the working class and its allies in a way that is compatible with the preservation of its independence. In this sense, its present political situation can only be transitory.

NOTES

1. FUIQ: Fédération des unions industrielles du Québec, formed in 1952 and representing some 30,000 members; it merged with the Fédération provinciale du travail du Québec (FPTQ) in 1957 to form what is now the FTQ.
2. In 1958, the FTQ joined in the proposal to form a new party that was initiated by the Canadian Labour Congress. Created in 1961, this party was called the New Democratic Party. But disagreements on constitutional issues and the organizational relationship between the Québec division and the pan-Canadian party quickly led to a deadlock in the new formation in Québec. It soon split into two organizations, a provincial wing of the federal NDP for federal elections, and a separate party for provincial elections called the Parti Socialiste du Québec. In the face of these problems, the FTQ took its distance from the process, from 1963 on. The Québec NDP and the PSQ never managed to develop, and the latter disappeared in 1968.
3. The major manifestations were discussed at length in the reports of the Laurendeau-Dunton Royal Commission on Bilingualism and Biculturalism.
4. This, in our opinion, is the primary reason why contemporary Québec nationalism marks a break in continuity with the philosophical and religious speculations and ultramontane themes that had persisted until then in the various nationalist currents.
5. In this respect the written contributions of acknowledged representatives of each of these currents in *L'Impasse*, edited by N. Laurin-Frenette and J.-F. Léonard (*Nouvelle Optique*, Montréal, 1980), are extremely revealing.
6. See, for example, the report by Marcel Pepin at the 1966 convention of the CSN, entitled *Une société bâtie pour l'homme*.
7. In the report to the CSN's 1970 convention, *Un camp de la liberté*, there was talk of "the collusion of the State with the economic power, [which] has given birth to an economic and political superpower" (reported by L. Favreau and P. L'Heureux, 1984:58).
8. See his report *Un seul front*, the opening speech at the FTQ's 12th convention, Montréal, 1971, pp. 15–16.
9. FRAP stood for Front d'action politique—Political Action Front. It is interesting to note, as Louise Quesnel-Ouellet does, that the union involvement in municipal politics corresponded in particular to "changes in the election rules in 1968 (in relation to universal suffrage and the holding of elections)" in the cities and municipalities under provincial legislation. These rules tended to encourage organized participation. See Louise Quesnel-Ouellet, "Les partis politiques locaux au Québec," in Vincent Lemieux, ed., *Personnel et partis politiques au Québec*, Boréal Express, Montréal 1982, especially pages 279–80.
10. Statement reproduced in *La Presse*, 29 August 1970.
11. CSN, *Élections générales, Québec: 29 octobre 1973*, Orientation No. 2, Montréal, 1973.
12. In this respect it is significant that the FRAP election program in 1970 was entitled *Les salariés au pouvoir*, while, as its name indicated, the RCM sought to appeal to all "citizens," and not to present itself as the spokesperson for "employees" alone. Marcel Perreault, the president of the Montréal Labour Council (FTQ), explained that the unions were supporting the RCM "despite the fact [that it] is not a workers' party" (Document at news conference of the Conseil régional intersyndical de Montréal, 7 November 1974).
13. Leaders of the CSN, for example, stated: "The labour movement could become something other than a machine for bread-and-butter issues if the collective proposal put forward by the PQ were

soon to result in concrete achievements...." "I don't see why the people in the construction industry wouldn't agree to make some concessions on work procedures (i.e., job and skills definitions)
if it would also enable them to spend less time unemployed." "I think the union membership
would agree to a combination of positions (in the health field) that would have been unthinkable
under the previous government..." (*Le Devoir*, 19 November 1979).
In February 1977 the FTQ opened a discussion on the following issues: "Do the members think it
is possible for their federation to undertake ... to reduce some demands to 'give the PQ a
chance'?" "Can we go so far as to promise voluntary restrictions on our wage demands? If so, on
what conditions?" (*Le monde ouvrier*, the FTQ newspaper, February 1977).

14. Although these reforms were assessed differently by the federations, the FTQ being more recep-
     tive as a general rule: e.g., occupational health and safety legislation, "antiscab" legislation, etc.

15. Starting, in our opinion, with a generalized recognition of multi-employer collective bargaining;
     given the economic structure of the province, a genuine new step forward for the unions would
     require a legal framework of this nature.

16. For example, at its 1977 convention, where it described the economic situation as the worst since
     the Depression, the CSN demanded the creation of economic incentive sectors using, where nec-
     essary, nationalizations, the establishment of a Québec banking system, disclosure requirements
     for corporations, etc. See Favreau and L'Heureux, 1984:128.

17. In their *Mémoire commun sur le projet de loi 53* [Joint brief on Bill 53], presented to the govern-
     ment in December 1977, for example, the three federations raised the idea of "opening the books"
     in the public service: making files and documents prepared by government employees, particu-
     larly those in the Ministry of Labour and the Workers' Compensation Board, available to be dis-
     tributed freely and contribute to public discussion; and separating the public service from the
     concerns of the governing party and bringing it more into touch with the population as a whole.
     Since it did not do this, the PQ was said to have failed to keep its election promises. (See p. 2 *et
     seq.*)

18. While Robert Burns (of the CSN) was a member of the first Lévesque cabinet, it was not until
     1979 that Clément Richard (CSN), Guy Chevrette (CEQ), Robert Dean (FTQ), etc., made their
     way in. Over the years the FTQ proved to be the federation that was most closely linked to the
     Parti Québécois. It is probably the federation to which the theory that is sketched herein applies
     most directly.

19. See Rouillard, 1989:379–80, for an explanation of the particular situation of the CEQ; the CSN
     officially supported the "yes" vote on April 11, 1980, in a special meeting of its Conseil con-
     fédéral; as for the FTQ, 2,500 delegates to a special convention voted almost unanimously on
     April 19, 1980 to support the "yes" pursuant to a proposal by the Conseil général.

20. The three federations were assessed before the Bélanger-Campeau Commission, and called
     for a referendum to be held on Québec's sovereignty in 1991. It may be observed, therefore, that
     the Québec union federations took a position in favour of independence by their own devices,
     rather than in response to proposals or initiatives of the PQ.

21. For a more detailed analysis, see Serge Denis, "Développement, tensions et lignes de clivage du
     mouvement ouvrier au Canada," in *Crise économique, transformations politiques et changements
     idéologiques*, Cahier de l'ACFAS No. 16, G. Bernier and G. Boismenu, eds., Montréal 1984, pp.
     373–98.

22. For example, through candidates from the labour movement, who would have entered themselves
     as potential candidates at PQ nomination meetings. This idea, which was mentioned to us during
     an interview with union members from northwestern Québec, did not go beyond token proposals,
     however.

23. *Le Monde ouvrier*, May–June 1990, p. 12.

24. This chapter had already gone to press when the October 26, 1992 referendum on the Charlot-
     tetown Accord was called. In keeping with the 25 year evolution of their constitutional positions
     and the importance accorded to these, Quebec labour unions unanimously and without internal
     dissent came out against the Accord, and campaigned actively for the "No" forces during the ref-
     erendum campaign.

REFERENCES

Archibald, C. (1983). *Un Québec corporatiste?* Asticou, Hull.

Bernier, G., and Boily, R. (1986). *Le Québec en chiffres, de 1850 à nos jours*, Collection Politique et
     Économie, Acfas, Montréal.

Brunelle, D., and Drouilly, P. (1985). "Analyse de la structure socio-professionnelle de la main-d'oeuvre québécoise," in *Interventions économiques*, nos. 14–15, pp. 233–60.

Carlos, S., and Latouche, D. (1976). "La composition de l'électorat péquiste," in Latouche, D., Lord, G., and Vaillancourt, J.-G., eds., *Le processus électoral au Québec: Les élections provinciales de 1970 et 1973*, HMH, Montréal.

CEQ (1974). *Documents du 24e congrès*, June-July, Québec.

CEQ (Bureau national) (1977). *Documents pour le Conseil général*, 14 March, Québec.

CEQ (1980). *Communiqué de presse*, 3 October, Québec.

CEQ (1990). Résolution générale du 32e congrès, 26–30 June, Québec.

CLC (1983). Special Colloquium, "Resolution d'action politique," March 5–8, Quebec.

Comité des douze (1973). *Évaluation de la réflextion collective sur le document "Ne comptons ..."* Cahier Orientation, CSN, Montréal.

CSN (1971). *Déclaration de principes*, Montréal.

CSN (1973). *Élections générales, Québec: 29 octobre 1973*, Orientation no. 2, Montréal.

CSN (exécutif de la) (1977). *Rapport d'orientation: la CSN aujourd'hui*, 48e congrès régulier, Montréal.

CSN (1979). *Cahier des résolutions*, congrès spécial, June 1–2, Montréal.

CSN (1982). "La faillite du gouvernement du Parti québécois," document soumis au Conseil confédéral, 17 December, Montréal.

CSN (1990). "Rapport du Comité exécutif," 55e congrès, 5–11 May, Montréal.

CSN-CEQ (1984). *L'histoire du mouvement ouvrier au Québec*, co-édition Confédération des syndicats nationaux et Centrale de l'enseignement du Québec, Montréal.

CSN-CEQ-FTQ (1977). *Mémoire commun sur le projet de loi 53*, December, Montréal.

CSN-CEQ-FTQ (1982) (with the Société Saint-Jean-Baptiste, section Montréal, le Mouvement national des Québécois-es and l'Alliance des professeur(e)s de Montréal). *Déclaration conjointe des présidents de la CSN, CEQ, FTQ, SSJB-M, MNQ et APM*, 11 December, Montréal.

CTC (1983). "Résolution d'action politique," Colloque spécial 'L'égalité maintenant,' 5–8 March, Québec.

Denis, R. (1979). *Luttes de classes et question nationale au Québec, 1948–1968*, PSI-Montréal, EDI-Paris.

Denis, R. (1989). "État fédéral et syndicalisme," in Bélanger, Y., and Brunelle, D., dir., *L'ère des libéraux*, PUQ, Québec.

Denis, S. (1984). "Développements, tensions et lignes de clivage du mouvement ouvrier au Canada," in Bernier, J., and Boismenu, G., dir., *Crise économique, transformations politiques et changements idéologiques*, cahier de l'Acfas, no. 16, Montréal, pp. 373–98.

Drouilly, P. (1990a). "Une analyse des résultats de 1985," pp. 105–10; (1990b) "L'élection du 25 septembre 1989," pp. 260–67 in Roch Denis, dir., *Québec: dix ans de crise constitutionnelle*, VLB éditeur, Montréal, 1990.

Favreau, L., and L'Heureux, P. (1984). *Le projet de société de la CSN*, CFP-Vie ouvrière, Montréal.

Fleury, G. (1984). *Évolution de la syndicalisation*, Centre de recherche et de statistiques sur le marché du travail, Montréal.

Fournier, M. (1979). *Communisme et anti-communisme au Québec, 1920–1950*, Albert Saint-Martin, Montréal.

Fraser, G. (1984). *Le Parti québécois*, Libre Expression, Montréal.

FTQ (1979). *La FTQ et la question nationale*, November, Montréal.

FTQ (1990). "Le temps de la souveraineté est venu," *La Presse*, 23 June, Montréal.

Hamilton, R., and Pinard, M. (1984). "The class bases of the Québec independence movement: conjectures and evidence," *Ethnic and Racial Studies*, vol. 7, no. 1, January, pp. 19–54.

Haupt, G. (1981). "Socialisme et syndicalisme," in *Jean Jaurès et la classe ouvrière*, Les éditions ouvrières, Paris, pp. 29–66.

Ingerman, S. (1983). "La syndicalisation dans le contexte économique québécois," in *La syndicalisation dans le secteur privé au Québec*, 38e Congrès des Relations industrielles de l'Université Laval, PUL, Québec, pp. 37–69.

Laberge, L. (1971). *Un seul front*, FTQ, Montréal.

Laberge, L. (1975). *Cible et force de frappe*, FTQ, Montréal.

Lamoureux, A. (1985). *Le NPD et le Québec*, Éditions du Parc, Montréal.

Larose, G. (1980). "Les syndicats et le référendum," in Laurin-Frenette, N., and Léonard, J-F., dir., *L'impasse*, Nouvelle Optique, Montréal.

Lavigne, M. (1992). "Les femmes et la Révolution tranquille, 30 ans après: bilan et perspectives," in Laford, M.-R., ed., *La Révolution tranquille, trante ans après: qu'en reste-t-il?*, Hull, Éditions de Lorraine.

Pepin, M. (1966). *Une société bâtie pour l'homme*, CSN, Montréal.

Pepin, M. (1970). *Un camp de la liberté*, CSN, Montréal.

Pepin, M. (1970). *Le deuxième front*; et *Pour une société bâtie pour l'homme*, 2e édition, CSN, Montréal.

Pepin, M. (1976). "Mémo à tous les syndicats affiliés," 10 February, CSN, Montréal.

Rouillard, J. (1989). *Histoire du syndicalisme québécois*, Boréal, Montréal.

Evolution of the Role of Central Agencies in the Québec Government, 1960–90

Jacques Bourgault
Université du Québec à Montréal

Stéphane Dion and James Iain Gow
Université de Montréal

The theme of central agencies is at the heart of modern discussions of administrative science, because specialists, from Frederick W. Taylor, Max Weber, and Henri Fayol, to contemporary royal commissions have recognized that a crucial form of specialization is that of the "staff" organization, *a unit that may plan, coordinate, control, organize, or assist the "line" agencies that deliver goods and services.*

This is a broad but classic definition, similar to those used in the literature of public administration (Ouellet, 1968; Gélinas, 1975). Within this framework, the composition of the group of central agencies may vary considerably, for the executive has considerable freedom to create and modify them at its convenience. Table 13.1 shows the timing of the creation of these agencies since 1960. While the majority of them have functions of planning, coordination, and control, they are not of equal importance. The essential core is composed of the Department of the Executive Council (the premier's department), the Department of Finance, both of which were created immediately after Confederation, and the Treasury Board, which in its present form dates from 1970. The heart of central administrative power is to be found in these agencies; on the political level, one should add the premier's private office, a group that has also existed since Confederation, but that has only taken a role in the substance of policies since 1960.

The other central agencies have more specialized functions. Some are attached to the premier or to the National Assembly (the Citizen's Protector), while others may be separate agencies (the Public Service Commission) or horizontal departments under the direction of a minister (Intergovernmental Affairs). Some have a relatively minor role, certainly much less important than that of a super "line" agency such as Hydro-Québec, but in total they represent an important directing and controlling power over the machinery of government.

Studying central agencies has many advantages for the comprehension of a government and of a society. More than any other institution, they reveal the style and the intentions of the governing party and, in particular, of the head of the government, who has considerable freedom to shape them as he or she pleases. The

Table 13.1
Québec Central Agencies Since 1960 According to Role

AGENCY/ROLE	PLAN	COORD.	ORGAN.	SERVICE	CONTROL	CONSULT.	INFO.
Council of Economic Orientation (1961–68)	X						
Dept. of Federal–Provincial Affairs (1961–67)	X	X					
Comptroller of the Treasury (1961)					X		
Office of Info. and Publicity (1961–71)		X					X
Public Service Commission (1965)				X	X		
Dept. of Intergovernmental Affairs (1967–84)	X	X					
General Secretariat of Government (1968)	X	X					
Citizen's Protector (1968)	X	X			X		
Dept. of Communications (1968)	X	X					X
Office of Planning and Development (1968/69)	X	X					
Planning Council (1969)						X	
Public Service Dept. (1969–83)	X	X					
Treasury Board (1970)	X	X	X		X		
Secretariats of Ministers of State (1976)	X	X					
Office of Recruitment and Selection (1978–83)		X		X			
Office of Human Resources (1983)	X	X		X			
Société immobilière du Québec (1983)		X		X			
Dept. of Canadian Intergovt. Affairs (1984)	X	X			X		
Dept. of International Relations (1984–88)	X	X					
Department of Supply and Services (1986)		X		X	X		
Dept. of International Affairs (1988)	X	X					

way they operate influences the entire political and administrative system and, by extension, society at large.

The purpose of this chapter is to describe and explain the events summarized in Table 13.1. We wish to recall the political context that led to the creation, the development, and sometimes, the disappearance of these agencies. The immediate subject is thus the evolution of the role of central agencies, but through them, the style of each government is revealed. They inform us about the evolution of the government of Québec.

THE 1960S: A DECADE OF CHANGE AND EXPERIMENTATION

The period of the Quiet Revolution under the Liberals (1960–66) and its prolongation under the Union Nationale (1966–70) provides ample confirmation that the desire to undertake new activities leads governments to create new administrative bodies. Equally interesting is the tentative nature of these changes. In hindsight, the 1960s appear to be a period of search during which many models were tried before being abandoned or revised.

Prior to 1960: Unstructured Paternalism

Before 1960, the Québec government had very few central agencies and those that had real political importance almost all dated from the 19th century. Power was in the hands of the premier and those he chose to consult, and the style of government and administration was paternalistic.

In the matter of structures, the basic framework was put in place during the early years of Confederation. The office of Clerk of the Executive Council (the cabinet in its formal guise) and the Department of the Treasury were created in 1867, as was the earliest version of the Treasury Board, a committee of three ministers that, despite having no formal powers, acted as the main agency of financial control (Gow, 1985). The estimates were prepared by the Treasury Department. In 1883, a reform occurred that gave the provincial auditor real independence from the executive, while continuing his participation in the control of public spending before and after payment. Then, in 1885, the position of the attorney general as government legal adviser was defined by law.

For the next eighty years, few new central agencies were created, and most of them were common services, such as the Bureau of Statistics (1912), the Provincial Archives (1920), the *Chambre de mécanographie* (data processing centre, 1936), the Purchasing Service (1939), and the Office of Publicity (1946). The only exception to this rule was the Civil Service Commission, created by the government of Adélard Godbout in 1943 to introduce and manage the merit system. Although Québec and New Brunswick shared the distinction of being the last two provinces to introduce such commissions (Scarrow, 1957), the new Québec commission was ahead of its time. Maurice Duplessis would not forgive the Liberals for firing so many Union Nationale supporters after the Liberal victory in 1939, and he was not of a mind to let an independent commission control appointments to the public service. He persuaded the three commissioners to resign and replaced them by his friend, Ernest Laforce, who presided alone over the commission until 1960.

Duplessis did not invent the paternalistic style of government—he continued it, and in some ways perfected it (Vigod, 1986:252–55; Black, 1977:333–34; Gow, 1986:278–80). The common agencies created during his successive mandates in the areas of purchasing and publicity only strengthened his hold over government contracts and other spending. However, the best sign of the amateur style of his government was the absence of the Clerk of the Executive Council from meetings of the cabinet. Without an agenda and without minutes, it was a throwback to a time when governments could function largely on an oral basis (Hamelin and Beaudoin, 1967:315; Ouellet, 1980:79).

The interesting point about the absence of systematic administration and the weakness of central agencies under Duplessis is that the premier knew exactly what he was doing. His determination not to be restricted in his decisions and activities by his colleagues or senior public servants is demonstrated by his refusal to allow deputy ministers to have any regular meetings among themselves (Bourgault, 1971:371).

The 1960s: The Quiet Revolution and After

Although the Lesage government was far from a unified body in its desire to modernize the state and society in Québec, the premier's interest in doing so may be charted by the central agencies he created or expanded. At the same time, most of these activities were in some way provisional, and the Union Nationale government of the years 1966 to 1970, although more conservative in outlook, created a greater number of central agencies (six as opposed to the Liberals' five).

Jean Lesage quickly put the cabinet on a more formal basis: the Clerk was in attendance, an agenda was circulated, and minutes were kept of cabinet proceedings (Hamelin and Beaudoin, 1967:315). This was only a reform of a procedural nature, however. For changes in the substance of policy and administrative decisions, other reforms were needed. Among other problems, there was the lack of research or planning units in the government departments. To meet this difficulty, one strategy was to create a record number of royal and other commissions of inquiry (Bonenfant, 1972). The major commissions initiated research studies and consulted the interested public widely. André Bazinet has interpreted this as a temporary device, noting that between 1960 and 1965 at least ten departments created planning units (Bazinet, 1976:110–15).

Lesage had shown that he meant to proceed quickly in his version of province-building when, at the federal–provincial first ministers' conference in Ottawa at the end of July 1960, he called for an end to shared-cost programs and the transfer of an increased share of personal and corporate income taxes from Ottawa to Québec. One of his first moves in building up the capacity of the Québec government in this area was the adoption in 1961 of legislation creating the *Department of Federal–Provincial Relations*, with a mandate to develop policies, coordinate government actions, and conduct research in this area. However, it took some time to organize the department, and it was not until 1963 that its first staff members were appointed. From that time on, however, the department's new deputy head, Claude Morin, was among the handful of powerful technocrats who caught the public's eye (Gow, 1986:352–53).

A principal source of policy support and advice during the early years of the Lesage regime was the *Council of Economic Orientation of Québec (COEQ)*, a combination staff agency and advisory body. In August 1960, Jean Lesage made use of a law adopted in 1943 during the Godbout regime, but never used, to appoint five members to this body. They, in turn, developed a new law that was adopted in 1961. The new council had fifteen members appointed by the government to represent business, labour, and the universities, as well as five nonvoting members drawn from the senior public service. Although its ambiguous status as both a planning and an advisory body eventually led the council to recommend separating the two roles, it was able to prepare a number of key dossiers for the Lesage government. This work was done, not by the prominent members of the council itself, but by working groups, directed by the ten permanent staff members, and drawing on the resources of the public service as well as representatives of outside interested groups. Through these groups the council was able to do the leading work on such dossiers as the *Société générale de financement*, the Quebec Pension Plan, the *Caisse de dépôt et placement*, the nationalization of electricity, and the creation of a government steel corporation. While the ambition to introduce indicative economic planning on the French model was abandoned in 1965, the council continued to work with the Department of Industry and Commerce in the preparation of national accounts for the province. Altogether, the council played an indispensable role in preparing key dossiers in the early years of the Lesage government (Conseil d'orientation économique, 1966; Roland Parenteau, 1970).

On the administrative side, another early reform of Jean Lesage was the transformation of the existing financial committee into a *Treasury Board*. Drawing on his experience as Parliamentary Secretary to the federal Minister of Finance, Lesage put the *Conseil de la trésorerie* on the basis of a permanent committee of the Executive Council in all matters of finance and most questions of personnel management, except the appointment of deputy ministers and those of equivalent rank. Control over expenditures was strengthened by the appointment of a Comptroller of the Treasury to monitor and control not only expenditures, but also contracts and other commitments.

While this reform greatly improved the financial management capacity of the government, it continued the tradition of staffing all these activities in the Finance Department. Thus, not only was the Finance Minister *ex officio* chairman of the Treasury Board, the staff work for the board was done by officials of the department and the Comptroller of the Treasury was located there. Even so, the intent to give greater importance to financial management was clear. For the first time, a separate Department of Revenue was created, thus liberating the Finance Department from the burdens of this vital, but routine task.

In personnel management, most reforms were launched before institutional changes were made. The existing Civil Service Commission was reorganized, and open competitions were generalized both for external recruitment and for promotions. At the same time, under the pressure of a newly formed group of public servants backed by the *Confédération des syndicats nationaux*, the government created a committee to examine the possibility of introducing collective bargaining in the civil service.

So, when a new Public Service Act was adopted in 1965, two diverging trends were in evidence. On the one hand, the Public Service Commission was made more autonomous and the merit system was reinforced. Although appointed by the government, commissioners were to remain in office until the age of 70 and their salaries could not be diminished. They might only be dismissed with the approval of the two houses of the legislature. While the commission lost responsibility for organization to the Finance Department, it retained many matters of a policy nature, most notably position classification, which led it to be involved in the early rounds of collective bargaining. It was left to the Union Nationale government to try to sort out these two roles, the technical guardian of the merit system and political direction of the public service.

The final example from this period is in many ways typical of the hopes and illusions of the 1960s. In 1961, the Lesage government proposed the creation of an *Office of Information and Publicity.* Although the law was adopted, it took three years and as many studies before the office began to operate. Almost immediately, it was involved in controversy, when, in March 1965, the director and one of his deputies resigned, alleging political interference (Gow, 1986:326). Several of its main functions were transferred to other institutions, and at the end of the Liberal regime, it appeared destined to disappear.

Thus in the Liberal years, the new central agencies reflect both new functions of government and the introduction of a more orderly approach to financial and personnel management. Much of the change had to be improvised, however, and it was left to the Union Nationale governments to consolidate these reforms.

The Union Nationale, 1966–70: Prudence and Consolidation

The Union Nationale years were almost evenly divided between the government of Daniel Johnson (1966–68) and, after his death, that of Jean-Jacques Bertrand (1968–70). Although very different in personal style, there was much continuity between these governments, since Bertrand tried to carry out the policies begun by Johnson. In every area previously mentioned, their governments consolidated or improved on what had gone before. Also, in a new departure, they introduced a provincial ombudsman, the Citizen's Protector (1968).

At the core of the administrative structure, the Union Nationale introduced two changes that were to have long-lasting effects. First, in 1968, Jean-Jacques Bertrand created the position of *Secretary General of the Government,* a position that expanded the role of the Clerk to that of the head of the public service. While this move looks in retrospect to have been inevitable, paving the way for much greater changes to come (Baccigalupo, 1978:159), it seems to have been done to meet the personal needs of Premier Bertrand. According to O'Neill and Benjamin (1978:79–83), Bertrand wanted both an orderly system of government and protection from his ministers, so he appointed his former deputy minister of justice, Julien Chouinard, to be the unique channel through which all had to pass to reach both himself and the cabinet. On the economic planning front, Johnson accepted the recommendation of the COEQ and divided its functions into an *Office of Planning* and an advisory body, the *Council of Planning* (1968). In 1969, the Office became the leading agency for regional development also, a subject that was to become its principal preoccupation in the future.

The creation of the *Department of Intergovernmental Affairs* in 1967 was both a consolidation and a new departure. While one of Daniel Johnson's major motives was to end the existing dispersal of responsibilities in this field, the primary objective was to allow Québec to occupy all the fields of jurisdiction that the Constitution accorded it (Gow, 1986:185). In this case, the premier was particularly concerned with the area of international cooperation (especially with France and francophone countries), a field that Johnson feared would fall under federal control unless Québec could assume its proper role. Although it was active in these three fields, external relations, international cooperation, and federal–provincial relations, the department remained divided, both in its structures and its outlook, between its federal–provincial and its external relations missions.

In matters of administrative management, the main developments under the UN concerned questions of personnel. The adoption of collective bargaining led the government to create a *Directorate of Labour Relations (Direction générale des relations de travail)*, but it took a while to decide where the labour relations function should be located. Following the UN party platform, Daniel Johnson proposed the creation of a Civil Service Department. However, the department was not actually created until 1969. In the meantime, Marcel Masse had served as *Minister of State for the Public Service* since 1966 aided by a team of senior public servants for purposes of collective bargaining. The new department was thus to be in charge of collective bargaining and the political dimension of personnel administration. However, its direction of this area was soon to be challenged by the remodelling of the Treasury Board the following year.

Under the UN, the *Office of Information and Publicity of Québec (OIPQ)* took on new life, with 50 percent more staff and a budget seven times as great in 1968–69 as in 1965–66. At the same time, the whole question of information and publicity remained controversial, leading the government to commission a special study on the subject by a public relations firm directed by two well-known party supporters, Jean Loiselle and Paul Gros d'Aillon. Their report, issued in 1969, recommended greater budgets for information and centralized control of the operation. At the same time, the government created a Department of Communications with both a technical line role and a coordinating responsibility, and the days of the OIPQ were numbered.

Thus, although the period under the Union Nationale was one of many changes to central agencies, most of these were in response to initiatives begun under Lesage. While both the ombudsman and the Department of Intergovernmental Affairs represented policy orientations of Daniel Johnson, the creation of the office of Secretary General of the Government appears to have been the result of the personal style of Jean-Jacques Bertrand.

THE 1970S: THE HIGH POINT OF CENTRAL AGENCIES

During the 1970s, central agencies in the Québec government reached their highest point of development. This occurred under the government of the Parti Québécois, and reflected both the managerial style of Premier Lévesque and the tasks at hand. Prior to that, there were few changes under the first governments of Robert Bourassa, a period when personal style predominated over the weight of business.

The Liberals, 1970–76: Politics and Personal Power

The government of Robert Bourassa from 1970 to 1976 has been called the era of the managers, as distinct from the era of the technocrats of the 1960s (Ambroise and Jacques, 1980:143). However, at the summit, it was a personal, not a systemic, conception of management that prevailed.

This government introduced sweeping reforms of the system of health and social services, the organization of the school boards of the province, and the system of recognized professions. It also transformed the Treasury Board, widening its mandate and increasing its powers. Henceforth the board had its own decision-making powers; it did not have to refer most of its decisions to the cabinet as a whole for approval. To its responsibilities in matters of finance, the board now acted for the cabinet in most matters of personnel administration and overall administrative policy. One of its priorities was the introduction of program budgeting, which was accomplished for the fiscal year 1973–74. While some interpreted the reinforced role of the Treasury Board as a sign of declining power for the recently created Department of the Public Service, the minister, Raymond Garneau, replied that the board was merely acting in the place of the cabinet in all these matters and that, at any rate, the Minister of the Public Service was *ex officio* vice-chairman of the board and that of the deputy minister of the public service as one of the three assistant secretaries of the board (Garneau, 1971).

In spite of these impressive reforms, Robert Bourassa did not want a collective style of government. He preferred to run things his way, frequently dealing directly with individual ministers rather than together. The early years of the Bourassa government were dominated by the *éminence grise* Paul Desrochers, who was neither *chef de cabinet* nor Secretary General, but merely a "special adviser" (O'Neill and Benjamin, 1978:114–17, 152–55; Baccigalupo, 1978:112–22).

The *General Secretariat* continued to develop, certainly. One of its new functions was highly controversial. In the midst of the October Crisis, in 1970, the government set up the CAD, the *Centre d'analyse et de documentation*, a kind of antiterrorism intelligence unit that compiled dossiers on as many as 30,000 individuals and 7,000 groups (O'Neill and Benjamin, 1978:123). Apparently never the object of a cabinet decision, the centre was unknown to the public until its existence was revealed in 1975. Its dossiers were destroyed by the PQ government after its election in 1976.

Relatively late in its existence, the government created in 1975 a system of permanent cabinet coordinating committees. The result of a proposal by the new Secretary General, Guy Coulombe, the committees were presided over by sectorial ministers who had portfolios of their own to administer. They covered the major preoccupations of the day: human resources, quality of life, natural resources, regional development, legislation, intergovernmental relations, and government administration (Baccigalupo, 1978:160–62).

Thus the Bourassa government had a relatively slim package of structures and practices to pass on to the Parti Québécois government after the 1976 election. The principal element was the new Treasury Board, followed by the idea of several cabinet committees covering the main functions of government. However, compared to its two predecessors, it changed the central administrative structure relatively little.

The Parti Québécois from 1976 to 1981: Collective Government

When the Parti Québécois defeated the Liberals in November 1976 on a platform of good government, it was faced with a major challenge. On the one hand, René Lévesque and his government had a substantial agenda they wanted to put into effect. On the other hand, except for Lévesque himself, no members of the cabinet had experience of government, although some, including Jacques Parizeau, Claude Morin, and Denis de Belleval, had first-hand, inside knowledge of the administration.

Thus it was that while Jacques Parizeau recommended adhering to the British model of a strong degree of individual responsibility for ministers, under the stewardship of the premier and the Minister of Finance, René Lévesque chose another option. Louis Bernard, whom Lévesque chose as his Secretary General, recommended a split-level government with strong coordinating capacities. All ordinary departments were organized in *standing committees of the cabinet*, each chaired by a minister of state, a senior member of the party who had no other executive responsibilities. Thus in 1976 there were four committees for economic development, social development, cultural development, and regional development. Their mandate was to plan and coordinate sectorial development. In 1979, a fifth committee on the status of women was added. Each committee was supported by a secretariat directed by an Associate Secretary General who, at that time, had the role and powers of a deputy minister (Baccigalupo, 1978:160–61; Bernard, 1987:61–89; Dion and Gow, 1989b:59–73; O'Neill and Benjamin, 1978:218–24).

There were three other standing committees of the cabinet, the Priorities Committee, Treasury Board, and the Committee on Legislation. Leaving aside the latter, which had a technical role, the other two committees were the heart of the system. The Priorities Committee was chaired by the premier and included the five ministers of state, and the ministers of finance and intergovernmental relations. This was the "inner cabinet" of the first Lévesque government, where the major arbitrations and resource allocations of the government took place. The Treasury Board retained its entire powers in the areas of preparation of the budgetary estimates and control of expenditure.

The system thus created required a good deal of discipline, but it was generally adhered to by the government. While ministers retained their right of direct access to the full cabinet, this right now had to be exercised through one of the committees. Ministers of state, while having no hierarchical control over their colleagues, had three sources of power: their membership in the Priorities Committee, their chairing of a coordinating committee, and direct responsibility for certain special dossiers, such as language legislation for Camille Laurin, health and safety in the workplace for Pierre Marois. Such a regime had the beneficial effects of obliging the ministers to negotiate openly among themselves and of preventing any one of them from obtaining special favours and advantages.

The one exception to this rule was the Minister of Finance, Jacques Parizeau. By keeping out of the development committees and from his key positions as President of the Treasury Board and member of the Priorities Committee, Parizeau retained a free hand to intervene in all debates. His colleagues later said that, by a combination of personal brilliance and strategic position, Parizeau came to dominate the Priorities Committee (Dion and Gow, 1989b:67). So while the committee system was an expression of the wish of the premier for a collective style of government, M. Lévesque also allowed Jacques Parizeau to have a predominant position.

This new style of government expanded the role of the Secretary General, who as the head of the premier's Department of the Executive Council holds the most senior position in the public service. The appointment of Louis Bernard in September 1977 was seen by all as a political appointment, in much the same manner as that of Michael Pitfield as Clerk of the Privy Council by Pierre Trudeau in Ottawa in January 1975. No one doubted the competency of Bernard, and he became the pivotal figure of the new system. The staffs of the various development committees came under his jurisdiction, the so-called deputy ministers of the ministers of state being in fact Associate Secretaries General. It is not surprising, therefore, that the size of the staff and the budget of the premier's department, already considerable under Bourassa, grew rapidly (the budget rose by 17 percent the first year, from $1.1 million to $1.6 million; Baccigalupo, 1978:171).

This was the system put in place by the Lévesque government during its first mandate. The only other important change to central agencies at this time was the creation in 1978 of a new agency for personnel management, the *Office of Recruitment and Selection for the Public Service*. Without changing the roles of the Treasury Board and the Public Service Department, the new law confided the active responsibility for recruitment and selection to the office, an expert but less autonomous body, while reserving the roles of appeals agent and watchdog of the merit principle to the autonomous Public Service Commission. Thus the Québec government had now four central agencies for personnel management, a luxury that it would not allow itself for very long (Bourgault, 1981).

The committee system was a product of both the ambitious tasks that the Parti Québécois had set itself and the personal style of René Lévesque. It also reflected the context of the first mandate, a context that was about to change dramatically.

THE 1980S: THE ERA OF THE GUARDIANS

The decade of the 1980s was, above all, a period of budgetary restraint. Priority was given to deficit reduction, productivity and employee evaluation, accountability of senior public servants, and a stricter wage policy. Governments tried to reinforce the "guardians" of the public purse (Finance and the Treasury Board) while, at the same time, increasing the discretionary powers of departments in the name of good management.

The Second Term of the Parti Québécois: The Limits to Development

Although it was on the losing side in the 1980 referendum, the Parti Québécois was re-elected on April 30, 1981. A recession was developing at that time that had a devastating effect on public finances, since it reduced revenues at the very moment when social expenditures were rising. The style of the government was profoundly affected by these events: program management was centralized, a moratorium on the creation of new institutions was introduced, severe budgetary restrictions led to freezes on wages and staff numbers and to measures to encourage voluntary departures by employees.

Managing downsizing led to tension and morosity within the governmental party, where many members with social-democratic leanings would have preferred to increase further the role of the state. Thus the government appeared divided on the socially unpopular measures that accompanied tighter financial management. Soon it would also be divided on constitutional matters, between orthodox *souverainistes* and those who wanted to follow Premier Lévesque in the *"beau risque"* of supporting Brian Mulroney and the Progressive Conservative Party in the federal general elections in 1984.

The Lévesque government rapidly modified its central organization in keeping with its new budgetary priorities. The two most spectacular transformations involved central agencies: first the disappearance of the full-time posts of the four ministers of state for development, and second, the reinforcement of the Treasury Board.

In 1982, the positions of minister of state exclusively devoted to the development and coordination of a sector of governmental activity were abolished. René Lévesque decided that the times were no longer suited to the development and introduction of major policy initiatives. At any event, the leading members of the government no longer wanted to be ministers of state, but asked rather to be appointed to head one of the major line departments, where real power and responsibility lay (Dion and Gow, 1989b). The interdepartmental cabinet committees were retained, but with a regular departmental minister as chair and a reduced secretariat. The result was an increase in power for traditional central agencies and, in particular, the Treasury Board.

The board acquired increased autonomy with the appointment in 1981 of Yves Bérubé as minister exclusively assigned to this portfolio. Prior to this, the Minister of Finance was also Chairman of the Treasury Board. Bérubé's mission was to hold the annual deficit at or below the threshold of three billion dollars. Year after year the board tightened its budgetary control over departments, first, in order to enforce the freeze on wages and spending introduced in 1982, and later, to impose compliance with the objectives of budgetary restraint.

The desire to reinforce budgetary control led the premier to attribute progressively to the Treasury Board the essential responsibilities in the management of human resources. After all, taken in the context of the entire public sector, more than two-thirds of public expenditures are devoted to wages and benefits. An amendment to the Public Service Act in 1981 gave to the board the mandate to develop human resources, in particular, by training program and responsibility for approving the regulations proposed by the Office of Recruitment and Selection. The following year the *Loi sur les conditions de travail du secteur public* charged the board with determining wages and other conditions of work (L.Q., 1982:c.45). In 1983, it was given the coordination of the program of voluntary departures of senior executives (Bourgault, 1990). However, the most important change occurred with the adoption in 1983 of the law abolishing the Civil Service Department and transferring to the Treasury Board its responsibilities for classification, staffing, codes of ethics and discipline, and above all, the negotiation, signature, execution, and interpretation of collective agreements involving civil servants (L.Q., 1983:c.55).

Behind these changes were three aspects of public sector labour relations. First, public sector unions had regularly short-circuited the Public Service Department in order to deal directly with the Treasury Board and, sometimes, the premier. Second, the government wished to unify the application of its personnel policies. Third, it wished to avoid the creation of precedents and special cases that the unions could then try to extend to the entire public sector.

Thus the Treasury Board gradually became the central agency for all aspects of the management of the public sector work force, including civil servants and employees of the education and health and welfare sectors. For example, the board was henceforth the body that approved the classification plans of managers in health and welfare establishments, which forbid any additional remuneration for heads of local institutions and which tried to introduce merit bonuses to managers in the school system. In this regard, some have qualified the 1983 act as a triumph for centralization under the Treasury Board (Bauer, 1989:53).

However, in spite of the extent of its new powers, the Treasury Board did not monopolize the field of personnel management. For one thing, the Public Service Commission kept its responsibilities as guardian of the merit system. Also, under the 1983 Act, the *Office of Human Resources* succeeded the Office of Recruitment and Selection, inheriting not only the main functions of that body, but also the role of adviser to the government on questions of human resources that had previously belonged to the Public Service Department. The new office also received former powers of the Public Service Commission concerning regulations governing recruitment competitions.

The 1983 Act thus aimed at centralizing personnel management. However, another objective was also apparent within the new framework, namely the transfer of powers and responsibilities to top and mid-level management in government departments and agencies. This aspect of the law marked the ascension of the rhetoric of management and productivity at the expense of the merit principle (Gow, 1984:100).

At the same time as it was consolidating its budgetary control and extending its responsibilities in personnel management, the Treasury Board was called upon to manage central government purchasing. In 1983, the Department of Public Works and Supply was abolished, the construction and management of government properties being allocated to a new public corporation (*La Société immobilière*), while that of purchasing went to the Treasury Board, for the sake of tighter expenditure control. So the board acquired the dominant role in both the preparation of regulations governing purchasing and the supervision of their execution. No matter where they turned, in matters of finance, personnel, or purchasing and supplies, departments now found the Treasury Board in their path.

The desire for increased control also led to the reinforcement of the powers of central agencies to supervise public corporations. Until this time, the government had left its corporations relatively free to set tariffs and determine the most appropriate framework for internal management. Now, in the spirit of the 1980s, the cabinet sought to integrate major public corporations into its overall management philosophy. To this end, it used a variety of means: legislative changes, closer supervision by the Secretariat of the Executive Council, and the deliberate use of appointments to the presidencies of corporations. In 1983, amendments to the law governing Hydro-Québec (L.Q., 1983:c.15) designated the government as the company's shareholder, and established its control over the investment program of Hydro-Québec and over the declaration (or not) of a dividend. In the same vein, both the *Société des Alcools* and *La Société des Loteries et Courses* found themselves obliged, by the Minister of Finance, to respect lower limits on the return on the government's investment.

Finally, another sign of concentration of power in the central agencies was the increased role given to the Secretariat for Administrative Reform and Senior Personnel, which is part of the General Secretariat of the government. Under the Public Service Act of 1983, deputy ministers, associate and assistant deputies, and others of equivalent rank were united in a corps of *Administrateurs d'État*. While its provisions did not innovate in granting the premier full powers in hiring, transferring, and firing these officials, having it all in writing for the first time underlined their dependency on those who advise the premier on these matters. This precarity was increased by the provision in the act that allowed for the appointment of individuals at this level on a contractual, fixed-term basis. Advising the premier on this subject also came under the responsibilities of the Secretariat for Senior Personnel, which increasingly manages the careers of senior officials.

Thus the contrast is striking between the place of central agencies during the first and second terms of the PQ government. Now, it was through their control functions that they strengthened their position, rather than through the development of new policies. No doubt these new priorities weakened the unity of a party that was obliged to manage austerity, where it had hoped to build a new Québec.

The Return of Robert Bourassa (1985 —): In Search of Productivity

The strong victory of the Liberal Party in the general elections of December 1985 brought Robert Bourassa to the head of a government that, according to its platform, intended to promote economic development and deficit reduction by reducing public expenditures, programs, and staffs and by introducing productivity control. The task was all the more necessary because the government was faced with new social demands in areas such as the protection of the environment. In these circumstances, the Québec public service, which had paradoxically helped to defeat the government at whose hands it had suffered wage cuts and repressive labour laws (Blais and Crête, 1989), was in for a big surprise.

No sooner was he in power than Premier Bourassa established three committees to recommend ways to reduce governmental expenses (the Gobeil Committee), to deregulate the economy (the Scowen Committee), and to privatize public corporations (the Fortier Committee). Their reports were often spectacular and ambitious, but the government only gave them limited application. The Gobeil Report, which was at once the most radical and the briefest, recommended the reduction of the number of government autonomous agencies from 202 to 116. In fact, the government did reduce their number to 184 after two years in office (Dion and Gow, 1989a:63–65), but their number rose again to reach 204 in April 1990 (Bourgault and Dion, 1990:47–48). The same trend was observed in the public service, where overall numbers declined from 53,927 in 1985 to 52,164 in 1988, before rising again to 52,835 in 1990.

Two characteristics of the managerial style of this government particularly concern central agencies: first, the determination to integrate political appointees into the governmental process, and second, the desire to reduce the burdens of central agencies in order that they might concentrate on their essential functions. The integration of political personnel took three forms under the Liberals. First, they made a much greater use of the post of *ministre délégué*, a sort of minister of state charged with the coordination of an interdepartmental policy field (Ouellet, 1980:76). The Liberals had thirteen such ministers in 1990, as opposed to one for the PQ government in 1980. The other two trends that concern us here are an increased politicization of the senior public service and reliance on ministers' private offices *(cabinets ministériels)*.

Politicization of the higher public service was not an invention of the Liberals in 1985, but they distinguished themselves by their use of former members of ministers' staffs—something the Parti Québécois could not do on the same scale, having been elected for the first time in 1976. The phenomenon first appeared in the case of the position of General Secretary to the Executive Council, the most senior position in the public service. Robert Bourassa imitated René Lévesque in appointing senior civil servants who were known both for distinguished administrative careers and for their affinities with the ideas of the government. To ensure the transition, the premier chose Roch Bolduc, a former deputy minister and Public Service Commissioner, who made no secret of his aversion for the principal policies of the PQ. Then, eighteen months later, he appointed Benoît Morin, who had worked in the private office of a Liberal minister in the 1970s. Moreover, in 1986, a Liberal *chef de cabinet* was transferred to the post of Associate Secretary General for Administrative Reform and Senior Personnel. This official prepares recommendations for appointments and renewals to discretionary positions and is consulted about the departure of deputy ministers and heads of agencies. Previously, this position had been occupied by career civil servants without political attachments.

These political appointments to the principal central agency had their repercussions in the departments as well. Robert Bourassa appointed in his first term five deputy ministers who had previously been members of ministers' office staffs and two more at the beginning of his second term (Bourgault and Dion, 1991). Moreover, recourse to contractual appointments rendered even more precarious the status of those chosen in this way (Bourgault and Dion, 1989:102–3).

The other means noted for ensuring political influence was the continued reliance on ministers' office staffs. In the opposition, the Liberals had criticized what they called the excessive importance given to these staffs and their political advisers (Plasse, 1981:334). In fact, the *cabinets ministériels* had even more members under the Liberals and, according to some observers, more influence (Johnson and Daigneault, 1988). From 1980 to 1990, the number of members (excluding clerical staff and constituency offices) rose from 182 to 258, an increase of 42 percent. The premier's chief of staff remained a very important figure, especially during the first term with Mario Bertrand, a friend and confidant of the premier, who left for the private sector in 1989. His successor, John Parisella, a party official and former member of the legislature, had not the same authority over ministers, a factor that reduced the strength of the premier's office as a central agency.

The other important trait of the Liberal style of the 1980s was the desire to trim the functions of certain central agencies in order to have them better concentrate on their basic mission. From the beginning of the first term, there was evidence of this strategy both in the organization of cabinet committees and within the Executive Council, the Treasury Board, and the Office of Human Resources.

Robert Bourassa maintained a streamlined version of the system of cabinet committees inherited from the Parti Québécois. He immediately put aside the Priorities Committee, which was too formal an arena for a premier who is known to prefer ad hoc consultations. The four development committees were reduced to three in number, in a manner that clearly demonstrated the priorities of this government: the two committees that were maintained were economic development and regional development, whereas social, cultural, education, and women's issues were merged in one committee on social and cultural affairs. Robert Bourassa has maintained this spare structure of standing committees, but he has had much more frequent recourse to ad hoc committees on policy problems or crisis management (as in the cases of Saint-Basile-Le-Grand, Saint-Amable, and Oka).

In a like manner, the Department of the Executive Council was slimmed down following the election of 1985. The premier soon transferred six committee secretariats to appropriate departments, in an effort to allow the General Secretariat to concentrate on its main tasks. Even so, the ebb and flow of issues and institutions pushed the number of secretariats attached to the department from nine in 1986 to thirteen in 1990, the newcomers being secretariats dealing with the family, planning, electoral reform, and *l'Ordre national du Québec*.

Under a government whose objectives stressed expenditure control and deficit reduction, the Treasury Board naturally had a prominent role. However, the massive transfer of powers that had strengthened it during the period from 1980 to 1985 meant that the most important changes it introduced were in its methods and operations.

For reasons both of efficiency and administrative doctrine, the board adopted a more flexible style of management, gradually transforming management regulations into policies, programs, and directives (Dion and Gow, 1989a:72). Within the framework of the 1983 Public Service Act, deputy ministers were responsible for personnel management in their departments. The Treasury Board also delegated further responsibilities to them in such areas as position evaluation and the organization of competitions. In return, the deputies from 1986 onward had to deposit with the board an annual review of their management of the personnel function.

In the area of public sector labour relations, the position of the board was considerably reinforced in 1986 by Bill 160, which, in addition to severely restricting the right to strike in health and welfare institutions, transformed the committees representing management in these sectors from full partners to advisers of the board.

Beyond financial management and personnel administration, the Treasury Board's success was more limited. After the election of 1985, the government let the board proceed with a major study of administrative reform launched in the last months of the Parti Québécois government under the name *Pour une rénovation de l'administration publique.* The process went as far as the publication in 1987 of a policy statement with the same name. However, the government seemed to have little interest in a broad-range reform of the public service, and deputy ministers rejected the enhancement of the role of the board, particularly the idea that they should be evaluated by it rather than by the Department of the Executive Council.

With the creation of the Department of Supply and Services in 1986, the Treasury Board was liberated from a part of its responsibilities in the area of contracts and purchasing. However, it would seem that a definitive division of labour between the board and the new department was not easy to achieve. Since the election of the Liberals in 1985, there have been numerous accusations that they had succumbed to their old habits of patronage. To meet these criticisms, the government created a task force to study the process of government contracting. Under the chairmanship of Louis Bernard, former Secretary General under the PQ, the committee recommended in May 1990, under the title *L'efficacité dans la transparence*, that leadership in this area should be clearly assigned to one or the other of these central agencies, either the Treasury Board or the Department of Supply and Services.

Another kind of centralization of financial management occurred in 1990, when the government decided to locate in the Finance Department all borrowing operations of Québec government agencies. The aim of the government was to save tens of millions of dollars in interest and commissions by the volume of activity thus created, but the immediate effect was to make government agencies more dependent on the timetable, the conditions, the standards, and the authorizations of the Department of Finance (A. Bernard, 1990:32–33).

Like the other central agencies, the Office of Human Resources has had to clarify its role. In 1986, it adopted a general policy statement that gave priority to service to its clients and the anticipation of needs in the area of human resources. More and more, it acts as a consultant and leader, leaving the role of controller to the Treasury Board and the Public Service Commission.

Finally, one should note the division of external relations into two separate departments in 1988, Intergovernmental Affairs and International Relations. Here again, the goal was to target better the interventions of each: on the one hand, to lay increasing stress on foreign trade and, on the other, to concentrate talent and energies on negotiation of a new arrangement with the rest of Canada.

In sum, the Liberal government was seeking, like its predecessor, to square the circle, that is, to join the centralization required by strict budgetary control with the decentralization required for flexible and adequate management. The results are mixed. With respect to budgetary control, the Liberal government began its second term with optimism, as its deficit seemed to be holding stable at less than $2 billion. Since then, however, the sudden rise in the deficit caused by the recession of 1990–91 has raised new doubts about the possibilities of achieving this objective. With respect to administrative devolution, it appears to have encountered some obstacles and generated some unforeseen side effects. On the one hand, deputy ministers have not fully exploited the possibilities of delegating responsibilities within their own organizations. On the other hand, the scope of discretionary powers delegated to departmental managers has raised questions about the fairness and impartiality of competitive appointments, if one is to believe the Public Service Commission (Commission de la fonction publique, 1990:12).

Thus the problems of administrative management are as difficult as ever, bedevilling a government that is otherwise preoccupied by the failure of the Meech Lake Accord, the crisis with native peoples, the health problems of the premier, and above all, the rise of pro-sovereignty sentiment.

CONCLUSION

Over the last three decades, the government of Québec has experienced a vast movement of administrative modernization. The frequent recourse to central agencies that has accompanied this movement has constantly faced the government with difficult choices, as it has elsewhere (Campbell, 1988). With hindsight, it is easy to draw up an evaluation.

This chapter has illustrated a general trend to centralization of administrative activities in Québec over the past thirty years. Politicians wanted more centralization to coordinate policy development, control the deficit, and make sure that the administration complied with their objectives. Senior officials in central agencies wanted more centralization to maintain consistency in administrative policies and integrate every administrative body in pursuit of the government's program.

The roles of central agencies have evolved not only by legislative changes, but also by many other processes, some political, others more administrative. Governments have used six different techniques to reinforce central agencies' powers: they have used *laws* to create agencies, such as the *Société immobilière,* or to increase their mandates and powers, as with the Treasury Board; they have used *executive discretionary decision powers* to create secretariats and staff those bodies; they have used *appointment processes* to give more influence to central secretariats in the choice of senior officials; they have given *more influence to the Department of the Executive Council,* by increasing the number of minister-delegate positions; they have given more influence to ministers over their departments by *enhancing the roles of ministers' private offices;* and they have used *administrative practices* such as performance appraisal of senior personnel in central agencies, to bind them more closely to their objectives.

In the 1960s and the 1970s Québec experienced steady expansion of the role of the public sector. The reinforcement of central agencies during this period served both to harmonize the new policies that were constantly being proposed by line departments and to develop other major policies as well. In this way, a critical mass of experts was brought together in the Office of Planning, the secretariats of the Executive Council, and at the Department of Finance. With no administrative responsibilities, freed from routine, and far from the pressures of vested interests, these experts were able to give free rein to imaginative policy development.

The apogee of this era of central agencies was reached with the creation of the posts of minister of state during the first term of the Parti Québécois government. Afterward, budgetary problems brought out the limits of this approach, limits that foretold the coming disenchantment with the planning ambitions of the 1960s. Far from the action, the experts working in central agencies appeared to departmental managers as abstract rationalists. The policies issuing from central agencies seemed unrealistic and inflexible, and their political and administrative heads were no longer able to impose their authority on departments seeking autonomy. The time came when prominent leaders of the government such as Camille Laurin and Bernard Landry deserted these agencies for key line departments, where action has tangible and visible results.

The time of budgetary difficulties also led to a major role for central agencies, but this time as controllers or guardians. Paradoxically, the first victim of the new order was a central agency: the Public Service Department. Caught between public sector unions, which regularly bypassed it to reach the real authority in financial matters, and the ever more stringent controls applied by the Treasury Board, the department had never really established its authority. Whether it be financial management, personnel management, or the negotiation of collective agreements, management was centred in one body, the Treasury Board, under the watchful eye of the Department of Finance and the premier.

In this period of restrictions, the challenge is to ensure absolute respect of the budgetary framework, while increasing the autonomy of managers within this framework. This is the dual, and sometimes conflicting, movement of centralization of financial control and managerial devolution that the government of Québec, like other governments (Aucoin, 1991) has been pursuing for a decade.

Thus, while everything is being done to reinforce the few guardians of the purse in the face of the enormous pressure to spend coming from line departments, more than ever attempts are being made to delegate responsibilities to their managers, who are urged to pursue the triple goals of excellence, productivity, and accountability. Whether or not this government has succeeded better than others in reconciling these requirements will no doubt be revealed as the 1990s progress.

REFERENCES

Ambroise, Antoine and Jacques, Jocelyn (1980), "L'appareil administratif," in G. Bergeron and R. Pelletier, eds., *L'État du Québec en devenir*, Montréal, Boréal Express, pp. 109–46.

Aucoin, Peter (1991), "The Politics and Management of Restraint Budgeting," in André Blais and Stéphane Dion, eds., *The Budgeting-Maximizing Bureaucrat: Appraisals and Evidence*, Pittsburgh: University of Pittsburgh Press, pp. 119–42.

Baccigalupo, Alain (1978), *Les grands rouages de la machine administrative québécoise*, Montréal: Agence d'Arc.

Bauer, Julien (1989), "La syndicalisation dans le secteur public québécois ou la longue marche vers la centralisation," *Administration publique québécoise: analyses sectorielles*, Québec: Presses de l'Université du Québec, pp. 35–61.

Bazinet, André (1976), *Les commissions d'enquête du Québec (1960–1966) comme organismes d'étude et de consultation*, M.A. thesis, Political Science, Université de Montréal.

Bernard, André (1990), "Les politiques gouvernementales," in Denis Monière, ed., *L'année politique au Québec, 1989–1990*, Montréal: Québec/Amérique, pp. 23–34.

Bernard, Louis (1987), *Réflexions sur l'art de se gouverner*, Montréal: Québec/Amérique.

Black, Conrad (1977), *Duplessis*, Toronto: McClelland and Stewart.

Blais, André and Crête, Jean (1989), "Can a Party Punish its Faithful Supporters? The Parti québécois and Public Sector Employees," *Canadian Public Administration*, 32:4, pp. 623–32.

Bonenfant, Jean-Charles (1972), "Les commissions d'enquête du Québec," *Annuaire du Québec 1972*, pp. 36–76.

Bourgault, Jacques (1971), *Les sous-ministres du Québec, de 1945 à nos jours*, M.A thesis, Political Science, Université de Montréal.

Bourgault, Jacques (1981), "L'organisation de l'administration publique québécoise, 1868–1980," *Annuaire du Québec, 1979–1980*, Québec: Bureau de la Statistique, pp. 121–37.

Bourgault, Jacques (1990), "Québec," in William A. Neilson, ed., *Getting the Pink Slip: Severances and Firings in the Senior Public Service*, Toronto: Institute of Public Administration of Canada.

Bourgault, Jacques and Dion, Stéphane (1989), "Les gouvernements antibureaucratiques face à la haute administration: une comparaison Québec–Canada," *Politiques et management public*, 7:2, pp. 97–118.

Bourgault, Jacques and Dion, Stéphane (1990), "L'administration publique," in Denis Monière, ed., *L'année politique, 1989–1990*, Montréal: Québec/Amérique, pp. 45–60.

Bourgault, Jacques and Dion, Stéphane (1991), "Haute fonction publique et changement de gouvernement au Québec: le cas des sous-ministres en titre (1976–1989)," *Politique*, 19, pp. 81–106.

Campbell, Colin (1988), "The Search for Coordination and Control: When and How Are Central Agencies the Answer?" in Colin Campbell and B. Guy Peters, *Organizing Governance, Governing Organizations*, Pittsburgh: University of Pittsburgh Press, pp. 55–75.

Commission de la fonction publique du Québec (1990), *Rapport annuel, 1989–1990*, Québec: Publications du Québec.

Conseil d'orientation économique du Québec (1966), *Le Conseil d'orientation économique, son statut, ses travaux*, Québec.

Conseil du trésor du Québec (1985), *Pour une rénovation de l'administration publique*, Québec.

Dion, Stéphane and Gow, James Iain (1989a), "L'administration publique", in Denis Monière, ed., *L'année politique au Québec, 1988–1989*, Montréal: Québec/Amérique, pp. 61–76.

Dion, Stéphane and Gow, James Iain (1989b), "The Budget Process Under the Parti Québécois, 1975(sic)–1985," in Allan M. Maslove, *Budgeting in the Provinces: Leadership and the Premiers*, Toronto: Institute of Public Administration of Canada, pp. 55–85.

Garneau, Raymond (1971), "La réforme de l'administration financière au Québec," *Canadian Public Administration*, 14:2, pp. 256–70.

Gélinas, André (1975). *Les organismes autonomes et centraux*, Montréal: Les Presses de l'Université du Québec.

Gow, James Iain (1984), "La réforme institutionnelle de la fonction publique de 1983: contexte, contenu et enjeux," *Politique*, 6, pp. 51–101.

Gow, James Iain (1985), "One Hundred Years of Quebec Administrative History, 1867–1970," *Canadian Public Administration*, 28:2, pp. 244–68.

Gow, James Iain (1986), *Histoire de l'administration publique québécoise, 1867–1970*, Montréal: Les Presses de l'Université de Montréal.

Hamelin, Jean and Beaudoin, Louise (1967), "Les cabinets provinciaux, 1867–1967," *Recherches sociographiques*, 8:3, pp. 299–318.

Johnson, Andrew F. and Daigneault, Jean (1988), "Liberal 'chefs de cabinets ministériels' in Québec: keeping politics in policy making," *Canadian Public Administration*, 31:4, pp. 501–16.

Lepage, Laurent (1989), "La construction de l'édifice scolaire québécois," in Yves Bélanger and Laurent Lepage, *L'administration publique québécoise, évolution sectorielle, 1960–1985*, Montréal: Les Presses de l'Université du Québec, pp. 85–104.

O'Neill, Pierre and Benjamin, Jacques (1978), *Les mandarins du pouvoir*, Montréal, Québec/Amérique.

Ouellet, Lionel (1968), "Concepts et techniques d'analyse des phénomènes administratifs," *Canadian Journal of Political Science*, 1:3, pp. 310–35.

Ouellet, Lionel (1980), "L'appareil gouvernemental et législatif," in G. Bergeron and R. Pelletier, eds., *L'État du Québec en devenir*, Montréal: Boréal Express, pp. 61–108.

Parenteau, Roland (1970), "L'expérience de la planification au Québec," *L'Actualité économique*, 25:4, pp. 679–96.

Plasse, Micheline (1981), "Les chefs de cabinets ministériels au Québec: la transition du gouvernement libéral au gouvernement péquiste (1976–1977)," *Canadian Journal of Political Science*, 14:2, pp. 309–55.

Scarrow, H.A. (1957), "Civil Service Commissions in the Canadian Provinces," *Journal of Politics*, 19, pp. 240–61.

Vigod, Bernard L. (1986), *Québec Before Duplessis*, Kingston and Montréal: McGill-Queen's University Press.

C H A P T E R *14*

State-Owned Enterprises in Québec: The Full Cycle, 1960–90*

Luc Bernier
École nationale d'administration publique, Montréal

INTRODUCTION

Quebec's state-owned enterprises (SOEs) act as bankers, traders, investors, and producers. They are in competition or cooperation with private enterprises in finance, forest, products, steel, mining, oil and gas, manufacturing, television broadcasting, and agriculture. Some of these SOEs have been making profits regularly, but some of them have lost billions of dollars. While some of them have been very useful instruments of policy implementation, successive governments have been unable to control many of them. Despite the fact that the government that was elected in 1985 clearly intended to sell them, SOEs have survived the privatization drive (Gouvernement du Québec, 1988b).

In this chapter, we will try to explain how Québec's state enterprises have survived. The Québec case offers a unique opportunity to study the use of state-owned enterprises over a thirty-year period. We have decided to study nine SOEs that were created between 1962 and 1975 under four different premiers representing the Union Nationale and the Liberal parties.[1] The Parti Québécois, in power between 1976 and 1985, also used SOEs extensively to foster economic development. The laws regarding these SOEs have often been modified, and seven out of the nine SOEs still exist despite having been considered for privatization. Profit, not a major concern for most of them ten years ago, is now a priority, if not "the number one priority." These SOEs have all evolved in a similar fashion over time in a changing environment, and can be studied as a group.

The SOEs studied here are: Caisse de dépôt et placement du Québec (CDPQ), la Société générale de financement (SGF), la Société de développement industriel (SDI), la Société québécoise d'initiatives agro-alimentaires (SOQUIA), la Sidérurgie québécoise (SIDBEC), Radio-Québec, la Société québécoise d'initiatives

---

*The author thanks Gladys Symons, Jeanne Laux, Jean Mercier, Alain-G. Gagnon, Louise Doré, and an anonymous assessor for their precious help in revising this paper.

pétrolières (SOQUIP), la Sociéte québécoise d'exploration minière (SOQUEM), and finally la Société de récupération, d'exploitation et de développement forestiers du Québec (REXFOR).[2] Hydro-Québec has been excluded from this research because it was never considered for privatization or a radical transformation, as was the case for the state enterprises studied here. Moreover, Hydro-Québec is very different from the other state enterprises because of its public utility and monopolistic nature and its size.[3]

State enterprises are the instruments used by governments to achieve their most commercially oriented activities. As Langford (1979:240) points out, a balance has to be struck between "the autonomy that the Crown corporation requires as an organizational form to perform the task it has been given, on the one hand, and the government's need to control and direct the corporation and Parliament's need to oversee and scrutinize it, on the other." The model proposed here suggests that studying SOE–state relations from the early days of the Quiet Revolution to the 1980s privatization drive might clarify how this difficulty can be overcome by governments. The institutional relations with the state in general, and with elected governments in particular, have secured SOEs' survival even better than their actual performance could have achieved. SOEs have developed a mythical vision of the Quiet Revolution to legitimate their existence, using the past in terms of the present, in order to survive.

THE USE OF STATE ENTERPRISES AS POLICY INSTRUMENTS

It has been generally argued that a lack of governmental control over state-owned enterprises exists (see Langford, 1979). Different factors can explain this fact: the reliance on international markets, capital, and technology, the mode of financing, or the nature of the activities of the firm (Laux and Molot, 1988; Hafsi and Koenig, 1988). But as Hafsi has explained, a lack of control actually exists only in portions of the cycle of relations between the state and SOEs (see Hafsi, 1981; Hafsi et al., 1987; and Hafsi and Koenig, 1988). According to this model, for state-owned enterprises, there are three possible modes of interaction with the state, which can be combined into a cycle. The state–SOE relationship evolves from mutual dependence and cooperation to autonomy via an adversarial stage.

For the purpose of this inquiry, the decision-making process of state-owned enterprises is divided in two subprocesses: one internal to the firm, the core process, and one involving external actors, the boundary process (Hafsi and Koenig, 1988:239). The phase of adversarial relations between the state and the SOE develops when the latter tries to protect its technical core from outside interference. "While this dual focus is important for all organizations, it is especially vital for SOEs, because of the permanent possibility of a devastating intervention from their principal, the government" (Hafsi, 1981:77). The two processes are linked. With the assurance that internal administrative tasks are reliably performed, public entrepreneurs can negotiate with the environment (all the institutions with which SOEs have relations) comfortably.

The cycle explains the evolution of the relation between state enterprises and the government, but does not explain why SOEs are created in the first place and how governments can regain control over them. The cycle studied by Hafsi has to be integrated into a longer time frame that includes the initial crisis where SOEs are created and ends with the second crisis that re-creates some "liability of new-ness" (Singh, Tucker, and House, 1986). During crises, organizations are established or reoriented. New solutions, in turn, develop their own inertia until challenged by the next crisis (Krasner, 1984). Although state-building can be a very peaceful process, it is not necessarily a linear process. Institutional structures do not respond in any rapid and fluid way to alterations in the domestic or international environment. Institutional change is episodic and dramatic, rather than continuous and incremental (Krasner, 1984:235). A transformation of the nature of the Quiet Revolution loosened the constraints of precedent and shook the accepted order until the recession in 1982 forced a re-evaluation of the institutions created since the 1960s.

In order to survive, any organization needs to be granted legitimacy by its institutional environment. SOEs' "appartenance" to the state diminishes the importance of technical coordination within them and amplifies the necessity of conforming to larger rules of the state. What matters is not what an SOE actually achieves, which may be loosely connected to its original charter, but the perception that it behaves according to the norms and expectations of the larger state apparatus. Direct control over the SOE does not exist as such; rather, compliance to prescribed behaviour ensures legitimation by the environment. In the long run, SOEs need to achieve both effectiveness and legitimacy. Effectiveness points to internal conditions and legitimacy to external ones. Effectiveness and legitimacy are not incompatible (Tolbert and Zucker, 1983). The influence of the environment varies over time, from strong at the beginning to weak later on.

SOEs provide a relatively independent base of operations for entrepreneurs in the public sector, providing managers with administrative power greater than that usually found within the regular departments. An entrepreneur is any person who takes primary responsibility for mobilizing people and other resources to build, manage, and give purpose to a public organization. "Entrepreneurs of the public variety engage in characteristic strategies of organizational design that simultaneously grant them high degrees of autonomy and flexibility, minimize external interference with core technologies, and which appear to be isomorphic with the most inclusive needs, wants, values and goals of crucial aspects of the task environment" (Lewis, 1980:9).

Public entrepreneurs move SOEs along their cycle of relations with the state toward more autonomy. This is as true of the founders of these organizations as it is of those who transform them later. They inevitably reduce the significance of the traditional political system and thereby alter the face of democratic government and politics (Lewis, 1980:237–41). Innovative programs are important, but strategies of implementation are at least equally critical. Entrepreneurs develop myths to explain the origins in terms of the present, identifying various social goals as technical ones and specifying how to pursue them. Myths become highly institutionalized, beyond the control of any individual participant and, consequently, must be taken for granted as legitimate, apart from evaluations of their impact on work outcomes (Meyer and Rowan, 1977:340–45).

State entrepreneurship, defined as a manifestation of an administrative will to intervene, occurs when the state operates enterprises as if they were private firms in a relatively uncontrolled market environment, in competition or collaboration with the private sector (Duvall and Freeman, 1983:570). The concept of the entrepreneur is an ideal type that is not necessarily applicable to individual cases. Only in a small organization can a single individual perform all entrepreneurial functions. In large organizations, the entrepreneur is, in essence, a combination of members of the organization, who all perform entrepreneurial functions.

State or public entrepreneurship can explain the fact that the state is switching from its role of landlord or rent collector to that of entrepreneur; and from its role as a source of subsidies for the private sector to that of direct competitor. Since the 1960s, governments in industrial countries have sought participation in viable rather than failing enterprises. State intervention has become more active and less defensive. The state no longer intervenes as an investor of last resort, but often as the initiator of investment (Laux and Molot, 1988). Figure 14.1 illustrates this tendency in the Canadian provinces. The number of SOEs created has grown rapidly since 1960 while their total assets have not increased as steadily.

SOEs in Québec have completed a full cycle, from the initial crisis to a second one that re-creates the conditions of newness and makes possible again a phase of cooperation. They were created during the early period of state-building, the Quiet Revolution. More than anywhere else in Canada, the bid in Québec for a relatively independent economy was placed in the hands of the provincial SOEs. They now constitute the most important network of state enterprises in the Canadian provinces (Gouvernement du Québec, 1986b). The liability of newness has been re-created by the privatization drive of the 1980s. This longer time frame allows us to study what goals SOEs pursue once they have had enough time to develop their organizational culture and how the managers that lead them have been able to secure their survival. The following section looks at this lengthy cycle in Québec.

STATE ENTREPRENEURSHIP IN QUÉBEC

What Does Québec Want State-Owned Enterprises to Do?

What was expected of state-owned enterprises in Québec during the 1960s and 1970s remains unclear if we rely solely on what the managers of these organizations understand. For them, SOEs in Québec were created to complete one another on a trial and error basis. The early policy proposals to establish the Société de developpement industriel and the Office du crédit industriel were actually to complement the already-existing Sociéte générale de financement and the Caisse de dépôt et placement du Québec.The SGF proposed various scenarios on how to establish the Sidérurgie québécoise (Parenteau, 1984). The creation of the Société Québécoise d'exploration minière complemented a sweeping form of mining laws in Quebec in 1965 that SIDBEC and the Sociéte nationale de l'amiante would continue a decade later (Gouvernement du Québec, 1966). Articles of the initial charter of the SGF set objectives that were later transmitted to the CDPQ (purchase of treasury bonds and use of savings), to the SDI (loans), or to the Centre de recherches industrielles du Québec (research services). The CDPQ was proposed in the report suggesting the pension policy (Gouvernement du Québec, 1964). The Société québécoise d'initiatives pétrolières replaced Hydro-Québec as an instrument for the implementation of energy policy in areas other than electricity, and the Société québécoise d'initiatives agro-alimentaires was set up to complete the programs of the SDI.

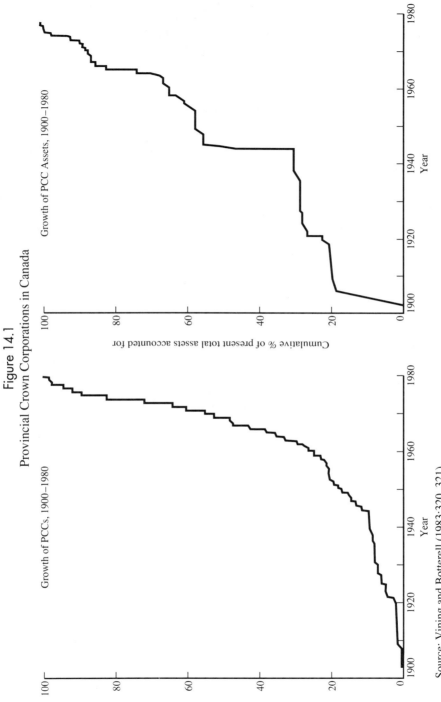

Figure 14.1
Provincial Crown Corporations in Canada

Growth of PCC Assets, 1900–1980

Growth of PCCs, 1900–1980

Source: Vining and Botterell (1983:320, 321).

These efforts could not be related to any major economic policy proposal until 1974. The structures created were similar, but the missions to fulfil were uncoordinated. The first broad economic policy proposal to be published in Québec was the Vézina Report (1974). This report suggested that SOEs could be better coordinated and that a global policy was needed. The report also stated explicitly that, instead of always re-evaluating the role of its SOEs, the state should give them the opportunity to be entrepreneurial. In practical terms, this meant that SOEs should be given the required resources and that administrative conditions should be established to ensure profitability.

The Vézina Report was followed in 1979 by *Challenges for Québec*, which suggested that the time had come to re-evaluate SOEs' orientations and controls. The authors added that the SOEs' activities should not be expanded, but specialized, and that they should work according to the rules and criteria of the private sector, i.e., competition and profitability. Consequently, it was suggested that SOEs should submit development plans for three and five years, that their charters should include the possibility of "directives" from government, and that the state should take charge of the cost of specific programs not intended to be profitable through subsidies.

Three years later, in *The Technology Conversion*, phase two of *Challenges for Québec*, the SOEs' future looked brighter. During the worst recession in fifty years, SOEs were given an important role to play. The SDI was supposed to be a major instrument in preparing Québec's economy for the next century by becoming active in tourism, advanced technology, and exports. The SGF, according to the report, should invest in biotechnology, a new area at the time. REXFOR, SOQUIA, SOQUEM, and SOQUIP should, the report said, be more entrepreneurial in a rapidly changing world economy. In three years, the SOEs returned to the agenda as necessary instruments of economic recovery.

The variability in economic policy proposals could also be observed in the charters of these organizations. The main characteristics of the charters of the SOEs is that they are in perpetual transformation. Figure 14.2 illustrates how often the charters of SOEs have been modified. These laws are often changed because they quickly become impossible to apply or because they are not precise enough. Under new governments or incumbents, early or late during their mandates, the three political parties in power between 1960 and 1986 have passed an important number of laws amending the charters of the nine SOEs under review.

The bulk of legislative activity concerning SOEs occurred after 1970. Counting the number of laws passed affecting SOEs is a crude indicator, as some of the modifications were minor. Several of the modifications have given clearer definition to the mandate of the various SOEs. For example, the task the SGF is supposed to fulfil has become more precise over the years. It shrank from encompassing the whole industry to dealing first with just three sectors and then with five. SOQUIP's mandate was also substantially modified in the early 1980s. Quite often amendments are made to SOEs' charters in order to acknowledge and legalize the growth of the activities of SOEs or to increase their equity. Legislation has followed administrative innovation, and is almost always more reactive than proactive. For example, from 1961 until 1973, the amendments to REXFOR's charter followed and legalized activities undertaken that went beyond its mandate.

Figure 14.2
Laws of the Province of Québec Creating or Amending the Charters of SOEs by Years, 1961–86

SOEs	61	62	63	64	65	66	67	68	69	70	71	72	73	74	75	76	77	78	79	80	81	82	83	84	85	86
Elections	I					G				G			I			G					I				G	
SGF		C					B		M		M	OB[1]	B			B	OB			B			OB	M		
CDPQ					C			M		O	M		M			M	M			M			M	M		M
SOQUEM					C						B		B			B				M				M	M	M
SIDBEC								C		M		B	B	B			OB			OB				M		
R-Q									C			M		B		B	B	OB	O							
REXFOR		C							C[3]	M		OB	OB	B		M	O	O			M	B	M	B	M	B
SOQUIP									C		M			B		B	O	B	M	OB					O	
SDI								C[2]					C				OB	OB					M	M	O	
SOQUIA															C		B		M				OB	M	M	O

Quiet Revolution

Legend

Elections
G: New government in power
I: Incumbent stays in power

C: Creation
M: Minor amendments on technicalities
O: Objectives changes for SOEs
B: Capital increases for SOEs

1. End of mixed enterprise
2. Creation of the OCI, ancestor of the SDI
3. Creation of the ancestor in 61

Source: Bernier (1989).

Development plans illustrate the same difficulty of controlling state-owned enterprises. Since the end of the 1970s, state-owned enterprises have been asked to produce development plans explaining what the SOEs intend to do, the investments planned, the resources required, etc. This puts the planning process in the hands of the SOEs instead of in the ministries. Development plans, which Parenteau (1984) sees as an additional source of control, can also be used by SOEs to simplify their relations with the state, reducing the turbulence of the environment.

In its 1985 political program, the Québec Liberal Party suggested that some SOEs should be privatized (PLQ, 1985:96–99). Once the Liberal Party took power, this electoral program was followed by two documents explaining in more detail the government's intentions. A year after the privatization process had been initiated, the government was already reconsidering the issue (Bernier, 1989b). What was supposed to be the sellout of the century was downgraded to a modest rationalization (see Molot, 1988). SOEs have been able to deviate from the rules suggested in these reports.

Drafting a development plan has been a soul-searching exercise for SOE managers involving several compromises. Mandates have indeed been narrowed, but they still exist, and in narrowing their mandates, SOEs have been able to legitimize their existence. In several SOEs (SOQUIP, SOQUEM, SIDBEC, Radio-Québec, REXFOR, SOQUIA), survival has meant drastic cuts in the number of employees.

Since the 1985 election, SOEs' mandates have been revised. For most of the SOEs, to survive privatization means a return to the basics. For SIDBEC, it means becoming a mini-mill, as was discussed along with other options in the 1960s. For the SDI, it means going back to the formula of 1968–71 (Gouvernement du Québec, 1986c). For SOQUEM also, it means to focus on exploration rather than production, as it did in the 1960s. SOQUIP's activities in western Canada have since been drastically reduced. New tasks have been defined, once again wide open to interpretation. SOEs now have to be "complementary." They are supposed to do what the private sector is unwilling or unable to do: a "negative" task definition.

It seems that the privatization-rationalization process has left SOEs at the beginning of a new cycle. However, state entrepreneurship is now acceptable according to the last energy policy proposal. SOQUIP's activities, along with those of Hydro-Québec, demonstrate that "the state is an entrepreneur on behalf of the collectivity" (translated from Gouvernement du Québec, 1988a:118). The policy is to be implemented through the use of SOEs. Moreover, the government asked Hydro-Québec to subsidize some research efforts done in universities because it is simpler to ask a state-owned enterprise to subsidize them than to reform the way universities are funded. SOEs are assigned ad hoc activities, as often occurred during the 1960s. REXFOR today receives special mandates outside its development plan just as it did in the early 1970s, and it is likely that with the recession deepening, REXFOR will be asked to rescue sawmills as it did during its early years. SOQUIA, like the SDI around 1970, has only a part-time president, worsening its lack of direction. Radio-Québec, on the other hand, has for the first time a clear sense of its mandate (see *Radio-Québec Maintenant*).

Managers need to insulate their activities from the vagaries of incoherent policy proposals and of politicians who are political weather vanes, to quote one manager. Managers in state-owned enterprises cannot base their decisions solely on the government-stated objectives. These objectives are too numerous and change too often. They base their decisions on a broader and more coherent set of objectives, those of the initial era from which SOEs emerged. To justify their decisions, they have found a rationale too strong to be attacked by politicians and deputy ministers: the myth of the Quiet Revolution as discussed below.

The Quiet Revolution Viewed by the SOEs

SOE managers do not perceive the development of their organizational mission as being the result of policy proposals and related documents published by the state, nor as being the result of governmental electoral programs. Managers believe that the turning points in the history of the SOE in which they work were the result of opportunities that they exploited, and not the result of government policies. Objectives, they say, have been determined based on these opportunities. They also share the perception that SOEs' objectives have been adapted to follow the ups and downs of the particular economic sectors.

What managers do know about the origins of the SOEs is the well-known story of what has since been called the "Quiet Revolution." In their own words, these enterprises were created in the "euphoria" of the Quiet Revolution, in its "stride," in its "fire," "dash," "wake," or "track," as they variously put it. They consider that it was the climate, the atmosphere, a feeling that state intervention in the economy was needed.

Managers refer to the slogan "Maîtres chez nous!" (masters in our own house), the 1962 Liberal electoral platform. For SOE managers, the other provinces were closely watching Québec. They speak of a new collective consciousness, a particular political and economic philosophy promoting the creation and control of economic instruments to foster economic development, and they speak of nationalism. SOEs were necessary because French Canadians did not control any significant economic institutions, and therefore Québec's economic development was decided elsewhere. Managers consider that what was important was to innovate, to change the structure of Québec's economy. There was no time for worrying about details when there was so much to do. With views such as these of what these organizations were allowed to do, it is no wonder that successive governments lost control over them.

Managers could rarely name the politicians who were associated with the creation of their SOE. They do not remember the name of the minister who in 1967 or 1969 proposed the charter of their SOE to parliament or suggested modifications in 1973. Managers prefer to link the emergence of SOEs with the political heroes of the early 1960s. The first one, as mentioned earlier, is Jean Lesage, the premier during the Quiet Revolution, who talked about Québec's "economic liberation" (Gouvernement du Québec, 1965). The second one is René Lévesque. The then Minister of Natural Resources was, according to the managers, the sponsoring minister for Hydro-Québec, SOQUEM, REXFOR, and for SIDBEC. The other people considered by the managers were then advisers or civil servants: people such as Michel Bélanger, André Marier, Roland Parenteau, and Jacques Parizeau. They were the technocrats around the ministers: Marier and Bélanger with Lévesque, and Parenteau and Parizeau closer to Lesage. These recollections demonstrate the small numbers of technocrats involved in state-building during the 1960s. They also show how interchangeable the roles were in these earlier phases of state-building.

The "euphoria" of the Quiet Revolution is, for most of these organizations, an interesting myth that has little to do with reality. The Quiet Revolution in Québec history encompasses a period of time that starts with the death of Maurice Duplessis in September 1959. The euphoric period is between 1960 and 1966, during the two mandates of Jean Lesage. The Quiet Revolution started as a movement to rupture with the past, with the Duplessis era. A protest movement cannot last for long, though already in 1965 the reformist fervour was diminishing (see Bergeron and Pelletier, 1980).

In fact, only three of the nine SOEs under study were created between 1960 and 1966: the SGF, the CDPQ, and SOQUEM. SIDBEC, although activated only in 1967–68, was the result of a debate initiated early during the Quiet Revolution. The others were created later, between 1969 and 1975. But even at SOQUIA, created in 1975, managers invoke the Quiet Revolution.

References to the Quiet Revolution do not explain why and how SOEs have been created. They do explain the persistence of certain elements of the organizational culture of SOEs over time. The Quiet Revolution is very useful as a source of legitimacy for SOEs in their relations with the government in power. References to the Quiet Revolution give SOE managers a mandate far broader than required to carry out their tasks, justifying the existence of SOEs in terms of Québec's uniqueness in North America.

SOEs had to escape the initial anarchy in order to become efficient. They had to escape environmental incertitude and develop their own sense of history. SOEs managers interpret the history of their respective organization not as a function of the changes in the laws and charters of the SOEs, but in terms of the main events linked to the technological core of their organizations: specific paths for specific organizations coming out of the same initial crisis but having to rationalize individually their existence and survival (see Bernier, 1989:ch. 5).

The major difficulties that faced SOEs in their early years are perceived by managers as external. The liability of newness comes from the lack of reputation in their governmental and industrial environments. To build a reputation takes time. Credibility implies the successful achievement of at least a few projects, and so organizations have to build a curriculum and a list of the things they have accomplished. The SDI can refer to the 3,500 enterprises it has helped in the past. The association with Culinar lends an aura of credibility to SOQUIA. Similarly, REXFOR has had very successful joint ventures: Taschereau, Tembec, F.F. Soucy, etc. SOQUEM, for its part, has been responsible for five important mining discoveries. The managers of SOEs can remind the government of these important stepping stones.

For SOEs, legitimation also implies making profits, as profits counteract the image that the public sector is inefficient. SOE managers perceive that their affiliation to the state decreases the legitimacy of their organizations. That is why they do not present themselves as part of the state. SOEs earned a substantial amount of money in the 1980s. The financial bleeding has been stopped, and even SIDBEC has been making profits for the last few years. The importance given to profitability also corresponds to the changing of the guard in SOEs. Economists, sociologists, or MBAs have replaced the engineers of the early days. The engineers, according to the present managers, were interested almost exclusively in the production aspect, while the newcomers give more attention to the commercial aspects.

For SOE managers, state intervention is still needed. To them, the situation has not changed to the extent that SOEs are not required anymore (Lebel, 1984b). SOEs have been part of the rapid evolution of Québec's state apparatus. For example, SOQUIA illustrates the evolution of the old Ministry of Agriculture into a modern department. From its initial involvement in colonization two decades earlier, the ministry became interested in the industrial transformation of farm products in the 1970s.

Québec SOEs in Hard Times

The organizational culture of Québec's SOEs has been deeply transformed by the push for privatization that has taken place over the last few years. One of the major consequences of this is that the environment is perceived as ambiguous again by SOE managers, making them feel insecure. Some management teams have been severely reduced: presidents have changed at Radio-Québec, SOQUEM, SOQUIA, SDI, REXFOR, and at the SGF three times. Nobody managing the SGF in 1981 was still in charge by 1986–87. The team that arrived with the 1978 shake-up had left by 1985. The same can be said of SOQUEM. Except for one executive, the 1985 management team was gone in 1988.

Privatization left some of these SOEs in far better financial health than they were before. The privatization drive has also given top management an occasion to impose changes that would not have been possible otherwise. It could be argued that the 1981–82 recession helped make possible some difficult surgery. The message was that SOEs should stand away from the limelight and that they should be profitable. In the words of one manager, SOEs do not exist to have opinions. SOEs that had become autonomous have been reminded of the limits of their autonomy. Seven of the nine SOEs discussed here were to be privatized or abolished according to one of the initial reports in 1985. By 1988, the privatization drive was over and SOEs still exist. Many in the SOEs feel that the government did not dare to privatize them completely and that they are starting a second cycle.

From the interviews conducted, it appears that communications with the government occur almost daily. The higher a manager climbs in the hierarchy of an SOE, the more frequent are his or her contacts with the minister and the state. The president is, according to the managers, the shock absorber or buffer in the system, more so than the board of directors. He or she contacts the sponsoring ministry every day and often has the most experience with state matters. By the time someone becomes president of an SOE, he or she knows or has known ten to fifteen ministers. Contacts are also very frequent for the deputy ministers, who are at the same hierarchical level as SOE presidents. As one former SOE president explains: "Even if you know the minister very well, you know that he or she will ask for more than just your advice. It is normal that, on a difficult question, he or she will ask the deputy minister, often located across the hall. So you had also better be close to the deputy minister." Contacts become more frequent in periods of crisis.

Table 14.1
Total Assets of State-Owned Enterprises in Québec
Before and After the Privatization Drive
(in thousand of current dollars)

	1985	1988
SGF	1,159,874	1,140,405
CDPQ	22,501,900	29,918,200
SIDBEC	529,234	554,635
SOQUEM	271,860	123,514
SOQUIA	58,137	87,207
REXFOR	158,282	212,677
SOQUIP	436,735	166,212
RADIO-QUÉBEC	47,628	48,272
SDI	146,972	435,919

Source: Gouvernement du Québec, 1988b, and Annual Reports of Radio-Québec (1984–85, 1987–88), SDI (1984–85, 1987–88), and CDPQ (1991).

Contacts do not mean control, however. There is little if any evidence, for example, to support claims that the investment policy of the CDPQ is influenced in a direct and systematic way by the political objectives of the government (Brooks and Tanguay, 1985). Another example, Radio-Québec's early growth, resulted from the sponsorship by the Ministry of Education. Contacts do not necessarily imply control because the ministries may lack the administrative ability to do so. Managers often complain about the low level of expertise of civil servants; they feel like experts or consultants working for the ministry. Managers have grievances about the time it takes ministries to decide on matters concerning SOEs or to give permission to invest. They understand that the ministry has far more factors to consider when making decisions, but still cannot understand why it always takes so long. This concerns them because business opportunities remain opportunities only for a short period of time, and investment opportunities have been lost because the ministry concerned was too slow. For example, Tanguay Industries, a subsidiary of SGF, had the opportunity to sell its products through the Caterpillar network. The opportunity was missed because SGF was not allowed to move Tanguay's small research team from the hinterland to Québec City in time to attract researchers and improve its products, as Caterpillar required. In general, it can be said that the state slows down decision-making and makes entrepreneurship more difficult.

SOE managers feel that they should be protected from politics. What a minister wants from his or her relations with SOEs is to know whether the SOE is going to get him or her in trouble or not. This risk-aversion attitude does not lead to entrepreneurship either. Also, ministers cannot wait for results very long: as one manager said, the long term for politicians is four years, and after a year and a half in power they only have a short-term perspective. Managers also resent that ministers can be pressured by unions or private companies. They see these pressures as negative, even though state-owned enterprises in Québec have had the time and the opportunities to develop their own grassroots support. They did not, however: there are no organized interest groups or political parties that are strong proponents of the use of SOEs, and both political parties that have been in power in the

1980s in Québec had privatization plans that differ very little. Neither trade unions, nor scholars, nor clients have demonstrated any strong support for SOEs. One development that has protected SOEs from political oversight has been the creation of a network of subsidiaries. In some cases, a subsidiary has been created to concentrate the common activities of other subsidiaries, such as Lignarex by REXFOR to manage marketing operations. In such subsidiaries, the political influence is further filtered; but the ultimate source of autonomy is profit. Profits silence critics. On the other hand, huge losses lead to very inadequate financing (on SIDBEC, see Parenteau, 1984). Over the last twenty-five years, SOEs have also developed joint ventures with private companies. The modernization of the provincial state apparatus made possible the emergence of entrepreneurship in Québec (Paquet, 1986). These business linkages have pushed them to emphasize profitability.

There is some evidence that, in some economic sectors, the emergence of state-owned enterprises has allowed the state of Québec to gain a relative autonomy over the formulation and implementation of its policies that it did not have previously. This is evident in the case of natural resources. Far more importantly, the CDPQ has made it possible for the state of Québec to gain some autonomy over its bonds and financial needs. The existence of SOEs means that the state of Québec can rely on a control over a minimum level of economic activity over all areas of its territory. The enterprises studied operate in unplanned markets and in direct competition with the private sector. They were created during an era of rapid institutional change in Québec society, and these state-owned enterprises have pursued a more consistent set of goals than the various governments with whom they have dealt since the Quiet Revolution.

The implementation cycle is not deterministic. State-owned enterprises that had failed initially have been rejuvenated by entrepreneurs. The first evaluations of the performance of state-owned enterprises in Québec were pessimistic (see Fournier, 1979), but the time frame of these evaluations was too short. Organizations need time to develop: for example, as one of the managers interviewed argues, it takes fifteen years to grind a steel mill like SIDBEC. Evaluations of implementation efforts should be done over relatively long periods.

The autonomy of public entrepreneurs in Québec is based on the need to reform and to catch up with development in North America as a whole. It is also based on their insulation in state-owned enterprises from political pressures and, to a lesser degree, on the linkages between Québec's economy and the world economy. In Québec's context, according to their managers, SOEs emerged as the only instrument available to a small state unable to control its various activities. The managers we interviewed consider that they fill a gap neither the state nor the private sector could fill. The state has to be, according to SOE managers, the engine of economic development (see Lebel, 1984a). National states might have other means to secure their relative autonomy, but, subnational states have fewer alternatives.

CONCLUSION

New structures such as SOEs originate in periods of crisis. Short bursts of rapid institutional change, such as the Quiet Revolution or the privatization trend of the

1980s, are followed by long periods of stasis. One difference between the two crises is that SOE management has developed an expertise in how to deal with their environment. SOEs, when created, are the instruments of policies that have yet to be definitively drafted. SOEs are created first and the objectives they ought to achieve are solidified later. Objectives are unclear at the beginning and are adjusted later as the process of institutionalization progresses. The development of a technological core takes time, as does attaining financial self-sufficiency.

Québec's successive governments have chosen this form of intervention because of the gap between the desire to intervene and the weakness of the resources, particularly human resources. Acknowledging this disparity, but willing to act quickly, the state chose to delegate responsibilities to autonomous organizations that were to achieve important parts of the activities the state wanted to undertake. Consequently, SOEs have to refer to objectives that they might share but that are ultimately the responsibility of the state (Parenteau, 1980:64–65). In one sense, SOEs have been created, in part, to avoid having to establish coherent and comprehensive policies (Parenteau, 1980:195). Verbs often used in stating SOEs' objectives are: "stimulate," "promote," "broaden," "participate," and "induce," verbs that leave a lot of room for interpretation. Measuring their fulfilment is difficult at best, and so the creation of an SOE often solves a problem mostly on a symbolic level.

From the informal exchanges in a relatively small state apparatus among SOE executives, deputy ministers, and a few ministers in the early 1960s, relations have become more statutory and documented. The development plan is the most consummate form of this 1980s way of doing things, one of the results being that SOEs are less open to ad hoc pressures because their mission is more firmly planned. The state has succeeded in instituting its processes in SOEs. The dramaturgy of exchanges (Ritti and Silver, 1986) is the one decided by the state. Once approved, the plan makes it more difficult for the state or the government to change the SOE's mandate, and decreases the frequency of interactions with the government. Later, SOE managers were able to patriate the planning process within SOEs and achieve some autonomy.

Profit is important for SOEs: it secures their autonomy and gives them legitimacy. Similarly, the training of French-Canadian managers and the emphasis on technology legitimates their existence. In stating the importance of Québec's economic development, SOE managers establish that they care about state objectives and comply with environmental expectations, although when it gets right down to it, SIDBEC produces steel, REXFOR cuts trees to make lumber, pulp, and paper, SOQUEM extracts minerals, the SGF has an aluminum smelter, etc.

The socioeconomic rationality in government and state intentions can be found in a reconstruction of the past, in a post-facto rationalization. When McRoberts (1988) writes that two primary strategies were pursued (the establishment of public enterprises and the strengthening of French-Canadian–owned enterprises), he explains what happened as it appeared twenty years later. Parenteau (1980), who was central to the process, argues, on the other hand, that the word "strategy" is too strong to characterize the development of SOEs in a small state where embryonic policies were drafted by small committees in which a few ministers and a few civil servants worked together. However, it is by linking their existence to the Quiet Revolution that SOEs have been able to survive the privatization drive of the 1980s. As Table 14.1 illustrates, most of the SOEs have continued to develop, although temporarily with a diminished autonomy.

NOTES

1. This chapter is part of a larger research program on state enterprises in Québec established with the financial help of the SSHRC. The empirical study is based on interviews with thirty-seven high-level officials in nine state-owned enterprises (see Figure 14.2) in Québec done during the spring of 1988. We used in-depth interviews, documentary and archival records. Essentially, documents and the survey helped us prepare the interviews with current and former executives and managers in Québec SOEs. For additional information on this research project, see Bernier (1989).

2. It is impossible to explain the history and describe every state enterprise studied. For background material on these enterprises, see McRoberts (1988), Bernier (1989), and Gouvernement du Québec (1986a, 1986b).

3. The reader interested in a similar analysis concerning Hydro-Québec should read Taieb Hafsi, and Christine Demers (1989), *Le Changement radical dans les organisations complexes: le cas d'Hydro-Québec*, Montréal: Gaëtan Morin.

REFERENCES

Bergeron, Gérard, and Réjean Pelletier, eds. (1980), *L'État du Québec en devenir*, Montréal: Boréal Express.

Bernier, Luc (1989), *Soldiers of Fortune: State-Owned Enterprises as Instruments of Public Policy*, Ph.D. dissertation, Northwestern University, Evanston, Illinois.

Brooks, Stephen, and A. Brian Tanguay (1985), "Québec's Caisse de dépôt et placement: tool of nationalism?" *Canadian Public Administration*, 28:99–119.

Duvall, Raymond D., and John R. Freeman (1983), "The Techno-Bureaucratic Elite and the Entrepreneurial State in Dependent Industrialization," *American Political Science Review*, 77:569–87.

Fournier, Pierre (1979), *Les Sociétés d'État et les objectifs économiques du Québec: une évaluation préliminaire*, Québec: Éditeur officiel.

Gouvernement du Québec (1964), *Rapport du Comité Interministériel d'Étude sur le régime des rentes du Québec.*

Gouvernement du Québec (1965), Assemblée nationale, "Notes du discours de l'honorable Jean Lesage prononcé en chambre le 9 juin 1965 lors de la présentation, en deuxième lecture, de la loi de la Caisse de dépôt et placement du Québec (bill 51)."

Gouvernement du Québec (1966), Ministère des richesses naturelles, Direction générale de la planification, *La politique minière du Québec: ses objectifs, son cadre, ses instruments.*

Gouvernement du Québec (1979), Ministère du Développement économique, *Challenges for Québec*, Québec: Éditeur officiel.

Gouvernement du Québec (1982), Ministère du Développement économique, *The Technology Conversion*, Québec: Éditeur officiel.

Gouvernement du Québec (1986a), Ministère des Finances, Ministre délégué à la Privatisation, *Privatisation de Sociétés d'État: Orientations et perspectives.*

Gouvernement du Québec (1986b), Rapport du comité sur la privatisation des sociétés d'État, *De la Révolution tranquille ... à l'an deux mille.*

Gouvernement du Québec (1986c), Ministère de l'industrie et du commerce, *Rapport du comité de révision des programmes d'aide de la SDI.*

Gouvernement du Québec (1987), Ministère des Finances, Ministre délégué aux Finances et à la Privatisation, *Rapport d'étape.*

Gouvernement du Québec (1988a), Ministère de l'Énergie et des Ressources, *l'Énergie, force motrice du développement économique: politique énergétique pour les années 1990.*

Gouvernement du Québec (1988b), Ministère des Finances, Cabinet du ministre délégué aux Finances et à la Privatisation, *Rapport d'étape, 1986–1988.*

Hafsi, Taieb (1981), *The Strategic Decision-Making Process in State-Owned Enterprises*, Ph.D. dissertation, Harvard University, unpublished.

Hafsi, Taieb, Moses N., Kiggundu, and Jan J. Jorgensen (1987), "Strategic Apex Configurations in State-Owned Enterprises," *Academy of Management Review*, 12:714–30.

Hafsi, Taieb, and C. Koenig (1988), "The State-SOE Relationship: Some Patterns," *Journal of Management Studies*, 25:235–49.

Krasner, Stephen D. (1984), "Approaches to the State: Alternative Conceptions and Historical Dynamics," *Comparative Politics*, 16:223–46.

Langford, John W. (1979), "Crown Corporations as Instruments of Policy," in G. Bruce Doern and Peter Aucoin, eds., *Public Policy in Canada: Organization, Process and Management*, Toronto: Macmillan:239–74.

Laux, Jeanne Kirk, and Maureen Appel Molot (1988), *State Capitalism: Public Enterprise in Canada*, Ithaca: Cornell University Press.

Lebel, Jean-Claude (1984a), "Un exemple de l'intervention de l'État dans la production industrielle: la SGF," *Forces*, no. 67:6–14.

Lebel, Jean-Claude (1984b), "Les Sociétés d'État au Québec: un outil indispensable," *Canadian Public Administration*, 27:253–61.

Lewis, Eugene (1980), *Public Entrepreneurship: Toward a Theory of Bureaucratic Political Power*, Bloomington: Indiana University Press.

McRoberts, Kenneth (1988), *Québec: Social Change and Political Crisis*, 3rd ed., Toronto: McClelland and Stewart.

Meyer, John W., and Brian Rowan (1977), "Institutionalized Organizations: Formal Structure as Myth and Ceremony," *American Journal of Sociology*, 83:340–63.

Molot, Maureen Appel (1988), "The Provinces and Privatization: Are the Provinces Really Getting Out of Business?" in Allan Tupper and G. Bruce Doern, eds., *Privatization, Public Policy and Public Corporations in Canada*, Halifax: Institute for Research on Public Policy:399–425.

Paquet, Gilles (1986), "Entrepreneurship canadien-français: mythes et réalités:" in *Mémoires de la Société Royale du Canada*, cinquième série, tome 1:151–78.

Parenteau, Roland (1980), "Les sociétés d'État: autonomie ou intégration," Montréal: École des HEC, document témoin de la recontre du 8 mai.

Parenteau, Roland (1984), "Les relations entre l'État et les entreprises publiques—Un exemple à ne pas suivre: Sidbec," *Gestion*, 9:7–16.

Parti Libéral du Québec (1985), Commission politique, *Maîtriser l'avenir: Programme politique*.

Radio-Québec (1985), *Radio-Québec Maintenant*, Montréal: Société de radio-télédiffusion du Québec.

Ritti, R. Richard, and Jonathan H. Silver (1986), "Early Processes of Institutionalization: The Dramaturgy of Exchange in Interorganizational Relations," *Administrative Science Quarterly*, 31:25–42.

Singh, Jitendra V., David J. Tucker, and Robert J. House (1986), "Organizational Legitimacy and the Liability of Newness," *Administrative Science Quarterly*, 171–93.

Tolbert, Pamela S., and Lynne G. Zucker (1983), "Institutional Sources of Change in the Formal Structure of Organizations: The Diffusion of Civil Service Reform, 1880–1935," *Administrative Science Quarterly*, 28:22–39.

Vézina, Jean (1974), *Une Politique économique québécoise*, Gouvernement du Québec, Ministère de l'Industrie et du Commerce.

Vining, Aidan R., and Robert Botterell (1983), "An Overview of the Origins, Growth, Size and Functions of Provincial Crown Corporations," in J. Prichard and S. Robert, eds., *Crown Corporations in Canada: The Calculus of Instrument Choice*, Toronto: Butterworths: 303–67.

Young, R.A., Philippe Faucher, and André Blais (1984), "The Concept of Province-Building: A Critique," *Canadian Journal of Political Science*, 17:783–818.

C H A P T E R *15*

Québec: An Expanding Foreign Policy*

Jean-Philippe Thérien
Université de Montréal

Louis Bélanger
and Guy Gosselin
Université Laval

This chapter gives a broad overview of Québec's international relations since the early 1960s. Using a conventional approach to foreign policy, the analysis will focus on intergovernmental relations, leaving aside the study of the transnationalization of activities in civil society. Of course, international relations do not, strictly speaking, constitute a new field of activity in Québec government policy (Hamelin, 1968). As we will see, however, the importance they have acquired lately is unprecedented.

An understanding of how Québec's international relations have developed must have as its basis an understanding of the structural transformations the world has gone through over the past half-century. Foremost among these changes is the general increase in interdependence between states (Keohane and Nye, 1989; Rosenau, 1980). This interdependence has been especially noticeable in the economic sector (Vernon, 1987:26–27), the period from the postwar era up to the present day having seen massive internationalization of production, trade, finance, and services. The globalization of markets has gradually emerged as the background to all choices made by political decision-makers. In Québec's case, the trend to market globalization has had all the more impact inasmuch as the province's economy is highly export-oriented.

Another element of the changing international environment can help shed light on the expansion of Québec's international relations: the increasing importance of nonstate actors (Mansbach et al., 1976; Taylor, 1984). Nonstate actors have grown in importance because the issues raised by the conduct of international relations have diversified. This process has occurred as centres of decision-making have

* Part of this chapter is based on material made available by the Projet d'analyse de la politique internationale du Québec (PARIQ) of the Centre québécois de relations internationales. PARIQ is a research project funded by the Fonds pour la formation de chercheurs et l'aide à la recherche. Research assistance was provided by Jean Plourde, Lyne Sauvageau, and Thomas Tessier.

dispersed, as social relationships have become transnational and as the sovereignty of the state has diminished. Many public and private nonstate actors have been actively involved in this fragmentation of power. The public ones can be subdivided according to whether their range of operation is supranational (international organizations) or subnational (federated states, provinces, municipalities). Falling within the second category, Québec obviously has fewer powers and responsibilities than a full sovereign state. Yet, in less than a generation, it has virtually succeeded in implementing a form of paradiplomacy (Duchacek, 1988:12–13; Soldatos, 1988:109).

One more element of the global political environment can account for the expansion of Québec's international relations: the transformation of the terms of membership in the world community. Certainly, the basic underlying properties of the international political system have changed little since the 17th century. The context, however, in which contemporary international relations develop has been greatly modified by the growing number of states that are fully recognized worldwide (Keating, 1990:29; Plischke, 1977). By demonstrating that the division of the world into a finite number of sovereign units was not written in stone, the changes of the postwar era have illustrated just how flexible the operating rules of the international diplomatic system can be (Holsti, 1988:88-89). These changes have since facilitated the rise of a specifically *Québécois* foreign policy.

The emergence of Québec's own international relations has thus been encouraged by certain general trends in the international environment. Still, if we consider how uniformly these trends have spread over the entire international political system, they cannot in themselves explain the specificity of Québec. The question is unavoidable: Why has Québec invested more energy into setting up an independent diplomatic service than most federated states—in particular compared to the other Canadian provinces? To answer this question, Québec's international relations must be understood within the context of Canadian politics and culture.

Within the Canadian federation, Québec is not in a position of strength. In sheer numbers alone this province barely makes up 26 percent of Canada's population, a proportion that, moreover, declines with each passing year. From a broader sociological viewpoint, Québec is part of a country whose dominant culture has been largely integrated into the worldwide hegemonic culture of its American neighbour. This asymmetry has strongly conditioned the province's political development (Tarlton, 1965), giving rise from the Quiet Revolution onward to a double process of "state-building" and "nation-building." On the one hand, Québec has acquired new levers for political influence and economic intervention. On the other, it has gradually come to define its own collective identity.

Some authors have already suggested that the extension of Québec's international activity falls within a logic of state modernization or "state-building" (Painchaud, 1980:352; Latouche, 1988). Latouche contends that the expansion of Québec's external relations has also met a need for "nation-building," a hypothesis that remains relatively unexplored to this day. Our wish here is to examine each of these intuitive explanations in greater detail and thus gain a deeper understanding of the question. The approach we will use recognizes that Québec's foreign policy is both a material and symbolic reality. From a material viewpoint, the Québec government has reinforced the trend to institutionalize state operations by providing an official framework for its international activities. Québec's foreign policy thus rests first of all on operational structures that ensure continuity of government action. From a symbolic viewpoint, international relations have also helped consolidate the "reserves of legitimacy" binding the state to civil society. Affirming Québec's international role has allowed the government to confirm the singularity of the province's interests and to highlight its status as a distinct society.

The analytical tools provided by the notions of state-building and nation-building will be used to examine some key aspects of the growth of Québec's international relations. We will thus examine how the machinery of Québec's foreign policy has been put in place, how relations with the *Francophonie* and the United States have developed, and how the issues of immigration and foreign trade have recently come to the forefront.

THE INSTITUTIONALIZATION OF A FIELD OF ACTIVITY

Québec's international activity has acquired an institutional form mainly through the signing of agreements with foreign partners, the setting up of a specialized bureaucracy, and the expansion of its network of permanent representation abroad. Among these means, the signing of *ententes* has played the most crucial role. It should be made clear from the outset that the Québec government calls ententes all agreements, minutes of meetings, exchanges of letters, and joint communiqués that are binding upon the province and a foreign government. These ententes have served several purposes: in addition to affirming Québec's own international role, they have given an official status to its cooperation and exchange with other countries while also legitimizing the creation of complex administrative structures.

The question of Québec's international status first came up when two such ententes were signed with France in February and November of 1965. These ententes, the first official mechanisms for cooperation between France and Québec, dealt with education and culture (Québec, 1984:4–8). The federal government reacted to Québec's initiative by signing in turn an umbrella agreement that was to encompass official relations between Québec City and Paris. A lively debate ensued over the legal standing of ententes signed by Québec: What was their exact status? The Québec government has always considered them to be bona fide international agreements, basing its interpretation on the principle of the international extension of provincial areas of jurisdiction—the "Gérin-Lajoie" doctrine (Gérin-Lajoie, 1965). The Canadian government for its part denies the binding nature under international law of the agreements signed by the provinces on the basis of the indivisibility of Canada's foreign policy (Canada, 1968a and 1968b). In any case, Québec's position opened a gap—not yet closed up—in Canadian legal doctrine (Jacomy-Millette, 1983).

Since the events of 1965, Québec has profited from a legal grey area acceptable to both parties and has gone on signing one entente after another, creating in this way an extensive network of official relationships. Analysis of 230 ententes signed by Québec from 1964 to 1989 shows that this network has continued to grow unabated. Its diversification is evident in the variety of areas of activity and in the number of partners involved (Figure 15.1). The fact that 60 percent of the ententes were signed with a sovereign state further emphasizes the government's wish to deal with other members of the international community on an equal footing.

By granting an official status to pre-existing contacts or by creating new external relationships (Beaudoin, 1977:448–58; Donneur, 1983), the international ententes helped to open up a new sphere of political involvement. A specialized bureaucracy arose in Québec City to occupy this sphere. It came into being through repeated attempts at centralization against the wishes of sectoral ministries that wanted to keep for themselves the international extension of their activities. The relative speed with which this whole process took place can be probably attributed to the combined effect of two factors. First, the pressure exerted by the general momentum of the Quiet Revolution had a telling impact. A class of politicians and senior civil servants realized how much their project of modernization could gain from a more direct access to resources of the international environment. Second, there was the deep undercurrent of political sentiment that in the Canadian constitutional context has encompassed Québec's ambitions to manage foreign policy in areas of its own jurisdiction. These factors—in addition to those that impel a state, if not to control, at least to direct the resources and constraints of its external environment—have helped make foreign affairs an issue of particular importance not only *for* the state but also, in Québec's case, *within* the state.

In the early 1960s, the first bureaucratic channels through which the government entered the area of external relations did not really distinguish between Canada and abroad. Also, Québec's international relations were at first subject to decentralized management involving various ministries. In the context of the times, they rapidly became instruments of interministerial competition, a phenomenon that Claude Morin has called "administrative nationalism" (1987:42). To coordinate all of this activity, the government set up in 1965 the interministerial Commission for External Relations (Commission interministérielle des relations extérieures), which brought together the deputy ministers of all ministries likely to develop international policy. In 1967, it was then decided to create the Ministry of Intergovernmental Affairs (the MAIG) by enlarging the mandate of the Ministry of Federal–Provincial Relations, which had been established in 1961. Within this new centralizing administrative entity, there began to emerge a sphere of involvement specific to international relations alongside that of federal–provincial relations.

The MAIG's development originally reflected a desire to coordinate different areas of activity, in keeping with the thinking behind major government programs on social, economic, and educational matters (Noda, 1988:152–61). A new strategy, however, came into being with the 1974 reform when the services of international cooperation were transferred to the MAIG from the Ministries of Education and Cultural Affairs. In addition to concerns over internal coordination, a desire arose to organize Québec's foreign policy along geographical lines. There developed alongside the division into *sectors* of the International Cooperation Branch (Direction générale de la coopération internationale) a pattern of regionalization overseen by the International Relations Branch (Direction générale des relations internationales). The latter initially had four divisions : "Europe," "The Americas," "Africa, Asia, and Oceania," and "International Organizations." In January 1979, further reform brought together under a single International Relations Branch three sectoral divisions in charge of policy evaluation and development and six regional divisions in charge of operation implementation and information gathering (a new division, "France," had been separated from "Europe," and the

Figure 15.1
Distribution of Ententes Signed by the Government of Quebec by Region and by Area of Activity, 1964–89
n=230

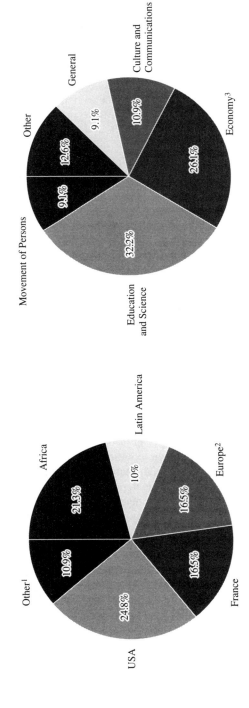

1. Multilateral ententes included.
2. France excluded.
3. Road and highway transportation included.

Source: Gouvernement du Quebec.

"Americas" division had been split in two: "United States" and "Latin America")
(Québec, 1980:4–5).

In 1985, the creation of the Ministry of International Relations (MRI) put an
end to the cohabitation of international relations and federal–provincial relations
under one roof. At the same time, the planning divisions set up along sectoral lines
disappeared; henceforth, ministerial action would proceed along geographical
lines. These two changes made the 1985 reform a decisive turning point in the process of identifying international affairs as a special field of political activity for
Québec. By setting up what was, for all intents and purposes, its own diplomatic
service, Québec sent to all concerned nationally and internationally a clear signal
of its intention to control international relations in areas under its jurisdiction.

Québec's international relations also became institutionalized through a better
harmonization of economic and political concerns. Not surprisingly, this trend
became more pronounced after the 1981–82 recession. Although the Ministry of
Industry and Trade had lost control over Québec's delegations abroad when the
MAIG was created, it nonetheless had maintained a role in Québec's international
economic relations by setting up its own External Relations Service (Service des
relations extérieures). This service later became first the International Services
Division (Direction des services internationaux), then the Québec Bureau of
External Trade (Office québécois du commerce extérieur), and finally, in 1983, a
ministry in its own right. In 1988, the Ministries of International Relations and
External Trade merged to become the Ministry of International Affairs (MAI).

The existence of a ministry with the exclusive mandate of planning, coordinating, and implementing international government policy (Québec, 1988a:art. 11–
18) is today part and parcel of Québec's civil service. This new ministry, with a
budget of almost $100 million, has two branches whose mandate is to conceive
and propose regional and sectoral policies. Another six branches are mandated to
ensure policy implementation on a regional basis. The branches in charge of relations with a region are split into subregional divisions, except for France and the
United States, which receive special attention and have their own branches.

The MAI also has full authority over Québec's permanent representation
abroad—a small-scale yet bona fide diplomatic network made up of twenty-six
"general delegations," "delegations," and "bureaus" that ensure ongoing contact
with key targets of Québec's international policy. When Jean Lesage came to
power in 1960, Québec already had an "agency" in New York City. It was, however, the opening in 1961 and 1962 of delegations in Paris and London that began
the steady build up of a network employing today more than 100 professionals.
This work force has focused its efforts on the two key areas of Québec's foreign
policy: the economy (including tourism and agriculture) and immigration (Table
15.1).

This gradual institutionalization of the government's power to act in international relations has clearly been in line with the expansion and reinforcement of
the Québec state. At the same time, it has also been part of a larger process of affirmation of national identity. We can never repeat too often that Québec is the one
Canadian province that has invested the most in fostering relationships with the
outside world. In fact, compared with the situation of any other federated state in
the world, Québec's experience appears to be highly uncommon. Over the past
thirty years, the transformations of Québec society have required modernization of

Table 15.1
Distribution of Quebec's Professional Staff Abroad by Region and by Main Area of Activity, 1989

REGION	NO. OF MISSIONS	MANAGEMENT AND ADMINISTRATION	CULTURE	ECONOMY	EDUCATION	IMMIGRATION	POLITICAL AND PUBLIC AFFAIRS	OTHER (cooperation)	TOTAL
Africa	1				1				1
Asia	4	2		9		9	1		2	23
Europe[1]	7	5.5		15	1	8	3.5	5	38
France	1	3	1	8	1	5	3	3	24
Latin America	5	3		4		3		1	11
Middle East	1					1			1
USA	7	5	1.5	20	1	2	6.5		36
TOTAL	26	18.5	2.5	56	4	28	14	11	134

[1] France excluded.

Source: Ministry of International Affairs, *Liste d'effectif au 31 mars 1989*, Internal document, 1990.

the state. Now it so happens that the activities of modern states tend more and more to be international in scope.

The emergence of the Québec nation on the world scene took place in the wake of a constitutional debate with Ottawa. Originally, Québec chose to develop its foreign policy because it was convinced that the federal government could not adequately pursue the international interests of Québec society, a view obviously not unrelated to the fact that the Department of External Affairs in Ottawa was traditionally an English-Canadian preserve. It was because of this mismatch between societal needs and institutional means that the Québec government has devoted so many resources to promoting its own international interests. Although the institutionalization of Québec's relations has gone through many changes, it has, interestingly enough, taken place in a context of continuity relatively free of strictly partisan interests.

Insofar as it has an international dimension, the collective identity of Quebeckers is based largely on the distinct nature of their state. The institutionalization of Québec's external relations thus illustrates the systematic overlap of nation-building and state-building. The means Québec has used to express its distinctness on the international scene have themselves reinforced a difference, which, in turn, has called for other means to be implemented.

THE FRANCOPHONIE: THE CORNERSTONE OF QUÉBEC'S EXTERNAL RELATIONS

First France and then the entire community of French-speaking countries have exerted a decisive influence on the direction and maturation of Québec's foreign policy. In short, the *Francophonie* has served as a catalyst for the expansion of Québec's external relations. Although Québec's commitment to the French-speaking world has sparked frequent clashes between the federal and Québec governments (Lalande, 1989; Morin, 1987), the Francophonie has nonetheless strongly contributed to consolidating Québec's place in international relations.

The Francophonie has, moreover, served to legitimize the Québec nation's wish for increased autonomy by enabling the province to project its distinctness abroad. The institutionalization of Québec's commitment to the Francophonie cannot be dissociated from the controversy, already mentioned, over the constitutional division of powers in external relations. Québec has constantly asserted its right to extend outside the country areas of jurisdiction the Constitution assigns it, notably education and culture. Its first moves into the French-speaking world were understandably made in these two areas. Furthermore, from the standpoint of political legitimacy, Québec has always maintained that as the sole French-speaking government in North America it had a duty to develop its external relations. Given Québec's cultural isolation, its opening up to the world would naturally be expected to favour those countries sharing its language. One analyst has even gone so far as to liken Québec's policy on the Francophonie to a virtual defence policy (Painchaud, 1988:204).

It was in this overall context that bilateral and multilateral relations were to develop with the Francophonie. On the bilateral level, permanent posts abroad have been successively opened in Paris (1961), Abidjan (1970), Brussels (1972), and Port-au-Prince (1976). All told, there are fewer permanent offices in the whole French-speaking world than in the United States alone. Yet, because of mutual distrust, the coexistence of Canada's and Québec's representatives in the French-speaking world has given rise to many diplomatic confrontations, as exemplified by the disputes over the establishment of links with France and Belgium. These recurring tensions, however, have not prevented Québec from setting up an extensive network of bilateral relations, especially with France. The annual meetings between the French and Québec prime ministers are the clearest sign of the priority both states give to strengthening their ties of cooperation. Since the mid-1960s, numerous ministerial visits by both parties have resulted in more than fifty agreements between France and Québec. Alongside governmental efforts, Franco-Québec cooperation has also been fostered by non- and paragovernmental organizations, the most important of which are the France–Québec Interuniversity Cooperation Centre (Centre de coopération interuniversitaire franco–québécoise), the Associations France–Québec and Québec–France, and the France–Québec Youth Bureau (Office franco–québécois pour la jeunesse). The last organization has had a particularly impressive impact: since its inception it has enabled more than 60,000 young people from France and Québec to participate in exchange programs.

In comparison with the expansion of bilateral ties, Québec's push to carve out a niche for itself in the multilateral networks of French-speaking states was to stir up tensions laden with far more emotion and significance. The province set a precedent in 1968 when, at the invitation of France, it attended the Conference of Education Ministers from French-speaking Countries (Conférence des ministres de l'Éducation nationale des pays francophones) (CONFEMEN) in Gabon. The federal government was highly upset over this incident and took steps to make sure it would never happen again. From 1969 on, Québec's representatives at this conference have attended as an integral part of the Canadian delegation under an arrangement between the two orders of government.

The Conferences of Niamey I (1969) and II (1970), which culminated in the creation of the Cultural and Technical Cooperation Agency (Agence de coopération culturelle et technique) (ACCT), put at odds more than ever the Canadian and Québec viewpoints. Ottawa pushed for an institution limited to sovereign states whereas Québec, supported by France, lobbied for one whose terms of membership would be more flexible. Thanks to the mediation of France, the dispute was finally resolved by the adoption of Article 3.3 of the agency's charter. This article allowed for the creation of a "participating government" status alongside the status of full-fledged member. In keeping with the provisions of Article 3.3 of the charter, an agreement was signed in 1971 between Ottawa and Québec City, thus confirming Québec's entry into the ACCT. Although the agreement did not grant the right to vote, it did recognize the right of Québec's representatives to express "the viewpoint of the government of Quebec on all matters falling within its areas of jurisdiction" (authors' translation) (Québec, 1988b:28–31).

The 1971 agreement was compromised at the end of the 1970s as public attention turned to a proposed summit of French-speaking heads of state. Against the wishes of the federal government, Québec insisted on being officially represented. This divergence of views repeatedly held up efforts to organize the first summit, thereby annoying a good many Africans who regarded this dispute as a squabble between "white big shots" (C. Morin, 1987:415). In 1980, Senegal scheduled a meeting of foreign affairs ministers to lay the groundwork for a summit, only to have to call it off at the last minute because of the Ottawa–Québec City dispute. The Conservatives' election in 1984 finally brought an end to the impasse by injecting a new way of thinking into federal–provincial relations.

An understanding reached in 1985 between the Canadian and Québec governments cleared the way for the first summit to be held in early 1986 by authorizing Québec's participation. The summit was to have two distinct parts: one devoted to the world political and economic situation, and the other to cooperation and development. However, in terms of the Canada–Québec division of powers, the summit was really split three ways. Proceedings thus followed two sets of rules during the first part—i.e., the world political and economic situation. On political issues, Québec could act only as an "interested observer." On economic issues, it could intervene "following consultation and with the agreement of the Prime Minister of Canada on a case-by-case basis." During the second part of the summit Québec had full right of participation, as it had at the ACCT (Québec, 1988b:32–33).

The 1985 understanding clearly had the effect of reinforcing Québec's power in the French-speaking world. This consolidation of Québec's external policy shows up for instance in the size of the budgets set aside for the institutions of the Francophonie. Québec allocates to them more than $5 million every year—a sum corresponding to approximately 20 percent of Ottawa's contribution. The somewhat broader recognition of Québec's right to intervene in international relations also helped to calm the constitutional wrangling between the Canadian and Québec governments (Bernier, 1988:68). The Paris, Québec City, and Dakar summits thus saw the two orders of government working hand-in-hand and even putting forward joint proposals, e.g., on environmental issues. Though still fragile, as shown by the controversy over organization of the first *Jeux de la Francophonie* in Morocco in 1989, the new climate of mutual trust could also be seen at the last general conference of the ACCT held that same year (Comeau, 1990:88). By jointly supporting, against France, the election of the Quebecker Jean-Louis Roy to the position of Secretary General, Canada and Québec demonstrated just how far their new partnership could go.

Besides the jurisdictional gains it made possible, the Francophonie has shaped Québec's identity by confirming the latter's status as a distinct society. It has enhanced Québec's opportunities to define and promote its own interests on the world scene. The Francophonie has contributed to making Québec's cultural assets known abroad, notably through the French-language television network TV-5. By fostering a feeling of belonging to a cultural community of more than forty states, it has also furthered a process of socialization through which Québec's political elite has grown accustomed to the workings of international relations. In addition to the meetings of the CONFEMEN and the CONFEJES (Conference of Ministers of Youth and Sports) (Conférence des ministres de la Jeunesse et des Sports), Québec has also attended numerous ministerial meetings on science and technology (1977), justice (1980 and 1989), culture (1981), scientific research and higher education (1983), and communications (1985).

The Francophonie has contributed on a broader level to training the Québec state in cooperation and development. Summit after summit, Québec has sought to promote expertise it could share with French-speaking developing countries. Energy know-how is looking to be the most promising area of need, as shown by the establishment in Québec City of the Energy Institute of French-speaking Countries (Institut de l'Énergie des pays francophones). Moreover, by its presence at the ACCT and the summits, Québec has become more aware of the benefits to be gained from using multilateralism as a means to manage international relationships. It is clear that in an international regime as strongly hierarchical as the Francophonie a small state like Québec naturally stands to gain from greater multilateralization in the regime's operation. On a symbolic but by no means negligible note, the Francophonie has also provided a political forum enabling the Québec government to express its views on such strategic issues as the Lebanese crisis, Third World debt, and changes in the price of raw materials.

Finally, the Francophonie has enabled Québec to internationalize the Canadian constitutional problem. The Québec government has thus succeeded in mobilizing external symbolic resources in order to maximize its political autonomy. In this perspective, France has clearly played a decisive role in the step-by-step affirmation of Québec's international identity. The special relationship between France and Québec has notably taken concrete form in the quasi-ambassadorial status accorded to Québec's delegation in Paris and to France's consulate general in Québec City. Throughout the confrontation between Québec City and Ottawa, France has taken a position broadly recognizing the legitimacy of Québec's aspirations as shown by General de Gaulle's statement of "Vive le Québec libre" (Long live free Québec) in 1967. Ottawa has denounced the French government's behaviour as unacceptable meddling in the country's internal affairs. France has replied to this criticism by maintaining that its policy is founded on the twin principles of noninterference and nonindifference (Portes, 1988:109). When all is said and done, it is undeniable that France's sympathies have broadly contributed to Québec's gaining the international standing it enjoys today.

The potential economic spin-offs from the Francophonie are no doubt limited (Soldatos, 1989:121). France, Quebec's largest French-speaking trading partner, absorbs only 1.7 percent of the province's exports. It stands only in sixth place among the province's external markets (Québec, 1989:965). As for French-speaking African countries, most of them remain in such a state of poverty as to be virtually insolvent. Nevertheless, from a political standpoint the Francophonie has contributed much to developing Québec's foreign relations. This bloc of countries has enabled the province to gain much prestige and visibility internationally. There may be even more gains to come since Québec, together with France, is seeking to promote the spread of the French language and culture into certain East European countries. For all these reasons, the French-speaking world still remains today the cornerstone of Québec diplomacy.

THE UNITED STATES: A NATURAL AND ONGOING PARTNERSHIP

In modern times, the United States, and not France, is the country with which Québec has had continuous relations the longest. Although these relations were initially centred in the private sector, they took on an increasingly public nature in the 1960s. They expanded continually from then on, particularly those established with state governments. Still, it was from 1976 on—after Québec's opening up to France and the Francophonie—that their institutional framework was consolidated as part of the Québec state's growing autonomy in the international sphere. All in all, Québec has always enjoyed close relations with its southern neighbour: from an economic standpoint, two-thirds of the province's international trade is done with the United States. Moreover, Quebeckers generally appreciate American cultural products, and large numbers of tourists cross the border in both directions. While the omnipresence of American culture has exerted a decisive influence on Québec's collective identity, political relations have extended the influence of American values even further into the Québec nation (Hero and Balthazar, 1988:199–202).

The multiple relationships between Québec and the United States came into being of their own accord and required little direct political support. Québec has nonetheless formalized these relationships one by one, putting the United States on an equal footing with France as one of its two most important partners on the international scene (Québec, 1985). Although the institutionalization of Québec's relationships with the United States has been developed steadily, the year 1976 marked a turning point. By electing that year a government committed to independence, Québec moved on to a more advanced stage of national affirmation and state development. In external policy-making, this change resulted in the new government leaning toward the United States.

In the postwar era, after the opening of the *Agence générale du Québec* in New York City in 1943, ministerial visits contributed to institutionalizing relations between Québec and the United States. The number of visits increased gradually and augmented at an even greater rate after the election of the Parti Québécois (PQ) in 1976 (authors' compilation). Until the early 1960s, the occasional visits of Québec premiers to New York were by and large private in nature. Premier Lesage was the first to turn them into a public event, thereby raising greatly their political profile. Despite the change in style, the visits by the premier and his ministers to the United States remained infrequent during the 1960s (eleven visits altogether). The visits increased in number perceptibly from 1970 to 1976 (twenty-eight visits) before reaching a high (160 visits) from 1976 to 1985 during the PQ's two terms of office. In his third term (1985–89), Robert Bourassa's ministers kept up a similar tempo (sixty-seven visits). In addition to this, of the fifty-seven ententes that were signed between Québec and the United States since 1960, about half of them were on the initiative of the PQ government. To provide a more precise picture of this rapprochement between Québec and the United States, it should be pointed out that about two-thirds of the ministerial visits and ententes gave top priority to economic issues (most others dealt with institutional, cultural and environmental issues) and that these contacts were made mostly with state governments rather than with Washington, the latter being involved only on rare occasions.

The *Agence générale du Québec* in New York City, which became a *Délégation générale* in 1961, was the sole mission Québec had in the United States until the end of the 1960s. Five other posts—three delegations and two bureaus—were established in 1969–70 in Chicago, Boston, Los Angeles, Lafayette, and Dallas (the Dallas bureau was closed in 1987). Later on, Québec opened an Atlanta bureau in 1977 and a Washington bureau in 1978. The Québec government reportedly wanted to use the latter for political lobbying purposes, but opposition from Ottawa resulted in the bureau being downgraded to a tourist information office (Lisée, 1990:307–12).

From 1976 on, the PQ government greatly enlarged the staff and mandate of Québec's permanent representatives in the United States. This strengthening of Québec's presence in the United States was undertaken in large part with the 1980 referendum in mind, but lasted beyond it. Québec sought to broaden the traditional economic and tourism-oriented role of its delegations. To correct the image that some English-Canadian journalists portrayed of it, which it considered deformed, Québec set up information services in most of its missions (Noda, 1988:326–31). By employing new means to defend its special interests it thus confirmed the importance of its relationship with the United States. In short, the government was getting ready to lead a vigorous campaign aimed at affirming the distinctness of the Québec nation and the legitimacy of its political agenda.

Solid institutional links have also been forged between Québec and some American states. In certain cases, these links have developed within bilateral structures, for example the annual summit meetings between the premier of Québec and the governors of New York and Massachusetts and the joint committees set up with the states of New York, Maine, and Vermont. In other cases, the links have taken shape within multilateral structures, these being all the more beneficial to the Québec government since they offer a more stable operational framework and a broader scope for extending its influence. Foremost among these structures is the Annual New England Governors and Eastern Canadian Premiers' Conference, which has met annually since 1973. Its wide-ranging agenda encompasses energy, the environment, transportation, tourism, trade, finance, economic development, fishing, forestry, agriculture, high technology, local history, and genealogy. At the heart of the proceedings are issues in which Québec has much at stake, namely energy and—more recently—the environment. Standing committees have been created on both issues. As the most important Canadian province at the conference, Québec has obviously played a leading role. Québec and Ontario also took part in meetings of the Council of Great Lakes Governors in the 1980s. This body has sought to promote greater coordination of the activities of the provinces and states within the framework of the Great Lakes Charter signed in 1985 (Lubin, 1986:30).

A United States division within the MAIG did not come into being until 1979. In the 1960s, relations with the United States came on the one hand under the Ministry of Industry and Trade, which oversaw Québec's delegations abroad, and on the other hand under the Ministry of Cultural Affairs, whose *Service du Canada français d'outre-frontières* worked to promote the diffusion of French culture to French-speaking groups across the continent. In 1974, the MAIG established an "Americas" division for all countries in the Western Hemisphere. Its financial resources, however, remained quite limited. The creation of the United States division in 1979 was accompanied by a large increase in staff as the number of personnel went from two to sixteen.

The government machinery that was put in place to structure Québec's relations with the United States has also legitimized the distinctness of the Québec nation. Until 1976, Québec's goals were largely confined to promoting its economic interests, seeking capital, and sponsoring a few cultural exchanges with Louisiana. Still, even before this watershed year, provincial authorities had emphasized on several occasions Québec's specificity. In 1962, Premier Lesage delivered before the Canadian Society of New York an important speech that put across vigorously the uniqueness of the political and social goals pursued by Québec's population and government. Not long after he was elected in 1970, Premier Bourassa hastened to tell Americans how much Québec society had progressed in recent years and how necessary it was to protect the language of the French-speaking majority. In September 1974, speaking before the Council on Foreign Relations, he went even further and insisted that the business community had to adapt to Québec's will "to become an integral element of the dynamism that animates the nations of North America while still preserving its indispensable cultural identity" (authors' translation) (Roy, 1977:502–07).

After 1976, the Québec government pursued its traditional goals of promoting the economy and developing relations with French-speaking and francophile communities. It also undertook to heighten understanding and improve the perception of Québec in the United States as well as to defend its political interests. When Lévesque made his first trip as premier outside Québec, he kicked off a series of public appearances aimed at the Americans by delivering a keynote speech on the PQ's program before the Economic Club of New York. Québec's strategy went on to take the form of "Operation America." This project, whose special budget required the joint efforts of five ministries, organized a series of ministerial visits and lasted throughout the eighteen months preceding the 1980 referendum. "Operation America" had two goals. First, its purpose was not so much to garner support for an independent Québec, but rather to bring the United States around to a position of not opposing such a prospect (C. Morin, 1987:275). Second, the Québec government wanted to rectify the image of the province that English-Canadian media were passing on to the Americans (Lisée, 1990:281–83 and 312–13; Noda, 1988:325–31). It therefore sought to reassure the business community by explaining as clearly as possible its political plans, underscoring in particular the democratic nature of these plans and the province's open attitude to foreign investment. While insisting on Quebec's cultural originality, i.e., its roots in both North American and French culture, government discourse at the time emphasized Québec's modernity and its capability to take relations with the outside world into its own hands.

In 1980, the Republicans took over the American administration and proved to be more open-minded toward the PQ than their Democrat predecessors (Lisée, 1990:408–19). Washington's change of attitude admittedly remained limited. On February 2, 1983, the American State Department issued an official statement rebuking Minister Bernard Landry for his talk about a possible common market between Québec, the United States, and Canada. The results of the 1980 referendum had a calming effect, though, and a new American stance could be discerned when President Reagan delivered a speech in Québec City during his 1985 meeting with Prime Minister Mulroney. Noting that Quebeckers had shown a double attachment to their province and Canada, the American president went on to profile their long historical development as a French-speaking North American community. Later, in keeping with previous policy choices, Québec vigorously supported the signing of the free trade agreement between Canada and the United States. For its part, the American business community, which had panicked in 1976 at the prospect of Québec attaining independence, reacted rather serenely as pro-sovereignty sentiment in the province rapidly mounted after the Meech Lake Accord died in June 1990 (Lisée, 1990:218).

Québec's relationship with the United States arose initially out of economic necessity. The two economies are highly interlinked and Québec has nothing to gain from antagonizing the Americans. Aside from some friction over trade in such products as pork, timber, asbestos, and hydroelectricity, as well as control of acid rain, the history of relations between Québec and the United States is not marred by many conflicts. In any case, fewer problems come up between Québec and the United States than between Canada and the United States. Québec feels less threatened by the United States than does the rest of Canada. Although Quebeckers and Americans share common values and the same way of life, Québec possesses a strong sense of cultural identity that, rightly or wrongly, gives it a feeling of protection from its powerful neighbour.

THE EMERGENCE OF NEW ISSUES

External Trade

Today, development of external trade permeates Québec's foreign policy in its entirety. It has not always been so. In the 1960s, government economic strategy sought rather more to reassure investors, mostly Americans, who were thought to be apprehensive of state interventionism and the risks of nationalization. Then, during the 1970s, the immense need for capital to finance construction of hydroelectric installations in northern Québec and the negative perception of the PQ government by the international financial community—especially after the nationalization of the General Dynamics asbestos mines—led to much effort to attract foreign investment. The early 1980s saw external trade emerge as a new priority. With the end of the 1981–82 recession, recovery of international trade and pressures for multilateral and continental free trade made Quebeckers more aware of how dependent their economy was on external markets. Government discourse has since emphasized more than ever the need to boost exports. It should be kept in mind that international exports make up about 16 percent of Québec's total production of goods and services, amounting to $23 billion in 1989 (Pélouas, 1991:C2).

Institutionalization of Québec's activity in international trade has been relatively recent. It mainly took place through the increased participation of the province in the Canadian decision-making process. Since federal decisions on international trading practices are not binding on any of the provinces when it comes to implementing treaties in areas falling within their jurisdiction, Ottawa had to bring the provinces into the policy-making process to make sure they do not obstruct its international commitments (Brown, 1991:85-100). It was in this context that mechanisms of federal–provincial coordination were created for the Tokyo Round negotiations (1973–79), just as they were for the Uruguay Round negotiations and the talks leading to the free trade agreement with the United States.

Besides taking part in Canadian policy-making, the Québec government influences external trade through various incentives. For example, the Ministry of International Affairs offers training in export development, provides aid for market research and development, and helps businesses to participate in different trade fairs, exhibitions, and foreign missions. Other government agencies offer more specialized aid programs. In keeping with the discourse of political decision-makers, there is an increasing tendency to integrate culture, communications, and even education into trade policy. Alongside the MAI's initiatives, two public corporations, the Corporation for Cultural Industries (Société générale des industries culturelles) and the Corporation for Educational Resource Development (Société d'exploitation des ressources éducatives du Québec), offer export aid programs. The general direction of all these agencies seems to indicate that external trade is becoming the instrument of choice for enlarging government participation in international affairs as well as a new axis for integrating foreign policy.

The growing importance of economic issues in Québec's international relations has served not only to strengthen the state, but also to help redefine the collective identity of the province. As one observer noted, in this nation-building process, the nation is increasingly perceived as a "pole of high-performance international competition" (authors' translation) (Létourneau, 1991:9). Generally speaking, on international economic questions Québec has been more open than Canada to the outside world. This openness was first shown toward foreign investment. The difference in attitude between Québec and Canada took on an especially political overtone when the PQ strongly opposed the protectionist policies behind the Foreign Investment Review Agency. Authorities in Québec took advantage of this dispute to denounce the obtuse nationalism of the Canadian government and to highlight tensions between Ottawa and Washington (J.-Y. Morin, 1982:8). On trade issues, Québec's position has also appeared to be more liberal than English Canada's. Unlike the neighbouring province of Ontario, whose economy is actually more dependent on exports, Québec strongly supported the proposed free trade agreement with the United States (Québec, 1988c). Solidly backed by the business community although opposed by the unions, the government's support for the free trade agreement expressed both a fear of American protectionism and a bias in favour of trade liberalization.

Much has been made over the past fifteen years of how Québec's economic elite has developed. This evolution has helped bring about a rather widely held social consensus on the relationship between general economic well-being and the expansion of trade. The government has done much to foster the creation of this consensus. It has acted first and foremost as a catalyst, one example being the round tables of joint consultation to which it invited various interest groups during the socioeconomic conferences "Québec in the World" of the early 1980s. Québec's desire for greater integration into world markets has since emerged as an increasingly important aspect of the province's identity.

Immigration

Control of immigration is a time-honoured element in the exercise of sovereignty. Québec's decision to enter this area in an increasingly sustained fashion since the Quiet Revolution has thus had much constitutional significance. Moreover, although immigration is an issue of foreign policy, the follow-up and social integration of immigrants is a matter of domestic policy. By familiarizing the French-speaking majority with other cultures, Québec's immigration policy has certainly contributed to defining a more tolerant and less inward-looking collective identity.

It was in 1965 that the government set up an immigration service under the Ministry of Cultural Affairs (Gow, 1986:224). This service went on to become a branch affiliated with the secretariat of the province. In 1968, the government created the Ministry of Immigration, transferring to it in 1969 eight immigrant counselling and training centres (COFI) previously under the Ministry of Education. In 1981, its mandate was broadened and the Ministry of Immigration became the Ministry of Cultural Communities and Immigration.

As Québec's immigration policy became institutionalized, the resources set aside for it expanded greatly. The ministry's staff went from thirty-five employees in 1969 to more than 600 in 1989. During the same time period, the number of bureaus located abroad grew from two to fourteen (six in Europe, three in Latin America, two in the United States, two in Asia, and one in the Middle East). The ministry, moreover, is still expanding the geographical range of its activities since it is now considering extending its network of operations to Eastern Europe (Québec, 1990a:90). Finally, the ministry's budget has avoided cuts in government spending, increasing from $ 2.8 million in 1969 to more than $40 million in 1989.

During its first decade of existence, the ministry needed to stake out its own range of operation with respect to the federal government. Relations between Ottawa and Québec City followed a path of development marked by a series of agreements: Cloutier-Lang (1971), Bienvenue-Andras (1975), and Couture-Cullen (1978). The first of these gave Québec's officials stationed abroad a role as information officers. The second required the federal government to take Québec's opinion into account when selecting immigrants. The third, much more binding, conceded to Québec the power to select immigrants abroad, leaving the federal government with control over only admission to the country.

The decentralization of decision-making in immigration was a cornerstone of the failed Meech Lake Accord. This accord, which put Québec's demands into constitutional form, provided for an increase in Québec's power to select immigrants in their countries of origin. It also gave Québec the possibility of receiving a share of Canada's immigration intake in proportion to the province's share of the total population, with the right to exceed this threshold by 5 percent (Hogg,

1988:66–68). It should be pointed out here that during the 1980–89 period the 200,000 immigrants to Québec made up only 17 percent of the total number of immigrants to Canada (Québec, 1990a:22).

The failure of Meech Lake did not stop the Québec government from going ahead and releasing, at the end of 1990, a wide-ranging policy statement on immigration. This document insisted, notably, on the need to improve the integration of immigrants. Above all else, it showed that immigration would henceforth constitute a strategic preoccupation within the provincial government's purview (Québec, 1990b). The policy statement helped to get matters moving since, only a few weeks after its release, the Canadian and Québec governments finally concluded an administrative agreement on all points in accordance with the provisions of the Meech Lake Accord (see Black and Hagen, in this volume).

Expansion of government activity in immigration has also enabled Québec to confirm its status as a distinct society. The very creation of the ministry took place at a time when Québec's linguistic crisis was coming to a head and when the demographic decline of the French-speaking majority was emerging as a major cause for concern. Socioeconomic integration of the immigrant population appeared quite early as a major policy goal for Québec in this area, with the result that the COFIs quickly became key instruments for familiarizing new arrivals with their culture of adoption. Nonetheless, it has only been by stages that *francisation* of immigrants has emerged as an unavoidable condition for their full insertion into Québec society. The insistence on francisation is stronger in the government's recent policy statement than it was before and illustrates the extent to which this goal ultimately constitutes a cornerstone of Québec's immigration policy. Moreover, the government's immigration policy has served to strengthen the international solidarity of the population of Québec. This spirit of internationalism has notably been exhibited in the acceptance of waves of immigrants from Chile, Vietnam, Haiti, and Turkey. It is noteworthy that, during the 1980s, Québec took in about half of all refugee claimants arriving in Canada.

Government involvement in immigration has opened up the frontiers of the state. By putting emphasis increasingly on improving the integration of immigrants and on the contribution they can make to economic development, it has also helped define a more outward-looking national identity.

CONCLUSION

Québec's international relations have greatly expanded over the past thirty years. This has come about primarily through step-by-step institutionalization of an international sphere of activity. The continuous growth and specialization of administrative structures devoted to management of international relations is in this respect highly noteworthy. From a geographical standpoint, Québec has focused its external policy on two countries: France and the United States. The choice of these partners stems from two different lines of reasoning: political and cultural in the first case, economic ones in the second. This duality corresponds in fact to a projection into the international arena of the generic components of political debate within the province. In terms of what is topical, new issues have taken the place of old ones. After culture and education, external trade and immigration have come to the forefront. This diversification of priorities mirrors an overriding concern for economic matters. It would have been difficult for the government to legitimize successfully the growth of its international relations other than by invoking economic arguments.

The gradual development of Québec's external relations cannot, of course, be fully understood without taking into account the Canadian political environment within which it has come about. On this point, it is worth repeating that Canada's Constitution contains ambiguities over the division of powers between the federal government and the provincial governments in the area of foreign policy. The existence of such ambiguities was a necessary legal condition for Québec to be able to enter the field of international relations. Depending on the times and the issues at stake, this constitutional context has sparked more or less heated tensions. In the final analysis, however, it has led to the negotiation of numerous political compromises between the federal government and the Québec government. The expansion of Québec's international relations has also been the product of a gap between the traditional interests of Canadian diplomacy and the growing expectations of the Québec government. Although absolute generalizations are hard to make on the subject, it is clear that Québec has historically identified less easily than the other provinces with the policies and image upheld by the federal government abroad.

Extending its external influence has ultimately become for Québec a way of better coming to terms with itself as a distinct society. Even though the question of international relations is a secondary one in the current constitutional debate, it has perceptibly contributed to shaping the difference between Québec and the rest of Canada. This is, moreover, the intuition underlying the central argument put forward in the preceding pages, i.e. that the processes of state-building and nation-building that have marked Québec's recent history entail an unavoidable international dimension. Québec, because of its asymmetrical position in the Canadian federation, has sought to obtain direct access to the material and symbolic resources of its international environment. These resources have in turn enabled it to consolidate a means of political control while helping it establish a better-defined collective identity.

In conclusion, it should be emphasized that the growth of Québec's foreign relations is the result not only of the province's own decisions, but also of developments in world politics. Québec's first moves into the international realm must certainly be interpreted as a deliberate undertaking. Nonetheless, from the 1970s on, the overall evolution of the international system has clearly helped to speed up the expansion of Québec's foreign policy. Growing interdependence has from this standpoint altered how the Québec government acts just as it has changed the behaviour of all other members of the international community. In any case, it is hard to imagine the politicians and officials who pioneered Québec's external policy as having been able to envisage how important this question would become in the course of time.

Amid the current uncertainties over Québec's constitutional future, one thing nonetheless seems assured. Whatever the exact nature of its political system, the province's external relations cannot help but go on developing. This prediction is based both on Québec's irreversible march toward greater political autonomy and on general trends in the international environment. In fact, the very future of Québec could be played out in the international arena. By the recognition it does or does not give Québec, the community of nations could determine the province's political status in the years to come.

REFERENCES

Beaudoin, L. (1977). "Origines et développement du rôle international du gouvernement du Québec," in P. Painchaud, ed., *Le Canada et le Québec sur la scène internationale*, Québec/Montréal: Centre québécois de relations internationales/Presses de l'Université du Québec, 441–70.

Bernier, I. (1988). "Les intérêts et les objectifs du Canada et du Québec," in Centre québécois de relations internationales, *Les Sommets francophones. Nouvel instrument de relations internationales*, Québec, 59–70.

Brown, D. (1991). "The Evolving Role of the Provinces in Canadian Trade Policy" in D. Brown and M. Smith, eds., *Canadian Federalism: Meeting Global Economic Challenges?* Kingston/Halifax: Institute of Intergovernmental Relations/Institute for Research on Public Policy, 81–128.

Canada (1968a). Secrétariat d'État aux Affaires extérieures, *Fédéralisme et conférences internationales sur l'éducation*, Ottawa: Imprimeur de la Reine.

Canada (1968b). Secrétariat d'État aux Affaires extérieures, *Fédéralisme et relations internationales*, Ottawa: Imprimeur de la Reine.

Comeau, P.-A. (1990). "Les relations internationales," in D. Monière, ed., *L'année politique au Québec, 1989–1990*, Montréal: Québec/Amérique, 83–90.

Donneur, A.P. et al. (1983). "L'évaluation des politiques en relations internationales: le cas de la coopération franco–québécoise en éducation," *Études internationales*, 14 (2), 237–54.

Duchacek, I.D. (1988). "Multicommunal and Bicommunal Polities and their International Relations," in I.D. Duchacek, D. Latouche, and G. Stevenson, eds., *Perforated Sovereignties and International Relations: Trans-Sovereign Contacts of Subnational Governments*, Westport: Greenwood Press, 3–28.

Gérin-Lajoie, P. (1965). *Allocution du ministre de l'Éducation, M. Paul Gérin-Lajoie, aux membres du corps consulaire de Montréal*, Montréal, 12 avril 1965.

Gow, J.I. (1986). *Histoire de l'administration publique québécoise, 1867–1970*, Montréal-Toronto: Presses de l'Université de Montréal/Institut d'administration publique du Canada.

Hamelin, J. (1968). "Québec et le monde extérieur," *Annuaire du Québec, 1968–1969*, Québec: Éditeur officiel, 2–36.

Hero, A.O., and Balthazar, L. (1988). *Contemporary Québec and the United States, 1960–1985*, Lanham: University Press of America.

Hogg, P.W. (1988). *Accord constitutionnel du Lac Meech. Texte annoté*, Toronto: Carswell.

Holsti, K.J. (1988). *International Politics. A Framework for Analysis*, 5th ed., Englewood Cliffs: Prentice Hall.

Jacomy-Millette, A. (1983). "Rapport canadien," *Revue belge de droit international*, 17 (1), 68-89.

Keating, T. (1990). "The State and International Relations," in D.G. Haglund and M.K. Hawes, eds., *World Politics: Power, Interdependence and Dependence*, Toronto: Harcourt Brace Jovanovich, 16–37.

Keohane, R. and Nye, J. (1989). *Power and Interdependence*, 2nd ed., Boston: Little, Brown.

Lalande, G. (1989). "La francophonie et la politique étrangère canadienne," in P. Painchaud, ed., *De Mackenzie King à Pierre Trudeau. Quarante ans de diplomatie canadienne*, Québec: Presses de l'Université Laval, 217–48.

Latouche, D. (1988). "State Building and Foreign Policy at the Subnational Level," in I.D. Duchacek, D. Latouche, and G. Stevenson, eds., *Perforated Sovereignties and International Relations: Trans-Sovereign Contacts of Subnational Governments*, Westport: Greenwood Press, 29–42.

Létourneau, J. (1991). "La nouvelle figure identitaire du Québécois. Essai sur la dimension symbolique d'un consensus social en voie d'émergence," Communication présentée au Colloque *Le Québec au carrefour de sa destinée: économie, politique, identité*, Londres.

Lisée, J.-F. (1990). *Dans l'oeil de l'aigle. Washington face au Québec*, Montréal: Boréal.

Lubin, M. (1986). "Québec–US Relations: An Overview," *American Review of Canadian Studies*, 16 (1), Spring, 25–39.

Mansbach, R., Ferguson, Y., and Lampert, D. (1976). *The Web of International Politics: Nonstate Actors in the Global System*, Englewood Cliffs: Prentice Hall.

Morin, C. (1987). *L'art de l'impossible. la diplomatie québécoise depuis 1960*, Montréal: Boréal.

Morin, J.-Y. (1982). *Text of an Address by the Vice Prime Minister of Québec and Minister of Intergovernmental Affairs, Mr. Jacques-Yvan Morin, Before the World Affairs Council of Northern California*, San Francisco, June 3rd, 1982.

Noda, S. (1988). *Les relations internationales du Québec de 1970 à 1980 : Comparaison des gou-vernements Bourassa et Lévesque*, Ph.D. dissertation, Department of History, Université de Montréal.

Painchaud, P. (1980). "L'État du Québec et le système international," in G. Bergeron and R. Pelletier, eds., *L'État du Québec en devenir*, Montréal: Boréal Express, 351–69.

Painchaud, P. (1988). "Le Québec et les sommets des pays francophones," in Centre québécois de rela-tions internationales, *Les Sommets francophones. Nouvel instrument de relations internationales*, Québec, 99–104.

Pelouas, A. (1991), "Plus tourné vers l'étranger, le Québec demeure malgré tout déficitaire dans ses échanges internationaux," *Le Devoir*, 1 February, p. C-2.

Plischke, E. (1977). *Microstates in World Affairs: Policy Problems and Options*, Washington: Ameri-can Enterprise Institute for Public Policy Research.

Portes, J. (1988). "Paris–Ottawa–Québec: A Unique Triangle," in I.D. Duchacek, D. Latouche, and G. Stevenson, eds., *Perforated Sovereignties and International Relations: Trans-Sovereign Con-tacts of Subnational Governments*, Westport: Greenwood Press, 103–18.

Québec,(1980). Ministère des Affaires intergouvernementales, *Rapport annuel, 1978-1979*, Québec: Éditeur officiel du Québec.

Québec (1984). Ministère des Relations internationales, *Recueil des ententes internationales du Québec*, Québec: Ministère des Communications.

Québec (1985). Ministère des Relations internationales, *Le Québec dans le monde ou le défi de l'inter-dépendance*, Québec.

Québec (1988a). Assemblée nationale, *Loi sur le ministère des Affaires internationales (Projet de loi 42)*, Québec: Éditeur officiel du Québec.

Québec (1988b). Ministère des Relations internationales, *Le Québec dans la francophonie*, Québec: Ministère des Communications.

Québec (1988c). Ministère du Commerce extérieur et du développement technologique, *L'accord de libre-échange entre le Canada et les États-Unis. Analyse dans une perspective québécoise*, Québec.

Québec (1989). Bureau de la statistique, *Le Québec statistique*, Québec.

Québec (1990a). Ministère des Communautés culturelles et de l'immigration, *Fiches synthèses pour la défense des crédits de 1990–1991*, Québec.

Québec (1990b), Ministère des Communautés culturelles et de l'Immigration, *Au Québec pour bâtir ensemble. Énoncé de politique en matière d'immigration et d'intégration*, Québec.

Rosenau, J. (1980). *The Study of Global Interdependence: Essays on the Transnationalization of World Affairs*, London: Pinter.

Roy, J.-L. (1977). "Les relations du Québec et des États-Unis (1945–1970)," in P. Painchaud, ed., *Le Canada et le Québec sur la scène internationale*, Québec/Montréal: Centre québécois de rela-tions internationales/Presses de l'Université du Québec, 497–514.

Soldatos, P. (1988). "Les relations internationales du Québec: la marque d'un déterminisme économique," in D. Monière, ed., *L'année politique au Québec, 1987–1988*, Montréal: Québec/ Amérique, 109–23.

Tarlton, C.D. (1965). "Symmetry and Asymmetry as Elements of Federalism: A Theoretical Specula-tion," *Journal of Politics*, 27, 861–75.

Taylor, P. (1984). *Nonstate Actors in International Politics: From Transregional to Substate Organiza-tions*, Boulder: Westview Press.

Vernon, R. (1987). "L'interdépendance globale dans une perspective historique," in OCDE, ed., *Inter-dépendance et coopération dans le monde de demain*, Paris: OCDE, 24–38.

P A R T

4

DEMOGRAPHY, ETHNICITY, AND LANGUAGE

Québec Immigration Politics and Policy: Historical and Contemporary Perspectives

Jerome H. Black
and
David Hagen
McGill University

INTRODUCTION

In February 1991, the Québec and federal governments signed a major agreement on immigration matters representing a significant additional step in the devolution of power in favour of the province. The agreement, which came into effect April 1, 1991, allowed Québec to gain complete control over the selection of independent immigrants, transferred total responsibility for language training and adaptation programs to the province, and stipulated that Québec could claim a share of future Canadian immigration intake up to 5 percent. This increase in powers and autonomy is not only unique among Canadian provinces, but is also markedly different from the norm found in most federal systems, where the central government has a jurisdictional monopoly with regard to immigration. The "distinctive" role that Québec has come to play in this increasingly important policy area is also paralleled by a steady growth of its bureaucratic structures. From humble beginnings as a tiny *Service d'immigration du Québec* in 1965, today's *Ministère des communautés culturelles et de l'immigration* (MCCI) has emerged as an important administrative and political entity.

Two months prior to the signing of the agreement, the Québec government published its first-ever comprehensive policy statement on immigration, the English version of which is entitled *Let's Build Québec Together* (1990).[1] The document confirmed the importance Québec attached to immigration as an element in its future development, but at the same time, was quite forthright about the problems and challenges that immigration posed. Principal among these was the need to reconcile the conflicting motivations behind immigrant recruitment. The desire to maximize the economic benefits associated with the selection of skilled or capital-endowed candidates often clashes with other imperatives, such as humanitarian

*The authors wish to thank the referees and Alain-G. Gagnon for their helpful comments. All translations are the authors'.

obligations, emphasis on the recruitment of francophones, or the use of immigration to offset demographic decline. Part of the solution to problems such as these lies in linking the nuts and bolts of immigration recruitment and selection to the wider concerns of integration and cultural pluralism. The articulation of these interrelationships and, more broadly, the commitment to policy development incorporating such considerations demonstrate not only the comprehensive character of the document but the generally sensible and realistic premises that underpin it. Furthermore, by presenting the statement as provincial policy reflective of the concern of the entire government, and not simply as MCCI policy, the Bourassa regime was clearly indicating the priority status now accorded the concerns and objectives embodied therein.

These recent developments contrast sharply with nearly a century of provincial inactivity in the immigration policy sector. This chapter seeks to provide an account of the reasons behind Québec's decision to assume a more interventionist posture in a field so long dominated by the federal government. The 1990 statement and the 1991 agreement represent a response to economic, social, and demographic imperatives that have only come to attain priority status on the political agenda in the course of the 1980s. The understanding of these initiatives should, however, include an appreciation of the fact that they are the fruit of a long evolution, the historical sources of which can be traced back to Confederation and beyond. Indeed, it is essential to understand these sources in order to grasp why through most of the 1960s and even into the 1970s, a period of otherwise unreserved and robust state activity, Québec proceeded with some hesitancy in the formulation of immigration policy and exhibited some restraint in pressing the federal government for a larger say. Historically based antipathy toward immigration, traditionally high levels of self-reproduction of the collectivity, and longstanding incoherency in the federal government's own approach to immigration are among the most important factors that will be cited for this belated "strong state" response.

Charting the historical development of Québec's approach to immigration will also reveal how alterations in the socioeconomic environment have had a bearing upon attitudes and policy. Often conflicting economic, demographic, and linguistic imperatives have combined in different ways over time to mould public attitudes to immigration in a particular way and to shape specific provincial policy responses. A historical approach also facilitates an appreciation of the effects of federalism on Québec's evolving preoccupation with immigration. This invites a better understanding of how Canadian federalism and its changing character have conditioned and complicated the nature of the debate on immigration within the province.

The next section opens up with a sketch of one of the most important of these conditioning factors, the constitutional division of powers over immigration as initially established in 1867. The analysis goes on, however, to trace the evolution of provincial orientations over the long period from 1867 to the end of World War II, and illustrates the attitudinal and ideological foundations underlying early provincial involvement and withdrawal. The section following explores the emergence of a new immigration-related discourse and events leading up to the establishment of the *Ministère de l'Immigration du Québec* in 1968. The first steps of the new ministry are examined next, followed by an analysis of provincial policy under the

Parti Québécois. A final section treats the period leading up to, and including, the new agreement and policy statement. A concluding section provides an opportunity for some reiteration and reflection.

FROM CONFEDERATION TO WORLD WAR II: INITIAL INVOLVEMENT AND WITHDRAWAL

Part of the understanding of the role that Québec has played in immigration matters derives from an appreciation of the formal constitutional setting and, in particular, section 95 of the Constitution Act of 1867, which grants concurrent powers in the field of immigration (and agriculture), but with federal paramountcy.[2] This provision for possible provincial legislative action is a readily understandable legacy of the involvement in these areas by the colonial governments and also follows from the necessity of allowing the new provinces some say in the settling of their sparsely populated lands (Vineberg, 1987:300). Yet, at the same time, the granting of ultimate authority to the federal government is quite explicit: the provincial legislatures may pass laws only if they do not conflict with existing federal legislation. Federal paramountcy and section 91(25), which confers upon the federal government jurisdiction over naturalization and aliens, form the basis for the observation that, in the design of the Constitution, the intention was to grant predominance to the federal government. On the other hand, provincial authority, owing to its jurisdictional prevalence in matters of property and civil rights, is less limited with regard to issues of immigrant integration and the provision of settlement assistance (Grey, 1984:5–6).

Even if the broader outlines of the constitutional context were relatively clear from the outset, it was not immediately obvious what specific roles the federal and provincial governments would come to play, nor evident how the relationship between them would evolve. The initial phase of federal–provincial interaction involved consultation, principally through the medium of federal–provincial conferences, which were held annually between 1868 and 1874. The first conference provided the momentum for Canada's first immigration act a year later and produced an agreement that allowed the provincial governments the right to appoint their own immigration agents abroad, independently of designated federal agents.

Several provinces, including Québec in 1871, did establish immigration offices overseas. From the beginning, Québec's orientation toward immigration was characterized by a blend of demographic, linguistic, and economic considerations. The recruitment of Catholic French-speaking immigrants, principally from France and Belgium, would help re-establish, it was argued, a demographic balance between the two linguistic groups that had been upset by waves of nonfrancophone immigration. The focal point of this concern was not only the populating of the province's unsettled reaches, but as well the settlement of francophones in western Canada. The latter dimension reflected a pan-Canadian orientation among many francophone elites, especially those within the church, who associated linguistic duality with the maintenance of political influence nation-wide. In both cases, however, the sought-after goal of colonization was manifested in the expressed preference for farmers who had capital and concrete agricultural skills. Endeavours to attract such immigrants were supported by transportation subsidies and by the possibility that immigrants, upon arrival, could draw upon food, accommodation, and employment services coordinated by agents operating in the province's two largest cities (Poitras, 1971:21–23).

By mid-decade, however, rivalry had come to characterize the way the overseas agents from the different governments operated, resulting, the 1874 federal–provincial conference concluded, in a "waste of strength and expense," as well as "an injuriously prejudicial effect on the minds of intending emigrants" (quoted in Vineberg, 1987:302). As a consequence, it was agreed that the provinces would give up their independent overseas agencies, but retain subagents attached to the federal offices. Québec reluctantly followed this course, but by 1883 had withdrawn its last agent; a second, largely unsuccessful attempt at recruiting was made between 1888 and 1892 (Poitras, 1971:16–19). The province also lessened its involvement in the area of integration and settlement; after 1879, many of the services that had been available to assist newly arrived immigrants were phased out (Poitras, 1971).

The inability of Québec to attract the kinds of immigrants it wanted helps explain why the province, gaining little for its expenditures, slowly pulled back in its recruitment efforts. Other explanations centre on two demographic—though contradictory—trends in the latter part of the 19th century, a high birthrate among French Canadians and the emigration of many *habitants* to the United States. High levels of fecundity compensated greatly for the essentially British character of immigration and thus lessened the preoccupation with using external recruitment to keep the demographic balance in check. Falling immigration levels, at least relative to pre-Confederation days, and the fact that after 1875 few British immigrants chose to settle in Québec served to strengthen further the compensatory role played by a high birthrate. Indeed, throughout this period, francophones came to comprise a larger proportion of the Québec population.

This was so in spite of a large-scale exodus of French Canadians to the United States—estimated to be about 200,000 Québécois in the 1870–90 period[3]—in search of better employment opportunities. The population loss was, nevertheless, significant enough to arouse deep concern and prompt attempts at curbing the outflow and repatriating those already gone. Championed by a clergy preoccupied with the spiritual well-being of emigrant "children of the soil" lost to the immoral manufacturing centres in New England (Poitras, 1971), the argument that money would be better spent on repatriation rather than on immigration struck a responsive note among the population at large. Repatriation thus largely became the centrepiece of Québec "immigration policy" as the 19th century drew to a close, although it, too, was largely ineffectual in realizing its aims.

In contrast, the federal government's efforts to draw immigrants, particularly farmers and farm workers for settlement in the West, did meet with more success. The aggressive recruitment campaign launched under the stewardship of Clifford Sifton, Minister of the Interior for the Laurier government from 1896 until 1905, attracted some three million people to Canada by 1914, although private enterprise also played a prominent role in recruitment and settlement efforts.[4]

Yet for many Canadians the recruitment effort was regarded as less than successful, for insufficient immigration from the traditional recruiting countries of Britain, the United States, and France had led Sifton to turn to the "peasant" countries of Eastern and Southern Europe. In Québec, many prominent figures, including Henri Bourassa, reacted bitterly to the influx of these "strangers," criticizing

Laurier's Liberals for deliberately choosing Jews from Poland and Russia, rather than francophones from Western Europe. To some extent, this hostility was driven by the impact such immigration was having in frustrating dreams of a pan-Canadian French–English dualism. But voice was also given to fears of outright assimilation, and many francophones even harboured suspicions that this was the result of a deliberate conspiracy, on par with the intent of the Durham Report, to overwhelm francophones in the country through massive British immigration.[5]

Although most immigrants went west, changes in the ethnic composition of Québec society, particularly in Montréal, were significant enough to cause concern. Fears for the purity of the French-Canadian "nation" led religious authorities to take measures limiting contact between immigrants and French Canadians. Immigrants of Catholic origin were isolated in ethnic parishes, a practice that actually encouraged the maintenance of ethnic ties and traditions, while non-Catholics were simply "abandoned" to the anglophone community (Helly, 1989).

Immigrants were also seen to pose a political threat. Whereas French Canadians had been largely conditioned to accept anglophone domination of provincial economic activity in exchange for control of political and religious institutions seen as vital to the survival of the French-Canadian collectivity, most immigrants were unwilling to accept second-class economic status for the sake of a political combat in which they felt they had no part. This became increasingly clear during the 1930s as growing numbers of Catholic immigrant families, disappointed with the inability of French-Canadian institutions to facilitate their economic insertion into provincial society, began sending their children to either Irish Catholic or Protestant English schools,[6] in some cases renouncing their faith to do so. This tendency only accelerated over time, doing little in the process to encourage the *rapprochement* of francophones and immigrants.

Although immigration dropped to a mere trickle during the 1930s, the economic crisis and the influence of fascist ideologies imported from Europe also fanned anti-immigrant sentiment, much of which focused against Québec's relatively large Jewish community. Antisemitism became a fact of life for Jews in the province, and those attempting to enter Canada to escape the horror of Nazism in Europe found their way blocked in part because of French-Canadian hostility (Abella and Troper, 1983; Anctil, in this volume). It was not until after World War II that signs of changing attitudes toward immigrants and immigration began to appear.

THE EARLY POSTWAR PERIOD: THE EMERGING NEW DISCOURSE

The postwar period was marked by a return, although not on the scale of the Sifton era, to high levels of immigration, as large numbers of European immigrants and refugees fled their war-ravaged continent. More than two million people entered Canada between 1951 and 1965, and while the majority of new arrivals chose Ontario as a destination, nearly 450,000 settled, at least initially, in Québec (Hill, 1987:209).

In spite of a continuing mix of hostility and indifference to immigration during this period,[7] there were nonetheless some signs of changing attitudes among a small, more progressive group of intellectuals. Many of the ideas that helped pave the way for the creation of an immigration ministry and that continue to inform

Québec immigration and ethnic policy-making to this day can trace their origins to this period. To be sure, these views were not widely shared—public opinion polls dating back that far show greater antipathy toward immigration on the part of French Canadians relative to English Canadians (Girard and Manègre, 1988:5–6; Humblet, 1976:132)—nor did they stimulate a great deal of immigration-related activity. Nevertheless, they represented a significant current of new thinking characterized by a more positive view about immigration.

Four specific, but overlapping, themes dominated the emerging discourse. One was a familiar, negative focus on the threat immigration posed to the demolinguistic balance between French and English Canada.The resurgence of an immigration inflow that was predominantly Anglo-Saxon and allophone reawakened fears of assimilation, moving some commentators to use, once again, the language of "conspiracy" to underscore their concerns. Conspiracy may seem a strong word given the federal government's approach to immigration policy, described by Ottawa itself as generally being made "in response to the events of the day" (Canada, 1974:1). However, in spite of the failure of the federal government to articulate clearly specific principles and objectives—a rather remarkable state of affairs given that immigration has been so central, in objective terms, to the country's evolution—francophone fears were justified by the "de facto" and persistent immigration imbalances. These concerns were compounded by Québec's relatively low levels of immigrant retention; many immigrants either left Québec shortly after their arrival or simply settled elsewhere in the country, a situation seen to swell further the ranks of the anglophone majority (Léger, 1954:414–15).

Integration comprised a second and, by contrast, a more positive theme. In spite of ongoing dissatisfaction with federal immigration policy, some new voices argued that carrying over that hostility into relationships with immigrants themselves only worsened the policy's impact on French Québec. As early as 1943, none other than Lionel Groulx was appealing for greater openness toward "New Canadians,"[8] a call taken up by others (Angers, 1954; Fugère, 1945; Léger, 1954), who felt that the problem of nonintegration of immigrants into the francophone community was largely the result of negative attitudes. Although the weak economic position of the francophone majority was recognized as early as 1945 as one of the principal reasons pushing allophone immigrants toward the anglophone minority community (Fugère, 1945), critics did not go so far as to challenge the economic structures of subordination that limited the integrative capacity of French-Canadian society. The narrower emphasis on the need for attitudinal change, important though it was, reflected the still nascent character of the new nationalist thought emerging in the 1950s (Helly, 1989:83).[9]

The integration issue was inextricably bound up with the question of education. The exodus of allophone immigrants from French-language schools, which had begun in the 1930s, only worsened during the late 1940s and the 1950s and prompted the *Commission des écoles catholiques de Montréal* (CECM) to establish in 1948 the *Comité des Néo-Canadiens* in an attempt to deal with the problem[10]. Efforts made to re-establish special programs for allophone immigrants ended in failure due to lack of government support, as well as internal CECM opposition and intense anglophone pressure, much of it from Irish Catholics, determined to maintain the clientele of their English Catholic schools (Behiels, 1986:48–51; Québec, 1967:37). Language courses for adults were slightly more successful,[11] but the minimal resources devoted to them limited their overall impact (de Jaham, 1980:5). Other private initiatives to promote immigrant adaptation were taken by various immigrant assistance societies, established most often under the auspices of the Catholic Church in response to appeals from Pope Pius XII for charitable actions on behalf of European Catholics displaced by the war (Harvey, 1987:21–22). However, these ventures, too, were limited in scope, and remained handicapped by the absence of both official and public support.

Provincial government disinterest in immigration was the final focus of those preoccupied with the evolution of the field. As already noted, apart from an initial post-Confederation flurry of provincial immigration-related activity, Québec had more or less left the field to the federal authorities. By the mid-1950s, many critics felt that this absence was no longer acceptable:

> Immigration is one of the principal factors conditioning the future of the French Canadian group. Now, eight years after the resumption of immigrant inflows, we have not yet been able to define a policy: we have not even been able, as a group, to establish the basics of a system of reception and assistance. (Léger, 1954:415)

In spite of a growing consensus on the need for government action among this group of critics, there was some debate on the appropriate scope of government activity. For some, government involvement principally meant immigrant reception, settlement assistance, and support for integration (Léger, 1954). However, briefs submitted to the Tremblay Commission on the Constitutional Future of Québec by the *Société d'aide aux immigrants* and the *Chambre de commerce de Montréal* in 1954, although strongly supportive of a comprehensive provincial policy in these areas, also argued in favour of the establishment of provincial recruitment offices in francophone countries with the potential to provide immigrants.

That the Duplessis regime turned a deaf ear to these calls is not surprising. After all, in pre–Quiet Revolution Québec, the provincial administration had been reluctant to act even in such exclusively provincial domains as education and social services (Latouche, 1989a:183–84). Furthermore, francophone second-class economic status and uncertain attitudes toward immigrants reflected the still ambiguous nature of Québec's political identity during this period, rendering action in the field even more unlikely.

Even with the arrival of the Lesage government in 1960, there were no sudden changes in immigration policy, as attention was largely focused on other matters more pressing in the short term (Harvey, 1987:25). Furthermore, the election of the Liberal administration coincided with a national economic downturn, which led to a sharp drop in immigration entries between 1961 and 1965 (Hawkins, 1988:100, 135); this, too, may have diverted attention from the policy sector.

As the decade drew to a close, however, a combination of events and a changing political context helped refocus attention on the immigration question, not only among longtime observers and critics, but also among a wider circle of decision-makers. Continuing low levels of francophone immigration,[12] ongoing anglicization of immigrants,[13] emerging awareness of the impact of a declining francophone birthrate, and increasing politicization of the language issue were all major trends that converged during this period to heighten preoccupation with immigration and integration matters. Moreover, immigration figures on the national level began to climb rapidly again, reaching over 900,000 between 1965 and 1970, while during the same period the proportion received by Québec dropped below 20 percent for the first time since the war (Hill, 1987:209).

Policy developments at the federal level also played a role. In 1966, the federal White Paper on immigration was released, heralding the complete elimination of openly discriminatory selection criteria—a process begun in 1962—and the establishment of a points system designed to facilitate the selection of immigrants in accordance with Canada's economic needs. While this policy did little to address francophone concerns regarding the prevailing ethnic imbalance in immigration, this focus on the economic impact of immigration did stimulate some attention on the part of provincial officials (Vineberg, 1987:307).

Prompted by these various developments, Québec made its first move back into the field of immigration with the 1965 establishment of its small *Service d'immigration du Québec* (SIQ). Initially housed within the *Ministère des affaires culturelles*, the SIQ was charged with researching potential avenues of provincial involvement, recommending appropriate accompanying administrative structures, and, later, with working toward the socioeconomic and cultural integration of immigrants. However, limited staff and budget curtailed the service's ability to carry out its mandate.[14]

Although then provincial minister Marcel Masse announced provincial intentions of creating a full-fledged immigration ministry as early as May 1967, the decision was no doubt further spurred on by the events in St. Leonard. In September 1967, the Catholic school board of this Montréal Island municipality adopted a resolution to abolish bilingual schools attended by children of the community's largely Italian immigrant population, and to transform them into unilingual French schools. The issue blew up into a major confrontation in 1968, when many Italians, backed by the Montréal anglophone community, led a movement demanding the opening of an English school. Whereas previous interest in the question had largely been restricted to elite circles, the issue of immigrant integration now received attention in a very public way. Several months after the incident, in November 1968, the *Ministère de l'immigration* (MIQ) was established, the first ministry of its kind in Canada to be devoted entirely to immigration.

It is not clear, however, that a full-fledged immigration administration was actually necessary to address the challenges thrust into the public eye by the linguistic crisis—particularly given that the province continued to defer to federal authority in most immigration matters. Ricardo Hill argues that "only the persistence of the 'nationalist' discourse seems to justify the amplitude of the provincial immigration apparatus on the administrative and organizational level" (1987:236), an observation that seems especially telling inasmuch as the kind of activities favoured by the new ministry early on could have been undertaken by the *Ministère de l'éducation du Québec* (MEQ) or by other ministries. Indeed, the *Centres d'orientation et de formation des immigrants* (COFIs), Québec's language-training facilities for adult immigrants, were initially under MEQ control after their establishment in 1968. The creation of the MIQ was likely meant to reassure Québec public opinion in the charged post–St. Leonard atmosphere (Hill, 1967:267). At the same time, its mere establishment spoke volumes about the distance covered by the increasingly dynamic Québec state in this period, as the strict noninterventionism of the Duplessis era gave way to a positive form of state involvement, driven by a new affirmative nationalism. At the same time, the ministry's low profile in the early years justifies queries about the practical importance it was accorded in the minds of decision-makers of the day.

The federal reaction to the establishment of the ministry, relatively favourable in spite of the arrival of Pierre Trudeau at the head of the federal Liberals (Hawkins, 1988:232), lends credence to the idea that provincial aims were initially modest. One author has suggested that the federal response is largely explained by the new ministry's expressed desire to collaborate with Ottawa (Latouche, 1989a:187). Indeed, provincial emphasis on adaptation programs and public education was in no way perceived as potentially menacing to the federal government, since these were areas where Ottawa took comparatively little initiative. Québec's lack of experience and a lack of consensus on measures to be taken may also explain the limited scope of these early steps (Harvey, 1987:25–26).

THE EARLY 1970S: A TIME OF TRANSITION

The Québec government's preoccupation with the integration and adaptation facets of immigration policy during this period is reflected in the organizational configuration of the ministry itself (Poitras, 1971:38–40). Most of the five principal bureaus within the MIQ were devoted, one way or another, to the provision of orientation, training, and social assistance services for immigrants and to the facilitation of a supportive environment of adaptation—the latter through an encouragement of ethnic community activities and the engendering of more sympathetic responses to immigrants by the Québec public at large. In contrast, only one service within one of the divisions concerned itself with recruitment matters, and this essentially amounted to the provision of information to prospective immigrants. This distinctly minor role accorded to overseas operations is also evident in the monopolization of the budget and resources by those bureaus and services involved in adaptation matters, though an equally important point to appreciate is the relatively small total budget the ministry had in these first few years. This was a time when the fledgling ministry commanded little status within the executive as a whole.

A small, but nonetheless important, first step toward a larger role was taken with the concluding of a Québec–Ottawa agreement, signed in 1971 by the respective ministers, Cloutier and Lang. The deal allowed Québec to station within certain overseas federal immigration bureaus "orientation agents," who could provide immigrants destined for Québec with additional counselling on working and living conditions in the province.[15] However, the agreement did little to alter the dominant position of the federal government in the crucial area of selection. Québec's input was limited to this strictly informational dimension and, indeed, Québec's officers had contact with the would-be immigrants only after they had already been chosen by federal officials. Still, by officially recognizing that the province had a legitimate interest in the selection process, the agreement, it could be argued, represented an important departure.

On the other hand, some quite vocal nationalist commentators, who were decrying the limited status commanded by the MIQ within government circles, regarded it as a step backward. For them, the Cloutier-Lang accord merely underscored the weakness of Québec's immigration policy, if not the fact that Québec lacked an immigration policy outright. Worse, because it gave the illusion that the province played a significant role overseas, the agreement constituted a decisive setback; in this sense, some viewed it as "pernicious" (e.g., Lemelin, 1971).

Such criticisms may have helped somewhat to focus more public attention on the subject. More important no doubt was the ongoing linguistic crisis, which was exacerbated in 1975 by Bill 22, the Bourassa government's ill-fated attempt to improve the status of the French language within the province and to address the language of education issue. By the middle of the decade, ministerial budgets and staff had increased significantly,[16] and the province manifested its desire to have more say in the selection of immigrants by requesting to renegotiate the Cloutier-Lang accord. A new immigration agreement was, in fact, signed in 1975 by the provincial minister Jean Bienvenue and his federal counterpart, Robert Andras. This second accord allowed MIQ officers to continue to play a counselling role, but more importantly, gave them some voice in the selection of those immigrants interested in heading to Québec. Though the province's input was purely advisory—final authority still belonged to federal officials—with the 1975 agreement, Québec could now claim, for the first time since the 19th century, some influence in the selection process.

Linguistic tensions form only part of the explanation for Québec's enhanced concern with all facets of immigration (including recruitment) as alarming demographic trends continued unabated. By the mid-1970s, fecundity rates among francophones had dropped below replacement levels (2.1 children per woman of childbearing age) (see Henripin in this volume). At the same time, negative migration flows were also slowing the growth rate of the Québec population. While this was mainly the result of the exodus of anglophones (a historical phenomenon that was to peak during the first mandate of the Parti Québécois), it was apparent that the ability of Québec to retain immigrants, never strong in the best of times, was on the decline as well. In conjunction with only a modest track record in attracting new arrivals, the immigration component of population growth as a problem and a challenge loomed ever larger.

Québec's interest in immigration was also piqued as it witnessed Ottawa grapple with weaknesses in its still largely ad hoc approach to immigration decision-making, made apparent by developments in the early 1970s.[17] Unforeseen new problems (especially the large-scale influx of undocumented and illegal aliens) underscored the inadequacy of the traditional approach and compelled serious consideration of more "modern" planning and management techniques. Canada could ill afford to continue relying on an outdated immigration act and a process lacking even a mechanism for controlling the total number of immigrants admitted. Québec, for its part, could hardly fail to take notice of the national debate on policy reform associated with the major immigration review that began in 1973 and culminated in 1977 with royal assent given to a new federal immigration act.

Ottawa's adoption of a planning-oriented approach, specifically highlighting the economic and demographic benefits to be derived from immigration, represented a potentially useful model that Québec could emulate. That the new legislation contained concrete provisions implicating the provinces in the federal planning and decision-making process was also important. One provision obliged the federal minister to consult with the provinces before annual announcements in Parliament were made about the number of immigrants to be admitted over a specified time period. Another feature provided for immigration agreements to be reached with the provinces. Indeed, these developments helped pave the way for the third contemporary Québec–Ottawa agreement on immigration.

THE PARTI QUÉBÉCOIS: CONSOLIDATING PROVINCIAL INVOLVEMENT

The Parti Québécois (PQ) victory in the 1976 election augured for a more muscular approach to immigration-related issues, and indeed the PQ administration has been recognized by several as carrying out a vital role in the development of the MIQ (Harvey, 1987:38; Rogel, 1989:30).

Such an interpretation has considerable merit. The signature of the Couture-Cullen accord in 1978, which allowed Québec a much larger role in the selection of certain categories of immigrants, and the passage of Bill 101 in 1977, which, although not aimed exclusively at immigrants, did much to steer them toward the francophone community, were major developments. The transformation of the MIQ into the *Ministère des communautés culturelles et de l'immigration* (MCCI) in 1981, as well as the release of the PQ government's ethnic policy, *Autant de façons d'être Québécois* (1981), the province's response to federal multiculturalism, also indicated continued evolution of the immigration dossier. However, the period merits attention not only for these developments, but also because it reveals more clearly some of the conflicting imperatives bearing on Québec policymakers.

The importance of the two PQ initiatives should not, however, be downplayed by a desire to point out these tensions. The passage of Bill 101, although strongly resisted by the immigrant community, irrevocably altered the linguistic power balance in Québec, putting a term to the severe crisis sparked several years earlier in St. Leonard. With the centrality of the French language established at school and, less conclusively, in the workplace, immigrants would henceforth be both obliged and encouraged to turn toward francophone society. By extension, this reinforcement of Québec's French character suggested the necessity for a change in the host society's own sense of identity from an essentially homogeneous self-image rooted in a monolithic Catholic tradition, to one accommodating and incorporating individuals from a variety of ethnic and racial origins.

The Couture-Cullen agreement gave Québec a decisive role in the selection of independent immigrants wishing to settle in the province. Although responsibility for selection was still to be shared by two tiers of government, the agreement gave Québec the right to establish the criteria governing the choice of applicants in this category, and permitted the province to override negative federal evaluations in certain circumstances. Canada maintained control over the definition of immigration categories (including refugees), establishment of national targets, and selection in the family category, as well as kept final say regarding actual admission to the country. Québec, however, was allowed to select refugees overseas, as well as to establish the norms governing the obligations of family sponsorship (Québec, 1978; Brossard and de Montigny, 1985:314–15).

Given the strained relations between the parties in power in Ottawa and Québec City in the late 1970s, it may seem odd that the federal government was willing to collaborate with the province in an area so long and unquestioningly under federal domination. This cooperation may have reflected a federal desire to manifest good will toward Québec (Brossard and de Montigny, 1985:316; Vineberg, 1987:313–14), or alternatively, may have been merely a question of pragmatism. From this latter perspective, effective immigration management, especially linked to labour market needs, simply necessitated intergovernmental collaboration (Hill, 1987; Latouche, 1989a:191).

Whatever the federal motivations, it is hardly necessary to detail the reasons for Québec's interest in such an agreement. Growing awareness of the impact of a federal immigration policy elaborated in the light of exclusively national concerns and lacking sensitivity to "regional" requirements helped crystallize a longstanding desire for change[18] (Bonin, 1990:142–43; Polèse, 1976). The new administrative entente promised the means by which the province could better tie its economic and cultural preoccupations to the selection process[19] (by expanding the presence of Québec immigration agents overseas, and by applying modified selection criteria[20]). Furthermore, this new emphasis on selection and recruitment implied a heightened international presence for the province, a presence that the government was anxious to develop in its push for greater autonomy.

In any event, the results flowing from the agreement, at least with regard to concrete language concerns, were rather mitigated. Although the revised selection criteria appeared to encourage francophone immigration, English-only entries actually increased steadily between 1980 and 1987 (Québec, 1989b). Conversely, French-only immigration, which had risen significantly during the early 1980s,[21] actually fell in 1984, dropping to 10 percent below English-only levels by 1986.

Québec, of course, can neither control factors that help determine patterns of international migration, nor escape the fact that the population basin of potential francophone immigrants is relatively small in comparison to that of English speakers and allophones. In addition, the economic climate of the recession years led to lower ceilings on immigrant entries in the Québec-controlled independent category, whereas entries in the family reunification and refugee categories grew steadily during this period,[22] partially as a result of the province's generous response to the plight of the Indo-Chinese.

Although the changing composition of immigration flows was placing increasing pressure on existing adaptation programs,[23] compensatory efforts were not automatic. For example, special programs to help immigrant children in the French-language school system were cut back severely in 1981 (Berthelot, 1990:117) While the recession no doubt helped create a climate of restraint, some critics also maintain that decreased support for such programs was consistent with the government's desire to reproduce the labour force at the lowest possible cost (e.g., Hill, 1987)—a motivation that ran counter to the integration mandate of the MIQ. The suggestion was that the early focus on linguistic fallout was giving way to economic preoccupations.

Conflicting tendencies are especially notable in the attitude of the PQ government toward the administration of the COFI. When the PQ arrived in power, jurisdiction over COFI programs was shared between provincial and federal authorities, as it had been since 1968. Federal officials, however, considered federally funded COFI programs (the only full-time adult language courses then offered by government in the province) as a form of job training and thus limited eligibility to adult newcomers who needed to achieve a certain knowledge of the French language to find employment (Québec, 1989a:3). As a result, immigrants whose knowledge of English was deemed sufficient for employment were often excluded (Hill, 1987:290).

Those attending these courses were also accorded an allowance paid by Ottawa. However, in 1978, the federal government abolished stipends for students in the family reunification and assisted relatives categories (de Jaham, 1980:54) in spite of the fact that arrivals in the former category were increasing steadily during this period.

The PQ initially reacted by voicing strong criticism of the federal government's emphasis on employability and the resulting eligibility restrictions, making it clear that Québec's special situation demanded widespread immigrant access to adaptation and French-language programs (Québec, MIQ, *Rapports annuels*, 1977:63, 1978:47). To compensate for this narrow federal focus, Québec increased funding for language training and did make some attempts to develop alternative programs for those unable to avail themselves of the federally financed program. Indeed, the largest increases in credits allocated to the MIQ by the PQ came at the end of the decade.

The provincial authorities also jumped in to grant substitute allowances to immigrants affected by the 1978 funding cut (de Jaham, 1980:31) and as well offered some financial aid to those not destined directly for the job market. However, the absence of any concentrated attempt to negotiate the transfer of full control over adaptation programs to the province and the quiet abandonment of these compensatory subsidies in 1981 suggest that Québec had decided to accept the status quo in order to avoid the financial burden involved in a domain nonetheless vital to its interests (Hill, 1987:290–91).[24] It was not until 1988 that a full-time, provincially funded program complete with stipend was established specifically for those ineligible for the federally subsidized courses (Québec, 1990b:7).

Disparities between discourse and policy also characterized two significant initiatives undertaken in 1981. The reorganization of the MIQ into the MCCI and the policy statement *Autant de façons d'être Québécois* (1981)—which, while proposing a societal model of convergence toward a central francophone culture,[25] also laid out goals of improved minority access to public services and public service employment—acknowledged the growing importance of Québec's ethnic and immigrant communities.

However, this recognition remained largely symbolic. Recession-connected funding restrictions admittedly limited public sector spending, but more significant was the fact that, despite increasing openness, major segments of francophone society had yet to come fully to terms with the idea of a multiethnic province, even one increasingly francophone in character. Many francophones appeared unprepared to share economic and political power so recently gained from the anglophone community, a sentiment reflected in the PQ's relatively weak follow-through on policy initiatives meant to increase minority participation in Québec francophone society[26] (Helly, 1989:89–90).

At the same time, the government displayed growing interest in the economic aspects of immigration, implementing, in 1983, an aggressive campaign to attract immigrant investors, particularly from Hong Kong (Delean, 1985; Emery, 1985). Québec selection seemed to insist "less on linguistic affinities than on the economic benefits ["rentabilité"] of immigrants" (Hill, 1987:336).

The second PQ mandate (1981–85) thus drew to a close on an ambivalent note. Recognition and support for ethnic groups had increased, whereas support for integration and adaptation programs had not kept pace with needs. As for the interest expressed in the economic gains to be made from special recruitment efforts, it coincided with an ideological shift within government circles as the PQ regime began to disengage the state from certain areas of activity, and to court more actively the private sector (Gagnon and Montcalm, 1990). Although the Bourassa Liberal regime elected at the end of 1985 was even more strongly committed to private sector development and state disengagement, provincial immigration policy was to evolve somewhat differently under the new government.

RECENT DEVELOPMENTS: EXTENDING PROVINCIAL INVOLVEMENT

The increased importance eventually accorded the immigration dossier by the Liberals can be at least partially traced to the way in which public debate over immigration-related issues has developed since the mid-1980s. With francophone fecundity rates hitting an all-time low of 1.35 in 1987 (Québec, 1990c:13), alarmist predictions on the future of Québec's francophone population, accompanied by calls for comprehensive "natalist" policies, were made by many of the province's demographers (Matthews, 1984; Paillé, 1989). These projections helped refocus public attention on the selection process, and on continuing high levels of English-speaking and allophone immigration at the very same time that both major provincial parties were stressing the need to increase entries for demographic reasons.[27]

Montréal has remained the centre of attention. Francophones have been leaving the city for the suburbs in increasing numbers while, at the same time, immigrant entries picked up after the end of the recession of the early 1980s. Concentrations of allophone children of ever-more diverse origins have grown considerably in Montréal-area French-language schools[28] and have not only rendered more concrete the reality of an increasingly visible multiethnic society, but as well have added new fuel to the language debate because of increased use of English in certain multiethnic schoolyards.[29] Incidents involving Montréal police and members of certain visible minority groups have also drawn attention to intergroup tensions.

In light of such changes, certain nationalist organizations such as the *Société Saint-Jean-Baptiste*, the *Mouvement national des québécois,* and the *Ligue d'action nationale* have called for increased francophone immigration and, in certain cases, for freezes on entries until Québec's capacity to integrate immigrants into the francophone community is "assured" (April, 1991). Echoes of past fears can be detected in concerns that immigrants from "nontraditional" sources are culturally less able to integrate into Québec society,[30] and thus pose a greater threat to the survival of francophone culture (McCall, 1991:2).

At the same time, representatives of ethnic and immigrant organizations, and certain francophone commentators, have increasingly pointed out that speaking French is but one of several dimensions of integration, and exclusion from the host society is still possible for the linguistically integrated (Cauchon, 1991; Piché, 1991). As one commentator put it, growing linguistic integration may actually be one of the principal roots of current tensions, for unlike Québec's anglophone minority, in many respects still a separate and self-sufficient community, allophone immigrants and their descendants are now demanding to be a part of a francophone collectivity still unsure of its newly achieved, and fragile, majority status (Llambias-Wolff, 1991). As Christopher McCall writes:

> Excluded by anglophones, francophones in their turn had to erect boundaries to be able to assure themselves of a certain social mobility or, at the least, a social space inside of which upward mobility in French becomes possible. If the precondition for access to this space is the capacity to work in French, the more immigrants learn French, the more there will be competition. This explains, in part, this ambiguity in the contemporary discourse on immigration. There is a tendency to reproduce ... the same desire for inclusion-exclusion that marked relations between francophones and anglophones. (1991:4)

In light of steady increases in immigration flows, such developments certainly seemed to invite some kind of government response. However, the Liberal's initial approach toward immigration, integration, and minority issues seemed to mimic the orientation taken by the PQ during its second mandate—a preoccupation with narrower economic dimensions within an overall context of restraint. Liberal funding of the MCCI even diminished from a total of $29.8 million in 1985–86 to $28.7 million in the following year.

This tendency was reversed, however, during the course of the two following years. In 1987–88, MCCI's budget was jacked up to $33.1 million, an increase of about 15 percent over the previous year, and this was followed, in turn, by an even greater hike, a total of $40.1 million allocated in 1988–89, representing a jump in funding of over 21 percent.[31] Not only is this expansion striking in absolute terms, but as well it contrasts with the Liberals' otherwise generally conservative approach to government. Fiscal restraint, privatization, and preoccupation with deficits remained hallmarks of the Bourassa regime, but in the closing years of the 1980s these preoccupations did not extend to MCCI and immigration and adaptation matters.

It is hard to escape the conclusion that these budgetary enhancements came about as the government reached a better understanding of the need to accord more attention to the growing problems surrounding immigration-connected challenges. The concrete steps taken by the MCCI to address these issues also illustrate a level of commitment that differentiates the latter 1980s from the first part of the decade.

Although the aggressive courting of immigrant investors begun under the PQ was stepped up under the Liberals, there were renewed attempts to deal with the questions of language and the place accorded to ethnic communities in Québec society. Efforts were made to increase the number of entries from the independent category—among whom, relative to the family class and refugee categories, generally greater proportions are French speaking—as well as to step up recruitment activities in Paris (Québec, 1990a:28). Access to French-language instruction was widened somewhat with the establishment of a new program in 1988–89 that provided financial assistance to immigrants ineligible for the federal program to learn French on a full-time basis.[32] Furthermore, some acknowledgment of the limits of strictly linguistic integration was evident in the announcement of renewed attempts at promoting affirmative action programs both within the private sector and the public service.

There was also increasing understanding of the need for what has since come to be termed a "moral contract," balancing the entitlement on the part of the host society to expect that immigration and ethnic groups recognize and develop an allegiance toward Québec's cultural and linguistic character with a reciprocating demonstration of respect and appreciation for the contribution of these groups to Québec society. The recognition that majority–minority relations have fallen quite short of the ideal embodied in the idea of such a contract prompted the introduction, in 1987, of a number of programs to assist community organizations that seek to foster less conflictual intergroup relations.

Paradoxically, this contrast in activity between the first few years of the Bourassa government and the last few does not extend to the broader question of winning greater control over immigration and adaptation programs from the federal government. As early as February 1985, the Liberals broke with past practice by incorporating demands for greater provincial autonomy within the context of constitutional reform. As part of the party's pre-election policy statement, the Liberals listed the entrenchment of a new immigration agreement as one of the five conditions that they believed were needed to be met before Québec would agree to sign the Constitution Act of 1982, something the PQ government had refused to do during the patriation exercise. Québec's five demands provided the basis for the process running up to the signing of the ill-fated Meech Lake Accord (see Gagnon in this volume).

If it had passed, the Constitution Amendment, 1987, would have obliged the federal government to conclude an agreement "relating to immigration or the temporary admission of aliens" with any province making such a request, although any pact would have had to respect the federal prerogative to determine the general classes of immigrants, the overall national levels of immigration, and categories of inadmissibility. Still, and a crucial point from the provincial perspective, passage of the amendment would have made it possible for a province to ensure constitutional protection. This is exactly what Québec had hoped to achieve with the deal that it reached with the federal government at Meech Lake. This agreement would have entrenched the principles of the Couture-Cullen agreement (confirming, among other things, Québec's authority to select independent immigrants), guaranteed that Québec receive an annual part of Canadian immigration that was at least in proportion to its share of the national population, with the right to exceed that level by 5 percent, and finally, provided for federal withdrawal—accompanied by financial compensation—from all immigrant reception and integration services in Québec. This latter feature would have allowed Québec significant latitude to expand and consolidate its integration programs in conformity with its own particular needs.

The failure of Meech Lake did not end the search for an agreement.While concerns about not appearing too yielding to Québec in the post-Meech political climate provoked some hesitation on the part of Ottawa, hard bargaining between Québec and federal officials over the devolution of powers to the province eventually did produce a new accord officially signed in February 1991. In essence, the provincial Immigration Minister, Monique Gagnon-Tremblay, and her federal counterpart, Barbara McDougall, put their names to a document that, while not the object of constitutional protection, differed little from the immigration section of the Meech Lake Accord. Québec did effectively obtain greater authority over the selection of independent immigrants and a right to receive up to 30 percent of the total Canadian immigrant inflow. The amount of compensation accompanying federal withdrawal from integration and reception programs was set at $332 million for the following four years.

While Québec and federal officials were hammering out this immigration agreement, MCCI was also busy preparing a new policy statement. The result was the 1990 document *Let's Build Québec Together*, released just weeks before the conclusion of the federal–provincial pact. Presented with much fanfare as a comprehensive policy declaration on behalf of the entire government, it purported to address the series of immigration and integration problems facing the province. In more concrete terms, the statement spelled out objectives in four overlapping policy domains centring on immigration per se, the promotion of French as a common language, full socioeconomic participation for immigrants and ethnic minorities, and the fostering of harmonious intergroup relationships. With regard to immigration, familiar preoccupations included boosting Québec's overall immigration totals, increasing the proportion of French-speaking immigrants, and maximizing the economic impact of immigration by assigning priority to the selection of newcomers in the independent category (goals nonetheless subject to the province's "receptive capacity").[33] The document does break some new ground in setting out target levels in each case. For example, at the same time that Québec aims to augment significantly its share of Canadian immigration, it also seeks to ensure, by 1995, that 40 percent of those arriving in Québec are French speaking. These are rather ambitious goals, considering that in 1989 the province took in only 17.7 percent of the Canadian total, of which portion only 28.3 percent were either francophone or had knowledge of French (Québec, 1990a). Moreover, any attempts to alter the existing patterns of immigration run up against the reality of an inherently small pool of potential francophone candidates. The virtual absence of recruiting offices in francophone Africa further circumscribes the recruitment pool.

Nevertheless, some of the measures proposed to accomplish the sought-after goals are promising. To boost immigration levels, for example, the government proposes the use of mobile missions to take advantage of fluctuating developments on the international scene,[34] whereas efforts to enhance the proportion of French speakers could include the allocation of more resources to the Québec immigration bureaus located in traditional francophone recruiting areas, the use of prospecting missions, and the assigning of more weight for knowledge of French in the selection process. As for maximizing the economic impact of immigration, closer coordination is promised with the business community of Québec and private consultants who help recruit business immigrants. The document also promises greater efforts to regionalize immigration in order to limit concentrations of new arrivals in Montréal and to stimulate regional development—an unlikely scenario given the severe economic difficulties facing many of the province's regions (see Bonin, 1991).

As far as promoting French-language usage is concerned, exclusive control over language training recently won by Québec should provide a great deal of scope for flexibility and innovation in the multiplication of French-language learning opportunities. The policy statement specifically proposes new endeavours, such as the establishment of correspondence courses and pilot projects for language instruction on the work-site. Also promised are greater francization efforts directed at small and medium-sized businesses where immigrants, and more generally minorities, tend to be concentrated. How effective these efforts will be remains to be seen, given the bilingual face of Montréal and the international importance of the English language.

The Québec government's commitment to encourage the full participation of immigrants and minorities, in order to avoid their marginalization, translates into a wide-ranging set of specific promises such as increased government-sponsored information and support services (e.g., job search assistance) as well as augmented funding for nongovernment organizations involved in immigrant adaptation. Of greater potential importance are pledges to expand employment opportunities through the use of affirmative action programs in both the private and public sectors. The fight against job and housing discrimination is, according to the government, another area of priority. These are challenging areas of engagement, requiring considerable resolve.

Finally, the Québec government's approach to the promotion of harmonious intergroup relationships is grounded in the recognition of a new moral contract based on the principle that "it takes two to tango" (Québec, 1990a:18). Immigrants and ethnic minorities must "appreciate the common heritage that is the history of Québec, its past and present culture and the foundations of its democratic traditions" (Québec, 1990a:77), and at the same time, the majority must be more accepting of cultural pluralism. The premise of reciprocation that underpins this "moral contract" has been praised by many commentators, and differs from the PQ principle of cultural convergence in the emphasis placed on obligations on the part of the host society.

Reaction to the policy package in its entirety was generally positive, with most commentary appreciative of the global approach it brought to bear on a complex set of issues that had traditionally been treated in piecemeal fashion. Most policy objectives achieved considerable support, as did many of the solutions proposed to realize them. However, some commentators in the press and at a parliamentary commission, struck to collect reactions to the policy, expressed some scepticism as to the will of the government to achieve the difficult goals it had set for itself (Lesage, 1991). Of course, in response the government could point to recent funding levels and projected budgetary allocations as evidence of its intention to carry through with its commitments. Aside from the will to act, however, there is also a question of government capacity to bring about proposed changes, for the state must also rely on the extensive cooperation of other actors to achieve such laudatory but elusive objectives as the establishment of moral contracts and reduced ethnic exclusion. For these reasons, it is simply too early to tell whether or not the government will succeed in meeting its goals. What can be said is that it at least has a blueprint for action.

CONCLUSION

One thing does seem clear, however, and that is that the Québec government intends to continue, for both economic and demographic reasons, to try to promote increases in immigration levels over the upcoming years. In this regard, the policy statement can perhaps also be seen as an attempt to lead public opinion into greater acceptance of the direction of current government effort. The July 1991 announcement of a freeze on immigration levels provides a lesson about the difficulty of doing so.

Nevertheless, viewed from a historical perspective, current levels of active governmental involvement represent a remarkable evolution of Québec's orientation toward immigration. As has been seen, Québec's long absence from the field can be traced, in part, to an anti-immigration reaction fuelled by the dynamics of Canadian dualism, a demographic situation long favourable to the self-generation of the French-Canadian population and a traditional ad hoc approach to immigrant policy-making on the part of the federal government. A more general explanation is the relative weakness of the pre-Quiet Revolution Québec state.

Much has changed, however, in the course of the past three decades. It was in the mid-1970s, for example, that the federal government finally moved decisively to develop more coherent policies of "immigration management," an action that partially explains Québec's enhanced interest in better controlling provincial immigration. Ottawa's determination to link immigration to economic policy, especially efforts made to synchronize more carefully the numbers and types of immigrants who were permitted entry with variable labour market requirements and to encourage the recruitment of immigrants with capital, no doubt served to stimulate at the provincial level similar sorts of concerns about the economic aspects of immigration.

Changing demographic trends have also placed new pressures on the province. Québec's traditionally high birthrate has now fallen to one of the lowest levels in the Western world, and the spectre of population decline is seen as a considerable threat on several fronts. Labour shortages would menace future economic growth and jeopardize the survival of already imperilled social programs, the result of a decline in workers' contributions to provincial coffers. In addition, a shrinking population would diminish Québec's relative political weight within the federation, including its ability to claim a large share of federal funds. Because of this, immigration, previously seen as "unnecessary" to population growth, has gained increasing attention as a focal point in the quest for population enhancement.

Linguistic conflict and the fact that Québec for a long time has not been as successful as some other provinces in retaining initially established immigrants further complicate the demographic challenge. The recruitment of French-speaking immigrants or, in the longer term, the integration of speakers of other languages into the francophone milieu, has become an important component of an overall strategy to preserve and promote a French-speaking society on the North American continent.

The response to these challenges was to evolve rapidly once the first steps back into the immigration field were taken in the last half of the 1960s. Initially, Québec's involvement was generally limited to reacting to integration issues, an orientation that did not call into question the federal government's dominance in the field. By the mid-1970s, however, Québec was claiming more say in the immigration selection process, in the interests of meeting economic and special cultural needs, and was beginning to adopt the same sorts of immigration management techniques recently developed by the federal government. These preoccupations became more pronounced in the 1980s at the same time that the reach of government extended into new areas related to immigration-driven social changes.

That Québec has come to exercise so much power in immigration vis-à-vis the central government—a situation that is unique among contemporary federal systems—could be used by some federalists as evidence that Québec's special needs, as the province defines them, can be accommodated within the confines of the Canadian federation. The recent immigration agreement could be cited as particularly convincing evidence in this regard. Nationalists, on the other hand, could, of course, point to the fact that the agreement does not have constitutional protection and that Québec is still vulnerable to federal authority. Continuing limitations on provincial control over family and refugee categories of immigration could also be noted as restrictions that an otherwise sovereign Québec would not have to endure.

However much federalists and nationalists may differ about the 1991 agreement, it is clear that Québec has acquired an unprecedented capacity to manage immigration and immigration-related affairs. The province has, at the same time, also assumed the kind of responsibility that all immigrant-receiving societies must face in dealing with the complex problems that are associated with immigration and integration issues. In Québec, given the province's distinctive position on the continent, the challenges are particularly demanding.

NOTES

1. The title of the document in French is *Au Québec pour bâtir ensemble*.
2. Section 95 of the Constitution Act, 1867, reads as follows: "In each Province the Legislature may make Laws in relation to Agriculture in the Province, and to Immigration into the Province; and it is hereby declared that the Parliament of Canada may from Time to Time make laws in relation to Agriculture in all or any of the Provinces, and to Immigration into all or any of the Provinces; and any Law of the Legislature of a Province relative to Agriculture or to Immigration shall have effect in and for the Province as long and as far only as it is not repugnant to any Act of the Parliament of Canada."
3. Another estimate places the number of emigrants at 900,000 between 1840 and 1930 (Landry, 1991:25).
4. Employment and travel agencies were given "finder's fees," for instance, and the Canadian Pacific Railway and Hudson Bay Company operated their own recruitment offices, selling available land to prospective settlers.
5. The words of Lord Durham with regard to the wish for English immigration are well remembered by francophones and understandably so: "The whole interior of the British dominions must ere long be filled with an English population, every year rapidly increasing its numerical superiority over the French... The French Canadians ... are and must be isolated in the midst of an Anglo-Saxon world" (quoted in Brossard, 1967:15).
6. Special classes for immigrant children where their native languages and history were taught alongside French were created for several immigrant groups between 1900–30. The *Commission des écoles catholiques de Montréal* decided to reduce the number of these classes in 1931, fearful that it would be eventually obliged to create separate schools, seen as a potential challenge to the fundamental dualism of Canadian society and reducing French-Canadian influence (Helly, 1989:77).
7. In 1944, Duplessis declared that a Union Nationale government would "prevent immigrants and foreigners from taking the place of our people on Quebec soil and combat all immigration projects as long as those of Canadian origin have not returned to civilian life and paid employment" (quoted in Helly, 1989:80). Hawkins also notes that federal authorities made several unsuccessful attempts to interest the province in greater federal–provincial cooperation during the 1950s (1988:225).
8. Groulx thought of forming alliances with allophone immigrants in the struggle with English Canada, since they, like the French Canadians, had no sentiment of attachment to Britain (Harvey, 1987:16).

9. Humblet also notes an economic basis for hostility—the heavy concentration of francophones in manual labour jobs placed them in direct competition with unskilled immigrant labour in a way largely unknown to Québec anglophones (1976:136).

10. Between 1931–32 and 1947–48, when the committee was founded, allophone enrolment in French-language schools decreased from 52.4 percent to 33.5 percent (Québec, 1967:29). Furthermore, some 10,000 to 12,000 non-Catholic francophone children were forced by confessional divisions into the Anglo-Protestant sector during the 1950s (Behiels, 1986:53–54).

11. Of the 50,000 students who attended these classes between 1948 and 1964, 90 percent were enrolled in French or bilingual classes. This high figure was partially due to the fact that program rules stipulated that those unable to manage in French were not permitted to attend classes exclusively in English (Québec, 1967:16).

12. The composition of Canadian postwar immigration—some 60 percent anglophone or Anglo-Saxon versus 3 percent francophone (Brossard, 1967:121)—was clearly disadvantageous to Québec and led one polemicist to describe it as a "trojan horse" introduced into the heart of French Canada (Morin, 1966:ix).

13. By the end of the decade, over 80 percent of immigrant children were in English-language schools (Hawkins, 1988:233).

14. In 1968, fewer than thirty-eight people were working for the service. Annual expenditures were less than $200,000 (Poitras, 1971:41).

15. This decision was no doubt meant to address a longstanding provincial grievance regarding the failure of federal immigration officers to sensitize candidates sufficiently to the realities of Canadian cultural dualism (Latouche, 1989a:187).

16. In 1975–76, the budget reached $12,099,300 and the MIQ staff tripled. A significant portion of the budgetary envelope came from federal sources (Québec, MIQ, *Rapports annuels*, 1976, 1981).

17. For some other reasons for Québec's increased interest in immigration see Latouche (1989a:188–89) and Vineberg (1987).

18. An obvious manifestation of this was the way points for knowledge of French or English were equally distributed under the old selection process, regardless of where in Canada a candidate for immigration intended to settle. Furthermore, the economically dominant position of Ontario meant that that province effectively dictated for the country as a whole the list of professions in demand (Polèse, 1976:10–14).

19. The wisdom of increased involvement in the selection process did not go unchallenged from within the MIQ, where at least one report expressed fears that an emphasis on selection would result in the negligence of essential integration programs (Hill, 1987:295).

20. Under the Couture-Cullen agreement, Québec elaborated its own point system, similar to that of the federal government, but awarded extra points for French and established its own categories of professions in demand (Grey, 1984:10; Helly, 1989:89).

21. This increase was largely due to a special program regularizing the status of a large number of Haitians in the province (Québec, 1989b).

22. In 1974, immigrants in the independent category made up 50 percent of new arrivals in Québec as compared to 25 percent in the family category and less than 1.0 percent in the refugee and designated categories. By 1984, arrivals in the family category had risen to nearly 47 percent and in the two humanitarian categories to over 17 percent of the total, whereas the number of independents had decreased by more than half (Labelle, 1989:7).

23. Between 1980 and 1988, 73.9 percent of immigrants were from so-called nontraditional source countries in Asia, South America, and to a much lesser extent, Africa (Québec, 1989b).

24. Bill 101 could also account for a certain shift away from the preoccupation with integration questions, and more particularly adult language programs in the measure that some saw it as "resolving" the language problem (Hagen, 1990).

25. The policy statement, a deliberate counter to the federal ideal of a multicultural mosaic of equal cultures (a vision seen as reducing the status of francophone culture to a level similar to that of other Canadian minority groups), was generally well received in Québec, but has been criticized for a certain ethnocentrism (Gay, 1985). Elsewhere, it has been suggested that the policy "supposes cultural change on the part of ethnic groups without analogous change on the part of the dominant community" (Constantinides, 1987:243).

26. No doubt, electoral calculations help explain why the number of ethnic organizations receiving provincial funding had increased from thirty-four to 336 between 1976 and 1985, with funding going from $600,000 to $3,000,000. The MCCI had also actively contributed to the construction of twenty-four ethnic community centres over that same period (*Gazette*, 1985). On the other hand, the committee struck to oversee the implementation of the more important equality of

access provisions in the 1981 ethnic policy was dissolved for financial reasons in 1984 in spite of the fact that progress toward the objectives laid out had been minimal (See Québec, 1984.)

27. A joint parliamentary committee of the National Assembly unanimously recommended upping levels in 1985 (*La Presse*, 26 September 1985:A2).

28. In 1976–77, only 27 percent of students born overseas were in French-language schools. By 1985, this figure had risen to 85 percent. In the same period, the percentage of allophones (Canadian and foreign born) in French schools grew from 30 percent to 57 percent (Proulx, 1985:1), and by 1985 allophones made up 30 percent of the total French sector school population (Tasso, 1985:63).

29. Continued use of English in many Montréal enterprises no doubt contributes to the maintenance of the language, as may a new sense of identity founded on multilingualism developing among second- and third-generation descendants of certain immigrant groups (Fortier, 1991).

30. For example, the brief presented by the CECM to the Bélanger-Campeau Commission argued for immigration of Judeo-Christian origin in order to limit such difficulties (Bissonnette, 1990:A8).

31. MCCI budget allocations were increased a further 17.9 percent for 1990–91 (Berger, 1990:A8).

32. This program was aimed particularly at women not destined for the job market and often isolated from the host society. In 1987, the government also negotiated a deal with Ottawa whereby the province would offer part-time French-language training for refugee claimants on Québec territory.

33. The document does, however, also clearly state the government's intention to maintain its commitment to the humanitarian engagements governing refugee and family category admissions.

34. For example, Québec has recently opened an office in Vienna in order to capitalize on the availability of French-speaking East Europeans seeking to leave for the West.

REFERENCES

Abella, Irving and Troper, H. (1983). *None Is Too Many: Canada and the Jews of Europe, 1933–1948.* Toronto: Lester & Orpen Dennys.

Anctil, Pierre. (1983). "Double majorité et multiplicité ethnoculturelle à Montréal." *Recherches sociographiques*, 25(3), 441–56.

———. (1986). "Introduction: le pluralisme au Québec." *Canadian Ethnic Studies*, 18 (2), 1–3.

Angers, François-Albert. (1954). "Le Canada français et l'immigration." *L'Action nationale*, 43(5), 423–40.

April, Pierre. (1991). "La SSJBM veut geler le niveau d'immigration." *Le Devoir*, 13 March 1991, A2.

Behiels, Michael. (1986). "The Commission des écoles catholiques de Montréal and the Neo-Canadian Question: 1947–1963." *Canadian Ethnic Studies*, 18 (2), 38–64.

Berger, François. (1990). "L'accord du Lac Meech permet au Québec d'accueillir plus d'immigrants." *La Presse*, 5 May 1990, A8.

Berthelot, Jocelyn. (1990). *Apprendre à vivre ensemble: immigration, société et éducation.* Montréal: Centrale de l'enseignement au Québec.

Bissonnette, Lise. (1990). "Appuyer le Mémo sans hésiter." *Le Devoir*, 16 November, 1990, A8.

Bonin, Daniel. (1990). "L'immigration au Québec en 1990; à l'heure des choix." In R.L. Watts and D.M. Brown, eds., *Canada: The State of the Federation.* Kingston: Institute of Intergovernmental Relations.

Brossard, Jacques. (1967). *L'immigration: les droits et pouvoirs du Canada et du Québec.* Montréal: Les Presses de l'Université de Montréal.

Brossard, Jacques and de Montigny, Yves. (1985). "L'immigration: ententes politiques et droit constitutionnel." *Thémis*, 19(3), 305–23.

Canada. (1974). *The Immigration Program.* Vol. 2. A Report of the Canadian Immigration and Population Study (Green Paper). Ottawa: Information Canada.

Cauchon, Paul. (1991). "Les cruelles limites de la francisation." *Le Devoir*, 21 February 1991, B1.

Constantinides, Stephanos. (1987). "Le fait français et la réalité multiculturelle au Québec." In *Le Québec français et l'école à clientèle pluriethnique: contributions à une réflexion.* Québec: Éditeur officiel du Québec, 229–66.

de Jaham, Bernard. (1980). *Les COFI: synthèse et projections* (mimeo).

Delean, Paul. (1985). "City Benefits from Hong Kong Investment." *The Gazette*, 20 February 1985, A3.

Émery, Claude. (1985). "Recrutement d'immigrants investisseurs." *Finance*, 4 March 1985, A4.

Fortier, Anne-Marie. (1991). "Les rapports conflictuels et la reproduction des identités minoritaires au Québec." Paper presented at the colloquium *Rapports conflictuels ethniques et nationaux: pratiques d'exclusion et d'inclusion*, June 13–14, 1991. Université de Montréal.

Fugère, Jean-Paul. (1945). "Le fait néo-canadien dans la vie montréalaise." *L'Action nationale*, 25(4), 354–68; 25(5), 445–58.

Gagnon, Alain-G. and Montcalm, Mary Beth (1990). *Québec: Beyond the Quiet Revolution.* Toronto: Nelson.

Gay, Daniel. (1985). "Réflexions critiques sur les politiques ethniques du gouvernement fédéral canadien et du gouvernement du Québec." *Revue internationale d'action communautaire*, 14 (54), 79–92.

Girard, S. and Manègre, J.F. (1988). *L'immigration et l'opinion publique: présentation des résultats de sondages d'opinion sur l'immigration au Québec et au Canada—1952 à 1988.* Montréal: Conseil des communautés culturelles et de l'immigration du Québec.

Grey, Julius. (1984). *Immigration Law in Canada.* Toronto: Butterworths.

Hagen, David. (1990). "The Development of the COFI in Quebec." Unpublished paper.

Harvey, Fernand. (1987). "La question de l'immigration au Québec: genèse historique." In *Le Québec français et l'école à clientèle pluriethnique: contributions à une réflexion.* Québec: Éditeur officiel du Québec, 1–55.

Hawkins, Freda. (1988). *Canada and Immigration: Public Policy and Public Concern.* Montréal: McGill-Queen's University Press.

Helly, Denise. (1989). "La perception de l'immigration au Québec, 1980–1985: contexte général de la mise en place d'une politique." In I. Lasvergnas, ed., *A/E.urages féministes.* Montréal: GIERF-CRF/Université du Québec à Montréal (Cahiers de recherche CRF-GIERF; Numéro spécial).

Hill, Ricardo. (1987). *Politiques d'immigration et reproduction sociale: Le cas du Québec.* Ph.D. thesis. Montréal: Université du Québec à Montréal.

Humblet, Jean-E. (1976). "Problématique de l'adaptation des immigrants au Québec." *Revue de l'Institut de sociologie*, 1(2), 119–46.

Labelle, Micheline. (1988) "La gestion fédérale de l'immigration internationale au Canada." In Y. Bélanger and D. Brunelle, eds., *L'ère des Libéraux: le pouvoir fédéral de 1963 à 1984.* Sillery: Presses de l'Université du Québec, 313–42.

Labelle, Micheline. (1989). "Les nouveaux arrivants." *Médium*, (32), 5–9.

Landry, J.E. (1991). "Les survenants." *Contact*, 5(3), 24–28.

Latouche, Daniel. (1989a). "Immigration, politique et société: le cas du Québec." In *Actes du Séminaire scientifique sur les tendances migratoires actuelles et l'insertion des migrants dans les pays de la francophonie*, (25–28 August 1987). Québec: Les publications du Québec, 179–96.

————. (1989b). "Le pluralisme ethnique et l'agenda public au Québec." *Revue internationale d'action communautaire*, 21(61), 11–26.

Léger, Jean-Marc. (1954). "Le devoir du Québec envers l'immigrant." *L'Action nationale*, 43(5), 410–22.

Lemelin, Claude. (1971). "Les placards du ministre Cloutier." *Le Devoir*, 19 May 1971, 4.

Lesage, Gilles. (1991). "Des immigrants oui, mais pas trop." *Le Devoir*, 30 April 1991, B1.

Llambias-Wolff, Jaime. (1991). "Le difficile tricotage de la nouvelle mosaïque." *Le Devoir*, 26 March 1991, B-8.

Matthews, George. (1984). *Le choc démographique.* Montréal: Boréal Express.

McCall, Christopher. (1991). "Enjeux et défis de l'immigration au Québec." Paper presented at the colloquium *Rapports conflictuels ethniques et nationaux: pratiques d'exclusion et d'inclusion*, June 13–14. Université de Montréal.

Morin, Rosaire. (1966). *L'immigration au Canada.* Montréal: Éditions de l'Action nationale.

Paillé, Michel. (1989). *Nouvelles tendances démolinguistiques dans l'île de Montréal.* Montréal: Conseil de la langue française (Notes et documents no. 71).

Piché, Victor. (1991). "La conception de l'intégration dans le discours démo-politique: inclusion ou exclusion." Paper presented at the colloquium *Rapports conflictuels ethniques et nationaux: pratiques d'exclusion et d'inclusion*, June 13–14, Université de Montréal.

Poitras, Rita. (1971). *Histoire de l'administration publique québécoise: secteur immigration* (mimeo).

Polèse, Mario. (1976). "Une analyse des incidences régionales de la politique canadienne d'immigration." Paper presented at the annual meeting of the Canadian Association of Geographers, 23–27 May.

Proulx, Jean-Pierre. (1985). "La majorité des anglophones fréquente l'école française." *Le Devoir*, 29 May 1985, 1.

Québec. (1967). *Rapport du Comité interministériel sur l'enseignement des langues aux néo-Canadiens.* MEQ and MAC.

————. (1969–81). *Rapports annuels*. MIQ.

————. (1978). Entente entre le Gouvernement du Canada et le Gouvernement du Québec portant sur la collaboration en matière d'immigration et sur la sélection des ressortissants étrangers qui souhaitent s'établir au Québec à titre permanent ou temporaire.

————. (1981). *Autant de façons d'être Québécois: plan d'action du gouvernement à l'intention des communautés culturelles.*

————. (1982–90). *Rapports annuels*. MCCI.

————. (1984). *Rapport d'activités pour la période du 1 novembre 1982 au 29 février 1984*. Comité d'implantation à l'intention des communautés culturelles.

————. (1989a). *La formation linguistique*. MCCI.

————. (1989b). *Le mouvement d'immigration au Québec depuis 1980*. MCCI.

————. (1990a). *Let's Build Québec Together*. MCCI.

————. (1990b). *Principales statistiques relatives aux activités de formation linguistique du MCCI, 1982–1983 à 1989–1990: synthèse et analyse des données*. MCCI.

————. (1990c). *Rôle de l'immigration internationale et l'avenir démographique du Québec*. MCCI.

Ramirez, Bruno. (1980). "L'immigration, la recomposition de classe, et la crise du marché du travail au Canada." *Cahiers du socialisme*, (6), 84–131.

Rogel, Jean-Pierre. (1989). *Le défi de l'immigration*. Québec: Institut québécois de recherche sur la culture.

Tasso, Lily. (1985). "Un forum sur l'école du Québec et l'éducation interculturelle." *La Presse*, 9 June 1985, 63.

Veltman, C. and Panneton, C. (1989). "L'intégration linguistique des immigrants allophones de la région métropolitaine de Montréal." In *Actes du Séminaire scientifique sur les tendances migratoires actuelles et l'insertion des migrants dans les pays de la francophonie* (25–28 August 1987). Québec: Les publications du Québec, 319–33.

Venne, Michel. (1991). "Du sang neuf qui vient de l'Est." *Le Devoir*, 28 February 1991, B1.

Vineberg, R.A. (1987). "Federal–Provincial Relations in Canadian Immigration." *Canadian Public Administration*, 30(2), 299–317.

17

Population Trends and Policies in Québec

Jacques Henripin
Université de Montréal

"Aging generates its own analgesic, its own non-conscience…"
–Alfred Sauvy, *Eléments de démographie* (Paris: P.U.F., 1976, p. 313)

We do not intend here to describe the Québec population, even in its principal aspects and trends. We shall rather focus on three or four major phenomena that are linked to important social problems. Some of these problems can already be seen, but the most challenging ones will develop within the next three or four decades, if recent trends do not change. In fact, these problems may arise even if things change for the better. In many instances, Québec will share these problems with the whole of the Western world, many of them reaching an unprecedented degree of severity.

This chapter will not, then, present any detailed analysis of mortality, nor will it describe regional or rural–urban distribution of the population. Suffice it to say that the province of Québec still has higher mortality rates than the rest of Canada, with one notable exception: infant mortality. Great progress has been made in the reduction of infant mortality, so much so that Québec is now in a better position than Canada as a whole, from this point of view. As to regional distribution, the strong concentration of anglophones and most minorities (except natives) in Montréal should be mentioned.

Fundamentally, we will deal with two major demographic phenomena and their effects:

1. the *very low fertility rate* that characterizes young adults, which will have two results: first, a very high proportion of older people and, then, around 2040, a rapid decline in the overall population;
2. *international immigration*, with its advantages (true or false), difficulties, and potential for modifying the ethnic and linguistic composition of the population.

Needless to say, a discussion of these phenomena will inevitably raise some important and perhaps controversial questions. In such a discussion, it is perhaps even more essential to remain cool-headed, so that the facts can be presented truthfully and objectively.

A VERY LOW FERTILITY RATE

If one single phenomenon characterizes the demographic makeup of the Québec population, it certainly is its surprisingly weak fertility, which is among the lowest in the world, along with those of West Germany and Italy. It is particularly remarkable in the case of Québec, because its population, until 1960, had an exceptionally high fertility rate. It is interesting to compare the long-term trends of Ontario and Québec, two provinces that have been quite similar in their social evolution. Table 17.1 presents the total fertility rate of both provinces for selected years from 1851 to 1988. That rate represents the number of children an average woman would bear during her lifetime, if she experienced, between the age of 15 and 50, the series of age-specific birthrates observed in a particular year for women of childbearing age. It is a good index for measuring long-term changes, but it is often difficult to interpret when short-term variations are considered.

From 1911 to 1937, Québec's fertility rate was about 50 percent higher than Ontario's. That over-fertility was called somewhat dramatically, "the revenge of the cradle"; it appeared only after 1871, and by 1961 it had totally disappeared, at least by comparison with Ontario.

The downward trend displayed in Table 17.1 is in no way unique to these two provinces. At about the same time, the majority of Western countries showed a similar trend. Nonetheless, in comparison with other industrial countries, Québec was a distinct society long before Premier Bourassa politicized the phrase. First, its fertility was particularly high from 1870 to 1960 due to many factors, the most important of which was probably the powerful influence of the Catholic clergy. As to the exceptionally depressed level of fertility since the beginning of the 1980s, there is no convincing explanation. It is not a characteristic exclusive to French

Table 17.1
Total Fertility Rates of Ontario and Quebec,
Selected Years, 1851 to 1988

YEAR	ONTARIO	QUÉBEC
1851	7.22 children	6.84 children
1871	6.77 children	6.41 children
1891	4.03 children	5.59 children
1911	3.66 children	5.44 children
1931	2.65 children	4.00 children
1937	2.16 children	3.27 children
1951	3.22 children	3.78 children
1961	2.74 children	3.70 children
1971	2.22 children	1.88 children
1981	1.63 children	1.61 children
1986	1.68 children	1.43 children
1988	1.70 children	1.50 children

Source: J. Henripin, *Trends and Factors of Fertility in Canada*, Ottawa: Queen's Printer, 1972, p. 30; and Statistics Canada, *Vital Statistics*, various annual reports.

Quebeckers: the particularly low fertility of Québec as compared to Ontario or to the rest of Canada is seen in the French, the English, and the other language groups (Lachapelle, 1991:201). The great French demographer Alfred Sauvy once noticed that among the countries affected by the unprecedented low levels of fertility, one finds all the noncommunist European countries that had suffered under fascist governments (Germany, Italy, Portugal, and Spain). Can freedom from Catholic doctrine have the same effect as the fall of fascism?

Let us note in passing that the province of Québec is distinctive in other ways: of all the provinces in Canada, it has by far the lowest proportion of married young adults, and the highest proportion of nonlegalized unions as well as of out-of-wedlock births. Certainly, all these manifestations of freedom are no appropriate soil for producing and raising children. It seems that it is not that easy for all societies to combine some aspects of freedom, affluence, and population reproduction.

A First Major Effect of Low Fertility: Aging

Population aging simply means that the proportion of younger people decreases and that of the elderly increases; at the same time, the proportion of adults increases also, but this change is mild compared to that of the two other age groups.

It is important for the reader to know the determinants of population aging. In the past, changes in the age composition of the population were due almost totally to fertility decline. For instance, and perhaps contrary to what common sense would dictate, fertility decline is responsible for the increase in the proportion of persons aged 65 and over, from 4.8 percent in 1901 to about 11 percent in 1990. In estimating the future proportion of the elderly, things are a little more complicated. Since future victories against mortality will mostly affect the elderly, both a mortality and a fertility decline would contribute to an increase in the proportion of the elderly; but fertility would still be the most important factor.

Let us now come to Québec's future prospects. Table 17.2 gives the percentage of three broad age groups in 1986 (according to the census) and in 2040, assuming that life expectancy is 78.5 years, that there is no migration, and with three hypotheses concerning the future level of fertility: the average number of children born to each woman is 1.17, 1.75, or 2.10. The latter number is the bare minimum that would ensure the replacement of a generation by the following one. An average of 1.75 children is approximately the number of children that Canadian women aged around 30 years in 1990 will bear during their lifetime. Québec women of the same generation will have less: about 1.6 children. The lowest level of fertility considered here might be typical of women of the same age in, for example, northern Italy.

One should note that:

1. The proportion of adults is exceptionally high in 1986. That is because recent low fertility has already reduced the proportion of young, whereas it has not yet produced its effect on the proportion of older people.
2. Even if the number of children born to each woman increased to 2.10 (which is quite higher than what was observed during the last two decades), the proportion of older people would, by the year 2040, be more than twice what it was in 1986.

3. With the Canadian level (1.75 children), there would be more people over 65 (26.6 percent) than young under 20. One can estimate that, with the Québec level (1.6 children), the proportion of elderly would be around 28.5 percent.

It is clear from what we have just seen that the full effect of the recent low fertility rate has not yet been felt, and that the population will age, no matter what the course of fertility is in the future. What will be the effects of this? It is difficult to predict, because no society has yet experienced any aging to the extent projected for the year 2040 in Table 17.2. We have never seen a society where the number of elderly is two or three times the number of those under age 20.

It is easier to evaluate some economic consequences in a very simple and meaningful way. In Table 17.3, some of the ratios reported give a good idea as to the possible variations in the burden of young and elderly on the adult population less than 65 years of age. The first two columns are ratios of elements taken from Table 17.2. Column 3 is the sum of them and also represents the number of young and elderly persons per 1,000 adults. It is clear that the burden will grow appreciably from 1986 (592 per 1,000) to 2040 (850 to 873 per 1,000), with no significant difference according to selected hypotheses, which is easily explained by the nearly constant proportion of adults in 2040. But simply to add up the number of young and elderly is fallacious, because it implies that the cost of persons in each age category is the same. That is far from true: private consumption is about double for an older person compared to a younger one; as to public expenditures, the ratio of older to younger persons is at least 2 if not 3 to 1. We have adopted the conservative ratio, and column 4 is the value of column 2 multiplied by 2. Added to column 1, it gives an estimate of the total burden to be borne by adults, which is certainly more accurate than the figures appearing in column 3.

The figures in Table 17.3 constitute an estimate of the real cost of dependants to adults: they represent, very roughly, the number of "equivalent children" that 1,000 adults have to supply with goods and services, supposing that persons under 20 and over 65 are dependent, and that an elderly costs twice as much as a youngster. According to results shown in the last column, the relative increase of the burden per adult, during this fifty-five-year period would be 47 percent if the higher

Table 17.2

Québec Population: Percentage Distribution by Age Groups in 1986 and in 2040, According to Three Levels of Fertility

AGE GROUPS	1986	2040		
		1.17 children	1.75 children	2.10 children
0–19 years	27.5%	11.9%	20.0%	24.7%
20–64 years	62.8%	53.7%	53.4%	54.1%
65+ years	9.7%	34.4%	26.6%	21.2%
Total	100.0%	100.0%	100.0%	100.0%

Note: Life expectancy at birth is 78.5 years and there is no migration.
Source: Bureau de la statistique du Québec, unpublished tables. The author is grateful to Mr. Normand Thibault for graciously supplying the results of the bureau's projections.

Table 17.3
Ratios of the Number of Young and Older
Persons to the Number of Adults, Québec, 1986
and 2040, According to Three Fertility Hypotheses
(number per 1,000 adults)

YEAR AND	<20/20-64	>65/20-64	col.1+col.2	col.2×2	col.1+col.4
NUMBER OF					
CHILDREN	1	2	3	4	5
PER WOMAN					
1986	438	154	592	308	846
2040					
2.10 children	457	393	850	786	1243
1.75 children	375	498	873	996	1371
1.17 children	222	641	863	1282	1504

fertility level was maintained, 62 percent with the middle level, and 84 percent with the lowest. So in any case, there seems to be no possibility of the cost borne by adults staying at the present level, or even at any level close to it.

Of course, there are more concrete and realistic procedures to appraise these kind of phenomena. For instance, in a recently published book, André Lux (1991:116–19) has calculated that the cost of a "pay-as-you-go" retirement plan giving a pension equal to 35 percent of the earned income would be: 6.78 percent of the salary with the 1986 age composition; 15.6 percent of the salary in 2041, if women have an average of 2.1 children; and 20.3 percent of the salary in 2041, if women have an average of 1.5 children. The increase in the contribution per worker from 1986 to 2041 would be: 133 percent if women have an average of 2.1 children; and 203 percent if women have an average of 1.5 children.

In an unpublished study just completed by the present author, changes in age composition between 1986 and 2040 would result in an increase in health expenditures *per worker* of about 160 percent if the fertility level was stabilized at 1.5 children per woman, and of about 100 percent if it was stabilized at 2.1 children. There is no doubt, then, that the future aging of the population will produce a tremendous increase in public expenditures and also in the overall costs of dependants on the adult population and, for that matter, on taxpayers. And all the more so if fertility rates do not recover.

Is there any way to solve this problem? Yes, at least partly. If one excludes any reduction of well-being, the following courses can be pursued:

- increasing women's labour force participation;
- raising the retirement age for both sexes;
- increasing the fertility rate;
- increasing efficiency in health care;
- improving health conditions, particularly in old age, when health costs are much heavier than for younger people.

We do not have the space here to comment on these suggestions in any detail. Let us just mention an interesting conclusion that can be drawn from research just completed: the cost per worker of health care would be reduced by 10 percent if *one* of the following measures were adopted:

* women's labour force participation increases by 40 percent;
* retirement age is raised by the equivalent of three full-time years for both sexes;
* the number of children born to each woman is increased by two-tenths of a child.

Even if all of these measures were taken, they would not compensate for the seemingly inevitable effect of the aging of the population during the next three or four decades. We have calculated that with the present quality of health care, and assuming that the pension plan ensures a pension of 25 percent of the salary for those who had been working for thirty-five full years, the following percentage of the net national income would be devoted to health care and our rather parsimonious pension plan: 26 percent if total fertility is 2.10 per woman; 33 percent if total fertility is 1.75 per woman; and 42 percent if total fertility is 1.17 per woman. In 1986, that percentage, for equivalent benefits, would have been 12 percent.

Some economists who have tackled these problems have suggested that a reasonable yearly increase in productivity could compensate for most, if not all, of the increased burden per adult that is to be expected. In fact, an increase of 1 percent per year corresponds to 64 percent after fifty years; and 2 percent, to 170 percent. Who could imagine a more enchanting scenario? But this is a flawed argument: if productivity increases in the whole economy, real salaries will increase. But what are health costs made of? Salaries! So the real cost of health care will increase as well, because there is no reason why salaries of health personnel would not rise along with the others. The only way to escape this cycle would be to find new medical treatments that would require less labour for the same curing effect.

As to the cost of pensions, the "productivity argument" implicitly assumes that pensions do not rise when salaries do. Perhaps there is some leeway here, but not very much, particularly if the pensions are modest like those we have supposed. Very curious reasoning indeed.

The Second Major Effect of Low Fertility: The Decline of Population

Obviously, if a population maintains a below-replacement fertility level, the number of people will diminish, unless the lack of births is compensated for by net immigration. Although this is rather straightforward in principle, two comments are worth mentioning. First, it takes time for the consequence to be evident. In Québec, for instance, the fertility level has been under the replacement level since 1970, but the population will start declining only around the year 2000; migrations played no role in this, since net migration has been negative. Second, different age groups do not see their numbers shrinking at the same time: school-age children started declining around 1970; young adults, those who get married, start their family, and so forth, started declining just after 1985; and the number of retirees will first increase drastically, and should not start declining much before 2030.

At what speed might the population decline, and how severe could the reduction be? Figure 17.1 illustrates the future evolution of total population up to 2086, according to four levels of fertility. To show just the effect of fertility, it is assumed that there is no migration and that life expectancy at birth is the same in all cases: it rises from 75 years in 1986 to 79.5 years in 2010, and does not vary afterward.

In the long run, a very low fertility rate will have a devastating effect. Even at the present level (1.6 children), the population would be only about four million by 2086. On the other hand, the replacement level (2.1 children) would bring the population to a little over eight million around 2020. Note that with a fertility of 1.8 children, which is approximately the present fertility rate of Canada as a whole and which seems to satisfy almost everyone, the rate of decline is about 7 percent per ten years. At this rate, the reduction would be 30 percent every half century. Figure 17.1 does not take migrations into account. In the past, Québec has had a *negative* net migration, so unless the balance becomes positive, one can expect that the prospects are even worse than what is shown in the figure.

It seems quite probable, then, that Québec will continue to lose some of its relative importance in Canada, at least in terms of its population. In a recent report, the Economic Council of Canada (1991:21) commented on a series of population projections calculated by Statistics Canada: all scenarios lead to a decrease in the percentage of the Canadian population residing in Québec by three to four percentage points, from 1990 to 2015. Of course, the situation may change, but one should note that two phenomena are acting against Québec: the low fertility rate and the negative net migration.

What can we say about the consequences of a decline in the population? Most economists who have analyzed this question tend to believe that population increase not only contributes to the reinforcement of consumer demand and to capital formation; it also lowers the average age of this capital and so favours a more dynamic functioning of the economy. Probably the most concrete illustration of this view is housing construction, which is obviously stimulated by increasing numbers of new families and young adults.

As to the probable decline of the relative importance of Quebeckers among Canadians, elementary reasoning leads to the conclusion that, whatever constitutional arrangements can be set up, political and economic power corresponds to numbers. What would be left of what is presently a more or less bilingual federal public service if Québec represented only 15 percent of the Canadian population (see Comeau, 1991:205–13)?

MIGRATIONS

Migration means more than just international immigration: international emigration and interprovincial migrations should be considered. They are too often absent in the arguments concerning the future of Québec society, especially regarding its linguistic composition. In general, Québec receives more in foreign immigrants than it loses in emigrants from Québec to other countries, although we have no direct information on international emigration. From 1966 to 1986, the annual number of foreign immigrants was 20,000; one-quarter spoke English as their mother tongue, one-third spoke French, and nearly 45 percent spoke another language (Lachapelle and Grenier, 1988:109; here, only the immigrants still remaining in Québec at the end of each five-year period are taken into account).

Figure 17.1
Future Population of Québec
According to Four Fertility Levels, 1981 to 2086
(without migrations)

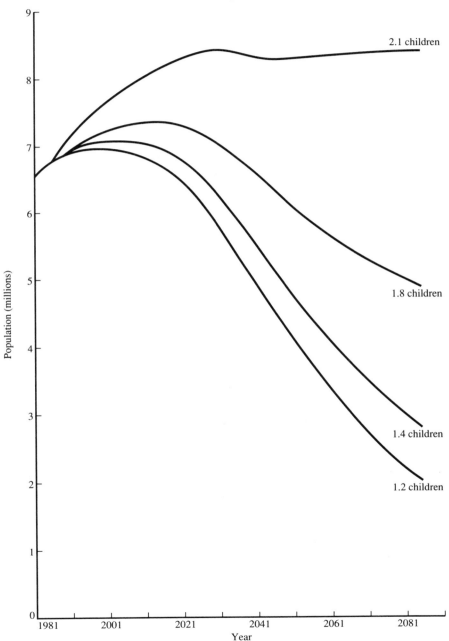

We have much better information on interprovincial migrants, thanks to Canadian censuses. Table 17.4 presents some useful data for the period 1966 to 1986, by five-year periods, and by mother tongue. All movements tend to slow down with time. Emigration from Québec to the rest of Canada was exceptionally high during 1976 to 1981; it is difficult not to link this with the election of the Parti Québécois and Law 101. But still there was an annual net loss of 12,600 during the period 1981 to 1986. Two-thirds of this loss can be attributed to those whose mother tongue is English. The average net loss of 12,600 anglophones per year from 1966 to 1986 represents 7 percent of the English-speaking population, which is about twice their natural increase (number of births less number of deaths). The positive balance of international migrations partly compensates for this loss, but on the whole the province of Québec loses out in its exchanges with the rest of the world.

Table 17.4
Annual Average Number of Migrants Between Québec and the Rest of Canada, 1965 to 1986, by Five-Year Periods, and by Mother Tongue
(number in thousands)

MIGRATION MOVEMENT AND PERIOD	TOTAL	ENGLISH	FRENCH	OTHERS
Rest of Canada to Québec:				
1966–1971	17.0	9.4	6.7	0.9
1971–1976	16.8	8.4	7.4	0.9
1976–1981	12.3	5.0	6.4	0.8
1981–1986	13.4	5.8	6.6	1.0
Average	14.9	7.2	6.8	0.9
Québec to Rest of Canada:				
1966–1971	32.1	19.8	9.4	2.9
1971–1976	29.2	18.8	8.3	2.1
1976–1981	40.6	26.3	10.0	4.3
1981–1986	26.0	14.1	9.2	2.7
Average	32.0	19.8	9.2	3.0
Net Migration:				
1966–1971	−15.1	−10.4	−2.7	−2.0
1971–1976	−12.4	−10.4	−0.9	−1.2
1976–1981	−28.3	−21.3	−3.6	−3.5
1981–1986	−12.6	−8.3	−2.6	−1.7
Average	−17.1	−12.6	−2.4	−2.1

Source: Réjean Lachapelle and Gilles Grenier, *Aspects linguistiques de l'évolution démographique au Canada*, Rapport au Secrétariat pour l'étude de l'évolution démographique et de son incidence sur la politique économique et sociale (Santé et bien-être Canada), 1988, p. 109.

International immigration has been proposed as a substitute for the missing births. For a few years now, one has witnessed a series of pleas and pressures in favour of doubling or even tripling the number of immigrants. Representatives of ethnic minorities, feminists, and even the Québec Department of Cultural Communities and Immigration added their voice to the concert. How can this be justified? As we have seen, Québec population will continue to increase for another decade or so and will then decline slowly; it is not until 2020 that the rate of decline will eventually become appreciable (see Figure 17.1). There is then no immediate *need* to increase the number of foreign immigrants, except those aged less than 20 years, who could reinforce the smaller generations born after 1970. Indeed, the only true substitutes for the lack of births would be orphaned babies.

The present writer is favourable to immigration. Canada and Québec should receive immigrants—and try to keep them—not because they need them for population growth, but because they are desirable for their talents, their energy, their knowledge, their cultural richness and diversity. Up to a point, they can compensate for the weak Canadian demography. But they cannot do the whole job. Why? Let us consider the case of Québec. First of all, full compensation would mean a rather unrealistic number of immigrants. Québec presently has a deficit of 30,000 births. That is the number that should be added to correspond to generation replacement. But Québec loses from one-half to two-thirds of its immigrants, so to add 30,000 persons to the population it would be necessary to receive from 60,000 to 90,000 immigrants every year on a continuous basis.

Can a city like Montréal absorb that? I say "Montréal" because that is where more than 85 percent of the newcomers settle (Paillé, 1989:32). In fact, they tend to concentrate on Montréal Island (80 percent of those who settle in Québec). The population of the island is about two million, and the 50,000 to 70,000 who would arrive every year would constitute between 2.4 and 3.6 percent of the population. The integration of such numbers would be, in the long run, an almost impossible job (see also Termote, 1991:161–65).

It is not necessary to engage in the difficult appraisal of the aptitude of the French Québec majority to be open to immigrants, for there is at least one easily observed problem that is far from being entirely solved: the adoption of English by most immigrants, against the will of the majority of the population and contrary to the government policy. During the 1968 to 1989 period, only 35 percent of immigrants who intended to settle in Québec knew some French (Ministère des communautés culturelles et de l'immigration, 1990:12). Moreover, among those whose mother tongue is neither English nor French, 70 percent chose English as their official language of adoption (either for themselves or for their children). Rightly or wrongly, this situation is emotionally charged, even if, as we shall see later, the percentage of the French-speaking population has been increasing continually for twenty years. What will happen after a few decades of annual immigration of, let us say, "only" 50,000 foreign immigrants? Such a number would most probably involve in the long run a reduction in the proportion of French-speaking people. Note also that such a flow would correspond to two million a year if the same proportion were to be let into the United States! In this country, it is at present only about 600,000 a year.

There is an effect of international immigration that is almost never mentioned, perhaps because it can be observed only over a long period: the change in the composition of the population regarding ethnicity. Over the last century in Québec, two important ethnic groups have been quite stable in their relative importance: the aboriginal peoples (1 percent of the total population) and the French (about 80 percent). The British comprised 20 percent around 1870 and are now only 8 percent; they were replaced by other ethnicities, which counted for 1 percent in 1870 and 12 percent in 1986 (Henripin, 1991:169–74). As to the future, a projection has been made by the Economic Council of Canada (1991:20): with the present level of immigration, from 1990 to 2015, the proportion of the Canadian population of non-European origin would increase from 4 to 10 percent. In Quebec, the percentage would probably be lower than that.

International immigration is the only domain that is the object of explicit and substantial policies associated with demographic preoccupations. Of course, we do not ignore health policies, but they are not, for the most part, related to population dynamics. Nor are the laws and programs concerning birth control and abortion. At the end of 1990, the Department of Cultural Communities and Immigration published a voluminous document doubly entitled: *Au Québec pour bâtir ensemble. Énoncé de politique en matière d' immigration et d' intégration.* The first part of the title (not to mention the very name of the department itself) is already an indication of the propagandistic character of the document. It contains useful information, and is well written and full of good sentiments. The reader gets a good idea of the direction in which the government intends to proceed, but is not told why. Statements on the absolute necessity to increase international immigration have to be accepted as true. Despite the difficulties of integrating the immigrants—and these difficulties are admitted here and there—the reader is assured that all the challenges will be met with success. And there is a very good reason for that: thanks to a recent agreement with the federal government, Québec is now (according at least to the above-mentioned document) the master of almost all the decisions and programs related to international immigration. It is expected that the readers and other authors of this volume have discovered many other examples of that pervading myth in Québec politics: if the Québec government has the power to intervene in a problem, the solution is already at hand.

Attributing questionable merits to immigration (of course, it also has real ones) is not unique to the Québec government. In fact, the same myth is found all over Canada among politicians as well as intellectuals. It is part of a new Canadian puritanism, along with an obsession for ecology and some other myths. By contrast, the Economic Council of Canada published (in 1991) a remarkably well-balanced report entitled *New Faces in the Crowd*, which is not without generosity and broadness of mind, and which avoids inundating the reader with unproven statements, wishful thinking, and sometimes fallacious arguments.

Returning to Québec's recent *Énoncé de politique,* an important, yet ambiguous if not fallacious passage has to be clarified (p. 10). The authors of the document compare two sets of hypotheses concerning future levels of immigration and fertility: one hypothesis is 55,000 immigrants per year and 1.8 children per woman; the other hypothesis is no immigration and the "present" level of fertility (the author probably had 1.4 children per woman in mind). The first hypothesis gives an average age of 42 years for the total population; the second, 48 years. That is probably correct, but the reader is inclined to believe that both factors are more or less equally responsible for the difference. The truth is that immigration has a rather small effect compared to that of fertility. On the whole, international immigration is a poor substitute for an increase in fertility. Let us quote the Economic Council of Canada's report (p. 1): "First, immigration is clearly not a simple substitute for natural increase as a method for raising Canada's population."

Demolinguistic Composition

As in Canada as a whole, the linguistic composition of Québec is more homogeneous than the ethnic mosaic. According to the 1986 census, 82.8 percent of the population was French speaking (mother tongue), 10.4 percent was English, and 6.8 percent spoke another language as their mother tongue. That differs greatly from a century ago, when about 20 percent were British and most probably spoke English. The proportion of French has been remarkably stable since 1870 (around 80 percent), diminishing somewhat with the arrival of large waves of immigrants and recovering when immigrants were scarce. It is the post–World War II wave that caused some anxiety among French Quebeckers. In fact, it did produce a small reduction of the proportion of French; not in favour of English though, as many thought, but to the benefit—a temporary benefit—of so-called allophones. But there was also a more fundamental reason for French Quebeckers to be worried.

As we said earlier, the proportion of French had been remarkably stable for a century, that is until the 1950s. That stability was the product of two main opposing forces: on the one hand, immigrants definitely reinforced the English "camp," either because they were English speaking, or because they adopted English as their new language; on the other hand, the French compensated by an important over-fertility. As we have seen, that over-fertility diminished progressively and finally disappeared during the 1960s (Lachapelle, 1991:201). So the century-old balance could not exist any more. At least that is what all scholars (including the present writer) concluded (Henripin, 1974:24–33). All demographers forecasted an eventual decrease in the proportion of French-speaking people in the province of Québec.

The conclusion, although quite logical, was erroneous, and for a very precise reason. Until 1977, demographers were supplied by Statistics Canada with good estimates of interprovincial migrations, but these estimates were not divided according to language. Demographers then had to make reasonable estimations as to their language distribution. The estimations were indeed reasonable, but quite far from reality. This was revealed for the first time in the summer of 1977, when the new data were extracted from the 1971 census and related to the period 1966 to 1971. One fact was striking: English-speaking Quebeckers were leaving the province in much larger numbers than was previously hypothesized. In fact, during that period, their propensity to leave for other provinces had been fifteen times that of the French (that is, of course, in proportion, not in absolute terms).

So the disappearing of the French over-fertility had been compensated for by an increase in the rate of emigration from Québec to the rest of Canada of members of the English-speaking community. No one realized this beforehand. The phenomenon was strong enough to produce a decline in the percentage of anglophones, which continued at least until the last census (1986), and most of the time not only did the percentage of anglophones decrease, but even their absolute numbers decreased. Allophones are also prone to leave Québec; their rate is four to five times that of the French (Lachapelle and Henripin, 1982:197).

Demographers then had to go back to the drawing-board, some finding that the chances of the French proportion decreasing were minimal (Lachapelle and Henripin, 1982:283–320). Three successive censuses showed an increase in the French-speaking proportion of the total population. This is true of the Montréal metropolitan area as well as of the whole province. Table 17.5 gives a good idea of the recent evolution, using two different concepts of language: "mother tongue" and "language most often spoken at home."

In this evolution one sees a decline in the English community. True, it continues to attract a large proportion of allophones, and this is clearly shown by the difference between the percentage of those with English as their *mother* tongue and the percentage of those with English as their *home* language (17.0 percent and 20.8 percent respectively in Montréal, 1986). This is not enough to maintain their absolute numbers. Table 17.6 shows the absolute numbers for Québec and Montréal according to the censuses. It seems that the drop in numbers has been minimal during the last period, and there is no compelling reason to believe that Montréal's English community is on the verge of disappearing. On the other hand, a serious threat of Québec secession might result in another departure of large number of English and "other" Quebeckers.

As to French Quebeckers, recent trends should convince them that their majority is rather safe and will continue to increase or at least stabilize. Of course, there are no guarantees; present trends are the result of many factors that could change. For instance, if the recently expressed plan of the Québec government to admit more than 40,000 foreign immigrants per year (Ministère des communautés culturelles et de l'immigration, 1990:40) is implemented, and if such a phenomenon persisted for a few decades, then we might see a significant diminution of the French majority. Such a policy would certainly be much more harmful for that majority than permitting some English or other languages on outdoor signs. For

Table 17.5
Population Distribution by Mother Tongue and Home
Language, Whole Province of Québec and Montréal
Metropolitan Area, 1971, 1981, and 1986

REGIONS AND LANGUAGES	MOTHER TONGUE			HOME LANGUAGE		
	1971	1981	1986	1971	1981	1986
QUÉBEC						
English	13.1	11.0	10.4	14.7	12.7	12.3
French	80.7	82.4	82.8	80.8	82.5	82.8
Others	6.2	6.6	6.8	4.5	4.8	4.9
MONTRÉAL						
English	21.7	18.2	17.0	24.9	21.7	20.8
French	66.3	68.8	69.6	66.3	69.0	69.7
Others	12.0	13.0	13.4	8.8	9.3	9.5

Source: J. Henripin, "The 1986 Census: Some Enduring Trends Abate," *Language and Society*, no. 24 (Fall 1988):7.

Table 17.6
Number of Anglophones (in thousands)

	MOTHER TONGUE			HOME LANGUAGE		
	1971	1981	1986	1971	1981	1986
Québec prov.	789	695	677	888	809	797
Montréal	538	522	496	717	615	600

Source: Censuses of Canada, particularly: Statistics Canada, *Census Canada 1986, Adjusted Language Data*, April 1988 (occasional publication).

the time being, however, if French is threatened in Québec, it is not for demographic reasons.

CONCLUSION

No country possesses an all-embracing population policy. Most Western industrialized countries limit themselves to international immigration policy. Despite some interesting declarations of the Québec premier and some programs to encourage parents to have more children, Québec is no exception to the generally practised modesty in population policy. But the simple fact that the premier has stated that his province's demographic situation is the greatest challenge that has to be tackled is uncommon among Western countries. Should governments engage in a so-called natalist policy? The word "natalist" horrifies some delicate minds who curiously associate it with some form of fascism. Let us then speak about measures intended to increase fertility, in all respect of individual freedom. Should governments intervene? Certainly, if there is some reason to believe that such an action might be effective.

A population is like a living being made up of organs, each of which must function to ensure survival and maintenance of health. If adults, who must produce the new members of society, do not fulfil this function adequately, the deficiency must be corrected rather than hastily turning to some prosthesis. In our context, the prosthesis is international immigration. Using immigration as the solution to an anemic fertility is giving an essential role to what should have a supporting role. Immigrants present other advantages: they are an enrichment of our culture in all walks of life. Integrating immigrants is a supplement of life and strength that society gives itself, or rather that is given to it by strangers. Immigrants should be invited and welcomed because their qualities are appreciated, not so that they can do work that is being neglected.

Quebeckers have to produce their own babies. What can be done about it? Certainly not only putting in place a few financial measures, such as increasing family allowances. First, those whose words are listened to (politicians, journalists, business and trade union leaders, artists, etc.) should express their views with regard to the undesirability of our very weak fertility rate. There is also a necessary precondition: relatively stable prospects for employment and adequate wages for young adults. That would require a better adjustment of our educational system to the needs of the labour market and less laxness in the whole teaching apparatus, including teachers' attitudes.

More specific measures should also be taken or at least tried. A whole chapter in one of this author's recent books is devoted to this (Henripin, 1989:121–33). One of the most important changes requires not so much just more money, but more imagination, and the renouncement of old practices: the reorganization of the working world so that raising children becomes more compatible with a working career, particularly for women, but also for men. Flexibility would be the key word. The school schedule and holidays should also cease to be fixed without any consideration for parents who are both working. Many services, both private and public, could be modified with the same purpose in mind. And, of course, more "classical" measures would have to be expanded: day-care centres (not necessarily subsidized) and family allowances are important examples. Income tax principles might also be questioned: Is there any justification for taxing the part of revenue that is devoted to the essential or normal needs of children?

The major difficulty probably lies in the fact that we still continue to consider children as free goods, that is, free (or almost) from the point of view of society. This is no longer true: children have become scarce, and society must pay for having a sufficient quantity and quality of them. This should not prevent society from improving the selection of foreign immigrants and the assistance given to them.

REFERENCES

Comeau, Paul-André (1991). "Declin démographique et prospective politique," in J. Henripin and Y. Martin, eds., *La population du Québec d'hier à demain*, Montréal: Les Presses de l'Université de Montréal, pp. 205–10.

Economic Council of Canada (1991). *Le nouveau visage du Canada*, Ottawa: Minister of Supply and Services (translated under the title "New Faces in the Crowd").

Henripin, Jacques (1972). *Trends and Factors of Fertility in Canada*, Ottawa: Queen's Printer, 1972.

Henripin, Jacques (1974). *L'immigration et le déséquilibre linguistique*, Étude sur l'immigration et les objectifs démographique du Canada, Ottawa: Information Canada.

Henripin, Jacques (1988). "The 1986 Census: Some Enduring Trends Abate," *Language and Society*, no. 24 (Fall 1988).

Henripin, Jacques (1989). *Naître ou ne pas être*, Québec: Institut québécois de recherche sur la culture.

Henripin, Jacques (1991). "Le peuplement non français et la diversité ethnique et linguistique," in Jacques Henripin and Yves Martin, eds., *La population du Québec d'hier à demain*, Montréal: Les Presses de l'Université de Montréal.

Lachapelle, Réjean (1991). "Quelques tendances démolinguistiques au Canada et au Québec," in Jacques Henripin and Yves Martin, eds., *La population du Québec d'hier à demain*, Montréal: Les Presses de l'Université de Montréal, pp. 191–204.

Lachapelle, Réjean, and Gilles Grenier (1988). *Aspects linguistiques de l'évolution démographique au Canada*, Rapport au Secrétariat pour l'étude de l'évolution démographique et de son incidence sur la politique économique et sociale (Santé et Bien-être Canada) (not published).

Lachapelle, Réjean, and Jacques Henripin (1982). *The Demolinguistic Situation in Canada: Past Trends and Future Prospects*, Montreal: Institute for Research on Public Policy.

Lux, André (1991). "Le poids du vieillissement: idéologies, paradoxes et stratégies," in Jacques Henripin and Yves Martin, eds., *La population du Québec d'hier à demain*, Montréal: Les Presses de l'Université de Montréal, pp. 109–38.

Ministère des communautés culturelles et de l'immigration, Québec Province (1990). *Énoncé de politique en matière d'immigration et d'intégration*, (also published in English).

Paillé, Michel (1989). *Nouvelles tendances démolinguistiques dans l'Île de Montréal, 1981–1996*. Québec: Conseil de la langue française.

Statistics Canada, *Vital Statistics* (annual reports).

Termote, Marc (1991). "Ce que pourrait être une politique de migration," in Jacques Henripin and Yves Martin, eds., *La population du Québec d'hier à demain*, Montréal: Les Presses de l'Université de Montréal, pp. 153–67.

Education and Politics in Québec: Adapting 19th-Century Structures to Face the Challenges of the 21st

Henry Milner
Vanier College

INTRODUCTION

No institution is more sensitive to, and responsible for, societal changes than the system of education. This chapter analyzes the recent developments in the primary and secondary school system in Québec (the Constitution of Canada assigns exclusive jurisdiction over education to the provinces) and relates these to wider issues. I focus on the Montréal area where almost one third of the 6.5 million Quebeckers reside, and on developments in the Montréal Catholic School Commission (CECM),[1] which runs the bulk of public schools (180 schools attended by 90,000 students) in the city of Montréal. The goal is to link current issues and circumstances to wider developments in Québec society.

Over one million students, one-quarter of Canada's school population, attend primary and secondary schools in Québec, and one in four of these resides on the Island of Montréal, Québec's metropolis. Just over half the population of the Island of Montréal lives within the city of Montréal; the remainder reside in twenty-eight other municipalities (see Figure 18.1). Public transit, police, and environmental programs are administered through a second tier, the Montréal Urban Community (CUM). Neither the CUM nor the municipalities have any say over education.

It is generally agreed that the situation in Montréal public schools is problematic—marked, on the one hand, by inadequacies in academic performance by the students and, on the other, by social problems reflecting wider societal developments. Of course, problems of these types are not limited to Montréal. Declining standards of academic achievement in U.S. high schools are well documented (e.g., Coleman et al., 1982), and similar trends have been noted in other Western societies. Levels of violence and social tension are higher in secondary schools in many American inner-cities than in Montréal. Nevertheless, the uniqueness of Québec's, and, especially Montréal's, ethnolinguistic situation is a contributing factor ιο the existence and particularity of the problems and, I shall argue, to the

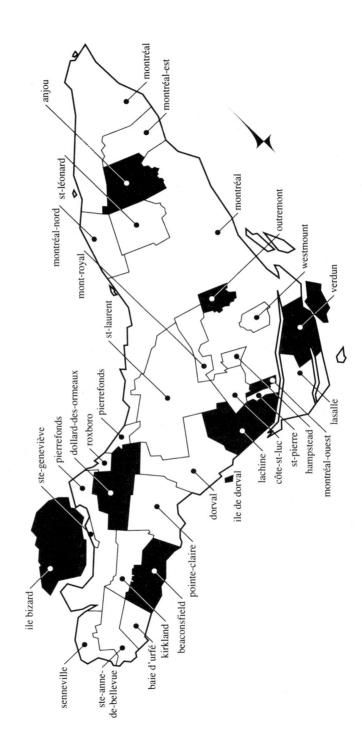

Figure 18.1
Territory of the Montréal Urban Community (CUM)

failure of the structures adequately to address them. This analysis of the workings of the educational structures places special emphasis on factors bearing upon parental and citizen participation on the premise that, in the long run, only through the effective channelling of the energies and resources of those affected can educational progress be achieved and sustained.

A PUBLIC EDUCATION SYSTEM IN TROUBLE: SOME SYMPTOMS

While the scientific literature has provided no foolproof method for comparing levels of educational performance across different societies, a number of indicators give credence to a frequently heard critical assessment of the performance of Québec's educational system (Balthazar and Bélanger, 1989; Migué and Marceau, 1989; Desbiens, 1989). One much discussed indicator these days is the length of the school year. A recent comparison places Québec tied with the United States at second lowest with 180 days (Barrett, 1990:79); moreover, if a 1990 report to the Québec Ministry of Education (MEQ) is accurate, the real average is closer to 170 than 180 days. Yet even with the short school year, in 1989, 45.8 percent of the boys and 31.9 percent of the girls dropped out before finishing high school (Demers, 1990). In addition, the MEQ revealed in 1990 that 30 percent of the 6,000 young people (aged 15 to 30) attending classes for illiterates had completed at least nine years of schooling (Léger, 1990).

There has long been great dissatisfaction with the quality of linguistic skills being acquired in Québec schools: various measures place at roughly one in five the proportion of high-school students whose French grammar is satisfactory (MEQ, 1990). National and international data analyses, which usually do not treat Québec distinctly from Canada as a whole, confirm this impression. A Statistics Canada study for the National Literacy Secretariat published in September 1990 revealed that 30 percent of high-school graduates do not have the reading skills, and 36 percent the numeracy skills, needed to meet most daily requirements. A comparison of the daily homework habits of 13 year olds found only 25 percent of Canadian students to average more than two hours, placing Canada last of the six countries surveyed (Sprout, 1990:50). Canadian high-school seniors placed last in chemistry and second to last in physics in the International Education Association ten-nation study (Sprout, 1990:51). In the Gallop (*National Geographic*) geography test (Grosvenor, 1989), young Canadians placed exactly in the middle of the ten-nation survey, while the Americans placed last.[2]

Within Québec, the performance of the CECM's students in French-language examinations in 1989–90 placed it 115th of 127 school commissions (Demers, 1990:34). This is not entirely unexpected since the CECM runs many of the inner-city multiethnic schools in the Montréal area. There is undeniably a link between academic performance and the social conditions of the school community. First of all, there is good reason to believe that these problems are related to the growing absence of middle-class families from Québec's 2,558 public schools due to their choosing instead to send their children to one of the 320 private elementary and secondary schools. Though private schools can and do serve a useful purpose in providing competition to the public schools, the situation in Québec has reached the point that this positive effect is more than counterbalanced by a negative one. In Québec, and especially in Montréal, the private schools drain resources out of the public education system to an inordinately large extent, depriving the public schools of needed active, caring parents, teachers, and administrators. Of the 1.1 million elementary and high-school students in Québec, 10 percent attend private schools (MEQ, 1989a), with over three-quarters of these at the high-school level. The highest concentration of private schools is found in the Montréal area, where demand for private schooling exceeds supply (Bernier, 1990). The proportion of Québec students in private schools is the highest among Canadian provinces— twice that of Ontario. In Ontario the proportion declined in the 1980s, while in Québec it rose over 15 percent.

While other factors help account for the low levels of participation in public education, there is definitely a causal relationship between these levels and the magnitude of the private-education sector. In effect, a classic vicious circle has set in making it impossible to distinguish cause from effect. Private schooling, it should be noted, is generously subsidized at roughly 60 percent and, therefore, not beyond the reach of even the lower strata of the middle class (see Bezeau, 1979). Given the opportunity, many (potentially) active parents pull their children out of the public schools in a desire to avoid the very problems that their active presence could have helped avert.

RELIGION AND THE DIVISIONS OF PUBLIC EDUCATIONAL STRUCTURES

At one level, the public schools' loss of human resources is a result of government policies subsidizing private education. At a deeper level, it is a manifestation of defects in the structure of Québec's educational system that impede it from addressing the problems faced by the schools. There are three dimensions to this predicament: the first is constitutional-legal, the second demographic, and the third political-administrative. Under the first heading we stress the constitutionally protected "confessional" nature of the Montréal public school system; the second takes in considerations of immigration, ethnic composition, and language; the third focuses especially on the effect of centralized bargaining.

The Island of Montréal is divided into six Catholic, and again into two Protestant, school-board territories, each subdivided into territorial constituencies represented by a school commissioner. These constituencies are unrelated to municipal districts, and school-board elections are held separately from municipal ones. (A map of the territories of the Montréal-area boards is provided in Figure 18.2). There can be no doubt that the complexity of this representational system inhibits citizen involvement in the educational system (see Milner, 1986). The confessional nature of the structure, which imposes upon people who do not identify themselves by religious affiliation the requirement of doing just that in order to get involved, compounds the problem. Consider the categories listed below, in a letter sent out in the Montréal area in Fall 1990 indicating whether the recipient was (in this case) an eligible Protestant-school-board (CEPGM-PSBGM) voter. No wonder turnout was so low.

1. Protestant, or neither Protestant nor Catholic and has no children of school-going age;
2. Protestant, or neither Protestant nor Catholic whose children attend schools belonging to the PSBGM;

3. Protestant, or neither Protestant nor Catholic whose children attend a school belonging to the PSBGM and a school belonging to another school commission;
4. Protestant, or neither Protestant nor Catholic whose children attend a private school or a school belonging to a board other than the PSBGM or the CECM.

A bit of historical background is in order here. Efforts by the Québec government to deconfessionalize the system, that is, to replace the separate Catholic and Protestant boards by French and English ones, have repeatedly failed—at least until now. Though the rapid modernization of Québec infrastructures in the 1960s (the "Quiet Revolution") was identified above all with the dramatic changes in education that it initiated, a key element of that reform never saw the light of day, leaving public education in Québec locally controlled by 175 Catholic and twenty-nine Protestant boards. In the Montréal area, the Catholic and Protestant boards administer a network of English as well as French schools. Elsewhere, with a few exceptions, Catholic schools are French, Protestant schools are English.

This structure is not only unwieldy, it is also expensive—Statistics Canada found that in 1982 it cost 38 percent less to educate a child in Ontario than in Québec. These excess costs are borne by the educational system, which pays for them in the form of outdated textbooks, poor buildings, and lack of equipment. A glaring manifestation of the resulting relative deprivation is found in a recent study of school libraries. The average number of books in Québec's schools is seven per student, compared with twenty in the United States and thirty-nine in Denmark. The low number is, in part, a residue of history: Québec educational development lagged, with the Ministry of Education only being set up in 1964. But financial constraints have made catching up impossible. Québec spent $5.27 per student on school library books in 1988 compared with $6.74 in the United States, $33.48 in Denmark, and $14 in the province of Manitoba (MEQ, Comité d'étude, 1989b:35–6).

The present structure, and the costs it entails, is the result of piecemeal modernizing reforms introduced since 1964 in the face of the failure to deconfessionalize the system. Both the Union Nationale government in the late 1960s and the Liberal administration of the 1970s sought to eliminate denominational boards in the Montréal area, as had been recommended in 1966 by the celebrated Parent Report. These bills were struck down by the courts based on section 93 of Canada's Constitution, the BNA Act, with its imprecise guarantees of denominational rights in education. As a result, Québec governments elected to retreat rather than face a cohesive and determined opposition of Protestant boards and Catholic *intégristes* (fundamentalists) ready to take to the courts. But pressure for legislative remedies did not let up, especially after adoption of language laws 22 and 101 in the mid-1970s required newcomers to send their children to French schools. This meant attending either the French Catholic schools—whatever the immigrants' religious beliefs—or the more secular French Protestant schools—where these existed.

Initiative for new reform attempts came from below. Parents, teachers, and administrators at Notre-Dame-des-Neiges, a Montréal elementary school, sought to create a pluralistic educational environment to serve a community ranging over immigrant groups from more than thirty different ethnic backgrounds to Université de Montréal staff. In 1979 the parents asked the CECM to revoke the school's status as a Catholic school. The request was refused, and the CECM's position

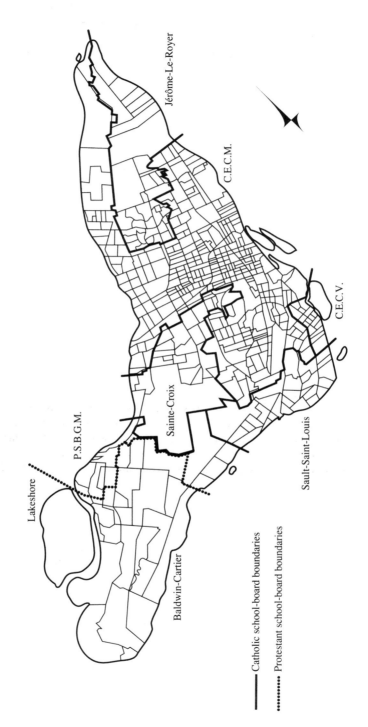

Figure 18.2
Montréal Area School-Board Territories (1986)

Source: Census Canada, 1986; prepared for the Montréal Island School Council by the mapping service of INRS-Urbanisation, 1990.

was subsequently upheld by the courts on constitutional grounds, thus bringing the issue back onto the political agenda. In 1982, Minister of Education Camille Laurin published his White Paper on School Reform, which proposed not only deconfessionalization, but also radical decentralization of school structures. In the modified version of his plan, Bill 40, presented to the Québec National Assembly in 1983, the denominational structures on the Island of Montréal were to be replaced with two separate linguistic structures, one serving the French schools, the other the English. Due to the opposition encountered, the provisions of Bill 40 were moderated further in 1984, and Laurin was replaced. Yet even this version, Bill 3, was in the end rejected as unconstitutional just after Laurin's Parti Québécois (PQ) was replaced by the Liberals at the end of 1985.

The new Liberal government reacted by drafting an even more moderate reform, Bill 107, which left in place all confessional privileges in the schools and provided for continued existence of confessional boards (the territorial boundaries of which were to be set according to requirements determined by the courts) alongside new linguistic ones in the Montréal area. Action was then delayed as the plan was referred to the courts. In September 1990, the Québec Court of Appeal ruled Bill 107 constitutional and, in a majority vote, found that the existing confessional boards, as such, had no constitutionally entrenched territorial rights beyond those applying throughout Québec, that of the religious minority to opt out of any public board and set up a "dissentient" board. This ruling was immediately appealed to the Supreme Court of Canada by the Protestant boards who claim their ownership of the existing schools' property to be constitutionally protected; their appeal, after some delay due to ongoing school-board elections, was endorsed by the CECM.

Developments in the CECM during this period have been especially noteworthy. The very low turnout for school-board elections in the 1970s and 1980s allowed *intégristes* to dominate the CECM (see Milner, 1986), a group out of step with the majority of Catholic School Commissioners as represented by the Québec Federation of Catholic School Commissions (FSCQ), which—to the outrage of the CECM—early in 1991 announced its intention to remove the epithet "Catholic" from its name. In turn, the policies and pronouncements of the CECM commissioners exacerbated the problems since (apart from wasting many badly needed dollars on legal fees to fight deconfessionalization) the system's resulting narrow confessional character (or, at least, image) deterred not only non-Catholics from sending their children to CECM schools, but also some liberal French-Canadian Catholics as well as many parents from various ethnic groups (Catholics and non-Catholics) unwilling to confide their children to a school environment they perceived as narrow and nonintegrative.

For an increasing number of middle-and upper-class families, lay private schools constitute the desired haven from the confessional Catholic system. For many immigrant families, though a still relatively small number of French-Canadian families, the Protestant (and de facto anglophone-run) schools serve the requisite function. This latter phenomenon is ironic since a major objective of the language legislation of the 1970s was to encourage the integration of these neo-Québécois families into the institutions of the majority. The French Catholic schools' (apparent) lack of openness drove many to schools run by the Protestant boards, which had the reputation of being more pluralistic,[3] and consequently, more French Protestant schools were opened to meet this demand. In the ten years to 1990, this sector went from less than 1,000 to almost 12,000 students—over one third of the total student population of the CEPGM. Since these students are concentrated in the lower grades, the number can be expected to rise to over 50 percent in the next few years. Already in 1986, 62 percent of the students in the French sector of the Protestant School Board of Greater Montréal (CEPGM) were nonfrancophone.

While it would be foolhardy to compare the overall quality of education in the Catholic and Protestant schools, one can say that the Protestant schools do enjoy a better academic reputation. Part of this is the residue of a past situation when school funding was denominational, with the Protestant schools thus having access to a greater tax base. But it is also, one suspects, due to the Protestant schools having attracted families with greater energies to invest in their children's education, energies lost to the Catholic schools. In sum, the inhibitions that confessional structures place upon popular involvement and the existence of safety valves in the form of Protestant and subsidized private schools have fed the vicious circle that both creates problems for the French Catholic schools and deprives them of resources for dealing with them.

Under these circumstances, it was no small feat in November 1990 to raise participation in the CECM elections to 15 percent[4] and, as a result, for supporters of deconfessionalization under the banner of the The Movement for a Modern and Open School (MEMO) to improve significantly on previous showings (see Milner, 1986) by winning ten of the twenty-one positions on the board. This leaves the intégristes in the Movement for a Confessional School (RSC) with a slim majority. However, their controversial leader, outgoing CECM chairman Michel Pallascio, was soundly defeated in his district.

LINGUISTIC DIVISIONS AND ETHNIC TENSIONS

Recent actions and statements by Pallascio are symptomatic of difficulties posed by the integration of nonfrancophone immigrants, the second dimension of the underlying problem. In the fall of 1989, the CECM commissioned a poll: one question read "Would you like to see immigrant children in separate schools?" (see Leclerc, 1990). A year later, in making public the RSC's position before the Bélanger-Campeau Commission on Québec's constitutional future, Pallascio called for preferences to be given to immigrants sharing Québec's "Judeo-Christian values." Representatives of neo-Québécois groups were understandably outraged, interpreting such gestures as evidence of lack of openness on the part of the Catholic school system.

Of course, the need to integrate large numbers of children from different cultural backgrounds with a different home language is a challenge faced by educational authorities in places other than Montréal. The added dimension, insofar as Québec and especially Montréal is concerned, is the fact that traditionally such newcomers have integrated via the English schools, seeing themselves as entrants to English-speaking North America. In that context, their being required as of the mid-1970s to send their children to French schools added a second layer to interethnic tensions.

It is important here to distinguish the CECM board from its teaching and administrative staff. On the whole, the staff has been positively oriented toward the integration of the immigrant students, and many individuals have worked hard in the task, especially in the "welcome classes" set up to teach them French and accommodate them to their new environment. The overall record remains a spotty one: the individuals concerned were often unprepared and lacked appropriate support from their political masters (see Ferland and Rocher, 1987; and Beauchesne and Hesler, 1987). An additional factor is the lack of experience of the francophone educational institutions at integrating a large number of non-francophones. Hence the extent to which the difficulties can be attributed to the particular constellation of leadership at the CECM during this period remains to be determined. Pallascio is no longer chairman, but though the opposition is much stronger, the RSC is still in control of the CECM.

The problems are compounded by the patterns of ethnic settlement. While Quebeckers whose mother tongue is neither French nor English make up only 7 percent of the population, they constitute almost 25 percent of that of the Island of Montréal, where 93 percent of new immigrants to Québec settle (Grandjean, 1990; see also Levine, 1990). On the island, the pattern tends to be a "mosaic" one: each of the groups concentrated in a particular part of the city, with certain areas coming to be known as especially "ethnic" in composition. In addition, apart from being mainly "visible" in skin colour and dress (70 percent of immigrants in the 1980s are estimated to be visible; Levine,1990), recent immigrants tend to be especially weak in resources, coming from poorer countries in Asia, Africa, and Central America (see Figures 18.3 and 18.4). In its January 1991 brief to the Québec National Assembly on immigration policy, the Montréal Island School Council, which represents the eight boards, predicted that soon 50 percent of island students would not be of French mother tongue, pointing to the fact that already in 1989 the majority in 13 percent of the schools were nonfrancophones (Grandjean, 1990).

Most of these forty or so schools are among the 100 (one-quarter of all schools on the island) designated as lying within zones of poverty, where 12 percent of children suffer from malnutrition (Léger, 1991). Most of these schools are also administered by the CECM. In all, 35 percent of CECM students have a mother tongue that is neither French nor English; in the lower grades, it is 50 percent. Many of these students attend "welcome classes," remedial French classes to enable them to join regular classes. In 1987, 20 percent of these students aged 12 to 16 were more than two years behind in their studies (Léger, 1991). To the difficulties inherent in integrating newcomers under these conditions is added the French–English tension. In many of the French schools where nonfrancophones are the majority, the common language of the students is English. Moreover, the families of many of these students still resent the obligation to educate their children in French (especially when the full range of English-language instruction is available to anglophone Canadians) since they believed they were immigrating to an English-speaking country. This resentment is reflected in the children's attitude toward their schools: reports of a systematic refusal to speak French among these children led the CECM in Spring 1990 to publicly consider (though not act) to oblige the use of French outside the classroom, a policy deemed undesirable by most, and unenforceable by everyone. The discussion, at least, brought the issue in

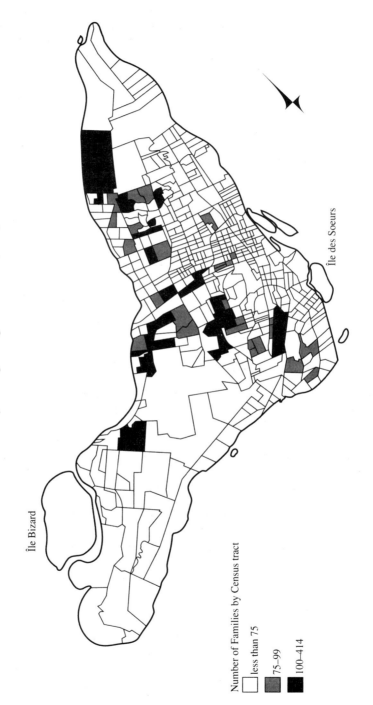

Figure 18.3
Poverty Among Immigrant Families (1985)

Number of Families by Census tract

☐ less than 75

▨ 75–99

■ 100–414

île Bizard

île des Soeurs

Families with at least one child under 13 with revenues under the Statistics Canada poverty line where the father (or single mother) was born outside Canada.
Source: Census Canada, 1986; prepared for the Montréal Island School Council by the mapping service of INRS-Urbanisation, 1989.

Figure 18.4

Non-French, Non-English-Speaking Immigrant Families (1985)

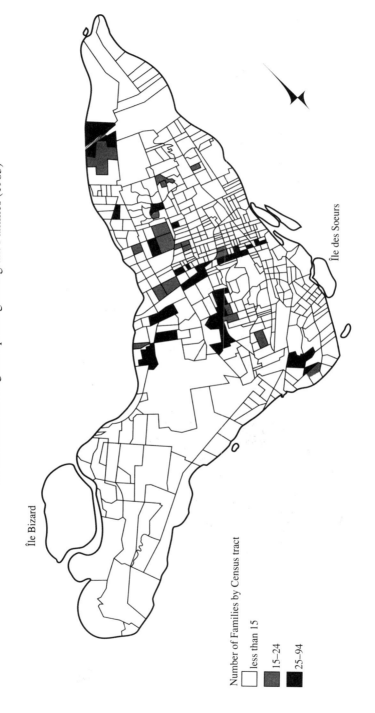

Île Bizard

Île des Soeurs

Number of Families by Census tract

less than 15

15–24

25–94

Families with at least one child under 13 where the mother speaks neither French nor English and where the father (or single mother) was born outside Canada.
Source: Census Canada, 1986; prepared for the Montréal Island School Council by the mapping service of INRS-Urbanisation, 1989.

the open, though it did nothing to enhance the already tarnished image of the CECM among the neo-Québécois.

A related though clearly separate phenomenon is the growing number of violent incidents in high schools, some of them linked to interethnic tensions (see Rioux, 1990). Yet clearly only a small part of the increase in the number of altercations in which knives, crowbars, baseball bats, etc. are brandished[5], is due to such tensions. Most of it is attributable to drugs and other antisocial forms of behaviour common among high-school-aged youth in the large urban centres.

BUREAUCRACY, LABOUR RELATIONS, AND EDUCATION

The third dimension in our analysis addresses a commonly expressed critique of public education based on the "public choice" approach to policy analysis. Public choice views the supply of public services within the neoclassical economic model and, therefore, the outcome of free choices in a competitive market as the optimum against which existing systems are measured and—necessarily—found wanting. In education this optimum takes the form of a voucher system that, it is presumed, minimizes public waste by maximizing consumer choice (see Chubb and Moe, 1988). Rather than enter the debate at the theoretical level, we note simply that, when public choice logic is applied to public services such as education, reality turns out to be more complex (see Witte, 1990). We argued above that there are negative as well as positive effects of the availability of private schooling in Québec. The primary consideration in the analysis presented here, that is, the investment of human resources into education, leads us to share the contention of public choice–oriented critics (e.g., Migué and Marceau, 1989; Desbiens: 1989) that an overcentralized bureaucratic apparatus frustrates parental and citizen participation. However, unlike these critics, we fear that further extension of private schooling through vouchers, which is in effect what the subsidies to private schools are (Bezeau, 1979), could exacerbate the problems by draining additional resources out of the public schools.

Public education in Québec is often regarded as characterized by excessive regulation from the centre. Nevertheless, inefficiency is not necessarily the result of overcentralization; it can rather be due to inadequate control from the centre combined with the perception that the rules are set by a distant and unresponsive bureaucracy. A recent manifestation of this is to be found in a cry of alarm registered by Michel Pagé, the Minister of Education early in 1991. He found it unacceptable that the school boards were being given additional funds for a staggeringly high number (144,000 in total) of students claimed by them to be suffering from learning disabilities, especially since the individual dossiers were sheltered by confidentiality. The problem here is not that decisions following rules set in Québec are insensitive to the needs of the local school community; indeed, a certain degree of insensitivity is inevitable if minimal standards and accepted accounting procedures are to be required, and if one wishes to reduce inequalities of expenditures per pupil (Bezeau, 1985). The problem is rather that the local school-board structures are insufficiently publicly (that is, visibly) accountable to an active school community as a counterweight to their accountability to the Ministry of Education. We have already seen how the confessional structure demobilizes the potentially active elements in the local community; we contend here that application of detailed province-wide collective agreements in education has a similar effect.

Lest what follows be misinterpreted, it is stated at the outset that centralized negotiation in itself is not the problem, not even centralized negotiations with teachers. Centralized negotiations can foster both economic productivity and social justice (Milner, 1989b), and centralized negotiations with public employees including teachers, as long as limited to salary and related conditions and within parameters set largely by private-sector negotiations, can complement this. In Québec, however, the public sector took the lead in centralized bargaining, and nowhere more than in education.

Earlier in this century Québec trade unions were relatively conservative in orientation, French-Canadian workers in the newly founded Catholic trade union confederation (CTCC) being discouraged from pushing their participation in industrial development too far lest they be themselves caught up in its underlying materialism (Milner, 1978). Though the CTCC grew more militant after World War II, it made little progress, running into the opposition of the reactionary Duplessis government and, generally, the conservative climate of the 1950s. The coming to power of Liberal Jean Lesage in 1960 marked a new era of cooperation between the newly deconfessionalized CTCC (which became the CSN under Jean Marchand) and the government. The Québec state and public-sector unionism mushroomed simultaneously. The newly established MEQ was made up almost entirely of unionized employees. Centralized public-sector bargaining became the norm by the end of the decade, just as the unions entered a new period of militancy. In the 1970s, province-wide teachers' negotiations were incorporated into a cartel, a negotiating "common front" of all public and parapublic employees. By then, radical, confrontation-oriented intellectuals had acquired leading positions, most notably in the Confederation of National Trade Unions (CSN) and the Québec Education Central (Centrale de l'enseignement du Québec/CEQ), composed of the teachers and other education employees, and thereby dominated the common front that undermined the Liberal government of Robert Bourassa (Milner, 1977).

The Lévesque government came to power in 1976 with a "favourable bias" toward unions as revealed in its early anti-strikebreaking legislation. The PQ hoped to put European-style concertation (structured labour–management cooperation along Scandinavian lines—see Tellier, 1977, 1978; Boisvert, 1980; and Tanguay in this volume) on the political agenda. Three "national" and more than thirty sectorial socioeconomic "summits," bringing together government, labour, and business, were convened. Yet, as with its 1980 referendum on sovereignty, the PQ proved to be ahead of its time. The CSN and CEQ were at times reticent even to sit down with their "class enemies." With the exceptions of the "corvée habitation," a jointly sponsored scheme to finance housing construction, and the Québec Federation of Labour's (FTQ) investment fund, the "Fonds de solidarité," the national summits produced no lasting achievement (Bellemare and Poulin-Simon, 1986). The "partners'" reticence was aggravated by the onset of the recession. In 1981 thousands of Québec companies went out of business; unemployment reached 15.5 percent, and the economy declined by 6.3 percent (Milner, 1986:103).

At the final national summit (1982), Premier René Lévesque sought to win the cooperation of the public and parapublic workers' unions in efforts to deal with these conditions, since there could be no question of raising the deficit to pay current expenditures (with the astronomical interest rates then prevailing), or cutting direct assistance to a population already suffering great hardship. Nonunionized employees (management staff, judges, doctors) saw their salaries frozen. But the common front of 300,000 unionized public and parapublic workers refused to forego even part of the 14 percent wage increase for the final year of the contract they had won. Put to the test, "concertation" had failed.

In response, the government in the summer of 1982 tabled a law under which $500 million would be recovered, once the contract had expired, in a three-month rollback at the start of 1983. For its part, the common front presented demands for the new contract, which explicitly ignored the economic crisis. After failing in its last-ditch appeal for top-level negotiations, the government rolled back the wages and imposed the provisions of the new contracts. The teachers' strike that ensued was the most dramatic conflict in the history of Québec education. By late February, the other groups, under the threat of severe back-to-work legislation, had returned to work: only the teachers were left on the picket lines. They had the most to lose since their contract included a complex hiring and seniority formula that had kept teacher numbers almost steady as the plummeting birthrate reduced student numbers by 29 percent through the 1970s. They refused to consider any modification of the staffing rules to take into account economic fluctuations or specific regional or local needs. The strike became a crusade over fundamental principle; and thus as bitter as any in recent memory. It was ended only with a harsh back-to-work law, the outcry against which polarized political parties even further and made the issue even more a crusade.

In the aftermath of the conflict, the PQ lost many active party members; the public-sector unions also proved weakened in the two subsequent negotiations with the new Liberal government under a resurrected Robert Bourassa, which compared to earlier rounds were virtual capitulations on the part of labour. But failure to win more contractual concessions should not be interpreted as adoption of a more cooperative attitude. Their crusade vanquished (betrayed, as many put it), teachers were left bitter and dispirited and, according to union pronouncements, suffering from low morale, overwork, and general frustration. Whatever the rights and wrongs of the situation, there can be no doubt that the climate created was one under which teachers and their unions were not predisposed to be cooperative when it came to participating on consultative bodies and or showing flexibility in the application of rules. Few today doubt that the inflexibility of the contracts, which, for example, place seniority above competence over subject matter in the allocation of teaching positions, has rendered the entire system insufficiently accountable. As one observer described it: "Centralized collective bargaining ... spawned a number of troublesome consequences that promote conflict.... Evaluation of teachers is practically impossible.... To some degree ... uniform procedure have replaced individual accountability and caused administrators to become apathetic" (Papale, 1981). Another observer described the process as an "arms race" between the government and the unions (Lauroesch, 1979). (These words were written, we should note, before the conflict of 1983.) In sum, it can safely be inferred that as a consequence of these practices, parental participation was discouraged and the flight to the private schools fostered.

Yet the picture is not uniformly bleak. Overall, the context in labour–management relations in Québec has changed with the ironical result that, having helped drive the PQ from power by spurning its overtures for concertation, labour has begun, with the PQ out of power, to redefine social democracy along cooperative Scandinavian lines. The more moderate private-sector-oriented Québec Federation of Labour (FTQ) is setting the tone. At its May 1990 convention, the CSN followed suit, publicly endorsing concertation with management and government.

The "Forum pour l'emploi" in November 1989 (see Milner, 1989a) proved an important turning point in the evolution toward concertation (and went largely unnoticed outside of French-speaking Québec). It brought together 1,500 participants from labour, business, government, and the voluntary sector to discuss ways of cooperating to reduce unemployment. A featured plenary on "the role of the partners in the labour market" gave top Québec business and labour leaders the chance to compare notes on "concertation, economic policy and employment" with representatives of Swedish business and labour. At the final plenary, the members of the board of the forum presented a joint declaration followed by testimonials from leading labour and business members. Of particular note was the strong commitment to work in concertation with employers expressed by Gérald Larose, president of the CSN. And, in an equally positive statement, Lorraine Pagé, president of the CEQ, acknowledged the deplorable state of the province's education system when it came to preparing young people for the work force of tomorrow—an assessment that emerged repeatedly from the workshop discussions—and pledged her organization to work with employers and administrators to do something about it.

It is inconceivable that a Québec teachers' union leader could have made such a statement a few years earlier. On matters concerning vocational education and training, it is not possible now, as was the norm in the 1970s and early 1980s, for teachers' unions simply to rule out cooperation with business. Of course, the extent to which the new verbal openness toward concertation translates into changing attitudes at the level of the schools and thereby leads to tangible progress is another question. There is no shortage of long-awaited improvements needed. For example, a recent report found that despite the great need for technically trained graduates, as compared to the tight labour market for those with general degrees, the proportion of CEGEP (junior college) students in this sector declined from 51 to 44 percent between 1980 and 1989. In the crucial areas of electrotechnology and data processing, the decline between 1984 and 1989 was 48.2 and 51.3 percent respectively. There were less than half as many graduate technicians as needed to fill the total of vacancies in civil and mechanical engineering, electronics, and control instrumentation (Brunet, 1991).

Bright spots at this point are local and sporadic. While no systematic information is available, reports of activities in several regions signal some encouraging developments. One such region lies to the southeast of Montréal with at least three functioning "tables de concertation éducation-industrie," one covering Granby-Bromont, another the Sorel-Tracy area, and a third the steel-based industries in the region. In each, representatives of the school boards and CEGEPs have been working with leading industrialists at providing the training needed, with varying degrees of success (Henripin, 1990). Obstacles noted include a certain inflexibility in the relevant administrative structures in the MEQ and other ministries, and the absence, so far, of the teachers' unions. It remains to be seen whether tripartite initiatives at the centre spawned by the continued work of the "Forum pour l'emploi" will trickle their way down to affect teacher attitudes at the base.

CONCLUSION

It is a fair guess that the teachers will be the last to change. But change is still likely, especially in those regions outside Montréal where local solidarity and cohesion means that the school system can be expected to adapt more readily to the changing needs of the population. This can be seen in the relative slowness of Montréal parents' committees to request the setting up of "orientation councils" in their schools as provided for under the new Education Act (77 percent, compared to 92 percent for the rest of the province; Morazain, 1990). These councils (on which parents must constitute the majority) are responsible for adopting the school's "educational project," rules of conduct, an ' policies concerning scheduling changes and off-school visits.[6] In general, Québec's evolution from confrontation toward concertation (Milner, 1990) faces the most significant impediments in Montréal. Beyond the confessional and overly complex nature of the structures of the public school systems in Montréal, there is the ethnic and sociocultural diversity that further dilutes local solidarities already weak due to the nature of cities in which teachers and other school employees are very unlikely to be themselves residents in the school community.[7]

What then of the future? If the analysis here presented is accurate, the problems can be seriously addressed only if structural obstacles to the mobilization of the needed energies can be removed. There is some ground for optimism: the Québec Court of Appeal ruling on Bill 107 has a reasonable chance of being upheld by the Supreme Court of Canada. This would—finally—pave the way for replacing the Catholic and Protestant boards by French and English ones. Such a development, although entailing serious problems of adjustment, should enhance the possibility of greater participation through the investment of more human resources in, and also free up more in the way of financial resources for, public education.

We cannot leave this discussion without at least touching upon a more profound constitutional change in the future, one certain to have a very pronounced effect on the education system. In the wake of the June 1990 failure of the Meech Lake Constitutional Accord to win the necessary Canadian support, Québec set up an enlarged parliamentary commission to consult the people and report on its constitutional future. The deliberations of the Bélanger-Campeau Commission, as well as the dramatic evolution of majority public opinion in Québec since 1989 in favour of sovereignty, suggest that change in relationship with Canada is in the offing. Two aspects of this relationship are of particular concern here. First is the fact that an inevitable new reallocation of powers will strengthen Québec's already powerful hold over education, with jurisdiction in all matters pertaining to education from day care to adult education. This includes different aspects of training and retraining, including unemployment insurance, as well as related areas such as broadcasting, immigration, and culture in order to ensure an overall coherence in policies that affect the dissemination of knowledge, information, and skills in

Québec. Such a reallocation, it should be noted, was endorsed by the "federalist" Québec Liberal Party at its March 1991 convention. It was not, however, achieved at the Charlottetown Accord in August 1992, both in Québec and Canada as a whole on October 26. Thus, only by declaring itself a sovereign state in a referendum will the people of Québec be in a position to establish independently educational structures in keeping with their needs.

Through these developments, newcomers will become clearer on the fact that they have settled in a distinct entity within or outside Canada, and that it is toward Québec that they must orient their primary efforts to integrate. While integration will always be difficult, the fading of the second dimension, that of newcomers' resentment over integrating into what they perceive to be a minority, should make for an improvement in the climate in which Québec education takes place.

The final issue, that of the participation of teachers and their unions in cooperative efforts at different levels to improve the education system, may also be affected by constitutional developments. Could the unleashing of greater participatory energies lessen the polarization that has characterized labour–management relations in this area? Ultimately, the success of a sovereign Québec in attaining its goals lies not in its constitutional relationship with Canada, but in its ability to build institutions that serve the long-term needs of its people by drawing upon their resources and energies. No institutions are more important in this endeavour than the schools. No institutions are beset by more problems and failings than the public schools, especially in the Montréal area. No greater test of that resolve is thus to be found.

We should not have too long to wait to assess the results. Whether in response to a Supreme Court ruling sustaining Bill 107, or to a new constitutional arrangement, Montréalers will be in a position to establish new public-school-board structures in keeping with present realities and future needs. The success of this endeavour not only in deconfessionalizing these institutions, but in restructuring the educational system to complement municipal institutions, and in this and other ways unleashing and channelling positive energies on the part of parents and educators, will be a crucial test. As we have seen all too clearly, there is a great deal that must be improved.

The educational problems will not wait. Are the words of the trade unionists, intellectuals, politicians, and business leaders who articulate Québec's collective aspirations for the 1990s merely rhetorical, or will they, this time, be able to work together to build institutions that will put these words into action?

NOTES

1. As a general rule, I use the English name of the agency or organization, but the French acronym, since this is usually the only one commonly known. Thus, in this case, I refer to the Montréal Catholic School Commission, but use the acronym "CECM" from its French title (La Commission des écoles catholiques de Montréal).

2. Unlike in Québec so far, there has been significant reaction in many American educational jurisdictions to these kinds of findings. Several states, for example, are moving to extend the number of days in the school year.

3. A former leading official of a major Protestant board put it rather succinctly in private conversation with the author. "We knew every time [CECM Chairman] Pallascio made one of his statements, because we would get a flurry of inquiries about registering in our schools."

4. This turnout in the highly contested CECM elections in 1990 represented a modest gain over the 12 percent in 1987. While turnout is somewhat higher in most other boards, in total, more than half the positions in Québec school-board elections are filled by acclamation.
5. For example, the minutes of the April 26, 1989 CECM commissioners' meeting quoted a student as claiming to have witnessed: "pistols in the lockers, knives being carried and in the lockers, crowbars and nightsticks in the schoolbags."
6. The teachers' unions, including not only the regional associations affiliated with the CEQ, but also groups outside the CEQ such as the Protestant and English Catholic teachers' organizations and CEGEP teachers' unions, have generally been less than warmly disposed toward efforts to increase parental power in the schools. A good test will come if and when MEMO, which is committed to such empowerment, takes control of the CECM, given that MEMO received moral and financial support from the CEQ's affiliate: l'Alliance des professeurs de Montréal.
7. Discussions with Alliance officials left the author with the distinct impression that most of their members live not only far from the schools where they teach, but in suburbs outside CECM territory altogether.

REFERENCES

Balthazar, Louis, and Bélanger, Jules (1989). *L'École détournée*. Montréal: Boréal.
Barrett, Michael J. (1990). "The Case for More School Days." *The Atlantic Monthly*, November, pp. 78–106.
Beaushesne, André, and Hesler, Hélène (1987). *L'école française à clientèle pluriethnique de l'Île de Montréal: situation du français et intégration psychosociale des élèves*. Montréal: Conseil de la langue française.
Bellemare, Diane, and Poulin-Simon, Lise (1986). *Le Défi du plein emploi*. Montréal: Albert Saint-Martin.
Bernier, Nicole France (1990). "Le secteur privé en croissance constant." *Le Devoir* (Publispécial: "écoles privées"), 16 November, pp. 4–5.
Bezeau, Lawrence M. (1979). "The Public Finance of Private Education in the Province of Québec." *Canadian Journal of Education*, 4(2), pp. 23–42.
——— (1985). "Level and Inequality of Per Pupil Expenditure as a Function of Finance Centralization." Paper presented at the Annual Meeting of the Canadian Society for the Study of Education (Montréal, May).
Boisvert, M.A. (1980). *Le Canada face à l'expérience des pays nordiques. Les implications économiques de la souveraineté-association*. Montréal: Presses de l'Université de Montréal.
Brunet, Alain (1991). "La formation technique au collégial: emplois nombreux, pénurie de diplomés." *La Presse*, 3 January, pp. 2–3.
Chubb, John E., and Moe, Terry M. (1988). *Politics, Markets, and American Schools*. Washington, D.C.: Brookings Institution.
Coleman, James S., Hoffer, Thomas, and Kilgore, Sally (1982). *High School Achievement*. New York: Basic Books.
Demers, Dominique (1990). "La CECM est-elle de bonne foi?" *L'Actualité*, 1 September, pp. 34–38.
Desbiens, Jean-Paul (1989). "Preface" to Migué, Jean-Luc, and Marceau, Richard (1989). *Le Monopole public de l'éducation*. Québec: Presses de l'Université du Québec.
Ferland, Mireille, and Rocher, Guy (1987). *La Loi 101 et l'école primaire à clientèle pluriethnique de l'Île de Montréal: perceptions des intervenants*. Montréal: Conseil de la langue française.
Grandjean, Patrick (1990). "Immigration: Le fait français dans l'île de Montréal menacé, selon le CSIM." *La Presse*, 22 January, p. B7.
Grosvenor, Gilbert (1989). "Superpowers not super in Geography." *National Geographic*, December, pp. 816–18.
Henripin, Marthe (1990). *Partenariat Éducation—Monde du travail 1,2,3*. Québec: Direction générale de la formation professionnelle, MEQ.
Lauroesch, William (1979). "Québec: Early Warning System for American Higher Education?" *Journal of Collective Negotiations in the Public Sector*, 8(4), pp. 333–38.
Leclerc, Jean-Claude (1990). "La bêtise d'un 'sondage.' " *Le Devoir*, 7 November.
Léger, Marie-France (1990). "Au Québec, le quart des 'analphabètes' ont plus d'une neuvième année de scolarité." *La Presse*, 27 November, p. A16.
———. (1991). "Il faut 56 millions pour les enfants pauvres et immigrants." *Le Presse*, 19 February, pp. A1–2.

Levine, Marc. V. (1990). *The Reconquest of Montreal: Language Policy and Social Change in a Bilingual City.* Philadelphia: Temple University Press.

MEQ (1989a). *Statistiques de l'éducation.* Direction générale de la recherche et du développement.

MEQ. Comité d'étude (1989b). *Les Bibliothèques scolaires québécoises.* Québec: May.

———. (1990). "La Qualité du français à l'école: une responsabilité partagée." *Avis au Ministre de l'Éducation.* October.

Migué, Jean-Luc, and Marceau, Richard (1989). *Le Monopole public de l'éducation.* Québec: Presses de l'Université du Québec.

Milner, Henry (1977). "The Rise and Fall of the Quebec Liberals: Some Contradictions in the Contemporary Quebec State," in L. Panitch, ed., *The Canadian State: Political Economy and Political Power.* Toronto: University of Toronto, Press, 1977.

———. (1978) *Politics in the New Québec.* Toronto: McClelland and Stewart.

———. (1986). *The Long Road to Reform: Restructuring Public Education in Québec.* Montréal: McGill-Queen's University Press.

———. (1989a). "Le Forum pour l'emploi: A Sign of Things to Come in Québec?" Paper presented at the 1989 meetings of ACSUS, San Francisco.

———. (1989b). *Sweden: Social Democracy in Practice.* Oxford: Oxford University Press.

———. (1990). "Québec in Retrospect: Beyond Political Nostalgia," *Québec Studies,* 11, pp. 75–82.

Morazain, Jeanne (1990). "Les parents ont-ils une influence réelle?" *Le Devoir* (Publispécial: "Éducation: école et démocratie"), 17 August, pp. c1, c1b.

Papale, Antimo (1981). "The Impact of Centralized Bargaining in Québec." *Phi Delta Kappan,* 63(4), pp. 250–51.

Rioux, Christiane (1990). "Ghettos, mode d'emploi." *L'Actualité,* 1 September, pp. 39–44.

Sprout, Alison L. (1990) "Do U.S. Schools Make the Grade?" *Fortune,* Spring, pp. 50–52.

Tellier, Luc Normand (1977). *Le Québec: État Nordique.* Montréal: Les Éditions Quinze.

———. (1978). *Étude des possibilités de rapprochement économique entre le Québec, le Canada, et les pays scandinaves.* Québec: Ministère des affaires intergouvernementales.

Witte, John F. (1990). "Understanding High School Achievement: After a Decade of Research, Do We Have Any Confident Policy Recommendations?" Paper presented at the 1990 meetings of the American Political Science Association, San Francisco.

English-Speaking Québec: The Emergence of a Disillusioned Minority

Ronald Rudin
Concordia University

In the 1989 Québec provincial election English-speaking Quebeckers[1] did something that they had never done before. While elections had been held in the province for nearly two centuries, there had never been a case of a general election in which most English speakers supported a party that was designed exclusively to address their particular grievances. In this case, roughly 70 percent of the members of the linguistic minority voted for candidates of the Equality Party, a newly formed party committed, among other things, to rolling back the various pieces of language legislation that had been introduced in Québec over the previous fifteen years. This commitment to "English rights" led the residents of four heavily English-speaking ridings in the western half of Montréal Island to elect Equality Party candidates to sit in the National Assembly.[2]

There certainly were other moments in the history of Québec at which English speakers distinguished themselves by giving the vast majority of their votes to a particular party.[3] In the years leading up to the rebellions of 1837, for instance, English speakers strongly supported the so-called Bureaucratic Party that was opposed to Louis-Joseph Papineau and his *Parti patriote*. The minority found itself supporting a party that sought gradual constitutional reform, and while this might have had particular appeal to the minority, the platform was not phrased in terms that could only appeal to English speakers (Ouellet, 1976:389). English speakers have also spoken with a single voice in various provincial elections throughout the post-Confederation era. The English-speaking minority provided almost no support to Honoré Mercier, the first openly nationalistic premier of the province, in the late 19th century; nor did it show much enthusiasm for the Union Nationale of Maurice Duplessis in the post–World War II era. As for the Parti Québécois, English speakers have never shown the least bit of interest from its inception in the late 1960s.

In all of these cases, the votes of English speakers went en bloc to the party that seemed the least hostile to their interests. In Mercier's time, this meant supporting the provincial Conservative Party, while in post–World War II Québec it has meant supporting the provincial Liberal Party. In none of these cases, however, did the English-speaking minority find itself opting en masse for political formations that were designed to serve its interests exclusively. For instance, while English speakers may have voted overwhelmingly for the provincial Liberals since the 1940s, they were joined in the process by large numbers of French speakers, so much so that the minority began to wonder whether its interests were being adequately served. These concerns were well founded since the leaders of the party understood both that English speakers made up a relatively insignificant part of the Liberals' base of support and, even more significantly, that the minority constituted an electorate with no other viable option.

English speakers indicated a certain discomfort with their relationship with the Liberals in the 1976 provincial election, which followed closely after the Liberal government's introduction of legislation to restrict the use of English. Incapable of supporting the other major party, the Parti Québécois, because of its *indépendantiste* leanings, the minority turned to the remnants of the Union Nationale, which was making one last effort to stay alive. There was nothing in the program of the Union Nationale that should have particularly appealed to English speakers other than the opportunity to express discontent with the Liberals. The strategy was hardly a successful one in that the votes that were taken away from the Liberals allowed the Parti Québécois to elect candidates in a number of ridings where the English were very much in the minority. In those ridings where they made up a sizable minority or even the majority of the voters, particularly in the western half of the Island of Montréal, their protest vote prevented the election of only a single Liberal candidate.

In the aftermath of further language legislation introduced by a Liberal government, English speakers were prepared to try a different gambit in the 1989 provincial election. In this case the issue that inflamed passions was Bill 178, which forbade the use of English on external commercial advertising.[4] Once more, if the minority wished to abandon the Liberals it was faced with the even more disagreeable option of supporting the Parti Québécois; and on this occasion there was not even a Union Nationale on the scene that might be employed to register the population's anger. It was in this context that the Equality Party was formed, claiming from the very start to be a vehicle for the disillusionment of the English-speaking minority. Other minor parties had been formed in the past, but they all quickly disappeared, having failed to gain more than a few votes; what was special about the Equality Party was that it managed to mobilize the *overwhelming majority* of the English-speaking electorate.

Such a political response could not have been mounted at any earlier moment in the history of English-speaking Québec. The following sections of this essay are designed to explain why such behaviour had not been possible over the previous 230 years. The first section deals with the period from the Conquest of Québec in 1759 to the coming of the Quiet Revolution in 1960. Over these two centuries English speakers rarely identified themselves as members of a minority. Accordingly, political mobilization in the defence of minority rights was inconceivable. The second section then deals with the period since the 1960s during which English speakers have been forced by circumstances to alter their self-image. Having finally come to recognize their minority status, English speakers quickly moved to equip themselves with the means to participate fully in a largely French-speaking world. In spite of the spectacular growth of bilingualism, many English speakers came to feel by the late 1980s that there was really nothing they could do that would allow them to be considered as legitimate Québécois. With the prospect of integration diminished, but with their minority status deeply ingrained, English speakers were prepared to use all of the means at their disposal, including a political party of their own, to fight for their interests.

A MINORITY IN FACT BUT NOT IN MIND

By and large, the immigrants who came to Québec to form part of the English mother tongue population arrived with no firm commitment to remain here for any length of time and with hardly any conception that they were coming to a territory, most of whose inhabitants spoke French. This was certainly the case for the earliest of English speakers, the businessmen of English and Scottish origins who followed the British army into this new part of the British Empire. They quickly came to dominate the fur trade in the late 18th century, and in the 19th century were active in the development of a transcontinental economy through their central role in the establishment and operation of banks, railways, and industries. By the start of the 20th century they had accumulated so much power that the part of Montréal where their magnificent residences were concentrated, the so-called Golden Square Mile, could boast the presence of the holders of three-quarters of the wealth in Canada.[5]

These businessmen lived in a community that was effectively sealed off from the French-speaking world that existed only kilometres to the east. They used their wealth to support a wide range of cultural and educational institutions, but these facilities were largely patronized by other English speakers. These men similarly had little reason to come into contact with French-speaking Québec in the daily operation of their businesses. Montréal had originally been chosen as a base of operations for British businessmen who were looking to secure profits from the Canadian hinterland that extended to the west. The city was attractive because it stood at the farthest point inland that could be reached by ships sailing the Atlantic. That Montréal was within a larger territory most of whose residents spoke French was of no particular interest to businessmen who perceived Québec, when they thought about it at all, as a feudal relic from the French regime that held few prospects for profit; by contrast, Ontario and later the Prairies were seen in a very different light.

The orientation of these businessmen was reflected in the affairs of the Bank of Montréal, which was established in 1817 largely to facilitate the movement of grain from Upper Canada to Montréal for subsequent shipment to Liverpool. As the 19th century progressed and the branches of the bank multiplied, relatively little effort was made to penetrate the province. When offices were established in Québec, however, the Bank of Montréal and other English-run banks tended to opt for towns with important English-speaking populations even when there were significant opportunities for investment within French-speaking communities. In addition, the Bank of Montréal had few French-speaking employees during the 19th century, and there was not a single francophone director of the bank from the 1840s until well into the 20th century (Rudin, 1985a:9–16).

Given the nature of both their private and public lives, English-speaking busi-nessmen had little reason to think about developments in Québec, and there cer-tainly was no reason why they should have conceived of themselves as members of a minority. Moreover, they had no sentimental attachment to prevent them from leaving when the economic attractions that had brought them to Montréal in the first place began to pale in the early 20th century. In the aftermath of World War I, the United States replaced Great Britain as the major source of foreign capital for Canada, with the result that Montréal lost one of its major functions as the hinge for an economy that extended to London to the east and to the Prairies to the west. Toronto soon assumed the role vis-à-vis American capital that Montréal had once occupied in terms of British funds. Industry began to concentrate in the Toronto region, the Toronto stock exchange came to supplant the Montreal exchange, and by the 1950s the construction of the St. Lawrence Seaway made it possible for ocean-going ships to avoid Montréal altogether, thus neutralizing one of the city's initial attractions. Accordingly, by the post–World War II era many firms had put a freeze on the expansion of their Montréal operations, and a few were starting to shift their affairs out of Montréal to Toronto.

In the 1970s such activities would receive sensationalistic coverage in the English press, but in the late 1940s and 1950s they were seldom discussed. Nev-ertheless, the ease with which the moves were made spoke volumes about the weak integration of these businessmen into the fabric of Québec society. Their businesses depended upon Montréal, narrowly defined, so that once the compara-tive advantages of the city dried up there was little to keep them here. But while there were signs of an exodus from Québec on the part of the English-speaking elite on the eve of the Quiet Revolution, the tendency for poorer members of the minority to leave when economic conditions seemed brighter elsewhere had been evident since the 19th century.

These "ordinary" English speakers came to Québec in a number of waves in the late 18th and the first half of the 19th centuries. The first of these immigrants were Americans who acquired land in the Eastern Townships and Ottawa Valley. Their ranks were supplemented, following the end of the Napoleonic wars, by the arrival of poor immigrants escaping from misery in both Scotland and Ireland. In the 1840s the newcomers were almost exclusively Irish immigrants fleeing from the potato famine. Due to these significant movements of population, English speak-ers constituted 25 percent of the population of Québec in 1851; after mid-century this percentage steadily declined to stand at 15 percent by the start of the 1960s (Rudin, 1985b:28).

The arrival of the Americans, Scots, and Irishmen had resulted in the rapid growth of the English-speaking population in the early 19th century; now the departure of these very same people or of their successors was largely responsible for the relative decline of the linguistic minority. Much like the English-speaking elite, these less prestigious immigrants had not come to Québec for any other rea-son than it provided a convenient stopping off spot in the search for greater wealth in North America. During their stay in Québec, they may have developed a close identification with their immediate community, which usually was populated by other English speakers. Unlike their French-speaking counterparts, however, they felt little attachment to the larger territory of Québec. In the case of the linguistic majority, this attachment did not necessarily preclude leaving the province.

Nevertheless, constrained by the potential threat to their language and culture, French speakers rarely travelled far from home, with the result that in the late 19th century they eschewed the newly opened lands of the Canadian Prairies for the nearby industrial towns of New England.

English speakers, on the other hand, once better prospects presented themselves elsewhere, felt no reason to stay either in or close to Québec. Accordingly, the English speakers of American ancestry in the Eastern Townships started to leave in substantial numbers in the late 1800s, with the residents of the Ottawa Valley following suit by the early 20th century. So dramatic was the exodus from the Townships that one journalist was moved to find a papist plot afoot (Sellar, 1974). Of course, there was no plot, but only the desire to exchange marginal land in Québec for what appeared to be better land in the Prairies (Little, 1980; Rudin, 1984). As for the Irish, they, too, slowly moved off to greener pastures, frequently to join their countrymen in the large Irish communities in American cities.

During their stay in Québec these English speakers, much like their co-linguists from the business community, generally remained isolated from the larger French-speaking population. In the Eastern Townships, for instance, English speakers were not evenly distributed across the landscape, but rather were concentrated in a few well-defined pockets. As a result, when the Québec educational system took shape in the mid-19th century and separate schools were established for Catholics and Protestants there were few communities in the region that required more than a single school (Rudin, 1985b:105). In the Eastern Townships most Catholics were French, and nearly all Protestants were English speakers, so that the apparent religious segregation reflected the existence of a certain linguistic segregation as well.

The situation of the Irish, particularly that of those who lived in Montréal and Québec City, was somewhat different in that they were largely Catholic. Nevertheless, even their sharing of a common religion with the French-speaking majority did not facilitate contact. In fact, from the very inception of public education in the two cities there were English schools established for the Irish, a situation that was found agreeable for both the Irish, who sought an English education to permit subsequent mobility, and for the French-Catholic hierarchy, which believed that the survival of the French-Catholic population was linked to its isolation from outsiders.

Weakly integrated into the province's institutions, the successors to the immigrants of the 19th century saw themselves as part of a larger English-speaking majority that populated North America, and when economic circumstances warranted they moved along. In the first half of the 20th century these departures were largely made up for, in terms of the demographic fortunes of the English-speaking population, by the resumption of significant immigration to Québec. What distinguished these immigrants from those who had preceded them, however, was the fact that they came to Québec speaking neither French nor English. Inevitably, in a generation or two the mother tongue brought with the immigrants would pass away; the question that remained was whether English or French would come to be the family's new mother tongue. The demographic fortunes of both the French- and English-speaking populations would be greatly influenced by such decisions.

Up to the depression, the most significant of these new immigrants were Jews who largely came to Québec speaking only Yiddish. Like the wealthy immigrants who had preceded them by more than a century, the Jews thought of the province solely in terms of Montréal, where they created their own community, reasonably well isolated from the French majority as they largely adopted English as the language to pass along to subsequent generations. This isolation was evident in the fact that by 1931 there were 30,000 Jews in Québec, more than 10 years of age, who spoke English in addition to their mother tongue, but only 112 who had adopted French as their second language (Rudin, 1985b:165). The adoption of English was, of course, a logical decision given that it was the vehicle for social mobility both in Montréal and across North America. Since there was a distinct possibility that the Jews might want to move elsewhere on the continent, facility in English provided a passport to leave Québec and to join Jewish communities elsewhere.

When Jewish immigration fell off in the 1930s, the slack was taken up by various other groups also coming from Europe, most notably the Greeks, Portuguese, and Italians. None of these groups integrated into the English-speaking population en bloc as had the Jews. For instance, the vast majority of Italians consistently passed along French as the mother tongue once the language from Europe had faded away. But even if only a small percentage of such immigrants formally "joined" the linguistic minority, they collectively constituted a significant, and growing, percentage of the post–World War II English-speaking population.

The Italians who passed along English to their children most likely first put a foot in the English stream by means of the "Irish" schools of the Montréal Catholic School Commission. There is some evidence to suggest that the French-Catholic hierarchy was no more enthusiastic about absorbing Italian and Portuguese children than it had been about taking on Irish pupils a century earlier (Taddeo and Taras, 1987). Be that as it may, the Italian parents who opted for English schools for their children made it quite clear in the early 1960s that the most important consideration in their decision was the desire to "facilitate moving to other parts of Canada" (Boissevain, 1970:38).

An Italian who opted for inserting a child into the English-speaking population of Québec was providing future generations with the means of leaving the province. This theme of mobility runs through the experience of all of the groups that contributed to the development of the linguistic minority in the two centuries following the Conquest. The members of these groups variously identified themselves as English Canadians, North Americans, Montréalers, Townshippers, Jews, or Italians; only rarely in the pre-1960 period did they see themselves as Quebeckers, a situation that is hardly surprising given their relative isolation from the French-speaking population. Accordingly, English speakers as a group had little incentive for thinking of themselves as members of a cohesive linguistic minority, much less to consider establishing a political party to champion their interests. This disinclination was further encouraged by the general absence of initiatives coming from Québec City that could be perceived as particularly threatening, but this would all change in the years beyond 1960.

COMING TO GRIPS WITH MINORITY STATUS

English speakers distinguished themselves in the two centuries following the Conquest by their predisposition to leave Québec if conditions appeared less than ideal, and they only reinforced this image in the decades following the election of

Jean Lesage as premier in 1960. But while the earlier exodus was relatively tranquil and almost totally ignored by the press, the departure of English speakers after 1960 became an emotionally charged issue as it was connected to the efforts on the part of a newly assertive Québec government to strengthen the role of French and of French speakers in the province.

The election of Lesage brought about the beginning of the Quiet Revolution, and with it a new role for the state, in the process triggering unprecedented expectations on the part of the linguistic majority. In short order, the Québec government, which had been seen as benign by the English-speaking population because of its laissez-faire approach to most issues, became a force to be reckoned with. Hydroelectric power was nationalized, a centralized educational system was created, and numerous new departments and agencies were established to encourage the social and economic well-being of the population. English speakers listened uneasily, however, as these reforms were trumpeted as efforts to make Quebeckers feel that they were "masters in their own house." The linguistic minority could not help but pick up on the fact that the new masters would be French; the fate of English speakers in this house remained ambiguous.

To many, the ambiguity was resolved by the demands that were being made upon Ottawa throughout the decade for increased powers to further the aims of the Quiet Revolution. Heretofore mainstream politicians such as René Lévesque, frustrated with the federal government's apparent unwillingness to consider fundamental changes, left the Québec Liberal Party and before the end of the decade had established the Parti Québécois as a vehicle for achieving the sovereignty of Québec. Still other Quebeckers took matters into their own hands, planting bombs and, in the case of the October Crisis of 1970, taking hostages to achieve "national liberation." Even the peaceful demonstrations in the streets that called for a "Québec aux Québécois" made it clear that English speakers were now operating within a new, and often hostile, environment.

Still, English speakers were left to wonder how all of these changes would effect their everyday lives. They received a small taste of what the future held in store in 1969 when the Catholic school commissioners in the Montréal suburb of St-Léonard declared that henceforth education would only be provided in French. Such an action stood to strike the substantial Italian community in the district very hard, since it would be deprived of access to English schools. More globally, English speakers understood that an interruption to the integration of groups such as the Italians into the English population would have grave consequences in the face of the ongoing departure of English speakers from the province. Throughout most of the 20th century the absolute growth of the linguistic minority had only been possible because of the integration of these immigrant groups; any interruption in the flow would have serious implications.

This doomsday scenario was avoided in 1969 by the passage by the Union Nationale government of relatively innocuous legislation (Bill 63) that did not fundamentally challenge the parents' right to educate their children in either French or English. The worst fears of English speakers came true, however, with the introduction of Bill 22 in 1974. By declaring that French was the only official language of the province, by restricting access to English schools to children who could pass an English proficiency test, and by introducing some very tentative attempts to make French the language of business in the province, English speakers, if they had not already done so, were forced to come to grips with the fact that they made up a minority within a largely French-speaking jurisdiction. This realization was only reinforced by the coming of the Parti Québécois to power in 1976 and the introduction in 1977 of Bill 101, which built upon the steps toward francization first taken in Bill 22.

In the short term, English speakers found it almost impossible to respond constructively to these challenges to their future. By the late 1970s English speakers had over two centuries of experience in identifying with their immediate neighbours when times were good and in leaving the province when better opportunities existed outside Québec. By contrast, they had almost no experience in lobbying to support their point of view as members of a minority within the province. Accordingly, in the late 1970s and early 1980s English speakers did what they did best, and left the province in unprecedented numbers. While mobility had always been one of the English speakers' distinguishing characteristics, between 1976 and 1986 the exodus took on unprecedented proportions, with the result that a population that had numbered roughly 800,000 in 1976 was reduced to 678,000 ten years later (Rudin, 1985b:30; Bourbeau, 1989:26).

Some individual English speakers and some directors of English-run businesses publicly proclaimed their unwillingness to remain in a province where there were restrictions upon the freedom of all citizens to use the language of their choosing in both the public and private sectors. To some in the French community such public declarations were interpreted as threats of blackmail against the use of the state as the majority saw fit. Both sides threw taunts at each other, while the media whipped up hysteria that may have sold newspapers but did little for restoring meaningful dialogue between the two linguistic groups.

Of course, it was difficult for the English-speaking population to advance a coherent view of its future role in Québec in the absence of any organization that might legitimately speak for it as a whole. The obstacles to the creation of such an organization were considerable: the absence of any tradition of lobbying as a Québec minority, together with the ethnic and regional diversity within the linguistic minority that made charting a common direction complicated, to say the least. There was a glimmer, however, that these problems had been surmounted with the establishment of Alliance Québec in 1982. While the organization could not avoid criticism that it did not represent all English speakers, it was accepted throughout most of the 1980s by the Québec government as the legitimate bargaining agent for English speakers. Through its constructive efforts, concrete gains were achieved such as the passage of legislation in 1986 that guaranteed English speakers health and social services in their own language.

By the mid-1980s the English-speaking population was looking for constructive ways to participate in the "new" Québec as those English speakers who had consciously chosen to remain worked at defining their new, and historically unprecedented, identity as members of a minority. Once the yelling and recriminations ended, it became clear that the minority had decided finally to invest considerable energy to function in the language of the majority. While the rate of bilingualism among English speakers had hovered around the 30 percent mark across most of the 20th century, it shot up from 37 percent to 53 percent between 1971 and 1981; by 1986 the figure was approaching 60 percent (Rudin, 1985b:282; Bourbeau, 1989:31).

While this increased bilingualism was partly a reflection of the departure of those who spoke only English, it was also attributable to the marked growth in the enrolment of English-speaking children in various French-language programs in the schools. In 1976 only 14 percent of these children were in either French-immersion programs, in which there was also teaching in English, or regular French schools where English would only be offered as a second language. By 1987 this figure had reached 35 percent, and by the close of the decade roughly 50 percent of all English-speaking students were enrolled.[6] It seems reasonable to assume that in the 1990s the traditional English school in which French is given relatively little emphasis will become the option for a shrinking minority of the population.

By the late 1980s there was a certain satisfaction on the part of English speakers that they had, in a relatively short time, shorn themselves of centuries of behaviour that had allowed them to ignore their true status within Québec. They were no longer the "White Rhodesians" that René Lévesque had once called them, but rather responsible citizens trying to follow the lead of the majority. While English speakers continued to leave, albeit in smaller numbers, those who stayed felt that they had made a commitment and were prepared to do what was necessary so that they and their children might function as real "Québécois." I was certainly convinced that a corner had been turned when I wrote, in 1985, that a new era in the history of English-speaking Québec had been entered (Rudin, 1985b:281).

Between the writing of those words and the 1989 provincial election something changed to permit the rise of the Equality Party. The trigger was no doubt the passage of Bill 178, which employed the "notwithstanding" clause of both the Québec and Canadian Charters of Rights to side-step a Supreme Court ruling that Bill 101's banning of bilingual commercial signs was unconstitutional. In a sense, then, Québec had simply returned to the situation in the immediate aftermath of the passage of Bill 101 more than a decade earlier. The difference was, however, that English speakers had changed, and more importantly, they thought that they deserved some respect for the changes that they had undergone. They were told that they had been doing all of the "right" things to be real Quebeckers; so why were their rights being suspended? Were they being told that no matter what they did they could never hope to be truly at home in Québec? Such a suspicion was certainly fuelled by the apparent inability of English speakers to penetrate the Québec civil service, even though most members of the minority were now equipped with the ability to function in French.

This sense of anxiety in the aftermath of the passage of Bill 178 was no doubt fuelled as well by the Meech Lake Accord, which had not yet died by the time of the 1989 Québec election. English speakers perceived that the provisions in the accord that empowered the Québec government to act as it saw fit to preserve the distinctiveness of Québec society would allow the passage of further Bill 178s, but without even the need to skirt the Québec and Canadian Charters of Rights. Curiously, as the Meech Lake agreement tottered toward collapse in the summer of 1990, English speakers started to become some of its warmest supporters as they correctly sensed that the defeat of the agreement could only result in Québec demands for even greater autonomy, and possibly even independence. No one writing in the spring of 1992 would want to predict the future. Suffice it to say that

English speakers would now gladly embrace the Meech Lake Accord over the other more threatening constitutional proposals of Québec's two main provincial parties.

In the fall of 1989, faced with both Bill 178 and the spectre of Meech Lake, English speakers voted en masse for the Equality Party. In the 1970s this population had found itself largely incapable of organizing any coherent response to the legislation that troubled it, but this was not the same population at the end of the 1980s. Reed Scowen, the chairman of Alliance Québec, was only slightly exaggerating the situation when he observed that a population that had traditionally had "no collective identity to speak of" now, due to the force of circumstances, had become a "community" (Scowen, 1991:25). One might argue that the word "community" is inappropriate for a population that is united only by a sense of grievance regarding linguistic issues. Nevertheless, Scowen was correct in observing that this was a population that now could be politically mobilized to defend what it perceived as its collective interests.

At the very least, English speakers had come to accept the fact that they constituted a coherent minority within Québec, quite independent of whatever competing identities they may have possessed. At the same time, the population by the close of the 1980s was in a churlish mood, feeling that it had been given little credit for having finally accommodated itself to the French fact. One might well ask whether a minority should be thanked for recognizing its true status after more than 200 years during which most of its members lived as if the French majority barely existed. Be that as it may, English speakers did feel betrayed, and while in the past they would have been incapable of mobilizing their forces for effective protest, they now had acquired the tools of organization that a minority requires to advance its interests. So when the Equality Party was launched it found a ready audience, although no one could have anticipated the level of support that it would garner in the 1989 election. As Scowen observed with some accuracy, "The creation and the success of the Equality Party [was] a logical consequence of the birth of a real Quebec English community" (Scowen, 1991:139).

CONCLUSION

The success of the Equality Party, however short-lived it might prove to be, provides a reasonably accurate reflection of the mood of the English-speaking population at the end of the 1980s. It is impossible to know what the future holds for English-speaking Québec; there are simply too many issues regarding both the place of Québec within Canada and that of English speakers within Québec that remain unresolved as this essay is being written. Nevertheless, as long as English speakers feel, rightly or wrongly, that there are obstacles to their acceptance as full-fledged members of Québec society, there will be room for the Equality Party or some other political formation with the same appeal.

Such a party would have had no attraction to the English-speaking population during the centuries during which it had failed to see itself as constituting a minority; nor would the party have had very much appeal during the brief period in the 1980s when English speakers perceived that they were successfully integrating themselves into Québec society. The political situation by the end of the 1980s dampened the minority's optimism about the future, and although there is no reason to believe that English speakers will turn their back on their efforts to operate in French, their support for the Equality Party indicated a certain disillusionment with developments in Québec. This malaise grew out of the realization that the simple ability to function in the language of the majority would not necessarily be rewarded in any tangible way. English speakers had not yet learned that a minority, by its very nature, cannot achieve its own goals when they are at odds with those of the majority. This was precisely the case in terms of the passage of Bill 178, which effectively pitted the interests of the majority against those of the minority. Inevitably, the minority will lose in such situations, no matter what efforts it has made to accommodate itself to its minority status. Until English speakers learn this lesson, there will be a place for an Equality Party.

NOTES

1. Throughout this essay the English-speaking population is defined as including all Quebeckers with English as their mother tongue.
2. A small number of English speakers, largely outside Montréal, also supported a second protest party, the Unity Party. Taken together the vote of the two parties would easily exceed 70 percent of the anglophone vote. See the calculations by Pierre Drouilly in *Le Devoir*, 4 October 1989.
3. Much of the historical background in this essay was first discussed in my *The Forgotten Quebecers* (Québec: Institut Québécois de recherche sur la culture, 1985).
4. While English would be accepted under certain circumstances on signs within commercial establishments, only French could be used externally.
5. Life in the Golden Square Mile at the start of this century has recently been chronicled by Margaret Westley in *Remembrance of Grandeur: The Anglo-Protestant Elite of Montreal, 1900–50* (Montréal: Libre Expression, 1990).
6. These figures were derived from *Clientèle scolaire des organismes d'enseignement* (Québec: Ministère de l'éducation, 1976–87).

REFERENCES

Boissevain, Jeremy (1970). *The Italians of Montreal*. Ottawa: Ministry of Supply and Services.

Bourbeau, Robert (1989). *Canada—A Linguistic Profile*. Ottawa: Ministry of Supply and Services.

Little, J.I. (1980). "Watching the Frontier Disappear." *Journal of Canadian Studies*, vol. 15, no. 4, pp. 93–111.

Ouellet, Fernand (1976). *Le Bas Canada*. Ottawa: Les éditions de l'Université d'Ottawa.

Rudin, Ronald (1984). "The Transformation of the Eastern Townships of Richard William Heneker." *Journal of Canadian Studies*, vol. 19, no. 3, pp. 32–49.

Rudin, Ronald (1985a). *Banking en français*. Toronto: University of Toronto Press.

Rudin, Ronald (1985b). *The Forgotten Quebecers*. Québec: Institut Québécois de recherche sur la culture.

Scowen, Reed (1991). *A Different Vision: The English in Québec in the 1990s*. Don Mills, Ont.: Maxwell Macmillan Canada.

Sellar, Robert (1974). *The Tragedy of Québec*. Toronto: University of Toronto Press.

Taddeo, Donat and Taras, Raymond (1987). *Le débat linguistique au Québec*. Montréal: Les Presses de l'Université de Montréal.

20

Québec and the Aboriginal Question*

Éric Gourdeau
Consultant, Québec City

INTRODUCTION

It is probably superfluous to remind the reader that the aboriginal question is in Québec a subject of great importance and acute actuality. Indeed, very few people, if any, will have forgotten the shocks produced by the Oka Crisis in the summer and autumn of 1990: Mohawk Amerindians at Kanasatake positioning during seventy-eight days behind barricades erected across a public secondary road leading to the site of the proposed development of a territory to which they had vainly claimed historical or ancestral rights; closing of Mercier Bridge by their Kahnawake Mohawk brothers, a gesture of solidarity that most seriously affected daily traffic for tens of thousands of Montréalers during a period of fifty-five days; humiliation of panicked political and judicial authorities forced to draw in their claws when faced with a small group of Warriors who succeeded in equating artificially their personal and not unselfish goals to the national objectives of frustrated autochthons throughout Canada; traumatic recourse by Québec to the Canadian Armed Forces; exaggerated and exacerbated judgments passed by inside and outside observers on the general attitude of Quebeckers toward Amerindians and Inuit.

True, all that did contribute to sensitizing various layers of the population that had remained indifferent, if not amorphous, to the aboriginal question in Québec; however, it is worthwhile mentioning that Québec, probably more steadily and seriously than any other provincial jurisdiction in Canada, has gradually developed over the last three decades an interesting and respectful policy to govern its relations with those aboriginal peoples who live in its territory. The triple purpose of this chapter is to present an overview of that policy, to underline some of its

---

*This chapter draws on an argument I made in "Québec and Aboriginal Peoples," pp. 109–25 in J. Anthony Long and Menno Boldt, eds., *Governments in Conflict? Provinces and Indian Nations in Canada* (Toronto: University of Toronto Press, 1988).

most significant aspects, and to discuss some current and emerging issues and problems.

THE QUÉBEC POLICY

Breaking Historical Indifference

Since the beginning of the 1960s successive provincial governments in Québec had to develop approaches, if not policies, to deal with Amerindians and Inuit who traditionally had been considered by Québec only as federal citizens. Indeed, in 1939 the Supreme Court of Canada even sanctioned the Québec government's position that, for the purposes of interpretation of the British North America Act of 1867, the Inuit must be considered Indians (Eskimos, [1939] S.C.R. 104). Hence, formulating governmental policies concerning the Inuit was believed by Québec to be the sole responsibility of Ottawa, as well as dispensating services normally falling under provincial jurisdiction (e.g. education, health, etc.).

With the advent of the 1960s, however, Québec was faced with requests for mining exploration and exploitation permits in the northern part of its territory, where virtually the only permanent residents were Inuit and Indians. In spite of its constitutional status as owner of the resources there, as in the rest of the province, Québec had no presence in the area except for having commissioned since the mid-1950s some hydrology surveys by private engineering firms for the Ministry of Hydraulic Resources. The ministry, when amalgamated with the Ministry of Mines, was to become in 1961 the new Ministry of Natural Resources, within which the General Directorship of Nouveau-Québec was created in April 1963 "to assume in the Nouveau-Québec territory, with the exception of those portions already linked with the organized Québec, the administration of all the government activities except those of Québec Provincial Police, Justice and Lands and Forest" (Order-in-Council, 1963:613).

Obviously, a government development policy for this territory had to take into account the aboriginal peoples who reside there, and especially the Inuit who live in the northernmost areas, where mining permits had been requested from Québec by private developers. Not surprisingly, then, the approach approved by the cabinet two months after the creation of the Direction Générale du Nouveau-Québec (DGNQ) centred on the role of the Inuit in the economic development of New Québec (Gourdeau,1963).

Implicit in this new approach of the Québec government—the government of the Quiet Revolution—was a complete reversal of its traditional position. Québec now considered in its best interest that the native inhabitants of the territory—well adapted to a remote and harsh environment—be called upon to play a major role in its modern development and be prepared accordingly. Provincial measures were taken in the areas of education, health, and professional training; physical and financial infrastructures were set up at the local level.

The Case of Inuit, Crees, and Naskapis

Another step in the building of Québec's native policy was reached in 1974 with the negotiation of the James Bay and Northern Québec Agreement, again in view of Québec's self-interests. This time, however, it was not the government that paternalistically decided to establish rules, ways, and means to secure the participation of the autochton in the development of its middle-north; on the contrary, the Québec government and its Hydroelectric Commission, having ignored the historical rights in the territory, were forced into negotiations by an injunction granted in the Superior Court of Québec to the beneficiaries of those rights, the Crees, the Inuit and the Naskapis (*Kanatewat et al. v. S. Baie James*, 1974). The result was a 500-odd-page agreement—the James Bay and Northern Québec Agreement—that spells out in detail what can be regarded as the comprehensive government policy toward the Inuit and the Crees. The Northeastern Québec Agreement in 1978 produced the same results with regards to the Naskapis.

What is strikingly new here, in terms of the policy-making process, is the fact that this policy, resulting from hard and tight negotiations over a two year period, did not emanate from the wisdom of nonaboriginal politicians and civil servants; it was jointly established by the governments and the beneficiaries of ancestral rights on the mandatory premise that it would explicitly recognize well-defined rights and provide for their implementation through specific regimes, mutually accepted and to be given legislative protection.

Additionally, this policy differs from the earlier one in that (1) it recognizes a key role for aboriginal nations in governing themselves and in the operation and the administration of their education, health, social services, and police; (2) it confers an economic value on their ancestral activities, thus permitting some essential elements of their cultural identity to survive and develop; (3) it provides them with large sums of money that they can use for community purposes as they see fit; and (4) it establishes clearly their title to *category I lands* in certain portions (albeit limited) of the 400,000 square mile area—two-thirds of Québec—covered by the agreements, and their exclusive rights both to trap on the entire territory and to hunt and fish on *category II lands*.

Québec's Overall Policy

A Québec comprehensive policy toward its whole autochthonous population was to be developed between 1978 and 1985. The policy-making process started with a three-day conference in Québec City in December 1978, bringing together government and status Amerindian representatives from all over the province. The 125 Amerindian participants delegated by nine nations and forty bands were able to acquaint themselves with the provincial government, to expose some of their problems, and to voice their concerns to the twelve ministers who actively participated, including the premier (*Rencontre*, 1978).

Not only did the aboriginal leaders take that occasion to signal, sometimes quite bluntly, historical and actual blockages to good relationships between them and the provincial government, they also expressed some fundamental preoccupations regarding the indefeasibility of their inherited collective rights: "We intend to make the Provincial government understand that we will *no longer* tolerate any government policy which has as its goal the extinguishment of our Indian rights..." (Delisle, 1979); about the judicial route they were always obliged to take in order to have their rights and interests respected: "Why is it that the only recourse to our problems of Jurisdiction and Aboriginal rights is through the

Courts?" (Dedam, 1979); and respecting their special status: "What date are you going to recognize our Nations as Nations?" (Delisle: 1979).

Following that get-together, new forms of autochthonous representation were put into place to establish dialogue with Québec. Of course, new forms of representation had already been established through the James Bay and Northern Québec Agreement (1975) and the Northeastern Québec Agreement (1978) in order for the 8,000 Crees, the 5,000 Inuit, and the 400 Naskapis to deal directly with the Québec government; in the case of the remaining 30,000 status Indians living in the province, however, the tutorship of the federal government over them was still omnipresent, and direct aboriginal representations to the Québec government were very rare, not to say nonexistent.

Representing 3,000 Attikameks and 7,000 Montagnais, the Conseil Attikamek-Montagnais (CAM) was the first native political organization to approach the Québec government, in the months following the Québec conference, for the purpose of negotiating land claims on the basis of their ancestral rights; then, in late 1982, status and nonstatus Indians together with the Inuit created a common front both to solicit from Québec the recognition of their rights as identified and defined in fifteen principles (see Appendix I) and to request the presence of Québec's premier at the first ministers' constitutional conference of April 1983 on "matters that directly affect the Aboriginal peoples of Canada, including the identification and definition of the rights of those peoples...."

Intensive preliminary discussions were held in 1980 and 1981, but real negotiations between the CAM and Québec stopped short of really starting, in spite of the fact that Québec had agreed, in contradiction with the federal policy, not to make the extinguishment of ancestral rights a precondition to the negotiations. One of the most important reasons, although it was never stated as such, for the CAM to postpone repeatedly meetings and discussions was most likely the hopes it entertained, like the other autochthonous organizations throughout Canada, that the coming conference of the first ministers, provided for in the Constitution Act of 1982, could reinforce their bargaining position through a constitutional entrenchment of the nature and reach of those aboriginal rights that were recognized and affirmed under article 35. As everyone knows, the 1983 first ministers' conference did not meet these hopes; but the Québec aboriginal common front succeeded in having Québec participate in that conference (as well as in the ensuing constitutional conferences of 1984, 1985, and 1987) in spite of its strong reluctance to partake in any official encounter held under the aegis of a Constitution that had been adopted against its formal and categoric opposition.

"Mr. Chairman, with all due respects, I am sure that you understand it is not because you called this conference that we are here today. The one and only reason that we are here is out of respect for the native peoples, above all, obviously, those living in Québec. Their elected representatives strongly insisted that we be present and, out of solidarity with them, but at our own risk somewhat, we decided to come." This was part of René Lévesque's opening statement at the First Ministers' Conference of 1983. (Statements and Interventions by Québec delegates, First Ministers' Conference, March 1983:9). In his concluding remarks at the 1985 conference, the premier committed his government to "remain associated with the present process, at least as long as the Aboriginal peoples of Québec feel that it is desirable" (SAGMAI, 1986).

Québec is probably the only province in Canada that has been "forced" into the Canadian constitutional exercise by aboriginal nations united for that purpose. This has caused them to work actively to orient Québec's policies toward Amerindians and Inuit and to appoint their own representatives on Québec's delegations to the first ministers' conferences. As a principle, and in fact, Québec's delegations to these conferences had to comprise a majority of autochthons. Although the 1983 conference did not make substantial progress toward the nature and range of native rights, it did entrench under article 35 an amendment that gives constitutional protection to the Cree, Naskapi, and Inuit rights recognized in the James Bay and Northern Québec Agreement and in the Northeastern Québec Agreement.

In late November of 1983, six months after the constitutional conference, a parliamentary commission was held in the Québec National Assembly to hear reports submitted by aboriginal bands, groups, and peoples on their rights and needs. These three-day hearings in the National Assembly permitted the provincial elected representatives to start building up a new conscience of the rights and needs of the aboriginal peoples of Québec and of the necessity to devise patterns that would help solve the problems mentioned and others to come. At the conclusion a feeling developed regarding the opportunity, if not the necessity, for an overall Québec policy toward its autochthons to be submitted to, and approved by, the National Assembly itself (*Rencontre*, 1984).

Formulation of the Policy

One and a half years later, on March 20, 1985, the National Assembly adopted the following resolution:

The National Assembly:

Recognizes the existence of the Abenaki, Algonquin, Attikamek, Cree, Huron, Micmac, Mohawk, Montagnais, Naskapi and Inuit nations in Québec;

Considers these agreements and all future agreements and accords of the same nature to have the same value as treaties;

Subscribes to the process whereby the Government has committed itself with the Aboriginal peoples to better identifying and defining their rights—a process which rests upon historical legitimacy and the importance for Québec society to establish harmonious relations with the natives, based on mutual trust and a respect for rights;

Urges the Government to pursue negotiations with the Aboriginal nations based on, *but not limited to*, the fifteen principles it approved on February 9, 1983, subsequent to proposals submitted to it on November 30, 1982, and to conclude with willing nations, or any of their constituent communities, agreements guaranteeing them the exercise of:

(a) the right to self-government within Québec;

(b) the right to their own language, culture and traditions;

(c) the right to own and control land;

(d) the right to hunt, fish, trap, harvest and participate in wildlife management;

(e) the right to participate in, and benefit from, the economic development of Québec, so as to enable them to develop as distinct nations having their own identity and exercising their rights within Québec;

Declares that the rights of Aboriginal peoples apply equally to men and women;
Affirms its will to protect, in its fundamental laws, the rights included in the agreements concluded with the Aboriginal nations of Québec; and agrees that a permanent parliamentary forum be established to enable the Aboriginal peoples to express their rights, needs and aspirations.

The fifteen principles alluded to in the resolution, adopted by the provincial cabinet in 1983, are reproduced in Appendix I. They were adopted as a response to the fifteen principles submitted by the Coalition of the Québec Aboriginal Organizations in November 1982 (*Rencontre*, 1983).

The Philosophy Behind the Policy

Like the policy toward Inuit, Crees, and Naskapis, the official policy as expressed in the 1985 resolution centres on the signing of negotiated agreements and the legal protection to be given them. But it differs in that it is not limited to negotiating when development projects urge settlement of land claims, and in that it is not premised on the extinguishing of aboriginal rights. Rather, the policy is based on the recognition by Québec of the special status of the Amerindians and the Inuit through Assembly legislation. When the Québec premier tabled the resolution before the April 1985 first minister's conference in Ottawa, he expressed the philosophy underlying Québec's approach and policy:

But finally, no matter what Aboriginal rights may be, no matter what their "constitutionalization" may be, it will always be of primary importance that such rights can be concretely exercised and in as much as possible be exercised harmoniously. It is evident that the tribunals will always have an important part to play in matters of safeguarding entrenched rights, but we must hope to be able to find together ways of defining our modes of coexistence by taking into account not only, and maybe not even principally, the sword of Damocles which the judicial system is, but, first and foremost, the fact that we live together, that we rub elbows, as it were, on a daily basis in a given territory. (SAGMAI, 1986)

As evidenced in this official declaration and in the resolution itself, the foundation of Québec's policy is the recognition of Amerindian and Inuit nations living in Québec and possessing a specific historical, linguistic, cultural, and social identity; the objective is to conclude social contracts permitting these nations to exercise their nationhood and their rights on provincial lands. Among those rights are, of course, those entrenched in the Canadian Constitution. There are also those that Québec may additionally recognize and even "entrench" in its own Constitution. The latter, while they cannot be capriciously and unilaterally modified, can be easily altered with the consent of the National Assembly and the aboriginal nation concerned, as evidenced by the numerous modifications already made to the various pieces of legislation adopted since 1978 to implement the James Bay and Northern Québec Agreement and the Northeastern Québec Agreement, most often at the request of the beneficiaries and always with their consent.

The present Québec policy on aboriginal matters, as expressed in the 1985 resolution and the fifteen principles of 1983, crystallized under a government different from the present one and those now in power voted unanimously against the adoption of the 1985 resolution when they constituted the Opposition in the National Assembly. Their stated reason for doing so, however, was not their opposition to the essence of the resolution, but that some representatives of aboriginal nations had manifested their dissatisfaction with the text, which they felt was not sufficiently precise, and too much restricted to a provincial approach, or even, in the case of a few aboriginal nations, their reluctance to see a provincial parliament, especially before the conclusion of the constitutional process, proclaiming a policy in aboriginal matters that "only the federal parliament would have the authority to do."

It can be said that interventions of Québec's ministers have since confirmed, though, the readiness of the present government not only to support constitutional entrenchment of aboriginal peoples' right to self-government, but also to negotiate agreements on how to implement that right within the province. Thus, in February 1986, the minister in charge of Canadian Intergovernmental Affairs, Gil Rémillard, ended his opening statement to a meeting of federal, provincial, and aboriginal representatives with these words:

> In closing let me reiterate that, while our government considers that the definition and affirmation of the Autochthons' right to self-government must receive constitutional protection, it also fully realizes that governing involves not only a population to administer but also a territory to exploit and some means of action.

> That is why the modalities to implement the Autochthons' right to self-government must be defined in negotiated agreement reached in mutual respect by the Autochthons, the Federal Government and the provinces.

> In this spirit, Mr. Chairman, we have accepted to participate in this conference and those to follow, in view of a most fruitful discussion on the constitutional recognition of the rights of the Autochthons of Canada, in particular those of Québec, to self-government.

Government Structural Pattern

SAGMAI

At the end of 1977, the Québec government made two decisions that affected its relationship structures with the Amerindians and Inuit residing in the province. *First*, it terminated the existence of the Direction Générale du Nouveau-Québec, which would in any case have become obsolete. Indeed, the DGNQ had been established in 1963 to look after the nonorganized parts of northern Québec. With the imminent adoption by the National Assembly of legislation foreseen in the James Bay and Northern Québec Agreement and the Northeastern Québec Agreement, the whole territory would be turned into a politically and socially organized region like any other part of the province. Consequently, the various departments of the administration had to regain the jurisdiction and responsibilities that had been transferred to the DGNQ. *Second*, the government decided that all sectors of the provincial administration would offer their services and programs to aboriginal peoples throughout the province, not only to those who were the beneficiaries of the James Bay and Northern Québec and the Northeastern Québec agreements. This decision was based on the underlying principle that the Indian and Inuit nations were the first to come here, to know, to tend, and to love the soil and the land they still inhabit. Not only have your nations survived all these years but they are now flourishing as never before. And that fact, in Québec as elsewhere, imposes strict demands on the rest of us because first settlers have specific rights that have to be recognized and since these have sort of been trampled on, to say the least, over a period of history. You also have the absolute right to share equally in all community or collective services that the population in general enjoys. (SAGMAI, 1981)

It is on the basis of that decision that a *Secrétariat des Activités Gouvernementales en Milieu Amérindien et Inuit* (SAGMAI) had been created on January 18, 1978. Placed under the sole and direct ministerial responsibility of Québec's premier, its mandate was to "assure the coordination and coherence of the governmental and paragovernmental interventions in Amerindian and Inuit milieux; elaborate, in consultation with those concerned, a comprehensive policy for Québec to be applied in the Amerindian and Inuit milieux; and supply those milieux with pertinent general information" (Order-in-Council:154–78).

Obviously, this mandate, while it gave a central role to SAGMAI, did not assign it direct administrative responsibilities for Québec's aboriginal peoples. SAGMAI was not created as a ministry or as a substitute for ministries, departments, and agencies to assume sectoral responsibilities. Rather, such responsibilities were left to the regular government structures, which had to extend their programs to aboriginal peoples and adapt them or create new ones in consideration of their status or their specific rights and needs.

When it adopted the order-in-council creating SAGMAI, the government concomitantly ordered a dozen "strategic" ministries to identify and establish within their respective structures at least one executive position, the holder of which would be considered to be the ministry's conscience in aboriginal matters—that is, the person who would ensure that programs and activities to serve Amerindians and Inuit were developed in consultation with them and were congruent with Québec's comprehensive policy toward aboriginal peoples.

In 1987, the name of SAGMAI was changed to SAA (Secrétariat aux Affaires Autochtones) (Order-in-Council:17-87), and while remaining in the ministry of the Executive Council—whose minister is the premier—it now operates under a Ministre délégué aux Affaires autochtones whose deputy is the Associate Secretary General of the Executive Council in charge of the Secrétariat.

Secrétariat Working Pattern

SAA uses a number of organizational means to fulfil its mandate. The ministerial coordinators' table mandatorily meets every month to assess progress, to set up, if needed, a multidisciplinary group to study new projects and requests presented by aboriginal peoples, and to exchange ideas and objectives respecting policies. The table is made up of the coordinators appointed by ministries and other government agencies to represent them in matters concerning aboriginal peoples. As mentioned above, when SAGMAI was created in 1978 some twelve ministerial coordinators were appointed by virtue of a cabinet directive; by mid-1986 their number had been voluntarily increased to twenty-five, demonstrating the interest of the various sectors of the Québec government in this institutionalized form of governmental coordination.

Ad hoc meetings are called by SAA in response to specific requests or on its own initiative to discuss new policies or to find solutions to specific problems. Most often, they occur at the request of aboriginal groups who feel unsatisfied with the regulations of some part of the provincial administration. Not infrequently, a ministry or agency, conscious of the need to coordinate its activities with other ministries, will ask SAA to convene interested parties. Such meetings are also called by SAA on its own initiative in order to assume mandates bestowed upon the Secrétariat by the government or the Treasury Board.

As copies of all proposed legislative and governmental projects are seen by the Associate Secretary General of the Executive Council responsible for SAA before being submitted to cabinet for approval, the Secrétariat can examine their eventual impact and, when needed, introduce modifications to ensure that governmental policies toward Amerindians and Inuit are respected.

Finally, SAA maintains a reference and documentation centre that aids Amerindians and Inuit as well as civil servants or other interested parties in obtaining information on matters involving aboriginal peoples. It also produces written and audio-visual information for Amerindians and Inuit. Its main publication is *Rencontre*, a quarterly magazine issued separately in English and French, which reaches every Amerindian and Inuit family in Québec. The purpose of *Rencontre*, which was first published in the spring of 1979, is threefold: to provide information on governmental and other institutions that may be of particular interest to aboriginal peoples; to give information on programs available to them; and to report on initiatives taken by and in the Amerindian and Inuit milieux. A translation of most texts into their respective mother tongues is inserted in the French issues reaching Montagnais and in the English issues reaching Cree and Inuit families.

SOME SIGNIFICANT ASPECTS
"Indianness"

In October 1980 the Québec government renounced the federal distinction between status and nonstatus Indians, and recognized as Indians, for the purpose of its own legislation and bylaws, all those who were Indians "by virtue of their ancestry and their belonging to the Amerindian Identity." This move was made in response to specific requests from the Native Women Association of Québec, who represented thousands of women deprived of their status.

Retroactive to January of that year, Amerindian women who had lost their legal status because of marriage to a non-Indian were eligible for the same exemption from provincial taxes as federally registered Indians. And, since 1981, the federal definition of "Indian" appearing in provincial orders-in-council has been erased and replaced by the words "a person of Indian ancestry." In other words, present Québec policy does not allow for a distinction to be made in its statutes between registered and nonregistered, de jure and de facto, or status and non-status Indians.

Since Québec also recognizes the reserve as the central place in which Amerindians will develop and master their destiny, its approach is not necessarily congruent with the aspirations of those Amerindians who have always lived off the reserves—children of Indians dispossessed of their "Indianness" by virtue of a federal statute and whom Québec has so far refused to consider as belonging to the Métis mentioned in Part II of the Constitution Act, 1982. In spite of that, Québec concurs with federal policies toward nonstatus Indians (for example, in housing) and has a policy of its own to help nonstatus Amerindians organize and implement certain projects. But so far the government's overall objective has been to favour a rapprochement of the nonstatus with the status Indians in order to preserve, if not restore, the integrity of the Amerindian nations.

As for the principle itself of the Reservation—the mode of Amerindian (not Inuit) settlement imposed by the British North America Act of 1867 and subsequent federal legislation—Québec did adopt an official policy (SAA; Decision 82-361) to favour its creation and/or enlargement as a residential place. (Following the James Bay and Northern Québec Agreement, Cree and Naskapi communities no longer constitute reservations, and their status is defined under the Cree-Naskapi Act and no longer under the Indian Act.)

It goes without saying that the reservation concept in the eyes of the Québec government—as was generally the case in the eyes of the other provincial governments—still represented at the end of the 1970s an outdated type of settlement, a sort of ghetto, whose legal status contributed somewhat to segregation and isolation from the surrounding milieux. At the same time, it had become quite obvious that the reservation had to be considered under a new light, that of its irreplaceable role in the affirmation and promotion of Indianness:

> Outside of James Bay and Northern Québec territory, an important part of the Indian reality is the reservation system. If you look at the perspective in the past, it was probably essential that the reservation system be set up; on the other hand, one must admit that the reservation system by itself, under outside tutorship, kind of helped alienate the two societies that we represent: your own, the first citizens, an historical fact, and ours growing up over the last two or three hundred years. You know, when the tutorship is more or less remote-controlled, even though it is a very conservative and there is this special status which is to other people somewhat like having foreign residents with completely different legal, tax and other alien ways of life as concerns legislation, regulation and sharing, it does help to hinder that kind of contact that I think you need if you are to really live together with a people, the surroundings and the environment.
>
> I don't want to be misunderstood, I am not attacking the concept of the reservation because for many of our Indian fellow citizens it was the only thing left that you could hang on to, like home, a strong tangible symbol of the heritage and of the closeness of your own people. What I am just trying to emphasize very briefly is that at least in part, the reservation set-up could explain a lot of the indifference and certainly a lot of the ignorance of the rest of the population, the human environment, in Québec as elsewhere throughout Canada, about Indian realities and problems. There is no question of suppressing or abolishing this system, whatever the political changes, but surely we have to build new links, new contacts, new lines of communication between those basic homes that you are attached to and the rest of our own society in Québec if we are to do away with the sort of psychological barrier which was built between us...."
> (SAGMAI, 1981)

Culture

The Québec government policy statement on cultural development published in 1978 (Québec, 1978) gives specific consideration to aboriginal peoples: "The indigenous Indians and Inuit living inside Québec's borders cannot be regarded as forming one or several minorities in the same light as groups whose members have come to the country more recently." Aboriginal peoples have the right to receive encouragement and financial assistance from the government in pursuing their objectives.

In 1977, the Charter of the French Language (Bill 101) had stated in its preamble that "The Assemblée Nationale recognizes to the Québec Amerindians and Inuit, descendants of the country's first inhabitants, their right to maintain and develop their original language and culture." It provided, in articles 87, 88, 95, and 96, particular forms of application in the case of aboriginal peoples. In short, Québec's official cultural policy recognizes the right of the aboriginal peoples living in Québec not only to maintain and develop their culture—which it also does for other minorities—but to remain culturally different from the rest of Québec society. A substantiation of this could already be found in the institutions created by, or to comply with, the James Bay and Northern Québec Agreement, through which Crees and Inuit may exercise the role of directing and administering their school boards' programs, activities, and operations.

A significant aspect of Québec's policy respecting the cultural development of Amerindians and Inuit is its traditional reference to the use of aboriginal languages in education, to which Québec has attached prime importance since the early 1960s. The very first educational policy to be applied in the north by DGNQ provided for instruction to be given only in Inuktitut, the Inuit language, in kindergarten and Grades 1 and 2—no English, no French. This policy was based principally on the assumption that the child's main tool in the learning process is the expression of his or her curiosity, and that educational policy not permitting the child to use his or her mother tongue—the only one he or she can function in at this early age—can cause mental development to be slowed and even somewhat paralyzed. The assumption was substantiated at least partly by a comparative analysis of drawings made by "Eskimo" preschool and Grade 2 students in Kuujjuaq, which revealed a certain blockage in those having attended schooling in an "alien" language (English) as compared to those that had not yet entered the school system.

Now that they are in control of their own education system, the Inuit, Crees, and Naskapis in Québec decide for themselves whether this policy should be maintained, modified, or abandoned. The government now has nothing to say in this regard. The results are far from uniform, since the decisions are made by local schools, parents, or communities whose approaches may differ, sometimes quite significantly. Elsewhere, Québec's support of aboriginal languages in schools has been used in reservation schools, especially in experiments being conducted by band-operated schools to make the vernacular language the language of instruction in the early grades.

In regard to general promotion of the vernacular languages, the policy of Québec has been to spend funds mostly where the original language was still regularly spoken in the communities and in answer to projects initiated in and by the milieu. In that respect, and because it is a unique achievement, the Inuit-only dictionary (27,000 words), realized over a period of ten years by Taamusi Qumaq of Povungnituk and published recently, is worthy of mention (Inuit Uqansillaringit, 1991).

Traditional Activities

In traditional activities such as hunting and fishing, the James Bay and Northern Québec Agreement has provided, among the compensatory measures to the Crees, for a truly innovative program, the Income Security Program, financed in its entirety by Québec (at an annual cost of nearly $14 million). The beneficiaries—some 35 percent of the total Cree population living in the territory—practising hunting, trapping, and fishing as their principal economic activity receive their income from a nongovernmental office created by Québec legislation and administered by the Crees. Since its passage in 1976, the Québec legislation has been twice amended, at the request of the Crees, to increase to 350,000 person-days the *maximum annual quota of 150,000* provided for in the James Bay and Northern Québec Agreement.

The program brings to its beneficiaries a rewarding and honourable substitute for welfare and traditional relief measures. Most important, it recognizes that traditional activities, when professionally practised, must be compensated. From this standpoint the program represents probably the most significant opportunity for each beneficiary to bring his or her contribution—even in financial terms—to the social evolution of the community without losing the essence of his or her identity and the land–person relationship. Using the land, as the ancestors did, fulfils an educational role among the people.

The corresponding program for the Inuit is community oriented, which distinguishes it from that of the Cree, but it is also based on the pursuit of traditional activities. The funds, which are entirely supplied by Québec (at an annual cost of over $2 million), are administered by the Kativik Regional Government, which, upon approving the projects submitted, channels them to local municipal governments for implementation. Since its inception the Québec Inuit hunting, fishing, and trapping support program has helped northern communities to finance a variety of local projects enhancing usage and exploitation of land and sea resources.

Self-Government

Three main types of governing institutions controlled by aboriginal peoples are operating in Québec by virtue of provincial legislation. Two of them, foreseen in the James Bay and Northern Québec Agreement (1975), involve Inuit, Cree, and Naskapi Indians and stem from tight negotiations with them; the third one results from a negotiation between Kahnawake Mohawk Indians and the Québec government (1984).

Of the institutions under the control of the Inuit in northern Québec, two are legally ethnic in nature: the Makivik Corporation, which is the trustee and administrator of the monetary compensation funds (approximately $90 million) awarded to the Inuit, their spouses, and descendants by the James Bay and Northern Québec Agreement, and the local land-holding corporations, which are the trustees and administrators of category I lands recognized by the agreement as being the property of the Inuit. The other governing institutions in Inuit territory (school boards, regional and local governments, health and social services boards, and regional police forces) legally are nonethnic. Their responsibilities and some of their jurisdiction apply to the entire territory and to all people living there, not only to the Inuit. In fact, however, those institutions are under Inuit control, since their administrative boards are elected by the whole population, which is 90 percent Inuit. In the case of the two ethnic institutions, the Makivik and the land-holding corporations, the autonomy of the Inuit is virtually complete. The only significant limitation imposed on it by law is that the Makivik cannot spend, over a twenty-year period (1975–95), more than 50 percent of the capital gradually received, plus accrued interest. Each of the other institutions reports to the Québec ministry responsible for the sector concerned. Thus, the Kativik School Board reports to the Ministry of Education, the Kativik Regional Government to Municipal Affairs, and so forth. In legal terms, the administrative authority of those institutions, under the de facto control of the Inuit, is extensive and surpasses in some respects that of similar governing institutions elsewhere in Québec.

This governing institution system, copied after "southern" patterns, has been consistently decried by a strong minority in the Québec Inuit population—represented by their association Inuit Tungavingat Nunamini—(ITN)—for failing, among other things, to provide them with enough autonomy to govern on the basis of their own priorities and allocate funds accordingly to the various sectors of activities. At the parliamentary commission of 1983 mentioned above, the government engaged to support a proposal of that nature that would be worked on and agreed by the Inuit "dissidents" and the signatories of the James Bay Agreement. Intense and lengthy discussions followed among them, and on October 1, 1987, a referendum was held in all the fourteen Inuit communities of northern Québec to select a task force charged with deciding on and preparing recommendations for the constitution and structure of an eventual regional government (*Rencontre*, 1987). On June 27, 1991, a protocol of understanding was signed by the Québec and Inuit representatives to finalize through negotiations a form of self-government for the residents of the Québec Nunavut territory. (SAA:memorandum).

Governing institutions under Cree and Nunavut control differ from those operating in the Inuit milieu. First, they are all legally of an ethnic nature—that is, their administrative authority in general applies only to the Crees and on lands reserved for them; second, some of these institutions have been established by provincial statute, others by federal statute.

The Cree School Board, the Cree Board of Health and Social Services, and the Cree Municipal Corporations (lands of category IB) are provincial legal creations and report to the Québec ministry concerned. The Band Councils are now placed under a specific federal statute, the Cree-Naskapi Act, to govern the day-to-day activities in category IA lands, where the local Cree population resides and lives. The Cree Compensation Board, created by provincial legislation within the Cree Regional Authority as trustee and administrator of the Cree funds, provided by the James Bay and Northern Québec Agreement, enjoys a degree of autonomy similar to that of Makivik in the case of the Inuit. So do the local Cree land-holding corporations, which own and possess in fee-simple category IB lands adjacent to category IA lands. Institutions governing the Crees, Inuit, and Naskapis resulted from negotiations undertaken almost twenty years ago, and most of them were legally created in the first part of 1978.

From that date on the government gradually introduced new elements in its Québec policy toward aboriginal peoples, largely through numerous exchanges with their representatives and their insistence on being treated not only with respect, but on the very basis of their rights. For example, even after the signing of the James Bay and Northern Québec Agreement and the Northeastern Québec Agreement, the government in 1980 indicated to the Conseil Attikamek-Montagnais that "it recognized *their right to their own philosophy* as regards educational and social services" (*Rencontre*, 1980). By early 1983 that position had changed: "The Aboriginal nations have *the right to have and control*, within the framework of agreements between them and the Government, such institutions as may correspond to their needs in matters of culture, education, language, health and social services as well as economic development" (see Appendix I).

It is within that context that an agreement was negotiated in 1984 between Québec and the Kahnawake Mohawk Indians on the construction and operation of a local hospital to be entirely financed by Québec. By virtue of its law of general application on health and social services, Québec could provide the required financing only through a provincial corporation specifically created for the purpose; the hospital and its operation would be subject to the provincial act regulating hospitals. Some of these clauses, of administrative nature, were irrelevant to the Kahnawake situation, and Québec was willing to amend its statute accordingly. But the Mohawk Council, in its pursuit of political autonomy, did not want to be governed by a provincial statute, even if it was amended. It wanted Québec to recognize the Mohawks' right to build, own, and operate the hospital according to its own rules and priorities.

The Mohawks were prepared, however, to negotiate an agreement that would recognize their right to self-government and at the same time fulfil the requirements of Québec's health policy. This is what was done. The Québec act respecting health and social services was amended by the National Assembly to state that, in the case of Kahnawake, the ad hoc negotiated agreement prevailed over any incompatible clause in provincial legislation. The agreement itself became a provincial statute, but not before the Mohawk Council of Kahnawake had given it formal approval. As a consequence, the organization and dispensation of health services and hospital administration are governed by an agreement that has the force of law for both Québec and Kahnawake and prevails over provincial laws of general application when there is conflict. Appendix II reproduces that agreement, which has been frequently referred to as a government-to-government agreement directly negotiated and signed between the Mohawks and the Québec government without any involvement of a third party.

CURRENT AND EMERGING ISSUES AND PROBLEMS
Land Claims
In the Indian Territory

To date, of ten Québec aboriginal nations, only three, or about 16,500 people, have had a land claim settlement: the Inuit (with a population of 6,000), the Crees

(10,000), and the Naskapis (500). There remain approximately 37,000 status Indians, living on federal reservations, who never surrendered any rights. Among them, about 20,000 Algonquins, Attikameks, and Montagnais live on reservations within or in the vicinity of the vast territory defined by the Royal Proclamation of 1763 as "Indian territory" in order to distinguish it from the "territory of the Government of Québec."

Twelve years ago the Montagnais and Attikamek nations united in order to negotiate a comprehensive settlement of their land claims. For the reasons mentioned earlier, discussions between them and the two governments (federal and provincial) have remained at a standstill. In all probability, however, they should be resumed soon, and, if so, the Algonquin nation could seize this occasion to demonstrate its interest. Indeed, the exercise of these three nations' rights, which would probably fall under section 35 of the Constitution Act, 1982, since they are historical (aboriginal) in their nature and have never been surrendered or extinguished, could give rise to international conflict in the absence of an agreed settlement.

Despite that, the Québec comprehensive policy will be more easily applied in the settlement of the Algonquin, Attikamek, and Montagnais land claims since (as was the case in James Bay and Northern Québec) there subsist, in and on the territory, rights of the type that are recognized and affirmed in the Canadian Constitution and obviously constituted, and constitute, mortgages on the lands to be developed or already developed. The exact nature and reach of these ill-defined rights and how they will be exercised must be stipulated in negotiated agreements. However, in spite of a certain similarity to James Bay, the present situation is different. At the request of the CAM, Québec already stated in 1980 its desire to find an alternative to the federal extinguishment-of-rights clause that appeared in the James Bay and Northern Québec Agreement and the Northeastern Québec Agreement. Throughout Canada, opposition by the First Nations themselves to the termination principle has been steadily growing and overtly affirmed and reaffirmed in the last decade, either publicly or before parliamentary commissions.

In the Government of Québec Territory

The remaining 17,000 Amerindians, members of the Abenaquis, Huron, Malecite, Micmac, and Mohawk nations, all live on or around reservations within that part of Québec designated by the Royal Proclamation of 1763 as "territory of the Government of Québec." Consequently, comprehensive land claims on their part are rather improbable, which does not mean that they will not fight to recuperate portions of territory originally allotted to them and "strangely" disposed of by their federal trustee, and to obtain from governments the recognition of fundamental rights allowing them to enjoy administrative autonomy and a certain degree of political autonomy, as well as to benefit from the development of the lands and resources they demand to possess, manage, or co-manage. Québec's comprehensive aboriginal policy, as officially proclaimed by the National Assembly, goes in this direction. So does federal policy, as was made clear during the first ministers' Conferences of 1983, 1984, and 1985 and in the report tabled in the House of Commons on November 3, 1983, by the Penner Committee (a parliamentary special committee created in 1982 to examine the matter of the Indian bands' political autonomy, which unanimously recommended enshrining in the Canadian Constitution the autochthons' right to self-government).

Other Claims

The "territorial component" of Québec's policy will be more difficult to apply to those Amerindian groups that are "without" comprehensive land claims. For example, some of them may want a land base large enough to ensure their self-controlled economic development, and to that end Québec should be ready, in view of its policy, to grant them exclusive use of certain portions of its territory. Provincial resistance, however, could be based on the fact that lands being thus reserved for the exclusive use of the Indians could be declared by the courts to have become federal lands by virtue of section 91(24) and would hence constitute a series of enclaves seriously threatening the integrity of Québec territory and the role of the provincial government in its development. The best way to cope with this potential problem would be for Québec to argue that the Canadian Constitution should be amended to ensure that provincial lands thus put aside for the exclusive benefit of the Indians—that is, lands similar to but possibly larger than those of the category IB type transferred to the James Bay Crees—would not fall under the constitutional authority of the federal government. Such an amendment was in fact brought into the Canadian Constitution in 1983 (art. 35:3), but only in regard to Cree, Inuit, and Naskapis freehold lands transferred to them by Québec under the James Bay Agreement.

The application of Québec policy will be more complex within the Québec territory as defined by the Royal Proclamation, since it is mainly here that urban and industrial development has taken place. There is hardly any important portion of land left "unoccupied" in the corridor zone along the St. Lawrence River officially assigned by the Royal Proclamation of 1763 to the government of Québec. It can be expected, however, that joint agreements will occur in this area between Québec and Amerindian nations in order to permit them to exercise their Indian rights—that is, those constitutionally recognized—or the rights of the Indians—that is, those formally recognized following negotiations or in line with Québec's or Canada's policy. Such agreements will probably be modelled on the Kahnawake Agreement appearing in Appendix II. They should at least reflect its "government-to-government" approach, which recognizes the political autonomy of the Amerindian nations.

Administrative Problems

The implementation of the legislative process of Québec's overall policy in aboriginal matters has been and will be confronted with internal administrative problems causing hesitations, delays, and postponements susceptible to entertain mistrust between a provincial government and the autochthonous nations. In part, such problems can be attributable to the fact that the administrative process, in spite of new specific structures put into place, can be blocked somewhat by a legislative process still largely based, as it were, on premises alien to the recognition of the autochthonous nations as distinct from any other groups in Québec in the area of collective rights.

To prevent administrative delays, postponements, and other complexities in the application of Québec's policy, it has been suggested that the National Assembly adopt a *loi-cadre*, "umbrella legislation," stating in clear terms, for the benefit of both the Amerindians and the Québec government's administrators, how its policy could be legally and concretely applied. It would state, among other things, that any agreement concluded between an aboriginal nation and the government can be ratified by the National Assembly, and that its provisions will thenceforth prevail over all incompatible parts of provincial legislation, even future ones unless they otherwise specify; in which case signatories to the agreements thus affected must be called before the National Assembly to express their viewpoints before final adoption. This *loi-cadre* would exempt devoted officials—sometimes overly zealous—from researching ad nauseam the entire provincial legislation in order to find parts of bills that must be amended before an agreement could be signed that was felt to be suitable by all parties.

To that effect a bill was introduced in the National Assembly early in 1987 (Assemblée Nationale du Québec, 1987), only to be withdrawn by its proponent, the Ministre délégué aux Affaires Autochtones, on the protest of aboriginal leaders whose unexpected opposition can seemingly be explained only by a lamentable lack of adequate information and/or some of their advisers' staunch resistance to the adoption of any provincial-only legislation in a domain under federal authority. Paradoxically, this withdrawal no doubt comforted those numerous civil servants who, for several years, had steadily opposed that kind of "special" treatment for the autochthons to be introduced in the regular legislative process.[1]

In any event, an efficient implementation of an overall provincial policy toward the autochthons—including that of Québec—calls for such a specific overall piece of legislation to accelerate the administrative process. In its absence, delays of implementation are reactivated more often than otherwise by a complex legislative process governing the adoption of the laws of general application.

The Financial Involvement

Another difficulty stems from the reticence of Québec to inject "provincial" funds, when needed, to implement its policy. The Oka case is an illuminating one in that respect. Since 1983, Québec had assured the Kanasatake Mohawks that, in view of its policy, it was ready to favour the creation of a reservation, along the terms of the 1982 decision, when requested. They preferred then to wait until the completion in Ottawa of a further study of their ancestral rights, the result of which, negative, was finally given them in 1987. Québec started to work on and to discuss a consolidation scheme that would permit the creation of the reservation. But Québec discarded the financing, at its own expense, of the costs involved in the required consolidation of lands, devoting its efforts to convincing the federal government to assume the cost; a federal government reluctant to do this in view of the precedent it would thus create (an Indian Reservation is normally a provincial land whose control and administration, not the property, is transferred by the province to the federal government for the exclusive benefit of the Indians). The result of this "set to partners" approach has postponed for months the solution implicit in the Québec policy. Perhaps the outburst of feelings generated by the Oka crisis has done more to sensitize the Québec population to the aboriginal cause than would have an early and rapid solution; but the Oka crisis revealed that lack of financial dedication and involvement from Québec was probably the main reason why its policy was not implemented as planned and the most important factor in the tragic development of the situation.

The Political Will

The reticence manifested by Québec to assume financial responsibilities in the settlement of the Oka case cannot be attributed to financial concerns, at least not principally. Indeed, the amounts involved were rather insignificant in terms of the total Québec budget; and they could not be viewed as a costly precedent since the Kanasatake band was the only one in Québec that needed an allocation of nonpublic lands for residential purposes.

One must look at a lack of political will to explain the attendant attitude of the government. While many sectors of the state apparel have resumed their relations with the aboriginal nations on the basis of the fifteen principles and the National Assembly resolution, the government itself, that is, the Cabinet, seems to have adopted a rather lukewarm approach to the aboriginal reality in Québec.

The process conducive to the desired harmonization of relations with the first occupants of the territory, following the James Bay and Northern Québec Agreement (1975) and the Northeastern Québec Agreement (1978), was a systematic one and featured a series of meetings between First Nations' representatives, the premier, and the elected members of the National Assembly under the preceding government. Obviously, the new cabinet did not attach, since 1986, the same importance to that process. Gradually, the new premier released himself from direct ministerial responsibility in aboriginal matters. He was absent from the fourth ministers' constitutional conference on aboriginal matters (1987), successively appointed three ministers over a period of six years to handle the Native Affairs Secrétariat, and has at times advocated the authority of the federal government and its tutorship role over the Indians to justify what would seem to be a lack of political will to put into action policies established and commitments made.

One of these commitments was the creation, announced in the National Assembly resolution of March 1985, of a permanent parliamentary forum to allow aboriginal nations' representatives to meet and dialogue with parliamentarians on their needs, rights, and aspirations. Seven years later, nothing has yet been done. Obviously, the government has preferred to rely on a few people, within the state apparel, to acquaint itself with the situation, instead of permitting a real evaluation of the aboriginal problem in Québec with the full involvement of all the interested parties.

This lack of political will has probably played a certain role in the present constitutional interplay between Québec and its aboriginal nations, although it must be noted that very few among their representatives have crusaded against Québec. They know about the recent history and about the most significant steps taken by Québec to recognize them as distinct nations entitled to their own governments and to encourage their development as such in Québec.

This, of course, cannot hide the fact that, in their fight to have the nature and reach of their rights enshrined in the Constitution, Québec aboriginals entertain real hopes in the outcome of constitutional battles fought by their colleagues from other parts of Canada. In the name of solidarity some of them have even endured being trapped somewhat by Canadian native leaders unaware of the situation in Québec and relaying messages passed on to them, more often than otherwise, by anti-Québec, non-native, and prejudiced speculators.

APPENDIX I
The Fifteen Principles*

On February 9, 1983, the Cabinet adopted the following 15 principles:

(1) Québec recognizes that the Aboriginal peoples of Québec constitute distinct nations, entitled to their own culture, language, traditions and customs, as well as having the right to determine, by themselves, the development of their own identity.

(2) It also recognizes the right of Aboriginal nations, within the framework of Québec legislation, to own and to control the lands that are attributed to them.

(3) These rights are to be exercised by them as part of the Québec community and hence could not imply rights of sovereignty that could affect the territorial integrity of Québec.

(4) The Aboriginal nations may exercise, on the lands agreed upon between them and the Government, hunting, fishing and trapping rights, the right to harvest fruit and game and to barter between themselves. Insofar as possible, their traditional occupations and needs are to be taken into account in designating these lands. The ways in which these rights may be exercised are to be defined in specific agreements concluded with each people.

(5) The Aboriginal nations have the right to take part in the economic development of Québec. The Government is also willing to recognize that they have the right to exploit to their own advantage, within the framework of existing legislation, the renewable and unrenewable resources of the lands allocated to them.

(6) The Aboriginal nations have the right, within the framework of existing legislation, to govern themselves on the lands allocated to them.

(7) The Aboriginal nations have the right to have and control, within the framework of agreements between them and the Government, such institutions as may correspond to their needs in matters of culture, education, language, health and social services as well as economic development.

(8) The Aboriginal nations are entitled, within the framework of laws of general application and of agreements between them and the Government, to benefit from public funds to encourage the pursuit of objectives they esteem to be fundamental.

(9) The rights recognized by Québec to the Aboriginal peoples are also recognized to women and men alike.

(10) From Québec's point of view, the protection of existing rights also includes the rights arising from agreements between Aboriginal peoples and Québec

*Cabinet decision 83-20, February 9, 1983, reproduced in "The Basis of the Québec Government's Policy on Aboriginal Peoples," published by the Gouvernement du Québec, SAA, Executive Council, March 1988.

concluded within the James Bay and Northern Québec Agreement and the Northeastern Québec Agreement are to be considered treaties with full effect.

(11) Québec is willing to consider that existing rights arising out of the Royal Proclamation of October 7, 1763, concerning Aboriginal nations be explicitly recognized within the framework of Québec legislation.

(12) Québec is willing to consider, case by case, the recognition of treaties signed outside Canada or before Confederation, Aboriginal title, as well as the rights of Aboriginal nations that would result therefrom.

(13) The Aboriginal nations of Québec, due to circumstances that are peculiar to them, may enjoy tax exemptions in accordance with terms agreed upon between them and the Government.

(14) Were the Government to legislate on matters related to the fundamental rights of the Aboriginal nations as recognized by Québec, it pledges to consult them through mechanisms to be determined between them and the Government.

(15) Once established, such mechanisms could be institutionalized so as to guarantee the participation of the Aboriginal nations in discussions pertaining to their fundamental rights.

APPENDIX II
Kahnawake–Québec Agreement

Agreement concerning the building and operation of a hospital centre in the Kahnawake Territory. *BETWEEN* THE KAHNAWAKE MOHAWKS represented by their elected Council, (hereinafter called "THE KAHNAWAKE MOHAWKS") *AND* LE GOUVERNEMENT DU QUÉBEC represented by Mr. René Lévesque, Prime Minister, and Mr. Camille Laurin, m.d., Minister of Social Affairs, (hereinafter called "LE GOUVERNEMENT").

CONSIDERING THAT LE GOUVERNEMENT has recognized:

a) THAT the Aboriginal Peoples of Québec constitute distinct nations, entitled to their own culture, language, traditional customs as well as having the right to determine, by themselves, the development of their own identity;

b) THAT the Aboriginal Nations have the right to have and control such institutions as may correspond to their needs in matters of culture, education, language, health and social services as well as economic development;

c) THAT the Aboriginal Nations are entitled, within the framework of agreements between them and LE GOUVERNEMENT, to benefit from public funds to encourage the pursuit of objectives they esteem to be fundamental.

CONSIDERING THAT THE KAHNAWAKE MOHAWKS have operated and continue to operate a hospital centre know as KATERI MEMORIAL HOSPITAL CENTRE in a building that is now beyond repair and that it is urgent to replace it by a modern building that is functional and provides security;

CONSIDERING THAT THE KAHNAWAKE MOHAWKS have shown their ability to maintain and operate a hospital centre and to offer quality health services, both short term and extended care, despite the inadequacies of the premises;

THE KAHNAWAKE MOHAWKS and LE GOUVERNEMENT hereby agree as follows:

1) THE KAHNAWAKE MOHAWKS AGREE:

a) to build on their Territory a hospital centre comprising 43 beds for long term care and nursing care including beds for multiple use or observation, in accordance with plans and specifications approved by both parties;

b) to entrust the operating of this hospital centre to the KATERI MEMORIAL HOSPITAL CENTRE, a non-profit organization registered with Québec Superior Court in 1955 and mandated for this purpose by the Council, and to take all the necessary steps to have this body abide by the ethics pertaining to health care and hospital services;

c) to allow the said organization to discuss, in its name, with the Minister of Social Affairs or his representatives, questions pertaining to annual budgets required to ensure the operating of the centre.

2) LE GOUVERNEMENT agrees:

a) to provide THE KAHNAWAKE MOHAWKS with the funds required for building the above-mentioned hospital centre;

b) to provide the annual budget required for operating the hospital centre, in accordance with the criteria and schedules agreed upon each year by the parties;

c) to provide the technical assistance and administrative support required by THE KAHNAWAKE MOHAWKS for operating the hospital centre.

3) The hospital centre will offer such health services as:

a) out-patient and minor emergency care

b) long term care

c) nursing care

d) community health services.

4) THE KAHNAWAKE MOHAWKS will supply the Minister of Social Affairs, at the end of the fiscal year, with the annual financial reports of the hospital centre, prepared by auditors as well as the usual periodical reports and will enable him or his representatives to carry out any verification required.

5) THE KAHNAWAKE MOHAWKS agree to receive in their hospital centre, inasmuch as beds are available, patients from outside the Territory.

6) LE GOUVERNEMENT could terminate annual funding for operating the hospital centre if the said centre were no longer used for the purposes described in paragraph 3 above or if the services it offers were no longer adequate.

7) THE KAHNAWAKE MOHAWKS agree to call for public tenders for the building of the hospital centre as soon as possible after the effective date of this agreement, to award the contract to the lowest tendered and to see to it that construction operations are in progress as quickly as possible in such a way as to be terminated, at the most, two years from the effective date of this agreement. Kahnawake Mohawks Tender Policy will apply (Appendix 1).

Constructors must have their principal place of business in Québec.

8) To give effect to this agreement THE KAHNAWAKE MOHAWKS agree to have a resolution adopted by their Council and LE GOUVERNEMENT to introduce legislation in the Assemblée nationale as soon as possible.

The Act will also provide that the Act respecting Health services and social services (Q.R.S. 1977, c. S-5) will apply to this new establishment, to the extent that it is not incompatible with the provisions of this agreement.

9) This agreement will come into effect as soon as the resolution and the Act mentioned in the preceding article will come into effect in conformity with the usual procedures.

Mohawk Council of Kahnawake Tender Policy

THAT the Mohawk Council of Kahnawake does state as its policy the following:

The intent of the Council is to promote fairness and priority in hiring Band Members in the allocating of contract work.

Any work to be performed which requires a contractor, must be made available to Band Members by way of Band public Tender.

Band Members shall be given priority for all contract work within the Mohawk Council operations, capital projects and its affiliate organizations.

The priority rests on the criteria that the work must be of same or superior quality as would be expected by any non-Indian contractor.

Where a Mohawk contractor cannot be found only then will non Mohawk contractors be invited to bid by Public tender.

Where there are bids from Mohawk and non Mohawk contractors, and the Mohawk member is outbidded by way of price, the Mohawk contractor will be given the option of meeting the bid within a (%) percent flexibility to be determined by the criteria of overall cost of work to be performed, provided no cost overruns will be incurred for that specific project.

APPLICATION

This policy applies to the Mohawk Council capital projects such as water & sewer, band buildings and the affiliates which are financed under the auspices of the Mohawk Council.

Tenders shall be posted (2) two weeks in advance for all projects, over $1,000, by public bulletin locations, and announced on the radio CKRK.

Tenders will contain the work requirements, time frame and related information.

Tenders will be decided upon by a tender committee made up of the following:

1) Council member
2) Band Manager
3) Operation Co-ordinator
4) Band Engineer

The general criteria will be quality of work, price of contract, time frame for completion of work, all of which must comply with the specific requirements of each project.

NOTES

1. For more information on the philosophical and administrative justification of the proposed legislation, see "Le Gouvernement et les nations Autochtones du Québec: Harmonisation des relations", pp. 50–55, SAA, Gouvernement du Québec, Conseil Exécutif

REFERENCES

Assemblée Nationale du Québec, Projet de loi 50; 1ère Session, 33ième législature, 1987.
Dedam, Anthony, "Discours et Ateliers", SAGMAI, 1979, p. 104.

Delisle, Andrew, "Discours et Ateliers," SAGMAI, 1979, pp. 64 and 65.

Gourdeau, Éric, "A Perspective on the Economic Development of New-Québec," paper presented before the Canadian Political Science Association, Learned Societies Convention, 1963, 13 pages, mimeographed document, Gouvernement du Québec, Ministère du conseil exécutif.

Inuit Uqansillaringit, Dictionary of definitions in Nunavik (Arctic Québec) Innuktitut (551 pp.), Avataq Cultural Institute, Montréal, 1991.

"Memorandum of Agreement between Québec and Nunavik Constitutional Committee," Gouvernement du Québec, Ministère du conseil exécutif, SAA, 3 pages.

Québec, *Politique du dévelopement culturel*, vol. 1, 1978, p. 86.

Rencontre, vol. 1, no. 1, 1978, 16 pages; Gouvernement du Québec, Ministère du Conseil exécutif, SAA.

Rencontre, vol. 2, no. 2, 1980, p. 4, SAA.

Rencontre, vol. 4, no. 3, March 1983, pp. 4 and 5 , SAA.

Rencontre, vol. 5, no. 3, March 1984 (report of the hearings pp. 9 to 12), SAA.

Rencontre, vol. 9, no. 2, December 1987, p. 4, SAA.

SAGMAI, "Discours et Ateliers," a reproduction of recorded interventions of the 13th, 14th, and 16th December 1978 encounter of the Québec Amerindians with the Québec government; French and English, 195 pages, SAA, Gouvernement du Québec, Conseil exécutif, 1979.

SAGMAI, (Sécretariat des Activités Gouvernementales en Milieu Amérindien et Inuit) "Address given by Premier René Lévesque before the National Association of Friendship Centres", Windsor Hotel, Montréal, June 16, 1978, pp. 5–7, Gouvernement du Québec, Ministère du conseil exécutif, SAGMAI, 1981.

SAGMAI, "Statements and Interventions by Québec Delegates, First Ministers' Conference of April 1985," Gouvernement du Québec, Ministère du conseil exécutif, 1986.

"Statements and Interventions by Québec Delegates, First Ministers' Conference," March 1983, p. 9; Gouvernement du Québec, Ministère du conseil exécutif, SAA.

Forging a Viable Partnership: The Montréal Jewish Community vis-à-vis the Québec State

Pierre Anctil
McGill University

Only recently has the Jewish community of Montréal become the object of serious research on the part of scholars. In the last ten years a number of studies have appeared that throw a much clearer light, both in terms of history and current sociology, on the Jewish contribution to Montréal (Abella, 1990; Anctil, 1988; Anctil and Caldwell, 1984; Berdugo-Cohen, 1987; Gottheil, 1988; Robinson, 1990; Rome and Langlais, 1986). The rather late appearance of as specific a field of study as Canadian Jewry (or Canadian immigrant history, for that matter) probably signals the extent to which Jews in Montréal have been marginalized in mainstream academic spheres and in society in general. The relative peripherization of third groups in Montréal (that is, groups of neither Franco-Catholic nor Anglo-Protestant origins) has tended to add considerably to the difficulties encountered when addressing the issue of their establishment and development in the metropolitan region itself. Nonetheless, researchers have uncovered a number of salient points that can serve as our point of departure. Equipped with a better understanding of the historical continuity of Montréal Jewry, we may be able to grasp the options that the community is currently facing in a changing Québec.

A THIRD SOLITUDE

A fundamental element of Canadian Jewish history is the fact that the mass migration of Jews began around the turn of the century, at a time when non-Christian settlers were few and far between in the country. Until this influx of Eastern European Yiddish-speaking Jews, which coincided with attempts to populate the vast empty expanses of the Prairies, Québécois society had not yet confronted the reality of having to integrate populations of a vastly different religious background. The Jews of this period were determined to gain access to the mechanisms of social mobility and formal participation in Canadian society, and tenaciously lobbied to this end. Evidently, this movement toward acceptance was not actualized overnight. As has generally been the case with most immigrant communities, it took many years for Jews to spell out the extent of their intentions. Some time was needed for a Canadian-born generation to appear, which could master at least one of the official languages and claim to have been reared and schooled in a Western context.

Montréal Jews could not escape the fact that to a Christian society they represented the challenge of a different spiritual and cultural tradition. As their numbers grew very rapidly in the city after 1905, Jews were obliged to begin assessing what it meant to face the entrenched rights of the Christian churches (Anctil, 1990). In the British North America Act of 1867, which had been negotiated at a time when fewer than 500 Jews lived in Montréal, the public school system of the province was defined as confessional in nature, and its administration was delegated to the various Christian denominations. In the field of education, the provincial government declared itself willing to act only as a remote, supervising presence, offering institutional channels to the discretionary power of the various churches. Article 93 of the British North America Act went even further in specifying that religious dissidence could be manifested in a Catholic or in a Protestant form only, thus leaving all other confessions in a political void.

Soon Montréal Jews began to take stock of the extent to which Québec society had defined itself as functioning within a dual context. Not only was education strictly a matter of provincial jurisdiction, but even within the Canadian Constitution the primacy of the two so-called founding religions had been specifically defined. Clearly, as Jews soon realized, the supreme law of the country had elected to protect linguistic and cultural minorities by defining them primarily in a religious frame of reference. By gaining control of that share of the educational system used by Catholics, the church authorities also obtained the direct responsibility in Québec of protecting the French character of their clientele. Similarly, it was widely understood that the Protestant institutions were awarded the sole task of safeguarding the anglophone and culturally specific British identity of the opposite segment of the population. Such a dual conception of society left non-Christians in the profoundly uncomfortable situation of having to achieve social mobility and cultural integration into Québec society, sometimes without any legal protection. As non-Catholics and non-Protestants, Jews could be expelled from the public schools without notice (which nearly happened in 1924) or had to resort to legal circumvolutions such as those provided by the David Bill of 1931 (Anctil, 1988:ch.4; Rome, 1975). As schools in Québec were necessarily invested with a confessional Christian character, similarly the vast majority of the institutions designed to serve the population in the areas of higher education, health services, social services, and cultural activities were also infused with a particular Christian spirit.

The exclusively dual nature of the constitutional arrangements of 1867 were brought to bear very heavily on the Jewish community of Montréal, which reacted in turn by attempting to define its own Jewish confessional sphere within Québec society. The immigrants of the first massive wave evidently had brought with them from Eastern Europe a very developed sense of communal responsibility. In all areas of literary, intellectual, and religious endeavour, Yiddish-speaking Jewish immigrants were able to re-create very rapidly in Montréal a relatively self-sustaining sphere (Roskies, 1990). Unlike the situation in the United States, where in the context of a rigid separation of church and state immigrants enjoyed some of the benefits of neutrally funded institutions, in Canada, and particularly in Québec, Jews were on the contrary encouraged to create parallel and exclusively Jewish organizational structures (Weinfeld, 1990). This trend toward erecting a separate Jewish polity within Canadian society has profoundly affected Jewish perception of their place vis-à-vis the state and of their capacity as a distinct cultural entity to influence the course of events in the political sphere.[1]

The 1930s were a particularly trying period for the Jewish community in Québec, at a time when the first generation of Canadian-born Jews was attempting to gain access to mainstream society while economic conditions were far from optimal. Abroad, notably in several European countries where fascist regimes had appeared, Jews were increasingly coming under the pressure of racist ideologies and discriminatory laws, a fact that deeply affected Canadian Jewry. In a more direct sense, Jews in Québec were encountering the deep-seated suspicion that was directed against them as recent immigrants, by both Catholics and Protestants, just as they were beginning their ascent out of the sweatshop sector and petty commerce.[2]

Although some Yiddish-language schools were established in Montréal in the 1910s in response to the needs of recent immigrants, most children of the Jewish newcomers eventually had to enter either of the two confessional school systems, as defined by the British North America Act of 1867. Financially speaking, Jews were not in a position to finance a universal Jewish day-school network. More importantly, most parents in the community felt that, notwithstanding their emotional attachment to Yiddish culture, the most profitable avenue for social mobility was to be found in the public institutions. The only real issue was therefore which of the two separate, confessional educational systems would be more amenable in Québec to a Jewish presence.

A provincial law in 1903 (before the massive influx of the early century) had directed Jews to the Protestant school system of Montréal. The reasons for this choice were multiple, the major one being the widely shared perception among immigrants that economic prosperity in Montréal was to be achieved through the English language. Integration into the Protestant school commissions of Montréal was not always smooth sailing for Jews in the interwar period, as history amply demonstrates, but at least a certain opening was maintained, making possible a gradual process of anglicization (Neamtan, 1940). On the other hand, Catholics (and the term must be understood to mean francophones) maintained a much more narrowly defined notion of confessionality in their school system, systematically refusing to entertain even the idea that non-Christians could attend their educational institutions (Huot, 1926; Dupont, 1973).

As a result of these attitudes of the various Christian denominations, by the 1950s Montréal Jews had become linguistically assimilated into the anglophone sphere. Admitted in the Protestant school system, most Canadian-born Jews were exposed to the British Victorian culture of the Anglo-Saxon population and often perceived their place in Québec through this prism. At the same time, although street-level contact between Jews and francophones was constant throughout this period, few members of the community were exposed to the institutional network that perpetuated French-Canadian culture or transmitted the French language from generation to generation (for an ethnographic description, consult Richler, 1969:ch.4). In the long run this meant that francophone nationalism, as it developed in the years before World War II and as it burst forth in a newly transformed shape in the early 1960s, would remain a phenomenon largely external to the experience of Montréal Jews. This unique situation—of immigrants being attracted to a demographic minority (albeit an economically and politically powerful one)—was not confined to the Jewish case. Except for the Italian-speaking community, which could claim a direct relationship to one of the basic components of French-Canadian identity, Catholicism, virtually all cultural communities in Montréal were attracted to the anglophone Protestant school system (Polèse, 1978). Even then, as the 1950s and 1960s wore on, Italian immigrants themselves were massively attracted on the Island of Montréal to the anglophone sector of the Catholic school commissions, where they felt their children would be better equipped linguistically to achieve social mobility (Boissevain, 1970; Taddeo and Taras, 1987).

THE NOT-SO-QUIET REVOLUTION

The injection into Montréal, starting in the mid-1950s, of a new contingent of Jewish immigrants of Sephardi (i.e., Middle Eastern or North African) origins did not significantly alter the linguistic pattern already well established by the 1930s (Lasry and Tapia, 1989). Although the *Sephardim* were francophone Jews, mostly from the former French protectorate of Morocco, their impact on the dominant *Ashkenazic* (i.e., East European) segment remained negligible until well into the 1970s. When francophone Québec society began to experience in the immediate postwar period the first signs of profound social and cultural change, Montréal anglophone Jews in general did not possess, for linguistic and institutional reasons, the social background needed to participate in the new movement. Although it had been in the making ideologically for at least one generation before the election of Jean Lesage in 1960, the Quiet Revolution appeared on the stage of Québec history with a resounding thunderclap, catching a largely unaware anglophone Montréal population off guard. The Jewish community was no exception. Events set in motion by the new Liberal administration were to have profound repercussions over the next twenty years on how Montréal Jews viewed their place in Québec society, forever modifying the linguistic and political environment to which they had learned to adapt as a religious and cultural minority.

Several of the reforms triggered by the Quiet Revolution did not directly affect Montréal Jews, at least not during the initial period when the desire for change and the will for political action were most evident. The creation of the Ministry of Education in 1964, the gradual takeover by the provincial administration of social and health institutions previously under church authority, and the rapid expansion of the francophone university network, to name but three of the most sweeping and visible innovations enacted under the leadership of Jean Lesage, were not aimed at the public bodies upon which Jews, either as a separate religious entity or as a largely anglophone community group, depended. In the early 1960s, the Québec government was concerned with dealing with the relative historical backwardness of the francophone social infrastructure, which in the eyes of Liberal planners accounted in large part for the subservient and fragile position that the linguistic majority occupied on the economic scale. Jews, largely associated with the better-endowed and socially well-equipped Anglo-Saxon Protestant community, did not initially find themselves affected by or at odds with the main objectives of the successive Québec governments of the 1960s. Moreover, because of their well-developed and diversified internal community structure, Jews were somewhat sheltered from direct state intervention. On the school front notably, in an area that was to become virtually a battlefield for Québec francophone nationalism, Jews could rest peacefully in the knowledge that they had gained inalienable historical rights as anglophones. By 1970, the overall majority of Jews in Montréal had been educated in the Protestant school system, a privilege that they could pass on to their children if they so wished. Virtually no other cultural minority in Québec could boast of enough seniority in the anglophone educational network to make the same claim.

However, the programmatic policies enacted during the Quiet Revolution and the long-term effects of years of rapid reform in the provincial civil service came to bear directly on the Jewish community of Montréal in two areas. It is a well-known fact that long before Jean Lesage, and even before the extended tenure of Maurice Duplessis, the financial and political weight of the provincial government of Québec amounted to little, especially in terms of the conduct of private business and in the socially sensitive spheres of education, health, and social welfare. With the Quiet Revolution and the emergence of a new francophone middle class, a provincial administration that had functioned within rather narrow confines was transformed into a full-fledged state apparatus:

> The role of the provincial government in Quebec's economy expanded dramatically after 1960. Public expenditures represented 17 percent of Quebec's gross domestic product in 1961; by 1983, that figure had climbed close to 30 percent. The provincial bureaucracy grew from around thirty thousand employees in 1960 to nearly a hundred thousand by 1980, and thousands more were employed in local health, education, and social service "parapublic" institutions funded by the provincial government. (Levine, 1990:151)

The overall strategy of this new francophone statist middle class was to compensate for perceived historical injustices and to correct a generally unfavourable balance of power in the economic marketplace by the use of the Québec state as a major lever of intervention. By controlling public policies in the provincial jurisdictions of education, culture, language, and public investment, francophones hoped to create a viable political base that could be used advantageously as an alternative to the otherwise solid Anglo-Protestant control of the private capitalist sector. As the pace of the Quiet Revolution accelerated, massive public investments were channelled directly or indirectly into certain key sectors of the Québec economy, such as hydroelectricity, public transportation in the Montréal region, educational infrastructure, and health institutions.

While the Québec state was rapidly developing in the 1960s and the francophone nationalist ideology was shedding its former traditional isolationism and self-confinement in favour of an assertive urban and capitalist perspective, Jews in Montréal soon realized that they were gradually being dragged into a debate to which they were not privy. As the two dominant ethnolinguistic communities engaged in a power struggle over the control of the political and economic sphere in Québec, Jews were witnessing dramatic changes in the social environment to which they had adapted as second- or third-generation immigrants. Clearly, pressures were being brought to bear by the Quiet Revolution on the Montréal Jewish institutional network that could not be avoided or simply ignored. Soon the organized leadership, which historically had tended to conduct the affairs of the community in relative isolation from the bulk of francophone society, came to a brutal awakening. It is true that for most of the 20th century Jews had sent at least one (usually Liberal) representative to the Québec National Assembly in each election. Before 1960, however, politicians such as Peter Bercovitch, Joseph Cohen, Louis Fitch, and more recently, Maurice Hartt did not hold key ministerial positions that would have confirmed their political stature outside of the Jewish community (Jedwab, 1986). Essentially, with the possible exception of the educational sphere, the Jewish polity in Montréal began to confront the various arms of the Quebec provincial state only as the Quiet Revolution was getting under way.

The first major encounter came with a reform of the funding policies for the province's private schools. Although the aim of the Minister of Education was to encourage the large confessional private francophone sector to adopt measures that would bring it in harmony with the newly redefined programs of the public school commissions, Jewish schools could not help but be caught in the net of state intervention. Institutions that had previously functioned either in association with the Protestant school board or in total independence (because of the willingness of Jewish parents to cover entirely the cost of a specifically Jewish curriculum) were forced to take into account the political orientations of the francophone majority.[3] A Private Education Act was passed in 1973 that left Jewish private schools no option but to apply directly to the Department of Education for funding, regardless of earlier arrangements. It soon became apparent that Jewish institutions that had relied essentially on the tested waters of private negotiations for their survival would now have to lobby a remote provincial bureaucracy in Québec City for the bulk of their funding: "This left the schools at the mercy of the minister and his/her agents, the civil servants. It soon became evident that the public interest would be defined in terms of the extent of instruction in French" (Elazar and Waller, 1990:126).

Indeed, already in the late 1960s, pressures were brought to bear by the Québec state on private nonfrancophone schools to improve their French-language curriculum and to insure that graduates of these institutions be fluently bilingual in the sense of the Canadian Official Languages Act of 1969. Administrative arrangements were worked out that guaranteed these institutions a high level of funding, in exchange for a fixed amount of French instruction each week, regardless of the cultural or confessional context. Because of its large private-school clientele, the prime recipient of these funds in the non-Catholic and non-Protestant world was the Jewish community, wherein approximately 8,000 children were enrolled in some twenty different institutions by the early 1970s (Shaffir, 1983). Armenian and Greek day schools were also included in the agreement, although much fewer students were affected in these communities. For the Jewish educational system in Montréal, which traditionally had been concerned neither with the integration of its graduates into the social fabric of francophone Québec nor with encouraging fluency in the French language, these sweeping changes came as an unpleasant surprise, to say the least.[4] The only choice afforded the Jewish school administrators was to either bypass government help and its 80 percent subsidy for the operational costs of the new state-defined secular curriculum, or bend to the reality of the Quiet Revolution. Realizing that the Jewish character of their school network would apparently remain untouched by the new policies, the educational leadership in most cases complied with government regulations early in the 1970s:

> Eventually [the Association of Jewish Day Schools president Ben] Beutel agreed to a total of 8 hours per week in French and 7 in English, with no changes in the 15 hours of Hebrew per week. The Association, with some misgivings, agreed to work out programs along these lines and the government also accepted the arrangement. But the agreement had no permanence, as was demonstrated when the PQ government later demanded 17 hours per week in French. In fact, by the end of the decade the schools were compelled to teach 14 hours per week in French. (Elazar and Waller, 1990:126–27)

Changes on the school front signalled other reorientations in Montréal Jewish communal life, notably in the health and social services sector where, in answer to discriminatory hiring practices, Jews had sought to establish a certain institutional independence as early as the 1930s. With the advent of the Quiet Revolution, the Québec state knocked insistently at the gates of the community to obtain some say in how private health organizations discharged their responsibilities. In 1972, a provincial bill was passed that proposed a reorganization of hospital, social, and welfare institutions, notably eliminating the possibility in this field of declaring an entirely private status. Just as the Québec government had advanced funds for private community schools in exchange for more French-language instruction, so it offered increased financial benefits to the Jewish health and social service sector in return for the sector's acceptance to play a more universal role in Québec society. Henceforth Jewish hospitals and convalescent homes in Montréal, among the best staffed and most efficient in the region, have been accepting non-Jewish patients and rendering services to all cultural communities, regardless of religious affiliation. This sudden shift in emphasis from the strictly Jewish to the broadly Québécois (which nevertheless did not destroy the Jewish quality of these health establishments) stunned some members of the community, whose frame of reference at the time of the Quiet Revolution owed much to the American model of private voluntary association. On a continental scale, the collectivist and centralizing efforts of the Québec government seemed too marginal a phenomenon in the minds of some Montréal Jewish leaders to elicit a favourable response.

LANGUAGE AS A POLITICAL TOOL

While the Jewish community experienced something like a shock treatment in its contacts with the emerging Québec state at the height of the Quiet Revolution, a new political context was being defined in the province that precipitated the sudden release of decades of social and cultural francophone frustrations at the hands of an Anglo-Saxon economic elite:

> As was the case around the world, the sixties were turbulent years in Montreal: it was a decade of street demonstrations, political agitations, riots and terrorism. But while racial divisions underlay the turmoil in American cities, and class tension surfaced in European cities, it was the linguistic cleavage that dominated Montreal life in those years. (Levine, 1990:39)

Despite the fact that Jews could hardly be held responsible at all for a situation the historical roots of which reached back to the 18th century and the British Conquest of New France, the language debate still hit the community with full force. Whether sheltered from the early warning signs because of its close association at the educational level with the Protestant school system, or overly confident that the federal regime would contain without great difficulty the francophone tide of discontent, Montréal Jews were abruptly called to reality in the mid-1970s when aggressive linguistic laws were passed in the Québec legislature. In the space of less than a decade the political climate among francophones had passed from benign laissez-faire to direct state regulation of public-language practices.

The major turning point for both Québec francophones and Montréal Jews came with the passing of Bill 22 in 1974 and with the election of the Parti Québécois in the November 1976 provincial elections (Caldwell and Waddell, 1982). Until then the Jewish community had felt rather secure in the belief that it could influence the Liberal cabinet and reasonably present its views on the linguistic question to the party in power. Indeed, the Jewish leadership had on many occasions presented its case to various public bodies, both in the provincial and federal spheres of jurisdiction, notably to the Laurendeau-Dunton Commission on bilingualism and biculturalism in the late 1960s and to the Québec Gendron Commission whose report was published in 1972 (Commission d'enquête sur la situation de la langue française au Québec, 1972:vol. 3). The community's stand was clear: it would welcome measures to encourage a flourishing of the French language and francophone culture in Québec, but would not accept the use of any coercive methods of legislation to that end. Among all the submissions presented to the Gendron Commission, the contribution of the Jewish community was probably among the very few that still shied away from supporting muscular state intervention policies in the protection of the French language in Québec.[5] In fact, by the early 1970s, large segments of public opinion in the province had become supportive of aggressive means of affirmation on the part of francophones. Several nationalist associations and interest groups were vigorously petitioning for the introduction of legislation to that effect.

Few Montréal Jews (at least at the leadership level) foresaw the possibility of the Parti Québécois' sweep to power in 1976.[6] The reversal of fortunes meant not only that Bill 22 would be replaced in the short run by a far more reaching *Charte de la langue française*; it also had the more dramatic effect of severing whatever ties and channels to Québec City the Jewish community had been cultivating over the years through the provincial Liberal Party. The PQ, largely a coalition of various francophone nationalist groups, could easily remain impervious to attempts by the Jewish community to influence its decisions, as it recruited its voters almost exclusively at the time from the francophone milieux. The Jewish reaction to the cataclysmic election of 1976, which can be measured partly by a series of opinions that were published in the wake of the event, shows in retrospect how far removed from the francophone political realities of the day portions of the community had drifted (see Richler, 1977; Wisse and Cotler, 1977; Waller and Weinfeld, 1981). In essence, while the conflict between the two linguistic and cultural majorities of Montréal had been raging throughout the 1960s and early 1970s, much of the Jewish leadership had counted on a reconciliation scenario based on the evocative strength of the Canadian national symbols. This thinly veiled reference to the manner in which the American Republic resolved its internal contradiction was soon to prove to be a futile and total misreading of Québec political reflexes (McRoberts, 1991).

The Jewish community remained essentially in a political purgatory from 1976 to 1985, when the provincial Liberal Party was returned to power. The PQ did not alter in any fundamental way the state interventionist ideology espoused by Québec governments at the onset of the Quiet Revolution, an ideology that had served to awaken abruptly Montréal Jewish institutions to the will of the francophone majority (Levine, 1990:7–8). On the linguistic front, however, the Lévesque government enacted laws and created state agencies that the Jewish leadership found offensive, i.e., contrary to the community's self-help principle and its freedom of expression. In choosing a vehicle for public expression, whether in signs, in addressing the marketplace, or in communications between bureaucrats and taxpayers, citizens now had to rely almost exclusively on the use of the French language. In a candid and rare intervention,[7] Victor Goldbloom, a former cabinet member in the Bourassa government of 1973–76, declared in 1982 that the Québec Jewish community, while vigorous in Montréal and solidly rooted in the province, ranked its state of mind as no more than "assez sereine." The problem, confessed Goldbloom, was that Jews could not easily conceive of themselves only as a cultural minority professing a divergent religious faith. The struggle between the anglophone and francophone segments of society in Montréal was obviously a matter beyond the immediate control of Jews that antedated their immigration by more than a century. Nonetheless, as an anglicized collectivity, argued Goldbloom, Jews could not remain indifferent to coercive measures destined to curb or limit the use of English in the public domain. The community was perhaps experiencing the linguistic policies of the PQ government with even more stress and dismay than the Anglo-Saxons themselves because of distinct historical memories:

> Does everything go beautifully in the best of worlds? Could I leave this picture without some shading? Not really. Quebec Jews benefit, as Jews, from a very great religious, social and cultural freedom. As mostly anglophones, however, they find excessive the constraints imposed with regards to signs and access to English schools. And they sometimes ask themselves: will knowing how to speak the French language always be enough to be a full-fledged Quebecker? The answer from the authorities is invariably yes and nobody doubts their sincerity, but one hears talk of isolated minor incidents which happen at lower levels of jurisdiction and which trouble the generally-held trust. (Goldbloom, 1982)

THE TEST OF LAW 178

Jewish opposition to francophone Québec nationalism abated during the 1960s, at least in the more enlightened segments of the community. The issue remained not whether francophones had a right to assert strongly their cultural and linguistic heritage, but whether some of the means chosen to achieve this end were legitimate and reasonable, given the presence in the province of a historically rooted anglophone minority. Three events that occurred within the last few years provide us with a clear understanding of how Jews view their role and position in the Québec of the 1990s and on which grounds they seek clarification, reassurances, and realignments vis-à-vis the provincial state. The first of these *moments de vérité* was the passing by the Bourassa government early in 1989 of a new linguistic law designed, not so much to alter the policies and regulations enforced by the Québec state on the language front since the late 1970s, but rather to maintain the momentum and preserve social peace. Late in 1988 the Supreme Court of Canada ruled on some of the constitutional aspects of Law 101, reaffirming the right of the province to take measures to protect the language and culture of the demographic majority, but striking down provisions that required commercial sign-postings to be in French only. The opinion of the court was that neither of the official languages of Canada could be prohibited as a vehicle for public expression even though one may require special protection. After intensive campaigns by francophone activists, the Liberals invoked the "notwithstanding" clause inscribed in the Canadian Charter of Rights and Freedoms and reinstated, with Law 178, the monopoly of French-language signs in the province. This legal strategy was supported by the vast majority of francophones (Lesage, 1988) who felt that the linguistic legislation put in place by the previous Lévesque governments remained the cornerstone of cultural security for a still-emerging collectivity and represented a widespread social consensus even in the more sensitive Montréal metropolitan region:

> Bill 101, while not initiating the *francisation* of the Montreal economy, clearly accelerated the process, forcing recalcitrant firms to adopt French systematically as the language of work and fostering an economic climate that increased the value of the French language in Montreal's labor and consumer markets. (Levine, 1990:207)

For the Jewish community, such a resolution of the linguistic dilemmas of Montréal was clearly unacceptable, not because it affected the ability of Jews to communicate with their fellow citizens in the marketplace,[8] or because Bill 178 signalled a drastic change of policy and a tightening of measures to protect the French language (which it did not), but because it constituted a breach of the human-rights guarantees of the Canadian Constitution. With varying degrees of indignation, Montréal Jews, as individuals and in their political alliances, were almost unanimous in denouncing Bill 178. The Canadian Jewish Congress (Québec Region),[9] which formulated perhaps the most coherent and moderate position within the community on this issue, insisted that the legal protection of individual rights must supersede all other political considerations "to demonstrate that it is not acceptable for any government to abrogate rights defined as fundamental by the highest court of the land" (Canadian Jewish Congress, Québec Region, 1989a).

The statements by the Canadian Jewish Congress (Québec Region) appeared to be all the more balanced since they reinstated the uncompromising will of the organized leadership in Montréal to commit itself to public policies designed to enhance, within the confines of the Canadian Charter of Rights, the development of the French language and culture in the province. For the first time in Montréal Jewish history, a clear, unequivocal position seemed to have been formulated that expressed the will of the community to cooperate with (or at least not interfere in any way with) the affirmation of the French fact in Québec, provided that individual rights be scrupulously respected by government authorities. The Congress, Québec Region, with such a straightforward policy in hand, could even afford to call to order individuals or minor organizations in the Montréal Jewish community who were reacting more emotionally or who simply fell back upon earlier and now inappropriate Jewish leadership stands:

> We will not succumb to extremists' points of view either within or outside our own community. We will continue to condemn such comments as those by Mr. Gerald Klein, co-founder of the Equality Party which compare Quebec to South Africa, as irresponsible and inflammatory. (Canadian Jewish Congress, Québec Region, 1989a:2)

The test of this new community policy came in the September 1989 provincial elections, which were called at a time when opposition to the Liberal government within the anglophone population ran very high. Indeed, two "Anglo" rights parties had appeared in the wake of the Supreme Court judgment of 1988 that sought to court voters dissatisfied with the Bourassa solution to the linguistic impasse in Québec. In the Montréal-based Equality Party, many Jewish Quebeckers saw an alternative to a Liberal Party that a majority of the community had supported for as long as they could remember. The lure of the Equality Party turned out to be particularly strong in the predominantly Jewish riding of D'Arcy McGee, where the leader of the party, Robert Libman (himself a member of the community), succeeded in distracting voters from their previously overwhelming attachment to Liberal candidates. Nevertheless, the Canadian Jewish Congress (Québec Region), in a *Political Action Guide* produced under the leadership of Joseph Benarrosh on the eve of the election and designed to "… sensitize candidates of all parties to the issues of concern to the Québec Jewish community and present the recommendations put forth by Canadian Jewish Congress, Québec region, on these matters" (Canadian Jewish Congress, Québec region, 1989b), reaffirmed the principles it had already laid out a few months earlier in the Bill 178 debate.

In an election when many Montréal Jews were tempted to equate both the protection of the rights of anglophones with those of the cultural communities of Québec and the encroachments on the freedom of expression in the English language with attacks on the Jewish entity itself, the Canadian Jewish Congress (Québec Region) stood firm in its recognition of the need for francophones to protect their linguistic heritage. French could be the object of special attention on the part of the state and receive legislature support, as long as collective right did not supersede the rights of individual citizens: "CJC, Québec Region, recognizes the preeminence of the French language but would urge that state promotion of the language of the majority not be pursued through the suspension of a fundamental right" (Canadian Jewish Congress, Québec Region, 1989b:6). This meant that the francophone majority, in the opinion of the CJC (QR), could proceed with its program of active support of French as the language of work and communication in the province, as long as the Charter of Rights remained pre-eminent. The CJC (QR), for example, supported in its *Political Action Guide* the long-sought-after radical nationalist demands for the creation of linguistic boards and the establishment of a nonconfessional public school system in the province (see Milner, in this volume). Moreover, it did not oppose the provisions in Bill 101 that directed immigrants to the French-language sectors of the existing school commissions. Quite the contrary, the CJC (QR) encouraged the Québec government to accelerate the pace of its efforts to integrate newcomers to the mainstream flow of francophone society, and applauded all measures designed to ensure that French speak-ers form a *société d'accueil* in the fullest sense of the word. In the mind of the emerging Jewish leadership of the 1990s, the future of the Montréal community rested in a Québec that, while finding comfort and strength in its francophone majority culture, makes every possible effort to recognize the various traditions and contributions of the cultural communities, all within the general framework of the pre-eminence of human rights.

The Jewish leadership still had certain specific requests to bring before the Québec state on the eve of the 1989 election. In a meeting with Premier Bourassa, held in June 1989, CJC (QR) officials stressed two points. They were: the improvement of channels of communications between minorities and all aspects of Québec's political life, and the "potential erosion of the Jewish character" of the community's institutional network (Canadian Jewish Congress, Québec Region, 1989a). Obviously, regardless of the party in power, these preoccupations will continue to occupy much of the energy of the Jewish organizational system in Montréal, at least as long as the ideological underpinnings of state intervention in Québec society remain unchanged. Meanwhile, a provincial election was held on September 25, 1989, in a climate reminiscent of the linguistic tensions of the mid-1970s. As in 1976, the anglophone population and the Jewish community in par-ticular registered a strong protest vote, electing four Equality Party candidates on the Island of Montréal (Boily, 1989; Drouilly, 1989). Once more one of the axioms of Jewish political life in Montréal was proven: individuals often choose not to follow too closely (or perhaps not at all) policies and guidelines emanating from the established leadership of the community. Nonetheless, since the election resulted in the return to power of the Liberal Party, with essentially an unchanged political platform, many Jews felt that voicing dissidence and dissatisfaction with the Bourassa regime was an important gesture in the context of Law 178 and the use of the "notwithstanding" clause. Perhaps, in the last analysis, such electoral behaviour on the part of Jews will prove to be a further element in forcing the leadership to define better its relationship to the Québec state.

THE CONSTITUTIONAL IMBROGLIO

Finally, one can assess the orientation of the Jewish polity in Montréal by its reac-tion to the current constitutional debate, as it has evolved since the demise in June 1990 of the Meech Lake Accord. Initially, except for individuals already commit-ted to partisan politics whose options were defined in advance, the Jewish com-munity had little objection to the position of the Bourassa government in the 1987 negotiations: "CJC, Québec Region, calls for a clearer definition of the concept of distinctiveness and its relationship to the equality provisions of the Charter" (Canadian Jewish Congress, Québec Region, 1989b:6). Now that events have led to an acceleration of the political tempo, with constitutional talks being defined along a radically new basis, the Jewish community has come forward with a state-ment regarding its future in Québec and in Canada. The occasion for this solemn declaration was a January 1991 hearing of the Bélanger-Campeau Commission (created in the summer of 1990). The Canadian Jewish Congress (Québec Region), Allied Jewish Community Services, and la Communauté sépharade du

Québec jointly expressed their intention to participate fully in the evolution of Québec society:

> The Jewish community of Quebec has been, is, and will remain a key component of Quebec society. As Jews and Quebecers, we understand the desire to retain and enhance one's language, culture and identity. The leadership of the Jewish community has consistently supported such efforts, documented in a series of briefs over many years. Quebec's Jews, like all Quebecers, regardless of origin, will play their part in shaping the evolving identity of Quebec. (Comité tripartite, 1990:1)

By 1991, Montréal Jews were referring to themselves as "Québécois" (Comité tripartite, 1990:2). What mattered most in the radically new context of the post-Meech Lake era, insisted the tripartite committee, was that Québec remain unfailingly committed to democratic ideals and to the preservation of human rights. For the organized leadership of the community and for the institutions they represented and managed, it was now possible to participate in the major political debates of Québec society, to examine all the constitutional solutions, and to do so in a serene and confident manner, providing that these human-rights guarantees were upheld. Of course, opinions in the community were diverse and allegiances to political parties multiple, to the point that any form of consensus or common front was impossible on most partisan questions. Most Jews in Montréal, however, were ready to recognize the legitimacy of a renewed and strengthened Québec state, providing that the proposed changes be achieved in a democratic context and that some form of confederalism be maintained with the rest of Canada:

> In our view, however, the large majority of our community would prefer a future constitutional arrangement in which Quebec would maintain important and significant links to Canada. We are certainly open to change and reform of the federal system. But an extreme reduction, and certainly the elimination of constitutional ties to Canada would likely find little support. (Comité tripartite, 1990:2)

The only other major point that the community sought to clarify vis-à-vis the Québec state in its submission to the Bélanger-Campeau Commission was the issue of the maintenance and possible aggrandizement of the Jewish network of institutions. Claiming a separate identity at the level of its religious traditions and world-wide diaspora network, the Jewish submission insisted on the right of Jews under any Québec regime to a community-centred social and cultural sphere, relatively free from the burden of centralized state intervention. This was deemed essential to the preservation of a strong Jewish identity and the perpetuation of certain specialized services to which no public instance could be held accountable, such as those pertaining to *kashrut* (i.e., observance of Jewish dietary laws) and *shekhita* (i.e., ritual slaughtering of animals) and religious education.

In essence, the tripartite submission of the institutionalized Jewish community called for the emergence of a pluralistic Québec.[10] For Jews, this meant first and foremost a Québec state that would be democratic, respectful of individual rights, and tolerant of the collective identities of its cultural communities. In other words, the tripartite Jewish presentation represented an appeal to the demographic majority to resist the temptation of monopolizing the Québec state for its own benefit, of turning the state into an instrument of cultural domination for the francophones. Formally invited to participate and to integrate themselves into a society where the

French language is emerging as the lingua franca of business and public affairs, Jews have found no insurmountable obstacle in adapting themselves to the new political circumstances, providing that their rights as individuals and their needs as a unique collectivity are recognized and enshrined by the state. Fundamentally, the publication in February 1991 by the Québec Liberal Party of the Allaire Report on constitutional matters did not alter this position, nor have the final conclusions of the Bélanger-Campeau Commission presented in March of the same year. Perhaps for the first time in a generation, that is, since the beginning of the Quiet Revolution thirty years ago, the Montréal Jewish community has achieved a coherent and definitive approach to the Québec state that is not only realistic in terms of the expectations of the francophone majority, but also capable of defining in a long-range perspective the community's interests in its most concise and essential form. Given the massive transformation of francophone Québec since the 1960s, the creation of an enlarged state bureaucratic structure, and the current reorientation of the nationalist movement, the Jewish position of the early 1990s will probably be far more likely to meet the demands of the current political conjuncture than any devised earlier.

This does not mean, of course, that Montréal Jews have come to this reorientation felicitously or, notably in the case of the anglophone Ashkenazi segment of the community, without much soul searching. Indeed, various observers have chosen the route of pessimism, as evidenced by the latest study on Canadian Jewry written by Daniel J. Elazar and Harold M. Waller: "Some Montreal Jews have found government policy to be too oppressive and onerous, and have moved away. The rest have been prepared to make accommodations up to now, though without enthusiasm" (Elazar and Waller, 1990:129). It would also be a mistake to assume that a position developed by the institutional leadership has necessarily been accepted at the individual level or even by a majority of the Montréal Jews. The community is far from monolithic in its response to issues that are not absolutely central to the survival of the Jewish identity itself, and the Québec debate certainly does not belong to that category. This may well signify that, with respect to the constitutional future, Jews may breach collective solidarity and choose as individuals and citizens of Québec to stand at opposite ends of the political spectrum, denouncing in public (as has been regularly the case in the last few months) the community's official position.[11] Whatever the outcome of the constitutional negotiations, Montréal Jews will indeed remain deeply committed to the Québec level of jurisdiction, whether reluctantly or in a spirit of cooperation and belonging. It remains for the community, and for Jews personally, either to achieve equanimity in this respect and amply participate in the democratic process and contribute to the various channels through which the Québec state operates, or to stand outside of the political arena, whatever the cost may be. This choice will most likely determine ultimately the question of whether the Jewish community of Montréal is viable and creative, or condemned to a gradual decline.[12]

NOTES

1. An excellent and up-to-date description of the Montréal Jewish community structure can be found in Elazar and Waller, 1990. See also Weinfeld, 1986.
2. A very detailed sociological study of this period was undertaken by Rosenberg, 1939.

3. According to the 1986 census, the Jewish community in Montréal numbers approximately 100,000 individuals. In 1989, there were thirteen full-time private Jewish schools in the Montréal region, serving 6,700 pupils, and eleven part-time supplementary education institutions serving 1,000 pupils. Sixty to 65 percent of the total Jewish school-age population is enrolled in the private Jewish day schools, primary level, and 35 percent in the secondary level. These percentages are among the highest in North America for any given Jewish community.
4. It must be added that before 1970, the francophone majority had shown a similar disinterest in bringing the Jews of Montréal into harmony with the pulse of Québec society.
5. See a document entitled: "Mémoire soumis par le Congrès juif canadien, région du Québec, à la Commission d'enquête sur la situation de la langue française ainsi que sur les droits linguistiques au Québec," August 1969; and another one entitled: "Allied Jewish Community Services, Cultural Services Division, Position Paper on Brief to be submitted by the Canadian Jewish Congress to the commission of Inquiry on Language Rights in Québec," Archives of Canadian Jewish Congress, Montréal.
6. See the memorandum to Leon Teitelbaum, from Ted Baker, November 5, 1976, and memorandum to Leon Teitelbaum from Mayer Levy, November 5, 1976. Archives of Canadian Jewish Congress, Montréal, Ted Baker collection.
7. Not all Montréal Jews at the time could present these matters in a rational perspective, as evidenced by other articles that appeared in the period (see Richler, 1983).
8. Most studies agree that the level of official bilingualism in the Montréal Jewish community reaches between 70 and 75 percent.
9. A very detailed description of the political role of the Canadian Jewish Congress in the Montréal community can be found in Elazar and Waller, 1990:chs. 4–5. The Québec region branch of the CJC enjoys a fair degree of autonomy and has often been far more sensitive to the issue of Québec nationalism than its parent body.
10. The other Jewish submission to the Bélanger-Campeau Commission, that of the B'nai Brith League for Human Rights, did not even mention the constitutional future of Québec society, concentrating solely on the issue of rights and freedoms.
11. The latest in a long series of such incidents has been sparked by the publication of Mordecai Richler's most controversial book to date on the Québec question: *Oh! Canada, Oh! Quebec, Requiem for a Divided Country* (Toronto: Penguin Books, 1992, 277 pp.). The text has triggered a bitter debate in the French-language press of Québec, but has also been the occasion of an acrimonious exchange of words between CJC (QR) and the author. See Michael Crelinsten, "Un portrait trompeur du Québec contemporain," in *Le Devoir*, September 24, 1991, pp. 3–8, and *The Canadian Jewish News*, April 2, 1992, pp. 4–5.
12. A recent development in the relationship between the Québec government and the Jewish community of Montréal highlighted how cooperation between the two entities can be advantageous to the latter. In April 1992, the Minister of Immigration and Cultural Communities signed an agreement whereby Jews from the former Soviet Union will be admitted to Québec as immigrants under a specific pilot project. The program will likely bring between 300 and 400 Jews to Montréal in 1992, and possibly more the following years if the venture is judged successful.

REFERENCES

Abella, Irving M. (1990). *A Coat of Many Colors*. Toronto: Lester & Orpen Dennys, 248 pp.
Anctil, Pierre (1988). *Le Rendez-vous manqué. Les Juifs de Montréal face au Québec de l'entre-deux-guerres*. Québec: Institut québécois de recherche sur la culture, 366 pp.
Anctil, Pierre (1990). "Ni Catholiques, ni Protestants: les Juifs de Montréal," in Jacques Portes, ed., *Le Fait français et l'histoire du Canada, XIXe et XXe siècle*. Paris: Société française d'histoire d'outre-mer, pp. 179–87.
Anctil, Pierre, and Gary Caldwell, eds. (1984). *Juifs et réalités juives au Québec*. Québec: Institut québécois de recherche sur la culture, 371 pp.
Berdugo-Cohen, Marie et al. (1987). *Juifs marocains à Montréal*. Montréal: VLB éditeur, 209 pp.
Boily, Robert et al. (1989). "Les Élections du 25 septembre," in *Le Devoir*, Montréal, October 12, p. 9; October 13, p. 9.
Boissevain, Jeremy (1970). *The Italians of Montreal: Social Adjustment in a Plural Society*. Ottawa: Minister of Supply and Services, Studies of the Royal Commission on Bilingualism and Biculturalism, no. 7, 87 pp.
Caldwell, Gary, and Éric Waddell, eds. (1982). *The English of Québec: From Majority to Minority Status*. Québec: Institut québécois de recherche sur la culture, 464 pp.

Canadian Jewish Congress, Québec Region (1989a). "The Québec Election and the Jewish Community, What Now?" in *Dialogue*, Montréal, vol. 1, no. 3, December, pp. 1–2.

Canadian Jewish Congress, Québec Region (1989b). *Provincial Election Political Action Guide*, Montréal, 12 pp.

Comité tripartite (1990). Brief Presented to the Parliamentary Commission Looking into the Political and Constitutional Future of Québec, Montréal, Canadian Jewish Congress (Québec Region) in collaboration with Allied Jewish Community Services of Montréal and the Communauté sépharade du Québec, 8 pp.

Commission d'enquête sur la situation de la langue française et sur les droits linguistiques au Québec (1972). *La Situation de la langue française au Québec*. Québec: Gouvernement du Québec, vol. III, "Les Groupes ethniques."

Drouilly, Pierre (1989). "Le Succès des Partis égalité et unité," in *Le Devoir*, Montréal, 4 October, p. 9.

Dupont, Antonin (1973). *Les Relations entre l'Église et l'État sous Louis-Alexandre Taschereau, 1920–36*. Montréal: Guérin, 366 pp.

Elazar, Daniel, and Harold M. Waller (1990). *Maintaining Consensus: The Canadian Jewish Polity in the Postwar World*. New York: University Press of America, 501 pp.

Goldbloom, Victor (1982). "Le Judaïsme québécois. Une Communauté vigoureuse, bien enracinée et assez sereine," in *Le Devoir*, Montréal, 8 April, pp. 36, 38.

Gottheil, Allen (1988). *Les Juifs progressistes au Québec*. Montréal: Éditions par ailleurs, 372 pp.

Huot, Antonio (1926). "La Question juive chez nous," in *L'Action catholique*, Québec, 17 May, p. 3; 18 May, p. 3; 19 May, p. 3.

Jedwab, Jack (1986). "Uniting Uptowners and Downtowners: The Jewish Electorate and Quebec Provincial Politics (1927–1939)," in *Canadian Ethnic Studies*, vol. XVIII, No. 2, pp. 7–19.

Lasry, Jean-Claude, and Claude Tapia, eds. (1989). *Les Juifs du Maghreb, diasporas contemporaines*. Montréal: Les Presses de l'Université de Montréal, Paris: L'Harmattan, 477 pp.

Lesage, Gilles (1988). "La Loi 101: une police d'assurance pour les francophones," in *Le Devoir*, Montréal, 20 June 1988, pp. 1, 8.

Levine, Marc V. (1990). *The Reconquest of Montreal: Language Policy and Social Change in a Bilingual City*. Philadelphia: Temple University Press, 285 pp.

McRoberts, Kenneth (1991). *English Canada and Quebec: Avoiding the Issue*. North York, Ont.: York University, Robarts Centre for Canadian Studies.

Neamtan, Hyman (1940). "The Rise and Fall of Jewish Attendance in the Protestant Schools of Greater Montreal," in *The Canadian Jewish Year Book, 1940–41*, Montréal, 11, pp. 180–96.

Polèse, Mario et al., eds. (1978). *La Géographie résidentielle des immigrants et des groupes ethniques: Montréal, 1971*. Montréal: INRS-Urbanisation, 42 pp.

Richler, Mordecai (1969). *The Street*. Toronto: McClelland and Stewart, 128 pp.

Richler, Mordecai (1977). "Oh Canada! Lament for a Divided Country," in *The Atlantic*, Boston, vol. 240, no. 6, December, pp. 41–55.

Richler, Mordecai (1983). "Quebec: Language Problems," in *The Atlantic*, Boston, vol. 251, no. 6, June, pp. 10, 14, 16–18, 20–21, 24.

Robinson, Ira et al., eds. (1990). *An Everyday Miracle: Yiddish Culture in Montreal*. Montréal: Véhicule Press, 169 pp.

Rome, David (1975). "On the Jewish School Question in Montreal, 1903–1931," in *Canadian Jewish Archives*, Montreal, new series, no. 3, 136 pp.

Rome, David, and Jacques Langlais (1986). *Juifs et Québécois français, 200 ans d'histoire commune*, Montréal: Fides, 286 pp.

Rosenberg, Louis (1939). *Canada's Jews: A Social and Economic Study of the Jews in Canada*. Montreal: Canadian Jewish Congress, 418 pp.

Roskies, David G. (1990). "Yiddish in Montreal: The Utopian Experiment," in Ira Robinson et al., eds., *An Everyday Miracle: Yiddish Culture in Montreal*. Montréal: Véhicule Press, pp. 22–38.

Shaffir, William (1983). "Hassidic Jews and Quebec Politics," in *The Jewish Journal of Sociology*, vol. XXV, no. 2, December, pp. 105–18.

Taddeo, Donat J., and Raymond C. Taras (1987). *Le Débat linguistique au Québec. La Communauté italienne et la langue d'enseignement*. Montréal: Les Presses de l'Université de Montréal, 246 pp.

Waller, Harold M., and Morton Weinfeld (1981). "The Jews of Quebec and 'Le Fait français,'" in M. Weinfeld, W. Shaffir, and I. Cotler, eds., *The Canadian Jewish Mosaic*. Toronto: John Wiley and Sons, pp. 415–39.

Weinfeld, Morton (1986). "The Jews of Quebec: An Overview," in Ronald S. Aigen and Gershon D. Hundert, eds., *Community and the Individual Jew*. Philadelphia: Reconstructionist Rabbinical College Press, pp. 85–109.

Weinfeld, Morton (1990). "Canadian Jews and Canadian Pluralism," in Seymour Martin Lipset, ed., *American Pluralism and the Jewish Community*. New Brunswick, N.J.: Transaction Books, pp. 89–106.

Wisse, Ruth R., and Irving Cotler (1977). "Québec's Jews: Caught in the Middle," in *Commentary*, vol. 64, no. 3, September, pp. 55–59.

P A R T

5

QUÉBEC
ECONOMY

Economic Development: From Family Enterprise to Big Business

Yves Bélanger
Université du Québec à Montréal

When we talk about Québec entrepreneurship, we tend to think mainly of the group of people and companies that presently control the Québec economy. These men and women are depicted as untiring pioneers who conquered hereto inaccessible economic spaces. Thanks to their determination, this new elite is perceived as a concrete embodiment of the movement of emancipation and liberation of the Québec people.

This epic vision of Québec development is pervasive in the economic literature, especially in the historical accounts of the achievements of the Quiet Revolution. This vision, however, has little to do with reality. Research has shown that the roots of Québec entrepreneurship can be traced to a much earlier period. Using statistics compiled by Jacques Viger around 1825, Fernand Ouellet concluded that francophones represented about 35 percent of the colony's bourgeois class at the beginning of the industrial era (Ouellet, 1971). Joanne Burgess showed how the footwear industry contributed to the rise of a francophone industrial class in the middle of the 19th century (Burgess, 1977). More recently, a remarkable study by Ronald Rudin demonstrated the strategic importance of francophone regional banks between 1900 and 1925 (Rudin, 1985). The emergence of the first large francophone fortunes at the beginning of this century have also been well documented by Ernest L'Heureux, and Émile Benoit (L'Heureux, 1930; and Benoit, 1925). The 1931 and 1941 censuses confirmed the existence of a significant local business elite: approximately 60 percent of the owners and managers in the Québec economy were francophones. A well-known study by André Raynauld revealed, however, that in the early 1960s the position of the francophone business class had deteriorated considerably (Raynauld, 1974).

The promoters of the economic liberation of Québec sent out distress signals during those difficult years. From Olivar Asselin to Jacques Parizeau, the objective was the same: "Let's take control of our economy." But the development of large firms being dependent upon economic and financial instruments that were inaccessible to Québec entrepreneurs, they inevitably perpetuated the model of the small and regional family enterprise, while anglophone capital for its part was creating large, modern corporations. In 1850, when small business was dominant, the struggle for control over the Québec economy had the language groups on a close to equal footing. The waves of economic concentration that culminated in the 1950s, and that were induced by American capital, provoked the loss of control of the more dynamic francophone companies, and widened the gap between francophone and anglophone capital.

The most recent evaluations put local francophone control over the province's economy at approximately 60 percent. In recent years, Québec entrepreneurship has undergone major transformations and is now made up of large industrial and financial firms that closely resemble those controlled by large anglophone capital. Many Québec francophone firms have acquired significant international status, after bypassing the Canadian market. What has spurred these radical changes in Québécois entrepreneurial structures?

The present chapter will attempt to answer this question, and will at the same time seek to contribute to a better understanding of the inner dynamics of the Québec business community. We will see that the rejection of the traditional model of development will bring many important and influential business leaders to participate in the transformation of society and the state. The first concrete results of this new orientation will appear after 1960. Small family empires will reach their peak, but this era of prosperity will be short-lived. The recession of the late 1960s will seriously undermine the economic foundations of the business elite. We will show that the difficulties of the private sector provoked substantial economic intervention by the state and its apparatus.

From that point on, a gradual movement toward concentration will take place and develop well into the 1970s. Large corporations will become dominant and a new generation of business leaders will emerge. These entrepreneurs will rely heavily on the nationalist policies of Robert Bourassa between 1970 and 1976, and of René Lévesque in the following years. The greater maturity achieved by francophone capital will eventually lead to significant changes in the role of the state.

THE APOGEE OF FAMILY ENTERPRISE

For business, the early 1960s proved quite favourable. The economy entered a period of prosperity, while at the same moment a government was elected in Québec that was the most interventionist and the most enthusiastic supporter of economic nationalism the province had known since Confederation. With the 1960 election, the broadening of the local market, preferential purchasing policies, the creation of new financial levers, and the adoption of measures to support Québec ownership and to encourage the formation of large local business concerns all became part of the dominant ideology of the new government.

Never, in fact, had Québec business leaders been more eagerly invited to participate in governmental power. Business associations were called upon to play an increasing role in devising governmental economic strategies. The main objective of the business elites, at that point, was clearly to strengthen local capital to make it more competitive and to adapt it to modern economic structures. The government channelled a significant portion of the new resources of the state toward private enterprise. Hence, francophone entrepreneurs were called upon, for the first time since the 19th century, to participate in defining the political parameters of the provincial economy.

At the same time that those ideas became dominant at the political level, a small number of the larger francophone family enterprises were expanding rapidly and appeared as the most logical contenders for the leadership of the Québec economy (Falardeau, 1965). For example, the Jean-Louis Lévesque group, with its conglomerate built around Trans-Canada Corporation and l'Industrielle, reached its peak after acquiring L.G. Beaubien in January 1963. Controlling assets of close to \$300 million, Lévesque's financial,[1] industrial,[2] and commercial[3] empire became a symbol of the success and economic emancipation of francophones.

Similarly, for the Brillant in Rimouski, the early 1960s were quite prosperous. The nationalization in 1962 of the Compagnie de pouvoir du Bas-St-Laurent for the sum of \$5 million gave the group the necessary cash flow to expand in other, more profitable areas. The most important transaction occurred in 1964, when Brillant took control of the Corporation d'expansion économique (Corpex). This move is indicative of the extent of the power of family enterprises at the time. Indeed, Corpex had symbolized for many years the march toward the modernization of the Québec economy. In the eyes of the nationalist intelligentsia, Corpex represented a financial lever to strengthen the economy and to create powerful industrial and financial empires. Even though the company did not achieve the goals of its founders, it was nonetheless, at the time of the takeover, one of the main focal points of regional economic forces.

Other family groups were expanding as well. The mining group controlled by the Beauchemin family, Sullivan Mines Inc., reached its peak in 1965–66.[4] In 1960, Bombardier successfully launched its snowmobile activities. In 1965–66, 45,000 units were sold. United Auto Parts, the Préfontaine family firm, pursued expansionist policies and its sales totalled more than \$40 million in the mid-1960s.

These family "success stories" were easy to explain. They were, to a large extent, the result of the movement toward concentration in the 1950s. With the help of the nationalist momentum, the state, and an expanding economy, these groups capitalized on their accumulated wealth and managed significant breakthroughs on the road to becoming large corporations. It has to be underlined, however, that francophone capital was still lagging behind. Since World War II, English Canadian and foreign capital had created giant corporations that far surpassed the nascent Québec financial or industrial groups (Government of Canada, 1971). In certain areas, and particularly in the financial sector, the gap was enormous (Bélanger, 1978). The early 1960s appeared nonetheless as the first stage of a transitional period that would lead to the creation of the first large francophone corporations. This phase allowed the more dynamic and prosperous local entrepreneurs to reach the limits of their financial potential. Those emerging conglomerates paved the way for a profound transformation of the mentality of the entrepreneurs, which in turn led to significant economic concentration and the development of new economic activities.

As regards concentration, the statistical data reproduced in Table 22.1 are quite eloquent. Between 1960 and 1970, the number of manufacturing firms dropped 15 percent, from 12,001 to 10,206. This movement towards concentration affected all areas, except a few rapid growth sectors such as metal fabricating,

Table 22.1
Industrial Concentration, Number of Manufacturing Companies by Industry Group, 1960–70

INDUSTRY GROUP	1960	1965	1970
Food and beverages	2,656	2,209	1,711
Tobacco products	22	20	16
Rubber products	33	30	182
Leather products	334	290	252
Textile mills	404	448	402
Knitting mills	209	227	190
Clothing industries	1,513	1,547	1,490
Wood industries	2,164	1,390	1,049
Furniture industries	726	778	766
Paper and allied products	195	209	208
Printing, publishing	987	1,022	1,028
Primary metals	117	106	96
Metal fabricating	709	917	975
Machinery	89	120	133
Transportation equipment	110	135	172
Electrical products	114	136	170
Non-metallic mineral products	407	414	328
Petroleum and coal products	15	17	19
Chemicals	368	342	325
Misc. manufacturing	781	790	664
Total	11,961	11,147	10,176

machinery, plastics, and electrical appliances. The drop is most noticeable in the wood industries, with a reduction of 59.2 percent in the number of manufacturing companies.

THE COLLAPSE OF FAMILY ENTERPRISE

Echoing the predictions of Gérard Filion, chief executive officer of the Société générale de financement, was an article in the Québec City daily *Le Soleil* titled: "Large industry will eventually kill family enterprise" (*Le Soleil,* 3 April 1964). According to Filion, this process would take twenty-five years and occur through mergers and acquisitions. His predictions were partially wrong, because, in less than ten years, St. James Street witnessed the complete overhaul of local economic structures, and many family empires collapsed.

Jean-Louis Lévesque seemed to be the first out of the gate. In May 1964, he announced his intention to sell l'Industrielle, one of Québec's most important insurance companies, to an American company. According to Lévesque, this transaction sought to guarantee the necessary funding to complete the purchase of L.G. Beaubien. Québec intellectual circles, led by Claude Ryan, desperately attempted to convince the management of l'Industrielle, which had more than a billion dollars in assets in 1964, to reverse its decision. Lévesque refused, and the sale was concluded at the price of $15 million, allowing the Americans to control 50.1 percent of the company. Following a protracted and intense public debate, in December 1969, the Québec government forced the "mutualization" (sale to the insured) of l'Industrielle, despite the strong objections of the stockholders. The sale of l'Industrielle had a detrimental effect on Lévesque's image.

Already in 1962–63, Lévesque had run into problems with Dupuis Frères. The Dupuis family company faced a shrinking market and found it increasingly difficult to compete with the large English Canadian retail outlets. Dupuis Frères returned briefly to a profit position in 1966–67, which was followed by a string of deficits. Jean-Louis Lévesque finally decided to sell the company. Despite many salvage attempts by the Caisse de dépôt et placement du Québec and other Québec financial groups, Dupuis Frères, the most prestigious symbol of the empire of Jean-Louis Lévesque, declared bankruptcy in 1978. In 1965, Jean-Louis Lévesque sold another subsidiary, the Corporation des Valeurs Trans-Canada, to a young Franco-Ontarian, Paul Desmarais, who, three years later, created Power Corporation. But contrary to Lévesque, Desmarais preferred to find most of his support and allies in the English-Canadian financial elite.

That same year, the Brillant family was once again in the limelight. At a time when large North American telephone conglomerates were attempting to take control of small independent rural telephone companies, Québec Telephone was offered $25 million by an American corporation for the sale of all its assets. At that point, the book value of the company stood at only $6 million! News of the transaction provoked a major political storm. Many parliamentarians asked for a public inquiry on the sale. In March 1966, the government passed legislation to block the sale and to force public hearings. The nationalist offensive failed, however, and the transaction was completed at the end of 1966.

In the fall of 1965, it was the turn of the Simard family to attract attention. Marine Industries, the jewel of the family enterprise, was threatened because of the potential loss of federal subsidies for shipbuilding. The Simards rapidly got rid of Marine and its subsidiaries, Foresteel and MIL Tag, and sold them to the Société générale de financement.

The situation of the family enterprises in Québec began to seriously deteriorate, however, with the 1968 recession. The first casualty was the Montréal daily *Métro Express*, founded by the Brillant family during the protracted strike at *La Presse* in 1964. The family financial holding Corpex was also encountering serious difficulties. Many of its key subsidiaries, including Simard-Beaudry and A. Bélanger, were incurring severe losses. In an attempt to strengthen its financial position, Corpex sought the support of English-Canadian financier Howard Webster. Additional financial problems forced it to sell its assets in the insurance company Les Prévoyants and in Québécair; the presence of Howard Webster became more and more pervasive. These moves were not sufficient to solve the financial difficulties of the Brillant. The following year, an additional five firms were sold to Hochigan Inc., another Webster company.

Probably the most important event in the decline of the large families, however, was the bankruptcy of the Marc Masson-Bienvenu group. Grandson of Joseph Masson on his mother's side, who was the first francophone vice-president of the Bank of Montréal, and on his father's side, of Tancrède Bienvenu, who reorganized the Provincial Bank, son of Achille Bienvenu, former vice-president of Catelli, and nephew of Paul Bienvenu, member of the board of directors of the Bank of Montréal, Marc Masson-Bienvenu started his business career at 21 years of age with the creation of the Maison Bienvenu. A few years later, the young financier set up Cofomo, a financial holding corporation specialized in small and medium-sized firms. Within ten years, he succeeded in building a strong financial group. In 1967, Cofomo controlled the Crédit St-Laurent, Phénix Finance, Sterling Finance Corp., St-Lawrence Credit Plan, Montréal Acceptance, the St-Laurent Life Insurance Company, and the Corporation foncière de Montréal (Canada, Statistics Canada, 1967). In addition, Cofomo acquired two companies with cash-flow problems, Labrador Finance and Crédit M.G. The overall value of his empire was estimated at approximately $50 million (Corporation foncière de Montréal, 1967).

Marc Masson-Bienvenu's problems started in March 1967 with the purchase of an important block of shares of British International Finance from Toronto financier Sinclair Stevens. This transaction gave Masson-Bienvenu the control of a company that was going to provoke his demise: the Western Bank. The curious history of this bank started in 1962, when Sinclair Stevens asked for a new bank charter, hoping to become the first financier in more than fifty years to be granted such a privilege. A few months earlier, the Porter Commission, created to study the situation in the banking sector and to propose changes in banking legislation, suggested that the creation of new banks would be beneficial. Of all the projects taking shape (the Maritime Bank, the Alberta Bank, the Continental Bank, etc.), the one involving the Western Bank seemed to have the most potential.

To increase their chances of success, the promoters obtained the cooperation of former Bank of Canada governor James Coyne, and offered him the presidency of the new bank. Coyne, however, lit the powder keg in 1967 by publicly accusing Sinclair Stevens of violating the bank's charter, by, among other things, attempting to draw foreign investors in the operation. The accusation provoked a stormy session in a House of Commons Committee, and led to the firing of Sinclair Stevens. Stevens quickly found himself in a difficult financial position, which left him no other choice but to sell his shares in the Western Bank.

Ten days before the deadline fixed by the creditors of Western Bank, Marc Masson-Bienvenu decided to purchase 50.2 percent of the capital stock of British International Finance (BIF) and obtained at the same time control of the Western Bank and its subsidiaries, including York Lambton. To pay off York Lambton's debt, Cofomo called upon Corpex, with which it established links in 1957, creating a de facto association between Aubert Brillant and the Western Bank initiative (Lépine, May 1969). At that point, Masson-Bienvenu's holdings passed the $120 million mark.

The Stevens-Coyne controversy became a power struggle between Coyne and Masson-Bienvenu and caused the dismissal of the former governor of the Bank of Canada. The new bank's problems led to at least three attempted takeovers by the western financial groups. Even Sinclair Stevens tried to exploit the chaotic situation by attempting a comeback.

The funds invested in the Western Bank dried up the financial resources of the Bienvenu group, and created cash flow problems in the two weak links of his empire, Labrador Acceptance and Crédit M.G. Marc Masson-Bienvenu opted for liquidation of his holdings in the Western Bank, but various legal proceedings and manoeuvres made him lose control of the bank before he could liquidate his assets. This did not prevent the Western Bank from becoming the first banking institution in the history of Canada from going bankrupt before opening day (Lemelin, March 1968).

The bankruptcy of the Western Bank provoked the disintegration of the Bienvenu group. In September 1967, Marc Masson-Bienvenu gave up control of Cofomo to Fridolin Simard and Aubert Brillant. The new management, however, was unsuccessful in turning the situation around, given that they were not able to obtain bank funding for a salvage operation. Cofomo filed for bankruptcy on 24 September 1968. Between October 1968 and January 1969, most of the subsidiaries followed suit (Miskew, January 1969). The collapse of Cofomo also had an impact on other Québec institutions. To avoid being dragged into the disaster, Corpex was restructured around Sogebry and moved away from Aubert Brillant. The latter filed for bankruptcy at the end of 1968.

In addition to depriving the provincial economy of one of its more significant financial institutions, the bankruptcy of Cofomo showed the tremendous vulnerability of private francophone capital in Québec. This vulnerability was due in large part to the weaknesses and insufficiencies of the local financial networks. In the case of Cofomo, a mistake of a few million dollars precipitated bankruptcy of two major holdings and disrupted the entire regional financial network. On the positive side, the problems of Cofomo and Corpex forced many participants on the Québec economic scene to become conscious of the limits of the private sector as it was structured at the time.

Most of the private entrepreneurs were never able to look beyond their immediate interests. An excellent example of the limits of the "group consciousness" of the financial and industrial private sector was provided by the attempted sale of La Prévoyance to U.S. interests in 1971. Involving once again Jean-Louis Lévesque, head of the Fond FIC (of which La Prévoyance was a subsidiary), the intended sale elicited strong negative reactions. Following this new episode in the long struggle for the protection of Québécois economic interests, a large part of the political elite lost faith in the traditional forms of administration and control, and turned to the state.

Indeed, in all circles, numerous voices supported the economic leadership of the state. Most Québec political parties adjusted their program accordingly (Bernier, 1975). The failure of the financial groups that we just described signalled the end of the era of family enterprise. And it is only from then on that Québec business started to undergo its own "Quiet Revolution".

THE QUÉBEC STATE AND THE RISE OF BIG BUSINESS

Thus it is in large part the weaknesses and failures of the Québec private sector that fuelled the debates over the role of the state in the economy. Indeed, the state created financial instruments which had a profound impact on the Québec economy. The Québec state initiated a preferential purchasing policy and an industrial development strategy whose objective was to stop the economic decline of the province and to reinforce the economic position of the local business class.

Table 22.2 demonstrates the growth in the assets of the main state corporations in Québec. At the beginning of 1965, only four major state corporations were in existence, totalling little more than $2.4 billion in assets. In 1970, eleven corpora-

Table 22.2
Assets held by the Main Québec State Corporations: 1964–80
(for fiscal years ending March 31)

CORPORATIONS	1964–65	1969–70	1974–75	1979–80
Raffinerie de sucre du Québec	3	3	13	14
Société générale de financement	22	49	201	824
Société des alcools du Québec	37	42	71	179
Hydro-Québec	2,351	3,658	5,814	15,505
Caisse de dépôt et placement	—	990	3,164	7,128
Sidbec	—	188(1)	355	972
Rexfor	—	3	58	41
SOQUEM	—	7	42	76
SOQUIP	—	1	76	103
SHQ	—	70	491	601
Société du parc industriel du centre du Québec	—	4	20	38
SDI	—	—	80	132
Société d'administration de l'Outaouais	—	—	17	45
CRIQ	—	—	10	14
Société de développement immobilier du Québec	—	—	27	62
SDBJ	—	—	52	67
Société de développement coopératif	—	—	—	8
SODIC	—	—	—	1
SNA	—	—	—	12
Total	2,431	5,015	10,491	25,822

(1) For fiscal year ending December 31 1970.
Source: Québec (prov.), *Comptes de la province de Québec et États financiers des entreprises du Gouvernement du Québec*, Québec, (1964-65) to (1979-80).

tions accounted for $5 billion in assets. In 1975, the sixteen main state firms, six of which were created by the Bourassa government, managed $10.5 billion in assets. In a ten-year period, the assets of the large state corporations quadrupled. The social and economic context of the 1960s, by encouraging a radical transformation of the Québec economy, opened the door to direct state interventions.

Even the Royal Commission on Bilingualism and Biculturalism, in its 1965 report, underlined the frustration generated by the economic inferiority of the Québécois. According to the commissioners, "the notion of equality implies considerably increased possibilities for the French Canadians in the public and private sectors of the economy" (Canada, 1965, p. xxxv).

The model of development put in place by the Lesage government was oriented toward greater provincial autonomy in the area of economic management and more independence with regard to companies under foreign control. The provincial government sought above all to strengthen local industrial and financial capital. The state apparatus became the "conscience" of Québécois firms. For the first time in history, francophone businessmen were invited to participate on a large scale in the definition of the province's economic policy. Even though they expressed concern over the state's growing intervention, including the nationalization of the province's hydro-electric companies, a large majority of local entrepreneurs reacted favourably to governmental initiatives granting them preferential treatment. They supported the creation of the Société générale de financement (SGF) in 1962, which was to become a "mixed" (public–private) holding corporation. In the area of forestry, local business groups backed the various measures to help the francophone-dominated wood industries. The creation of an Office de crédit industriel (OCI) in 1967 was a direct response to the complaints of francophone industrialists that the various existing funding agencies were mainly destined to support large Canadian capital. Through the OCI and eventually the Société de développement industriel (SDI), a new group of small and medium-sized corporations progressively replaced the family entreprises of the 1950s.

Thus, following the collapse of family enterprise, it was around the state that the new guard ("la garde montante") organized. Hydro-Québec, the Caisse de dépôt, and the SGF were to become the Québec government's major instruments to orchestrate economic renewal. Later, SIDBEC (1968), SOQUIP (1969), CRIQ (1969), and SDI (1970) allowed the state to play a preponderant role in the promotion of regional economic forces in many sectors of the economy. It is largely because, with few exceptions, francophone entrepreneurship was incapable of creating a significant network of large, modern, and competitive business firms that the state intervened. The primary objective was not to increase the economic powers of the state, but rather to stimulate and develop a local private economic base.

The Caisse de dépôt played a particularly important role in restructuring local capital. In 1969, for example, it initiated the creation of Provigo, a large retail food chain that was built around three small existing distributors. The Caisse not only participated financially in the operation, but laid the groundwork which allowed the new company to gain access to the stock market. Various acquisitions culminated in 1977 with the purchase of food giant M. Loeb. Here again, the Caisse played a key role in supporting Provigo.

In the 1970s, the Caisse participated in a large number of transactions with the objective of creating new industrial groups. It supported the purchase of Québec Poultry by the Coopérative Fédérée in 1975, the creation of Omnimedic in 1973, and the acquisition of Câblevision Nationale from U.S. interests. La Caisse also joined with SGF to allow Bombardier to purchase MLW-Worthington.

Although quite different, the role of the SDI in funding "dynamic" small and medium-sized firms was of crucial importance. In the space of a few years, the SDI invested several hundred million dollars in loans, subsidies, and capital stock of over a thousand companies. Through its programs centred on the transformation of the industrial structure and on job creation, it contributed significantly to opening up perspectives for firms in Québec's regions (Québec, Ministère du Développement économique, 1979).

Hydro-Québec also played a key role in the development of francophone corporations. A few years after the nationalizations, the new state monopoly succeeded through a preferential buying policy and contract allocations (James Bay, Churchill Falls) in stimulating the growth of many local firms in the areas of electrical equipment and hydroelectricity. Engineering firms are a good example of a sector which benefited from Hydro-Québec's policies. Before nationalization, most of the engineering work was allocated to American or English-Canadian firms. Nascent francophone firms obtained most of the contracts for the Manicouagan and James Bay developments. As a result, firms such as SNC, Lavalin,

ABBDL, and Warren Rousseau experienced very rapid growth and were eventually able to compete for international contracts. SNC, for example, increased its assets from $7 to $78.5 million, and its employees from 500 to 2,000 in the 1969 to 1975 period. As a result, three Québec firms were ranked among the top five hydroelectric engineering companies in the world (Québec, OPDQ, 1981).

Here are a few other examples. In 1969–70, American food giant Beatrice Foods attempted to buy out Vachon Inc., a small but dynamic food processor from Beauce region. The Québec government's reaction was instantaneous. The Department of Industry and Commerce succeeded in attracting the interest of Mouvement Desjardins, but the Loi des Caisses d'épargne et de crédit did not authorize the cooperative to invest in capital stock. In 1971, the law was changed (Bill 91), and the Mouvement Desjardins created the Société d'investissement Desjardins (SID). Under the aegis of SID, Vachon became Culinar, one of the most powerful manufacturing groups in the food sector in Québec.

Government support, especially that of the Caisse, the SDI, the SGF, and Rexfor, was also vital in helping local firms to invest in the forest products sector. By providing funding and eliminating the pulp and paper giant's monopoly on woodcutting rights, the state made possible the rapid development of firms such as Normick Perron, La Vérendrye, Papier Cascade, Tembec, Industries Tanguay, and Forex-Leroy (Québec, Ministère des Terres et Forêts, 1972).

The picture would not be complete without examining the considerable role played by the cooperative movement, which, in many ways, best reflected the ideals of the "Quiet Revolution." Not only did the cooperative sector provide support for the developing Québécois firms, but it regrouped, concentrated, and diversified its activities. In a few short years, particularly in the financial and agricultural products sectors, cooperative firms came to occupy leadership positions. The Mouvement Desjardins, the Caisses d'entraide économique, the Fédérée, the Coopérative agricole de Granby, the Coopérative agricole du Bas St-Laurent, and the Coopérative agricole du Sud-Est du Québec all became powerful industrial, commercial, and financial groups, and symbols of the economic renaissance of francophones.

The overall success of the Québec government's efforts to support the development of large francophone corporations should not distract from the fact that it took a significant amount of time for the government to enact coherent economic policies. Many initiatives in the 1960s failed, including the much vaunted attempt by the Conseil d'orientation économique du Québec (COEQ) to devise an economic plan for the province. Several state corporations, including the SGF, adopted strategies of indiscriminate support for local firms. As a result, resources were wasted in attempts to bolster firms in declining industries or with no long-term growth potential.

In the 1970s, state intervention, at the global as well as at the crown corporation level, became more focused and more coherent. The emphasis was clearly placed on developing large and competitive firms in areas where growth potential and international perspectives seemed optimal. Increasingly, Québec firms were encouraged to seek international partnership and consortium arrangements. It was felt important that the provincial economy should be more integrated into the continental economy. The Descoteaux and Tetley reports in 1974 clearly and explicitly articulated the Québec government's economic objectives and strategies: a policy of economic nationalism based on the development of large francophone conglomerates able to operate in the continental and international context (Gouvernement du Québec, MIC, 1974, and Gouvernement du Québec, Conseil exécutif, 1974).

THE EVOLUTION OF FRANCOPHONE CAPITAL

The remarkable evolution of francophone Québécois capital was documented by the province's department of Industry and Commerce in 1975. Focussing on the evolution and the structure of the ownership of Québec manufacturing firms, the study made six main points:

1. As can be seen in Table 22.3, Québec francophones were dominant in two industries, wood and furniture, and had a strong presence in five others: food and beverages, leather, metal products, transport equipment, and mineral products.
2. Other parts of the study indicate that growth was evident in five sectors. The francophone share in transport equipment increased from 5.1 percent in 1961 to 35 percent in 1973, in large part because of Bombardier's rapid development. In the rubber and plastics sectors, francophone capital increased from 6.1 percent to 21.4 percent. In printing and editing, francophone ownership rose to 44.6 percent from 28.2 percent, partly as a result of the growth of Quebecor and Unimedia. Led by Shockbeton and various glass manufacturers, the francophone share in nonmetallic mineral products doubled from 15.8 percent to 32.3 percent. And finally the creation of the state steel complex SIDBEC allowed francophones to increase their participation in primary metals from 7.1 percent in 1961 to 21.2 in 1973.
3. As a result of this growth, the percentage of outputs controlled by francophones rose rapidly to the detriment of Canadian and American capital. It progressed to 23.4 percent in 1973 from 16.4 percent in 1961.
4. In comparaison with the 1961 study, industrial concentration had also increased substantially. More and more francophone-held companies were part of the group of the larger corporations. In sectors such as wood, printing, and editing, they clearly dominated the market.
5. Francophone investments and assets, however, remained heavily concentrated in the traditional sectors, such as wood (27.2 percent), food and agricultural products (17 percent), and nonmetallic mineral products (11.4 percent).
6. Francophone investments tended to be concentrated geographically in the Montréal and Québec City regions. In 1973, these two regions accounted for 65 percent of all investments.

It thus seemed clear that the policies followed during the Quiet Revolution allowed a marked improvement in the place of francophone capital in the Québec economy. Québécois firms succeeded not only in strengthening their traditional positions in finance, commerce, food and beverages, and wood and furniture, but also in penetrating new sectors, such as transport equipment, plastics, and primary metals, from which they had been almost absent in the past.

Table 22.3
Distribution of Manufacturing Companies According to Ethnic Group, by Industrial Sector
Québec, 1973 (%)

	FRANCO- PHONE	ANGLO- PHONE	CANADIAN	FOREIGN	TOTAL
Food and beverages	80.4	6.4	4.6	8.6	100
Tobacco products	—	18.2	9.1	72.7	100
Rubber products	48.7	29.2	5.5	16.6	100
Leather products	50.2	37.1	3.4	9.3	100
Textile mills	20.4	63.2	3.2	13.2	100
Knitting mills	18.6	72.9	—	8.5	100
Clothing industries	19.7	77.1	0.9	2.3	100
Wood industries	83.1	12.1	1.1	3.7	100
Furniture industries	62.8	32.1	3.8	1.3	100
Paper and allied products	25.8	41.2	10.5	22.5	100
Printing, publishing	65.8	28.1	3.9	2.2	100
Primary metals	28.6	23.4	19.4	28.6	100
Metal fabricating	58.9	27.9	5.8	7.4	100
Machinery	33.5	41.9	1.1	23.5	100
Transportation equipment	77.6	6.2	5.2	11.0	100
Electrical products	25.4	24.9	10.1	39.6	100
Non-metallic mineral pr.	71.1	11.4	4.1	13.4	100
Petroleum and coal pr.	25.0	—	—	75.0	100
Chemicals	14.8	19.9	3.8	61.5	100
Misc. manufacturing	37.2	41.4	7.5	13.9	100
Total	52.8	33.3	4.0	9.9	100

Source: Québec (prov.), Department of Industry and Commerce, Direction des politiques industrielles, *Caractères ethniques de l'investissement au Québec*, 1973-74, p. 41.

THE GROWTH OF THE FINANCIAL SECTOR

The development of a manufacturing sector under francophone control required the financial resources of the state, but also of the private sector. At the beginning of the 1960s, Québec financial institutions were small, fragile, and conservative. In a word, they were not prepared for the radical economic transformations that were required.

The modernization of the francophone financial network was more than likely the most important event of the 1960–70 decade. For many years, proponents of increased Québec control over its economic development underlined the fundamental importance of an increase in local control over savings. The investment policies of the large Canadian financial institutions, and particularly of the insurance companies, drained a large part of local savings out of the province (Loranger, 1961). The difficulty for the Québécois entrepreneurs to obtain adequate financing was probably the main reason for the initial economic thrust of the Quiet Revolution. By and large, in the 1960s the government's efforts met with little success. In 1965, the five largest Canadian banks still controlled most of the province's savings.

An interesting experience was attempted in 1962. With the objective of funding more adequately medium-sized companies, the Conseil d'expansion économique and the National Bank devised a plan to create a new industrial bank. Various local financial institutions joined in the project, including the Canadian National Bank with a 35 percent participation, and began to channel funds to Québec companies. The new financial institution, called Roynat, was slow to get off the ground. In 1966, it had only $5.6 million worth of capital.

The Québec government's entry into the financial world was not without difficulties. It should be remembered that since 1929 a financial group directed by A.E. Ames and the Bank of Montréal had exercised a monopoly on the province's financing. The efforts by Maurice Duplessis during the 1950s to initiate the creation of a competing group only served to open up a modest market share for francophone dealers. The nationalization of the private hydroelectric firms in 1963 provided the opportunity for the partial breakup of the cartel. Initially the Bank of Montréal–Ames group attempted to boycott the bond issue that was intended to finance the nationalization. It backed down when the government began negotiations with an American dealer (Moreau, 1981:55). In 1963, a year later, the group once again boycotted a Hydro–Québec bond issue. Supported by René Lévesque, then Minister of Natural Resources, Hydro–Québec took the initiative of creating a new financial group headed by the Royal Bank, the Canadian National Bank, Greenshields, and René T. Leclerc, a francophone broker.

In January 1964, after a major struggle within the Québec cabinet opposing George Marler to the Lesage-Lévesque-Kierans trio, a new policy was adopted. The two managing groups would take turns in managing Québec issues. This would allow the Québec government somewhat more freedom in negotiating the terms of its bond issues. By and large, however, this episode underlined the weak position of the francophone brokers and convinced the government that the rules of the game needed to be changed to give a more strategic position to Québécois financial institutions.

A major turning point was provided by the creation of the Régie des rentes in 1964 and the Caisse de dépôt et placement du Québec in 1965, following a bitter squabble with Ottawa, which wanted Québec to participate in the Canada Pension Plan. In its mandate, the Caisse was given the tasks of intervening to stabilize the Québec financial market, and of channelling part of its capital to support the development of the local economy and of Québécois firms. In a few short years, the Caisse accumulated the largest capital stock portfolio in Canada (Fournier, 1977). Its financial clout allowed it to become a major buyer of Québec government bonds, which resulted in a considerable lessening of Québec's dependency on Canadian financial markets.

The controversy surrounding the Caisse as well as its considerable success convinced Québec politicians of the necessity of a profound restructuring of the regional financial networks. The Caisse's experience demonstrated that it was possible and advantageous for the Québec economy to regionalize savings by channelling them into Québec-based firms. From that moment on, various government departments embarked upon the task of devising a provincial financial strategy. This process culminated in 1969 with the publication of the Parizeau Report (Québec (prov.), Comité d'étude sur les institutions financières, 1969).

Between 1960 and 1970, the Québec financial sector also developed around the controversial issue of the financial cooperatives and particularly the Caisses d'épargne et de crédit. For many years previously, the cooperative movement had been asking for new powers in order to diversify and broaden its operations. The adoption of Bill 8 in 1963 revised the legislation regulating the Caisses d'épargne et de crédit and eliminated a certain number of obstacles to their development. Financial cooperatives were henceforth authorized to participate in the ownership of other cooperatives, were given the right to own SGF capital stock, and were allowed to diversify their operations toward fiduciary activities. Despite the opposition of the chartered banks, the Mouvement Desjardins was thus allowed to take control of the Fiducie du Québec and the insurance company La Sécurité.

The reaction of the federal government was contained in the report of the Porter Commission. In 1945, the McDougal Commission had recommended that cooperatives be exempt from income tax, and the federal government had accepted this principle (Canada, Commission of Inquiry on the Cooperatives, 1945). The Porter Commission, however, recommended that the cooperatives should be taxed once again (Canada, Royal Commission of Inquiry on the Banking and Financial System). Québec counterattacked in 1965, when the Bélanger Commission proposed that the exemption be maintained (Québec (prov.), Commission royale d'enquête sur la fiscalité, 1965). Two years later, the Carter Commission suggested that cooperatives should be taxed at the same rate as private corporations.

From then on, the controversy took on a political dimension, with Québec seeking to confirm its jurisdiction over the Caisses d'épargne et de crédit. In order to prepare for an eventual struggle, the government gave Deputy Minister Jacques Parizeau the mandate to prepare a strategy for managing provincial financial resources. More precisely, Parizeau was mandated to study the legislation governing non banking institutions, to inquire into their activities, and to examine the impact of federal legislation. Four years later, the committee recommended major legislative changes in order to consolidate the regional financial network, to improve the competitive position of the cooperative sector vis à vis the banks, to favour a higher degree of concentration, and to ensure better protection for the consumers and investors. The Parizeau Report also broadened the role of the Caisse de dépôt, giving it more power to intervene directly in the ownership and control of private corporations.

As a result of the election of Robert Bourassa's Liberals in 1970, some of the more "nationalist" recommendations were not implemented. The influence of the Parizeau Report was nonetheless important. As indicated earlier, the Société d'investissement Desjardins (SID) was created in 1971, following the passage of legislation allowing more freedom of manoeuver for the Caisses d'épargne et de crédit. By granting more powers to the Fédération de Québec des Caisses populaires Desjardins, the new law accelerated the process of centralization and concentration in the cooperative movement, allowing the management to increase its overall control (Office de planification et de développement du Québec, 1975). The new legislative environment rapidly improved the situation of the cooperative sector in the financial arena. Already in 1970, the Caisses were the main competitors of the banks, controlling 18.5 percent of total savings, compared to 24.7 percent for the banks. In 1975, their share of savings went up to 22.8 percent as compared with 24.1 percent for the banks. Then, in 1976, with the development of SID and CID (Crédit industriel Desjardins), the Caisses became the major financial institution in the province.

In 1974, the government introduced Bill 7, which aimed at ensuring that a greater share of provincial savings channelled into the insurance industry be reinvested in the province. Already in the 1950 to 1974 period, the market share of francophone insurance companies had increased from 15 percent to 30 percent, with the Canadian institutions dropping from 39 percent to 34 percent. The new legislation accelerated the process by favouring the development and concentration of regional firms. Nonetheless, it is probably in the investment dealers industry that the Bourassa government had the most significant impact. In 1969, a major North American wave of concentration and buyouts threatened many Canadian investment dealers. The following year, a federal government task force proposed that support measures be adopted to protect Canadian capital in the sector (Canada, Comité d'étude sur les besoins et les sources de capital de l'industrie canadienne des valeurs mobilières, 1970). Given that the recommendations of the task force were perceived in Québec as favouring the development of the Toronto and Vancouver stock exchanges to the detriment of Montréal, whose stock exchange had been declining in recent years, the Québec government decided to react. In June 1970, the cabinet announced the creation of a provincial task force presided by Louis-Philippe Bouchard, then Deputy Minister of Financial Institutions, Companies, and Cooperatives. The report was highly critical of the federal government proposals, claiming that they were not adapted to Québec's particular needs, and proposed a series of measures to consolidate the position of local investment dealers and to regionalize the activities of the Montréal stock exchange.

Some of the ensuing legislation had immediate effects for Québec investment dealers. In 1972, the cabinet changed the rules of the games for the financing of the government and its agencies, and brought in four Québec-based investment dealers in the managing group. Given that the governmental market (including the Caisse de dépôt) was the largest on the Montréal stock exchange, the new policies led to the rapid growth of local firms.

Thus, the various measures to support the development of local financial institutions and to increase vastly the accumulation of indigenous Québec-based capital played a key role in augmenting local economic power and industrial development. Québec savings were more and more channelled into new local industrial projects and the modernization of existing firms. In the end, the growth of Québécois financial institutions was the launching pad for many powerful regional economic groups. The strategy pursued until 1975 allowed for the concentration, diversification, and growth of local firms. Francophone capital was not only strengthened, but transformed. The main objectives were a more dynamic and a more regionalized Québec economy.

After 1976, the new Parti Québécois government pursued even more aggressively the same objective of supporting what Jacques Parizeau called "la garde montante." The level of concentration among Québec firms increased, and so did their control of the internal market. They began as well to become more active on the international markets. Nonetheless, an overwhelming majority of Québec businessmen refused the sovereignty option put forward by the Parti Québécois in 1980, preferring to maintain the Canadian federal link.

The 1981–83 recession made Québec-based business acutely aware of the vulnerability of the Québec economy and of the need to pursue and rejuvenate governmental support for the local private sector. Neoliberal pressures in favour of less government intervention have probably had less impact in Québec than in the rest of Canada, probably contributing to opening up new areas of conflict between Québec and the federal government.

Québec business interests are now at the crossroads. In large part as a result of the support of the provincial state, they have succeeded in modernizing their structures and in taking control of an important part of the local economy. This is no longer sufficient, however. To survive and to continue to prosper in a global economic framework, Québec business needs to expand its markets. Efforts to penetrate the Canadian market in other provinces have often led to disappointing results. The initial impacts of the free trade agreement with the U.S. have been less than spectacular, especially in the context of the recession. At present, business is seeking government support that is unambiguous and unhampered by federal–provincial conflicts and contradictions. To this end, they have repeatedly called, since the failure of the Meech Lake Accord in 1990, for a clarification of the constitutional status of Québec.

NOTES

1. Including l'Industrielle, Lévesque-Beaubien, La Prévoyance, Crédit Interprovincial, Corporation de valeurs Trans-Canada.
2. Fashion Craft, Alfred Lambert, Fred A. L'Allemand, Slater Shoes, Daoust-Lalonde.
3. Dupuis frères, Quincaillerie Durand, Palais du commerce, Chaussures Trans-Canada, Payette radio, etc.
4. At that date, Sullivan owned five active mines and employed more than 1,000 workers.

REFERENCES

Bélanger, Y. (1978). "Capital bancaire et fractions de classe au Québec," in P. Fournier, ed., *Le capitalisme au Québec.* Montréal: Editions coopératives Albert St-Martin.
Benoit, E. (1925). "Monographies économiques." Montréal: *Le Devoir.*
Bernier, R. et al. (1975). *Une certaine révolution tranquille.* Montréal: Éditions La Presse.
Burgess, J. (1977). "L'industrie de la chaussure à Montréal: 1840–1870." *Revue d'histoire de l'Amérique française*, 31–2.
Canada (1945). *Rapport de la Commission d'enquête sur les coopératives.* Ottawa: Queen's Printer.
Canada (1964). *Rapport de la Commission d'enquête sur le système bancaire et financier.* Ottawa: Queen's Printer.
Canada (1965). *Royal Commission of Inquiry on Bilingualism and Biculturalism.* Ottawa: Queen's Printer.
Canada. Statistics Canada (1967). *Liens de parenté entre les corporations.* Ottawa: Queen's Printer.
Canada (1970). *Rapport du Comité d'étude sur les besoins et les sources de capital de l'industrie canadienne des valeurs mobilières.* Toronto.
Canada. Department of Consumer and Corporate Affairs (1971). *Concentration dans les industries manufacturières du Canada.* Ottawa: Queen's Printer.
Corporation foncière de Montréal (1967). *Annual Report.* Montréal: CFM.
Falardeau, J.C. (1965). "L'origine et l'ascension des hommes d'affaires dans la société canadienne-française." *Recherches sociographiques*, 6 (1).
Fournier, P. (1977). *Les sociétés d'État et les objectifs économiques du Québec: une évaluation préliminaire.* Québec: Éditeur officiel du Québec.
Gagnon, Gabriel and Luc Martin, eds., (1973). *Québec 1960-1980, la crise du développement.* Montréal: Hurtubise-HMH.

Lemelin, C. (1968, 20 March). "Les difficultés financières de Cofomo mettent en péril d'autres institutions financières." Montréal: *Le Devoir*.

Lépine, N. (1969, 21 May). "Une réclamation de 12$ millions contre les directeurs de Cofomo." Montréal: *Le Devoir*.

L'Heureux, E. (1930). "La participation des Canadiens français à la vie économique." *L'Action nationale*.

Loranger, J.G. (1961). *La concentration financière des entreprises au Canada*. Montréal, Ph.D. thesis, Hautes Études Commerciales: Université de Montréal.

Miskew, B. (1969, 8 January). "Le sort de la Banque de l'Ouest a eu quelque chose à voir dans l'effondrement de l'empire financier de Marc Masson-Bienvenu." Québec: *Le Soleil*.

Moreau, F. (1981). *Le capital financier québécois*. Montréal: Éditions coopératives Albert St-Martin.

Office de planification et de développement du Québec (1975). *Profil du mouvement coopératif au Québec*. Québec: Éditeur officiel du Québec.

Office de planification et de développement du Québec (1981). *Les activités des sociétés québécoises de génie-conseil et leur effet d'entraînement*. Québec: Éditeur officiel du Québec.

Ouellet, F. (1971). *Histoire économique et sociale du Québec 1760–1850*. Montréal: Fides.

Québec (prov.) (1965). *Rapport de la Commission d'enquête sur la fiscalité*. Québec: Gouvernement du Québec.

Québec (prov.) (1969). *Comité d'étude sur les institutions financières*. Québec: Éditeur officiel du Québec.

Québec (prov.) Department of Lands and Forests (1972). *Exposé sur la politique forestière*. Québec: Éditeur officiel du Québec.

Québec (prov.) Department of Industry and Commerce (1974). *Une politique économique québécoise*. Québec: Éditeur officiel du Québec.

Québec (prov.) Department of Industry and Commerce (1978). *Caractères ethniques de l'investissement au Québec, 1973–1974*. Québec: Mimeo.

Québec (prov.) Department of Economic Development (1979). *Bâtir le Québec, Énoncé de politique économique*. Québec: Éditeur officiel du Québec.

Raynauld, A. (1974). *La propriété des entreprises au Québec*. Montréal: Presses de l'Université de Montréal.

Rudin, R. (1985). *Banking en français: The French Banks of Québec 1835–1925*. Toronto: University of Toronto Press.

The Economic Status of the French Language and Francophones in Québec*

François Vaillancourt
Université de Montréal

INTRODUCTION

The purpose of this chapter is to describe the economic status, and its recent evolution, of the French language and of francophones in Québec and to indicate how various factors may explain these changes. This is of interest in the context of a book entitled *Québec: State and Society* for two reasons. First, the French nature of Québec is an important dimension of the difference between Québec and the remainder of Canada and North America, with the economic status of francophones, along with their demographic status, often the subject of public attention and debate. Second, specific public policy initiatives (Bills 22, 101, and 178) have addressed the issue of the status of French in Québec and it is therefore appropriate to examine their impact, if any.

This paper is divided into three parts. In the first part we present briefly the economic approach to languages and the key features of language policies in Québec. In the second, we examine how the status of francophones and French has evolved in Québec since 1960. In the third, we examine how these changes may be explained.

THE ECONOMICS OF LANGUAGE AND THE LANGUAGE POLICIES IN QUÉBEC

This first part is divided in two sections. The first one briefly presents the economic approach to language, while the second outlines the chronology and key features of federal and Québec language policies over the 1969–90 period.

---

*The author thanks a referee for useful comments on a previous version of this chapter.

The Economics of Language: A Summary Presentation

There is a fair body of literature on the economics of language presented in part in Vaillancourt (1983) and Vaillancourt (1985). The main theoretical findings of that literature can be summarized as follows (Vaillancourt, 1989:73–74):

1. Languages, like other knowledge and skills gained through work experience or formal education in such subjects as mathematics and history, are human capital (Vaillancourt 1980; 1983). However, it is a child's parents who decide which language he or she will first learn. Generally, this decision is not a choice per se, because the vast majority of parents, given their language skills, can offer only one "choice" of language to their children. This "mother tongue" is usually, but not necessarily, the same language that the child uses in his or her first years in school. It is also the means used by the child to acquire other useful knowledge. It is clear, therefore, that the acquisition of complete linguistic human capital (the ability to understand and use) is essential if the child is to learn to perform various other skills, and that language is an input in the production of human capital. But language is also used as a substitute for and complement to other types of human capital. It is a complement because it enables individuals to make use of their other skills in serving employers and families. And it is a substitute because, by improving language skills, one can obtain jobs that would otherwise not be accessible, such as editor or publisher (thorough or intensive knowledge) or translator (broad or extensive knowledge).

2. The decision to learn a second language or to give one's children the opportunity to learn a second language is influenced in part by economic factors, that is, the anticipated benefits of the investment (learning the second language), and the cost of the investment (Vaillancourt 1983; Grenier and Vaillancourt 1983). We say that this decision is only partly influenced by economic factors because non-economic considerations—an individual's flair for languages or the desire to preserve or rediscover one's ethnic roots—can also influence one's choice. The return on the linguistic investment is determined by the anticipated duration and extent of use of the second language. The cost of learning depends on how the learning time in question might otherwise be spent (acquiring other types of human capital, work, leisure, or domestic output).

3. The value of a given language in economic terms is determined by the degree to which it is used in various tasks, occupations and sectors of activity, which in turn is dictated by the law of supply and demand with respect to that language. In the labour market, which is the primary market in this process, the demand for a language is determined by the choices made by employers. These choices vary according to employers' individual language skills, the languages used in their market(s), and the language(s) of the technological inputs they use. The supply of language attributes is relatively stable at any given point because it is determined by past investments made partly on the basis of the anticipated value of a given language. These anticipated values can change more rapidly than the laws that reflect societal evolution (Vaillancourt 1979).

In this paper it is the first and third findings that are used to explain and then measure the value of a language. Figure 23.1 summarizes the main determinants of the value of a language. The factors identified in Figure 23.1 will determine the

Figure 23.1
Analytical Framework of the Economics of Language:
Relationship Between Language Acquisition,
Language Use, and Socioeconomic Factors

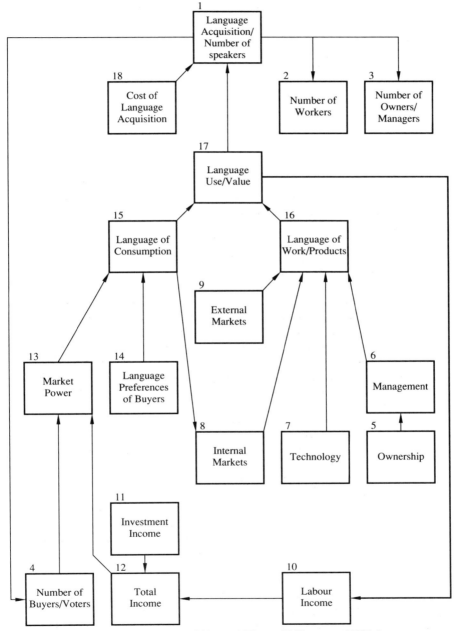

Source: Adapted from Vaillancourt (1989a, p. 167); see Vaillancourt (1991a).

location of the supply and demand curve for a given language at a given point in time and for a given society. The interaction of these two curves will determine the quantity used and value (implicit price of a language).

Language Policies in Québec, 1969–90

Both the federal and Québec governments have put forward since 1969 language policies aimed at the promotion of the French language in either Canada as a whole or in Québec. The more constraining policies were put forward by the Québec government in Bills 22 and 101. A chronology of these language policies is presented in Table 23.1, while the main features of Bill 22 (1974), Bill 101 (1977) and current (1990) language policies are presented in Table 23.2

Table 23.1
A Chronology of Key Events in Language Policies, Québec, 1969–90

1969	An Act to promote the French Language (Bill 63) is adopted.
	Official Languages Act is adopted (Federal).
1974	Official Language Act (Bill 22) is adopted.
1977	Charter of French Language is adopted (Bill 101).
1982	Constitution Act (Federal) adopted. Includes provisions on language of education for minorities (Article 23).
1983	Minor amendments (Bill 57) to Bill 101.
1986	Health and Social Services Act (Bill 142) providing for English-language services adopted.
1988	Supreme Court strikes down French-only signs requirement of Bill 101.
	New Official Languages Act adopted (Federal).
1989	Bill 178 reinstates part of French-only signs requirement.

Source: Derived from "Federal and Provincial Linguistic Dates," *Language and Society* (28), Summer 1989, R-31.

THE STATUS OF FRANCOPHONES AND FRENCH IN QUÉBEC

This second part of the paper is divided into three sections. In the first, evidence is presented on three of the determinants of the language of work identified in Figure 23.1: markets, ownership, and management. In the second, we present evidence on the use of French in the labour market and on the remuneration of that attribute. In the third, we examine the income and thus market power of francophones.

The Determinants of the Language of Work

As Table 23.3 shows, the importance of the French-speaking market for Québec firms has increased from 1970 to 1985. This is due both to an increase in the mean income of francophones (see Table 23.9) and to an increase in their share of the population.

Francophones have also increased their ownership of Québec's economy as shown in Table 23.4 and partly as a result, their share of management jobs, as shown in Table 23.5, over the 1960–90 period. As a result, one expects an increase in the use and remuneration in the workplace of French.

Table 23.2
A Comparison of the Main Features of Bill 22, Bill 101, and 1990 Language Policies in Québec

	BILL 22 (1974)	BILL 101 (1977)	STATUS IN 1990
Language of business:	French or bilingual documents (bills, instructions, etc.) and store signs	French or bilingual documents and French-only signs for stores (with some exceptions)	Bill 178 (1989) allows a greater use of English on indoor signs
Language of education:	Access to English-language schools is on the basis of language tests administered to children	Access to English schools is restricted to children of parents who attended English elementary schools in *Québec*	Article 23 of the 1982 Constitution Act (Federal) allows children whose parents attended English schools in *Canada* access to English schools
Language of work:	Increased use of French through francization programs and hiring of "francophones" is required of firms doing business with the Québec government	Increased use of French through francization programs that firms of fifty employees or more must implement	Unchanged
Language requirements for professionals:	—	Members of professional corporations (nurses, engineers, M.D., etc.) must demonstrate proficiency in French to attain the right to practise	Unchanged
Language of Public Services:	—	Individuals may be served in languages other than French	Bill 142 (1986) extends services in English
Main language bodies:	Régie de la langue française	Office de la langue française, Conseil de la langue française, Commission de protection de la langue française	Unchanged

Source: Vaillancourt, 1991.

Table 23.3
The Significance of the Francophone Market for Québec Businesses, 1970, 1980, and 1985, in Percentage of Total Market

| | INTERNAL MARKET | | EXTERNAL MARKET | | OVERALL |
| | SHARE | USE OF FRENCH | SHARE | USE OF FRENCH | USE OF FRENCH |
	(a)	(b)	(c)	(d)	(e)
1970	62.0	75.7	38.0	8.3	50.1
1980	58.0	80.8	42.0	9.6	50.9
1985	60.0	81.8	40.0	10.0	53.8

Note: a + c = 100 percent; (a x b) + (c x d) = e.
Source: Vaillancourt (1988), Table 2.4 for 1970 and 1980, and Vaillancourt (1991), Table 2.4 for 1985.

Table 23.4
Ownership by Language Groups of Various Sectors of the Québec Economy in 1961, 1978, and 1987

| | PERCENTAGE OF TOTAL EMPLOYMENT UNDER | | | | | | | | |
| | FRANCOPHONE CONTROL (CANADIAN) | | | ANGLOPHONE CONTROL (CANADIAN) | | | FOREIGN CONTROL | | |
SECTOR	1961	1978	1987	1961	1978	1987	1961	1978	1987
Agriculture	91.3	91.8	87.5	8.7	8.2	12.2	0[1]	0[1]	0.3
Forestry	—[2]	33.4	92.3	—[2]	28.9	7.7	—[2]	37.7	0
Mining	6.5	17.8	35.0	53.1	18.1	40.4	40.4	64.9	24.6
Manufacturing	21.7	27.8	39.3	47.0	38.6	38.2	31.3	33.5	22.5
Construction	50.7	74.4	75.5	35.2	18.5	21.8	14.1	7.1	2.7
Transportation, communications, and public services	36.4	42.2	44.9	55.3	53.4	50.2	8.3	4.4	4.9
Commerce	50.4	51.0	57.8	39.5	32.0	34.0	11.5	17.0	8.2
Finance, insurance, and real estate	25.8	44.8	58.2	53.1	43.1	34.6	21.1	12.1	7.2
Services	71.4	75.0	75.7	28.6	21.2	21.6	0[1]	3.8	2.7
Government	51.8	67.2	67.2	47.7	32.8	33.0	0.5	0[1]	0[1]
Total	47.1	54.8	61.6	39.3	31.2	30.8	13.6	13.9	7.8

[1]Hypothesis.
[2]Not calculated. Note that the nature of the data for this sector varies through time in such a manner that intertemporal comparisons are difficult.
Source: Vaillancourt and Carpentier (1989), Table 3.2.

Table 23.5
Percentage of Francophones in Management
Positions in Québec, 1964–86

STUDY	YEAR	%	YEAR	%
Bernard et al.[1]	1971	72.5	1978	74.8
Secor[2]	1964	69.0	1979	75.0
Sauvé/Champagne[3]	1975	19.3	1981	25.4
Board of Trade[4]	1967	65.6	1979	81.7
Vaillancourt[5]	1971	64.9	1981	75.8
Vaillancourt[6]	1971	64.9	1986	77.6

Sources and Notes

[1]Data drawn from Bernard et al. (1979:116), Table 30. Data for 1971 were drawn from the census, and for 1978, from a study of 3,893 individuals in the province of Québec. Individuals were categorized by mother tongue.

[2]Secor, Inc. (1980:43). Percentages refer to Québec divisions as reflected in a study of nineteen manufacturing firms controlled by anglophones. Figures for 1964 were drawn from Morrison (1970).

[3]The figure for 1976 was reported by Champagne (1983:43) from Sauvé's data (1978), which in turn were based on a 1975 study of 104 companies with 1,000 or more employees in Québec. Champagne's data were based on a 1981 study of 134 companies with 1,000 or more employees. Both studies focused on senior managers. If anglophone firms alone are considered—91 in 1975 and 101 in 1981—the proportions were 9.2 percent and 13.7 percent.

[4]Montréal Board of Trace (n.d.). The percentage shown represents the nonweighted proportion of senior, middle, and junior management positions held by francophones in Québec regional offices.

[5]Vaillancourt (1988), Tables B-26, B-28, B-30, and B-32. Individuals are categorized by mother tongue.

[6]Vaillancourt (1991), Tables B-14 and B-16 for 1985 and note 5 for 1971. Individuals are categorized by mother tongue with individuals with both English and French as mother tongue not included in the francophone group.

The Value and Use of French as the Language of Work

As argued above, the value and use of French as the language of work should have increased in Québec in the 1970 to 1990 period. Table 23.6 presents evidence on the impact of language skills on the earnings of Québec residents. It shows that the returns to French have increased from 1970 to 1985, particularly from 1970 to 1980 and more so for men than women. Table 23.7 presents evidence on the use of French in the workplace and Table 23.8 on language skills required from candidates for managerial and engineering employment. Both tables show an improvement in the status of French in the 1970s and 1980s.

The Income and Market Power of Francophones

As shown in Figure 23.1, the investment and labour income of language groups, along with transfer payments, will determine their total income, which in turn affects their market power. Table 23.9 shows that the share of income received by francophones and French speakers has increased in Québec from 1970 to 1985. One explanation of this is the increase in labour income from 1970 to 1986 (Table 23.10), and even from 1960 to 1970 (Table 23.11) as documented in the case of men.

Table 23.6
Effects of Basic Individual Attributes on Employment Income
for Men and Women in Québec, 1970–85 (percentages)

FACTORS	MEN			WOMEN		
	1970	1980	1985	1970	1980	1985
Linguistic factors						
(reference: unilingual francophones)						
Unilingual anglophones	10.11	-7.16	-12.76	0	-4.60	0
Bilingual anglophones	16.99	0	-3.53	0	0	0
Bilingual francophones	12.61	5.11	5.91	9.73	7.50	9.07
English-speaking allophones	0	-16.27	-21.01	0	0	0
French-speaking allophones	0	-20.03	-25.11	22.82	0	-9.47
Bilingual allophones	6.025	-6.41	-9.08	11.10	0	5.32
Other allophones	-17.64	-45.11	-33.12	0	0	0
Anglophones/francophones	-	-	-9.87	-	-	0
Standardization factors						
Education						
(reference: primary 1–4 years)						
Primary (5–8) years	5.87	-13.25	0	0	-11.48	-14.47
Secondary (9–10 years)	19.98	-6.44	7.43	0	0	-8.79
Secondary (11–13 years)	35.61	13.46	31.20	35.06	22.71	19.30
University (1–2 years)	68.34	25.82	49.09	73.66	58.08	50.58
University (3–4 years)	119.30	63.41	90.25	135.05	86.51	89.14
University (5 years or more)	140.35	90.74	130.93	152.27	128.70	114.68
Experience (years)	6.15	5.95	7.11	2.06	2.00	4.86
Experience^2	-0.093	-0.09	-0.11	-0.03	-0.03	-0.08
Weeks worked (each additional week)	3.37	3.53	3.64	4.10	4.35	4.27
Percentage of Variance explained (R^2)	49.10	49.54	50.87	46.71	50.26	49.04

Notes: These effects are calculated using a log-linear equation with employment income as the dependent variable. It was estimated using the 1971–81 and 1986 census micro data files for individuals with a positive employment income.

A "0" indicates a coefficient not significantly different from zero using as a cutoff point a t-statistics of 1.65.

In the 1986 census database, some individuals are classified as having two mother tongues (English/French). This is not the case for the 1971 or 1981 database.

Source: For 1970 and 1980: Vaillancourt (1988), Table 3.2; for 1985: Vaillancourt (1991), Table 3.2.

Table 23.7
Use of French in the Workplace in Québec, 1970, 1979, and 1989

1970–79	PERCENTAGE OF WORK TIME FRENCH IS USED	
	FRANCOPHONES	ANGLOPHONES
1970	87.0	17.0
1979	90.0	37.0
1989	92.0	40.0

Source: For 1970–79: Vaillancourt (1982); for 1989: calculations by the author.

Table 23.8
Language Skills Required in Newspaper Ads for Managers
and Engineers, Montréal, 1964, 1970, 1979, and 1984

LANGUAGE SKILLS REQUIRED:	FRENCH ONLY		ENGLISH AND FRENCH		ENGLISH ONLY	
EMPLOYMENT AS:	Managers	Engineers	Managers	Engineers	Managers	Engineers
1964	31	12	40	16	29	72
1970	27	27	39	21	34	52
1979	36	43	44	37	20	20
1984	31	35	49	29	20	36

Source: For 1964–79: Vaillancourt and Daneau (1981); for 1984: Archambault (1988).

Table 23.9
Average Income and Share of Total Income by Language Group, 1990

	1970		1980		1985	
LANGUAGE GROUP	MEAN INCOME $	SHARE OF INCOME %	MEAN INCOME $	SHARE OF INCOME %	MEAN INCOME $	SHARE OF INCOME %
Anglophones, unilingual	4,447	9.2	10,677	4.7	14,748	3.8
Anglophones, bilingual	5,760	8.6	13,475	8.1	8,550	6.7
Francophones, unilingual	2,627	37.5	8,543	42.4	11,603	41.6
Francophones, bilingual	5,056	37.2	14,420	37.7	18,790	38.1
Allophones, anglophones	4,000	2.7	10,404	2.0	13,254	1.7
Allophones, francophones	3,374	1.0	8,764	1.0	10,470	1.1
Allophones, bilingual	5,161	3.3	13,225	4.1	16,852	4.7
Allophones, other	2,127	0.5	5,045	0.3	6,652	0.3
Anglophones/ francophones	—	—			14,183	2.0

Note: Shares may not add to 100% because of rounding.
Source: Vaillancourt (1988 and 1991), Table 2.2.

Table 23.10
Average Employment Income for Men and Women in Québec, 1970, 1980, and 1985

LANGUAGE GROUPS (MOTHER TONGUE)	Men						Women					
	1970		1980		1985		1970		1980		1985	
	$	RRC	$	RRC	$	RRC	$	RRC	$	RRC	$	RRC
Unilingual anglophones	8,171	1.59	17,635	1.22	23,924	1.24	3,835	1.24	10,271	1.17	14,335	1.21
Bilingual anglophones	8,938	1.74	19,562	1.36	26,078	1.36	3,956	1.28	10,759	1.22	14,449	1.22
Unilingual francophones	5,136	—	14,408	—	14,235	—	3,097	—	8,801	—	1,802	—
Bilingual francophones	7,363	1.43	19,547	1.36	25,923	1.35	3,842	1.24	11,195	1.27	14,718	1.25
English-speaking allophones	6,462	1.26	15,637	1.09	20,504	1.07	3,329	1.07	9,753	1.11	12,927	1.10
French-speaking allophones	5,430	1.06	13,287	0.92	17,664	0.92	3,241	1.05	8,191	0.93	9,918	0.84
Bilingual allophones	7,481	1.46	17,946	1.25	23,729	1.23	3,881	1.25	10,868	1.23	14,060	1.19
Other allophones	4,229	0.82	10,003	0.69	12,666	0.66	2,343	0.76	7,539	0.86	8,539	0.72
Anglophones / francophones	—	—	—	—	21,705	1.13	—	—	—	—	13,182	1.12

RRC: Ratio to reference category (unilingual francophone). For example, 1970 earnings of unilingual male anglophones were 59 percent higher than those of unilingual francophones.

Note: In the 1986 census database, some individuals are classified as having two mother tongues (English/French). This is not the case for the 1971 or 1981 database.

Source: For 1970 and 1980: Vaillancourt (1988), Table 3.1; for 1985: Vaillancourt (1991), Table 3.1.

Table 23.11
Québec, Mean Wages and Salaries by
Ethnic Group, 1960 and 1970,
Male Nonagricultural Sector

Ethnic origin	1960 $	1970 $
British	$4,940	$7,909
Dutch	$4,891	$9,122
French	$3,185	$6,009
German	$4,254	$8,396
Hungarian	$3,537	$6,670
Italian	$2,938	$6,214
Jewish	$4,851	$9,506
Polish	$3,984	$7,586
Ukrainian	$3,733	$6,416
All groups	$3,469	$6,374

Source: Vaillancourt (1978).

THE SOURCES OF CHANGE IN THE STATUS OF FRANCOPHONES AND FRENCH IN QUÉBEC

In this last part of the paper we examine how the improvement in the status of francophones and French in Québec from 1960 to 1990 can be explained. Using the demand–supply framework presented in the first part of the paper, one can see that the increase in the use (price) of French in the workplace in Québec can come about either through an increase (decrease) in the supply of French-speaking workers, or through an increase in the demand for French-speaking workers. Let us examine each possibility in turn.

Changes in Supply

As Table 23.12 shows, the share of Québec's labour force that is francophone or nonfrancophone but French speaking has increased from 1971 to 1986. There is also, as shown in Table 23.13, an increase in the schooling, and thus quality, of the francophone workers which makes them more easily employable. Both forces should increase the supply and thus use of French, but reduce its value in the labour force. Since there was an increase in the value of French, there must also have been an increase in the demand for French.

In our opinion, the increased demand for French and the decreased demand for English can be attributed to five factors:

♦ the growth (measured in numbers of employees) of the public and parapublic sector relative to the private sector;

♦ growing employment under francophone control in the private sector (Table 23.4);

♦ growth in the disposable income of francophones (Table 23.9) who prefer to purchase goods and services in French;

♦ language legislation, which encouraged some firms to implement francization programs; these laws had little impact on the economic status of

Québec's two language groups for two reasons: first, by 1970, a substantial proportion of francophones were already working in French; second, many decisions to implement francization programs were made before the language legislation was enacted (Lacroix and Vaillancourt, 1981);

• the transfer of some head-office functions outside Québec for various reasons (boom in western Canada, concern over Québec nationalism), which reduced the relative demand for English.

Table 23.12
Share of Francophones and French-Speaking Earners, Québec, 1971, 1981, and 1986 (percent)

	1971	1981	1986
Francophones (mother tongue)	78.4	81.4	82.8
Nonfrancophone French Speakers	10.6	12.3	12.2
Other	11.0	6.7	5.0
Total	100.0	100.0	100.0

Note: In 1986 individuals with English and French as their mother tongue are assigned to the francophone group.
Source: For 1971 and 1981: Vaillancourt (1988), Tables B-1, 3, 5, and 7; for 1986: Vaillancourt (1990), Tables B-1 and 3.

Table 23.13
Schooling Level of Francophone Earners, Québec, 1971, 1981, and 1986

SCHOOLING LEVEL	1971	1981	1986
Primary	39.1	19.8	13.6
Secondary	50.5	64.4	63.9
Post-Secondary	10.4	15.8	22.5
Total	100.0	100.0	100.0

Source: For 1971 and 1981: Vaillancourt (1988), Tables B-9, 11, 13, and 15; for 1986: Vaillancourt (1990), Tables B-5 and 7.

CONCLUSION

The main conclusion of this paper is that the socioeconomic status of French and francophones in Québec has improved from 1960 to 1990. Indeed, the returns to knowing French on the labour market are higher than those to knowing English in 1980 and 1985. The issue has now become how to ensure the economic prosperity of Québec and thus of francophones in the 21st century. Various policies, but in particular human resources policies (population, education and training, health, etc.), will play a role in this. These policies must take into account the fact that the continued existence of a French-speaking Québec requires a sufficient number of French speakers regrouped together in this small territory. They must also take into account the lower mobility of Québec francophones in terms of out-migration compared to the mobility of Québec anglophones and Canadian residents. This lower mobility is the result of both cultural choices and economic forces and explains in part the policies of various Québec governments (e.g., Caisse de dépôt, state-owned corporations, etc.) and francophone federal politicians (e.g., the creation of the Department of Regional Economic Expansion) that attempt to attract mobile capital to immobile francophone workers in Québec. A complementary policy is the opening of foreign markets, such as the U.S. market, to Québec firms through means such as the 1989 free trade agreement.

In terms of language policies, we have argued elsewhere (Vaillancourt, 1989) that the objectives of Québec's language policies should be as follows:

1. to ensure that French is the common language of oral communication in the internal Québec market;
2. to allow the use of other languages in combination with French for written communication (for example, on forms and signs);
3. to allow companies to use the optimum combination of languages to serve their external markets;
4. to promote learning of English by all francophones;
5. to require or promote learning of French by all nonfrancophones, depending on their place of birth and age.

These objectives are designed to ease language-related tensions in the anglophone (point 2) and francophone (points 1 and 5) communities, while enhancing the competitive position of the Québec economy in international markets (points 3 and 4). They would require a compromise between, on the one hand, greater internal visibility and wider use in external markets of the English language, and on the other, greater use of French in the internal market.

In order to achieve the objectives set out above, the following measures seem appropriate:

1. Business and public and private organizations operating in the Québec market should be able to serve their clientele in French at all times. This means that elected officials (for example, the members of school boards and municipal councils) and individual employees of businesses and public-sector institutions (hospitals, CEGEPs, universities, and so on) should be proficient in French. Anglophones who do not speak French would pay a price: they would have to learn French within a reasonable period (three to five years), or lose their jobs. This policy would send a very clear message about the economic value of the French language in Québec. Of course, businesses and services could still serve their customers in English or any other language if they so desired.
2. Signs, labels, and forms would be in French, but could also be in one or more other languages, which would provide suitable visibility for those languages and still take nothing away from French.
3. Francization programs would be maintained, but requirements relating to the use of French could be altered over time as technologies and markets evolve. The *optimum* use of French, rather than the maximum, would be sought, that is, a level of use that maximizes both private interest (profits) and public benefits (externalities) associated with the use of French.

4. Francophones could attend the senior primary grades, in an English school or a full-immersion program, for one year, which would give all francophones a better opportunity to learn English than they now have. This policy would increase slightly the risk of assimilation, but it would also enhance economic opportunities for Québec francophones.

5. All children born in Québec would be required to take the junior primary grades in French, in either a French-language school or an immersion program. This policy would perhaps lower somewhat the quality of English spoken by some of these nonfrancophones, but when combined with improvements in the teaching of French in English-language schools, it would ensure that they have an adequate knowledge of French to satisfy the requirements of the policy on businesses and services. The cost of such a policy would be low. School-age nonfrancophones born outside Québec would, on arriving in the province, be required to demonstrate fluency in French or to attend school in French until this was achieved (two years?). Adults would have the opportunity, but not an obligation, to study French on a full-time basis for six months at government expense (living allowance and free courses). This series of policies would mean that the requirement that individual employees be able to use French in order to serve the Québec market would not be excessively constraining.

All things considered, we believe that these objectives and measures would ensure that French occupies its rightful place in the internal Québec market, and would therefore enhance its profitability and vitality. They would make francophones feel more secure and induce them to accept more fully a more visible English-speaking community, as well as the acquisition and use of English to serve markets outside the province.

REFERENCES

Archambault, Y., "Offres d'emploi annoncées dans les quotidiens et exigences linguistiques requises à l'embauche," Québec: Conseil de la langue française, 1988, mimeo.

Béland, Paul, *L'usage du français au travail: situations et tendances*, Québec, Conseil de la langue française, 1991.

Bernard, P., A. Demers, D. Grenier, and J. Renaud, *L'évolution de la situation linguistique et socio-économique des francophones et des non-francophones au Québec*, Montréal: Office de la langue française, 1971–78, 1979.

Champagne, R., *Évolution de la présence francophone parmi les hauts dirigeants des grandes entreprises québécoises entre 1976 et 1982*, Montréal: Office de la langue française, 1983.

Grenier, G., and F. Vaillancourt, "An Economic Perspective on Learning a Second Language" (with Gilles Grenier), *Journal of Multilingual and Multicultural Development*, 4(6), 1983, pp. 471–83.

Lacroix, Robert, and F. Vaillancourt, *Les revenus et la langue au Québec (1970–1978)*, Québec: Conseil de la langue française, Collection Dossiers, 1981, 176 pages.

Monnier, D., *L'usage du français au travail*, Québec: Conseil de la langue française, 1983.

Montréal Board of Trade, "Enquête sur les personnes dans les niveaux de direction des entreprises de la région de Montréal dont la langue maternelle est le français," Montréal: mimeo, undated text.

Morrison, N., *Corporate Adaptability to Bilingualism and Biculturalism*, Ottawa: Queen's Printer, 1970.

Sauvé, M., "Les Canadiens français et la direction des entreprises au Québec," *Commerce*, September 1978.

Secor, Inc., "La présence francophone dans la grande entreprise manufacturière", 1964–1979," Montréal: mimeo, 1980.

Vaillancourt, F., "Revenus et langues, Québec, 1961–1971," *Journal of Canadian Studies*, 13, Spring 1978, pp. 63–69.

————, "La situation démographique et socioéconomique des francophones du Québec," *Canadian Public Policy*, 5, Autumn 1979, pp. 542–52.

————, *Difference in Earnings by Language Groups in Québec 1970: An Economic Analysis*, Québec: Centre international de recherche sur le bilinguisme, Publication B-90, 1980 (Ph.D. thesis, Queen's University, 1978), 238 pages.

————, "Le statut socio-économique des francophones et du français au Québec à la fin des années 1970," *Revue de l'Association canadienne d'éducation de langue française*, 11, August 1982, pp. 9–13.

————, "The Economics of Language and Language Planning," *Language Problems and Language Planning*, 7, Summer 1983, pp. 162–78.

————, "Les écrits en économie de la langue: brève revue et introduction du recueil," dans *Économie et Langue: un recueil de textes*, F. Vaillancourt, ed., Québec: Conseil de la langue française, 1985, pp. 13–25.

————, *Langue et disparités de statut économique au Québec: 1970 et 1980*, Québec: Conseil de la langue française, Collection Dossiers, 1988, 230 pages.

————, "Demolinguistic Trends and Canadian Institutions: An Economic Perspective," in *Demolinguistic Trends and the Evolution of Canadian Institutions, Canadian Issues* (special issue), Association for Canadian Studies, Montréal, 1989, pp. 73–92.

————, "The Economics of Language: An Empirical Evaluation of Some Theoretical Predictions," *Slovene Studies*, 11, 1–2, 1989a, pp. 167–75.

————, "Langue et statut économique au Québec: 1980-1985," Conseil de la langue française, 1991.

————, "Language and Public Policy in Canada and the United States: An Economic Perspective," in *Immigration, Language and Ethnicity: Canada and the United States*, B. Chiswick, ed., Washington: American Enterprise Institute, 1991, pp. 179–228.

————, "The Economics of Language: Theory, Empiricism and Application to the Asian Pacific," *Journal of Asia Pacific Communications*, 2, 1991a.

Vaillancourt, F., and J. Carpentier, "Le contrôle de l'économie du Québec: la place des francophones en 1987 et son évolution depuis 1961," Montréal: Office de la langue française, 1989, 91 pages.

Vaillancourt, F., and A. Daneau "L'évolution des exigences linguistiques pour les postes de cadres et d'ingénieur au Québec de 1970 à 1979," *Gestion*, 6, April 1981, pp. 22–25.

Politics in a High-Unemployment Society*

Alain Noël
Université de Montréal

"We can go on criticizing, and say it doesn't make sense. It's true that it doesn't make sense."

–Gérald Tremblay, Québec Industry, Commerce, and Technology Minister

In Québec, more than 1.2 million persons live under the poverty line.[1] The Mont-réal region alone counts more persons facing poverty than the four Atlantic provinces together. Of all the metropolitan areas in Canada, only those of Trois-Rivières and Sherbrooke—also in Québec—have worse records. In the city of Montréal proper, once Canada's metropolis, the situation is even more dramatic: almost a third of the population lives in poverty (Tremblay and Van Schendel, 1991:340-47; Pépin, 1991). In 117 out of the 154 primary schools of the Montréal Catholic School Commission (CECM), over 20 percent of the pupils live in poor families. In some of these schools, teachers avoid giving exams at the end of the month because too many children come to school hungry and unable to concentrate (Demers, 1990:42; André Noël, 1990).[2]

Why is poverty so important in contemporary Québec? So much has been said about the development of a modern Québec state and the rise of a successful francophone business class that one would expect better results. Have the poor been ignored in the process? Many think so. From their point of view, the Quiet Revolution and the changes that followed have been made by elites mostly interested in their own economic and political situation. Fascinated by business and by constitutional subtleties, these elites would be largely oblivious to the growing poverty of a province they govern unchallenged (see Pelletier, 1991; Resnick, 1990:32). Like any legend, this one contains some truth. It is correct, for instance, to say that

*I thank André Blais, Gérard Boismenu, Stéphane Dion, Alain-G. Gagnon, Marie-France Le Blanc, Henry Milner, Tim Thompson, and two anonymous referees for their comments on earlier versions of this chapter. I also wish to acknowledge the financial assistance of the CAFIR (Université de Montréal).

Québec's new business class is not particularly inclined to discuss social justice. But that alone explains little. Where in the world is business at the forefront of the fight against poverty?

Québec society is not poor simply because it has self-serving elites, and it will not change by some miraculous conversion of those in power. Poverty and unemployment are complex social and political problems rooted in history, institutions, and public policies. In Québec as elsewhere, change on such questions is less a matter of good will than an outcome of broad social and political conflicts around economic growth, income distribution, and state intervention. To understand the current situation, it is thus necessary to account for Québec's history as a poor province, to explain the specific difficulties experienced in the 1980s, and to identify the social and political forces likely to have an impact in the years to come.

For more than a century, Québec has had lower wages and higher unemployment rates than its neighbours (except for the Maritimes). The first part of this chapter discusses the origins and the implications of this historical condition. It shows, in particular, how Québec's early rural poverty and its specificity as a French society in North America contributed to create a high-unemployment, low-wage labour market. In turn, this economic condition shaped Québec politics and made effective policy responses difficult.

After World War II, and even more so in the 1960s and 1970s, Québec's situation began to improve. Many problems nevertheless remained, and the 1980s brought important setbacks. The second part of the chapter attempts to establish what happened in the 1960s and 1970s, and why, in particular, Québec caught up with Ontario during these years. The third part moves to the 1980s and discusses the return of an important unemployment gap between Ontario and Québec, during the very years when the Québec economy was supposed to be changing for the better. The evolution of this last decade shows the limits and the fragility of what has been accomplished thus far.

The fourth and last part completes the analysis with a discussion of the politics of poverty and unemployment in the 1990s. While the exact policy outcome cannot be predicted, it is possible to identify the main social forces and the policies they are likely to advocate. Beyond a vague consensus on the need to do something, three alternatives seem to be emerging: the liberal or neoliberal policy option, which offers the status quo or policies inspired by the United States, the neocorporatist option, inspired by Germany, and the full-employment option, whose main reference is Sweden. While the first option is likely to prevail in the short term, the other two should have lasting influence. The chapter's conclusion briefly assesses the significance of the poverty/unemployment debate for the years to come. In the 1990s and probably beyond, this debate is likely to define much of Québec politics.

A LOW-WAGE REGION IN A HIGH-WAGE CONTINENT

The Québec farmer, wrote in the late 1930s University of Chicago sociologist Everett C. Hughes, "is not poverty-stricken" but,

> he is not so likely as is his English-speaking rural compatriot of Ontario to own an automobile or a radio, to have a telephone, or to take a city newspaper. The road

before his house is not so good. The district school is a poorer structure. The teacher
has less training and is worse paid. (1943:4)

In the cities, the situation was similar: "The telephone, the automobile, and the
radio all are less frequent in Québec, rural and urban, than in Ontario" (1943:189).
This relative poverty, observed Hughes, mostly affected French Canadians. In the
small industrial city he studied, "19 percent of the French gainfully employed
males" owned a car, while 52 percent of the English did (188-89). On the eve of
World War II, when Hughes did the field work for his *French Canada in Transition*, French Canadians appeared to him as a relatively poor ethnic group in a relatively poor province.

This poverty was not transitory. It had long been a fact of life in Québec, and
was not about to disappear. From the second half of the 19th century to the 1980s,
Québec maintained lower incomes per capita and higher unemployment rates than
Ontario (McRoberts, 1979:298; Raynauld, 1961:32 and 63; Economic Council of
Canada, 1977:35; Gouin and Chouinard, 1989:161–62). Within Québec itself,
francophones traditionally predominated in the low-skilled, low-paying jobs,
while anglophones prevailed in skilled and management occupations (McRoberts,
1988:67–68). This linguistic division of labour made Québec francophones one of
the poorest ethnic groups in the province. In 1961, they earned about 66 percent of
the average income obtained by Quebeckers of British origins. At the time, personal bilingualism did not correct the disparities. On average, a bilingual francophone earned less than a bilingual anglophone, and they both had lower incomes
than a unilingual anglophone. "Ethnic origin," noted the Royal Commission on
Bilingualism and Biculturalism, appears to have "a greater impact on incomes
than does linguistic knowledge" (1969:21–23). Only in the early 1980s did the gap
between Québec francophones and anglophones diminish enough to appear minor
compared to income disparities affecting other categories of the population
(women, natives, and recent immigrants in particular; Boulet and Lavallée,
1983:66; S. Langlois, 1990:259).[3]

The economic "inferiority" of both the province and its francophone majority
has been the object of numerous debates among historians and social scientists.
Early explanations focused on factors specific to the province, such as the debilitating consequences of the British Conquest of 1760, the traditionalism of French-
Canadian culture, or the anti-industrial bias of the early Montréal merchants (for a
critical introduction, see Durocher and Linteau, 1971; McCallum, 1980:121).
These cultural explanations were problematic on many counts. Contrary to what is
often believed, before 1960 Québec was not a rural, traditional society impervious
to change and industrialization. With Ontario, the province constituted the urban,
industrial core of Canada. As early as 1915, more than half of Québec's population
lived in cities, and during the 1930s and early 1940s, the province was actually
more urban than Ontario (McRoberts, 1988:72; Salée, 1990:89). Closely integrated, the economies of the two provinces fluctuated together and grew at the
same pace. "We are far," observed economist André Raynauld, "from an autarchic
province of Québec, from those images of an economy closed on itself" (my translation, Raynauld, 1961:46–52).

True enough, an equivalent growth rate could not eliminate the initial gap
between the two central provinces, and Québec's linguistic division of labour also

persisted. In a recent discussion, historian Fernand Ouellet underlines these two problems to salvage the old cultural interpretation (1990). Cultural deficiencies, however, can hardly explain the persistence of an initial disadvantage. If culture were the mainspring of economic growth, the parallel evolution of the two provinces would suggest they had the same, not different, cultures.

Cultural explanations prove unhelpful because they pose the problem of economic and social change in simplistic, dichotomous terms. From this point of view, a society can only be backward or advanced, traditional or modern, underdeveloped or normal.[4] Québec's problem, however, was not backwardness. After all, few countries in the world matched the province's level of development.[5] Québec's difficulties were not absolute but relative: it was a low-wage region in a high-wage continent, and francophones disproportionately bore the brunt of this situation. Culture may have played a role, but economic and institutional factors explain most of the disparities.

Consider, first, Québec's status as a low-wage region. As mentioned above, the gap between Québec and Ontario goes back to the 19th century (Raynauld, 1961:63). At the time, the main economic activity was agriculture. In 1850, about two-thirds of the Canadian population lived on a farm (McCallum, 1980:50). The farmer's situation, however, differed markedly in the two Canadas. In Lower Canada (now Québec), farmers were poor and pessimistic about future possibilities, while in Upper Canada (now Ontario), they prospered and had every reason to be confident (Norrie and Owram, 1991:150–52 and 174–85).

Traditionally, the plight of Québec farmers was linked to their conservatism. "The Québec *habitant*," asserts John Isbister, "was a peasant, poor and self-sufficient, not a man of business." Ignorant of modern technologies and approaches, Québec farmers would have been responsible for their own difficulties (Isbister, 1987:67). In fact, Québec and Ontario farmers faced very different agricultural conditions. The land and climate of pre-Confederation Ontario "were admirably suited to the growing of wheat," a commodity that could profitably be exported (McCallum, 1980:3–9). By contrast, Québec's climatic conditions did not permit wheat crops abundant enough for exports. With no obvious commercial substitute, Québec farmers persisted in growing wheat or reverted to "a subsistence level of farming characterized by periodic food shortages, declining living standards, and mounting debt" (McCallum, 1980:29–34).

Every year between 1850 and 1867, Ontario farmers earned in cash sales from three to five times more than did their Québec counterparts (McCallum, 1980:5). This early advantage had three major consequences for Ontario. First, it stimulated the province's economic growth and created favorable conditions for industrialization. Second, it best equipped Ontario farmers to make the transition out of wheat after Confederation. Third, it made Ontario a high-wage labour market.

The most obvious contribution of the wheat surplus was its positive impact on Ontario's urban and industrial development. Farmers spent most of their income locally, and a variety of small industries benefited from these expenditures. Sawmills, flour mills, tanneries, blacksmiths, and the like prospered and sometimes grew into small manufactures (McCallum, 1980:90–91). The impact of the wheat surplus best appears in the contrasted evolutions of Toronto, Hamilton, Kingston, and Bytown (now Ottawa). While the first two benefited from the prosperity of their wheat-growing back country, the latter two, remote from the best agricultural lands, remained small lumber towns: "in 1830 Kingston had a larger population than York [later Toronto] and about four times as many people as Hamilton; by 1851 it had been surpassed by Hamilton and had less than 40 percent of the population of Toronto" (McCallum, 1980:67). In Québec, many merchants and artisans failed because local farmers could not afford their goods or services, and towns grew slowly, like the lumber-based communities of eastern Ontario. Still a major commercial city, Montréal progressed with little contributions from the province's agriculture (McCallum, 1980:70–74).

After Confederation, soil exhaustion and competition from more productive Prairie producers forced farmers to shift to new commodities such as fruits and vegetables, meat, and dairy products. With well-established farms, savings, and a now prosperous domestic market, Ontario farmers made the transition successfully. For Québec farmers, indebted and far from the best markets, the same transition proved more difficult (McCallum, 1980:45–53; Isbister, 1987:68–69; Pomfret, 1987).

In sum, Ontario's geographical advantage provided the province with capital, prosperous farms, and fledging towns and industries, while Québec agriculture failed to generate a commercial surplus. In these conditions, Québec's development was bound to lag behind that of Ontario. The most surprising, notes John Isbister, was that Québec's disadvantage had so little effect (1987:69). Bestowed with unequal resources, the two provinces grew at about the same pace (Raynauld, 1961:46–52). Resource endowments, modern economics teaches us, do not determine economic growth (Economic Council of Canada, 1977:23–25). Québec and Ontario had highly integrated economies. Natural resources, manufactured goods, technologies, and capital circulated freely, and business conditions were similar (Raynauld, 1961:52). The key difference was in each province's labour market. From its past, Québec inherited a low-wage market.

In a predominantly agricultural economy, the income of farmers has a strong influence on the level of industrial wages. When good land is scarce and farmers are poor, the supply of persons willing to accept poorly paid unskilled industrial jobs is high. By opposition, when good land is abundant and farmers are prosperous, unskilled labour is relatively unavailable and expensive (Raynauld, 1961:202–3). If workers and industries moved freely from one region to the other, the income differences between the low-wage and the high-wage region could eventually disappear. Labour and capital markets, however, never function perfectly. Between 1830 and 1930, about one million Quebeckers left the province to seek a better life in the United States (Rouillard, 1985:11). Others moved west, to Ontario and beyond (Faucher, 1964). Québec unemployment and underemployment nevertheless remained high and, added to low farm incomes, continued to pressure wages downward (Raynauld, 1961:203–4; McCallum, 1980:117–18).

Québec's situation as a low-wage economy in a high-wage continent favoured investments in sectors such as textiles and clothing, which required an abundance of cheap, unskilled labour. Less productive than sectors using more capital, these industries paid low wages and reproduced Québec's initial disadvantage. André Raynauld suggests that with slower population growth this disadvantage would have diminished gradually (1961:213–15). Recent studies on regional development show, however, that early disparities tend to last irrespective of demographic trends. Québec's legacy of high unemployment levels, low manufacturing productivity, and low wages endured for a long period (Economic Council of Canada, 1977; Altman, 1988).

The province's relative poverty was a key factor in the constitution of a linguistic division of labour. With the Conquest, the elites of New France had lost their power, their imperial markets, and their financial networks, and a new class of Anglo-Saxon merchants based in Montréal had taken over the lucrative fur and, later, lumber trades. Excluded from the colony's main economic activities, French-Canadian merchants were largely confined to the relatively poor domestic market (Saint-Germain, 1973:356–77; Sales, 1979:290–91). After Confederation, they were further marginalized by the rise of large, modern corporations and the influx of American capital (Bélanger and Fournier, 1987:17–36). Alone, the predominance of anglophone business would have been sufficient to generate a linguistic division of labour: managers and workers did not speak the same language. Ownership, however, does not explain the poor representation of francophones at intermediary levels. Modern multinational firms prove business can operate in any local language. One would even think there are advantages in doing so. Was business efficiency well served when firms with a francophone work force employed unilingual anglophones at the lowest managerial levels? Why did such a choice prevail in so many industries for such a long period?

Explanations for these hiring policies have alternatively stressed cultural factors, educational levels, linguistic skills, and discrimination. Appeals to culture and education are the least convincing. Presumed differences in values suffer too many exceptions and fail to account for the rise and decline of the linguistic division of labour (Boulet, 1980:42). As for educational levels, studies have shown anglophones could receive promotions without training, while education did not guarantee advancement for francophones (McRoberts, 1979:305). The notion of linguistic skills provides a more plausible explanation. From an economic point of view, language is a skill demanded by employers. For many years, in Québec, the demand for English fluency exceeded the supply. Bilingual francophones filled some of the positions demanding a good knowledge of English, but necessarily remained disadvantaged compared to anglophones. The latter benefited from this situation and received higher incomes, until social changes, the rise of francophone firms, and language policies made the demand for French fluency rise (Vaillancourt, 1986, and Chapter 23 in this volume; McRoberts, 1979:305–6). This explanation fits the evidence better than cultural accounts. It explains, in particular, why disparities widened with industrialization. Some aspects of the question, however, remain problematic. The economic explanation assumes firms determine the language of each position in a rational fashion, with considerations on the language used by managers, clients, and workers (Vaillancourt, 1986:405–7). Many practices appear unwarranted by such rational calculations. The predominance of unilingual anglophones as foremen and security agents in firms with a francophone work force, for instance, does not seem to maximize efficiency (on these cases, see Hughes, 1943:54–59). In such cases, hiring decisions seem to have more to do with discrimination than with skills or optimality.

Contrary to what economists often believe, the market logic does not eliminate discrimination. In fact, labour markets often reinforce prejudices by giving stable structures to transitory ethnic preferences (Wright, 1986:189). Consider Québec's situation at the beginning of this century. A surplus of unskilled labour lowered real wages for the majority. At the same time, as in any industrializing economy managerial and industrial skills remained scarce. Firms often had to attract specialists and skilled workers from Europe and the United States. "Each new industry," observed Everett C. Hughes in the town he studied, "has brought in new managers, who, although of the same language and religion as the earlier English settlers, are as little kin to them as to the local French families" (1943:32). Experienced, mobile, and demanded in many places, these outsiders functioned in a distinct labour market, something like a high-wage enclave in a low-wage economy. In ethnically divided societies, such labour market divisions tend to endure because ethnicity becomes a code for both employers and workers. In the American South, for instance, a factor totally irrelevant to efficiency—race—became central in the labour market because the first skilled workers were whites brought from outside the low-wage regional economy. As long as employers continued to associate skills to ethnicity, the code remained self-confirming: victims of discrimination had no reason to acquire skills that employers would not recognize (Wright, 1986:158 and 189–94). Thus, while the skilled workers imported by Ontario firms tended to blend with the local work force, the Québec labour market remained segmented (on Ontario, see Heron, 1988:74–87). Skilled or not, Québec anglophones gained access to the high-wage segment of the market by virtue of their identity, while skilled francophones often remained tied to the low-wage segment, for the same reason. Needless to say, anglophones did everything they could to avoid being associated with those at the wrong end of the labour market. The Irish, for instance, downplayed a Catholicism that associated them with poorly paid French Canadians (Hughes, 1943:119).

The fate of Québec and of the province's francophones was thus largely determined by early disadvantages confirmed year after year by the working of institutional and market forces. In the American South, regional poverty and labour market discrimination were only defeated with political interventions aimed at changing the rules of the game. From the 1930s to the 1960s, federal measures and trade union pressures helped raise wages to the national level, and in the 1960s the civil rights movement completed this evolution by eliminating segregation. No longer a low-wage enclave, the South shifted, with the support of the different states, toward a capital-intensive, modern economic structure (Wright, 1986:250–68). Québec's evolution after World War II bears some resemblance to that of the American South. Political forces transformed Québec's economy and, in many ways, improved the situation. By the 1980s, for instance, productivity and wage levels had risen almost to national levels. The province's evolution, however, left some important problems unresolved, notably growing rates of unemployment and poverty.

OUT OF LOW WAGES

After World War II, the legacy of Québec's past as a low-wage, high-unemployment region was still very much in evidence. With high economic growth rates, stimulated by the war and by the postwar domestic boom, the unemployment rate remained remarkably low for a few years (Noël, 1987:99–100; Fortin, 1991:200). Yet, in the words of economist François-Albert Angers, Québec remained the province of textiles, and Ontario the province of iron and steel. The wartime demand for metal and chemical products generated new manufacturing activities in Québec, but these activities subsided with the end of the war. The province's heavy industry mostly captured the excess business Ontario firms could not keep during boom time, only to lose it in hard times (Angers, 1952:338; Boismenu, 1981:131 and 149). Outside the traditional labour-intensive activities, the Québec economy functioned as a complement to that of Ontario, as a secondary labour market that absorbed the shocks during cyclical downturns. Near full employment during the war and immediately after, Québec was the first to feel the full impact of the early 1950s recession.[6]

Federal macroeconomic policies compounded Québec's industrial and labour-market difficulties. More preoccupied by the threat of inflation than by unemployment, the federal government maintained a "passive orientation" and "tolerated" a secular rise in the unemployment rate (Campbell, 1991:6–14). At 1.8 percent in 1948, Québec's unemployment rate rose to around 4 percent between 1956 and 1966, 6.6 percent in 1974, 9.6 percent in 1979, and 10.1 percent in 1990.[7] Compared to Ontario, the province also maintained a low employment–population ratio, which means that many persons who would have worked in Ontario did not in Québec. These persons did not increase the unemployment rate because they were "discouraged" job-seekers, people who decided to stay out of the labour market. The ranks of the "discouraged" increased alongside the unemployment rate, and the gap between the employment–population ratios of the two central provinces more than doubled between the 1940s and the 1980s (Dépatie, 1971; Fortin, 1991:200–201).

Québec's relative disadvantage also persisted with respect to incomes. Between the war and the end of the 1950s, real wages increased considerably, but the gap with Ontario continued basically unchanged (Boismenu, 1981:305). From the 1930s to the late 1950s, Québec's per capita income never exceeded 72 percent of Ontario's (Raynauld, 1961:210). Yet, things had started to change. Maintained by Québec's high rates of unemployment and underemployment, the overall income gap between the two provinces masked modest improvements in manufacturing and for those who were employed in general (Raynauld, 1961:200). New factors were at play in the workplace that would eventually upset long-entrenched disparities.

World War II gave rise to the first explicit social and political attack against the Québec/Ontario income gap. The war effort brought the federal government to intervene heavily into the labour market, with controls on employment, wages, and working conditions. In a labour shortage situation, Ottawa planned production and froze wages to avoid conflicts and inflation. No longer a "natural" market outcome, income distribution became for the first time the result of an explicit political decision to freeze existing market disparities (MacDowell, 1983:16–21). In Québec, where wartime full employment created an unprecedented occasion to obtain better wages, the federal wage policy appeared particularly unfair. Québec workers, argued a Montréal steelworkers union local in 1941, have as much a right as workers in other provinces to an equivalent standard of living (Gérin-Lajoie, 1982:35). Tradition, still argued the Québec steelworkers in 1945, should not justify inequity:"there is a gross injustice," they pleaded to the War Labour Board, "when employees working on the same kind of machinery, performing the same operations giving about the same output and producing similar goods sold on the same market at the same price, are not receiving the same rates of pay" (Québec Steelworkers, quoted in Cardin, 1992:342). Numerous attempts, backed by national unions who felt undermined by lower wages in one region, failed to win a unique contract for the entire steel industry, but they opened the way, after the war, to "pattern bargaining," a bargaining procedure using national coordination to lower regional disparities (Gérin-Lajoie, 1982:35–45). Until the early 1960s, pattern bargaining and recurrent demands for national contracts, or at least national standards, failed to eliminate Québec's wage disadvantage, which persisted in most industries (Raynauld, 1961:200–205). Yet, a breach had been opened. No longer accepted as natural and necessary, Québec's low-wage status was now challenged by workers and their unions. In the most unionized industries Québec workers were beginning to catch up with those of Ontario (Ostry, 1960; Raynauld, 1961:245). In the almost totally organized pulp and paper industry, for instance, average wages became almost identical in the two provinces around 1950 (Charland, 1990:292).[8]

The real breakthrough came after 1960, when union militancy and state intervention definitively changed the rules of the game. In Western Europe and North America, the unprecedented rapid and stable economic growth of the 1950s and early 1960s created the conditions for new social and political demands in the 1960s. In many ways, the decade was a watershed: state interventions multiplied, welfare programs expanded, trade unions grew and became increasingly militant, and a host of new social movements redefined the politics and culture of advanced capitalist countries (Wee, 1987:62–84; Heclo, 1981:394–98). In Québec, the steady growth and the fiscal conservatism of the 1950s gave the Liberal government elected in 1960 the margin of manoeuvre to implement changes along similar lines (Lipsig-Mummé, 1984:299). "For a few years," notes Kenneth McRoberts, "*all* seemed possible" (1988:130). Committed to state intervention, the Liberals modernized and expanded the civil service, and gave it a host of new mandates, in economic development, education, health, welfare, and cultural matters.

In ten years, during the 1960s, the civil service almost doubled its work force, public enterprises multiplied, and parapublic institutions in education, health, and social services expanded considerably (Gow, 1986:331–34). The public sector became a primary source of employment for a new generation of workers, who were educated, mostly white-collar, and often of blue-collar family origin (Lipsig-Mummé, 1984:300; Gow, 1986:336). This new generation of service employees massively joined trade unions. Everywhere in Canada, public sector workers were organizing. In 1961, Canadian public sector unions counted 183,000 members, or one union member out of eight; ten years later they had 572,000 members, and by 1981, 1,500,000, by then 40 percent of the country's union membership (Kumar, 1986:115). In Québec, these new union members had high expectations. In 1961, public sector workers earned on average 25 percent less than private sector ones, and from a government committed to expand and improve the civil service, they expected better wages and working conditions (Rouillard, 1989a:377).

At the outset, the new Liberal government was ambivalent toward trade unions. Close to a labour movement that supported its program of state intervention and modernization, it was committed to reform the Labour Code, but not to the extent of granting full collective bargaining rights to its own employees: "the Queen," affirmed Premier Jean Lesage, "does not negotiate with her subjects" (McRoberts, 1988:159–61). Trade union leaders themselves were not convinced all public employees should have the right to strike. Pressures from union members themselves, expressed most vividly in a series of illegal strikes in 1963 and 1964, pushed them to demand full collective bargaining rights, which the government granted in two steps, in 1964 and 1965 (Rouillard, 1989a:298–300). The new Labour Code was almost unprecedented in North America. Only Saskatchewan had given similar rights to public sector employees, in 1944 when the CCF was first elected, and that reform had little impact.[9] The adoption of Québec's new Labour Code, on the contrary, and the militancy of Québec federal public sector workers, rapidly led to similar changes in Ottawa and in other provinces (Panitch and Swartz, 1988:24). Taking full advantage of their newly won rights, Québec public sector employees made major gains and forced the government to react. In an attempt to control the process and, in particular, to avoid whipsawing tactics (where concessions obtained from a weak institution became a precedent for other negotiations), the Québec government centralized collective bargaining to an extent that was unparalleled in North America (Bauer, 1989:44; Conseil du Trésor, 1985). In reaction, traditionally divided trade unions created a "Common Front," and the successive rounds of public sector collective bargaining became a confrontational negotiation over wages that affected the entire province.

Québec's unique industrial relations framework generated an equally unique economic and social outcome. This framework, observed economist Robert Lacroix, so much increased the profitability of public sector strikes that a low level of militancy would have been surprising (1987:106). Not only were public sector workers militant, but collectively, they sought to transform Québec society. Trade unions defined the "Common Front" as an instrument to correct, if not eliminate, market-determined wage inequities. The successive "Common Fronts" shared three aims: first, reducing inequalities within the public sector, between the best and the lowest paid; second, guaranteeing that public sector workers benefited from economic growth and improved their income over time; and third, pulling up wages in the private sector, in particular for those at the bottom of the scale (Beaucage, 1989:57–59). In Ontario, public sector unions acted conservatively because the wage settlements that pulled up all wages were established by private sector unions in the high-wage manufacturing industries. In Québec, by contrast, the low wages that still prevailed in manufacturing gave public sector unions the leading role. More frequent than in Ontario, private sector strikes seemed to follow in the wake of public sector settlements (Rouillard, 1983:221–22; Lacroix, 1987:107).

Between 1971 and 1983, the Common Front successfully reduced wage differences in the public sector (by about 15 to 20 percent), and it significantly improved the real wages of its members (Beaucage, 1989:76–79). More importantly, it appears to have succeeded with respect to its third, most unlikely, objective: improving wages in the private sector. In the 1970s, the wage increases obtained by the Common Front influenced private sector wage settlements by encouraging private sector trade union militancy and pulling up comparable wages, especially in smaller communities (Lacroix, 1987:104–7). In Canada, this evolution was unique (Riddell, 1986:25–27). Public sector trade unions succeeded where international unions had failed during and after the war: they imposed something like an incomes policy aimed at ending Québec's low-wage status

(Boismenu, 1990:179-80). By the beginning of the 1980s, as Figure 24.1 indicates, Québec public and private sector workers had reached wage parity with those of Ontario (Fortin, 1991:210–11). In low-wage manufacturing industries such as clothing or textiles, Québec wages even surpassed those of Ontario, and proportionally there were more low-wage workers in Ontario than in Québec (Cousineau, Lacroix, and Vaillancourt, 1982:79; Cournoyer, 1988:102).

Trade union pressures were not the only determinant of this evolution. The development of income security and the concomitant rise of the minimum wage in the 1960s and 1970s also improved wages, particularly those of the lowest paid in the private sector. Convinced the minimum wage should maintain work incentives and provide an income sufficiently above what welfare programs guaranteed, the Québec government increased it regularly between 1965 and 1978 (Boivin, 1987:137–40). In 1970, the province still had a lower minimum wage than Ontario; by 1978, its rates were 18 percent higher, thanks to a large extent to Ontario's conservatism (Fortin, 1980:46). This relatively high minimum wage pushed up all wages, especially those just above the minimum, prevalent in manufacturing industries such as clothing or services such as hotels and restaurants (Fortin, 1978:45). At the same time, the 1960s reforms in education and the active promotion of French in the workplace opened better opportunities at the top and ended the old linguistic division of labour (Vaillancourt, 1986).[10] A host of welfare, labour market, education, and linguistic policies thus reinforced the impact of

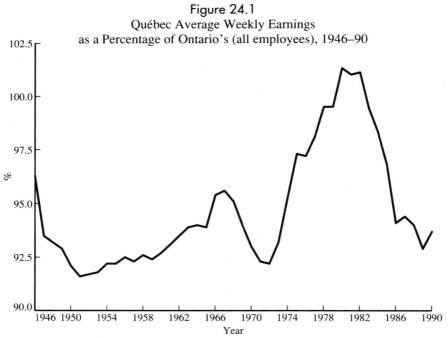

Figure 24.1
Québec Average Weekly Earnings
as a Percentage of Ontario's (all employees), 1946–90

Source: Statistics Canada, *Historical Statistics of Canada,* 2nd ed. (11-516), *Canada Year Book* (11-202), and *Perspectives on Labour and Income* (75-001).

trade union militancy. Together, these various interventions constituted a deliberate, yet unplanned, attempt to end both of Québec's long-lasting economic "inferiorities," an attempt that almost succeeded.

TWO QUÉBECS IN ONE

Wage increases obtained by trade union militancy and government intervention can have a positive effect on productivity if they compel employers to upgrade their capital equipment, improve their organizational methods, and better train their employees (Freeman and Medoff, 1984:162–80). When this happens, better incomes are justified by the economy's increased capacity to generate wealth, and steady economic growth, high levels of employment, and stable prices can be achieved. If, on the other hand, productivity gains lag behind wage increases, higher wages may put some firms out of business and create unemployment, often at the expense of the most vulnerable, less mobile workers (Cousineau, Lacroix, and Vaillancourt, 1982:125–26). For trade unions and progressive governments, this situation constitutes a dilemma. On one hand, the acceptance of low wages may become self-perpetuating and prevent investments necessary to guarantee competitiveness against producers benefiting from still lower wages. On the other hand, nothing guarantees sustained wage pressures will foster investments rather than increase unemployment. Unable to control or even predict business decisions, trade unions and governments can follow three strategies. They can pursue wage gains and equality without worrying about employment, they can forgo a broader conception of solidarity and seek sector-specific wage gains tied to productivity and employment, or they can accept wage moderation in exchange for guarantees of social justice and high employment levels. Labour movements always hesitate between these three approaches because each one entails losses on one front (Swenson, 1989:111–28).

In Québec, in the 1960s and 1970s, more emphasis was put on incomes and equality than on employment, and wage gains and greater equality probably contributed to a rising unemployment rate. Economic estimates indicate, however, that the impact of wages on unemployment remained very small (Fortin, 1991:210). In retrospect, trade union militancy appears warranted: in the 1980s, most of what had been gained was lost and, yet, unemployment continued to rise. Minimum wage increases became a rarity and failed to protect low-paid workers against inflation, most major collective agreements established wage increases below the inflation rate, and the Québec/Ontario income gap returned to its 1973 level, when Québec per capita wages were at 93 percent of Ontario's (McRoberts, 1988:371; R. Langlois, 1990:28–29; Fortin, 1991:210–11 and 227). Logically, notes economist Pierre Fortin, if wage losses did not bring higher employment, wage gains cannot be the root cause of unemployment (1991:211).

The attempts to eliminate the traditional Québec/Ontario wage disparity and to raise Québec's lowest wages have probably contributed to increase unemployment. The real culprit, however, lies elsewhere. Between the 1950s and the 1980s, the unemployment rate increased everywhere in Canada, largely as a result of federal macroeconomic policies. The Canadian government never made full employment a priority. Inflation and perceived threats of inflation have regularly been met with restrictive policies that increased the unemployment rate without solving the inflation problem (Noël, 1990; Fortin, 1991:217). After 1975, price stability practically became the sole policy objective, and the federal government proved willing to induce recessions and let unemployment increase by as much as five percentage points to deal with inflation. The 1981–82 recession, for instance, was to a large extent deliberate (Campbell, 1991:12–14). The problem with this approach is that recessions are not simply temporary economic downturns. They permanently destroy the jobs of people who may never find another stable situation, because they are in the wrong place, have the wrong skills or are deemed too old or otherwise inadequate (Kaliski, 1987). Recessions, economists say, have a "ratchet effect": each one leaves the "good times" unemployment rate higher than it used to be. In Québec, this "ratchet effect" proved particularly disastrous. Driven by the threat of inflation in Metropolitan Toronto, federal macroeconomic policies generated downturns while unemployment was still high in Québec: the Economic Council of Canada estimated in 1977 that "for every ten people put out of work by recession in Ontario, there [were] twenty-nine in the Atlantic region and twenty in Québec" (1977:99). Recessions hurt more, and durably, an economy still far from full employment and more dependent on vulnerable, labour-intensive industries (Fortin, 1991:218-19).

Regular recessions also had adverse effects on the financial position of governments. The federal deficit, for instance, increased dramatically as a result of the 1981–82 recession (Bloskie, 1989). After the recession, high interest payments on the debt and discretionary tax reductions maintained the deficit at a high level, in spite of stable social program spending (Mimoto and Cross, 1991). In Québec, the 1981–82 recession also reduced revenues and pushed up the need for social spending. Confronted with heightened financial constraints, the provincial government shifted its priorities, and "a period of relative spending freedom" gave way to "an era of severe restrictions" (Dion and Gow, 1989:82). Ironically, very much an outcome of policies of austerity, high budget deficits encouraged more of the same policies.

In Europe and North America, the 1960s and early 1970s constituted something like a golden age of improved incomes and rising productivity. State intervention and collective bargaining sustained economic growth and created the conditions for a steady rise of productivity and real wages (Temin, 1989:126–28). Canadian wages rose to the level of American wages, while Québec caught up with Ontario, and productivity figures converged (Boismenu, 1990:181). Steadily increasing incomes and high levels of employment generated inflationary pressures that, in countries where the left was weak, led governments to adopt stop-and-go policies detrimental to both employment and price stability (Cameron, 1984). Until the 1970s, the tendency of centrist and conservative governments to disregard the employment objective was held in check by electoral considerations. The 1973 oil shock lifted these political constraints. Because it appeared as an international disaster and seemed to dissociate economic difficulties from domestic policies, the oil shock "decreased the electoral risks of allowing unemployment to increase and tempted many governments into using unemployment as a cure for inflation" (Korpi, 1991:336). One after the other, advanced capitalist countries abandoned the ambivalent policy orientations of the 1960s and early 1970s, and turned decidedly to the right. Macroeconomic policies were designed with little regard for unemployment, the expansion of welfare programs was abandoned, and trade unions faced mounting opposition (Boyer, 1986:210–25). This policy shift was most explicit in countries such as Great Britain, the United States, and Canada, where the commitment to full employment was the weakest, where economic difficulties appeared most pronounced, and where the electoral system allowed conservative parties to rule without coalitions (Castles, 1990).

Québec's conservative 1950s and activist 1960s evolved in tune with politics in all of North America and Western Europe. So did the 1980s, when individualistic and market values took centre stage. From the 1980 referendum to its electoral defeat in 1985, the Parti Québécois government gradually became more conservative. The PQ's vision of a sovereign and interventionist state was defeated twice in two years: first during the referendum, when electors denied the Québec government a mandate to negotiate sovereignty-association, and second in 1982, when the constitutional agreement reached without Québec ended the province's long-lasting drive to obtain more responsibilities. Left without a clear strategy, the Lévesque government also faced in 1981–82 what became "by far the worst recession Canadians have experienced since the Second World War" (Royal Commission, 1985:44). Largely determined by outside forces, in particular by federal policies, the recession and the financial difficulties it created gave credence to a new discourse stressing the limits of state intervention and of welfare programs, and the need for concessions from public sector trade unions (McRoberts, 1988:356–65). For ten years in the 1980s, provincial and federal policies would combine with new business strategies to increase unemployment, underemployment, and poverty. As a result, in less than a decade Québec society lost much of the ground gained after the Quiet Revolution and become sufficiently polarized to be characterized as "two Québecs in one" (Conseil des affaires sociales, 1989; see Figure 24.1 and Figure 24.2).

While unemployment rates rose, Ottawa and Québec redefined their welfare and labour market programs to limit state intervention and reduce social benefits. The two levels of government did not dismantle the welfare state, but circumscribed and restricted most programs (Houle, 1990:432). Income security measures, for instance, became less generous and less accessible, making the jobless poorer and more likely to accept unstable and badly paid employment. In the 1960s, the Québec government raised the minimum wage to maintain work incentives; by the 1980s, it mostly reduced the income of able-to-work welfare recipients who refused jobs that failed to provide an escape from poverty (Conseil des affaires sociales, 1990:39–47; R. Langlois, 1990:78–85). At the same time, taxation became more regressive, more favourable to high-income earners and less advantageous for the poor. The poor now spend more of their resources than the rich to reduce the federal deficit (R. Langlois, 1990:88). Finally, a host of social programs have been restricted. In constant dollars, Québec spent 15.3 percent less on primary and secondary education in 1988 than in 1981. Hospitals, low-cost housing, children protection, social services for those in difficulties, every aspect of the welfare state was constrained by dwindling resources, at a time when needs had rarely been so important (R. Langlois, 1990:79–81).

Policies also changed with respect to trade unions. In both the federal and the provincial public sectors, collective bargaining gradually gave place to laws of exception and settlements by decree (Panitch and Swartz, 1988). In 1982, the Lévesque government went as far as suspending the Québec Charter of Human

Figure 24.2
Unemployment Rates, Québec and Ontario, 1946–90
(percent)

Source: Statistics Canada, *Historical Statistics of Canada,* 2nd ed. (11-516)
and *Historical Labour Fource Statistics* (71-201).

Rights and Freedoms to impose reduced wages and stricter working conditions to 320,000 public sector employees (McRoberts, 1988:371–75; Rouillard, 1989a:388–93). In the following years numerous conflicts were ended with similar, if less spectacular, legislative measures, and public sector wages fell in real terms, increasing less rapidly than the inflation rate. In the private sector, wage increases were slightly superior, but still behind the inflation rate (Rouillard, 1989b:162; Blais and Vaillancourt, 1989:37–38). In the 1980s, workers stopped benefiting from economic growth and gradually lost ground. By the end of the decade, the share of wage-earners in Québec's total income had shrunk to a proportion not seen in more than twenty years (Rouillard, 1990:126). Wage moderation did not even prevent union avoidance strategies. In the public as well as the private sector, high unemployment rates and weaker unions facilitated the rise of new forms of employment characterized by their instability. For many young Quebeckers, regular jobs providing a full-time, full-year, stable situation with a single employer appeared to be a thing of the past. Forty percent of the jobs created since 1975 were part-time jobs, many of which were accepted by people seeking full-time employment. Short-term work, self-employment, and temporary-help agency work also multiplied, so that by 1986, hardly half of the Québec work force held regular full-time jobs (Tremblay, 1990:81-98). In most cases, nonstandard jobs yielded low and insecure incomes, poor working conditions, and few marginal benefits. Together, they strongly contributed to the 1980s polarization of incomes, visible in Québec and Canada as well as in the United States (Economic Council of Canada, 1990:11–18).

With little state commitment to full employment, income security, minimum working conditions and welfare, with unions unable to protect the workers' share of the total income, and with the rise of precarious employment, Québec society was bound to change. The income gap between Québec and Ontario reappeared, the province once again became a high-unemployment labour market, and poverty reached unprecedented proportions (see Figures 24.1 and 24.2 above). In 1973, Québec's rate of poverty gave the province the fifth rank among the provinces; by 1986, the province had dropped to the eight rank, far behind Ontario and close to the two provinces with the highest poverty rates, Newfoundland and Saskatchewan. The root cause of this situation was Québec's low employment/population ratio, or in other words its high rates of unemployment and underemployment (Ministère de la main-d'oeuvre, de la sécurité du revenu et de la formation professionnelle, 1990:200–205). Essentially a policy outcome, high unemployment was used to justify lower minimum wages, revisions in welfare programs, and concessions from trade unions. It also contributed to the rise of non-standard, low-wage employment. The end result was a polarized society, best described by the Conseil des affaires sociales as "two Québecs in one" (Conseil des affaires sociales, 1989).

By 1989, the Montréal area counted three times more organizations distributing food to the poor than in 1970. These 374 organizations still failed to meet the demand, in a region where, they estimated, one person out of five did not have enough to eat. Only a "conspiracy of silence," denounced the "Table de concertation sur la faim à Montréal," could explain the general lack of concern for such a situation (R. Langlois, 1990:10–11). For most of the 1980s, the elites of Québec celebrated their economic achievements. The creation of an original institutional network, the development of francophone business, the virtual elimination of the linguistic division of labour, and the overall rise of productivity were no mean accomplishments. They masked, however, not only growing disparities, but problems that risked undermining everything achieved earlier. In 1989, when the Conseil des affaires sociales published *Deux Québec dans un*, few worried about unemployment, poverty, the decline of many regions and industries, and the overall fragility of the Québec economy. Soon, most would.

SWEDEN, GERMANY, OR THE UNITED STATES?

In September 1991, Québec Industry, Commerce, and Technology Minister Gérald Tremblay declared the province's economy "in a state of emergency." Of all the OECD countries, he noted, only Ireland and Spain had worst unemployment rates than Québec in the 1980s, and if we add to the unemployed those who are able to work but receive social assistance, we can say one worker out of five failed to contribute to economic growth. At the same time, thousands of positions remained vacant for lack of qualified applicants. Almost 40 percent of Québec's youth quit high school without a degree, and the same proportion of the adult population had difficulties reading simple material. Business invested almost nothing in training, and proved unable to modernize capacities and improve productivity. Canada ranked twenty-second out of twenty-four OECD countries for productivity gains between 1961 and 1990, and confronted with strong international competitors, entire industrial sectors collapsed. Québec governments, the Liberal minister concluded, had to push forward major changes, or face the prospect of managing the increasingly severe economic crises of a society sinking into poverty (Tremblay, 1991b and 1991c).

The Liberal minister's call of emergency did not fall on deaf ears. Editorialists, politicians of different stripes, business associations, trade unions, and various individuals and groups praised the minister for speaking like politicians in power rarely do and for exposing the disastrous state of Québec's economy (see, for instance, Dubuc, 1991b; Picher, 1991). Most interesting was the attitude of business. Two weeks earlier, Québec's most important business association, the *Conseil du patronat du Québec*, had itself denounced the province's "intolerable" unemployment situation, and called for a "Rendez-vous économique" between business, trade unions, and other groups (Cauchon, 1991). Held a week after Tremblay's speech, the "Rendez-vous" showed a remarkable unity of purpose between business and labour, who agreed on various policy recommendations and on forty-eight specific projects aimed at strengthening, without state subsidies, different industrial sectors (Turcotte, 1991; Lefebvre, 1991).

Belatedly, Québec's business leaders were discovering that economic success and international competitiveness have little to do with low wages and unfettered labour markets and owed much instead to policies aimed at developing high value-added industries, a qualified work force, and cooperative industrial relations (on these questions, see Block, 1987). That a deep recession and a general sense of losing ground were required to bring about this awareness did not lessen the importance of the shift in attitudes. But, of course, as mentioned above, the fight against unemployment and poverty depends on much more than elite attitudes. The recent and still fragile consensus on unemployment and poverty hides crucial differences in the reading of the situation and the conception of solutions. It also leaves unanswered the most difficult questions, those related to the choices, concessions, and compromises the main social actors would have to make to create new institutional arrangements.

Everybody is for economic growth and against unemployment, for social justice and against poverty. Disagreements begin when social actors discuss how to reach these goals. In Québec, the contending options can be narrowed down to three different policy visions. First, there is the liberal vision,[11] traditionally predominant in Québec and Canada, whereby free markets and economic growth should in the long run provide a solution to poverty and unemployment. Second, the social-democratic vision, which aims at making full employment the absolute policy priority and is best advocated in Québec by the *Forum pour l'emploi*. And third, the neocorporatist vision of a more organized and concerted market economy, proposed by Gérald Tremblay and likely to be quite influential.

Typical of the United States, Britain, and Canada, the liberal vision had many years to prove its worth and it failed. In Québec as in the rest of Canada, the liberal policies of the 1980s yielded high unemployment, low productivity gains, polarized incomes, and all the social problems associated with poverty. In retrospect, this outcome was hardly surprising. In every country faithful to the liberal vision, the neglect of unemployment and the preference for low wages, insecure employment, and strict welfare programs produced similar results (Leborgne and Lipietz, 1990; Harrison and Bluestone, 1990). In Québec, the liberal vision has nevertheless remained powerful. The federal government, most of the Québec Liberal Party, and business in general continue to accept its basic tenets. Invited to react to Tremblay's discourse on Québec's economic difficulties, Jean Corbeil, federal ˙minister responsible for Montréal's economic development, explained Montréalers themselves should find solutions and create their own jobs. The federal government could do nothing except reducing the deficit (Presse canadienne, 1991). Likewise, Daniel Johnson, the Québec minister responsible for the Montréal area, proposed nothing more concrete than to support export-oriented business and foreign investments (Venne, 1991; Lessard, 1991a). In the same vein, then Québec education minister Michel Pagé announced the government would seek a reduction in the high-school drop-out rate, but did not propose any concrete measures besides giving greater autonomy to school boards (Gruda, 1991; Sheppard, 1991). For its part, the federal government announced it would spend unemployment-insurance surplus funds on training the same year it reduced its overall contribution to education and training (Girard, 1991; Lessard, 1991b). Overall, the strategies of the Conservatives and of the Québec Liberals remained faithful to the liberal vision (see Lesage, 1991). The PQ opposition critique for Industry, Commerce, and Technology, Pauline Marois, was not wrong to conclude Gérald Tremblay's assessment and proposals were taking the minister away from the economic philosophy of his own government (Marois, 1991).

The opposite stance consists in making full employment an institutionalized priority. Associated with social democracy, this vision is also possible within a conservative framework. Sharing a strong political commitment to maintain full-employment, countries as different as Sweden, Norway, Switzerland, Austria, and Japan have been able to obtain both high levels of employment and low inflation rates, even in the 1980s (Therborn, 1986). In these countries, macroeconomic policies are designed to avoid costly cyclical downturns, active labour market policies are used to retrain workers displaced by international competition and economic change, and various forms of industrial relations arrangements are used to maintain wage and price stability. In Québec, a full-employment strategy was first advocated by two economists, Diane Bellemare and Lise Poulin-Simon, who tried to convince social actors, political parties, and governments that a new policy orientation was both desirable and feasible (1983 and 1986). Their ideas proved appealing because they addressed a longstanding issue of Québec politics and could draw on the examples of successful small countries. Trade unions and progressive elements of the business sector organized in November 1989 a *Forum sur l'emploi* to discuss the possibility of adopting this new approach. Unions, business associations, and representatives from community organizations, governments, and various associations opened a broad discussion on the question, and short of concrete results, they at least created a meeting point and an institutional structure supportive of a new economic vision (Milner, 1990/91:80). The Parti Québécois also embraced the full-employment vision (Parti Québécois, 1991:80-97). One may question the depth of this commitment, but at least the full-employment objective now occupies a central place in Québec politics. The opposition, major groups, and some of the francophone press now support the idea (Dubuc, 1991a). Even the very liberal Economic Council of Canada admitted, before being dismantled, the approach may serve Canada better than the traditional vision (Conseil économique du Canada, 1990:41–64).

A third vision occupies the space between liberalism and full employment, a complex and more ambiguous one, not easily subsumed under a few principles. The central component of this third approach is neo-corporatism and the best model is contemporary Germany. Compared to the liberal vision, this approach preserves the essentials of welfare programs and collective bargaining, and it maintains a premium on full-time, regular employment. It does not, however, give priority to full employment. In Germany, for instance, the commitment to full employment was abandoned in the 1980s and unemployment rose almost as high as in Canada (Bellemare and Poulin-Simon, 1986:395–410). At the same time, "there was no large-scale attack on the programs of the welfare state or the position of the unions," and a marked polarization of incomes was avoided (Katzenstein, 1989a:8; Myles, 1991:362). High unemployment rates excluded a significant part of the work force from the labour market, inflated welfare costs, and discouraged investment, but they did not transform industrial relations. Still strong, trade unions compelled employers to seek competitiveness through productivity gains and cooperation rather than low wages and precarious employment. As a result, Germany maintained a highly competitive industry, able if not to create enough jobs, at least to generate good and well-paid ones in sufficient number to cover rising welfare costs (Esping-Andersen, 1990:186; Mahon, 1987:52). The foundations of Germany's strategy lay in a working tradition of neo-corporatism, but alone concertation between business and labour would have been insufficient. Germany "prospered," writes Peter Katzenstein, "because of the density of its institutional life." Collective bargaining, cooperation in the workplace, welfare programs, vocational training, industrial policy, all aspects of German life are structured so that change only occurs "in small doses." External pressures and unprecedented events are filtered and absorbed through stable institutions aimed at reducing uncertainty, risk, and resistance to change (1989b:346).

In April 1991, Gérald Tremblay called upon business and labour to create a Québec version of the German model. To promote quality, training, and technological development, the Industry, Commerce, and Technology minister suggested firms guarantee jobs, training, and investment to their employees in exchange for long, flexible, no-strike collective agreements (Le Cours, 1991; Tremblay, 1991a). Trade unions and business reacted prudently. Business associations noted such a model seemed foreign to North American business traditions, and trade unions called for broader discussions, at the industry level. Some local precedents were nevertheless established. At the Sammi-Atlas steel company and at Marine Industries of Sorel, Tremblay convinced employers and workers to sign flexible, long-term agreements with job guarantees (Gibbon, 1991a and 1991b; April, 1991). At about the same time, in an unprecedented display of wage moderation, public sector unions accepted a six-month wage freeze for 1992 (Berger, 1991).

In Québec, many factors militate in favour of reforms inspired by the German model. Years of state intervention in various domains have created in Québec a density of institutional structures and networks that could be compared to that of Germany (see Latouche, 1990:149, 181-82, and 282; and Katzenstein, 1989b). Most obvious are the financial structures that re-create in North America something like European-style "universal banking": in Québec, governmental, private, cooperative, and union-based financial institutions act together in various ways to foster economic development, to support industrial policies, or to prevent foreign takeovers (Courchene and Wolfe, 1990:10–11). Likewise, with more than 40 percent of the work force organized, a rate comparable to that of Germany before unification, Québec trade unions are the most powerful in North America. In the last two years, union membership still increased, even in the private sector, while almost everywhere it fell (Tremblay and Van Schendel, 1991:561–63; Fournier, 1990). State intervention and trade union strength gave rise to an equally organized business, willing to coordinate on political issues and to participate in concertation efforts (Boivin and Guilbault, 1989:112–20). In the past, concertation efforts have been rightly criticized for being too centred on governmental objectives and overall unfruitful (Tanguay, 1984). Trade unions and business have nevertheless continued to support the idea (Guénard, 1991). At the very least, they estimate, concertation brought the other side to consider new dimensions of economic development: trade unions started to pay more attention to productivity and competitiveness; employers began to accept the importance of skills and training (Jalbert, 1990:353–56). Six months of discussions at the Bélanger-Campeau Commission seem to have contributed to this process, and it encouraged the rare unanimity shown by the *Conseil du Patronat du Québec* and trade unions at the September 1991 "Rendez-vous" (see Nadeau, 1991:73; Turcotte, 1991).

Of the three visions outlined here, the first one, the liberal vision, seems the most likely because it constitutes the "default" option, the choice sheer inertia would impose. Liberalism predominates at the federal level, and in Québec it remains the preferred option of business and of most Liberals, including the premier. It has strong supporters in the Parti Québécois as well. Recent welfare reforms that facilitated the rise of precarious work, for instance, were inspired by a White Paper prepared by Jacques Parizeau when he was finance minister (Bissonnette, 1988; Boismenu and Rocher, 1986). In principle, the PQ is committed to full employment, but this commitment remains untested. During the last electoral campaign, the party hardly even raised the poverty issue (Picher, 1989). In a country with a strong liberal tradition, the litmus test for change will come not from political discourses, but from concrete measures regarding the unemployed, the poor, welfare, education, and trade unionism.

At the same time, there are good reasons to believe Québec could move toward one of the other two visions. Industrial relations observers note the province "is an anomaly in the area of consultation where labour, management and government appear to have a strong, shared understanding for working together" (Kumar and Ryan, quoted in Milner, 1990/91:79). Years of conflicts have left trade unions and business sufficiently strong and organized to consider broad compromises (Francoeur, 1991). Québec's historical disadvantages, its smallness, and the fragility of its economy have also encouraged a search for consensus and flexibility typical of small European states (Courchene, 1991:50; Katzenstein, 1985). But concertation does not mean full employment. A successful "Québec Inc." is more likely to look like the German model, a model that combines competitiveness with high unemployment. For the social-democratic vision to prevail, a commitment to full employment would have to be institutionalized, cast in concrete by major programs and institutions. The countries that successfully maintained full employment designed all their major policies around this goal (Therborn, 1986:110–11). Even there, consistently pursuing this strategy proved increasingly difficult in recent years, in part because the internationalization of the money and capital markets made important policy instruments obsolete (Kurzer, 1991; Scharpf, 1991:244–55). To conclude, nothing prevents Québec from institutionalizing full employment, but given the forces in presence a more or less liberal variant of the German model seems the most likely outcome for the coming years.

CONCLUSION

Quebeckers paid a heavy price for their province's unfavourable beginnings. Endowed with comparatively poor agricultural resources, Québec developed early as a low-wage, high-unemployment economy. Without access to the main financial and commercial networks, francophones occupied a marginal place in industry, and they were confined to the lower segments of a linguistically divided labour market. After World War II, international unions led the effort to bring wages up to national levels, but an industrial structure dominated by low-wage manufacturing made the task almost impossible outside a few modern sectors.

It was only with the Quiet Revolution that this situation changed. An interventionist state committed to modernization, education, welfare, and the use of French in the workplace combined with a militant trade union movement bent on erasing the long-lasting income gap between Québec and Ontario. Together, state intervention and labour militancy eliminated the linguistic division of labour and the income disparities it perpetuated, improved the living conditions of the poor, and brought real wages to the Ontario level. Income disparities decreased, productivity came near the Ontario level, and Québec society changed into a modern service economy equipped with institutional resources unique in North America.

With the 1981–82 recession, everything changed once again, this time in reverse. Like Britain and the United States, Québec and Canada turned right. Concerns for social justice were replaced by market imperatives, welfare programs were circumscribed, and trade unions went into retreat. In the public sector, laws of exception made the strike weapon less effective, while in the private sector, the rise of nonstandard employment prevented the unionization of large categories of the population, especially the youth and women (see Lipsig-Mummé and Roy, 1989). Amid the ostentatious chorus of a new business class singing its success, unemployment and poverty silently reached new heights.

In 1990–91, Canada entered into its second major recession in less than ten years. This time even "winners" were hurt. The problems of Raymond Malenfant, the businessman who denounced state intervention but never missed a subsidy, and the fall of Lavalin, one of Québec's two giant engineering firms, were the most spectacular of a series of retreats that forced all sectors of society to acknowledge the limitations of ten years of liberal policies and practices (Gagnon, 1991; McKenna and Gibbon, 1991). A new discourse, best publicized by Industry, Commerce, and Technology Minister Gérald Tremblay, emerged, a call for concertation for the sake of training, productivity, and competitiveness. Rooted in Québec's specific social arrangements, this new discourse seems plausible because it refers to the experience of numerous European countries that have refused the liberal vision, even in the 1980s (see Garrett and Lange, 1991). In Québec, however, the full content of this approach has yet to be defined.

Québec business remains confident in the province's liberal traditions, labour seeks full employment, and the main political parties hesitate somewhere between liberalism and variants of German-style corporatism. Disagreements on Québec's constitutional status reflect these orientations: the liberal vision would be reinforced by a constitutional status quo that would make any transformation unlikely. Independence, on the other hand, would impose institutional adjustments and make new arrangements easier to reach. Independence alone, of course, hardly guarantees anything.

Plagued by poverty and unemployment, Québec nevertheless constitutes a rich society, one of the richest in the world. When recessions are over, it is easy for voters and politicians to forget social problems they would rather not see (Blais and Deschênes, 1989). "Green," wrote Lise Bissonnette during the 1989 Québec electoral campaign, "is the fashion color of this election, and ugly welfare grey is not about to compete" (1989). Are recent concerns for poverty and unemployment temporary or superficial ? After all, the Bélanger-Campeau Commission on Québec's political and constitutional future made little room for the unemployed and the poor (see Front Commun des personnes assistées sociales du Québec, 1991). Only time will tell.

In an essay on political cycles, American historian Arthur M. Schlesinger, Jr. notes how the United States episodically shifted from "the politics of public purpose ... to the politics of private interests," and then back from conservatism to "idealism and reform" (1986:32). The conservative 1920s were followed by the reformist 1930s, the staid 1950s by the 1960s, and the ebullient 1960s and 1970s by Ronald Reagan's 1980s. In this century, Québec politics evolved at roughly the same pace as American politics, and produced similar cycles of public and private concerns. These cycles are poorly understood, and time patterns do not allow predictions.[12] They nevertheless teach us that political attitudes and orientations usually prove transitory. In Québec, as in the United States, the 1990s do not have to be like the 1980s.

NOTES

1. This evaluation is for 1986; in 1991 the situation was probably worse (R. Langlois, 1990:34; Pépin, 1991). Statistics Canada defines the poverty line as a situation where more than 58.5 percent of one's income before tax is spent on food, housing, and clothing (the average family spends 38.5 percent of its income before tax on these necessities) (Tremblay and Van Schendel, 1991:341).

2. At the end of May 1991, the Ministry of Education announced new programs to provide food in the schools. Lise Bissonnette, editor of *Le Devoir*, noted that although necessary, these measures acknowledged the impact of poverty without addressing the problem itself (Bissonnette, 1991).

3. The remaining gap is explained by differences in education levels between the two groups. In 1980, at equivalent levels of education, francophones actually had a small advantage over anglophones (the reverse was true as late as 1970; Conseil de la langue française, 1991:60–63).

4. Such dichotomies, often used in the past to characterize Third World countries, have been broadly rejected by social scientists, in favour of more modest, historically specific models (see Migdal, 1983; Tilly, 1984).

5. In 1953, Québec's per capita income was low compared to Canada and the United States, but higher than that of any other country in the world (Raynauld, 1961:54).

6. On the concept of a secondary labour market see Piore and Sabel, 1984:56–57.

7. In 1991, the unemployment rate rose above 12 percent, but this may well be a recession peak akin to the 13.9 percent experienced in 1983. The 10 percent of 1990 is probably closer to what is now the permanent rate (Fortin, 1991:200; Juneau, 1991:A8).
8. Québec hourly wages, however, remained somewhat lower. Québec workers worked longer hours to compensate (Charland, 1990:293 and 345).
9. "There was never even a threat of a strike by government employees in Saskatchewan for thirty years after the law allowed it" (Goldenberg, 1990:296). This quiescence is only partly explained by the cooperation the labour movement and the CCF government felt they had to maintain in an environment hostile to socialism, since the defeat of the CCF in 1964 was not followed by increased strike activities (see Horowitz, 1968:145, and Richards and Pratt, 1979:143–44).
10. "While barely 50 percent of young Quebeckers—and even less, of course, among franco-phones—reached grade 9 in 1960, now 95 percent do. Furthermore, in 1982 almost 15 percent go through university, instead of only 4 percent in 1960" (Fortin, 1982:5).
11. The word "liberal" is used here in the European sense and describes the pro-market view shared by centrist and right-wing parties. Only in the United States is the term "liberal" associated with the left.
12. Although in 1949, Schlesinger's father, also a historian, estimated postwar conservatism would end "in 1962, with a possible margin of a year or two in either direction" and that "the next con-servative epoch" would "commence around 1978" (1986:24–25)!

REFERENCES

Altman, M. (1988). "Economic Development with High Wages: An Historical Perspective." *Explorations in Economic History*, 25 (2), 198–224.

Angers, F.-A. (1952). "Progrès industriels du Québec." *L'actualité économique*, 28 (2), 332–38.

April, P. (1991, June 27). "Tremblay exige un nouveau contrat social de la CSN afin de sauver MIL Davie." *Le Devoir*, 5.

Bauer, J. (1989). "La syndicalisation dans le secteur public québécois ou la longue marche vers la cen-tralisation." In Y. Bélanger and L. Lepage, eds., *L'administration publique québécoise: évolutions sectorielles, 1960-1985* (pp. 35–61). Montréal: Presses de l'Université du Québec.

Beaucage, A. (1989). *Syndicats, salaires et conjoncture économique: l'expérience des fronts communs du secteur public québécois de 1971 à 1983*. Sillery: Presses de l'Université du Québec.

Bélanger, Y., and P. Fournier (1987). *L'entreprise québécoise: développement historique et dynamique contemporaine*. Montréal: Hurtubise HMH.

Bellemare, D., and L. Poulin-Simon (1983). *Le plein-emploi: pourquoi?* Montréal: Presses de l'Uni-versité du Québec.

Bellemare, D., and L. Poulin-Simon (1986). *Le défi du plein-emploi*. Montréal: Éditions Saint-Martin.

Berger, F. (1991, April 27). "L'acceptation syndicale d'un gel de salaires inaugure-t-elle un 'partena-riat'?" *La Presse*, B6.

Bissonnette, L. (1988, March 5). "Parizeau Twists Toward Centre." *The Globe and Mail*, D2.

Bissonnette, L. (1989, September 2). "Social Issues Fail to Stir Well-Heeled Voters." *The Globe and Mail*, D2.

Bissonnette, L. (1991, May 29). "Après le petit déjeuner." *Le Devoir*, A8.

Blais, A., and L. Deschênes (1989). "L'économie en rose." *Recherches sociographiques*, 30 (1), 101–9.

Blais, A., and F. Vaillancourt (1989). "Le budget." In D. Monière, ed., *L'année politique au Québec, 1987–1988* (pp. 33–40). Montréal: Québec-Amérique.

Block, F. (1987). "Rethinking the Political Economy of the Welfare State." In F. Block et al., eds., *The Mean Season: The Attack on the Welfare State* (pp. 109–60). New York: Pantheon.

Bloskie, C. (1989, November). "An Overview of Different Measures of Government Deficits and Debt." In *Canadian Economic Observer* (pp. 3.1–3.20). Ottawa: Statistics Canada.

Boismenu, G. (1981). *Le duplessisme: politique économique et rapports de force, 1944–1960*. Mont-réal: Presses de l'Université de Montréal.

Boismenu, G. (1990). "L'État et la régulation du rapport salarial depuis 1945." In G. Boismenu and D. Drache, eds., *Politique et régulation: modèle de développement et trajectoire canadienne* (pp. 155–203). Montréal: Méridien.

Boismenu, G., and F. Rocher (1986). "Vers une réorientation des politiques sociales au Canada?" *Revue internationale d'action communautaire*, 15/56, 119–30.

Boivin, J. (1987). *Essai d'interprétation de la transformation du rapport salarial et de sa gestion éta-tique au Québec, 1960-1976*. Unpublished M.Sc. thesis, Département de science politique, Uni-versité de Montréal.

Boivin, J., and J. Guilbault (1989). *Les relations patronales-syndicales*, 2nd ed. Boucherville: Gaëtan Morin.

Boulet, J.-A. (1980). *La langue et le revenu du travail à Montréal*. Ottawa: Approvisionnements et Services Canada (Étude préparée pour le Conseil économique du Canada).

Boulet, J.-A., and L. Lavallée (1983). *L'évolution des disparités linguistiques de revenus de travail au Canada de 1970 à 1980*, Paper 245, Ottawa: Economic Council of Canada.

Boyer, R. (1986). "Segmentations ou solidarité, déclin ou redressement: quel modèle pour l'Europe?" In R. Boyer ed., *La flexibilité du travail en Europe* (pp. 201–304). Paris: La Découverte.

Cameron, D.R. (1984). "The Politics and Economics of the Business Cycle." In T. Ferguson and J. Rogers, eds., *The Political Economy: Readings in the Politics and Economics of American Public Policy* (pp. 237–62). New York: M.E. Sharpe.

Campbell, R.M. (1991). *The Full-Employment Objective in Canada, 1945–85: Historical, Conceptual, and Comparative Perspectives.* Study prepared for the Economic Council of Canada, Ottawa: Minister of Supply and Services.

Cardin, J.-F. (1992). *Travailleurs industriels et syndicalisme en période de prospérité: conditions de vie et conscience ouvrière des métallos montréalais durant la guerre et l'après-guerre (1940–1960)*. Unpublished Ph.D. thesis, Département d'histoire, Université de Montréal.

Castles, F.G. (1990). "The Dynamics of Policy Change: What Happened to the English-Speaking Nations in the 1980s." *European Journal of Political Research*, 18(5), 491–513.

Cauchon, P. (1991, August 28). "Le CPQ juge 'intolérable' la situation de l'emploi." *Le Devoir*, 5.

Charland, J.-P. (1990). *Les pâtes et papiers au Québec, 1880–1980: technologies, travail et travailleurs*. Québec: Institut québécois de recherche sur la culture.

Conseil de la langue française (1991). *Indicateurs de la situation linguistique au Québec*. Québec: Conseil de la langue française.

Conseil des affaires sociales (1989). *Deux Québec dans un: rapport sur le développement social et démographique*. Boucherville: Gaëtan Morin.

Conseil des affaires sociales (1990). *Agir ensemble: rapport sur le développement*. Boucherville: Gaëtan Morin.

Conseil du Trésor (1985). *Rapport Cadieux-Bernier: Régime de relations de travail dans le secteur public de certains pays industrialisés*. Québec: Gouvernement du Québec.

Conseil économique du Canada (1990). *Une décennie de transitions*. Vingt-septième exposé annuel, Ottawa: Ministère des approvisionnements et services.

Courchene, T.J. (1991). "Forever Amber." In D.E. Smith, P. MacKinnon, and J.C. Courtney, eds., *After Meech Lake: Lessons for the Future* (pp. 33–60). Saskatoon: Fifth House Publishers.

Courchene, T.J., and R. Wolfe (1990). "Québec Inc.: Overview and Implications." In T.J. Courchene, ed., *Québec Inc.: Foreign Takeovers, Competition/Merger Policy and Universal Banking* (pp. 3–16). Kingston: School of Policy Studies, Queen's University.

Cournoyer, M. (1988). "Les caractéristiques principales des personnes à bas salaires au Québec." *Interventions économiques*, 19, 93–107.

Cousineau, J.-M., R. Lacroix, and F. Vaillancourt (1982). *Les marchés du travail de Montréal et Toronto*. Montréal: École des Hautes Études Commerciales.

Demers, D. (1990, September 15). "La capitale des pauvres." *L'actualité*, 40–44.

Dépatie, R. (1971). "Essai d'évaluation de l'ampleur réelle du chômage au Québec." *L'actualité économique*, 47(3), 534–48.

Dion, S., and J.I. Gow (1989). "The Budget Process under the Parti Québécois, 1975–1985." In A.M. Maslove, ed., *Budgeting in the Provinces: Leadership and the Premiers* (pp. 55–85). Toronto: The Institute of Public Administration of Canada.

Dubuc, A. (1991a, August 18). "Le temps du plein-emploi." *La Presse*, B2.

Dubuc, A. (1991b, September 12). "Avant de sombrer, une deuxième Révolution tranquille." *La Presse*, B2.

Durocher, R., and P.-A. Linteau, eds. (1971). *Le "retard" du Québec et l'infériorité économique des Canadiens français*. Montréal: Boréal.

Economic Council of Canada (1977). *Living Together: A Study of Regional Disparities*. Ottawa: Minister of Supply and Services.

Economic Council of Canada (1990). *Good Jobs, Bad Jobs: Employment in the Service Economy*. Ottawa: Minister of Supply and Services.

Esping-Andersen, G. (1990). *The Three Worlds of Welfare Capitalism*. Princeton: Princeton University Press.

Faucher, A. (1964). "L'émigration des Canadiens français au XIXe siècle: position du problème et perspectives." *Recherches sociographiques*, 5(3), 277–317.

Fortin, P. (1978). *Une évaluation de l'effet de la politique québécoise du salaire minimum sur la production, l'emploi, les prix et la répartition des revenus.* Étude présentée à la Commission du salaire minimum et au Secrétariat du Comité ministériel permanent du développement économique. Québec: Ministère du travail et de la main-d'oeuvre.

Fortin, P. (1980). *Chômage, inflation et régulation de la conjoncture au Québec.* Montréal: Institut de recherches C.D. Howe.

Fortin, P. (1982). *Economic Growth in Québec (1978–80): The Human Capital Connection.* Policy Study no. 82-4, Institute for Policy Analysis, University of Toronto.

Fortin, P. (1991). "La question de l'emploi au Québec: la photo et le film." In *Eléments d'analyse économique pertinents à la révision du statut politique et constitutionnel du Québec* (pp. 167–241). Document de travail numéro 1, Québec: Commission sur l'avenir politique et constitutionnel du Québec.

Fournier, L. (1990, May 1). "Remontée syndicale au Québec?" *Le Devoir,* 7.

Francoeur, J. (1991, October 15). "Un syndicalisme en santé." *Le Devoir,* 14.

Freeman, R.B., and J.L. Medoff (1984). *What Do Unions Do?* New York: Basic Books.

Front commun des personnes assistées sociales du Québec (1991). "Mémoire présenté à la Commission sur l'avenir politique et constitutionnel du Québec," Québec.

Gagnon, L. (1991, October 10). "La garde tombante." *La Presse,* B3.

Garrett, G., and P. Lange (1991). "Political Responses to Interdependence: What's 'Left' for the Left?" *International Organization,* 45(4), 539–64.

Gérin-Lajoie, J. (1982). *Les Métallos, 1936–1981.* Montréal: Boréal.

Gibbon, A. (1991a, April 9). "Atlas Gets Labour Peace in $ 500-Million Expansion." *The Globe and Mail,* B1.

Gibbon, A. (1991b, July 5). "Workers Vow Not to Strike." *The Globe and Mail,* B3.

Girard, M. (1991, August 30). "Ottawa réduit le budget de l'éducation dans les provinces." *La Presse,* B4.

Goldenberg, S. B. (1990). "Strikes Against the Government: An Overview of the Canadian Experience." In J.A. Willes, ed., *Labour Relations in Canada: Readings and Cases* (pp. 294–99). Scarborough: Prentice-Hall.

Gouin, P., and Y. Chouinard (1989). "L'évolution socio-économique du Québec depuis la récession de 1982." In *Le Québec statistique* (pp. 145–69). Québec: Publications du Québec.

Gow, J.I. (1986). *Histoire de l'administration publique québécoise, 1867–1970.* Montréal: Les Presses de l'Université de Montréal.

Gruda, A. (1991, September 11). "Les voeux pieux du ministre Pagé." *La Presse,* B2.

Guénard, M. (1991). "Contrat social: Gérald Tremblay entre le banc d'essai ... et le pilori." *Magazine Avenir,* May, 3-14.

Harrison, B., and B. Bluestone (1990). "Wage Polarization in the US and the 'Flexibility' Debate." *Cambridge Journal of Economics,* 14(3), 351–73.

Heclo, H. (1981). "Toward a New Welfare State?" In P. Flora and A.J. Heidenheimer, eds., *The Development of Welfare States in Europe and America* (pp. 383–406). New Brunswick: Transaction Books.

Heron, C. (1988). *Working in Steel: The Early Years in Canada, 1883–1935.* Toronto: McClelland and Stewart.

Horowitz, G. (1968). *Canadian Labour in Politics.* Toronto: University of Toronto Press.

Houle, F. (1990). "Economic Renewal and Social Policy." In A.-G. Gagnon and J.P. Bickerton, eds., *Canadian Politics: An Introduction to the Discipline* (pp. 424–45). Peterborough: Broadview Press.

Hughes, Everett C. (1943). *French Canada in Transition.* Chicago: University of Chicago Press.

Isbister, J. (1987). "Agriculture, Balanced Growth, and Social Change in Central Canada Since 1850: An Interpretation." In D. McCalla, ed., *Perspectives on Canadian Economic History* (pp. 58–80). Toronto: Copp Clark Pitman.

Jalbert, P. (1990). *La concertation comme mode étatique de gestion des rapports sociaux.* Unpublished Ph.D. thesis, Département de science politique, Université de Montréal.

Juneau, A. (1991, February 13). "La plaie du chômage." *Le Devoir,* A8.

Kaliski, S.F. (1987). "Accounting for Unemployment: A Labour Market Perspective." *Canadian Journal of Economics,* 20(4), 665–93.

Katzenstein, P.J. (1985). *Small States in World Markets: Industrial Policy in Europe.* Ithaca: Cornell University Press.

Katzenstein, P.J. (1989a). "Industry in a Changing West Germany." In P.J. Katzenstein, ed., *Industry and Politics in West Germany: Toward the Third Republic* (pp. 3–29). Ithaca: Cornell University Press.

Katzenstein, P. J. (1989b). "Stability and Change in the Emerging Third Republic." In P.J. Katzenstein, ed., *Industry and Politics in West Germany: Toward the Third Republic* (pp. 307–53). Ithaca: Cornell University Press.

Korpi, W. (1991). "Political and Economic Explanations for Unemployment: A Cross–National and Long-Term Analysis." *British Journal of Political Science*, 21(3), 315–48.

Kumar, P. (1986). "Union Growth in Canada: Retrospect and Prospect." In W.C. Riddell, ed., *Canadian Labour Relations* (pp. 95–160). Studies for the Royal Commission on the Economic Union and Development Prospects for Canada, Volume 16, Toronto: University of Toronto Press.

Kurzer, P. (1991). "Unemployment in Open Economies: The Impact of Trade, Finance and European Integration." *Comparative Political Studies*, 24(1), 3–30.

Lacroix, Robert (1987). *Les grèves au Canada: causes et conséquences*. Montréal: Les Presses de l'Université de Montréal.

Langlois, R. (1990). *S'appauvrir dans un pays riche*. Montréal: Saint-Martin.

Langlois, S. (1990). "Inégalités sociales." In S. Langlois, ed., *La société québécoise en tendances, 1960–1990* (pp. 257–60). Québec: Institut québécois de recherche sur la culture.

Latouche, D. (1990). *Le bazar: des anciens Canadiens aux nouveaux Québécois*. Montréal: Boréal.

Leborgne, D. and A. Lipietz (1990). "Pour éviter l'Europe à deux vitesses." *Travail et société* 15 (2), 189–210.

Le Cours, R. (1991, April 5). "Travail: Québec veut instaurer 'le modèle allemand.' " *La Presse*, A1.

Lefebvre, M. (1991, September 23). "La façon québécoise de s'en sortir." *Le Devoir*, 12.

Lesage, G. (1991, October 11). "Remettre le Québec à l'ouvrage." *Le Devoir*, A7.

Lessard, D. (1991a, September 19). "Pour relancer Montréal, exportations et investissements étrangers." *La Presse*, A3.

Lessard, D. (1991b, September 19). "55 millions dans la formation: Ottawa court-circuite Québec." *La Presse*, A1.

Lipsig-Mummé, C. (1984). "The Web of Dependence: Québec Unions in Politics Before 1976." In A.-G. Gagnon , ed., *Québec: State and Society* (pp. 286–313). Toronto: Methuen.

Lipsig-Mummé, C., and R. Roy (1989). "La population syndiquée au Québec." *Labour/Le Travail*, 23, 119–57.

MacDowell, L.S. (1983). *"Remember Kirkland Lake:" The Gold Miners' Strike of 1941–42*. Toronto: University of Toronto Press.

Mahon, R. (1987). "From Fordism to ? New Technology, Labour Markets and Unions." *Economic and Industrial Democracy*, 8(1), 5–60.

Marois, P. (1991, September 19). "Économie en état d'urgence: 'Il ne faut pas en rester aux voeux pieux!' ", *La Presse*, B3.

McCallum, J. (1980). *Unequal Beginnings: Agriculture and Economic Development in Québec and Ontario until 1870*. Toronto: University of Toronto Press.

McKenna, B. and A. Gibbon (1991, January 29). "Few Bright Spots Seen for Québec Economy." *The Globe and Mail*, B18.

McRoberts, K. (1979). "Internal Colonialism: The Case of Québec." *Ethnic and Racial Studies*, 2 (3), 293–318.

McRoberts, K. (1988). *Québec: Social Change and Political Crisis*, 3rd ed. Toronto: McClelland and Stewart.

Migdal, J.S. (1983). "Studying the Politics of Development and Change: The State of the Art." In A.W. Finifter, ed., *Political Science: The State of the Discipline* (pp. 30–38) Washington, D.C.: APSA.

Milner, H. (1990/91). "Québec in Retrospect: Beyond Political Nostalgia." *Québec Studies*, 11, 75–82.

Mimoto, H., and P. Cross (1991, June). "The Growth of the Federal Debt." In *Canadian Economic Observer* (pp. 3.1–3.18). Ottawa: Statistics Canada.

Ministère de la main-d'oeuvre, de la sécurité du revenu et de la formation professionnelle (1990). *La pauvreté au Québec: situation récente et évolution de 1973 à 1986*. Québec: Les publications du Québec.

Myles, J. (1991). "Post-Industrialism and the Service Economy." In D. Drache and M.S. Gertler, eds., *The New Era of Global Competition: State Policy and Market Power* (pp. 351–66). Montréal: McGill-Queen's University Press.

Nadeau, J.M. (1991, August). "L'homme à tout faire du patronat." *L'actualité*, 61–73.

Noël, A. (1987). "L'après guerre au Canada: politiques keynésiennes ou nouvelles formes de régulation?" In G. Boismenu and G. Dostaler, eds., *La 'Théorie générale' et le keynésianisme* (pp. 91–107). Montréal: ACFAS.

Noël, A. (1990). "Jobs! Jobs! Jobs! The Political Management of Unemployment." In A.-G. Gagnon and J.P. Bickerton, eds., *Canadian Politics: An Introduction to the Discipline* (pp. 446–70). Peterborough: Broadview Press.

Noël, André (1990, November 3). "On ne peut plus parler de poches de pauvreté à Montréal, mais de poches d'aisance." *La Presse*, B5.

Norrie, K., and D. Owram (1991). *A History of the Canadian Economy*. Toronto: Harcourt Brace Jovanovich.

Ostry, S. (1960). "Inter-Establishment Dispersion of Occupational Wage Rates, Ontario and Québec, 1957." *Canadian Journal of Economics and Political Science*, 26(2), 277–88.

Ouellet, F. (1990). "The Quiet Revolution: A Turning Point." In T.S. Axworthy and P.E. Trudeau, eds., *Towards a Just Society: The Trudeau Years* (pp. 313–41). Markham, Ont.: Viking.

Panitch, L., and D. Swartz (1988). *The Assault on Trade Union Freedoms: From Consent to Coercion Revisited*. Toronto: Garamond.

Parti Québécois (1991). *Programme du Parti Québécois, édition 1991*. Montréal: Parti Québécois.

Pelletier, G. (1991). "Du pain avant les jeux, même constitutionnels." *Cité libre*, 19 (1), 5–6.

Pépin, A. (1991, March 28). "La pauvreté gagne du terrain dans la région de Montréal." *La Presse*, B1.

Picher, C. (1989, September 2). "Cette pauvreté dont personne ne parle..." *La Presse*, B1.

Picher, C. (1991, September 12). "La saine colère d'un ministre tranquille." *La Presse*, D1.

Piore, M., and C. Sabel (1984). *The Second Industrial Divide: Possibilities for Prosperity*. New York: Basic Books.

Pomfret, R. (1987). "The Mechanization of Reaping in Nineteenth-Century Ontario: A Case Study of the Pace and Causes of the Diffusion of Embodied Technical Change." In D. McCalla, ed., *Perspectives on Canadian Economic History* (pp. 81–95). Toronto: Copp Clark Pitman.

Presse canadienne (1991, September 19). "Ottawa invite les Montréalais à créer leurs propres emplois." *La Presse*, D3.

Raynauld, A. (1961). *Croissance et structure économiques de la province de Québec*. Québec: Ministère de l'industrie et du commerce.

Resnick, P. (1990). *Letters to a Québécois Friend*. Montréal: McGill-Queen's University Press.

Richards, J., and L. Pratt (1979). *Prairie Capitalism: Power and Influence in the New West*. Toronto: McClelland and Stewart.

Riddell, W.C. (1986). "Canadian Labour Relations: An Overview." In W.C. Riddell, ed., *Canadian Labour Relations* (pp. 1–93). Studies for the Royal Commission on the Economic Union and Development Prospects for Canada, Volume 16, Toronto: University of Toronto Press.

Rouillard, J. (1983). "Le militantisme des travailleurs au Québec et en Ontario, niveau de syndicalisation et mouvement de grève." *Revue d'histoire de l'Amérique française* 37 (2), 201–25.

Rouillard, J. (1985). *Ah les Etats! Les travailleurs canadiens-français dans l'industrie textile de la Nouvelle-Angleterre d'après le témoignage des derniers migrants*. Montréal: Boréal.

Rouillard, J. (1989a). *Histoire du syndicalisme au Québec: des origines à nos jours*. Montréal: Boréal.

Rouillard, J. (1989b). "Le mouvement syndical." In D. Monière, ed., *L'année politique au Québec, 1987–1988* (pp. 149–64). Montréal: Québec-Amérique.

Rouillard, J. (1990). "Le mouvement syndical." In D. Monière, ed., *L'année politique au Québec, 1989–1990* (pp. 125–34). Montréal: Québec-Amérique.

Royal Commission on Bilingualism and Biculturalism (1969). *Report*, Volume 3A. Ottawa: Queen's Printer.

Royal Commission on the Economic Union and Development Prospects for Canada (1985). *Report*, Volume 2. Ottawa: Minister of Supply and Services.

Saint-Germain, M. (1973). *Une économie à libérer: Le Québec analysé dans ses structures économiques*. Montréal: Presses de l'Université de Montréal.

Salée, D. (1990). "Reposer la question du Québec? Notes critiques sur l'imagination sociologique." *Politique*, 18, 83–106.

Sales, A. (1979). *La bourgeoisie industrielle au Québec*. Montréal: Les Presses de l'Université de Montréal.

Scharpf, F.W. (1991). *Crisis and Choice in European Social Democracy*. Ithaca: Cornell University Press.

Schlesinger, Arthur M., Jr. (1986). *The Cycles of American History*. Boston: Houghton Mifflin.

Sheppard, R. (1991, September 12). "Let Distinct Flowers Bloom." *The Globe and Mail*, A17.

Swenson, P. (1989). *Fair Shares: Unions, Pay, and Politics in Sweden and West Germany*. Ithaca: Cornell University Press.

Tanguay, A.B. (1984). "Concerted Action in Québec, 1976–1983: Dialogue of the Deaf." In A.-G. Gagnon, ed., *Québec: State and Society* (pp. 365–85). Toronto: Methuen.

Temin, P. (1989). *Lessons from the Great Depression*. Cambridge: M.I.T. Press.

Therborn, G. (1986). *Why Some Peoples Are More Unemployed Than Others*. London: Verso.

Tilly, C. (1984). *Big Structures, Large Processes, Huge Comparisons*. New York: Russell Sage Foundation.

Tremblay, D.-G. (1990). *L'emploi en devenir.* Québec: Institut québécois de recherche sur la culture.

Tremblay, D.-G., and V. Van Schendel, (1991). *Économie du Québec et de ses régions.* Montréal: Saint-Martin.

Tremblay, G. (1991a, April 17). "Les entreprises doivent créer un nouveau modèle de succès au Québec." *La Presse*, B3.

Tremblay, G. (1991b, September 11). "Nous vivons dans une économie en état d'urgence!" *La Presse*, B3.

Tremblay, G. (1991c, September 12). "Économie en état d'urgence: Tremblay propose des solutions." *La Presse*, B3.

Turcotte, C. (1991, September 19). "La situation économique alerte patrons et syndicats." *Le Devoir*, A1.

Vaillancourt, F. (1986). "Le français, les francophones et les législations linguistiques au Québec: une analyse économique." In G. Lapointe and M. Amyot, eds., *L'état de la langue française au Québec: bilan et prospective* (pp. 397–452). Québec: Conseil de la langue française.

Venne, M. (1991, September 19). "Johnson croit que c'est aux Montréalais à trouver remède à leur mal économique." *Le Devoir*, A1.

Wee, H. (1987). *Prosperity and Upheaval: The World Economy, 1945–1980.* Berkeley: University of California Press.

Wright, Gavin (1986). *Old South, New South: Revolutions in the Southern Economy Since the Civil War.* New York: Basic Books.

Continental Strategy: Québec in North America

François Rocher
Carleton University

Québec cannot ignore its destiny in the North American continent. This issue is multifaceted, involving not only the economic and commercial relations which link Québec and its partners (the other Canadian provinces and the United States), but also the political dimensions that influence the nature and depth of these relations. The question to be answered is: How successful has Québec been in its continental integration in view of future stakes? If, due to circumstance, Québec has maintained privileged links with its commercial partners, it has done so through a variety of means over the years. Historically, the federal government and the internal political dynamic of Québec have determined the way in which Québec has regarded its continental position. While accepting as inevitable the constraints imposed by this reality, Québec has recently sought to redefine these parameters.

The stakes for Québec, given this continental factor, raise four questions that will be addressed in this chapter. First, what is the extent of the continental integration of Québec? This question refers to the structure of the economic ties which link Québec and its continental partners. In this connection it is necessary to evaluate not only the importance of the commercial relations, but also the implied restraints. Second, what structural conditions influence the integration of Québec into the continental economy? Québec's economic development is characterized by a double dependence: on Canada, and on the American market, whose importance cannot be underestimated. Historically, this situation has imposed limits on Québec's political options. Third, in what way have the different governments in Québec, notably since World War II, managed politically the increasing continental links, and integrated this reality into their economic programs? The answers to this question, as we shall see, are numerous and often contradictory. Lastly, what are the socioeconomic ramifications of Québec's adhesion to the federal strategy regarding the adoption of the Canada–U.S. Free Trade Agreement?

Québec's strategy toward continental integration cannot be explained away as merely the adhesion of the political and economic elites to neoliberal theses: it represents a phase in Québec's nationalist ideology marked by a maturation of the francophone business elite seeking increased integration into the Canadian and American markets. The continental strategy is therefore situated within a reconfiguration of power in Québec that takes into account the new imperatives imposed by the global economy and the structural constraints placed on Québec's economy.

OVERVIEW OF QUÉBEC'S COMMERCIAL TRADE

The Québec economy, like that of Canada, is fundamentally open. Commercial trade with other provinces and with foreign markets makes up an important part of the province's gross domestic product. Exports to other provinces and countries represent about 40 percent of Québec's GDP. This ratio is one of the highest among countries with market economies. A study of Québec's position in a continental economy cannot, however, be limited solely to Québec–U.S. economic ties. The economic ties that link Québec to the Canadian market, and those that influence the way in which Québec can determine its economic future, must also be considered. As well, the degree of integration of the Québec economy within the entire North American economy must be established in order to demonstrate its strengths and weaknesses. The latter condition determines, to a great extent, the constraints that Québec has to face not only with regard to its ties with the United States, but also with the rest of Canada.

During the preceding decades, commercial trade has evolved in a global context marked on the one hand by a globalization of national economies and, on the other, by rapid technological change which in recent years has necessitated improving the competitive position of these economies. Québec cannot isolate itself from this process, and its geographic proximity to the United States results, in the same way as for the rest of Canada, in a reduction of its ability to manoeuvre (Rocher, 1988:197–220). Québec's international exports for 1987 amounted to about $20 billion. However, despite an increase in the actual dollar value of Québec's exports, its contribution to Canada's international exports was less than in previous years, falling from 22.5 percent in 1968 to 16.2 percent in 1987 (Québec, 1988a:9). Similarly, Québec's exports to the United States represented only 16 percent of all Canadian exports to that country, compared to 27 percent in 1965. Thus, even if Québec's economy is relatively open, it is still vulnerable.

To obtain an accurate picture of Québec's commercial trade, several aspects must be considered, four of which merit particular attention in the context of Québec's exports. First, Québec's commercial trade is directed increasingly toward the United States. In 1980 the United States was already receiving 58 percent of Québec's exports; by 1987, this figure had risen to 72 percent. While this was close to the same proportion as Canadian exports to the United States for the same year, Québec's exports were clearly more concentrated than those of Canada: the ten principal products represented close to 50 percent of total international exports, and the twenty-five principal products represented more than 68 percent. For Canada, these proportions were 32 percent and 54 percent respectively. Québec exports more noncomestible consumer products (49.3 percent) than finished noncomestible products (37.3 percent). It should be noted that Québec's international exports were concentrated in three groups of products: pulp and paper (24.3 percent of total exports), metals and minerals (22.7 percent), and transport material (17.3 percent). Similarly, exports to the United States showed a high level of concentration: primarily paper products (17.3 percent), aluminum and alloys (11.5 percent), and automobiles and auto parts (5.8 percent) (Québec, 1988a:9). On the other hand, although Québec's exports remain concentrated in certain sectors, between 1968 and 1989 finished products rose from 24 to 40 percent of total exports. Québec sells abroad (not exclusively to the United States) a number of finished products such as telecommunications equipment, aviation engines and parts, machinery and office products, airplanes, and a variety of paper products (Pélouas, 1991:C-2). Exports thus tend to be diverse, although products based on natural resources remain the most important. The popular image that Québec simply exports raw materials and imports finished products no longer does justice to the complexity of Québec's economy (Proulx and Shipman, 1986:79).

Second, exports from Québec to the United States are geographically concentrated: in 1987, the Atlantic and New England regions and the central northeast received more than 72 percent of Québec's exports destined for the United States. By comparison, Canada's exports to these three regions in the United States were in the order of 69 percent, of which 40 percent was to the northeast, because of the automobiles that Canada sends to the United States. The geographic proximity of regional U.S. markets thus appears to play a key role.

Third, the importance of exports produced by small and medium-sized businesses (SMB) in Canada and the United States should not be underestimated. Between 1975 and 1986, these exports rose from $6.6 billion to $16.8 billion. Furthermore, the relative importance of SMB exports to international markets rose from 4.4 percent in 1975 to 7.4 percent in 1984. In 1984, the United States received 78 percent of goods exported by SMBs. As is the case with total exports, the products exported by Québec SMBs are highly concentrated: seven industrial groups were responsible for two-thirds of international exports in 1984, consisting of wood (15.3 percent), food and beverages (14.6 percent), manufacturing machinery (9.8 percent), electrical products (6.8 percent), clothing (6.7 percent), rubber and plastics (6.7 percent), and metal products (5.5 percent) (Québec, 1988b:182–88). Even though SMBs concentrate on the domestic market, it should be noted that their activities consist largely of subcontracting for large businesses whose products tend to be destined for export.

Finally, though Québec exports are increasingly destined for the American market, it is important to stress the fact that the Québec economy has traditionally relied heavily upon the Canadian market. In 1984, exports to foreign countries amounted to 21.3 percent of deliveries, compared to 26.5 percent destined for other provinces. In light of these figures, it can be seen that in regard to the "continental" market in the broad sense, Québec depends to a greater extent on the other provinces than on the United States. By comparison, Ontario relies more upon its southern neighbour, primarily because of the importance of automobile parts arising from the Autopact. In fact, Québec is the province that is most dependent upon the internal Canadian market, while Ontario is two percentage points under the national average of 19 percent (Raynauld, 1990:13). The situation is the same for Québec SMBs, the majority of whose products go to other Canadian provinces for a total of close to 75 percent of exports. Ontario alone receives a little less than two-thirds of products exported by Québec SMBs to other provinces.

These facts must, however, be considered in the larger context of recent developments. It should be noted that over a considerable period, Québec's international exports have increased at the expense of products destined for the domestic market. This phenomenon reflects the liberalization of trade arising from the General Agreement on Tariffs and Trade (GATT). As a result, during the period 1974–85, international exports grew at a rate of 30 percent per annum compared to a growth of only 3 percent per annum for interprovincial exports (Pélouas, 1991:C-2). It could be concluded that this tendency would increase as a result of the free trade agreement with the United States, which has the effect of decreasing the importance of interprovincial trade. In other words, if this trend continues, Québec will focus more on foreign markets for its exports than on other provinces. However, since this phenomenon applies equally to the other provinces, Québec continues, to depend more on the Canadian market than do the other provinces. In 1984, this market made up 55 percent of Québec's total exports, as compared to 35.5 percent for Ontario. Obviously, Ontario constitutes Québec's major trading partner. In 1984, this market represented 15 percent of Québec's manufactured exports, 33 percent of total exports, and 61 percent of exports, to other provinces (Raynauld, 1990:15).

The structure of exports is therefore strongly influenced by the continental market, and the dependence of Québec upon the Canadian and American markets should not be underestimated. The situation with regard to imports, however, is somewhat different. In 1987, the value of Québec's international imports amounted to $23.2 billion. Imports, however, are more diversified than exports: close to 48 percent of Québec's imports came from the United States, while 26 percent of the products purchased abroad by Québec came from Western Europe. Québec imports mainly finished products (58.4 percent of imports). The principal imports are automobiles and auto parts, which alone amounted to 15 percent of total imports and represented more than 20.5 percent of imports from the United States. These imports are highly concentrated: in 1987 the four principal products amounted to 27.4 percent of total imports. Besides automobiles, Québec imported a large quantity of metal and mineral products (14.4 percent) as well as machinery and tools (11.8 percent) (Québec, 1988a:56–59).

The structure of trade relations between Canada and the United States is characterized by an atypical phenomenon within industrialized countries, namely the importance of intrafirm trade. At the end of the 1970s, close to 60 percent of Canadian exports were carried out within the framework of intrafirm trade. Similarly, in 1978, 72 percent of Canadian exports were effected by branch plants of foreign companies. Although similar figures are not available for Québec, it is probable, given the principal export products, that its intrafirm trade is comparable to that of the rest of Canada, though possibly less than that of Ontario. It can therefore be assumed that intrafirm trade represents between 50 and 60 percent of Québec's exports (Perron, 1985:19–20). This assumption is all the more likely in view of the fact that Québec's exports are strongly concentrated in a few enterprises controlled for the most part by American interests (Bonin, 1984:22–23).

In short, the level of interdependence of Québec's economy on the continental economy proves to be very high. In light of the asymmetry of the economies, it is even possible to speak of a relation of double dependence: first, interprovincial trade constitutes an important element of Québec's economy, though in view of Québec's strengthened economic relations with foreign markets, its dependence on the Canadian market will gradually decrease; second, trade relations between

Québec and the United States have developed strongly, notably with regard to exports. This fact reflects not only the extroverted nature of Québec's economy, but also its dependence with regard to trade with its principal partners. Québec's economy is thus particularly vulnerable to economic slowdowns that may arise in the United States, and to fluctuations in the demand for raw materials. In this connection, the problems encountered by the asbestos industry provide an excellent example. The weakness in domestic demand in the United States during periods of economic downturn contributes to a limited growth in imports and an increase in Québec's exports. This illustrates the vulnerability of the Québec economy to changes in economic conditions affecting its principal foreign trading partner.

STRUCTURAL DIMENSIONS OF CONTINENTAL RELATIONS

To acknowledge only the quantitative importance of Québec's commercial relations on a continental scale presents an incomplete picture of the facts. The structural constraints and consequently the qualitative order faced by Québec's economy raise a number of questions as to the nature of the ever-increasing continental integration. We have already noted that Québec's exports are strongly concentrated, that they are oriented principally toward the northeastern United States, that interprovincial trade is very important, and that intrafirm trade probably occupies a place of prime importance in the structure of Québec's trade. All these elements illustrate Québec's dependence on its principal trading partners and the fragility of its foreign trade due to its high level of concentration. Two other indicators show the extent of the constraints that affect Québec's economy in the continental framework: namely, the composition and structure of the manufacturing sector, and the degree of specialization and control of ownership of companies by foreign interests.

The Québec economy has for some time been characterized by its structural dependence on Canada as a whole, which is itself economically dominated by the United States (Henry, 1976:295). In fact, as we shall see, the integration of Québec into the Canadian economy was effected by the creation of a truncated industrial structure. Québec's particular problems can also be attributed to other phenomena, notably the shift of continental economic activity toward the West and the behaviour of foreign companies. These various factors have at different times influenced the economic development of Québec and have contributed to the attenuation of Québec's advantages in comparison to other regions.

When trade between Canada and the United Kingdom was at its height, Québec possessed an advantage of location over Ontario, constituting as it does a gateway to Canada. With the decline of the United Kingdom's trading empire and the increasing trade along the north–south axis, concentrated particularly in the Great Lakes region, Ontario was able to seize the market west of Montréal. This situation contributed to the marginalization of Québec's economy in relation to the principal North American market (Fréchette, Jouandet-Bernadat, and Vézina, 1975, p. 91; Gagnon and Montcalm, 1982:32–33). The importance of foreign investment, mainly American, increased Ontario's geographic advantage. American investment in the Canadian market was in response to the National Policy adopted by Ottawa in 1879, which imposed significant trade tariff barriers. Moreover, because of Canada's wealth of natural resources, many foreign companies took advantage of the opportunity to assure themselves of a good source of supply. This is not to say that Québec did not receive a share of foreign investment. However, its share was proportionately lower and came from companies in New England, which was itself in decline in relation to the Great Lakes region. In other words, the integration of the Québec economy into the continental economy took place under very different conditions from that of Ontario.

Québec's economic development was also influenced by a combination of economic policies adopted by the federal government to accelerate the growth of the Canadian economy. The impact of these policies on the regions, however, was unequal. In fact, they favoured Ontario to the detriment of Québec. Some examples are: the construction of the St. Lawrence Seaway (1959), which had the effect of diminishing Québec's advantages in transport; the national policy on gas (1961), which eroded Québec's gas industry; the Autopact (1965), which concentrated the automobile industry in Ontario; the federal regional economic development policy (1969), which did nothing to modify the structural weaknesses of the Québec economy; restrictive monetary policies, which were adopted at various times, essentially in response to economic conditions in Ontario; and public investment by the federal government, which was primarily concentrated in Ontario.

It can thus be said that overall the Québec industrial structure has historically been undermined by factors over which Québec had little influence. Thus, the principal comparative advantages still at Québec's disposal are the abundance of natural resources and low-cost hydroelectricity. Until the mid-1970s, Québec also benefited from the availability of low-cost labour. Furthermore, the importance of traditional industries in Québec (textiles, clothing, hosiery, leather, shoes, etc.) should not be overlooked. Québec's industrial structure is characterized by its concentration in labour-intensive sectors, its unskilled labour, and its weak investment level. As a result, Québec producers are in a weak position, and are often unable to compete outside the Canadian market, which is itself protected by tariff and non-tariff barriers against imports from newly industrialized countries that have the advantage of cheap labour, and from the United States, with its many large enterprises. Although during the last decade the situation of industries in the traditional sectors improved as a result of the modernization of a number of them and the disappearance of the less competitive ones, these industries nevertheless continued to account for a larger number of workers than Québec's share of the gross provincial product (Hero and Balthazar, 1988:308-9). Furthermore, these industries have historically benefited from considerable tariff protection, making their integration into the continental economy even more difficult. In fact, a reduction of trade barriers would result in a relocation of these industries to the United States because of its technologically advanced firms, or to the newly industrialized countries, where there is abundant cheap labour (Proulx, Dulude, and Rabeau, 1978:380).

Québec's export of manufactured goods to other provinces and other countries clearly demonstrates the importance of the weight of the Canadian and foreign markets. In 1986, the principal manufactured products exported to other provinces, in order of importance, were: food and beverages (11.3 percent of total manufactured goods), chemical industry (11 percent), paper and related products (9.7 percent), clothing (9.3 percent), electrical appliances and equipment (8.3 percent), base metals (7.3 percent), and textiles (7.1 percent). Among these, a number of sectors that are considered "traditional" occupy leading positions. The concentration of exports to foreign countries differs considerably. A high level of concentration can be found in some products: transportation material (25.4 percent, due to the Autopact), paper and related products (24.5 percent), and base metals (19 percent), while traditional sectors occupy only a small place.

The extent of Canada's trade barriers explains in part Québec's dependence on Ontario in matters of trade: the manufacturing enterprises that evolved in protected sectors sent close to two-thirds of their production to other parts of Canada, with Ontario alone receiving over one-half of this. The high degree of protection of the Canadian market results in Québec sending more of its products to Ontario than to the United States and, overall, more to other parts of Canada than to all other countries. In other words, the Canadian tariff structure has contributed to making Québec a society that is economically dependent on the rest of Canada. The opening of markets will result in the restructuring of traditional sector industries through consolidation and modernization of installations, which will in turn lead to a loss of jobs and the growth of the tertiary sector of the economy.

The question of foreign ownership of companies must be considered among the structural dimensions of the continental integration of Québec's economy. The distribution of control among the different types of employers in Québec can be ascertained by sector and subsector of economic activity as well as for the economy as a whole. In the latter case, it is interesting to note that in 1987, in the private sector, 56.3 percent of jobs were under French-Canadian control, 33.6 percent under English-Canadian control, and 10 percent under foreign control. If the public sector is included, however, the number of jobs under French-Canadian control increases markedly at the expense of the other two groups, with the proportions changing to 61.6 percent, 30.6 percent, and 7.8 percent respectively (Vaillancourt and Carpentier, 1989:37, 39; also Vaillancourt, in this volume).

Overall, jobs under francophone control are predominant in the primary and tertiary sectors. The situation in the manufacturing sector varies considerably according to the subsector of activity. Thus, with the exception of the subsector of mines, quarries, and gas wells, where in 1987 jobs controlled by francophones were only at a level of 35 per cent, ownership was essentially francophone in the primary sector. The situation is slightly different in the manufacturing sector where francophones control only 39.3 percent of jobs. They controlled almost all the forest industry, however (90.4 percent), and were in a favourable position in many other sectors: furniture (65.9 percent), printing and publishing (60.8 percent), food and beverages (54.2 percent), nonmetal mineral products (51.2 percent), and metal products (50.3 percent). English Canadians controlled the tobacco industry (99.3 percent), the chemical industry (60.7 percent), gas and coal products (56.7 percent), and occupied an important place in the subsectors of electrical products (47.2 percent), transport equipment (43.9 percent), and various other equipment (43.1 percent). Ownership in the tertiary sector indicates that francophones play an influential role in the areas of public utility services (notably due to the presence of Hydro-Québec), retail (61.7 percent), finance (56.8 percent), insurance (47.2 percent), and real estate (65.8 percent) (Vaillancourt and Carpentier, 1989:21–26).

These figures demonstrate the importance of the role now played by francophones in the Québec economy. Clearly, in certain sectors the presence of English-

Canadian and foreign interests remains significant. Nevertheless, during the last few decades, there has been a considerable change in the extent of francophone ownership, notably an important increase in sectors such as financial institutions, manufacturing, construction, mining and transport, communications, and public utilities. It is interesting to note that between 1961 and 1978 these gains were made at the expense of English Canadians, whereas between 1978 and 1987 they were primarily at the expense of foreigners. This steady growth has been sustained since the start of the 1960s by the modernization and consolidation of the Québec public sector, the intervention of the state in the private sector, and the emergence of francophone entrepreneurs. It has also led to a greater diversification of economic opportunities for francophones who were previously relatively confined to traditional sectors with little security (Sales, 1979:182–86).

This growth has modified the structure of francophone entrepreneurship, which is in a better position to insert itself into the continental economic framework. As a result, several Québec companies are now capable of competing with Canadian and foreign corporations. The consolidation of the position of companies controlled by francophones, notably in the sectors of natural resources (wood, pulp and paper, energy) and manufacturing, has taken place in the most competitive areas. These achievements have been made possible in part through the emergence of financial power in Québec and the involvement of its financial institutions in financing companies (Moreau, 1981:105–13). Furthermore, and in some ways paradoxically, the crisis of the early 1980s favoured the move towards the concentration and consolidation of companies, particularly in the tertiary sector, which in turn contributed to the improved conditions. In short, the changes in the structure of ownership of Québec's economy favouring francophone entrepreneurs have permitted many of them to become involved in the wave of internationalization of capital and encouraged their expansion, notably within the North American market (Bélanger and Fournier, 1987:175–81; also, Bélanger in this volume).

In spite of these changes affecting the structure of ownership, Québec's economy remains in a fragile position. Indeed, the new role played in the economy by Québec francophones has not substantially modified the structural problems that the province continues to face. Although the situation seems to have improved, it should be noted that at the end of the 1970s, companies owned by francophones were smaller, had a lower labour productivity rate, paid lower salaries, and served primarily the local market. In other words, compared with English-Canadian or foreign-owned businesses, francophone businesses sold a smaller proportion of their products outside the province. In 1979, they were responsible for only 15 percent of total exports from Québec, while foreign companies dominated the export sector (Raynauld and Vaillancourt, 1984:120–23). Thus, even if a certain number of large francophone companies are ready to face the continentalization of the economy, it should be noted that francophone entrepreneurs are primarily concentrated in SMBs, which are characterized by their presence in the traditional industries of consumer goods, retail, construction, services, and subcontracting. They therefore serve the needs of local and regional markets (Sales and Bélanger, 1985:58–61).

In short, if the situation has improved for a number of francophone entrepreneurs in Québec, this does not necessarily indicate a definitive reinforcement of Québec's industrial and commercial structure. On the contrary, this structure has changed little over the last two decades, with the traditional sectors, which are the object of considerable competition, remaining significant.

POLITICAL STRATEGIES AND THE CONTINENTAL REALITY

Although Québec's dependence vis-à-vis the continental market has been well established for some time, public authorities have only recently taken it into account in planning their strategies for economic development.

The postwar economic policy was influenced by the regime of Maurice Duplessis and the Union Nationale. In fact, Duplessis was pursuing a line of action already established by his predecessors (Roby, 1976). The popular philosophy of the era was simple: the state must reduce to a minimum its direct intervention in economic activities, while at the same time supporting their growth by ensuring favourable social and material conditions. Up to the end of the 1950s, this position reflected government policy, which favoured foreign investment and accorded important territorial concessions to foreign investors in order to stimulate the exploitation of natural resources. The emphasis placed on the exploitation of these resources by foreign companies, predominantly American, was aimed at encouraging the growth of the manufacturing sector. This strategy thus followed an accumulation model that relied on direct foreign investment as the impetus for economic development and that can be explained by the structural conditions of Québec's economy, namely, a limited domestic market and the weakness of the local financial institutions necessary to support local investment. The strategy available at that time consisted of looking toward the continental market to obtain the economic stimulus necessary for industrialization and the creation of jobs. Continental integration of Québec's economy was not solely the result of the policy of economic liberalism put forward by Duplessis, but was also strongly encouraged by the government, which saw in it a way to revitalize Québec's economy. Thus the government actively solicited American investment both for the manufacturing and natural resources sectors, and readily accepted dependence on the United States (Boismenu, 1981:125).

The election victory of the Liberal Party in 1960 marked the start of the Quiet Revolution. Although continental economic integration was not the prime objective of a number of the adopted reforms, the issue did have an impact on the way in which Québec was to deal with its principal trading partner. On the one hand, Québec's economy had many characteristics similar to those of underdeveloped countries: according to Gaudet, "the province lacked the coherent and well-integrated interindustry trade structure vital to any well-developed economy" (Gaudet, 1980:251). On the other hand, by taking into account the weakness of the socioeconomic status of Québec francophones as opposed to the domination exercised by the anglophone bourgeoisie in large industries and in the financial and commercial sectors, the Québec state sought not so much to challenge the objectives of capitalism as to promote the development of a francophone bourgeoisie. Furthermore, in reaction to a policy that had previously welcomed American investment, some now contested, in the name of nationalism, the overexploitation of Québec's natural resources and began to call for state intervention in this sector.

In the face of foreign domination of Québec's economy, the state appeared as an effective means of intervention to limit this large foreign presence, to facilitate the accession to managerial positions of francophones, and ultimately, to strengthen the foundations of a francophone bourgeoisie. To this end, the new political elite established a number of public institutions that permitted members of the new middle class to occupy technical and managerial positions in, for example, Hydro-Québec, the Société générale de financement, the Caisse de dépôt et placement, etc. In effect, the state sought to support SMBs operated primarily by francophones (Pelletier, 1989:202–3; Bernier, in this volume). This arose essentially from a desire to take control of an economy largely controlled by foreign and English-Canadian capital (Raynauld, 1974:81). The project of nationalization of electricity put forward by the Liberal Party in 1962 thus played a part in the process of the economic liberation of Québec. The collective takeover of an important natural resource became the first milestone in a process of "decolonization" of the economy. It is important to note, however, that the nationalization of electricity applied only to the sectors of production and distribution of electricity for use by the public. Production of hydroelectricity by companies for industrial activities remained under private control. Thus, Québec did not appropriate all hydroelectricity resources, but left the responsibility of exploiting dams for industrial purposes to individual companies (generally monopolistic companies held by foreign interests such as Alcan). These dams represented 30 percent of total production in Québec (Brunelle, 1978:145). Moreover, in order to limit Québec's vulnerability to foreign control, a number of crown corporations were created. They became central to governmental economic strategy and the promotion of the economic status of francophones (Montcalm and Gagnon, 1990:352).

This process raised the problem of reconciling the continued need for foreign capital and the desire to promote a larger integration of these new investments within Québec's economy. In effect, the policy pursued by the Québec state from this point for several decades attempted simultaneously to increase Québécois control over both the economy and foreign investment. In other words, the aim was to demonstrate that Québec nationalism could be compatible with a large increase in foreign capital. Thus, Québec has consistently refused to attribute its economic problems to the presence of foreign investments. It has, however, always insisted that economic development should not continue to depend exclusively on the capacity to attract foreign capital.

Contrary to the economic nationalism that was evident in Canada in reports such as those of Gordon (1958), Watkins (1968), and Gray (1972), the government of Québec was primarily concerned with encouraging its own economy rather than limiting by legislation the nature and extent of the influx of American capital into Québec (Gaudet, 1980:253–54). Thus, Québec's reaction to the adoption of the law creating the Foreign Investment Review Agency (FIRA) was to call attention to the lack of consideration by the federal government of the regional implications of such an initiative. The Québec government feared that the criteria adopted would contribute to the reinforcement of the existing industrial structure to the detriment of Québec's efforts to modify its own industrial structure and to stimulate the participation of Québec entrepreneurs in the process. Opposition in Québec to the federal policy reflected a prioritization of growth over the limitation of foreign investment. This attitude reflects the specific nature of Québec's economy. Foreign investment continues to be perceived as necessary to maintain the rate of growth in the economy and to increase Québec's margin of manoeuvrability in relation to English Canada. This line of thought has been followed by successive governments since that of Jean Lesage, including the Liberal government under Bourassa between the years 1970 and 1976, which sought an even larger increase in foreign investment.

The Parti Québécois government published two position papers on economic policy, setting out the basis of its industrial strategy (Québec, 1979 and 1982). The promotion of Québec capital, particularly in the base sectors of the economy, constituted one of the government's priorities. In keeping with the line of economic nationalism, two prime objectives were: the growth of Québec capital in certain key sectors of the domestic market (telecommunications, transport, finance, metals), and the increase in Québec's capacity to export (Romulus and Deblock, 1985:202–3). The two principal bases of this strategy, however, were in the areas of natural resources and hydroelectricity. Thus, the intention to increase the presence of Québec interests in the area of ownership was clearly aimed at the area of natural resources. However, while government policy sought to encourage local entrepreneurship, it was never stated that this would be done at the expense of foreign investors. The intention, among other things, was to encourage the integration of foreign companies, to increase Québec content in products, and to assist the access of Québec businesses to purchasing networks and multinational investment (Romulus and Deblock, 1985:203). Moreover, as Bonin emphasized, "nowhere in Québec's industrial policy has the contribution expected from foreign-owned firms or from foreign relations in general been clearly stated," adding further that "the absence of an international perspective is noticeable in both documents" (Bonin, 1984:35–36).

Although state interventionism was directed toward all sectors of activity, the most notable results were in those of natural resources, with the strongest growth in francophone capital in the past twenty years being in the sectors of forestry and mines: jobs under foreign control in the forestry sector declined from 37.7 percent in 1978 to 0 percent in 1987, while jobs in the mining sector in the same period declined from 64.9 percent to 24.6 percent (Vaillancourt and Carpentier, 1989:53). This exceptional growth in the role of francophones was attributable in large part to the state strategy in the 1960s, which was directed toward the implementation of the necessary infrastructures to improve the exploitation of natural resources. When Québec created a number of public enterprises in a variety of economic sectors, the area of natural resources was not overlooked. In this connection, we find the Société québécoise d'exploration minière (SOQUEM), la Société québécoise d'initiative pétrolière (SOQUIP), la Société de récupération et d'exploitation forestière (Rexfor), la Sidérurgie du Québec (SIDBEC), and la Société de développement de la Baie James (SDBJ). These numerous state corporations made it possible for Québec to control the exploitation of its natural resources more effectively. Today, the favoured market for these natural resources remains the United States, but their domestic exploitation no longer depends on foreign strategies.

In short, government strategy is aimed not so much at decreasing Québec's dependency on the American market as at ensuring that francophones occupy better positions in the Québec economy. The growth of jobs under francophone control can be seen in the takeover of foreign companies, either by the state (the acquisition of the Asbestos Corporation and other asbestos mines by francophones; control of Domtar acquired by the Caisse de dépôt et placement), by other enterprises (control of paper companies acquired by Cascades), or by the expansion of certain companies (Noranda, Cambior).

Government management of Québec's economic dependency on the continental economy has also taken other forms. The government of Québec has established a number of delegations in the United States (notably in New York, Boston, Chicago, Los Angeles, and Atlanta). Among their tasks are the promotion of commercial trade, research into new technologies, and identification of businesses interested in investing in Québec. In addition, these delegations offer technical assistance to Québec business people who are interested in penetrating the American market (Québec, 1988b:188–90). These Québec initiatives were taken in response to complaints by the francophone business community about a lack of commitment and assistance from Ottawa, in particular when competing with producers from other Canadian provinces (Balthazar, 1984:223).

Even if the opening of Québec's economy to foreign influence was seen by some as a deterrent to indigenous economic development (Parenteau, 1970:679–96), those interested in the growth of Québec–United States commercial relations stressed the advantages of an open continental framework compared to the constraints imposed by the Canadian policy, which historically emphasized the east–west axis. For this reason, in 1983, the PQ minister of international trade, Bernard Landry, declared himself in favour of a common market between Québec and the United States. The arguments put forward stressed the desire to lower the cost of imported products by reducing tariffs as well as the desire to further integrate the markets, which would in turn translate into a larger integration of the production process (Perron, 1985:24). The Americans, however, rejected Québec's overtures, claiming that they preferred to deal with Canada as a whole, in other words with the federal government, rather than with one of the provincial governments (Balthazar, 1984:220). Since Québec was unable to deal directly with the American government, the free trade project presented by the Mulroney government was therefore seen by certain Québec nationalists as a valid alternative.

The Québec debate surrounding free trade has always been linked to the question of the nature of the economic relations between Québec and the rest of Canada. Two problems are raised in this connection. First, the increased economic relations along the north–south axis calls for a review of the traditional east–west axis. Furthermore, the debate must be situated within the dynamic imposed by the Canadian constitution. It may appear surprising to link this latter issue with the debate on free trade, but it should be remembered that the central government established a balance between the elimination of interprovincial trade barriers, which contribute to the fragmentation of the Canadian industrial structure, and the implementation of free trade with the United States. Thus, Québec's specific economic problems have always led its governments to demand a larger margin of manoeuvrability not only in regard to the administration of federal policies, but also with respect to the actual sharing of constitutional powers. The positions presented by the PQ and the Québec Liberal Party to the hearings of the Macdonald Commission (1982–85) concerning economic union and free trade reiterated these two problems with some variations.

In its brief to the hearings of the Macdonald Commission, the PQ stressed the need for the Québec government to have complete control over the policy areas of manpower, education, and professional training in order to redress the inequalities arising from the lower mobility of its population (PQ, 1983:28–30). In this sense, Québec's strategy opposed to a certain extent the Canadian view, which encourages the mobility of manpower to meet the availability of jobs. Québec emphasized instead the creation of jobs in Québec to re-establish the balance of the labour market. With this in mind, the PQ demanded a decentralization of powers. The agreement in principle of many nationalists, including Jacques Parizeau and Bernard Landry, to a free trade policy can be seen as an attempt to reinforce Québec's economic relations with the United States, without a resultant reduction in Québec's powers to the benefit of the federal government. Moreover, *Péquistes* made a strategic calculation that would in the long run be favourable for Québec sovereignty. Since the natural flow of commerce follows the north–south axis more than the east–west axis, the latter having been imposed to a certain extent through the protectionist measures of the National Policy, a return to the natural axis could result in a considerable increase in Canada's economic base. This would permit Québec at some point in the future to dissociate itself from Canada. The reshaping of Canada's economic sphere could thus in the long run be favourable to sovereigntist goals.

If the arguments of the PQ revolve essentially around the centralization–decentralization debate, the position of the Québec Liberal Party is primarily aimed at making recommendations with a view to guaranteeing a Canadian common market. However, in order to achieve this, the Liberal Party rejects the establishment of new constitutional rules limiting the powers of the provincial government (Bourassa, 1984:21–22). Thus, for the Liberal Party, it is not a question of Québec putting aside the economic levers essential for its development. In fact, the Liberal Party has not always been in favour of free trade. When Bourassa was leader of the Opposition, he expressed certain concerns regarding the possibility of an economic union evolving into first a political union, and then a monetary union. However, the leader of the Liberal Party softened his position, since negotiations led toward trade liberalization on a sectoral basis from which culture had been excluded and that, furthermore, involved a period of transition. Free trade, then, would not bring about a political association (Blouin, 1986:101). Moreover, the Liberal Party felt that an open entente dealing with liberalized trade could offer Québec producers improved and guaranteed access to the American market. Finally, the Liberals declared that if elected, they would not push economic integration to the point of conferring on the central government a predominant role in defining the interventionist strategies of the Québec state.

Once in power, the Liberal Party maintained this policy. During the free trade debate, Québec placed limits on the extent of continental integration by basing its position on three points, namely: the integral respect of Québec's constitutional framework and jurisdiction; the need to conserve a sufficient margin of manoeuvrability to reinforce the industrial and technological base, particularly with regard to SMBs that are most vulnerable; and the need to provide for periods of transition assistance programs for those sectors most affected by the new economic agreement.

The need to establish a sufficiently lengthy transition period was based on the recognition of the disparity between the Québec and American economies and the fact that Canada possesses a higher level of protection. Moreover, when Québec speaks of the need to maintain a sufficient margin of manoeuvrability, this refers to its ability to intervene in market mechanisms, particularly with regard to aid programs for companies and regional development. The possibility of maintaining these policies implied that the Canadian government was attempting to negotiate the "grandfather" clause in such a way that governments could continue to support economic development through more generally accessible programs. This right to intervene should not be seen as a clause allowing the American government to take advantage of these safeguard measures (Blouin, 1986:70–74).

In view of the implications of free trade on Canada's political sovereignty, and consequently on that of Québec, and in view of the changes that it will impose on state interventionism, Brunelle and Deblock have noted that this continental strategy can be seen as contradictory to the nationalist theses that favour dependence on the state (Brunelle and Deblock, 1989:131–32). The shift away from this view can be explained by, among other things, the rejection of state interventionism that occurred after the Quiet Revolution. It can thus be said that the continental option is a reconfiguration of the nationalism of the 1960s and 1970s, which was based on public measures of intervention in the economy, society, and culture.

NEONATIONALISM AND CONTINENTAL INTEGRATION

It is tempting to liken the position of the free trade proponents to that of neoliberals who extol a return to market forces alone as a means of regulating the economy and society. However, the debate that took place in Québec on this question never favoured a return to the unconditional open-door strategy put forward throughout the period that preceded the Quiet Revolution, under the Duplessis regime.

The support of a large portion of the Québec business class for the continentalist strategy demonstrated the new maturity of the francophone business elite and the need for a structural affirmation. It was in this spirit that the Québec business class backed the Mulroney–Reagan entente throughout the federal election campaign of 1988. Thus, in response to the negative publicity created by the central Québec unions, the business sector created the *Regroupement pour le libre-échange* and financed a publicity campaign in support of this option. Nevertheless, the position of the large business associations illustrates the complexity of the debate. In view of the structural problems of Québec's economy, it is not surprising that businesses evolving in weak sectors put pressure on the large businesses to moderate their support.

It would be an exaggeration to argue that the business community unanimously supports the continentalist option. Important rifts can be detected in the bourgeoisie, both in Canada and in Québec. In this connection, two points should be stressed. On the one hand, many studies have shown that the impact of free trade would vary according to sector. Thus, according to the Québec minister of Industry and Commerce, of eighteen sectors examined, free trade would benefit four industries (nonmetallic minerals, sporting goods, tiles and linoleum, wood products); affect negatively twelve (printing and publishing, jewellery, instruments, plastic and rubber, electrical products, computers, metals, base metals transformation, footwear, machinery, furniture, and clothing); and would not affect the remaining two (agricultural and related products, toys and games) (Blouin, 1986:102–3). Furthermore, the majority of general indicators, such as increases in exports, the proportion of the population with higher education, research and development, and expenditure on fixed assets, point to the problems that Québec will face with increased competition. The weaker businesses are obviously not enthusiastic about the idea of facing new competition in a market in which they have traditionally been dominant, or where they have had a significant lead. On the other hand, in addition to the number of probable winners and losers, the division in the business class also occurs between businesses already oriented toward the continental market exporting directly or indirectly as subcontracting firms linked with this market, and others that serve primarily the domestic market (Rocher, 1991). In other words, not all large businesses will profit from the tightening of commercial ties with the United States, just as a number of SMBs will benefit from this strategy, since they are already oriented toward the continental market. In this connection, it is possibly the agents of these enterprises who have successfully dominated the public debate on free trade and imposed their views on other elements of the Québec business class. These same agents represent the "garde montante," namely francophone entrepreneurs who are in a position not only to influence the local market, but also to occupy a privileged place within the continental economy, and for some of them, within the international economy.

The support of the business world was conditional on the adoption of government measures for the smooth transition toward continental integration. To this end, and in order to minimize the negative effects of free trade, the representatives of this group requested government aid for businesses in weaker competitive sectors and assistance in meeting changes in technology (Guay, 1989:154–55). Many of those involved in the debate, among them the Conseil du patronat du Québec (CPQ), called upon the government to create information centres to prepare the work force for changes, to adopt a labour policy, and to support businesses in weaker sectors (CPQ, 1988:8). The business world furthermore demanded that the government develop strategies of intervention in various sectors, notably in the area of technological modernization of industrial equipment and financing of universities, in order to confront a continental economy.

Ideologically, the business class has displayed a continentalist approach which, however, acknowledges the necessity of obtaining support from the state. This is seen as necessary for the advancement of business and the improvement of its competitive capacity. It would thus be incorrect to view the trend toward free trade simply as neoliberalism. Moreover, the business class felt that in light of the internal adjustments that would result from the opening of the Québec market to American firms, the state must play a role of primary importance in supporting Québec business in its attempt to penetrate the American market and in protecting the economy and society (Brunelle and Deblock, 1987:32).

If aid to business is always put forward as a condition for the opening of the Québec market, it nevertheless remains true that behind this strategy there is a desire on the part of business to see a reduction in the role of the state, in particular with regard to the programs that make up the safety-net of social security for the population as a whole. Although this question was not discussed within the framework of the free trade agreement, for many Québec entrepreneurs the fiscal role of the state in financing these programs constitutes a factor that could harm their competitiveness. In this context, the alternatives are simple: either the state must reduce its programs in sectors of social policy and health, or transfer the costs to the users or the taxpayers. The business milieu intervened to stress the importance of education as an essential element for improving the efficiency of business in the context of the "virage technologique." However, the CPQ has strongly advocated raising tuition fees and allowing universities to set their own rates, even if this results in certain departments being closed in institutions that are less productive. In other words, if the business world is favourable to state intervention, it is essentially in selected areas based on the criteria of their adaptability to new conditions imposed by continental, and indeed international, economy.

Overall, therefore, it can be said that the position of the business class in regard to the continental economy is neonationalist. It supports state action to assist Québec businesses in adjusting to contemporary realities, on condition that there are as few constraints as possible. Moreover, the process of continental integration is perceived as a means of reinforcing the bases of francophone capital in the long run. From this point of view, it is of little consequence that this capital consists primarily of SMBs, many of which are involved in subcontracting. Despite the success enjoyed by some large francophone corporations in fields such as engineering, vehicles for public transport, and paper, it should not be forgotten that the majority of francophone capital is to be found elsewhere. Furthermore, although Québec's present overtures toward the United States, unlike those of Duplessis, are far from unconditional, the importance of foreign investment in Québec, which although declining is still considerable, has never been questioned. The success of the continental option in Québec can be attributed to the "garde montante," which in this debate sided with leading elements of the Canadian business class and which was able to convince Canadian and Québec politicians of the validity of their position.

CONCLUSION

Québec has continually endeavoured to assume its place in the continental economy. It has had to do so within a political framework that has maintained regional inequality and negatively influenced the development of the industrial structure of Québec, which historically has had numerous problem sectors. Québec's continental insertion has thus been influenced by a number of factors that have limited the political options available to mitigate undesirable economic effects. In fact, the structure of Québec's exports is largely determined by the continental market.

Québec is one of the Canadian provinces exporting the most to the Canadian market, although this tendency is decreasing. Moreover, Québec's exports to the United States are strongly concentrated, while imports are noticeably more diversified. This highlights the sensitivity of the Québec export base to changes in the economy affecting its principal trading partner. This situation is all the more significant since Québec deals with American border states, which are themselves faced with problems of marginalization because of the transfer of the principal centres of growth to the West Coast. Furthermore, the extent of English-Canadian and American control over Québec's economy, together with the need to find foreign capital to finance important public investments, contributes to limiting the state's margin of manoeuvrability to reduce the dependency of Québec's economy on the continental market. Reducing Québec's economic dependency has never been considered in either autarkic or closed-economy terms, since Québec's geo-economic situation rules out these alternatives.

The strategy adopted by the Québec government in regard to continental integration is characterized by two positions. The first, which was that of Duplessis and his predecessors, was to accept foreign investment indiscriminately and with a minimum of constraint. This option was adopted in line with the perception of state intervention as the outcome of classical liberalism. The second, which was adopted at the time of the Quiet Revolution and which was adhered to by successive governments, sought not so much to limit Québec's economic dependence on the continental economy, as to ensure that francophone capital would play a larger part in such an economy. In other words, it was not a matter of radically transforming the economic and industrial fabric of Québec, although this objective had been supported from time to time under the label "virage technologique," but rather of increasing the socioeconomic status of francophones through an interventionist state that also sought to mitigate the negative effects of the endemic structural weakness of Québec's economy. In the final analysis, the success of francophone capital over the past few decades has only slightly modified the industrial structure of Québec and partly solved its problems. The fact that Québec embarked willingly on the same free trade strategy as the federal government may appear as something of a paradox, but it reflects the vision created by the growth of francophone control of capital in Québec's economy. This new reality has encouraged the voluntarist attitude of the business class, proud of its gains and convinced that the future will continue to offer the same successes. Moreover, it reflects Québec's desire to distance itself from Canada's economic sphere, whose constraints are seen as having a negative influence on its economy. Hence the poor opinion of federal economic development policies, which are seen by many as favouring Ontario at the expense of Québec. Québec is therefore interested in developing economic relations with the rest of Canada on a similar basis as the ties between Québec and the United States.

In conclusion, it is not Québec's aim to break off the ties that constitute its continental integration. Instead, it seeks to review the various options to ensure that Québec capital, rather than English-Canadian capital, will benefit. In this process, the Québec state has an important role to play. Given the particular conditions of Québec's economy and the francophone capital on which it is based, Québec's business class will continue to demand state support, preferably on its own terms.

REFERENCES

Balthazar, L. (1984). "Québec's Policies Toward the United States," in A.O. Hero, Jr. and M. Daneau, eds., *Problems and Opportunities in U.S.–Québec Relations*. Boulder and London: Westview Press, pp. 220–48.

Bélanger, Y. and Fournier, P. (1987). *L'entreprise québécoise*. La Salle: Hurtubise HMH.

Blouin, J. (1986). *Le libre-échange vraiment libre?* Québec: Institut québécois de recherche sur la culture.

Boismenu, G. (1981). *Le duplessisme*. Montréal, Presses de l'Université de Montréal.

Bonin, B. (1984). "U.S.–Québec Economic Relations: Some Interactions Between Trade and Investment," in A.O. Hero, Jr. and M. Daneau, eds., *Problems and Opportunities in U.S.–Québec Relations*. Boulder and London: Westview Press, pp. 17–38.

Bourassa, R. (1984). *Mémoire* présenté par le Parti libéral du Québec devant la Commission sur l'union économique. Mimeo, February.

Brunelle, D. (1978). *La désillusion tranquille*. Montréal: Éditions Hurtubise HMH.

Brunelle, D. and Deblock, C. (1987). "Défenseurs et adversaires du libre-échange avec les U.S.A.: Étude des positions des parties au Canada," in P.J. Hamel, *Un marché, deux sociétés?* 2e partie. Montréal: A.C.F.A.S., "Les cahiers scientifiques," pp. 25–41.

Brunelle, D. and Deblock, C. (1989). *Le libre-échange par défaut.* Montréal, VLB Éditeur.

Conseil du patronat du Québec. (1988). *Des améliorations possibles dans un climat conjoncturel favorable.* Éléments de discussion pour une rencontre avec le caucus du Parti libéral et du Parti québécois à l'Assemblée nationale. November.

Fréchette, P., Jouandet-Bernadat, R. and Vézina, J.P. (1975). *L'économie du Québec.* Montréal: Éditions HRW.

Gagnon, A.-G. and Montcalm, M.B. (1982). "Peripheralization and Québec Unrest." *Journal of Canadian Studies,* 17(2), 32–42.

Gaudet, G. (1980). "Forces Underlying the Evolution of Natural Resource Policies in Québec," in C.E. Beigie and A.O. Hero, eds., *Natural Resources in U.S.–Canadian Relations,* Volume I, The Evolution of Policies and Issues. Boulder: Westview Press, pp. 242–65.

Guay, J.-H. (1989). "Le patronat," in D. Monière, ed., *L'année politique au Québec, 1988–1989.* Montréal: Québec/Amérique, pp. 153–59.

Henry, J. (1976). "La dépendance structurelle du Québec dans un Canada dominé par les États-Unis," in R. Tremblay, ed., *L'économie québécoise.* Montréal: Les Presses de l'Université du Québec, pp. 295–311.

Hero, A.O. and Balthazar, L. (1988). *Contemporary Québec and the United States, 1960–1985.* Lanham and London: University Press of America.

Montcalm, M.B. and Gagnon, A.-G. (1990). "Québec in the Continental Economy," in A.-G. Gagnon and J.P. Bickerton, eds., *Canadian Politics: An Introduction to the Discipline.* Peterborough: Broadview Press, pp. 345–59.

Moreau, F. (1981). *Le capital financier québécois.* Laval: Éditions coopératives Albert Saint-Martin.

Niosi, J. (1979). "The New French-Canadian Bourgeoisie." *Studies in Political Economy,* l, 113–61.

Parenteau, R. (1970). "L'expérience de la planification au Québec (1960–1969)." *L'Actualité économique,* 45(4), January–March, pp. 679–96.

Parti Québécois. (1983). *Mémoire* présenté à la Commission d'enquête sur l'union économique canadienne, Conseil exécutif national. Mimeo, December.

Pelletier, R. (1989). *Partis politiques et société québécoise. De Duplessis à Bourassa, 1944–1970.* Montréal: Québec/Amérique.

Pélouas, A. (1991). "Plus tourné vers l'étranger, le Québec demeure malgré tout déficitaire dans ses échanges internationaux." *Le Devoir,* February 1, C-2.

Perron, B. (1985). "Les contraintes dans les relations entre le Québec et les États-Unis." *Politique,* 7, Winter, 9–31.

Proulx, P.P. and Shipman, W.D. (1986). "Trade Relations Among Québec, the Atlantic Provinces, and New England," in W.D. Shipman, ed., *Trade and Investment Across the Northeast Boundary: Québec, the Atlantic Provinces, and New England.* Montreal: Institute for Research on Public Policy, 47–84.

Proulx, P.P., Dulude, L. and Rabeau, Y. (1978). *Étude des relations commerciales Québec–USA, Québec–Canada.* Québec: Gouvernement du Québec, Ministère des affaires intergouvernementales.

Québec. (1979). *Bâtir le Québec.* Québec: Éditeur officiel.

Québec. (1982). *La virage technologique.* Québec: Éditeur officiel.

Québec. (1987). *La libéralisation des échanges avec les États-Unis. Une Perspective québécoise.* Québec. Mimeo, April.

Québec. (1988a). Bureau de la statistique du Québec, *Commerce international du Québec. Édition 1988.* Québec: Éditeur officiel.

Québec. (1988b). Report by the Ministre délégué aux PME 1987, *The State of Small and Medium-Sized Businesses in Québec.* Québec: Éditeur officiel.

Raynauld, A. (1974). *La propriété des entreprises au Québec, les années 60.* Montréal: Presses de l'Université de Montréal.

Raynauld, A. (1990). *Les enjeux économiques de la souveraineté.* Mémoire soumis au Conseil du patronat du Québec, October.

Raynauld, A. and Vaillancourt, F. (1984). *L'appartenance des entreprises: le cas du Québec en 1978.* Québec: Éditeur officiel.

Roby, Y. (1976). *Les Québécois et les investissements américains, 1918–1929.* Québec: Presses de l'Université Laval.

Rocher, F. (1987). "Fédéralisme et libre-échange: vers une restructuration centralisée de l'Etat canadien," in C. Deblock and M. Couture, eds., *Un marché, deux sociétés?*, lère partie. Montréal: A.C.F.A.S., "Les cahiers scientifiques," pp. 151–68.

Rocher, F. (1988). "Économie canadienne et marché international: entre l'écartèlement et l'alignement," in C. Deblock and R. Arteau, eds., *La politique économique canadienne à l'épreuve du continentalisme*. Montréal: A.C.F.A.S., "Politique et économie," pp. 197–220.

Rocher, F. (1991). "Canadian Business, Free Trade and the Rhetoric of Economic Continentalization." *Studies in Political Economy*, 35, Summer, pp. 135–54.

Romulus, M. and Deblock, C. (1985). "État, politique et développement industriel du Québec." *Interventions économiques*, 14/15, Spring, 293-330.

Sales, A. (1979). *La bourgeoisie industrielle au Québec*. Montréal: Presses de l'Université de Montréal.

Sales, A. and Bélanger, N. (1985). *Décideurs et qestionnaires*. Québec: Éditeur officiel.

Vaillancourt, F. and Carpentier, J. (1989). *Le contrôle de l'économie du Québec: la place des francophones en 1987 et son évolution depuis 1961*. Québec: Gouvernement du Québec, Office de la langue française.

I

Major Themes for the Study of *Québec: State and Society*—An Annotated Bibliography

Scott Evans and Tim Thomas
Carleton University

QUÉBEC ECONOMY

Brunelle, Dorval, and Christian Deblock. *Le libre-échange par défaut* (Montréal: VLB, 1989).

Among examinations of free trade and the broader continentalization of North American economy, Brunelle and Deblock have written one of the few works that reserve a section of their study to analyze Québec specifically. While Québec is not central to the work, the chapter "L'axe Québec–États-Unis" examines debates within Québec over closer economic linkages with other geopolitical units and the implications within the context of global economic transformation and the strategy of continentalization. Moreover, the discussion of the process of negotiation and possible alternatives for adapting to this "inevitable" transformation of the economy informs the reader not only about the federal role within this process, but also depicts the implications for Québec and the other provinces. However, one should be cautious when considering their generalizations on the historical relations between the United States and Canada.

Gagnon, Alain-G., and Mary Beth Montcalm. *Québec: Beyond the Quiet Revolution* (Scarborough: Nelson Canada, 1990).

This text extends to the present day the economic peripheralization thesis first established by Faucher and Lamontagne to explain Québec's economic and cultural development in the 19th century. In previous work, Gagnon and Montcalm have argued that the inability of the federal government to reverse the negative repercussions of global economic trends has reinforced the belief on the part of the Québécois that their provincial government is the only effective means of protecting Québec's interests. This text establishes Québec's economic peripheralization by tracing large capital movements in the North American economy and then asserts that this, more than language policy or nationalism, has been the major factor in the transformation of Québec. It is asserted that the ensuing reliance on the Québec state as the vehicle to combat these negative economic trends, and its attempts, in turn, to generate indigenous economic and entrepreneurial activities, has resulted in the capturing of Québec nationalism by the forces of neoconservatism and the Québec business community. Along the way, the book provides some solid analyses of the province's union movement, its language policies, and its constitutional relations with the rest of Canada.

Milner, Henry, and Sheilagh Hodgins. *The Decolonization of Québec: An Analysis of Left-Wing Nationalism* (Toronto: McClelland and Stewart, 1973).

Written about the 1960s and 1970s, this text uses a political economy approach to explain the growth in popularity of the separatist option. Using Gonick's metropolis–hinterland analysis, Milner situates Ontario as the centre and Québec as the periphery, with historical outcome being influenced by this relationship. Interestingly, Milner notes that even when Québec was home to manufacturing industries they were usually labour intensive (textiles) as opposed to the higher–paying, technical nature of Ontario's industry.

Rioux, Marcel. *Le besoin et le désir* (Montréal: Les Éditions de l'Hexagone, 1984).

Rioux is important in that he expresses a perspective that runs counter to Québec's contemporary political discourse: that of the cultural conservative. He might even be considered as a Québécois George Grant except that he is ideologically grounded in socialism rather than toryism and his impact upon his intellectual community has not been as powerful. Using a sociological analysis in this text, Rioux warns of the deleterious effects capitalist society and its corresponding modes of production can have upon a culture and its institutions, especially its system of education. With particular reference to Québec, he argues that in contemporary societies that are rapidly modernizing, rather than adapting techniques to their own cultural needs, technique and rationality become societal ends in themselves.

IDENTITY, SYMBOLS, AND VISIONS

Boismenu, Gérard, Laurent Mailhot, and Jacques Rouillard, eds., *Le Québec en textes: Anthologie, 1940–1986* (Montréal: Boréal, 1986).

If one were to rely on a synoptic account of the various debates and transformations that have developed in Québec since the 1940s, this anthology would be an excellent choice for those who read French. On a historical level, there is a careful balance between the prominent Québec writers who have examined the socioeconomic transformations of Québec and those who look at ideological conflicts and developments. There is also an attempt to include examples of those who write from a federalist perspective (e.g., Pierre Elliott Trudeau), as well as the nationalist position. One of the book's weaknesses is its lack of material on formal political institutions in Québec and their relation to ideological and socioeconomic factors discussed elsewhere in the compilation. Another problem is the truncated nature of many of the selections, which is the necessary result of trying to provide such a representative view of the many debates. The articles that examine the state do so from a political economy or sociological perspective. The absence of the institutional perspective is, however, offset by the attempt to examine the experiential dimension through selections by artists such as Michel Tremblay and Robert Charlebois. The section on social movements provides much needed insights into the internal workings of Québec society and its concomitant political movements.

Cook, Ramsay. *Canada and the French-Canadian Question* (Toronto: Macmillan, 1966).

Cook remains one of the few English-speaking historians who have systematically attempted to analyze the relationship between Québec, French Canadians, and the rest of Canada. While the book does not draw from the experience of Québec politics in the late 1970s and 1980s, it does provide a historical context and highlights the relevance of this context for understanding what may be considered consistent problems between the French and English elements within Canada.

Dufour, Christian. *Le défi québécois* (Montréal: Les Éditions de l'Hexagone, 1989).
Dufour, Christian. *A Canadian Challenge—Le défi québécois* (Halifax: The Institute for Research on Public Policy, 1990, and, Lantzville, B.C.: Oolichan Books, 1990).

This text calls for some kind of convergence between Québécois and English-Canadian nationalism in order that both cultures might be able to survive their confrontation with increased continentalism. Such a convergence can only be achieved through mutual understanding and the clear communication of the cultural aspirations of both groups by their leadership. Dufour feels English Canada, to date, has been unable to articulate its nationalist content. Dufour argues that although these two forms of nationalism manifest themselves in many different ways, ultimately they can only be truly understood through an examination of their historical origins. Through such an examination Dufour concludes that a possible method for convergence might be to highlight the similarities of both forms of nationalism, such as their mutual fear of absorption by a larger group, which has already forcibly altered their cultural circumstances.

Latouche, Daniel. *Le Canada et le Québec: Un essai rétrospectif et prospectif* (Ottawa: Ministre des approvisionnements et services, 1986).
Latouche, Daniel. *Canada and Québec, Past and Future: An Essay* (Toronto: University of Toronto Press, 1986).

In a somewhat eclectic and iconoclastic fashion, Latouche uses this book to expound his position regarding Québec's relationship with the rest of Canada. Stated succinctly, his premise is that because Québec is such a formative part of Canada and because it is so inextricably linked with Canada in so many ways, Canada cannot help but become more receptive to the Québécois vision, particularly with respect to greater spatial sovereignty or jurisdictional autonomy.

Monière, Denis. *Ideologies in Québec: The Historical Development* (Toronto: University of Toronto Press, 1981).

According to Monière, ideology can be defined as a system of concepts, images, myths, and representations that in any given society supports a specific hierarchy of values and certain patterns of individual and collective behaviour. In the end, the mode of production of material existence determines any historical change in ideologies. Incorporating such a framework to explain the ideological development of Québec, Monière argues that following the 1837 revolt Québec experienced a hundred years of the ideology of survival, agriculturalism, messianism, and antistatism. This ideological perspective was not challenged until the development in the 19th century of capitalist-style farming and industrialization, which countered the legitimizing ideology of petty producers. The text asserts that in the case of the Quiet Revolution, it was the direct challenge to the petite bourgeoisie by their urban counterparts that permitted the state to replace the church as the main institution of the collectivity.

Resnick, Philip. *Letters to a Québécois Friend, with a reply by Daniel Latouche* (Montréal: McGill-Queen's University Press, 1990).

A fascinating debate between two rival visions of the contemporary Canadian situation and the linguistic, constitutional, and economic implications. Resnick recognizes the interdependence of these categories and expresses themes reminiscent of George Grant in his indignation over the free trade agreement and the apparent insensitivity on the part of Québec to the English-Canadian perspective. Daniel Latouche, Resnick's Québécois respondent, expresses surprise that such a monolithic English-Canadian viewpoint has ever existed, and although he welcomes Resnick to the world of nationalism and believes it will lead to more honest dialogue, he warns that English-Canadian visions have been numerous in form and have rarely, if ever, corresponded to the Québécois vision of reality.

Weinmann, Heinz. *Du Canada au Québec, Généalogie d'une histoire* (Montréal: Les Éditions de l'Hexagone, 1987).

This text constitutes an excellent study of the political thought of Québec. It attempts to capture the Québec "primal" through an examination of Québec history and the first Québécois encounter with the land and its native peoples. In the same vein as much of the Canadian political thought literature, the text examines the literature and mythology of Québec. Included in this examination are events such as the Conquest, the "beheading" of Québec society, and other important Québécois "moments" that have contributed to the founding myth and that help explain the evolution of the modern psyche of Québec.

QUÉBEC NATIONALISM

Behiels, Michael D. *Prelude to Québec's Quiet Revolution: Liberalism Versus Neo-Nationalism, 1945–1960* (Toronto: University of Toronto Press, 1985).

Behiels attempts to explain the roots of the Quiet Revolution by examining the fifteen years leading up to its occurrence and the streams of thought that were emerging in Québec during that time. He argues that two ideological movements emerged in Québec after World War II to challenge tenets of traditional French-Canadian political culture. One group included Trudeau and other dedicated, young social democrats and liberals, and the other, the neonationalists, included André Laurendeau and various politically concerned, young journalists and intellectuals. Essentially, Behiels's main premise is that it was the clash between these two groups that produced the Quiet Revolution. They had a common goal in the fight against Duplessis, yet at the same time they had different views about what Québec or the new Québec should be, and the legacy of this confrontation is still being felt today.

Cook, Ramsay. *Canada, Québec, and the Uses of Nationalism* (Toronto: McClelland and Stewart, 1986).

In many respects, this work represents a sophisticated attempt at examining the nature of Québec nationalism in the broader cultural context of Canada. Unlike Cook's earlier work, this examination avoids the overriding central Canadian emphasis that characterized his analysis of the "Québec Question." Cook achieves a balance by comparing the internal and external tensions engendered by nationalism in Québec and similarities within different regions of Canada. While the connection between chapters is less smooth than one would expect from a scholar of this stature, the Québec question remains a central linking theme. Cook brings greater depth to his analysis by including cultural material that incorporates regional mythologies and symbols.

Fournier, Pierre. *Autopsie du lac Meech: la Souveraineté est-elle inévitable?* (Montréal: VLB, 1990).
Fournier, Pierre. *A Meech Lake Post-Mortem: Is Québec Sovereignty Inevitable?* (Montréal: McGill-Queen's University Press, 1991).

This text offers a concise description of the events surrounding the Meech Lake Accord. It successfully demonstrates how these events have allowed for the dominant theme of Québec to be enhanced to such an extent that even Québec's principal economic actors such as the Conseil du patronat are calling for some form of greater sovereignty. Fournier emphasizes, however, that the mood of contemporary Québec is not driven solely by the private sector, but that in fact there is a consensus among all of its main societal and political actors.

Kwavnick, David, ed. *The Tremblay Report* (Toronto: McClelland and Stewart, 1973).

Kwavnick provides a manageable abridgment of the five-volume report first published in 1954. This report remains an essential document outlining the philosophical and moral foundation of a Catholic French-Canadian society prior to the Quiet Revolution. More specifically, the report links the fundamental relationship between constitutional and jurisdictional matters and their relevance to the protection and promotion of French-Canadian culture. While initially concerned with federal–provincial jurisdiction over direct taxation, the strong constitutional position of the federal government required the commission to formulate an argument justifying exclusive provincial jurisdiction on moral and sociological grounds.

This involved a systematic effort to discuss the significance of culture in the moral and spiritual development of society, and the role the state must play in promoting the cultural institutions guiding social transformation. In this context, the state, while subject to the moral guidance of cultural institutions such as the Catholic Church, requires guaranteed access to resources with which to fulfil its assigned tasks. The argument contained in the Tremblay Report provides a summary of the dominant tendency of traditional Québec nationalism and its conceptualization of society, culture, and the state.

Trudeau, Pierre Elliott. *Federalism and the French Canadians* (Toronto: Macmillan, 1968).

This collection of essays provides the classic response to Québec nationalism from the perspective of a federalist. Trudeau provides an articulate notion of federalism and advances an analysis of the relationship between Canada and Québec that rejects many of the traditional analyses of Québec nationalists. The philosophical underpinnings of Trudeau's conception of federalism and its practice still remain the intellectual source of many in Québec who oppose those suggesting either complete separation or a radical transformation of federal institutions.

Vallières, Pierre. *White Niggers of America* (Toronto: McClelland and Stewart, 1971).

Written by one of the founders of the FLQ during the 1960s, this text provides one of the ideological responses to the cultural division of labour and the noticeable economic inequities that existed between linguistic groups in Québec. Revolutionary in its language, the text is a testimony not only of the psychological anguish that results from socioeconomic repression, but of the psychological consequences of the ideological repression of the Church prior to the Quiet Revolution. This book remains the best expression of many of the ideological sentiments that fuelled the Quiet Revolution.

STATE, SOCIETY, AND POLITICS

Bélanger, Yves, and Laurent Lepage, eds. *L'administration publique québécoise: évolutions sectorielles, 1960–1985* (Sillery, Québec: Presses de l'Université du Québec, 1989).

Although less unified than other historical analyses of the organizational structure of the state, the essays in this collection provide thematic coverage of more contemporary developments. Emphasizing a descriptive approach, the majority of essays focus on the process of centralization and barriers to government action. The essays' authors are also very conscious of the tensions between politics and bureaucracy.

Gagnon, Alain-G., ed. *Québec: State and Society*, 1st ed. (Toronto: Methuen Publications, 1984).

An ambitious work that studies Québec politics using a variety of analytic methods. Incorporating an interesting blend of class analysis, history, statistical work, geopolitics, and political economy, the text examines the roles played by markets, political parties, Québec's business interests, and the state itself in influencing the socioeconomic status of Québec and the various political strategies and forms of nationalism that have subsequently emerged.

Godbout, Jacques. *La participation contre la démocratie* (Montréal: Éditions Saint-Martin, 1983).

Essentially this is a study of the relationship between technocrats and elected officials in Québec society. Godbout's research focuses upon citizen political participation in Québec, and he concludes that the democratic participation of this society's "grassroots" is becoming increasingly important.

Gow, James Iain. *Histoire de l'administration publique québécoise, 1867–1970* (Montréal: Les Presses de l'Université de Montréal, 1986).

Gow's historical examination provides sufficient detail for those wanting to know the organizational structure of the state and the historical tension between politics and bureaucracy. While the density of the material may be daunting for some, the chapter breakdown permits the selection of those historical periods that are of interest. Appendices provide historical data on revenue and expenditures, with helpful tables chronicling the evolution of administrative structures.

Guindon, Hubert. *Québec Society: Tradition, Modernity, and Nationhood* (Toronto: University of Toronto Press, 1988).

In this collection of past essays, Guindon describes Québec's Quiet Revolution as a bureaucratic revolution launched by an emerging francophone middle class using the apparatus of the state. Guindon observes that through the technique of overcrowding the state, this middle class also succeeded in achieving a form of social revolution as well in that their efforts resulted in a transformed societal mentality or an alteration of Québec's political culture. Guindon's observations with respect to the creation of the technocratic middle class and the form of nationalism that it spurned clarify this particular scholar's role as the progenitor of the debate found in the developmental thesis of the early 1960s and in the Marxist literature discussing the actual role and position of Québec's bourgeoisie and petite bourgeoisie.

Langlois, Simon et al. *La société québécoise en tendances, 1960–1990* (Québec: Institut québécois de recherche sur la culture, 1990).

An important tool in the discussion of social and political transformation is longitudinal measures that indicate shifts or changes across time. This work provides readily accessible measures for those wanting to examine the changing nature of Québec society at the socioeconomic, institutional, and the attitudinal levels. Chapters are divided into well-defined areas, and there are summaries describing each of the dominant trends, followed by more detailed tables that provide the numerical indicators available for further analysis. Another helpful feature is the inclusion of the principal scholarly sources that have dealt with each trend in more detail. The provision of tables, trend summaries, and chapter bibliographies makes this a valuable resource for both English-speaking and French-speaking students.

McRoberts, Kenneth. *Québec: Social Change and Political Crisis*, 3rd ed. (Toronto: McClelland and Stewart, 1988).

McRoberts has the advantage of building upon two previous editions by extending his analysis into the 1980s and addressing some of the current interpretations and models purporting to explain the transformation of Québec. The principal argument continues to look at Québec from a developmental perspective, emphasizing the unique factors affecting its modernization and concomitant political conflict. These factors are identified as the political and economic dependence of Québec on Ontario and the United States, a cultural division of labour, a skewed class structure within the francophone community, Canadian federal institutions, and the historical national consciousness of Québec francophones. In the context of this framework, McRoberts provides a very adequate description of the transformation of the Québec state and the events and actors (i.e., the new middle class and organized labour) that shaped this development. Underscored is the transformation of Québec nationalism and the fact that many of the inherent factors that have historically generated nationalist political agendas (i.e., the pre-1960s Catholic society or the post-1960s interventionist state) remain latent in Québec society and may result in new and equally significant nationalist political projects.

Monière, Denis, ed. *L'année politique au Québec, 1987–1988* (Montréal: Le Devoir–Québec/Amérique, 1989).

This volume is the beginning of a grand Québec version of the *Canadian Annual Review of Politics and Public Affairs*. There are short essays written by experts in the field covering standard topics for 1987–88 such as legislative activity, parties, public administration, organized labour, and public opinion. Other essays examining more topical issues such as the Meech Lake Accord and the language question are taking on a more polemical style. For students trying to chart developments, the chronologies on political events and legislative bills provide a useful starting point.

Trudeau, Pierre Elliott, ed. *The Asbestos Strike*, trans. James Boake (Toronto: James Lewis and Samuel, 1974).

Essays by Trudeau, Fernand Dumont, and Gérard Dion provide an excellent background for understanding the political developments and forces confronting Québec prior to the Quiet Revolution. Although polemical in nature, Trudeau's account of the ideological and institutional forces impeding Québec's "material progress" provides a very compelling argument that represents an important tendency within the anti-Duplessis forces prior to the 1960s. While other essays discuss the particulars of the Asbestos Strike, essays by Dumont and Dion analyze the broader historical tensions and developments within labour and the church and their relation to the strike. In both instances the strike is viewed as an important watershed in the changing nature and role of the labour movement and the church in Québec society and politics.

Vaillancourt, Yves. *L'Évolution des politiques sociales au Québec, 1940–1960* (Montréal: Presses de l'Université de Montréal, 1988).

The development of health and social programs is a generic element of the modern welfare state. Vaillancourt provides a careful examination of the formative period of the modern Québec state by analyzing the failure of the Union Nationale to counter the federal government, which was omnipresent in the field of Québec's social policy prior to the 1960s. The description and critique of specific programs such as health, social assistance, and income maintenance prior to 1960 is the strongest quality of this study. Vaillancourt's conclusions concerning the alliance of class fractions that prevented the development of the Québec state prior to 1960 are less developed. However, this study does provide an important look at the "passive" beginnings of the modern Québec state and the federal–provincial dynamic in the area of social policy.

FORMS OF REPRESENTATION

Dumont, Micheline, Michèle Jean, Marie Lavigne, and Jennifer Stoddart (The Clio Collective) *Québec Women: A History*, trans. Roger Gannon and Rosalind Gill. (Toronto: The Women's Press, 1987).

Most of the emerging studies in this area are involved in giving a historical and contemporary meaning to the lives and struggles of women in Québec. In effect, this means revealing the political and socioeconomic relations within Québec society that have acted to constrain and exploit women. This study provides a chronological account of the changing roles and struggles of women in Québec from 1617 to 1979, and it does so in a manner that is both readable and informative. Interspersed in the historical narrative are boxes of text that personalize the historical account or infuse the narrative with critical passages from historical events or documents.

Lavigne, Marie, and Yolande Pinard. *Travailleuses et féministes: Les femmes dans la société québécoise* (Montréal: Boréal Express, 1983).

Except for the theoretical essay by Nicole Laurin-Frenette, this compilation is more thematic, providing a critical analysis of particular developments or case studies. While the historical range varies, many are worth reading for their insights in contemporary struggles within the women's movement. This is particularly true for the synthesis of the "Bilan historique" by Lavigne and Pinard and the essays on politics and labour by Francine Fournier and Mona-Josée Gagnon respectively.

Raboy, Marc, ed. *Old Passions, New Visions: Social Movements and Political Activism in Québec*, trans. Robert Chodos (Toronto: Between the Lines, 1986).

Raboy has not only compiled some important primary documents portraying the energy and direction of many of the social movements in contemporary Québec, he has also provided English-speaking students with an important window into the dynamic culture and politics that are not generally accessible to English-speaking, non-Québec audiences. The section titled "Reflections" contains synoptic articles giving an overview of alternative politics related to feminism, labour, immigrant culture, and the peace movement. However, it is the sections "Positions" and "Debates" that provide an informative look at the political agendas and conflicts informing new movements in Québec. Documents such as Gisèle Tremblay's "A Women's Manifesto," the "Ecologist Manifesto" of Les Ami-e-s de la Terre de Québec, and the English working class "Black Rock Manifesto" of the Verdun Black Rock Cultural Group suggest some of the diverse perspectives and forces mobilizing in Québec. Round-table discussions on the role of the left, organized labour, and the PQ provide an insightful glimpse of the current dilemmas facing activists and the difficult task of forging consensus and practical alternatives.

DEMOGRAPHY, ETHNICITY, AND LANGUAGE

Coleman, William D. *The Independence Movement in Québec, 1945–1980* (Toronto: University of Toronto Press, 1984).

Coleman examines the modernization of Québec society, and his principal concern is with the ideological impact of this process. His conclusions in this regard make this text an important read for cultural conservatives and for those who have followed the political thought of Marcel Rioux. Coleman argues that by the late 1960s, with the reform of educational and social welfare institutions and the withdrawal of the church into more spiritual realms, the most evident distinguishing characteristic of Québec became its language. Having established this observation, Coleman then proceeds to suggest that although it had previously acted as a barrier, the French language's recent adaptation to economic life in Québec and its subsequent integration of the language of technology have enabled it to perform as a vehicle for the integration of Québec society and its value system into the dominant culture of North America.

Levine, Marc. *The Reconquest of Montréal: Language Policy and Social Change in a Bilingual City* (Philadelphia: Temple University Press, 1990).

The cultural and economic importance of Montréal makes it an integral factor when attempting to understand the transformation of Québec society and Québec politics. Levine examines the way in which public policy has been used to break the autonomy of English-language institutions and the accommodation between anglophone economic elites and francophone politicians which has historically protected the interests of the anglophone minority. The analysis of this question does not rest with economic explanation, but attempts to look at the unequal distribution of resources (i.e., cultural division of labour) in the context of the struggle for linguistic survival and cultural affirmation. The tensions of this struggle underscore the underlying dynamic that remains a critical characteristic of Québec and fundamental to the problems associated with a territorial solution to the Québec question.

QUÉBEC AND COMPARATIVE POLITICS

Dyck, Rand. *Provincial Politics in Canada* (Scarborough: Prentice-Hall, 1986).

The comparative nature of Dyck's work on provincial politics provides students with a good descriptive introduction to the historical, institutional, cultural, and political environment of each of the provinces. While the analytical component of Dyck's work is thin, he does provide a very helpful comparative framework from which the development and context of Québec politics can be contrasted with that of the other provinces. The general lack of sophisticated comparative analysis in the Québec literature means that Dyck's systematic treatment of specified themes provides a broader context for those trying to locate Québec politics within a provincial milieu. The conclusions Dyck draws raise the fundamental question of regionalism, but for Québec specialists the linking of Québec and Ontario (i.e., central Canada) fails to address what many would consider the "specificity" of the political projects and developments that continue to transform and inform Québec society.

Legaré, Anne, and Nicole Morf. *La société distincte de l'État: Québec–Canada, 1930–1980* (Montréal: Éditions Hurtubise HMH, 1989).

Although they are not specifically concerned with Québec, in their historical analysis of Canada's passage from the laissez-faire, economic liberal form of the state to its more interventionist form after the depression, these authors argue that the Québec state is an integral part of the Canadian state. Legaré and Morf's structuralist approach leads to their assertion that Québec partakes of the structural unity of the Canadian state, and the national question within this relationship is just a way of structuring the Canadian state and the exchanges between its two orders of government. Essentially, they argue that the Canadian state and federalism in Canada are perpetually in crisis because of the antagonism between the two orders of the state. Paradoxically though, they conclude that this antagonism is also what makes the Canadian state unique and united because of the provincial states' inability to muster a common front against the federal state.

Lemieux, Vincent, and Raymond Hudon. *Patronage et politique au Québec, 1944–1972* (Sillery, Québec: Éditions du Boréal Express, 1975).

Methodologically, this study is a compilation of the results of a series of interviews conducted in a small Québec locality. The text's first chapter is quite theoretical and its authors are ambitiously attempting to use their Québec-based case study as a vehicle for discovering the characteristics of patronage inherent in politics. By focusing on the locality, its people, local elites, and political parties, they in effect examine the structure and evolution of patronage in order to make conclusions about the process in which patronage relationships tend to be established.

Linteau, Paul-André, René Durocher, and Jean-Claude Robert. *Histoire du Québec contemporain, Volume I: De la Conféderation à la crise, 1867–1929* (Montréal: Les Éditions du Boréal Express, 1979).
Linteau, Paul-André, René Durocher, and Jean-Claude Robert. *Québec: A History, 1867–1929* (Toronto: James Lorimer, 1983).

This text includes a primarily structural analysis of Québec society since the 19th century encompassing virtually every societal dimension such as ideology, economy, politics, culture, religion, etc. The authors' principal assertion emanating from this comprehensive analysis is that Québec is a society like any other, and although culturally distinct, it has gone through a normal process of modernization similar to that experienced by any other part of the country.

Linteau, Paul André, René Durocher, Jean-Claude Robert, and François Ricard. *Histoire du Québec contemporain, Volume II: Le Québec depuis 1930* (Montréal: Les Éditions du Boréal Express, 1986).
Linteau, Paul André, René Durocher, Jean-Claude Robert, and François Ricard. *Quebec Since 1960* (Toronto: James Lorimer, 1991).

This second text resumes the themes undertaken in the first and simply updates them to the mid-1980s.

Renaud, Gilbert. *À l'ombre du rationalisme: la société québécoise de sa dépendance à sa quotidienneté* (Montréal: Éditions Saint-Martin, 1984).

Renaud looks at the construction or the emergence of the Québec state and how the technocratic discourse has powerfully informed this particular process. He believes that this influence has resulted in the creation of a programmed society where everything is submitted to the dictates of the technocratic mind. The dominance of this discourse, according to Renaud, is the result of the Quiet Revolution and the ensuing rise to prominence of the bureaucracy and liberalism. In his analysis of Québec's development and shifting modes of production, he says that what is interesting about Québec is that although it is part of the modernity of North America, at the same time it is also a dependent society, which makes its management doubly complex for the state. Basically, this is an excellent examination of what Renaud feels is an imposition of the technocratic logic upon Québec society.

The Québec Charter
of
Human Rights and Freedoms

An act adopted on June 27th, 1975 by the National Assembly of Québec to

- **promote** the rights of individuals, of groups and of the community in Québec;

- **encourage** respect towards all and the accountability of each individual for others and for the common weal;

- **help** individuals and groups to attain recognition of their rights and to exercise such rights;

- **guard** against discrimination and exploitation.

The Charter: the symbol of the values held by the Québec Community

"The aim of the Charter," as stated in the introduction to Bill 50, "is to solemnly declare the fundamental human rights and freedoms so that they be guaranteed by the collective will and better protected against violation". In practice, it is the aim of the Charter to set rules governing relations between citizens based on human dignity, and to designate the rights and privileges essential to the development of each human being.

Among the reasons for the adoption of the Charter, are the growing complexity of individual relationships, the increasing intervention of Government in the daily lives of its citizens, the proliferation of laws and of situations where individual rights and liberties are threatened, the pervasive spread of computers and its intrusion in private life, the increasingly cosmopolitan character of our cities. The Bill, moreover, outlines that human rights are indissociable from general welfare and are the basis of justice and peace. The Government thus recognizes that the respect of human rights is essential to the establishment of harmonious social relations and the maintaining of social peace. To sum up, the Charter is the symbol of the values held by the Quebec Community."[1]

---

1 Excerpt from a Government statement summarizing the aims of the Charter, issued October 29, 1974, on the occasion of the first reading of Bill 50.

Summary to find a specific item in the Charter

Charte des droits et libertés de la personne
Préambule

Whereas every human being possesses intrinsic rights and freedoms designed to ensure his protection and development;

Whereas all human beings are equal in worth and dignity, and are entitled to equal protection of the law;

Whereas respect for the dignity of the human being and recognition of his rights and freedoms constitute the foundation of justice and peace;

Whereas the rights and freedoms of the human person are inseparable from the rights and freedoms of others and from the common well-being;

Whereas it is expedient to solemnly declare the fundamental human rights and freedoms in a Charter, so that they may be guaranteed by the collective will and better protected against any violation;

Therefore, Her Majesty, with the advice and consent of the National Assembly of Québec, enacts as follows:

Part I - Human rights and freedoms

Chapter I - Fundamental freedoms and rights

1. Every human being has a right to life, and to personal security, inviolability and freedom.

He also possesses juridical personality.

2. Every human being whose life is in peril has a right to assistance.

Every person must come to the aid of anyone whose life is in peril, either personally or calling for aid, by giving him the necessary and immediate physical assistance, unless it involves danger to himself or a third person, or he has another valid reason.

3. Every person is the possessor of the fundamental freedoms, including freedom of conscience, freedom of religion, freedom of opinion, freedom of expression, freedom of peaceful assembly and freedom of association.

4. Every person has a right to the safeguard of his dignity, honour and reputation.

5. Every person has a right to respect for his private life.

6. Every person has a right to the peaceful enjoyment and free disposition of his property, except to the extent provided by law.

7. A person's home is inviolable.

8. No one may enter upon the property of another or take anything therefrom without his express or implied consent.

9. Every person has a right to non-disclosure of confidential information.

No person bound to professional secrecy by law and no priest or other minister of religion may, even in judicial proceedings, disclose confidential information revealed to him by reason of his position or profession, unless he is authorized to do so by the person who confided such information to him or by an express provision of law.

The Tribunal must, *ex officio*, ensure that professional secrecy is respected.

9.1 In exercising his fundamental freedoms and rights, a person shall maintain a proper regard for democratic values, public order and the general well-being of the citizens of Québec.

In this respect, the scope of the freedoms and rights, and limits to their exercise, may be fixed by law.

Chapter 1.1 - Right to equal recognition and exercise of rights and freedoms

10.   Every person has a right to full and equal recognition and exercise of his human rights and freedoms, without distinction, exclusion or preference based on race, colour, sex, pregnancy, sexual orientation, civil status, age except as provided by law, religion, political convictions, language, ethnic or national origin, social condition, a handicap or the use of any means to palliate a handicap.

Discrimination exists where such a distinction, exclusion or preference has the effect of nullifying or impairing such right.

10.1 No one may harass a person on the basis of any ground mentioned in section 10.

11.   No one may distribute, publish or publicly exhibit a notice, symbol or sign involving discrimination, or authorize anyone to do so.

12.   No one may, through discrimination, refuse to make a juridical act concerning goods or services ordinarily offered to the public.

13.   No one may in a juridical act stipulate a clause involving discrimination. Such a clause is deemed without effect.

14.   The prohibitions contemplated in sections 12 and 13 do not apply to the person who leases a room situated in a dwelling if the lessor or his family resides in such dwelling, leases only one room and does not advertise the room for lease by a notice or any other public means of solicitation.

15.   No one may, through discrimination, inhibit the access of another to public transportation or a public place, such as a commercial establishment, hotel, restaurant, theatre, cinema, park, camping ground or trailer park, or his obtaining the goods and services available there.

16.   No one may practise discrimination in respect of the hiring, apprenticeship, duration of the probationary period, vocational training, promotion, transfer, displacement, laying-off, suspension, dismissal or conditions of employment of a person or in the establishment or categories of classes of employment.

17.   No one may practise discrimination in respect of the admission, enjoyment of benefits, suspension or expulsion of a person to, of or from an association of employers or employees or any professional corporation or association of persons carrying on the same occupation.

18.   No employment bureau may practise discrimination in respect of the reception, classification or processing of a job application or in any document intended for submitting an application to a prospective employer.

18.1 No one may, in an employment application form or employment interview, require a person to give information regarding any ground mentioned in section 10 unless the information is useful for the application of section 20 or the implementation of an affirmative action program in existence at the time of the application.

18.2 No one may dismiss, refuse to hire or otherwise penalize a person in his employment owing to the mere fact that he was convicted of a penal or criminal offence, if the offence was in no way connected with the employment or if the person has obtain a pardon for the offence.

19. Every employer must, without discrimination, grant equal salary or wages to the members of his personnel who perform equivalent work at the same place.

A difference in salary or wages based on experience, seniority, years of service, merit, productivity or overtime is not considered discriminatory if such criteria are common to all members of the personnel.

20. A distinction, exclusion or preference based on the aptitudes or qualifications required for an employment, or justified by the charitable, philanthropic, religious, political or educational nature of a non-profit institution or of an institution devoted exclusively to the well-being of an ethnic group, is deemed non-discriminatory.

Not in force
Similarly, under an insurance or pension contract, a social benefits plan or a retirement, pension or insurance plan, or under a public pension or public insurance plan, a distinction, exclusion or preference based on risk determining factors or actuarial data fixed by regulation is deemed non-discriminatory.

Chapter II - Political rights

21. Every person has a right of petition to the National Assembly for the redress of grievances.

22. Every person legally capable and qualified has the right to be a candidate and to vote at an election.

Chapter III - Judicial rights

23. Every person has a right to a full and equal, public and fair hearing by an independent and impartial tribunal, for the determination of his rights and obligations or of the merits of any charge brought against him.

The tribunal may decide to sit in camera, however, in the interest of morality or public order.

Furthermore, in proceedings in family cases, sittings in first instance are held in camera unless the tribunal decides otherwise on the motion of any person and if it deems it expedient in the interests of justice.

24. No one may be deprived of his liberty or of his rights except on grounds provided by law and in accordance with prescribed procedure.

24.1 No one may be subjected to unreasonable search or seizure.

25. Every person arrested or detained must be treated with humanity and with the respect due to the human person.

26. Every person confined to a house of detention has the right to separate treatment appropriate to his sex, his age and his physical or mental condition.

27. Every person confined to a house of detention while awaiting the outcome of his trial has the rights to be kept apart, until final judgment, from prisoners serving sentence.

28. Every person arrested or detained has a right to be promptly informed, in a language he understands, of the grounds of his arrest or detention.

28.1 Every accused person has a right to be promptly informed of the specific offence with which he is charged.

29. Every person arrested or detained has a right to immediately advise his next of kin thereof and to have recourse to the assistance of an advocate. He has a right to be informed promptly of those rights.

30. Every person arrested or detained must be brought promptly before the competent tribunal or released.

31. No person arrested or detained may be deprived without just cause of the right to be released on undertaking, with or without deposit or surety, to appear before the tribunal at the appointed time.

32. Every person deprived of his liberty has a right or recourse to habeas corpus.

32.1 Every accused person has a right to be tried within a reasonable time.

33. Every accused person is presumed innocent until proven guilty according to law.

33.1 No accused person may be compelled to testify against himself at his trial.

34. Every person has a right to be represented by an advocate or to be assisted by one before any tribunal.

35. Every accused person has a right to a full and complete defence and has the right to examine and cross-examine witnesses.

36. Every accused person has a right to be assisted free of charge by an interpreter if he does not understand the language used at the hearing or if he is deaf.

37. No accused person may be held guilty on account of any act or omission which at the time when it was committed, did not constitute a violation of the law.

37.1 No person may be tried again for an offence of which he has been acquitted or of which he has been found guilty by a judgment that has acquired status as res judicata.

37.2 Where the punishment for an offence has been varied between the time of Commission and the time of sentencing, the accused person has a right to the lesser punishment.

38. No testimony before a tribunal may be used to incriminate the person who gives it, except in a prosecution for perjury or for the giving of contradictory evidence.

Chapter IV - Economic and social rights

39. Every child has a right to the protection, security and attention that his parents or the persons acting in their stead are capable of providing.

40. Every person has a right, to the extent and according to the standards provided for by law, to free public education.

41. Parents or the persons acting in their stead have a right to require that, in the public educational establishments, their children receive a religious or moral education in conformity with their convictions, within the framework of the curricula provided for by law.

42. Parents or the persons acting in their stead have a right to choose private educational establishments for their children, provided such establishments comply with the standards prescribed or approved by virtue of the law.

43.   Persons belonging to ethnic minorities have a right to maintain and develop their own cultural interests with the other members of their group.

44.   Every person has a right to information to the extent provided by law.

45.   Every person in need has a right, for himself and his family, to measures of financial assistance and to social measures provided for by law, susceptible of ensuring such person an acceptable standard of living.

46.   Every person who works has a right, in accordance with the law, to fair and reasonable conditions of employment which have proper regard for his health, safety and physical well-being.

47.   Husband and wife have, in the marriage, the same rights, obligations and responsibilities.

Together they provide the moral guidance and material support of the family and the education of their common offspring.

48.   Every aged person and every handicapped person has a right to protection against any form of exploitation.

Such a person also has a right to the protection and security that must be provided to him by his family or the persons acting in their stead.

Chapter V - Special and Interpretative provisions

49.   Any unlawful interference with any right or freedom recognized by this Charter entitles the victim to obtain the cessation of such interference and compensation for the moral or material prejudice resulting therefrom.

In case of unlawful and intentional interference, the tribunal may, in addition, condemn the person guilty of it to exemplary damages.

50.   The Charter shall not be so interpreted as to suppress or limit the enjoyment or exercise of any human right or freedom not enumerated herein.

51.   The Charter shall not be so interpreted as to extend, limit or amend the scope of a provision of law except to the extent provided in section 52.

52.   No provision of any Act, even subsequent to the Charter, may derogate from sections 1 to 38, except so far as provided by those sections, unless such Act expressly states that it applies despite the Charter.

53.   If any doubt arises in the interpretation of a provision of the act, it shall be resolved in keeping with the intent of the Charter.

54.   The Charter binds the Crown.

55.   The Charter affects those matters that come under the legislative authority of Québec.

56.1 In sections 9, 23, 30, 31, 34 and 38, in Chapter III of Part II and in Part IV, the word "tribunal" includes a coroner, a fire investigation commissioner, an inquiry commission, and any person or agency exercising quasi-judicial functions.

2. In section 19, the words "salary" and "wages" include the compensations or benefits or pecuniary value connected with the employment.

3. In the Charter, the word "law" or "act" includes a regulation, a decree, an ordinance or an order in council made under the authority of any act.

PART II - Commission des droits de la personne

Chapter I - Constitution

57.   A body, hereinafter called "the Commission" is established under the name of "Commission des droits de la personne".

58.   The Commission shall be composed of a least seven members, one of whom shall be the president, and another, the vice-president. They shall be appointed by the National Assembly upon the motion of the Prime Minister, for a term not exceeding ten years.

Such appointments must be approved by two-thirds of the members of National Assembly.

The term of office, once determined, shall not be reduced.

59.   The Government shall fix the salary and the conditions of employment or, as the case may be, the additional salary, fees or allowance of each member of the Commission.

Their salary, additional salary, fees and allowances, once determined, shall not be reduced.

60.   The members of the Commission shall remain in office until they are replaced, except int he case of resignation.

61.   The Commission may establish a complaints committee composed of three of its members designated in writing by the Commission and delegate certain responsibilities to it by regulation.

62.   The Commission shall appoint the personnel it requires for the performance of its functions; their number shall be determined by the Government; they may be dismissed by order of the Government but only on the recommendation of the Commission.

The Commission may, in writing, give to a person other than a member of its personnel the mandate to either make an investigation or endeavour to effect a settlement between the parties under the terms of subparagraph 1 or 2 of the second paragraph of section 71, with the obligation to report to the Commission within a specified time.

For the arbitration of a matter, the Commission shall designate an arbitrator to act alone from among persons having notable experience and expertise in, sensitivity to and interest for matters or human rights and freedoms and included in the panel of arbitrators established periodically by the Government according to the recruitment and selection procedure prescribed by government regulation. The arbitrator shall act in accordance with the rules set out in Book VII, except Chapter II of Title I, of the Code of Civil Procedure, adapted as required.

No person having taken part in the investigation may be given the mandate to endeavour to effect a settlement or act as an arbitrator except with the consent of the parties.

63.   The Government shall establish standards and scales applicable to the remuneration or allowances and other conditions of employment to be borne by the Commission in respect of its personnel, its mandataries and the arbitrators it designates.

64.   Before entering office, the members and mandataries of the Commission, the members of its personnel and the arbitrators designated by it shall make the oaths or solemn affirmations provided in Schedule I before the President of the National Assembly in the case of the members of the Commission and before the president of the Commission in all other cases.

65.   The president and the vice-president shall devote their time exclusively to the duties of their office.

66.   The president is responsible for the administration and management of the affairs of the Commission within the scope of the regulations, governing the administration of this Charter. He may, by delegation, exercise the powers of the Commission under section 61, the second and third paragraphs of section 62 and the first paragraph of section 77.

The president shall preside the sittings of the Commission.

67. The vice-president shall *ex officio* and temporarily, replace the president if he is absent or unable to act or if the office of president is vacant. If the vice-president, while he is called upon to replace the president, is himself absent or unable to act, or if the office of vice-president is vacant, the Government shall designate another member of the Commission to replace him temporarily and, if need be, shall fix the additional salary, fees or allowances of that other member.

68. In no case may the Commission, any member or mandatary of the Commission, any member of its personnel or a complaints committee established by the Commission be prosecuted for any omission or any act done in good faith in the performance of his or its duties.

Moreover, they are, for the purposes of an investigation, vested with the powers and immunity of commissioners appointed under the Act respecting public inquiry commissions (R.S.Q., chapter C-37), except the power to order imprisonment.

69. The Commission shall have its seat in the city of Québec or Montréal as the Government may decide by an order which shall come into force upon publication in the *Gazette officielle du Québec;* it shall also have an office in the other city.

The Commission may establish offices anywhere in Québec.

It may hold its sittings anywhere in Québec.

70. The Commission may make by-laws for its internal management.

Chapter II - Functions

71. The Commission shall promote and uphold, by every appropriate measure, the principles enunciated in this Charter.

The responsibilities of the Commission include, without being limited to, the following:

(1) to make a non-adversary investigation, on its own initiative or following receipt of a complaint, into any situation which appears to the Commission to be either a case of discrimination within the meaning of sections 10 to 19, including a case contemplated by section 86, or a violation of the right of aged or handicapped persons against exploitation enunciated in the first paragraph of section 48;

(2) to foster a settlement between a person whose rights allegedly have been violated, or the person or organization representing him, and the person to whom the violation is attributed;

(3) to report to the Public Curator any case it becomes aware of in the exercise of its functions where, in its opinion, protective supervision within the jurisdiction of the Public Curator is required;

(4) to develop and conduct a program of public information and education designed to promote an understanding and acceptance of the object and provisions of this Charter;

(5) to direct and encourage research and publications relating to fundamental rights and freedoms;

(6) to point out any provision in the laws of Québec that may be contrary to this Charter and make the appropriate recommendations to the Government;

(7) to receive and examine suggestions, recommendations and requests made to it concerning human rights and freedoms, possibly by inviting any interested person or body of persons to present his or its views before the Commission where it believes that the interest of the public or of a body of persons so requires, with a view to making the appropriate recommendations to the Government;

(8) to cooperate with any organization, dedicated to the promotion of human rights and freedoms in or outside Québec;

(9) to make an investigation into any act of reprisal or attempted reprisals and into any other act or omission which, in the opinion of the Commission, constitutes an offence under this Charter, and report its findings to the Attorney General.

72. The Commission, its members, personnel and mandataries and any complaints committee established by the Commission shall lend their assistance to any person, group or organization requesting it for the carrying out of the objects within the jurisdiction of the of the Commission under Chapter III of this Part, Parts III and IV and the regulations hereunder.

They shall, in addition, lend their assistance for the drafting of any complaint, any settlement reached between parties or any applications that must be made in writing to the Commission.

73. Not later than 31 March each year, the Commission shall submit to the President of the National Assembly a report on its activities and recommendations for the preceding calendar year.

The report shall be tabled in the National Assembly if it is in session or, if it is not, within 30 days after the opening of the next session. The report shall be published and distributed by the Québec Official Publisher on the terms determined by order of the Government.

Chapter III - Complaints

74. Any person who believes he has been the victim of a violation of rights that is within the sphere of investigation of the Commission may file a complaint with the Commission. If several persons believe they have suffered a violation of their rights in similar circumstances, they may form a group to file a complaint.

Every complaint must be made in writing.

A complaint may be filed on behalf of a victim or group of victims by any organization dedicated to the defence of human rights and freedoms or to the welfare of a group of persons. The written consent of the victim or victims is required except in the case of exploitation of aged persons or handicapped persons contemplated by the first paragraph of section 48.

75 The Public Protector shall transmit to the Commission every complaint he receives that is within the sphere of investigation of the Commission, unless the complainant objects thereto.

Any complaint transmitted to the Commission is deemed to be received by the Commission on the day it is filed with the Public Protector.

76. Prescription of any civil action respecting the facts alleged in a complaint or revealed by means of an investigation is suspended from the day the complaint is filed with the Commission or the day an investigation is commenced by the Commission on its own initiative until the earliest of

(1)   the day on which a settlement is reached between the parties;

(2)   the day on which the victim and the complainant are notified that the Commission is referring the matter to a tribunal;

(3)   the day on which the victim or the complainant personally institutes proceedings in regard to one of the remedies provided for in sections 49 and 80; and

(4)   the day on which the victim and the complainant are notified that the Commission refuses or is ceasing to act.

77. The Commission shall refuse or cease to act in favour of the victim where

(1)   the victim or the complainant so requests, subject to the Commission's ascertaining that such request is made freely and voluntarily;

(2)   the victim or the complainant has, on the basis of the same facts, personally pursued one of the remedies provided for in sections 49 and 80.

The Commission may refuse or cease to act in favour of the victim where

(1)   the complaint is based on acts or omissions the last of which occurred more than two years before the filing of the complaint;

(2)   the victim or the complainant does not have a sufficient interest;

(3)   the complaint is frivolous, vexatious or made in bad faith;

(4)   the victim or the complainant has, on the basis of the same facts, personally pursued a remedy other than those provided for in sections 49 and 80.

The decision of the Commission shall state in writing the reasons on which it is based and indicate any remedy which the Commission may consider appropriate; it shall be notified to the victim and the complainant.

78.   The Commission shall seek, in respect of every situation reported in the complaint or revealed in the course of the investigation, any evidence allowing it to decide whether it is expedient to foster the negotiation of a settlement between the parties, to propose the submission of the dispute to arbitration or to refer any unsettled issue to a tribunal.

The Commission may cease to act where it believes it would be futile to seek further evidence or where the evidence collected is insufficient. Its decision shall state in writing the reasons on which it is based and indicate any remedy which the Commission may consider appropriate; it shall be notified to the victim and the complainant. Where the Commission decides to cease to act, it shall give notice thereof to any person to whom a violation of rights is attributed in the complaint.

79.   Where a settlement is reached between the parties, it shall be evidenced in writing.

If no settlement is possible, the Commission shall again propose arbitration to the parties; it may also propose to the parties, taking into account the public interest and the interest of the victim, any measure of redress, such as the admission of the violation of a right, the cessation of the act complained of, the performance of any act or the payment of compensation or exemplary damages, within such time as it fixes.

80.   Where the parties will not agree to negotiation of a settlement or to arbitration of the dispute or where the proposal of the Commission has not been implemented to its satisfaction within the allotted time, the Commission may apply to a tribunal to obtain, where consistent with the public interest, any appropriate measure against the person at fault or to demand, in favour of the victim, any measure of redress it considers appropriate at that time.

81. Where the Commission has reason to believe that the life, health or safety of a person involved in a case of discrimination or exploitation is threatened or that any evidence or clue pertaining to such a case could be lost, it may apply to a tribunal for any emergency measure capable of putting an end to the threat or risk of loss.

82. The Commission may also apply to a tribunal for any appropriate measure against any person who attempts to take or takes reprisals against a person, group or organization having an interest in the handling of a case of discrimination or exploitation or having participated therein either as the victim, the complainant, a witness or otherwise.

The Commission may, in particular, request the tribunal to order that, on such date as it deems fair and expedient under the circumstances, the injured person be instated in the position or dwelling he would have occupied had it not been for the contravention.

83. Where the Commission applies to a tribunal, pursuant to sections 80 to 82, for measures for a person's benefit, it must obtain the person's written consent, except in the case of a person contemplated by the first paragraph of section 48.

84. Where, following the filing of a complaint, the Commission exercises its discretionary power not to submit an application to a tribunal to pursue, for a person's benefit, a remedy provided for in sections 80 to 82, it shall notify the complainant of its decision, stating the reasons on which it is based.

Within 90 days after he receives such notification, the complainant may, at his own expense, submit an application to the Human Rights Tribunal to pursue such remedy and, in that case, he is, for the pursuit of the remedy, substituted by operation of law for the Commission with the same effects as if the remedy had been pursued by the Commission.

85. The victim may intervene at any stage of proceedings to which the Commission is party pursuant to sections 80 to 82 and in which he has an interest. If the victim does intervene, the Commission cannot bring an appeal without his consent.

Subject to the second paragraph of section III, the victim may personally pursue the remedies provided for in sections 80 to 82 or bring an appeal, even though he was not party to the proceedings in first instance.

In all such cases, the Commission shall give the victim access to the record which concerns him.

Part III - Affirmative action programs

86. The object of an affirmative action program is to remedy the situation of persons belonging to groups discriminated against in employment, or in the sector of education or of health services and other services generally available to the public.

An affirmative action program is deemed non-discriminatory if it is established in conformity with the Charter.

87. *Not in force*

Every affirmative action program must be approved by the Commission, unless it is imposed by order of a tribunal.

The Commission shall, on request, lend assistance for the devising of an affirmative action program.

88. If, after investigation, the Commission confirms the existence of a situation involving discrimination referred to in section 86, it may propose the implementation of an affirmative action program within such time as it may fix.

Where its proposal has not been followed, the Commission may apply to a tribunal and, on proof of the existence of a situation contemplated in section 86, obtain, within the time fixed by the tribunal, an order to devise and implement a program. The program thus devised is filed with the tribunal which may, in accordance with the Charter, make the modifications it considers appropriate.

89. The Commission shall supervise the administration of the affirmative action programs. It may make investigations and require reports.

90. Where the Commission becomes aware that an affirmative action program has not been implemented within the alloted time or is not being complied with, it may, in the case of a program it has approved, withdraw its approval or, if it proposed implementation of the program, it may apply to a tribunal in accordance with the second paragraph of section 88.

91. A program contemplated in section 88 may be modified, postponed or cancelled if new facts warrant it.

If the Commission and the person required or having consented to implement the affirmative action program agree on its modification, postponement or cancellation, the agreement shall be evidenced in writing.

Failing agreement, either party may request the tribunal to which the Commission has applied pursuant to the second paragraph of section 88 to decide whether the new facts warrant the modification, postponement or cancellation of the program.

All modifications must conform to the Charter.

92.   The Government must require its departments and agencies to implement affirmative action programs within such time as it may fix.

Sections 86 to 92 do not apply to the programs contemplated in this section. The programs must, however, be the object of a consultation with the Commission before being implemented.

Part IV - Confidentiality

93.   Notwithstanding sections 9 and 83 of the Act respecting access to documents held by public bodies and the protection of personal information (R.S.Q. Chapter A-2.1), any information or document furnished voluntarily to the Commission and held by it for the purposes of the devising or implementation of or compliance with an affirmative action program is confidential and may be used only for the purposes for which it was furnished; it shall not be disclosed or used otherwise, except with the consent of the person or organization having furnished it.

No such information or document may be revealed before a tribunal by or on behalf of the Commission or, despite paragraph 9 of section 71, reported to the Attorney General, except with the consent of the person or organization having furnished the information or document to the Commission and the consent of the parties to the dispute.

This section shall not be construed as limiting the power to compel the person or organization, by way of a summons, warrant or order, to communicate any information or document relating to an affirmative action program.

94.   Nothing said or written in the course of the negotiation of a settlement pursuant to section 78 may be revealed, even in judicial proceedings, except with the consent of the parties to the negotiation and the parties to the dispute.

95.   Subject to article 61 of the Code of Penal Procedure (1987, chapter 96), no member or mandatary of the Commission or member of its personnel may be compelled to give testimony before a tribunal as to information obtained in the performance of his duties or to produce a document containing any such information, except for the purpose of ascertaining whether it is confidential.

96.   No civil action may be taken by reason or in consequence of the publication of a report emanating from the Commission or the publication, in good faith, of an abstract from or summary of such a report.

Part V - Regulations

97. The Government, by regulation:

(1) may fix the actuarial data and the risk determining factors that are non-discriminatory under an insurance or pension contract, a social benefits plan or a retirement, pension or insurance plan, or a public pension or public insurance plan, determine in which cases and according to what kind of contract or plan the date and factors are deemed non-discriminatory, and make, for the purposes of those contracts and plans, every provision incident to the application of the principle of non-discrimination and the rules relating to the notion of spouse;

(2) may fix the criteria, norms, scales, conditions or modalities applicable for the devising, implementation or carrying out of affirmative action programs, define their limits and determine anything necessary or useful for those purposes;

(3) shall prescribe the procedure for the recruitment and selection of persons apt for designation to the function of arbitrator or appointment to the function of assessor with the Human Rights Tribunal.

The regulation made under subparagraph 3 of the first paragraph shall, among other things:

(1) determine the minimum proportion of advocates that must be maintained on the panel provided for in the third paragraph of section 62;

(2) determine the forms of publicity that must be used for the purpose of establishing such panel;

(3) determine the manner in which a person may apply;

(4) authorize the Minister of Justice to form a selection committee charged with evaluating the aptitude of applicants and advising him as to applicants and to fix the composition and mode of appointment of the members of the committee;

(5) determine the criteria of selection on which the committee is to base its decisions, the information it may require of applicants and the consultations it may make;

(6) prescribe that the panel of persons apt for designation to the function of arbitrator or appointment to the function of assessor with the Human Rights Tribunal be recorded in a register established for that purpose at the Ministère de la Justice.

The members of a selection committee receive no remuneration except in such cases, on such conditions and to such extent as may be determined by the Government. They are, however, entitled to reimbursement for expenses incurred in the performance of their duties, on the conditions and to the extent determined by the Government.

98. The Government, after consultation with the Commission, shall publish the draft regulation in the *Gazette officielle du Québec* with a notice stating the time after which the draft will be tabled before the Standing Committee on Institutions and stating that it may be adopted on the expiry of 45 days after the Committee reports to the National Assembly.

The Government may subsequently amend the draft regulation. It must, in that case, publish the amended draft regulation in the *Gazette officielle du Québec* with a notice stating that it will be adopted without amendment at the expiry of 45 days after the publication.

99. The Commission, by regulation,

(1)   may delegate to a complaints committee established under section 61 such responsibilities as it indicates;

(2)   shall prescribe the other rules, procedures, terms or conditions applicable with respect to the mechanisms provided for in Chapters II and III of Part II and in Parts III and IV, including the form and content of the related reports.

Every regulation hereunder is subject to the approval of the Government; the Government may, when granting its approval, amend the regulation.

Part VI - Human Rights Tribunal

Chapter I - Establishment and organization

100. The Human Rights Tribunal, referred to in this Part as the "Tribunal", is hereby established.

101. The Tribunal is composed of not fewer than seven members, including a president and assessors, appointed by the Government. The president shall be chosen, after consultation with the chief judge of the Court of Québec, from among the judges of that court having notable experience and expertise in, sensitivity to and interest for matters of human rights and freedoms; the assessors shall be chosen from among the persons included in the panel provided for in the third paragraph of section 62.

The term of office of the members of the Tribunal is five years. It may be renewed for a shorter determined time.

The Government shall establish the standards and scales governing the remuneration and conditions of employment or, where applicable, the allowances of the assessors.

102. Before entering office, the members shall make the oaths or solemn affirmations provided in Schedule II; the president shall do so before the chief judge of the Court of Québec and the other members, before the president.

103. The Government may, on the request of the president and after consultation with the chief judge of the Court of Québec, designate another judge of that court having notable experience and expertise in, sensitivity to and interest for matters of human rights and freedoms to sit as a member of the Tribunal either to hear and decide an application or for a determined period.

104. To hear an application, the Tribunal shall sit in a division composed of three members, that is, the judge presiding the division and two assessors assisting him, designated by the president. The member presiding the division shall decide the application alone.

However, a preliminary or incidental application or an application under section 81 or 82 shall be heard and decided by the president or by the judge to whom he refers the application; such an application shall be referred to a division of the Tribunal in the cases determined by the rules of procedure and practice or where the president so decides.

105. The clerk and staff of the Court of Québec of the district in which an application is filed or in which the Tribunal or a division or member of the Tribunal sits shall provide it or him with the services they usually provide to the Court of Québec itself.

The bailiffs are *ex officio* bailiffs of the Tribunal and may make a return to the Tribunal, under their oath of office, of any service made by them.

106. The president of the Tribunal shall devote his time exclusively to the duties of his office. His duties include

(1) fostering a consensus among the members concerning the general orientation of the Tribunal;

(2) coordinating the work of the Tribunal and distributing it among the members; the members shall, in that regard, comply with his orders and directives and see to their proper implementation;

(3) prescribing a code of ethics and ensuring that it is observed. The code of ethics shall come into force 15 days after its publication in the *Gazette officielle du Québec* or at any later date indicated therein.

107. A judge designated under section 103 shall replace the president if he is absent or unable to act or if the office of president is vacant.

108. A judge of the Tribunal, even if no longer in office, shall render a decision on every application heard by him. If no decision is rendered within 90 days, the application shall be referred by the president to another judge of the Tribunal with the consent of the parties or heard anew.

109. Except on a question of jurisdiction, no recourse provided for in articles 33 and 834 to 850 of the Code of Civil Procedure may be exercised nor any injunction granted against the Tribunal, its president or any other member acting in its or his official capacity.

A judge of the Court of Appeal may, upon a motion, annul summarily any decision, order or injunction issued or granted contrary to the first paragraph.

110. The president of the Tribunal may, with the assistance of the majority of the other members, adopt such rules of procedure and practice as are considered necessary for the performance of the functions of the Tribunal.

Chapter II - Jurisdiction and powers

111. The Tribunal is competent to hear and dispose of any application submitted under section 80, 81 or 82, in particular in matters of employment or housing or in connection with goods and services generally available to the public, and any application submitted under section 88, 90 or 91 in respect of an affirmative action program.

Only the Commission may initially submit an application to the Tribunal to pursue any of the remedies provided for in any of the said sections, subject to the substitution provided for in section 84 in favour of a complainant and to the pursuit of the remedy provided for in section 91 by a person on whom the Tribunal has previously imposed an affirmative action program.

112. The Tribunal and its divisions and judges are, in the performance of their functions, vested with the powers and immunity of commissioners appointed under the Act respecting public inquiry commissions, except the power to impose imprisonment.

113. In the absence of an applicable rule of procedure and practice, the Tribunal may, on the basis of the Code of Civil Procedure, adapted as required, render such rulings and orders of procedure and practice as the performance of its functions may require.

Moreover, in the absence of a provision applicable to a particular case, the Tribunal may, in a matter submitted to it, prescribe with the same effect any act or formality which could have been prescribed in the rules of procedure and practice.

Chapter III - Proof and procedure

114. Every application shall be submitted to the Tribunal in writing and served in accordance with the rules provided in the Code of Civil Procedure, unless it is made in the course of a hearing. Where the said Code provides that a mode of service requires authorization, it may be obtained from the Tribunal.

The application shall be filed at the office of the Court of Québec in the judicial district where the person on whom the conclusions of the application may be imposed or, in the case of the implementation of an affirmative action program, the person on whom the program has been or may be imposed has his domicile or, failing that, his residence or principal place of business.

115. Within 15 days of the filing of an application other than an application referred to in the second paragraph of section 104, the plaintiff shall file a factum setting out his pretensions, which the Tribunal shall serve on every interested person or organization wishing to do so may file a factum of his or its own, which the Tribunal shall serve on the plaintiff.

Failure to comply with this section on the part of the plaintiff may entail the dismissal of the application.

116. The Commission, the victim, the group of victims, the complainant before the Commission any person or organization on whom or which an application is served and the person on whom an affirmative action program has been or may be imposed are parties to the application by operation of law and may intervene at any time before the execution of the decision.

Any other person, group or organization may, at any time before the execution of the decision, become a party to the application if the Tribunal is satisfied that he or it has a sufficient interest to intervene, however, the person, group or organization must obtain leave from the Tribunal each time he or it wishes to produce, examine or cross-examine witnesses, or examine any evidence in the record and comment or refute it.

117. An application may be amended at any time before the decision on the conditions the Tribunal deems necessary to safeguard the rights of all parties. However, except with the consent of the parties, no amendment which would result in an entirely new application unrelated to the original shall be allowed.

118. Any party may, before the hearing or at any time before the decision provided he shows that he has been diligent, request the recusation of any member of the Tribunal. The request shall be addressed to the president of the Tribunal who shall rule upon the request or refer it to a judge of the Tribunal, in particular where the request concerns him personally.

Any member of the Tribunal who is aware of a valid ground of recusation to which he is liable is bound to make and file in the record a written declaration thereof.

119. The Tribunal shall sit in the judicial district at the office of which the application was filed.

However, the president of the Tribunal and the member presiding the division to which the application is referred may decide, on their own initiative or on the request of a party, that the hearing shall be held in another judicial district if the public interest and the interest of the parties so require.

120. On his own initiative or on request, the president of the Tribunal or the member designated by him to preside the hearing shall fix the date of the hearing.

The Tribunal shall give written notice of the hearing to every party and to his attorney, unless the party has waived his right thereto, not less than one clear day before the hearing in the case of an application under the second paragraph of section 104 and not less than 10 clear days before the hearing in all other cases. The notice shall set out:

(1)   the purpose of the hearing;

(2)   the date, time and place of the hearing;

(3)   the right of every party to be assisted or represented by an advocate;

(4)   the right of every party to waive a *viva voce* hearing and present his views in writing;

(5)   the right of every party to request that the hearing be held *in camera* or that an order be issued banning or restricting the disclosure, publication or release of any information or document;

(6)   the power of the Tribunal to hear the application and to render any decision or issue any order without further time or notice, despite the default or absence of any party or of his attorney.

121. The Tribunal may, on its own initiative or on request and in the interest of morality or public order, ban or restrict the disclosure, publication or release of any information or document it indicates, to preserve the confidentiality of the source of the information or document or to protect a person's rights and freedoms.

122. The Tribunal may hear the application and render a decision or issue an order despite the absence of a party or his attorney who, although duly notified of the hearing, fails to present himself on the day of the hearing at the appointed time and place, refuses to be heard or fails to present his views in writing as required.

The Tribunal is required to postpone the hearing, however, if the absent party or attorney has given the Tribunal a valid excuse for his absence.

123. The Tribunal, though bound by the general principles of justice, may admit any evidence useful and relevant to the application submitted to it and allow any means of proof.

The Tribunal is not bound by the special rules of evidence applicable in civil matters, except to the extent determined in this Part.

124. Depositions shall be recorded unless the parties agree expressly to dispense with recording.

Chapter IV - Decision and execution

125. Every decision of the Tribunal must be rendered in writing and filed at the office of the Court of Québec where the application was filed. It shall contain, in addition to the purview, a statement of any ban or restriction on the disclosure, publication or release of any information or document it indicates and the reasons therefore.

Subject to any such ban or restriction, any person may, at his expense, obtain a copy of or extract from the decision.

126. The Tribunal may, in a final decision, condemn one of the parties who appeared in the proceedings to the payment of the costs and disbursements or apportion them among them as it determines.

127. The Tribunal may, without any formality, correct a decision it has rendered which contains an error in writing or in calculation or any other clerical error provided that the decision has not been executed or appealed from.

128. The Tribunal may, on its own initiative or on the request of an interested person or organization, revise or revoke any decision it has rendered provided that it has not been executed or appealed from,

(1) where a new fact is discovered which, if it had been known in due time, might have justified a different decision;

(2) where an interested person or organization was unable, for reasons deemed sufficient, to be heard;

(3) where a substantive or procedural defect is likely to invalidate the decision.

However, in the case described in subparagraph 3 of the first paragraph, a judge of the Tribunal cannot revise or revoke a decision rendered on an application heard by him.

129. The clerk of the Court of Québec of the district where the application was filed shall cause every final decision to be served on all parties who appeared in the proceedings and on all parties contemplated by the first paragraph of section 116, as soon as it is filed at the office of the Court.

However, where a decision is rendered in the presence of a party or his attorney, it is deemed to be served on them on being so rendered.

130. A decision of the Tribunal condemning a person to pay a sum of money becomes executory as a judgment of the Court of Québec or the Superior Court, according to their respective jurisdictions, and has all the effects thereof from the date of its filing at the office of the Court of Québec or of its homologation in Superior Court.

Homologation of the decision is obtained by the filing by the clerk of the Court of Québec of the district where the decision of the Tribunal was filed of a certified copy of the decision at the office of the prothonotary of the Superior Court of the district where the condemned person has his domicile or, failing that, his residence or principal place of business.

A final decision of the Tribunal other than a decision described in the first paragraph is executory upon the expiry of the time for appeal, in accordance with the terms and conditions set out in the decision, unless the Tribunal orders provisional execution of the decision upon its service or at any specified later date.

Any other decision of the Tribunal is executory upon its service and notwithstanding appeal, unless the appeal tribunal orders otherwise.

131. Every person who fails to comply with a decision of the Tribunal which has been duly served on him and which does not require to be homologated in Superior Court is guilty of contempt of court and may be condemned, with or without imprisonment for not over one year, and without prejudice to any suit for damages, to a fine not exceeding $50 000.

Every person who contravenes a ban or restriction on disclosure, publication or release imposed by a decision of the Tribunal rendered under section 121 is liable to the same sanction, except that the amount of the fine shall not exceed $5 000.

Chapter V- Appeal

132. Any final decision of the Tribunal may be appealed from to the Court of Appeal with leave from one of the judges thereof.

133. Subject to section 85, the rules relating to appeals set out in the Code of Civil Procedure, adapted as required, apply to any appeal under this Chapter.

Part VII - Final provisions

134. Every person is guilty of an offence

(1) who contravenes any of sections 10 to 19 or the first paragraph of section 48;

(2) who, being a member or mandatary of the Commission or a member of its personnel, reveals, without being duly authorized to do so, anything of which he has gained knowledge in the performance of his duties;

(3) who attempts to obstruct or obstructs the Commission, a complaints committee, a member or mandatary of the Commission or a member of its personnel in the performance of its or his duties;

(4) who contravenes a ban or restriction on the disclosure, publication or release of any information or document contemplated by Part IV or by any regulation under section 99;

(5) who attempts to take or takes reprisals as described in section 82.

135. If a corporation commits an offence referred to in section 134, any officer, director, employee or representative of such corporation who prescribed or authorized the committing of the offence, or who consented thereto or acquiesced or participated therein, is deemed to be a party to the offence whether or not the corporation has been prosecuted or found guilty.

136. Penal proceedings under this Charter are instituted by the Commission or by the Attorney General or the person authorized by him for that purpose.

137. Sections 11, 13, 16, 17 and 19 of this Charter do not apply to pension plans, retirement plans, life insurance plans or any other plan or scheme of social benefits unless the discrimination is founded on race, colour, religion, political convictions, language, ethnic or national origin or social condition.

138. The Minister of Justice has charge of the application of this Charter.

To the owner of this book

We hope that you have enjoyed *Québec: State and Society, Second Edition* and we would like to know as much about your experiences as you would care to offer. Only through your comments and those of others can we learn how to make this a better text for future readers.

School _____ Your instructor's name _____

Course _____ Was the text required? _____ Recommended? _____

1. What did you like the most about *Québec: State and Society, Second Edition?*

_____

_____

_____

2. How useful was this text for your course?

_____

_____

_____

3. Do you have any recommendations for ways to improve the next edition of this text?

_____

_____

_____

4. In the space below or in a separate letter, please write any other comments you have about the book. (For example, please feel free to comment on reading level, writing style, terminology, design features, and learning aids.)

_____

_____

_____

Optional

Your
name _____ Date _____

May Nelson Canada quote you, either in promotion for *Québec: State and Society, Second Edition* or in future publishing ventures?

Yes _____ No _____

Thanks!

- FOLD HERE -

MAIL ⮞ POSTE

Canada Post Corporation / Société canadienne des postes

Postage paid
if mailed in Canada

Port payé
si posté au Canada

Business
Reply

Réponse
d'affaires

0107077099   01

Nelson

TAPE SHUT

0107077099-M1K5G4-BR01

Nelson Canada
College Editorial Department
1120 Birchmount Rd.
Scarborough, ON M1K 9Z9

PLEASE TAPE SHUT. DO NOT STAPLE.